The Official RED BOOK™

A GUIDE BOOK OF

UNITED STATES COINS

R. S. YEOMAN

EDITED BY

KENNETH BRESSETT

58th Edition

*Fully Illustrated Catalog
and Retail Valuation List
1616 to Date*

A BRIEF HISTORY OF AMERICAN COINAGE
EARLY AMERICAN COINS AND TOKENS
EARLY MINT ISSUES   REGULAR MINT ISSUES   PROOFS
PRIVATE, STATE AND TERRITORIAL GOLD
SILVER AND GOLD COMMEMORATIVE ISSUES
PATTERNS   HARD TIMES TOKENS

THE OFFICIAL RED BOOK is a registered
trademark of Whitman Publishing, LLC.
Library of Congress Catalog Card No.: 47-22284

The publisher of this book does not deal in coins; the values shown here are not offers to sell or buy but are included only as general information. Descriptions of coins are based on the most accurate data available, but could contain beliefs that may change with further research or discoveries.

www.whitman**books**.com

No part of this book may be reproduced or copied in any form without written permission from the publisher. Prices listed in this book may not be used in any form of computer data base or program without written permission from the publisher.

For a complete listing of numismatic reference
books, supplies and storage products,
visit us at www.whitman**books**.com

COLLECT HISTORY

The United States Mint is proud to present the new Westward Journey Nickel Series™ commemorating the bicentennials of the Louisiana Purchase and Lewis and Clark expedition. This limited series will feature new reverse designs for the nickel in 2004 and 2005, and will be included in several exciting new products.

For more information about this new series and other fine products, come to the source—the United States Mint.

For genuine United States Mint products visit **www.usmint.gov** or call **1-800-USA-MINT**

UNITED STATES MINT

CONTRIBUTORS TO THE FIFTY-EIGHTH EDITION

Special Consultants: Q. David Bowers,
Philip Bressett, Jeff Garrett, Tom Hallenbeck, and Robert Rhue

Gary Adkins
David Akers
John Albanese
Buddy Alleva
Dr. Richard S. Appel
Michael Aron
Richard M. August
Richard A. Bagg, Ph.D.
Mitchell A. Battino
Lee J. Bellisario
Jack Beymor
Mark R. Borckardt
J. H. Cline
Elizabeth W. Coggan
Alan R. Cohen
Gary Cohen
Marc Crane
John West Dannreuther
Tom DeLorey
Silvano Di Genova
Kenneth Duncan
Sheridan Downey
Col. Steven Ellsworth
John Feigenbaum
Dennis M. Gillio
Ronald J. Gillio
Ira M. Goldberg
Lawrence S. Goldberg

Kenneth M. Goldman
J. R. Grellman
Ron Guth
James Halperin
John Hamrick
Gene L. Henry
Karl D. Hirtzinger
Jesse Iskowitz
Steve Ivy
James J. Jelinski
A. M. Kagin
Donald H. Kagin
Bradley S. Karoleff
John J. Kraljevich, Jr.
Richard A. Lecce
Robert B. Lecce
Julian M. Leidman
David Leventhal
Stuart Levine
Kevin Lipton
Denis W. Loring
Andy Lustig
Chris McCawley
Robert T. McIntire
Dwight N. Manley
Harry Miller
Lee S. Minshull
Robert Mish

Scott P. Mitchell
Michael C. Moline
Paul Montgomery
Richard Nachbar
Chris Napolitano
Paul Nugget
John M. Pack
Robert M. Paul
William P. Paul
Joel Rettew, Jr.
Robert J. Rhue
Tom Rinaldo
Maurice Rosen
Leonard R. Saunders
Mary Sauvain
Cherie Schoeps
Richard J. Schwary
James A. Simek
Richard E. Snow
William J. Spencer
David M. Sundman
Anthony J. Swiatek
Anthony Terranova
Jerry Treglia
Frank E. Van Valen
Fred Weinberg
Douglas Winter
Mark S. Yaffe

Special credit is due to the following for service and data in this book:
Stewart Blay, Roger W. Burdette, Columbus-America Discovery Group, Charles Davis, Bill Fivaz, George Fuld, Charles Hoskins, Robert W. Julian, David W. Lange, G. J. Lawson, Andy Lustig, Arnold Margolis, J. P. Martin, Eric P. Newman, Margaret Olsen, Doug Plasencia, Len Roosmalen, P. Scott Rubin, Dr. Paul Rynearson, Neil Shafer, Robert W. Shippee, Arlie Slabaugh, Mark R. Vitunic, Holland Wallace, Weimar White, John Whitney, and John Wright.

Special credit is due to the following for service in the past editions of the Guide Book:
Philip E. Benedetti, George H. Blenker, Larry Brigs, Bob Entlich, Dennis J. Forgue, Harry J. Forman, Mike Fuljenz, Henry G. Garrett, William G. Gay, Harry Gittelson, Brian H. Hendelson, John W. Highfill, Robert H. Jacobs, Stanley Kesselman, Jerry Kimmel, Mike Kliman, Paul L. Koppenhaver, Ed Leventhal, Glenn E. Miller, Beth O. Piper, John C. Porter, Joel D. Rettew, Mike Ringo, Gerald R. Scherer, Jr., J. S. Schreiber, Hugh J. Sconyers, Robert R. Shaw, Thomas J. Smith, Paul Spiegel, Maurice A. Storck, Sr., Charles Surasky, Mark Van Winkle, Russell P. Vaughn,

Special photo credits are due to the following:
American Numismatic Rarities, Douglas F. Bird, Bill Fivaz, Ira & Larry Goldberg Coins & Collectibles, Tom Mulvaney, the Museum of the American Numismatic Association, Numismatic Guaranty Corporation (NGC), Brent Pogue, the Smithsonian Institution, heritagecoins.com, Spectrum, Stack's Rare Coins of New York, Superior Galleries, and Anthony Swiatek.

THE PURPOSE OF THIS BOOK

Coin values shown in this book are retail prices averaged from data supplied by the listed contributors approximately two months prior to publication. The coin market is so active in some categories that values can easily change during that period. Values listed are shown as a guide and are not intended to serve as a price-list for any dealer's stock. A dash appearing in a price column indicates the existence of coins in that grade where there are no current sales or auction records. The dash does not necessarily mean that such coins are excessively rare. Italicized prices indicate unsettled or speculative values. A number of listings of rare coins do not have prices or dashes in certain grades. This indicates that they are not available or not believed to exist in those grades.

Prices rise when: 1. The economic trend is inflationary and speculators turn to tangible assets as a hedge, or when the number of collectors increases, while coin supplies remain stationary or decrease through attrition or melting. 2. Dealers replace their stocks of coins only from collectors or other dealers, who expect a profit over what they originally paid. 3. Speculators attempt to influence the market through selective buying. 4. Bullion gold and silver prices rise.

Prices decline when: 1. Changes in collecting habits, or economic conditions, alter demand for certain coins. 2. Speculators sell in large quantities. 3. Hoards or large holdings are suddenly released and cannot be quickly absorbed by the normal market. 4. Bullion gold and silver prices decline.

Those who edit, contribute to, and publish this book advocate the collecting of coins for pleasure and educational benefits. A secondary consideration is that of investment, the profits from which are usually realized over the long term based on careful purchases.

The Handbook of United States Coins by R. S. Yeoman, Whitman Publishing, LLC, Atlanta, GA, contains average prices dealers will pay for these coins, and is obtainable through most coin dealers, hobby shops, bookstores and the Internet

THE SPANISH MILLED DOLLAR

The Spanish Milled Dollar valued at 8 reales, otherwise known as the "pillar dollar" or "piece of eight," has been given a place in romantic fiction unequaled by any other coin.

This time-honored piece and its fractional parts of 1/2 and 1 real, 2 and 4 reales were the principal coins of the American colonists, and were the forerunners of our own silver dollar and its fractional divisions. Thomas Jefferson even recommended to the Continental Congress on September 2, 1776 that the new country adopt the silver "Spanish Milled dollar" as our monetary unit of value.

The coin shown above bears the M mintmark for Mexico City. Similar pieces with other mintmarks were struck in Bolivia, Chile, Colombia, Guatemala and Peru. Average value for an 8 reales of common date and mint is about $150.00 in Fine to Very Fine condition. Dates range from 1732 to 1772.

Note: Many modern copies of the 8 reales exist. These are produced mostly as souvenirs and have little or no value.

CONDITION OF COINS
Essential elements of the A.N.A. grading system

ABOUT GOOD (AG-3) —Very heavily worn with portions of lettering, date and legends worn smooth. The date may be barely readable.

GOOD (G-4)—Heavily worn with design visible but faint in areas. Many details are flat.

VERY GOOD (VG-8) —Well worn with main features clear and bold although rather flat.

FINE (F-12) —Moderate to considerable even wear. Entire design is bold with overall pleasing appearance.

VERY FINE (VF-20) —Shows moderate wear on high points of design. All major details are clear.

CHOICE VERY FINE (VF-30) —Light even wear on the surface and highest parts of the design. All lettering and major features are sharp.

EXTREMELY FINE (EF-40) — Design is lightly worn throughout, but all features are sharp and well defined. Traces of luster may show.

CHOICE EXTREMELY FINE (EF-45)—Light overall wear shows on highest points. All design details are very sharp. Some of the mint luster is evident.

ABOUT UNCIRCULATED (AU-50)—Has traces of light wear on many of the high points. At least half of the mint luster is still present.

CHOICE ABOUT UNCIRCULATED (AU-55)—Evidence of friction on design high points. Most of mint luster remains.

MINT STATE — The terms Mint State (MS) and Uncirculated (Unc.) are interchangeably used to describe coins showing no trace of wear. Such coins may vary to some degree because of blemishes, toning or slight imperfections as described in the following subdivisions.

UNCIRCULATED (MS-60)—Has no trace of wear but may show a number of contact marks, and surface may be spotted or lack some luster.

UNCIRCULATED (MS-63) —Some distracting contact marks or blemishes in prime focal areas. Luster may be impaired.

CHOICE UNCIRCULATED (MS-65) — An above average Uncirculated coin that may be brilliant or lightly toned and has very few contact marks on the surface or rim. MS-67 through MS-62 indicate a slightly higher or lower grade of preservation.

PERFECT UNCIRCULATED (MS-70) — Perfect new condition, showing no trace of wear. The finest quality possible, with no evidence of scratches, handling or contact with other coins. Very few regular issue coins are ever found in this condition.

PROOF (PF-60) —Surface may have several contact marks, hairlines or light rubs. Luster may be dull and eye appeal lacking.

ATTRACTIVE PROOF (PF-63) — Reflective surfaces with only a few blemishes in secondary focal places. No major flaws.

CHOICE PROOF (PF-65) —Brilliant surfaces with no noticable blemishes or flaws. Few scattered barely noticeable marks or hairlines.

IMPORTANT: Damaged coins, such as those that are bent, corroded, scratched, holed, nicked, stained, or mutilated, are worth less than those without defects. Flawless uncirculated coins are generally worth more than values quoted in this book. Slightly worn coins ("sliders") that have been cleaned and conditioned ("whizzed") to simulate uncirculated luster are worth considerably less than perfect pieces.

Unlike damage inflicted after striking, manufacturing defects do not always lessen values. Examples are: Colonial coins with planchet flaws and weakly struck designs; early silver and gold with weight adjustment "file marks" (parallel cuts made prior to striking); and coins with "lint marks" (dust or other foreign matter which may mar the surface during striking).

Brief guides to grading are placed before each major coin type in this book.

RARE COINS AS AN INVESTMENT

Investing in rare coins can be a rewarding experience for anyone who approaches the calling armed with the right attitude and background knowledge about this exciting field. It can just as easily become a costly mistake for anyone who attempts to profit from coins without giving serious thought to the idiosyncrasies of this unique market.

The best advice given to anyone considering investing in rare coins is to use common sense. No thinking person would consider buying a diamond ring from a street peddler, or an art masterpiece at a garage sale. It is just the same with rare coins, and the more careful you are in selecting a qualified dealer and making an educated evaluation of the coins that you purchased, the greater will be your chance of making a profitable investment.

The opportunities for successful collecting and investing in quality numismatic items are as great today as at any time in the past. Inexperienced buyers can now purchase coins that have been graded and authenticated by third-party services to assure the quality of each item. Coins that are independently graded by these professional services are sealed in plastic holders, called slabs, to identify and protect them. There is also more written information available for beginners than ever before. The pricing of rare coins is very competitive in today's widespread market where profit margins are often lower than in the past.

The shift in emphasis from collecting to investing has created a new market and demand for coins resulting in more stringent grading methods, and pricing geared to the perceived rarity of coins in various levels of uncirculated perfection. Coins in high grades of condition that have been certified and encapsulated (slabbed) may be valued at multiples of similar coins that have not been so graded. The "raw" (non-serviced) coins that are listed in this catalog are valued at what collectors normally pay for such items without encapsulation, and in many cases will be lower than what is charged for "investment" (slabbed) coins.

For hundreds of years rare coins and precious metals have proven themselves to be an excellent hedge against inflation and source of ready money in times of disaster. There is no reason to think that this will change in the future. Gone are the days when coin collecting was only a passive hobby for those who would study the history and artistry of these enjoyable objects. It has now grown into an activity where speculation on the future demand for rare coins has made them a part of many investment portfolios.

With this change in attitude about collecting has come a measure of concern for those who purchase coins without the background or experience necessary to avoid costly mistakes in accepting overpriced or overgraded coins that simply are not worth what is charged for them. This is especially true of coins that are offered for sale or at auction over the Internet where it is often not possible to examine the items carefully enough to determine authenticity or grade. Extreme caution is advised for anyone considering an investment in expensive coins. Investigate the person or firm with whom you are dealing. Seek professional non-biased help with grading determinations. Satisfy yourself that the coins you select authentic and are not priced considerably higher than is being charged by other dealers.

Protecting valuable coins from deterioration is an important part of investing. They should also be insured and kept in a secure place. The best protection for keeping coins pristine is to store them in an inert, airtight plastic holder, (the encapsulated 'slabs' are a good example), and away from paper products, cigarette smoke, wood, natural rubber, paint and textiles such as wool or felt. Humidity greater than 75% can also be harmful and should be avoided.

Collectors and investors alike can profit by investigating the background and history of the coins they buy. Coins are a mirror of history and art that tell the story of mankind over the past 2,600 years, reflecting economic struggles, wars, prosperity and creativity of every major nation on earth. We are but the custodians of these historical relics, and must appreciate and care for them while in our possession. Those who treat rare coins with the consideration and respect they deserve will profit in many ways, not the least of which can be in the form of a sound financial return on one's investment of time and money.

═ AN INTRODUCTION TO UNITED STATES COINS ═

Money of the Early Americans

The saga of American money covers a period of nearly four centuries from 1620 to the present. It began when the early European settlers in New England started trading with Native Americans for furs and commodities that could be exported to England. The furs, tobacco and lumber exports were used to purchase needed items that could not be produced locally. Trade was carried on with the Indians through the use of barter and strings of wampum, which were fashioned from mussel shells in the form of beads. Beaver skins, wampum, and in Virginia, tobacco, soon became the commonly accepted local media of exchange for all other available commodities that were not traded by barter. The immigrants, in fact, had little use for coined money at first, but when merchandise arrived from Europe, coins were usually demanded in payment for goods.

Nearly all foreign coins were accepted for purchases. The most popular were French louis, English guineas, German thalers, Dutch ducats, and various Spanish coins, including doubloons and particularly the Spanish milled dollar, or piece of eight. The piece of eight continued to be a standard money unit throughout the entire colonial period. Even after the Revolutionary War ended in 1783, and the United States Mint was established in 1792, the Spanish dollar and its fractional parts circulated in this country with official sanction until 1857. One real equaled 12 1/2 cents and was known as a "bit." A quarter of the dollar thus became known as "two bits," a term that is still understood to mean twenty-five cents.

England consistently ignored the plight of its American colonists and made no effort to provide gold or silver coins, or small change in any form for their convenience. The English mercantile system relied on exports from the colonies, and sought to control trade by limiting the amount of "hard" money paid to them. Under these restraints, the colonists were only able to trade with England for necessities, and were left with very little coinage that could be used in other countries. The foreign coins that were sometimes available were a valuable commodity for purchases outside of the normal English trade.

As a remedy for the dearth of circulating coinage a wide assortment of foreign coins, and tokens were pressed into use, but only a very few were made in this country prior to 1783. Copper coins known as "Hogge Money" (from their design, see page 21) were privately made for the Sommer Islands, now known as Bermuda, about the year 1616. The first coins minted for the colonies in America were made by John Hull in Boston for the Massachusetts Bay Colony. The General Court of the colony granted him authority to begin coinage, despite the possibility of objection and recrimination by the King of

England. Starting in 1652 the Massachusetts minter began producing the famous N.E., Willow, Oak and Pine Tree shillings, with their fractional parts, for the convenience of the colonists. The importance of this venture, which defied the English law, and lasted from 1652 to 1682, was in a sense the first declaration of independence for the colonies.

As time passed, coins and tokens of many types were introduced and employed by the colonists to supplement their use of barter. Lord Baltimore was responsible for a small issue of silver pieces, which were struck in England in 1659 and sent to Maryland for use there. Mark Newby imported from Ireland, coins known as St. Patrick's Halfpence for use in the province of New Jersey in 1682. Coins dated 1722 to 1724, known as Rosa Americana and Hibernia coppers, were produced by William Wood in England and were widely circulated in America. There were also a few issues of uncertain date and origin, such as the New Yorke Token, the Hibernia-Voce Populi, and the Elephant Tokens, which likely circulated among the early settlers.

Enterprising American individuals were responsible for some of the other copper pieces that circulated during the eighteenth century. The Gloucester Token, about which little is known, was one of these. Samuel and John Higley of Granby, Connecticut, made an interesting series of threepence pieces during the period from 1737 to 1739. J. Chalmers, a silversmith in Annapolis, Maryland, issued silver shillings, sixpence, and threepence pieces in 1783. In 1787 Ephraim Brasher, a New York goldsmith, struck a gold piece of the value of a doubloon (about $15.00 in New York currency). Standish Barry of Baltimore, Maryland, made a curious silver token threepence in 1790.

Still other tokens, struck in England, reached our shores in Revolutionary times and were for the most part speculative ventures. These much-needed, small-denomination coppers were readily circulated because of the great scarcity of fractional coins. Included in this category were the Nova Constellatio coppers and various English Merchant's tokens.

During the period of turmoil following America's War of Independence, from about 1781 to 1794, still more English copper pieces were added to the great variety of coins and tokens employed in the new nation. It was a time when Americans were suffering from post-war economic depression, a shortage of currency, high taxes and foreclosures from bankruptcies. In 1787 the Nova Eboracs pieces, known as New York Coppers, the Georgius Triumpho coppers, and the Auctori Plebis tokens found their way into circulation as small change, despite their unofficial nature.

Collectors of colonial coins also include other pieces that are interesting because of their close association with early America and its first president. These consists of the Kentucky, Myddelton and Franklin Press tokens, and those pieces bearing the portrait of George Washington. Although most of these pieces are dated from 1783 to 1795, many of them were made in England around the turn of the century, and few of them actually circulated in the United States.

Coinage of the States

The Articles of Confederation, adopted March 1, 1781, provided that Congress should have the sole right to regulate the alloy and value of coin struck by its own authority or by that of the respective states. Each state, therefore, had the right to coin money with Congress serving as a regulating authority. New Hampshire was the first state to consider coinage, but few if any of their copper coins were placed in circulation. The only specimens known bear the date 1776.

In the period from 1785 to 1788, Vermont, Connecticut, and New Jersey granted coining privileges to companies or individuals. Massachusetts erected its own mint in Boston where copper coins were produced in 1787 and 1788. A number of interesting types and varieties of these state issues, most of which were struck in fairly large quantities, are still extant, and form the basis for many present day collections and museum exhibits of early American coins.

The Beginnings of United States Coinage

Throughout the years, from 1620 to 1776, Americans were forced to rely on numerous European coins and denominations that had to be converted to some common value to facilitate transactions. Further compounding this mathematical obstacle was the variation of values from one colony to another. Merchants became accustomed to using the Spanish dollar and its fractional parts, the real, the medio (half-real), and other similar denominations. In time those coins became more familiar to them than the old English coins that were always scarce. It was only natural, therefore, that when a national coinage was under consideration a dollar-size coin was the first choice.

Contracts, currency statutes, and prices in the colonies were usually quoted in English pounds or Spanish dollars. In 1767 Maryland took the lead and produced paper money that was denominated in dollars. Connecticut, Massachusetts, and Virginia soon passed laws making Spanish coins a legal tender. The first issue of Continental paper money May 10, 1775, offers further evidence that the dollar was to be our basic money unit, for it provided that the notes should be payable in "Spanish Milled Dollars or the value thereof in gold or silver."

The Assistant Financier of the Confederation, Gouverneur Morris, proposed a decimal coinage ratio designed to make conversion of various foreign currencies easier to compute in terms of a dollar-size unit. His plan was incorporated in a report presented by Robert Morris, Superintendent of Finance, to the Congress, January 15, 1782. Plans for a mint were advanced, and a uniform national currency to relieve the confused money conditions was outlined. Morris's unit, 1/1440 of a dollar, was calculated to agree without a fraction with all the different valuations of the Spanish Milled Dollar in the various States. Although a government mint was approved February 21, 1782, no immediate action was taken. During 1784 Thomas Jefferson, then a member of the House of Representatives, brought in a report concerning the plan, and expressed disagreement with Morris' complicated money unit. He advocated the simple dollar unit because he believed the dollar was already as familiar and convenient a unit of value as the British pound. He favored the decimal system and remarked that, "The most easy ratio of multiplication and division is that of ten. George Washington referred to it as 'a measure, which in my opinion, has become indispensably necessary."

The Grand Committee in May 1785 recommended a gold five-dollar piece; a dollar of silver with fractional coins, of the same metal, in denominations of half, quarter, tenth, and twentieth parts of a dollar; and copper pieces valued at one-hundredth and one two-hundredth of a dollar.

In 1783 Robert Morris submitted a series of pattern pieces in silver that were designed by Benjamin Dudley to carry out the decimal idea for United States money. These are known as the Nova Constellatio Patterns and consist of the "Mark" or 1,000 units, the "Quint" or 500 units, the "Bit" or 100 units, and a copper "five." The unit was to be a quarter grain of silver. This was not the first attempt at a dollar coin, for the Continental Currency piece of dollar size, dated 1776, had been struck in such metals as brass, pewter, and silver. The variety in silver possibly saw limited service as a dollar, although there is a theory that the Continental Congress considered circulating pewter pieces as an emergency token coinage.

Congress gave formal approval to the basic dollar unit and decimal coinage ratio in its resolution of August 8, 1786, but other more pressing matters delayed further action. Not until the Constitutional Convention of 1787 had placed the country on firm ground and the new nation had elected George Washington President, did the Congress again turn attention to the subject of currency, a mint, and a coinage system.

The Massachusetts cents and half cents struck in 1787 and 1788 were the first official coins to bear a stated value in terms of decimal parts of the dollar unit in this country. The cent represented a hundredth part of a Spanish dollar.

The first federally authorized coin was the Fugio Cent, sometimes called the Franklin cent, as he is believed to have supplied the design and composed the legends. This piece, similar in design to the Continental Currency dollar of 1776, was privately struck in 1787 by contract with the government.

Alexander Hamilton, then Secretary of the Treasury, reported his views on monetary matters January 21, 1791. He concurred in all essentials with the decimal subdivisions and multiples of the dollar contained in the earlier resolutions and urged the use of both gold and silver in our standard money.

Congress passed a resolution March 3, 1791, that a mint be established and authorized President Washington to engage artists and procure machinery for the making of coins. No immediate steps were taken, but when President Washington delivered his third annual address, he recommended immediate establishment of a mint.

On April 2, 1792, a bill was finally passed providing "that the money of account of the United States should be expressed in dollars or units, dismes or tenths, cents or hundredths, and milles or thousandths; a disme being the tenth part of a dollar, a cent the hundredth part of a dollar, a mille the thousandth part of a dollar..."

Denominations specified in the act were as follows:

	Value of	Grains Pure	Grains Standard
Gold Eagle	$10.00	247 - 4/8	270
Gold Half Eagle	5.00	123 - 6/8	135
Gold Quarter Eagle	2.50	61 - 7/8	67 - 4/8
Silver Dollar	1.00	371 - 4/16	416
Silver Half Dollar	.50	185 - 10/16	208
Silver Quarter Dollar	.25	92 - 13/16	104
Silver Disme (dime)	.10	37 - 2/16	41 - 3/5
Silver Half Disme	.05	18 - 9/16	20 - 4/5
Copper Cent	.01	11 pennyweights	
Copper Half Cent	.005	5 1/2 pennyweights	

The word "pure" meant unalloyed metal; "standard" meant, in the case of gold, 11/12 fine or 11 parts pure metal to one part alloy, which was mixed with the pure metal to improve the wearing qualities of the coins. The fineness for silver coins was 1485/1664 or approximately 892.43 thousandths, in contrast with the gold coins of 22 karats, or 916 2/3 thousandths fine.

The law also provided for free coinage of gold and silver coins at the fixed ratio of 15 to one, and a token coinage of copper cents and half cents. Under the free coinage provision no charge was to be made for converting gold or silver bullion into coins "weight for weight." At the depositor's option, however, he could demand an immediate exchange of coins for his bullion, for which privilege a deduction of one-half of one percent was to be imposed.

President Washington appointed David Rittenhouse, a well-known philosopher and scientist, as the first Director of the Mint. Construction began on a mint building nearly four months after the passage of the Act of April 2, 1792. The building was located on Seventh Street near Arch in Philadelphia.

The first coin struck by the government was the half disme. Fifteen hundred of these pieces were produced during the month of July 1792 before the mint was completed. Washington supplied some of his own silver in the form of bullion or tableware in the value of about one hundred dollars to make those first coins. A few dismes also were also struck at this time or a short while later. Silver and gold for coinage was to be supplied by the public, but copper for cents and half cents had to be provided by the government. This was accomplished by the Act of May 8, 1792 when the purchase of not over 150 tons was authorized. On September 11, 1792, six pounds of old copper were purchased, and probably used for the striking of patterns. Thereafter,planchets with upset rims for cents and half cents were purchased from Boulton of Birmingham, England from 1798 to 1838.

Several pattern coins were prepared in 1792 before regular mint operations commenced. Patterns are test or trial pieces intended to show the size, form and design of proposed coins. These included the silvercenter cent by Henry Voigt, a smaller piece than that of regular issue. The small plug of silver, worth about three-quarters of a cent, was evidently intended to bring the intrinsic value of the coin up to the value of one cent and permit production of a coin of more convenient size. Alexander Hamilton had mentioned a year before that the proposed "intrinsic value" cent would be too large, and suggested that the amount of copper could be reduced and a trace of silver added. The pattern cent with a silver center may have been designed to conform to this recommendation.

The cents by Robert Birch are equally interesting. These patterns are identified by their legends that read "liberty parent of science and industry" and "to be esteemed be useful." The quarter with an eagle on the reverse side by Joseph Wright belongs among the 1792 patterns devised before regular issues were struck.

The Bank of Maryland deposited the first silver, sending $80,715.731/2 in French coins to the mint July 18, 1794. Moses Brown, a Boston merchant, deposited the first gold in the form of ingots, February 12, 1795, amounting to $2,276.22, receiving silver coin in payment. The first coins transferred to the Treasurer consisted of 11,178 cents on March 1, 1793. The first return of coined silver was made on October 15, 1794, and the first gold coins, 744 half eagles, were delivered July 31, 1795. The early mint was constantly vigilant to see that the weight of these early coins was up to standard. Blank planchets were filed and adjusted prior to striking, and many of the coins made prior to 1836 show file marks and blemishes.

Regular Mint Issues

Cents and half-cents exclusively were coined during the year 1793, and by 1799 approximately $50,000 in these coins had been placed in circulation. This amount proved insufficient for the requirements of commerce, and small denomination coins of the states and of foreign countries continued in use well into the nineteenth century.

One of the most serious problems confronting the commercial interests prior to 1857 was the failure of the government to provide a sufficient volume of circulating coins. The fault, contrary to popular opinion at the time, did not lie with any lack of effort on the part of the mint. Other circumstances tended to interfere with the expected steady flow of new coinage into the channels of trade.

Free circulation of United States gold and silver coins was greatly hindered by speculators. For example, worn Spanish dollars of reduced weight and value were easily exchanged for U. S. silver dollars, which meant the export of most of the new dollars as fast as they were minted, and a complete loss to American trade channels.

Gold coins failed to circulate for similar reasons. The ratio of 15 to 1 between gold and silver was close to the world ratio when Alexander Hamilton recommended it in 1791, but by 1799 the ratio in European commercial centers had reached 153/4 to 1. At this rate the undervalued gold coins tended to flow out of the country, or were melted for bullion. After 1800, therefore, United States gold coins were rarely seen in general circulation. As no remedy could be found, coinage of the gold eagle and the silver dollar was suspended by President Jefferson in 1804 and 1806, respectively. It is generally conceded that the silver dollar was discontinued in 1804, although the last coins minted for the period were dated 1803.

Lacking gold coins and silver dollars, the half dollar became the desirable coin for large transactions, bank reserves, and foreign payments. Until 1830, in fact, half dollars circulated very little as they were mainly transferred from bank to bank. This will account for the relatively good supply of half dollars of this period that is still available to collectors in better than average condition. A senate committee of 1830 reported that United States silver coins were considered so much bullion and were accordingly "lost to the community as coins."

There was only a negligible coinage of quarters, dimes, and half dimes from 1794 to 1834. It has been estimated that there was less than one piece for each person in the country in the year 1830. This period has been described as one of nondescript currency made up of banknotes, underweight foreign gold coins, foreign silver coins of many varieties, and domestic fractional silver coins. Paper money of that time was equally distressing. Privately issued bank notes often had no backing and were apt to be worthless at the time of redemption. In this period before national paper money commenced in 1861, notes of the so-called "wildcat banks" flooded the country and were much more common than silver coins.

On June 28, 1834, a new law was passed reducing the weight of standard gold, which had the effect of placing our money on a gold standard. Trade and finance were greatly benefited by this act, which also proved a boon to the gold mines of Georgia and North Carolina. Branch mints in Dahlonega, Georgia, and

Charlotte, North Carolina, were established in 1838 to handle the newly mined gold at the source. The Templeton Reid and Bechtler issues of private gold coins were struck in this area.

The law of January 18, 1837, completely revised and standardized the mint and coinage laws. Legal standards, mint charges, legal tender, mint procedure, tolerance in coin weights, accounting methods, a bullion fund, standardization of gold and silver coins to 900 thousandths fine, and other desirable regulations were covered by the new legislation. Results of importance to the collector were the changes in type for the various coin denominations and the resumption of coinage of the eagle in 1838 and larger quantities of silver dollars in 1840.

Prior to Andrew Jackson's election as President in 1829, the Second Bank of the United States had complete control over the nation's currency. In 1832 Jackson vetoed a bill rechartering the bank, and transferred government deposits to state banks. The action took away some stability from an already shaky economy and eventually led to a national financial collapse. By 1834 the country was so deprived of circulating coinage that merchants resorted to making their own "hard times tokens" to facilitate trade. The few available government coins were hoarded or traded at a premium for the unreliable private paper money.

The California gold discovery in 1848 was responsible for an interesting series of private, state, and territorial gold issues in the Western states, culminating in the establishment of a branch mint at San Francisco in 1854.

Two new regular gold issues were adopted in 1849. In that year the double eagle and gold dollar joined our American family of coins. The California gold fields greatly influenced the world gold market, making the exportation of silver profitable. For example, the silver in two half dollars was worth $1.03 1/2 in gold. The newly introduced gold dollars soon took over the burden and hastened the disappearance of silver coins from trade channels. This was the situation when the new three-cent postage rate brought about the bill authorized by Congress March 3, 1851, calling for the coinage of a silver three-cent piece in 1851. This was our country's first subsidiary coin, for its value was intrinsically 86% of its face value, as an expedient designed to prevent its withdrawal from circulation.

The three-dollar gold piece was authorized by the act of February 21, 1853. It was never a popular or necessary coin because of the existing $2.50 and $5.00 coins; it nevertheless was issued regularly from 1854 until 1889.

On February 21, 1853, fractional silver coins were made subsidiary by reducing the weights of all silver pieces, excepting the dollar. As the coins were now worth less than their face value, free coinage of silver was prohibited, and the mint was authorized to purchase its silver requirements on its own account using the bullion fund of the mint, and, according to law, "the profit of said coinage shall be...transferred to the account of the treasury of the United States."

To identify the new lightweight pieces, arrows were placed at the date on all silver coins except three-cent pieces, where arrows were added to the reverse, and dollars, which were not marked in any way. On the quarters and half dollars of 1853 rays were added on the reverse side to denote the change of weight. In 1854 the rays were removed, and in 1856 the arrows disappeared from all but the silver three-cent coins. Production of silver coins in large quantities during this period greatly relieved the demands on gold dollars and three-cent pieces. Consequently, for the first time in our nation's history there was a sufficient supply of fractional coins in general circulation to facilitate commerce.

The Coinage Act of February 21, 1857 was designed primarily to reform the copper coinage. No matter how interesting and valuable the large cents and half cents may have become in the eyes of the modern collector, they were unpopular with the public because of their size, and cost the mint too much to produce.

The new law abolished the half-cent piece, and reduced the size and changed the design of the cent. The new Flying Eagle cent contained 88% copper and 12% nickel. Several hundred experimental cents were stamped from dies bearing the date 1856 although no authority for the issue existed before 1857. Other important effects of the law were the retirement of the Spanish silver coins from circulation, and dispersal of the new cents in such excessive quantities as to create a nuisance to business houses, particularly in the eastern cities. The Indian head device replaced the Flying Eagle in 1859, and in 1864 the weight of the cent was further reduced and its composition changed to a proportion of 95% copper and 5% tin and zinc. This bronze composition was the standard for our cent except for the years 1943, and 1944 to 1946. In 1962 the alloy was changed to 95% copper and 5% zinc. In 1982 the composition was changed to 97.5% zinc and 2.5% copper.

The abundance of copper coins turned to scarcity following the outbreak of the Civil War. Anticipation of a scarcity of hard money, and depreciation of the paper money was sufficient to induce hoarding. The large volume of greenbacks in circulation caused a premium on gold, and subsidiary silver, as a result of the sudden depreciation, quickly vanished from circulation. As an expediency, some people made use of postage stamps for small change. Merchants, banks and individuals produced a wide variety of small denomination paper scrip and promissory notes to meet their needs. In 1862 the government produced its first issue of "Postage currency" and subsequent fractional notes. In 1863 a great number of privately issued copper tokens appeared to help fill the vacuum. As with the tokens of 1837, they were of two general classes, tradesmen's tokens and imitations of official cents. Many of the latter were political or patriotic in character and carried slogans typical of the times. They not only served as a medium of exchange, but also often advertised a merchant or product, and were usually produced at a profit.

The Coinage Act of April 22, 1864, which affected changes in the cent, provided also for the new bronze two-cent piece. The Act, moreover, provided legal tender status for these two coins up to ten times their value. The two-cent piece was the first coin to bear the motto "In God We Trust". The new coin was at first readily accepted by the public, but proved an unnecessary denomination because of the competing three-cent coins, and production was halted after only nine years. Treasury Secretary Salmon P. Chase had issued a great many currency notes of three-cent denomination early in 1865. The nickel interests seized upon this circumstance to fight for a new three-cent coin for redemption of the paper money. A law was quickly passed and signed by President Abraham Lincoln on March 3, 1865, providing for a three-cent coin of 75-25 copper-nickel composition. Our country then possessed two types of three-cent pieces, although neither was seriously needed The nickel three-cent piece was struck continuously until 1889; the three-cent silver until 1873.

The new copper-nickel alloy ratio was selected for the five-cent coin, adopted May 16, 1866, to be thereafter known as a "nickel." Again, the people had a coin denomination available to them in two forms. The silver half dime, like the three-cent piece, was retired from service in 1873 as a conservative measure.

The great influx of silver from the Comstock Load deposit in Nevada increased the nation's supply of silver coins and taxed the Philadelphia Mint's capacity for production. Pressure from silver mine interests in Nevada influenced the opening of a special mint in Carson City to assay and mint silver locally rather than having it shipped to Philadelphia. Production was inefficient, costly and slow. By 1893 the load was virtually depleted and minting activities ceased.

The Law of March 3, 1871, was a redemption measure and was passed to provide a means for the disposal to the United States Treasury of millions of minor coins, which had accumulated in the hands of postmasters, merchants, and others. Small-denomination coins, because of this new law, were placed on an equal footing with silver and could be redeemed when presented in lots of twenty dollars.

There was a general revision of the coinage laws in 1873. Several years of study and debate preceded the final enactment. The legislative history of the bill occupies hundreds of pages of the Congressional Globe, and the result was considered by many a clumsy attempt and a failure. The law has sometimes been referred to as the "Crime of '73." One consequence of the bill, which achieved final enactment February 12, 1873, was the elimination of the silver dollar. In its stead, the Trade dollar of greater weight was provided for use in commerce with the Orient in competition with the Mexican dollar. The legal tender provision, which gave the Trade dollar currency within our borders, was repealed the following year to avoid profiteering from buying them overseas at a reduced rate. The Trade dollar was thus the only United States coin ever demonetized even for a short time. Through an oversight, it was reinstated under the Coinage Act of 1965.

It may be a surprise to some collectors to learn that silver dollars had not circulated to any great extent in the United States after 1803. The coin had been turned out steadily since 1840, but for various reasons such as exportation, melting, and holding in bank vaults, the dollar was virtually an unknown coin. The Law of 1873 in effect demonetized silver and committed our country to gold as a single standard. The silver mining interests came to realize what had occurred a little later, and the ensuing quarter century of political and monetary history was filled with their voluble protests. There was a constant bitter struggle for the return to bimetallism.

From an economic point of view the inadequate supply of gold was responsible for a gradual decline in prices worldwide. This brought about a gradual business depression in our country, particularly in the South and Middle West. Private silver interests influenced great sections of the West for bimetallism as a remedy for the failing price level. Authorities have concluded that a worldwide adoption of bimetallism would have improved economic conditions, but the United States alone proceeding to place its money on a double standard at the old 16 to 1 ratio would have led only to a worse situation.

Of particular importance to collectors, were those features of the Law of 1873 that affected the status and physical properties of the individual coins. The weight of the half-dollar, quarter, and dime, was slightly changed and arrows were placed at the date for the ensuing two years to indicate the difference in weight. Silver three-cent pieces, half-dimes, and two-cent pieces were abolished by the act, and the manufacture of minor coins was restricted to the Mint at Philadelphia.

The short-lived twenty-cent piece was authorized March 3, 1875. It was created for the Western states where the Spanish "bit" had become equivalent to a U. S. dime. The five-cent piece did not circulate there, so when a quarter was offered for a "bit" purchase, only a dime change was returned. The so-called "double dime" was frequently confused with the quarter-dollar and was only issued for circulation in 1875 and 1876.

On February 28, 1878, Congress passed the Bland-Allison Act that restored legal-tender character to silver money and required the treasury to purchase at market price $2,000,000 to $4,000,000 worth of silver each month and to coin it into silver dollars at a ratio to gold of 16 to 1. Proponents of "free silver" contended that with more money in circulation, workers would receive higher wages. Business leaders argued for the gold standard and against free silver because they believed that inflation would cheapen the value of money. The Act was called by all "a wretched compromise."

The North and East so disliked the silver dollars that they did not actively circulate there and eventually found their way back to the Treasury, mostly through tax payments. Treasury Secretary Manning transferred ownership to the people and removed them from Treasury holdings by the simple expedient of issuing silver certificates in small bills to effect a wide circulation.

The Bland-Allison Act was repealed in 1890 and the Sherman Act took its place. Under this new law 4,500,000 ounces of silver per month could be paid for with Treasury Notes that were to be legal tender, and redeemable in gold or silver dollars coined from the bullion purchased. Important in this case was the fact that the notes were constantly being redeemed for gold that was mainly exported. The measure was actually a government subsidy for a few influential silver miners and as such it was marked for failure, and was hastily repealed. The Bland-Allison Act and the Sherman Act added a total of 570 million silver dollars to our monetary stocks.

The "Gold Standard Act" of 1900 again gave our country a single standard, but reaffirmed the fiction that the silver dollar was a standard coin. It still enjoyed unlimited legal tender, but was as much a subsidiary coin, practically speaking, as the dime, for its value in terms of standard gold, even before the gold surrender executive order, was far below its face value.

The lapse in coinage after 1904 and until 1921 was due to lack of demand. Legislation authorizing further metal supplies for silver dollars was not forthcoming until 1918 when the Pittman Act provided silver for more dollars.

Before the first World War the value of gold was equal to the value of gold coined into money. In order to encourage a steady flow of gold to the mints, the government (with the exception of the period 1853-1873) had adopted a policy of gratuitous coinage. The cost of converting gold into coin had generally been considered an expense chargeable to the government.

In practice the mint made fine bars for commercial use or mint bars for coinage at its discretion. The bars in later years were stored in vaults and gold or silver certificates issued in place of the coins.

On April 5, 1933 President Roosevelt issued an order prohibiting banks from paying out gold and gold certificates without permission, and gold currency was thus kept for reserve purposes. The law was intended to stabilize the value of gold. In effect, it removed all gold from circulation and prevented it from being hoarded or even saved by collectors. Gold imports and newly mined domestic gold could be sold only to the government. Gold bullion and coins may now be collected and saved by anyone as all restrictions were removed in 1975.

Under the Coinage Act of 1965, the composition of dimes, quarters and half dollars was changed to eliminate or reduce the silver content of these coins because the price of silver had risen to above their face value. The replacement "clad" dimes and quarters were composed of an outer layer of copper-nickel (75% copper and 25% nickel) bonded to an inner core of pure copper. Beginning in 1971 the half dollar and dollar composition was changed to that of the dime and quarter. All silver clad coins have an outer layer of 80% silver bonded to an inner core of 21% silver, with a total content of 40% silver.

By the Law of September 26, 1890, changes in designs of United States coins cannot be made more often than once every twenty-five years without Congressional approval. Since that date, there have been design changes in all denominations and there have been many gold and silver commemorative issues. In 1999, a ten-year program was started to honor each of the individual States by using special designs on the reverse of the quarter. These factors, and a growing awareness of the value and historical importance of older coins, are largely responsible for the ever-increasing interest in coin collecting.

QUANTITIES OF COINS STRUCK

Collectors are cautioned that mint reports are not always reliable for estimating the rarity of coins. In the early years of the mint, dies of previous years were often used until they became worn or broken.

It should also be emphasized that quantities reported, particularly for gold and silver, cover the number of coins struck and have no reference to the quantity reaching actual circulation. Many issues were deposited in the treasury as backing for paper currency and were later melted.

The rarity of gold pieces struck before 1834, particularly half eagles, can be traced to the fact that the gold content was reduced in 1834, making previous issues greater in value than face, causing melting and re-minting.

The quantities reported by the mint of three dollar gold pieces from 1873 to 1877 and half cents from 1832 to 1836 are subject to doubt.

Coinage figures shown for 1964 through 1966 are for coins bearing those dates. Some of them were struck in more than one year and at various mints, both with and without mintmarks. In recent years, mintage figures reported by the Mint have been revised several times and remain uncertain as to precise amounts.

Mint quantities are shown adjacent to each date throughout the book. Figures shown in italic are estimates based on the most accurate information available. PROOF TOTALS ARE SHOWN IN PARENTHESES.

ABBREVIATIONS USED IN THIS BOOK:

Word or phrase	Abbreviation	Word or phrase	Abbreviation
Open 3	Op 3	New Reverse	New
Closed 3	Cl 3	with arrows	/arrows
Large Date	LgDt	Normal	Nml
Small Date	SmDt	Square	Sq
Doubled Die Obverse	DblDieObv	Large Stars	LgS
S over D	S/D	Large Letters	LgL
D over S	D/S	Medium Letters	MedL
over horizontal D	/HozD	Small Letters	SmL
Doubled eye	DblEye	Counterstamped	CTSP
3 over 2	3/2	Long Worm	Lworm
Normal Date	NmlDt	Small Letter Reverse	SmLetRev
(any overs)	/word or number	50c over UNI	50c/UNI
No drapery	NoDrap	Close Date	ClDt
Partial drapery	PartDrap	Wide Date	WdDt
Proof	Pf	Small head	SmHd
Tail feathers	Feathers	Large head	LgHd
Old Reverse	Old		

A star (★) throughout the colonial section indicates that struck copies exist.

Copies of certain American issues were made after 1850 to provide facsimiles of rarer issues which would otherwise be unobtainable. A star has been placed adjacent to those pieces of which deceptive copies exist. Many crude imitations have also been made in recent years, as well as forgeries intended to deceive collectors. THE SPECIMENS ILLUSTRATED ARE GENUINE.

I. THE BRITISH COLONIES IN AMERICA
SOMMER ISLANDS (Bermuda)

This coinage, the first struck for the English colonies in America, was issued about 1616. The coins were known as "Hogge Money" or "Hoggies."

The pieces were made of copper lightly silvered, in four denominations: shilling, sixpence, threepence and twopence, indicated by Roman numerals. The hog is the main device and appears on the obverse side of each. SOMMER ISLANDS is inscribed within beaded circles. The reverse shows a full-rigged galleon with the flag of St. George on each of four masts.

The islands were named for Sir George Sommers who was shipwrecked there in 1609 while enroute to the Virginia Plantations. Shakespeare's *The Tempest* was possibly based on this incident.

The Bermuda Islands, as they are known today, were named for Juan Bermudez who is believed to have stopped there in 1515. A few hogs which he carried for delivery to the West Indies were left behind. When Sommers and his party arrived, the islands were overrun with the animals which served as a welcome source of food for the expedition.

Twopence   Threepence

Sixpence   Large Portholes   Small Portholes

Shilling ★   Small Sail   Large Sail

	G	VG	F	VF	EF
Twopence,LgS between legs	$3,000.	$4,250.	$8,500.	$16,000.	$25,000.
Twopence, SmS between legs	3,000.	4,250.	8,500.	16,000.	25,000.
Threepence *(Very Rare)*	—	—	50,000.	75,000.	—
Sixpence, Sm portholes	2,500.	4,000.	7,000.	17,000.	27,500.
Sixpence, Lg portholes	2,500.	4,000.	7,000.	17,000.	27,500.
Shilling, Sm sail	3,200.	5,000.	12,000.	27,500.	50,000.
Shilling, Lg sail	3,500.	6,000.	13,000.	30,000.	55,000.

MASSACHUSETTS
"NEW ENGLAND" COINAGE (1652)

The earliest authorized medium of exchange in the New England settlements was wampum. The General Court of Massachusetts in 1637 ordered "that wampamege should passe at 6 a penny for any sume under 12 d." Wampum consisted of shells of various colors ground to the size of a grain of corn. A hole was drilled through each piece so it could be strung on leather thongs for convenience and adornment.

Corn, pelts, and bullets were frequently used in lieu of coins, which were rarely available. Silver and gold coins brought over from England, Holland and other countries tended to flow back across the Atlantic to purchase needed supplies. The colonists thus left to their own resources dealt with the friendly Native Americans in kind. In 1661 the law making wampum legal tender was repealed.

Agitation for a standard coinage reached its height in 1651. England, recovering from a civil war between the Puritans and Royalists, ignored the colonists, who took matters into their own hands in 1652.

The General Court in 1652 ordered the first metallic currency to be struck in the English Americas (the Spaniards had established a mint in Mexico City in 1535), the New England silver threepence, sixpence, and shilling. Silver bullion was procured principally from the West Indies. The mint was located in Boston, Massachusetts, and John Hull was appointed mintmaster; his assistant was Robert Sanderson (or Saunderson). At first, Hull received one shilling threepence for every twenty shillings coined as his compensation. This fee was adjusted several times during his term as mintmaster.

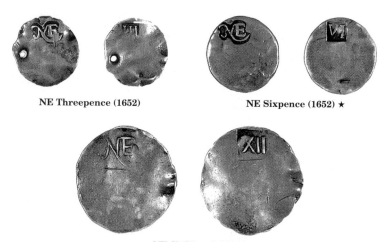

NE Threepence (1652)

NE Sixpence (1652) ★

NE Shilling (1652) ★

Note: Early American coins are rare in conditions better than those listed and are consequently valued much higher.

	G	VG	F	VF
NE Threepence (*Unique*)				—
NE Sixpence *(8 known)*	$15,000.	$27,500.	$45,000.	$110,000.
NE Shilling	17,500.	30,000.	50,000.	125,000.

WILLOW TREE COINAGE (1653-1660)

The simplicity of the design on the N.E. coins invited counterfeiting and clipping of the edges. Therefore, they were soon replaced by the Willow, Oak and Pine Tree series. The Willow Tree coins were struck from 1653 to 1660, the Oak Trees 1660 to 1667, and the Pine Trees 1667 to 1682. All of them (with the exception of the Oak Tree twopence) bore the date 1652, which gives them the appearance of having been struck after the English civil war, when Cromwell was in power.

The coinage was abandoned in 1682; a proposal to renew coinage in 1686 was rejected by the General Court.

Early American coins were produced from handmade dies which are often individually distinctive. The great number of die varieties which can be found and identified are of interest to collectors who value each according to individual rarity. Values shown for type coins in this catalog are for the most common die variety.

Threepence   **Sixpence**

Shilling

	FA	G	VG	F	VF
Willow Tree Threepence 1652 *(3 known)*		—	—	—	—
Willow Tree Sixpence 1652 *(14 known)*	4,000.	10,000.	20,000.	40,000.	85,000.
Willow Tree Shilling 1652	5,000.	12,500.	20,000.	45,000.	100,000.

OAK TREE COINAGE (1660-1667)

Twopence ★   **Threepence**

	G	VG	F	VF	EF	AU
Oak Tree Twopence 1662, Sm 2	$450.	$825.	$1,700.	$3,300.	$5,800.	$8,000.
Oak Tree Twopence 1662, Lg 2	450.	825.	1,700.	3,300.	5,800.	8,000.
Oak Tree Threepence 1652, no IN on obv	500.	875.	2,100.	4,750.	7,000.	9,000.
Oak Tree Threepence 1652, IN on obv	500.	900.	2,200.	5,000.	8,500.	12,000.

Sixpence   Shilling ★

	G	VG	F	VF	EF	AU
Oak Tree Sixpence 1652, IN on rev	$500.	$900.	$2,500.	$5,500.	$9,500.	$13,500.
Oak Tree Sixpence 1652, IN on obv................	500.	900.	2,400.	5,000.	9,000.	13,000.
Oak Tree Shilling 1652, IN at left	550.	1,000.	2,700.	5,300.	8,500.	11,500.
Oak Tree Shilling 1652, IN at bottom..............	550.	1,000.	2,400.	4,750.	8,250.	11,000.
Oak Tree Shilling 1652, ANDO	750.	1,500.	3,500.	7,000.	11,000.	15,000.
Oak Tree Shilling 1652, Spiny tree	550.	1,000.	2,300.	4,500.	8,000.	10,500.

PINE TREE COINAGE (1667-1682)

The first Pine Tree coins were minted on the same size planchets as the Oak Tree pieces. Subsequent issues of the shilling were narrower and thicker to conform to the size of English coins.

Threepence ★   Sixpence ★

Shilling, Large Planchet (1667-1674) ★   Shilling, Small Planchet (1675-1682)

	G	VG	F	VF	EF	AU
Pine Tree Threepence 1652, pellets at trunk	$350.	$625.	$1,250.	$2,500.	$5,200.	$7,500.
Pine Tree Threepence 1652, w/o pellets	350.	625.	1,250.	2,500.	5,200.	7,500.
Pine Tree Sixpence 1652, pellets at trunk	400.	750.	1,500.	3,000.	5,750.	7,800.
Pine Tree Sixpence 1652, w/o pellets	400.	775.	1,600.	3,200.	6,000.	8,000.
Pine Tree Shillings 1652—Large Planchet (27-31mm diameter)						
1652 Shilling, pellets at trunk	500.	850.	1,800.	3,750.	6,750.	9,500.
1652 Shilling, w/o pellets at trunk	500.	850.	1,800.	3,750.	6,750.	9,500.
1652 Shilling, no H in MASATUSETS	600.	1,300.	2,700.	4,750.	10,000.	13,500.
1652 Shilling, rev. N in legend	625.	1,400.	2,800.	4,900.	10,500.	14,000.
1652 Shilling monogrammed NE in legend	550.	1,200.	1,900.	4,200.	7,250.	10,000.
Pine Tree Shillings 1652—Small Planchet (22-26mm diameter)						
1652 Shilling, Sm planchet	400.	750.	1,600.	3,200.	6,250.	9,000.

MARYLAND

Cecil Calvert, the second Lord Baltimore, inherited from his father nearly absolute control over Maryland. Cecil believed he had the right to coin money for the colony and in 1659 he ordered shillings, sixpences and groats (four-penny pieces) from the Royal Mint in London and shipped samples to his brother Philip in Maryland, who was then his secretary for the colony. Cecil's right to strike coins was challenged but upheld by Cromwell's government. The whole issue was small, and while his coins circulated in Maryland at first, by 1700 they had largely disappeared.

Calvert's coins bear his portrait on the obverse, with a Latin legend calling him "Lord of Mary's Land." The reverses bear his family coat of arms and the denomination in Roman numerals. There are several die varieties of each. Many of these coins are found holed and repaired. The copper penny or denarium is the rarest denomination, with only five known specimens.

Penny (denarium) ★

Fourpence (groat)

Sixpence

Lord Baltimore Shilling

	G	VG	F	VF	EF	AU
Penny (copper) *(Ex. Rare)*	—	—	—	—	—	—
Fourpence	$1,300.	$2,700.	$5,500.	$11,000.	$16,000.	$25,000.
Sixpence	1,250.	2,000.	4,000.	6,250.	10,500.	15,000.
Shilling	1,600.	2,750.	5,700.	11,500.	17,000.	20,000.

NEW JERSEY
ST. PATRICK OR MARK NEWBY COINAGE

Mark Newby, who came to America from Dublin, Ireland, in November 1681, brought copper pieces believed by numismatists to have been struck in Dublin c. 1663-1672. These are called St. Patrick coppers.

The coinage was made legal tender by the General Assembly of New Jersey in May, 1682. The legislature did not specify which size piece could circulate, only that the coin was to be worth a halfpenny in trade. Most numismatists believe the larger size coin was intended. However, as many more farthing size pieces are known than halfpennies, some believe that the smaller size piece was meant. Copper coins often circulated in the colonies at twice what they would have been worth in England.

The obverses show a crowned king kneeling playing a harp. The legend FLOREAT REX (May the King prosper) is separated by a crown. The reverse side of the halfpence shows St. Patrick with a crozier in his left hand and a trefoil in his right, surrounded by people. At his left is a shield. The legend is ECCE GREX (Behold the flock). The farthing reverse shows St. Patrick driving away reptiles and serpents, as he holds a Metropolitan cross in his left hand. The legend reads QUIESCAT PLEBS (May the people be at ease).

The large size piece, called a halfpenny, bears the arms of the City of Dublin on the shield on the reverse; the smaller size piece, called a farthing, does not. All of these pieces have a reeded edge.

The decorative brass insert found on the coinage, usually over the crown on the obverse, was put there to make counterfeiting more difficult. On some pieces this decoration has been removed or does not show. Numerous die variations exist.

St. Patrick "Farthing"

St. Patrick "Halfpenny"

	G	VG	F	VF	EF	AU
St. Patrick "Farthing"	$50.	$140.	$450.	$1,500.	$3,000.	$5,500.
Similar, halo around saint's head	200.	550.	1,500.	2,750.	—	—
Similar, no C in QUIESCAT	250.	700.	1,750.	3,500.	—	—
St. Patrick "Farthing" - Silver	1,000.	1,750.	3,000.	4,500.	6,500.	8,500.
St. Patrick "Farthing" - Gold				(Unique)		
St. Patrick "Halfpenny"	180.	450.	1,000.	2,250.	5,000.	—

II. COINAGE AUTHORIZED BY ROYAL PATENT
AMERICAN PLANTATIONS TOKEN

These tokens struck in nearly pure tin were the first authorized coinage for the British colonies in America. They were made under a franchise granted in 1688 to Richard Holt. Bright, unblemished specimens are more valuable. Restrikes were made about 1828 from original dies.

	G	F	EF	AU	UNC
(1688) James II Plantation Token Farthing,					
1/24 PART REAL - Tin	$200.	$400.	$1,100.	$1,400.	$3,000.
1/24 PART REAL - Tin ET. HB. REX	200.	475.	1,200.	1,750.	3,600.
1/24 PART REAL - Tin, Sidewise 4 in 24 .	300.	900.	2,750.	4,300.	—
1/24 PART REAL - Tin, Arms transposed	350.	1,100.	4,000.	—	—
1/24 PART REAL - Restrike	100.	250.	600.	850.	1,500.

William Wood, an Englishman, obtained a patent from George I to make tokens for Ireland and the American Colonies.

The first pieces struck were undated; others bear the dates 1722, 1723, 1724 and 1733. The Rosa Americana pieces were issued in three denominations, halfpenny, penny and twopence, and were intended for America. This type had a full-blown rose on the reverse with the words ROSA AMERICANA UTILE DULCI (American Rose — useful and pleasant).

The obverse, common to both Rosa Americana and Hibernia pieces, shows the head of George I and the legend GEORGIUS D:G: MAG: BRI: FRA: ET. HIB: REX. (George, by the Grace of God, King of Great Britain, France and Ireland) or abbreviations thereof. Rosa Americana tokens, however, were rejected by the American colonists. The coins are made of a brass composition of 75% copper, 24.7% zinc and .3% silver, sometimes mistakenly referred to as Bath metal.

	VG	F	VF	EF	AU	UNC
Twopence (no date) motto in ribbon (illustrated)	$135.	$300.	$600.	$1,000.	$2,200.	$3,800.
Twopence (no date) motto without ribbon (3 known)	—	—	—			

	VG	F	VF	EF	AU	UNC
1722 Halfpenny VTILE DVLCI	.800.	2,200.	3,400.	—	—	
1722 Halfpenny D.G.REX ROSA AMERI. UTILE DULCI	.135.	240.	475.	950.	1,650.	3,200.
1722 Halfpenny DEI GRATIA REX UTILE DULCI	.135.	240.	450.	850.	1,600.	3,000.

	VG	F	VF	EF	AU	UNC
1722 Penny GEORGIVS				—	—	
1722 Penny VTILE DVLCI	135.	240.	450.	900.	2,000.	3,750.
1722 Penny UTILE DULCI	135.	240.	385.	850.	1,550.	3,000.

	VG	F	VF	EF	AU	UNC
1722 Twopence, period after REX	$135.	$265.	$500.	$1,000.	$1,950.	$3,600.
1722 Twopence, no period after REX	135.	265.	500.	1,000.	1,950.	3,600.

1723 Halfpenny, uncrowned rose	800.	1,400.	2,800.	4,000.	—	—
1723 Halfpenny	100.	140.	350.	800.	1,650.	3,000.

1723 Penny	95.	135.	300.	700.	1,250.	2,750.
1723 Twopence (illustrated)	135.	265.	450.	1,000.	1,750.	3,250.

1724, 4/3 Penny (Pattern) DEI GRATIA				6,000.	9,000.	—
1724, 4/3 Penny (Pattern) D GRATIA				7,000.	12,500.	—
1724 Penny (undated) ROSA: SINE: SPINA.*(3 known)*				9,000.	14,500.	—

ROSA AMERICANA

	EF	UNC
1724 Twopence (Pattern)	$11,000.	—

The 1733 twopence is a pattern piece and bears the bust of George II facing to the left. It was issued by the successors to the coinage patent, as William Wood had died in 1730.

	EF	UNC
1733 Twopence (Pattern) Pf	24,000.	—

WOOD'S HIBERNIA COINAGE

The type intended for Ireland had a seated figure with a harp on the reverse side and the word HIBERNIA. Denominations struck were halfpenny and farthing with dates 1722, 1723 and 1724. Hibernia coins were unpopular in Ireland, so many of them were sent to the American colonies.

| First Type | Second Type | 1723 over 22 |

	VG	F	VF	EF	AU	UNC
1722 Farthing, D: G: REX	$200.	$400.	$800.	$1,500.	$2,000.	$3,200.
1722 Halfpenny, D: G: REX, rocks at right (Pattern)	1,800.	4,000.				
1722 Halfpenny, first type, harp at left	100.	150.	300.	600.	850.	1,300.
1722 Halfpenny, second type, harp at right	65.	100.	200.	375.	500.	900.
1722 Halfpenny, second type, DEII (blunder)	125.	250.	500.	900.	1,200.	1,750.
1723 Farthing - D:G:REX	100.	135.	225.	500.	650.	900.
1723 Farthing - DEI. GRATIA. REX	55.	75.	135.	275.	400.	700.
1723 Farthing - Silver pattern	1,100.	1,600.	2,750.	4,000.	5,000.	6,500.

1724 Hibernia Farthing **1723 Hibernia Halfpenny**

	VG	F	VF	EF	AU	UNC
1723 over 22 Halfpenny	$70.	$125.	$300.	$600.	$900.	$1,400.
1723 Halfpenny	35.	65.	115.	275.	400.	700.
1723 Halfpenny - Silver pattern	—	—	—	—	—	—
1724 Farthing	90.	190.	350.	750.	1,000.	1,600.
1724 Halfpenny	70.	120.	275.	650.	900.	1,500.
1724 Halfpenny, DEI above head	115.	230.	650.	1,000.	1,250.	1,800.

VIRGINIA HALFPENNY

In 1773 coinage of a copper halfpenny was authorized for Virginia by the Crown. The pattern in Proof struck on a large planchet with wide milled border is often referred to as a penny.

The silver piece dated 1774 is referred to as a shilling, but may have been a pattern or trial for a halfpenny or a guinea.

Red uncirculated pieces without spots are worth considerably more.

	VG	F	VF	EF	AU	UNC
1773 Halfpenny, period after GEORGIVS	$40.	$95.	$180.	$325.	$500.	$900.
1773 Halfpenny, no period after GEORGIVS	.50.	100.	200.	350.	550.	1,100.

	Proof
1773 "Penny"	$10,000.

Proof
1774 "Shilling" *(6 known)* . . . . $24,000.

III. EARLY AMERICAN TOKENS

Struck in America or England for use
by American Merchants

LONDON ELEPHANT TOKENS

The London Elephant tokens were struck circa 1672-1694. Although undated, two examples are known struck over 1672 British halfpennies. Most are struck in copper, but one is made of brass. The legend on this piece, GOD PRESERVE LONDON, is probably just a general plea for divine aid and not a specific reference to the outbreak of plague in 1665 or the great fire of 1666.

These pieces were not struck for the colonies, and probably did not circulate widely in America, although a few may have been carried here by colonists. They are associated with the 1694 Carolina and New England Elephant tokens, through a shared obverse die.

	VG	F	VF	EF	AU	UNC
(1694) Halfpenny, GOD PRESERVE LONDON .... (Thick planchet)	$225.	$425.	$750.	$1,400.	$2,000.	$3,000.
(1694) Halfpenny, GOD PRESERVE LONDON .... (Thin planchet)	325.	650.	1,450.	2,700.	3,800.	6,000.
(1694) Halfpenny, GOD PRESERVE LONDON .... (Diagonals in center of shield)	350.	700.	1,800.	3,200.	4,200.	6,800.
(1694) Halfpenny, similar. .... Variety -Sword in second quarter of shield	—	—	8,000.	—	—	—
(1694) Halfpenny LON DON	600.	1,600.	2,500.	4,200.	7,400.	10,500.

CAROLINA AND NEW ENGLAND ELEPHANT TOKENS

Although no law is known authorizing coinage for Carolina, two very interesting pieces known as Elephant Tokens were made with the date 1694. These copper tokens were of halfpenny denomination. The reverse reads GOD PRESERVE CAROLINA AND THE LORDS PROPRIETERS 1694.

The second and more common variety has the last word spelled PRO-PRIETORS. The correction was made on the original die, for the E shows plainly beneath the O. The elephant's tusks nearly touch the milling on the second variety.

CAROLINA ELEPHANT TOKENS

The Carolina pieces were probably struck in England and perhaps intended only as tokens, or possibly as advertising to heighten interest in the Carolina Plantation.

Like the Carolina Tokens, the New England Elephant Tokens were believed to have been struck in England as a promotional piece to increase interest in the American colonies.

	VG	F	VF	EF
1694 PROPRIETERS	$4,000.	$5,500.	$9,500.	$16,500.
1694 PROPRIETERS, O OVER E	3,500.	4,800.	8,000.	13,500.

NEW ENGLAND ELEPHANT TOKEN

	VG	F	VF	EF
1694 NEW ENGLAND	$18,000.	$25,000.	$38,000.	$50,000.

THE NEW YORKE IN AMERICA TOKEN

This is a farthing or halfpenny token intended for New York, issued by Francis Lovelace, who was governor from 1668 until 1673. The token uses the older spelling with a final "e", which predominated before 1710. The obverse shows Cupid pursuing the butterfly-winged Psyche, a rebus on the name Lovelace. The reverse shows an eagle, displayed, on a staff in fesse, raguly, which is identical to the crest of the Lovelace arms. In weight, fabric and die axis the tokens are similar to the 1670 farthing tokens of Bristol, England, where they may have been struck. There is no evidence that any of these pieces ever circulated in America.

	VG	F	VF
Brass (undated)	$4,500.	$9,500	$15,000.
Pewter (undated)	5,000.	12,000.	20,000.

GLOUCESTER TOKENS

S. S. Crosby, in his book *The Early Coins of America*, stated that this coin appears to have been intended as a pattern for a shilling; a private coinage by Richard Dawson of Gloucester (county), Virginia. The only specimens known are struck in brass, although the denomination XII indicates that a silver coinage (one shilling) may have been planned. The building may represent some public building, possibly the court house.

Although neither of the two known examples shows the full legends, combining the pieces shows GLOVCESTER COVRTHOVSE VIRGINIA / RIGHAVLT DAWSON-.ANNO.DOM. 1714. This recent discovery has provided a new interpretation of the legends, as a Righault family once owned land near the Gloucester Courthouse. A similar, but somewhat smaller piece dated 1715 exists. The condition of this unique piece is too poor for positive attribution.

	F
1714 Shilling (brass) *(2 known)*	$50,000.

HIGLEY OR GRANBY COPPERS

Dr. Samuel Higley owned a private copper mine near Granby, Connecticut. He worked the mine as an individual, smelting his own ore and making his own dies for the coins that he issued. After his death in 1737 his brother John continued the coinage.

The Higley coppers were never officially authorized. All the tokens were made of pure copper. There were seven obverse and four reverse dies. The first issue, in 1737, bore the legend THE VALUE OF THREEPENCE. After a time the quantity exceeded the local demand, and a protest arose against the value of the piece. Higley, a resourceful individual, promptly created a new design, still with the Roman III, but with the inscription VALUE ME AS YOU PLEASE. On the reverse appeared the words I AM GOOD COPPER.

(Electrotypes and Casts Exist)

★

	G	VG	F	VF
1737 THE • VALVE • OF • THREE • PENCE.— 3 Hammers — CONNECTICVT	$7,000.	$12,500.	$25,000.	$60,000.
1737 THE • VALVE • OF • THREE • PENCE.— 3 Hammers — I • AM • GOOD • COPPER	7,500.	13,500.	26,000.	62,000.
1737 VALUE • ME • AS • YOU • PLEASE — 3 Hammers — I • AM • GOOD • COPPER	7,000.	12,500.	25,000.	60,000.

A star (★) throughout the colonial section indicates that struck copies exist. All specimens illustrated are genuine.

HIGLEY OR GRANBY COPPERS

	G	VG	F	VF
1737 VALVE ME AS YOU PLEASE - 3 Hammers - I • AM • GOOD • COPPER	(Ex.Rare)			
(1737) VALUE ME AS YOU PLEASE - BROAD AXE - J • CUT • MY • WAY • THROUGH .	$7,000.	$12,000.	$25,000.	$60,000.
(1737) THE • WHEEL • GOES • ROUND, Rev. as above (*Unique*)			75,000.	
1739 VALUE ME AS YOU PLEASE - Broad Axe - J • CUT • MY • WAY • THROUGH ...	9,000.	15,000.	30,000.	75,000.

HIBERNIA-VOCE POPULI

These coins, struck in the year 1760, were prepared by Roche, of King Street, Dublin, who was at that period engaged in the manufacture of buttons for the army. Like other Irish tokens, some of these pieces found their way to Colonial America and possibly circulated in the colonies with numerous other counterfeit halfpence and "bungtown tokens."

There are two distinct issues. The first, with a "short bust" on the obverse, range in weight from 87 to 120 grains. The second, with a "long bust" on the obverse, range in weight from 129 to 154 grains. Most of the "long bust" varieties have the letter P on the obverse. None of the "short bust" varieties bear the letter P and judging from their weight may have been contemporary counterfeits.

Large Letter Variety
Farthing 1760

Halfpenny "P" before face

Halfpenny

VOOE POPULI

HIBERNIA-VOCE POPULI

	G	VG	F	VF	EF	AU	UNC
1760 Farthing, LgL	$175.	$250.	$500.	$1,100.	$2,100.	$3,500.	$6,500.
1760 Farthing, SmL	600.	1,000.	2,000.	5,000.	9,000.	—	—
1760 Halfpenny	60.	100.	145.	300.	600.	1,000.	2,000.
1760 Halfpenny, VOOE POPULI . . .	70.	125.	200.	375.	650.	1,200.	2,750.
1760 Halfpenny, P below bust	90.	150.	250.	500.	1,200.	2,500.	5,000.
1760 Halfpenny, P in front of face .	90.	140.	235.	450.	1,000.	2,100.	4,500.

PITT TOKENS

William Pitt, who endeared himself to America, is the subject of these pieces, probably intended as commemorative medalets. The so-called half-penny served as currency during a shortage of regular coinage. The reverse legend refers to Pitt's efforts to have the Stamp Act repealed. The Pitt far-thing-size tokens, struck in brass or copper are rare.

	VG	F	VF	EF	AU	UNC
1766 Farthing		$6,000.	$16,000.	$24,000.	—	—
1766 Halfpenny	325.	600.	1,250.	2,400.	3,800.	5,750.
1766 Halfpenny, silvered			1,800.	3,500.	5,500.	8,500.

RHODE ISLAND SHIP MEDAL

The obverse type shows the flagship of British Admiral Howe at anchor, while the reverse depicts the retreat of American forces from Rhode Island in 1778. The inscriptions show that it was meant for a Dutch speaking audience. It is believed the token was struck in England c. 1779-1780 for the Dutch market, as propaganda to persuade the Dutch not to sign the Treaty of Armed Neutrality (December, 1780). Specimens are known in brass, copper, and pewter.

**1778-1779
Rhode Island
Ship Medal**

	VF	EF	AU	UNC
VLUGTENDE (FLEEING) BELOW SHIP		$13,000.		
WREATH BELOW SHIP	950.	1,700.	2,500.	3,750.
WITHOUT WREATH BELOW SHIP	850.	1,500.	2,100.	3,100

.*Values shown are for brass or copper pieces. Those struck in pewter are all rare and valued higher.

J. CHALMERS — Annapolis, Maryland

John Chalmers, a silversmith, struck a series of silver tokens at Annapolis in 1783. The shortage of change and the refusal of the people to use underweight cut Spanish coins, or "bits," prompted the issuance of these pieces.

On the Chalmers threepence and shilling obverses two clasped hands are shown, symbolizing unity of the several states; the reverse of the threepence has a branch encircled by a wreath. A star within a wreath is placed on the obverse of the sixpence, with hands clasped upon a cross utilized as the reverse type. On this denomination, the designer's initials TS (for Thomas Sparrow, a fellow silversmith of Chalmers) can be found in the crescents which terminate the horizontal arm of the cross. The reverse of the more common shilling varieties displays two doves competing for a worm underneath a hedge and a snake. There are only a few known examples of the shilling type with thirteen interlinked rings from which a liberty cap on pole arises.

	VG	F	VF	EF	AU
1783 Threepence	$1,100.	$2,400.	$3,500.	$7,000.	$9,000.
1783 Sixpence, SmDt	1,800.	3,100.	5,500.	12,000.	15,000.
1783 Sixpence, LgDt	1,700.	3,000.	5,200.	11,000.	14,000.

1783 Shilling, Birds, Long worm (illustrated)	1,000.	2,000.	3,800.	6,800.	9,000.
1783 Shilling, Birds, Short worm	1,000.	2,000.	3,600.	6,500.	8,500.
1783 Shilling, Rings design	—	—	40,000.	—	—

IV. THE FRENCH COLONIES

None of the coins of the French regime is strictly American. They were all general issues for the French colonies of the New World. The coinage of 1670 was authorized by an edict of Louis XIV dated February 19, 1670, for use in New France, Acadia, the French settlements in Newfoundland, and the French West Indies. The copper of 1717 to 1722 was authorized by edicts of 1716 and 1721 for use in New France, Louisiana, and the French West Indies.

ISSUE OF 1670

The coinage of 1670 consisted of silver 5 and 15 sols and copper 2 deniers or "double." A total of 200,000 of the 5 sols and 40,000 of the 15 sols, was struck at Paris. Nantes was to have coined the copper, but did not; the reasons for this may never be known, since the archives of the Nantes mint before 1700 were destroyed. The only known specimen is a pattern struck at Paris. The silver coins were raised in value by a third in 1672 to keep them circulating, but in vain. They rapidly disappeared, and by 1680 none was to be seen. Later they were restored to their original value. This rare plan should not be confused with the common 1670A 1/12 ecu with reverse legend: SIT. NOMEN. DOMINI. BENEDICTUM.

The 1670-A Double de l'Amerique Françoise was struck in the Paris Mint along with the 5 and 15 sols denominations of the same date. All three were intended to circulate in France's North American colonies. Probably due to an engraving error, very few 1670-A doubles were actually struck. Today, only one specimen is known to survive.

Copper Double   **Silver 5 Sols**

	VG	F	VF	EF	UNC
Copper Double 1670 *(Unique)*			—		
5 Sols 1670-A (200,000)	$450.	$850.	$1,750.	$3,600.	$6,000.
15 Sols 1670-A (40,000)	8,500.	20,000.	35,000.	60,000.	—

COINAGE OF 1717-1720

The copper 6 and 12 deniers of 1717 were authorized by an edict of Louis XV dated December 1716, to be struck at Perpignan (mintmark Q). The order could not be carried out, for the supply of copper was too brassy. A second attempt in 1720 also failed, probably for the same reason.

"COLONIES" and No Crowned Arms on Reverse Copper

	Fine	E. Fine
6 Deniers 1717 Q, ...		*(Ex. Rare)*
12 DENIERS 1717 Q, ...		$35,000.

Crowned Arms on Reverse

	Fine	E. Fine
6 DENIERS 1720-A	$125.	$600.
20 Sols, silver 1720-A	275.	900.

BILLON COINAGE

The piece of 30 deniers was called a *mousquetaire*, and was coined at Metz and Lyon. The 15 deniers was coined only at Metz. The sou marque and half were coined at almost every French mint, those of Paris being commonest. The half sou of 1740 is the only commonly available date. Specimens of the sou marque dated after 1760 were not used in North America. A unique specimen of the 1712AA 30 deniers is known in the size and weight of the 15 deniers coins.

30 Deniers "Mousquetaire"   **Sou Marque (24 Deniers)**

	VG	F	VF	EF	UNC
15 Deniers 1711-1713AA	$110.	$240.	$475.	$950.	$2,000.
30 Deniers 1709-1713AA	65.	125.	250.	550.	1,200.
30 Deniers 1709-1713D	65.	125.	250.	550.	1,200.
Half sou marque 1738-1748, various mints	60.	110.	225.	500.	1,200.
Sou marque 1738-1760, various mints	50.	85.	135.	300.	500.

The copper coinage of 1721-1722 was authorized by an edict of Louis XV dated June 1721. The coins were struck on copper blanks imported from Sweden. Rouen and La Rochelle struck pieces of 9 deniers in 1721 and 1722. New France received 534,000 pieces, mostly from the mint of La Rochelle, but only 8,180 were successfully put into circulation as the colonists disliked copper. In 1726 the rest of the issue was sent back to France.

COPPER SOU OR NINE DENIERS

	VG	F	VF
1721-B (Rouen)	$150.	$325.	$650.
1721-H (La Rochelle)	75.	150.	350.
1722-H	75.	150.	350.
1722-H, 2/1	125.	250.	475.

FRENCH COLONIES IN GENERAL

Coined for use in the French colonies and only unofficially circulated in Louisiana along with other foreign coins and tokens. Most were counterstamped RF (République Française) for use in the West Indies. The mintmark A signifies the Paris Mint.

	VG	VF	EF	AU
1767 French Colonies, Sou	$80.	$300.	$600.	$1,350.
1767 French Colonies, Sou. with RF	60.	150.	350.	650.

V. SPECULATIVE ISSUES, TOKENS & PATTERNS
THE CONTINENTAL CURRENCY

The Continental Currency pieces probably had some value at the time they were issued, but the exact nature of their monetary role is still unclear. They were the first silver dollar-sized coins ever proposed for the United States. One obverse die was engraved by someone whose initials were E.G. (undoubtedly Elisha Gallaudet) and is marked with his signature EG FECIT. Studies of the coinage show that there may have been two separate emissions made at different mints. The link design on the reverse was suggested by Benjamin Franklin.

Varieties result from differences in the spelling of the word CURRENCY and the addition of EG FECIT on the obverse. These coins were struck in pewter, brass and silver. Pewter pieces probably served as a dollar, substituting for paper currency of this design that was never issued. Brass and silver pieces may have been experimental or patterns. Pewter pieces in original bright Uncirculated condition are worth an additional premium.

Numerous copies and replicas of these coins have been made over the years. Authentication is recommended for all pieces.

"CURRENCY"

★

	G	F	VF	EF	AU	UNC
1776 CURENCY, Pewter (2 varieties) ..	$3,500.	$6,000.	$12,000.	$16,000.	$21,000.	$33,000.
1776 CURENCY, Brass (2 varieties) ...	10,000.	18,000.	30,000.	45,000.	—	—
1776 CURENCY, Silver		200,000.	300,000.			
1776 CURRENCY, Pewter	3,750.	6,500.	13,000.	18,000.	23,000.	35,000.
1776 CURRENCY, Pewter, EG FECIT ...	3,750.	6,500.	13,000.	19,000.	24,000.	36,000.
1776 CURRENCY, Silver, EG FECIT	—	—	—	—	—	—
1776 CURRENCEY, Pewter	—	—	—	—	75,000.	—
1776 CURRENCY - Ornament after date	—	—	—	—		

NOVA CONSTELLATIO COPPERS

The Nova Constellatio coppers dated 1783 and 1785 and without denomination were struck in fairly large quantities in Birmingham, England beginning in 1785 and were shipped to New York where they entered circulation. Apparently they were a private coinage venture undertaken by Constable, Rucker & Co., a trading business formed by William Constable, John Rucker, Robert Morris and Gouverneur Morris as equal partners. The designs and legends were copied from the denominated patterns dated 1783 made in Philadelphia. A few additional coppers dated 1786 were made by an inferior die sinker.

NOVA CONSTELLATIO COPPERS

1783
"CONSTELLATIO"
Pointed Rays, Small U.S.

V.Good	$85.
Fine	185.
V. Fine	375.
E. Fine	850.
A. Unc..	1,500.
Unc..	3,000.

1783
"CONSTELLATIO"
Pointed Rays, Large U.S.

V.Good	$90.
Fine	200.
V. Fine	450.
E. Fine	1,000.
A. Unc.	2,250.
Unc.	4,200.

1783
"CONSTELATIO"
Blunt Rays

V.Good	$90.
Fine	200.
V. Fine	400.
E. Fine	925.
A. Unc.	1,800.
Unc.	3,400.

1785
"CONSTELATIO"
Blunt Rays

V.Good	$90.
Fine	200.
V. Fine	450.
E. Fine	1,000.
A. Unc.	2,200.
Unc.	3,700.

1785
"CONSTELLATIO"
Pointed Rays

V.Good	$85.
Fine	185.
V. Fine	400.
E. Fine	900.
A. Unc.	1,650.
Unc.	3,100.

1785 Similar, SmClDt		**VG** $250.	**F** $600.	**VF** $2,250.
1786 Similar, SmDt	*(Very Rare)*	—		

NOVA CONSTELLATIO PATTERNS

These Nova Constellatio pieces undoubtedly represent the first patterns for a coinage of the United States. They were designed by Benjamin Dudley for Gouverneur Morris to carry out his ideas for a decimal coinage system. The 1000 unit designation he called a "mark," the 500 a "quint." These denominations, together with the small 100 unit piece, were designed to standardize the many different coin values among the several states. These pattern pieces represent the first attempt at a decimal ratio, and were the forerunners of our present system of money values. Neither the proposed denominations nor the coins advanced beyond the pattern stage. These unique pieces are all dated 1783. There are two types of the "quint." The enigmatic copper "five" was first brought to the attention of collectors in 1980.

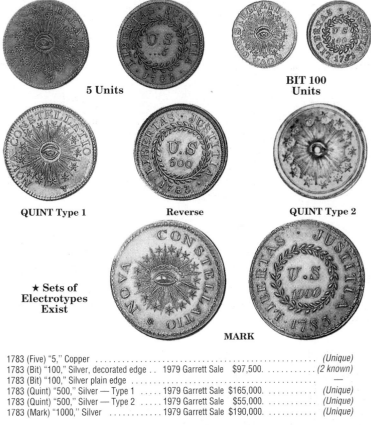

5 Units

BIT 100
Units

QUINT Type 1   Reverse   QUINT Type 2

★ Sets of
Electrotypes
Exist

MARK

1783 (Five) "5," Copper	. . . .		*(Unique)*
1783 (Bit) "100," Silver, decorated edge . .	1979 Garrett Sale	$97,500.	*(2 known)*
1783 (Bit) "100," Silver plain edge	. . . .		—
1783 (Quint) "500," Silver — Type 1	. . . . . 1979 Garrett Sale	$165,000.	*(Unique)*
1783 (Quint) "500," Silver — Type 2	. . . . . 1979 Garrett Sale	$55,000.	*(Unique)*
1783 (Mark) "1000," Silver	. . . . 1979 Garrett Sale	$190,000.	*(Unique)*

IMMUNE COLUMBIA PIECES

These are considered experimental or pattern pieces. No laws describing them are known. There are several types with the seated figure of Justice device. These dies were possibly the work of George Wyon. The Immune Columbia device with liberty cap and scale replaced the LIBERTAS and JUSTITIA on the Nova Constellatio coppers.

IMMUNE COLUMBIA PIECES

	VF
1785 Copper, 13 stars	$15,000.
1785 Silver, 13 stars	24,000.

1785 Ptd. Rays CONSTELLATIO
Copper. Extra star in reverse legend
VF .... $15,000.
1785 Blunt Rays CONSTELLATIO
Copper ... *(2 known)* —
Gold .... *(Unique)* —
A gold specimen in the National Coin
Collection was acquired from collector
Matthew A. Stickney in exchange for an
1804 dollar.

1785
George III Obverse
Good .. $2,750. **Fine** ..... $5,500.
1785
Vermon Auctori Obverse
Good .. $4,000. **Fine** ..... $7,000.

1787
IMMUNIS COLUMBIA
Eagle Reverse

V.Good	$550.
Fine	1,200.
V.Fine	2,750.
E. Fine	5,000.
A. Unc.	7,500.

This piece is believed to be a prototype for federal coinage. Evidence shows that some of these pieces were coined sometime after 1787.

CONFEDERATIO COPPERS

The Confederatio Coppers are experimental or pattern pieces. This will explain why the die with the CONFEDERATIO legend was combined with other designs such as bust of George Washington, Libertas et Justitia of 1785, Immunis Columbia of 1786, the New York "Excelsiors," Inimica Tyrannis Americana and others. There were in all thirteen dies struck in fourteen combinations. Some of the dies may have been made by George Wyon of Birmingham, England.

There are two types of the Confederatio reverse. In one instance the stars are contained in a small circle; in the other larger stars are in a larger circle.

CONFEDERATIO COPPERS

Typical Obverse

Small Circle Reverse ★

Large Circle Reverse

	VF
1785 Stars in Sm circle, various obverses	$24,000.
1785 Stars in Sm circle, struck in silver	—
1785 Stars in Lg circle, various obverses	22,000.

SPECULATIVE PATTERNS

The motto and shield design used on some of these patterns was later adopted for use on the New Jersey copper coins.

1786 IMMUNIS COLUMBIA

Eagle Reverse

Shield Reverse

1786 IMMUNIS COLUMBIA, eagle rev.	35,000.
1786 IMMUNIS COLUMBIA, shield rev.	25,000.

1786 (No date) Washington obv., shield reverse	253,000.
1786 Eagle obverse, shield reverse	37,500.
1786 Washington obverse, eagle reverse (*Unique*)	—

VI. COINAGE OF THE STATES
NEW HAMPSHIRE

New Hampshire was the first of the states to consider the subject of coinage following the Declaration of Independence.

William Moulton was empowered to make a limited quantity of coins of pure copper authorized by the State House of Representatives in 1776. Although cast patterns were prepared, it is believed that they were not approved. Little of the proposed coinage was ever actually circulated.

Other purported patterns are of doubtful origin. These include a unique engraved piece and a rare struck piece with large initials WM on the reverse.

	VG
1776 New Hampshire copper	$20,000.

MASSACHUSETTS
MASSACHUSETTS UNOFFICIAL COPPERS

Nothing is known regarding the origin of the Pine Tree piece dated 1776. The obverse has a crude pine tree with the letters 1d LM at its base; Inscription, MASSACHUSETTS STATE. The reverse has a figure probably intended to represent the Goddess of Liberty, seated on a globe and holding a liberty cap and staff. A dog sits at her feet. The legend LIBERTY AND VIRTUE surrounds the figure.

1776 Pine Tree copper *(Unique)* .... —

A similar piece, probably from the same source, has a Native American with bow on the obverse, and seated figure on the reverse.

1776 Indian copper (*Unique*) —

MASSACHUSETTS UNOFFICIAL COPPERS

This piece is sometimes called the "Janus Copper." There are three heads facing left, front and right on the obverse with the inscription STATE OF MASSA. 1/2 D. The reverse shows the Goddess of Liberty facing right, resting against a globe inscribed GODDESS LIBERTY 1776.

1776 Halfpenny, 3 heads on obverse (*Unique*) .... $42,000.

MASSACHUSETTS AUTHORIZED ISSUES

An "Act for establishing a mint for the coinage of gold, silver and copper" was passed by the Massachusetts General Court October 17, 1786. The next year the Council directed that the design should incorporate "the figure of an Indian with a bow and arrow and a star at one side, with the word 'Commonwealth,' the reverse, a spread eagle with the words 'of Massachusetts A.D. 1787'."

The coinage of Massachusetts copper cents and half cents in 1787 and 1788 was under the direction of Joshua Witherle. These were the first coins bearing the denomination *cent* as established by Congress. Many varieties exist, the most valuable being that with arrows in the eagle's right talon.

Most of the dies for these coppers were made by Joseph Callender. Jacob Perkins of Newburyport also engraved some of the dies.

The mint was abandoned early in 1789 in compliance with the newly ratified constitution.

Half Cent

	Obverse	Arrows in Eagle's Right Talon	Arrows in Left Talon

	G	F	VF	EF	AU	UNC
1787 Half Cent	$85.	$210.	$475.	$1,050.	$1,900.	$3,250.
1787 Cent, arrows in right talon	5,000.	15,000.	—	—	—	—
1787 Cent, arrows in left talon	75.	200.	450.	1,000.	2,100.	4,200.
1787 Cent, "horn" *(die break)* from eagle's head......	75.	200.	450.	1,000.	2,200.	5,000.

1788 Half Cent

Good	$100.
Fine	250.
V. Fine	500.
E. Fine	1,050.
A. Unc	2,200.
Unc.	3,400.

1788 Cent
Period after Massachusetts

Good	80.
Fine	220.
V. Fine	450.
E. Fine	1,000.
A. Unc	2,100.
Unc.	4,000.

No period after Massachusetts

Good	95.
Fine	225.
V. Fine	600.
E. Fine	1,250.
A. Unc	2,400.
Unc.	4,700.

Early American coins were produced from handmade dies which are often individually distinctive. The great number of die varieties which can be found and identified are of interest to collectors who value each according to individual rarity. Values shown for type coins in this catalog are for the most common die variety.

CONNECTICUT

Authority for establishing a mint near New Haven was granted by the State to Samuel Bishop, Joseph Hopkins, James Hillhouse and John Goodrich in 1785.

Available records indicate that most of the Connecticut coppers were coined under a sub-contract by Samuel Broome and Jeremiah Platt, former New York merchants. Abel Buell and James Atlee were probably the principal die-sinkers.

1785 Copper
Bust Facing Right

Good	$55.
V. Good	85.
Fine	200.
V. Fine	600.
E. Fine	1,400.

1785 Copper
African Head

Good	$70.
V. Good	135.
Fine	450.
V. Fine	1,100.
E. Fine	2,750.

1785 Copper
Bust Facing Left

Good	$200.
V. Good	350.
Fine	600.
V. Fine	1,400.
E. Fine	2,800.

1786 Copper
ETLIB INDE

Good	$75.
V. Good	150.
Fine	350.
V. Fine	800.
E. Fine	1,800.

1786 Copper
Large Head Facing Right

Good	$90.
V. Good	225.
Fine	600.
V. Fine	2,000.
E. Fine	4,000.

1786 Copper
Mailed Bust Facing Left

Good	$55.
V. Good	85.
Fine	175.
V. Fine	500.
E. Fine	1,100

1786 Copper
Mailed Bust Facing Left
Hercules Head

Good	$100.
V. Good	150.
Fine	500.
V. Fine	1,500.
E. Fine	3,500.

**1786 Copper
Draped Bust**

Good	$85.
V. Good	175.
Fine	375.
V. Fine	900.
E. Fine	2,200.

The Connecticut coppers, especially those dated 1787 and 1788, were usually crudely struck and on imperfect planchets.

**1787 Copper
Small Head Facing Right
ETLIB INDE** →

Good	$100.
V. Good	175.
Fine	375.
V. Fine	1,250.
E. Fine	2,800

**1787 Copper
Liberty Seated Right**

2 known .... —

**1787 Copper
Mailed Bust Facing Right
INDE ET LIB**

Good	$110.
V. Good	175.
Fine	450.
V. Fine	2,000.

← **1787 Muttonhead Variety**

Good	90.
V. Good	150.
Fine	400.
V. Fine	1,400.
E. Fine	3,000.
A. Fine	7,500.

	G	VG	F	VF	EF	AU
1787 Mailed bust facing left	$50.	$85.	$160.	$500.	$1,400.	$2,500.
1787 Mailed bust facing left, Laughing Head variety	50.	100.	175.	550.	1,600.	2,750.
1787 Mailed bust facing left, Hercules Head (see 1786)	300.	600.	1,250.	3,000.	4,250.	—
1787 Mailed bust facing left, dated 1787 over 1877	80.	160.	500.	1,400.	3,500.	—
1787 Mailed bust facing left, dated 1787 over 1788	120.	200.	675.	1,600.	3,750.	—

1787 Mailed bust facing left, Horned Bust variety ..	45.	70.	150.	400.	1,050.	2,000.
1787 Mailed bust facing left, CONNECT variety ...	50.	110.	230.	650.	1,600.	2,500.

	G	**VG**	**F**	**VF**	**EF**	**AU**
1787 Draped bust facing left	$45.	$75.	$125.	$375.	$850.	$1,750.
1787 Draped bust facing left, AUCIORI variety	45.	75.	150.	450.	1,000.	2,100.
1787 Draped bust facing left, AUCTOPI variety	55.	90.	200.	650.	1,600.	2,800.
1787 Draped bust facing left, AUCTOBI variety	55.	90.	200.	600.	1,500.	2,700.
1787 Draped bust facing left, CONNFC variety	50.	75.	160.	500.	1,100.	2,100.
1787 Draped bust facing left, CONNLC variety	75.	175.	350.	800.	1,700.	3,000.
1787 Draped bust facing left, FNDE variety . .	55.	85.	175.	500.	1,200.	2,400.
1787 Mailed bust facing left, ETLIR variety . .	50.	75.	150.	500.	1,200.	2,400.
1787 Mailed bust facing left, ETIIB variety . . .	55.	80.	150.	500.	1,200.	2,400.
1787 GEORGIVS III obv., Rev. as below	1,000.	2,000.	4,500.	—	—	—

1788 Mailed bust facing right	45.	90.	200.	550.	1,250.	2,500.
1788 GEORGIVS III obv. Rev. as above	110.	200.	500.	1,300.	2,500.	—
1788 SmHd (see 1787 page 48)	900.	2,000.	3,200.	7,500.	—	—

1788 Mailed bust facing left	45.	70.	160.	500.	1,000.	2,000.
1788 Mailed bust facing left, CONNLC	60.	125.	275.	650.	1,800.	3,200.

CONNECTICUT

	G	VG	F	VF	EF	AU
1788 Draped bust facing left	$50.	$75.	$200.	$500.	$1,100.	$2,200.
1788 Draped bust facing left, CONNLC variety	85.	200.	500.	1,200.	2,000.	3,500.
1788 Draped bust, INDL ET LIB variety	80.	140.	325.	750.	1,600.	3,000.

NEW YORK
THE BRASHER DOUBLOON

Perhaps the most famous pieces coined before establishment of the U.S. Mint at Philadelphia were those produced by the well-known goldsmith and jeweler, Ephraim Brasher, who was a neighbor and friend of George Washington, in New York.

The gold pieces Brasher made weighed about 408 grains and were valued at $15 in New York currency. They were approximately equal to the Spanish doubloon which was equal to 16 Spanish dollars.

Pieces known as "Lima Style" doubloons were dated 1742, but it is almost certain that they were produced in 1786, and were the first efforts of Brasher to make a circulating coin for local use. Neither of the two known specimens show the full legends, but weight, gold content and punch mark are all identical to the other Brasher coins.

An original design was used on the 1787 doubloon with an eagle on one side and the arms of New York on the other. In addition to his impressed hallmark, Brasher's name appears in small letters on each of his coins. The unique 1787 gold half doubloon is struck from doubloon dies on an undersized planchet that weighs half as much as the larger coins.

It is uncertain why Brasher produced these pieces. He was later commissioned to test and verify other gold coins then in circulation. His hallmark EB was punched on each coin as evidence of his testing and its value. In some cases the foreign coins have been weight-adjusted by clipping.

"1742" (1786) Lima style gold doubloon .... *(2 known)*

1787 New York gold doubloon, punch of breast (*Unique*) .... $625,000.
1787 New York doubloon, punch on wings. .... 725,000.
1787 New York gold half doubloon, Smithsonian Collection(*Unique*) ....
Various foreign gold coins with Brasher's EB hallmark ....4,000. to 8,000.

COPPER COINAGE

Several individuals petitioned the New York legislature in early 1787 for the right to coin copper for the state, but a coinage was never authorized. Instead a law was passed to regulate the copper coins already in use. Nevertheless, various unauthorized copper coins were issued within the state, principally by two private mints.

One firm, known as Machin's Mills, was located at the mills of Thomas Machin near Newburgh. Shortly after this mint was formed, on April 18, 1787, it was merged with the Rupert, Vermont mint operated by Reuben Harmon, Jr. Harmon held a coinage grant from the Republic of Vermont. The combined partnership agreed to conduct their business in New York, Vermont, Connecticut, or elsewhere if they could benefit by it.

The operations at Machin's Mills were conducted in secret and were looked upon with suspicion by the local residents. They minted several varieties of imitation George III halfpence, and coppers of Connecticut, Vermont and New Jersey.

The other mints, located in or near New York City, were operated by John Bailey and Ephraim Brasher. They had petitioned the legislature on February 12, 1787 for a franchise to coin copper. The extent of their partnership, if any, and details of their operation are not known. Studies of the state coinage show that they produced primarily the EXCELSIOR and NOVA EBORAC pieces of New York, and the "running fox" New Jersey coppers.

(Believed to be the bust of Washington.)

	G	VG	F	VF
1786 NON VI VIRTUTE VICI	$3,750.	$5,000.	$8,000.	$18,000.

A star (★) throughout the colonial section indicates that struck copies exist. The specimens illustrated are genuine.

★

	G	F	VF	EF
1787 EXCELSIOR copper, eagle on globe, facing right	$1,600.	$4,900.	$11,500.	$24,000.
1787 EXCELSIOR copper, eagle on globe, facing left	1,600.	4,500.	10,500.	22,000.

1787 Large Eagle on reverse—Arrows and branch
transposed .... $26,000.

★

1787 George Clinton
Good	$5,500.
Fine	14,000.
V. Fine	24,000.

1787
Indian and N.Y. Arms
Good	$3,850.
Fine	9,000.
V. Fine	19,000.
E. Fine	35,000.

★

**1787
Indian and Eagle
on Globe**

Good ....$6,250.
Fine ....18,000.
V. Fine ....32,000.
E. Fine ....60,000.

★

**1787 Indian and George III
Reverse (3 known)**
V. Good ....$15,000.

IMITATION BRITISH HALFPENCE
(Machin's Mills and other Coinage 1786-1789)

The most common coin used for small transactions in early America was the copper British halfpenny. Wide acceptance and the non-legal tender status of these copper coins made them a prime choice for unauthorized reproduction by private individuals. Many such counterfeits were made in this country by casting or other crude methods. Some were made in England and imported to this country. Pieces dated 1781 and 1785 seem to have been made specifically for this purpose, while others were circulated in both countries.

During the American state coinage era, James F. Atlee and/or others engraved dies used to mint unauthorized lightweight imitation British halfpence. These American-made British halfpence have the same devices, legends and in some cases the same dates as genuine regal halfpence. There are three distinct groups of these halfpence, all linked to the regular state coinage. The first group was probably struck in New York City prior to 1786. Group two was minted in New York City in association with John Bailey and Ephraim Brasher during the first half of 1787. The third group was struck at Machin's Mills during the second half of 1787 and into 1788. Pieces dated 1784 are believed to have been struck elsewhere in New England.

Dates used on these pieces were often evasive and are: 1771, 1772 and 1774-1776 for group one; 1747 and 1787 for group two; and 1776, 1778, 1787 and 1788 for group three. Pieces generally attributed to Atlee can be identified by a single outline in the crosses (British Union) of Britannia's shield and large triangular denticles along the coin's circumference. These pieces are not to be confused with the similar English made George III counterfeits, some of which have identical dates, or genuine British halfpence, dated 1770 to 1775.

GROUP I   **GROUP II**   **GROUP III**

Machin's Mills Copper Halfpenny

GEORGIVS/BRITANNIA

	G	VG	F	VF	EF	AU
1747 GEORGIVS II	$150.	$275.	$650.	$2,000.	$3,700.	—
1771 GEORGIVS III	90.	140.	350.	900.	2,500.	4,250.
1772 GEORGIVS III	90.	160.	450.	1,000.	3,000.	5,500.
1772 GEORGIUS III	200.	375.	850.	2,250.	4,000.	—
1774 GEORGIVS III	65.	120.	300.	850.	2,300.	4,000.
1774 GEORGIUS III	80.	160.	350.	950.	2,600.	4,200.
1775 GEORGIVS III	80.	130.	300.	900.	2,300.	3,800.
1776 GEORGIVS III	160.	285.	700.	1,500.	3,200.	—
1776 SmDt - CEORCIVS	750.	1,800.	4,000.	8,750.	—	—
1778 GEORGIVS III	75.	125.	300.	800.	2,600.	4,200.
1784 GEORGIVS III	300.	650.	1,450.	2,500.	—	—
1787 GEORGIVS III	65.	110.	250.	700.	2,100.	3,600.
1788 GEORGIVS III	70.	120.	300.	800.	2,400.	3,800.

See related George III combinations under Connecticut, Vermont, and New York.

NOVA EBORAC COINAGE FOR NEW YORK

1787 NOVA EBORAC
**Reverse Seated
Figure Facing Right**

Good	$110.
Fine	350.
V. Fine	925.
E. Fine	2,000.
A. Unc	3,250.

1787 NOVA EBORAC
Reverse Seated
Figure Facing Left

Good	$100.
Fine	325.
V. Fine	825.
E. Fine	1,600.
A. Unc	2,750.

[54]

NEW YORK

1787
NOVA EBORAC
Small Head

Fair	$800.
Good	2,200.
Fine	6,000.
V. Fine	13,500.

1787
NOVA EBORAC
Large Head

Fair	$150.
Good	475.
Fine	1,400.
V. Fine	4,500.

NEW JERSEY

On June 1, 1786, the New Jersey Colonial legislature granted to Thomas Goadsby, Albion Cox and Walter Mould authority to coin some three million coppers weighing six pennyweight and six grains apiece, not later than June 1788, on condition that they delivered to the Treasurer of the State, "one-tenth part of the full sum they shall strike and coin," in quarterly install-ments. These coppers were to pass current at 15 to the shilling.

In an operation of this kind the contractors purchased the metal and assumed all expenses of coining. The difference between these expenses and the total face value of the coins issued represented the profit.

Later Goadsby and Cox asked authority to coin two-thirds of the total independently. Their petition was granted November 22, 1786. Mould was known to have produced his coins at Morristown, while Cox (and probably Goadsby) operated in Rahway. Coins were also minted in Elizabethtown and New York.

The series offers many varieties. The obverse shows a horse's head with plow and the legend NOVA CAESAREA (New Jersey). The reverse has a United States shield and legend E PLURIBUS UNUM (One composed of many).

1786 Date Under Draw Bar
No Coulter

1786 Date Under Plow
No Coulter

	G	F	VF
1786 Date under draw bar, no coulter		25,000.	50,000.
1786 Date under plow, no coulter	300.	1,200.	4,000.

Narrow Shield

Wide Shield

	G	F	VF	EF	AU
1786 Narrow Shield, straight plow beam	$50.	$200.	$500.	$1,200.	$2,000.
1786 Narrow Shield, curved plow beam	50.	200.	550.	1,300.	2,200.
1786 Wide Shield	65.	225.	600.	1,800.	2,750.
1786 Wide Shield, bridle variety	65.	225.	600.	1,800.	2,750.

Pluribs Variety, Lg. Planchet   **Small Planchet**

Outlined Shield

	G	F	VF	EF	AU
1787 Pronounced outline to shield	55.	200.	525.	1,100.	1,900.
1787 Sm planchet, plain shield	55.	200.	500.	1,000.	1,800.
1787 Lg planchet, plain shield	60.	200.	650.	1,500.	2,300.
1787 Lg planchet, plain shield, PLURIBS variety . .	100.	435.	1,150.	2,900.	5,000.
1787 Similar, second U over S in PLURIBUS	175.	450.	1,250.	2,900.	5,000.
1787 Similar, PLURIRUS variety	150.	375.	850.	2,300.	3,250.
1787, Date over 1887	400.	1,500.	3,000.	6,000.	—
1787 "Camel head" variety (snout in high relief) . . .	65.	200.	650.	1,300.	2,200.

Camel Head   **Serpent Head**

Fox Variety

	G	F	VF	EF	AU
1787 Serpent head variety	80.	325.	1,100.	2,750.	4,500.
1787 WM above plow		—			
1788 Horse's head facing right	55.	185.	525.	1,150.	2,000.
1788 Horse's head facing right,					
running fox before legend	100.	400.	1,500.	3,500.	6,750.
1788 Similar, fox, indistinct coulter	400.	1,700.	4,500.	9,500.	—
1788 Horse's head facing left	350.	1,200.	3,250.	6,000.	—

Many varieties of these coins exist.
Some have a sprig of three leaves above the plow.

VERMONT

Reuben Harmon, Jr., of Rupert, Vermont, was granted permission to coin copper pieces for a period of two years beginning July 1, 1785. The well-known Vermont plow coppers were first produced in that year. The franchise was extended for eight years in 1786.

Harmon's mint was located in the northeast corner of Rupert near a stream known as Millbrook. Col. William Coley, a New York goldsmith, made the first dies.

Some of the late issues were made near Newburgh, N.Y. by the Machin's Mills coiners.

1785 IMMUNE COLUMBIA

	G	VG	F	VF	EF	AU
1785 IMMUNE COLUMBIA	$4,000.	$5,000.	$7,000.	$20,000.	—	—
1785 VERMONTS	$225.	$500.	$1,000.	$2,500.	$6,500.	—
1785 VERMONTIS	250.	600.	1,200.	2,750.	7,500.	—

1786 VERMONTENSIUM

	G	VG	F	VF	EF	AU
1786 VERMONTENSIUM	$200.	400.	800.	2,000.	3,500.	7,000.

1786 Baby Head

	G	VG	F	VF	EF	AU
1786 Baby head	$275.	500.	1,000.	3,600.	7,000.	—

1786 Bust Left　　　　**1787 Bust Left**

	G	VG	F	VF	EF	AU
1786 Bust left ....$140.		$300.	$750.	$2,000.	$3,700.	—
1787 Bust left ....3,500.		7,500.	15,000.	25,000.	—	

1787 BRITANNIA

The reverse of this coin is always weak.

1787 BRITANNIA ....90.	125.	250.	550.	1,400.	2,750.

1787, 1788 Bust Right (Several Varieties)

1787 Bust right (Several var.)	125.	200.	475.	1,100.	2,200.	3,750.
1788 (Several Var.)	100.	150.	375.	8,50.	1,450.	2,750.
1788 Backward C in AUCTORI	3,500.	5,000.	9,000.	—	—	
1788 *ET LIB* *INDE	300.	600.	1,200.	3,750.	10,000.	—

1788 GEORGIVS III REX

This piece should not be confused with the common English halfpence with similar design and reverse legend BRITANNIA.

1788 GEORGIVS III REX	400.	750.	2,000.	3,800.	9,000.	—

　　Most Vermont coppers are struck on poor and defective planchets. Well struck coins on smooth full planchets command higher prices.

VII. PRIVATE TOKENS AFTER CONFEDERATION
NORTH AMERICAN TOKEN

This piece was struck in Dublin, Ireland. The obverse shows the seated figure of Hibernia facing left. The date of issue is believed to have been much later than that shown on the token.

Like many Irish tokens, this issue found its way to America in limited quantities and was accepted near the Canadian border.

1781 Copper or Brass

VG	F	VF	EF
$55.	$120.	$275.	$650.

BAR "COPPER"

The Bar "Copper" is undated and of uncertain origin. It has thirteen parallel and unconnected bars on one side. On the other side is the large roman letter USA monogram. The design was supposedly copied from a Continental button.

The significance of the design is clearly defined by its extreme simplicity. The separate thirteen states (bars) unite into a single entity as symbolized by the interlocking letters (USA).

This piece is believed to have first circulated in New York during November, 1785, and may have been made in England.

On the less valuable struck copy made by J. A. Bolen (c. 1862) the A passes under, instead of over, the S.

	VG	F	VF	EF	AU
Undated (about 1785) Bar "Copper"	$900.	$1,800.	$3,000.	$4,000.	$5,500.

AUCTORI PLEBIS TOKEN

This token is sometimes included with the coins of Connecticut as it greatly resembles issues of that state. It was struck in England by an unknown maker, possibly for use in America.

1787
AUCTORI PLEBIS

Good	$85.
V. Good	150.
Fine	275.
V. Fine	600.
E. Fine	1,150.
A. Unc.	2,000.
Unc.	5,000.

MOTT STORE CARD

This item has long been considered as an early token because of its date 1789. Some scholars believe it was most likely produced c. 1809 as a commemorative of the founding of the Mott Company, and probably served as a business card. The firm, operated by Jordan Mott, was located at 240 Water Street, a fashionable section of New York at that time.

	F	VF	EF	AU	UNC
"1789" Mott Token, thick planchet	$250.	$425.	$800.	$1,350.	$2,000.
"1789" Mott Token, thin planchet	350.	600.	1,300.	2,200.	3,000.
"1789" Mott Token, entire edge engrailed	450.	700.	1,750.	2,900.	4,500.

STANDISH BARRY, BALTIMORE, MARYLAND

Standish Barry, a Baltimore silversmith, circulated a silver threepence in 1790. He was a watch and clockmaker, engraver and later a silversmith. The tokens were believed to have been an advertising venture at a time when small change was scarce. The precise date, July 4, 90, on this piece may indicate that Barry intended to commemorate Independence Day, but there are no records to substantiate this belief. The head shown on the obverse is probably that of George Washington. The legend BALTIMORE TOWN JULY 4, 90 appears in the border. STANDISH BARRY THREE PENCE is on the reverse.

	F	VF
1790 Threepence	$8,500.	$18,000.

ALBANY CHURCH PENNY

The First Presbyterian Church of Albany, New York authorized an issue of one thousand copper uniface tokens in 1790. These passed at twelve to a shilling and were used to stop contributions of worn and counterfeit coppers. Two varieties were made, one with the addition of a large D above the word CHURCH.

	VG	F
(1790) Without D	$5,500.	$11,000.
(1790) With D added	4,500.	10,000.

KENTUCKY TOKEN

These tokens were struck in England about 1792-94. Each star in the triangle represents a state, identified by its initial letter. These pieces are usually called Kentucky Cents because the letter K (for Kentucky) happens to be at the top. Some of the edges are plain; others are engrailed with an oblique reeding, and some have the edge lettered: "PAYABLE IN LANCASTER LONDON OR BRISTOL," or "PAYABLE AT BEDWORTH NUNEATON OR HINKLEY."

	VF	EF	AU	UNC
Copper, (1792-94) plain edge	$200.	$375.	$550.	$975.
Copper, engrailed edge	500.	800.	1,400.	2,800.
Copper, lettered edge PAYABLE AT BEDWORTH, etc.	—	—	—	—
COPPER, lettered edge PAYABLE IN LANCASTER, etc.	225.	425.	650.	1,100.
COPPER, lettered edge PAYABLE AT I. FIELDING, etc.	—	—	—	—

FRANKLIN PRESS

This piece is an English tradesman's token but, being associated with Benjamin Franklin, has accordingly been included in American collections.

	VF	EF	AU	UNC
1794 Franklin Press Token	$250.	$425.	$650.	$1,100.
Similar edge: AN ASYLUM, etc.	(Unique)			
Similar edge: diagonally reeded	(Unique)			

TALBOT, ALLUM & LEE CENTS

Talbot, Allum & Lee, engaged in the India trade and located at 241 Pearl Street, New York, placed a large quantity of English-made coppers in circulation during 1794 and 1795. ONE CENT appears on the 1794 issue, and the legend PAYABLE AT THE STORE OF on the edge. The denomination is not found on the 1795 reverse but the edge legend was changed to read: WE PROMISE TO PAY THE

TALBOT, ALLUM & LEE CENTS

BEARER ONE CENT. Rare plain edge specimens of both dates exist. Exceptional pieces have edge ornamented or with lettering CAMBRIDGE BEDFORD AND HUNTINGDON.X.X.

1794 Cent with NEW YORK

V. Good	$80.
V. Fine	250.
E. Fine	425.
A. Unc.	700.
Unc.	1,400.

1794 Cent Without NEW YORK

V. Good	450.
V. Fine	1,400.
E. Fine	3,300.
A. Unc.	4,300.
Unc.	6,500.

1795 Cent

V. Good	$75.
V. Fine	225.
E. Fine	375.
A. Unc.	600.
Unc.	1,100.

MYDDELTON TOKENS

These tokens were struck at the Soho Mint of Boulton and Watt near Birmingham, England, but they were never actually issued for circulation in Kentucky. They are unsurpassed in beauty and design by any piece of this period.

1796 Myddelton Token

	Proof
Copper	$10,000.
Silver	10,000.

COPPER COMPANY OF UPPER CANADA

The obverse of this piece is the same as the Myddelton token. The new reverse legend was apparently intended for Canadian circulation, or it was used to give the token credibility and display the designer's skill.

	Proof
1796 Copper	$6,000.

CASTORLAND MEDAL

These medals or "jetons" are dated 1796 and allude to a proposed French settlement known as Castorland in Carthage, New York, at the time of the French Revolution. They were given to directors of the colonizing company for their attendance at board meetings.

Copy dies are still available and have been used at the Paris Mint for restriking throughout the years. Restrikes have a more modern look. Their metallic content (in French) is impressed on the edge: ARGENT (silver), CUIVRE (copper), and OR (gold).

	AU	UNC
1796 Silver original (Reeded edge, unbroken dies)	$5,000.	$7,500.
1796 Silver or bronze (original dies, reverse rusted and broken)	150.	275.
(1796) Silver restrike. (Paris Mint edge marks)	25.	60.
(1796) Bronze restike. (Paris Mint edge marks)	15.	35.

NEW YORK THEATRE TOKEN

Token penny issued by Skidmore of London illustrating the Park Theatre, New York c. 1797.

	AU	UNC
Penny, THE THEATRE AT NEW YORK AMERICA	$6,500.	$11,000.

NEW SPAIN (TEXAS) JOLA

These copper tokens were authorized by the military governor of San Antonio in 1818. Eight thousand pieces were coined by José Antonio de la Garza (JAG). Large and small planchet varieties exist, and all are very rare.

	F	VF	EF
1818 1/2 Real	$4,000.	$6,500.	$13,000.

NORTH WEST COMPANY TOKEN

These tokens were probably valued at one beaver and struck in Birmingham in 1820 by John Walker & Co. All but two known specimens are holed, and most have been found in the region of the lower Columbia River valley in Oregon.

1820 Copper or Brass
- Good .... $500.
- V. Good .... 1,500.
- Fine .... 2,750.
- V. Fine .... 4,750.

VIII. WASHINGTON PIECES

An interesting series of coins and tokens dated from 1783 to 1795 bear the portrait of George Washington. The likenesses in most instances were faithfully reproduced and were designed to honor Washington. Many of these pieces were of English origin and made later than the dates indicate.

The legends generally signify a strong unity among the states and a marked display of patriotism which pervaded the new nation during that period. We find among these tokens an employment of what were soon to become our official coin devices, namely, the American eagle, the United States shield and stars. The denomination *one cent* is used in several instances, while on some of the English pieces *halfpenny* will be found. Several of these pieces were private patterns for proposed coinage contracts.

GEORGIVS TRIUMPHO TOKEN

Although the head shown on this token bears a strong resemblance to that on some coins of George III, many collectors consider the Georgivs Triumpho (Triumphant George) a token intended to commemorate the successful termination of the Revolutionary War.

The reverse side shows the Goddess of Liberty behind a framework of thirteen bars and fleur de lis. She holds an olive branch in her right hand and staff of liberty in her left. VOCE POPOLI (By the Voice of the People) 1783.

1783 GEORGIVS TRIUMPHO	
V. Good	$100.
Fine	250.
V. Fine	575.
E. Fine	1,100.
A. Unc.	2,000.
Unc.	4,500.

**Military Bust
Large Military Bust
Point of Bust
Close to W
(illustrated)**

	F	VF	EF	AU	UNC
1783 Lg military bust	$80.	$160.	$375.	$900.	$2,250.
1783 Sm military bust, plain edge	85.	175.	450.	1,000.	2,750.
1783 Sm military bust, engrailed edge	110.	250.	600.	1,500.	3,250.

1783 Draped bust, no button (illustrated)	85.	175.	400.	800.	2,000.
1783 Draped bust, with button on drapery at neck	130.	325.	600.	975.	4,000.

		Proof
1783 Draped bust. Copper restrike, plain edge	....	$775.
1783 Draped bust. Copper restrike, engrailed edge	....	550.
1783 Draped bust. Silver restrike, engrailed edge	....	1,350.

1783
UNITY STATES

V. Good	$90.
V. Fine	240.
E. Fine	475.
A. Unc.	950.
Unc.	2,100.

Undated Double Head Cent

Fine	$90.
V. Fine	225.
E. Fine	475.
A. Unc.	950.
Unc.	2,500.

Satirical medal
presumably of
American origin.

1784 Ugly head — Copper

.................$14,850.

1784 Ugly head — Pewter ..*(Unique)*

1791 Cent
Edge Lettered: UNITED STATES OF AMERICA . ★

	Fine	E. Fine	A. Unc.	Unc.
1791 Cent, lg eagle (date on obverse)	$400.	$800.	$1,500.	$2,500.
1791 Cent, sm eagle (date on reverse)	425.	850.	1,750.	2,800.

1791 Liverpool
Halfpenny
Lettered Edge

Fine	$1,200.
E. Fine	3,250.
A. Unc.	5,500.

1792 Eagle with Stars
Copper . . . . —
Silver . . . . —
2004 Stack's Auction $115,000
Gold *(Unique)* . . . . —

Eagle reverse with
"Washington Born Virginia"
obverse *(3 known)* . . . . . . —

(1792) Undated Cent "WASHINGTON BORN VIRGINIA"				1792 Cent "WASHINGTON PRESIDENT"		
	VG	F	VF		VG	F	VF
Copper	$1,600.	$3,000.	$5,500.	Plain edge	$1,750.	$4,750.	$7,500.
Silver	—	—	—	Lettered edge . .	—	—	—

Uniface restrike of obverse exists, made from transfer dies by Albert Collis, 1959.

GETZ PATTERNS

    Dies engraved by Peter Getz of Lancaster, Pennsylvania were probably intended for the half dollar and cent, but were rejected by the president who did not want his portrait on the first United States coinage.

★

	VG	F	VF	EF
1792 Small eagle Silver . . 2004 Stack's Auction . . . $241,500	—	—	—	—
1792 Small eagle Copper	$4,750	$8,500	$1,600	$27,000
2004 Stack's Auction . . $54,625				
1792 Small eagle Copper, Ornamented edge				
(circles and squares) . . 2004 Stack's Auction . . .$149,500	—	—	—	—
1792 Small eagle Silver	—	—	—	—
Ornamented edge . . . . 2004 Stack's Auction . . .$391,000				
1792 Large eagle Silver . . 2004 Stack's Auction . . . $34,500	—	—	—	—

WASHINGTON PIECES

1792 Cent
Roman Head

Lettered Edge:
UNITED STATES OF
AMERICA

2004 Stack's Auction $32,200

1793 Ship
Halfpenny

Lettered Edge

Fine	$200.
V. Fine	375.
E. Fine	725.
A. Unc.	1,000.
Unc.	2,500.
Plain edge (Rare)	—

1795 Halfpenny
Grate Token

(Large coat buttons
variety illustrated.)

	VF	EF	AU	UNC
1795 Lg buttons, lettered edge	$400.	$800.	$1,400.	$2,100.
1795 Lg buttons, reeded edge	200.	400.	600.	900.
1795 Sm buttons, reeded edge	250.	500.	750.	1,300.

LIBERTY AND SECURITY TOKENS

	F	VF	EF	AU
1795 Halfpenny, plain edge	$135.	$275.	$600.	$1,100.
1795 Halfpenny, LONDON edge	125.	250.	550.	975.
1795 Halfpenny, BIRMINGHAM edge	135.	300.	650.	1,200.
1795 Halfpenny, ASYLUM EDGE	250.	550.	1,300.	2,000.
1795 Penny, ASYLUM edge	—	—		

WASHINGTON PIECES

Liberty and Security (1795)

	F	VF	EF	AU	UNC
Undated Liberty and Security penny	$275.	$500.	$950.	$1,600.	$3,000.
Same, corded outer rims	550.	900.	1,950.	3,300.	—

SUCCESS MEDALS

	F	VF	EF	AU	UNC
SUCCESS medal, Lg Plain or reeded edge	$250.	$500.	$900.	$2,100.	$3,500.
SUCCESS medal Sm Plain or reeded edge	300.	600.	1,150.	2,200.	3,750.

These pieces are struck in copper or brass and are believed to have been made in the mid nineteenth century. Specimens with original silvering are rare and valued 20 to 50 percent higher. Varieties exist.

NORTH WALES HALFPENNY

	G	F	VF	EF
1795 NORTH WALES Halfpenny	$100.	$250.	$550.	$1,250.
1795 Lettered edge	500.	1,300.	2,500.	—
1795 Two stars at each side of harp	1,000.	3,600.	—	

The first coins issued by authority of the United States were the "Fugio" cents. Entries in the Journal of Congress supply interesting information about proceedings relating to this coinage.

Saturday, April 21, 1787. ...

"That the board of treasury be authorized to contract for three hundred tons of copper coin of the federal standard, agreeable to the proposition of Mr. James Jarvis... That it be coined at the expense of the contractor, etc."

On Friday, July 6, 1787, there was "Resolved, that the board of treasury direct the contractor for the copper coinage to stamp on one side of each piece the following device, viz: thirteen circles linked together, a small circle in the middle, with the words 'United States,' around it; and in the centre, the words 'We are one'; on the other side of the same piece the following device, viz: a dial with the hours expressed on the face of it; a meridian sun above on one side of which is the word 'Fugio,' (The intended meaning is, 'time flies') and on the other the year in figures '1787', below the dial, the words 'Mind Your Business.' "

The legends have been credited to Benjamin Franklin, and the coin, as a consequence, has sometimes been referred to as the Franklin Cent.

These cents were coined in New Haven, Conn., and possibly elsewhere. Most of the copper used in this coinage came from military stores. It is believed to have been the copper bands which held together the powder kegs sent to us by the French. The dies were made by Abel Buell of New Haven.

1787 WITH POINTED RAYS

Cross after date

American Congress Pattern

	VG	F	VF	EF	AU	UNC
Obv. no cinquefoils. Cross after date.						
Rev. Rays and AMERICAN CONGRESS			—	$175,000.		
Rev. label with raised rims				*(Ex. Rare)*		
Rev. STATES UNITED	$650.	$1,200.	$3,200.	—	—	—
Rev. UNITED STATES	625.	1,100.	3,000.	—	—	—

Cinquefoil after date

Note: The following types with pointed rays have regular obverses punctuated with four cinquefoils (five-leafed ornament.)

	VG	F	VF	EF	AU	UNC
STATES UNITED at sides of circle,						
Cinquefoils on label	$225.	$400.	$725.	$1,200.	$1,600.	$2,500.
STATES UNITED, 1 over horiz. 1	350.	800.	1,750.	3,500.		
UNITED STATES, 1 over horiz. 1	325.	700.	1,500.	3,000.		
UNITED STATES at sides of circle	235.	425.	750.	1,400.	1,750.	2,800.

THE FUGIO CENTS

	VG	F	VF	EF	AU	UNC
STATES UNITED, Label with raised rims, . Large letters in WE ARE ONE	$450.	$800.	$2,000.	$4,750.	$8,000.	$15,000.
STATES UNITED, 8 pointed stars on label	450.	650.	1,100.	2,250.	4,000.	—
UNITED above, STATES below. (Rare) . . .	—	—	—	—	—	—

1787 WITH CLUB RAYS

	VG	F	VF	EF	AU
Club Rays. Rounded ends	$425.	$850.	$1,900.	$3,600.	$5,500.
Club Rays. Concave ends to rays: . . . . FUCIO (C instead of G). *(Ex. Rare)*	3,200.	6,750.	16,000.		
Club Rays. Concave ends. FUGIO, UNITED STATES . .	3,700.	7,700.	18,000.	—	—
Club Rays. Similar, STATES UNITED Reverse	—	—		—	—

New Haven "Restrike," note narrow rings

	EF	AU	UNC
Gold *(2 known)*	—	—	—
Silver	$1,000.	$1,400.	$2,400.
Copper or brass	350.	500.	750.

So-called New Haven "restrikes" are believed to have been made from dies created in the 1860s. A story was circulated at that time that these were old dies found by 14-year old C. Wylls Betts in 1858 on the site of the Broom & Platt store in New Haven, where the original coins were made.

BIBLIOGRAPHY

Breen, Walter. *Encyclopedia of U.S. and Colonial Coins*. New York 1988.
Carlotto, Tony. *The Copper Coins of Vermont*. Chelsea, MI 1998.
Crosby, S. S. *The Early Coins of America*. Boston 1875 (reprinted 1945, 1965, 1974, 1983).
Kessler, Alan. *The Fugio Cents*. Newtonville, Massachusetts 1976.
Maris, Edward. *A Historic Sketch of the Coins of New Jersey*. Philadelphia 1881 (reprinted 1925, 1974, 1987).
Miller, Henry C. and Hillyer Ryder. *The State Coinages of New England*. New York 1920.
Nelson, Philip. *The Coinage of William Wood 1722-1733*. London 1903 (reprinted 1959).
Newman, Eric P. *Coinage for Colonial Virginia*. New York 1957.
Studies on Money in Early America. American Numismatic Society. New York 1976.
Noe, Sydney P. *The New England and Willow Tree Coinage of Massachusetts*. New York 1943. *The Oak Tree Coinage of Massachusetts*. New York 1947, and *The Pine Tree Coinage of Massachusetts*. New York 1952. (all reprinted 1973).
Rulau, Russell and George Fuld. *Medallic Portraits of Washington*. Iola, Wisconsin 1999.
Wurtzbach, Carl. *Massachusetts Colonial Silver Money 1937*.

X. FIRST UNITED STATES MINT ISSUES

Many members of the House favored a representation of the President's head on the obverse of each coin; others considered the idea a monarchical practice. Washington is believed to have expressed disapproval of the use of his portrait on our coins.

The majority considered a figure emblematic of Liberty more appropriate and the Senate finally concurred in this opinion. Robert Birch was an engraver employed at designing proposed devices for our coins. He, perhaps together with others, engraved the dies for the disme and half disme. He has also been associated with a large copper cent of unusual design known as the Birch Cent.

1792 SILVER CENTER CENT

	VF
Cent. Silver Center — *(13 known. A unique specimen has no silver plug)*	$150,000.
Cent. No silver center *(8 known)*	150,000.

1792 BIRCH CENT

Copper—Plain edge *(Unique)*
Copper—Lettered edge to be esteemed * BE USEFUL * *(8 known)*
  (Unc. 200,000) .... $200,000.
Copper—Lettered edge TO BE ESTEEMED BE USEFUL * *(2 known)*
White Metal—G*W.Pt. (George Washington President) .... 250,000.
  below wreath. *(Unique)*

1792 HALF DISME

	G	VG	F	VF	EF	AU
Silver	$10,000.	$17,500.	$25,000.	$37,500.	$52,500.	$100,000.
Copper *(Unique)*	—	—	—	—	—	—

	EF	UNC
Silver *(3 known)*	$350,000.	—
Copper *(about 15 known)*	150,000.	300,000.

1792 PATTERN QUARTER DOLLAR

Joseph Wright, an accomplished artist in the private sector, designed this attractive pattern quarter dollar intended for the original United States coins. He was George Washington's choice for the position of first Chief Engraver of the United States Mint, and designed the 1793 Liberty Cap Cent in that capacity, but died in 1793 before being confirmed by Congress. Unique uniface trials of the quarter dollar pattern obverse and reverse also exist.

Copper . . . . (2 known)
White Metal . . . . (4 known)

MINTS AND MINT MARKS

Mint marks are small letters designating where coins were made. Coins struck at Philadelphia before 1979 (except 1942-1945 five-cent pieces) do not have a mint mark. Starting in 1979 a letter P was used on the dollar, and thereafter on all other denominations except the cent. Mint mark position is on the reverse of nearly all coins prior to 1965 (the cent is an exception), and on the obverse after 1967. Letters used are as follows:

C — Charlotte, North Carolina (gold coins only). 1838-1861.

CC — Carson City, Nevada. 1870-1893.

D — Dahlonega, Georgia (gold coins only). 1838-1861.

D — Denver, Colorado. 1906 to date.

O — New Orleans, Louisiana. 1838-1909.

P — Philadelphia, Pennsylvania. 1793 to date.

S — San Francisco, California. 1854 to date.

W — West Point, New York. 1984 to date.

All dies for United States coins were made at the Philadelphia Mint prior to 1996. Some dies are now made at the Denver Mint. Dies for use at other mints are made with the appropriate mint mark before they are shipped to those mints. Because this was a hand operation prior to 1985, the exact positioning and size of the mint mark may vary slightly, depending on where and how deeply the punch was impressed. This also accounts for double-punched and superimposed mint marks such as the 1938 D over D, and D over S Buffalo nickels. Polishing of dies may also alter the apparent size of fine details. Occasionally the mint mark is inadvertently left off a die sent to a branch mint, as was the case with some of the recent Proof dimes. Similarly, some 1982 dimes without mint mark, were made as business strikes. The mint mark "M" was used on coins made in Manila for the Philippines 1925-1941.

Prior to 1900, punches for mint marks varied greatly in size. This is particularly noticeable in the 1850 to 1880 period in which the letters range from very small to very large. An attempt to standardize sizes started in 1892 with the Barber series, but exceptions are seen in the 1892 O half dollar and 1905 O dime, both of which have normal and "microscopic" mint marks. A more or less standard size small mint mark was used on all minor coins starting in 1909, and on all dimes, quarters and halves after the Barber series was replaced in 1916. Slight variations in mint mark size occur through 1945 with notable differences in 1928, when small and large S mint marks were used.

In recent years a single D or S punch has been used to mark all branch mint dies. The change to the larger D for Denver coins occurred in 1933. Nickels, dimes, half dollars and dollars of 1934 exist with either the old, smaller size mint mark or the new, larger size D. All other denominations of 1934 and after are standard. The San Francisco mint mark was changed to larger size during 1941 and, with the exception of the half dollar, all 1941 S coins are known with either small or large size mint marks. Halves were not changed until 1942, and the 1942 S and 1943 S pieces exist both ways. The 1945 S dime with "microscopic" S is an unexplained use of a punch originally intended for Philippine coins 1907-1920. In 1979 the punches were replaced. Varieties of some 1979 coins appear with either the old or new shaped S or D. The S punch was again replaced in 1982 with a more distinct letter.

Mint mark application technique for Proof coins was changed in 1985, and for business strike production in 1990-91, when the letter was applied directly to the production hub rather than being hand punched on each working die. At the same time all the mint mark letters were made much larger and clearer than those of previous years.

PROOF COINS

A "Proof" is a specimen striking of coinage for presentation, souvenir, exhibition, or numismatic purposes. Pre-1968 Proofs were made only at the Philadelphia Mint except in a few rare instances in which presentation pieces were struck at branch mints. Current Proofs are made at San Francisco and West Point.

The term "Proof" refers to the method of manufacture and not the condition of a coin. Regular production coins in mint state have coruscating, frosty luster, soft details, and minor imperfections. Proof coins can usually be distinguished by their sharpness of detail, high wire edge, and extremely brilliant, mirrorlike surface. All Proofs are originally sold by the mint at a premium.

Very few Proof coins were made prior to 1856. Because of their rarity and infrequent sales, they are not all listed in this catalog.

Frosted Proofs were issued prior to 1936 and starting again in the late 1970's. These have a brilliant mirrorlike field with contrasting dull or frosted design.

Matte Proofs have a granular "sandblast" surface instead of the mirror finish. Matte Proof cents, nickels, and gold coins were issued from 1908 to 1916; a few 1921 and 1922 silver dollars were also struck in this manner.

Brilliant Proofs have been issued from 1936 to date. These have a uniformly brilliant mirrorlike surface and sharp, high relief details.

"Prooflike" coins are occasionally seen. These are specimens from the first few impressions of regular coinage dies from any mint. They are not true Proofs, but may have most of the characteristics of a Proof coin and generally command a premium. Collectors should beware of coins that have been buffed to look like Proofs; magnification will reveal polishing lines and lack of detail.

How A Proof Coin Is Made...

Selected dies are inspected for perfection and are highly polished and cleaned. They are again wiped clean or polished after every 15 to 25 impressions and are replaced frequently to avoid imperfections from worn dies. Coinage blanks are polished and cleaned to assure high quality in striking. They are then hand fed into the coinage press one at a time, each blank receiving two or more blows from the dies to bring up sharp, high relief details. The coinage operation is done at slow speed with extra pressure. Finished Proofs are individually inspected and are handled by gloves or tongs. They also receive a final inspection by packers before being sonically sealed in special plastic cases.

After a lapse of twenty years, Proof coins were struck at the Philadelphia Mint from 1936 to 1942 inclusive. In 1942, when the composition of the five-cent piece was changed, there were two types of this denomination available to collectors. The striking of Proof coins was temporarily suspended from 1943 to 1949, and again from 1965 to 1967; during the latter period special mint sets were struck. Proof sets were resumed in 1968. They are available during the year of issue from: The United States Mint, Customer Service Center, 10003 Derekwood Lane, Lanham, MD 20706.

Sets from 1936 through 1972 include the cent, nickel, dime, quarter and half; from 1973 through 1981 the dollar was also included, and again from 2000 on. Regular Proof sets issued from 1982 to 1998 contain the cent through half dollar. Special sets containing commemorative coins were sold at an additional premium. Beginning in 1999 sets contain five different statehood quarters. 1999 Proof dollars were sold separately.

Values are for sets in average unspotted condition.

Year Minted	Sets Minted	Issue Price	Current Value
1936	(3,837)	$1.89	$6,000.
1937	(5,542)	1.89	3,500.
1938	(8,045)	1.89	1,800.
1939	(8,795)	1.89	1,750.
1940	(11,246)	1.89	1,400.
1941	(15,287)	1.89	1,500.
1942 Both nickels	(21,120)	1.89	1,400.
1942 One nickel		1.89	1,250.
1950	(51,386)	2.10	650.
1951	(57,500)	2.10	600.
1952	(81,980)	2.10	325.
1953	(128,800)	2.10	310.
1954	(233,300)	2.10	175.
1955 Box pack	(378,200)	2.10	150.
1955 Flat pack ....Included above		2.10	175.

PROOF SETS

Year Minted	Sets Minted	Issue Price	Current Value
1956	(669,384)	$2.10	$75.
1957	(1,247,952)	2.10	38.
1958	(875,652)	2.10	80.
1959	(1,149,291)	2.10	30.
1960 with lg. date 1 cent	(1,691,602)	2.10	22.
1960 with sm. date 1 cent	Included above	2.10	60.
1961	(3,028,244)	2.10	12.
1962	(3,218,019)	2.10	12.
1963	(3,075,645)	2.10	16.
1964	(3,950,762)	2.10	12.
1968S	(3,041,506)	5.00	9.
1968S 10 cent w/o mint mark	Included above	5.00	10,000.
1969S	(2,934,631)	5.00	8.
1970S	(2,632,810)	5.00	18.
1970S with sm. date 1 cent	Included above	5.00	125.
1970S 10 cent w/o mint mark (est 2,200)	Included above	5.00	1,700.
1971S	(3,220,733)	5.00	7.
1971S 5 cent w/o mint mark (est 1,655)	Included above	5.00	1,500.
1972S	(3,260,996)	5.00	6.
1973S	(2,760,339)	7.00	14.
1974S	(2,612,568)	7.00	12.
1975S (with 1976 25 cent, 50 cent, $1)	(2,845,450)	7.00	16.
1975S 10 cent w/o mint mark	Included above	7.00	45,000.
1976S	(4,149,730)	7.00	10.
1976S 3 pc. set	(3,998,621)	15.00	20.
1977S	(3,251,152)	9.00	10.
1978S	(3,127,781)	9.00	11.
1979S Filled S	(3,677,175)	9.00	12.
1979S Clear S	Included above	9.00	140.
1980S	(3,554,806)	10.00	12.
1981S Filled S	(4,063,083)	11.00	11.
1981S Clear S (all coins)	Included above	11.00	375.
1982S	(3,857,479)	11.00	6.
1983S	(3,138,765)	11.00	8.
1983S 10 cent w/o mint mark	Included above	11.00	1,300.
1983S Prestige Set (Olympic dollar)	(140,361)	59.00	100.
1984S	(2,748,430)	11.00	13.
1984S Prestige Set (Olympic dollar)	(316,680)	59.00	25.
1985S	(3,362,821)	11.00	8.
1986S	(2,411,180)	11.00	22.
1986S Prestige Set (Statue 50 cent, 1$)	(599,317)	48.50	35.
1987S	(3,792,233)	11.00	7.
1987S Prestige Set (Constitution dollar)	(435,495)	45.00	23.
1988S	(3,031,287)	11.00	12.
1988S Prestige Set (Olympic dollar)	(231,661)	45.00	35.
1989S	(3,009,107)	11.00	12.
1989S Prestige Set (Congressional 50 cent, $1)	Included above	45.00	40.
1990S	(2,793,433)	11.00	12.
1990S with no-S 1 cent proof set	(3,555)	11.00	6,000.
1990S with no-S 1 cent Prestige set	Included above	45.00	6,200.
1990S Prestige Set (Eisenhower dollar)	(506,126)	45.00	32.
1991S	(2,610,833)	11.00	18.
1991 Prestige Set (Mt. Rushmore 50 cent, $1)	(256,954)	59.00	80.
1992S	(2,675,618)	11.00	10.
1992S Prestige Set (Olympic 50 cent, $1)	(183,293)	56.00	90.
1992S Silver	(1,009,586)	21.00	18.
1992S Silver Premier Set	(308,055)	37.00	19.
1993S	(2,409,394)	12.50	16.
1993S Prestige Set (Madison 50 cent, $1)	(224,045)	57.00	50.
1993S Silver	(570,213)	21.00	40.
1993S Silver Premier Set	(191,140)	37.50	42.
1994S	(2,308,701)	12.50	25.
1994S Prestige Set (World Cup 50 cent, $1)	(175,893)	$57.00	$56.
1994S Silver	(636,009)	21.00	44.

[75]

PROOF SETS

Year Minted	Sets Minted	Issue Price	Current Value
1994S Silver Premier Set	(149,320)	$37.50	$47.
1995S	(2,010,384)	12.50	90.
1995S Prestige Set (Civil War 50 cent, $1)	(107,112)	57.00	275.
1995S Silver	(549,878)	21.00	110.
1995S Silver Premier Set	(130,107)	37.50	110.
1996S	(1,695,244)	12.50	18.
1996S Prestige Set (Olympic 50 cent, $1)	(55,000)	57.00	500.
1996S Silver	(623,655)	21.00	50.
1996S Silver Premier Set	(151,366)	37.50	55.
1997S	(1,975,000)	12.50	62.
1997S Prestige Set (Botanic $1)	(80,000)	48.00	200.
1997S Silver	(605,473)	21.00	100.
1997S Silver Premier Set	(136,205)	37.50	100.
1998S	(2,086,507)	12.50	38.
1998S Silver	(638,134)	21.00	45.
1998S Silver Premier Set	(240,658)	37.50	45.
1999S 9 piece set	(2,543,401)	19.95	90.
1999S 5 piece quarter set	(1,169,958)	13.95	60.
1999S Silver 9 piece set	(804,565)	31.95	275.
2000S 10 piece set	(3,082,483)	19.95	22.
2000S 5 piece quarter set	(937,600)	13.95	18.
2000S Silver 10 piece set	(965,421)	31.95	40.
2001S 10 piece set	(2,294,043)	19.95	75.
2001S 5 piece quarter set	(799,231)	13.95	40.
2001S Silver 10 piece set	(889,697)	31.95	125.
2002S 10 piece set	(2,277,720)	19.95	50.
2002S 5 piece quarter set	(761,000)	13.95	30.
2002S Silver 10 piece set	(888,826)	31.95	80.
2003S 10 piece set		19.95	20.
2003S 5 piece quarter set		13.95	14.
2003S Silver 10 piece set		31.95	32.
2004S Silver 5 piece quarter set		23.95	24.

UNCIRCULATED MINT SETS

Official Mint Sets are specially packaged by the government for sale to collectors. They contain uncirculated specimens of each year's coins for every denomination issued from each mint. Unlike the Proof sets, these are normal coins intended for circulation and are not minted with any special consideration for quality. Coins struck only as Proofs are not included.

Uncirculated sets sold by the Treasury from 1947 through 1958 contained two examples of each regular-issue coin. These were packaged in cardboard holders that did not protect the coins from tarnish. Nicely preserved early sets generally command a 10 to 20 percent premium above listed values. No official mint sets were produced in 1950, 1982 or 1983.

Since 1959 sets have been sealed in a protective plastic envelope. In 1965, 1966 and 1967, Special Mint Sets of higher than normal quality were made as a substitute for Proof sets which were not made during that period. Similar specimen sets dated 1964 are reported to exist. The 1966 and 1967 sets were packaged in hard plastic holders.

Privately assembled mint sets, and souvenir sets produced for sale at the Philadelphia or Denver mints, or for special occasions, are valued according to the individual pieces they contain. Only the official government sealed full sets are included in the following list.

Current year sets may be ordered by telephoning 1-800-USA MINT.

Year Minted	Sets Minted	Issue Price	Face Value	Current Value
1947 P-D-S	(5,000)	$4.87	$4.46	$1,300.00
1948 P-D-S	(6,000)	4.92	4.46	650.00
1949 P-D-S	(5,000)	5.45	4.96	900.00
1951 P-D-S	8,654	6.75	5.46	900.00
1952 P-D-S	11,499	6.14	5.46	800.00
1953 P-D-S	15,538	6.14	5.46	600.00
1954 P-D-S	25,599	6.19	5.46	300.00
1955 P-D-S	49,656	3.57	2.86	190.00
1956 P-D	45,475	3.34	2.64	175.00
1957 P-D	34,324	4.40	3.64	250.00
1958 P-D	50,314	4.43	3.64	175.00

UNCIRCULATED MINT SETS

Year Minted	Sets Minted	Issue Price	Face Value	Current Value
1959 P-D	187,000	$2.40	$1.82	$50.00
1960 P-D	260,485	2.40	1.82	27.00
1961 P-D	223,704	2.40	1.82	48.00
1962 P-D	385,285	2.40	1.82	20.00
1963 P-D	606,612	2.40	1.82	15.00
1964 P-D	1,008,108	2.40	1.82	13.00
1968 P-D-S	2,105,128	2.50	1.33	5.00
1969 P-D-S	1,817,392	2.50	1.33	7.00
1970 P-D-S Lg. date 1 cent ...	2,038,134	2.50	1.33	20.00
1970 P-D-S Sm. date 1 cent ...		2.50	1.33	50.00
1971 P-D-S‡	2,193,396	3.50	1.83	4.50
1972 P-D-S‡	2,750,000	3.50	1.83	4.50
1973 P-D-S	1,767,691	6.00	3.83	25.00
1974 P-D-S	1,975,981	6.00	3.83	8.00
1973 P-D (w/1976 25c, 50c, $1)	1,921,488	6.00	3.82	12.00
1776-1976 (3 pieces)	4,908,319	9.00	1.75	18.00
1976 P-D	1,892,513	6.00	3.82	12.00
1977 P-D	2,006,869	7.00	3.82	9.00
1978 P-D	2,162,609	7.00	3.82	10.00
1979 P-D*	2,526,000	8.00	3.82	8.00
1980 P-D-S	2,815,066	9.00	4.82	8.00
1981 P-D-S	2,908,145	11.00	4.82	18.00
1984 P-D	1,832,857	7.00	1.82	7.00
1985 P-D	1,710,571	7.00	1.82	9.00
1986 P-D	1,153,536	7.00	1.82	25.00
1987 P-D	2,890,758	7.00	1.82	9.00
1988 P-D	1,646,204	7.00	1.82	9.00
1989 P-D	1,987,915	7.00	1.82	8.00
1990 P-D	1,809,184	7.00	1.82	7.00
1991 P-D	1,352,101	7.00	1.82	13.00
1992 P-D	1,500,143	7.00	1.82	8.00
1993 P-D	1,297,431	8.00	1.82	12.00
1994 P-D	1,234,813	8.00	1.82	12.00
1995 P-D	1,038,787	8.00	1.82	27.00
1996 P-D plus 1996W dime ...	1,457,949	8.00	1.92	24.00
1997 P-D	950,473	8.00	1.82	40.00
1998 P-D	1,187,325	8.00	1.82	19.00
1999 P-D (18 pieces)	1,243,867	14.95	3.82	40.00
2000 P-D (20 pieces)	1,416,000	14.95	5.82	19.00
2001 P-D (20 pieces)	1,113,623	14.95	5.82	24.00
2002 P-D (20 pieces)	1,139,388	14.95	5.82	19.00
2003 P-D (20 pieces)		14.95	5.82	30.00
2004 P-D (22 pieces)		16.95	5.92	19.00

‡ Dollar not included.
* S mint dollar not included.

SPECIAL MINT SETS

1965 ....(2,360,000)		$4.00	$0.91	$14.00
1966 ....(2,261,583)		4.00	0.91	15.00
1967 ....(1,863,344)		4.00	0.91	22.00

SOUVENIR SETS

Uncirculated sets were packaged and sold at Philadelphia and Denver gift shops in 1982 and 1983 in place of the "official mint sets" which were not made in those years. A bronze mint medal is packaged with each set. Similar sets were also made in other years.

1982P		$4.00	$0.91	$25.00
1982D		4.00	0.91	20.00
1983P		4.00	0.91	40.00
1983D		4.00	0.91	30.00

UNITED STATES REGULAR ISSUES
HALF CENTS — 1793-1857

The half cent is the lowest face value coin struck by the United States. All half cents are scarce, and this series is beginning to enjoy the popularity of large cents and certain other early series. Prices for the common dates and varieties have remained at reasonable levels for many years.

This denomination was authorized to be coined April 2, 1792. Originally the weight was to have been 132 grains, but this was changed to 104 grains by the Act of January 14, 1793, before coinage commenced. The weight was again changed to 84 grains January 26, 1796 by presidential proclamation in conformity with the Act of March 3, 1795. Coinage was discontinued by the Act of February 21, 1857. All were coined at the Philadelphia Mint.

There were various intermissions in coinage. During the period from 1836 to 1848, coinage consisted entirely of Proofs and in very small quantities, causing a very noticeable lapse in the series for most collectors. While 1796 is the most valuable date, the original and restrike Proofs of 1831, 1836, and 1840 through 1848, along with other rare varieties, are all to difficult to obtain.

+ or – indicates change from previous year	TYPE COIN VALUES									
	G-4	F-12	EF-40	AU-50	MS-60	MS-63	MS-65	PF-60	PF-63	PF-65
Flowing Hair 1793 ......1,850.+	4,500.+	15,000.+	20,000.+	*30,000.+*	*50,000.+*	*100,000.+*				
Liberty Cap 1794-1797 ....250.	700.+	3,000.+	4,800.+	10,000.+	15,000.+	*50,000.+*				
Draped Bust 1800-1808 ....50.+	80.+	225.	500.+	1,000.+	2,500.+	8,000.+				
Classic Head 1809-1835 ....30.	50.	85.+	150.+	250.+	450.	2,400.+	5,000.+	4,500.+	8,500.+
Coronet Head 1840-1857 ...32.+	55.+	85.+	135.+	225.+	400.+	2,000.+	2,300.+	4,500.+	7,750.+

LIBERTY CAP TYPE 1793-1797

AG-3 ABOUT GOOD—*Clear enough to identify.*
G-4 GOOD—*Outline of bust clear, no details. Date readable. Reverse lettering incomplete.*
VG-8 VERY GOOD—*Some hair details. Reverse lettering complete.*
F-12 FINE—*Most of hair detail shows. Leaves worn but all visible.*
VF-20 VERY FINE—*Hair near ear and forehead worn, other areas distinct. Some details in leaves show.*
EF-40 EXTREMELY FINE—*Light wear on highest parts of head and wreath.*
AU-50 ABOUT UNCIRCULATED—*Only a trace of wear shows on Liberty's face.*

Values shown are for coins with attractive surfaces and color consistent with the amount of normal wear. Minor imperfections are permissible for grades below Fine. Coins that are porous, corroded, or similarly defective are worth significantly lower prices.

Head Facing Left 1793

Designer, probably Joseph Wright; weight 6.74 grams; composition: copper; approx. diameter 22 mm; edge: TWO HUNDRED FOR A DOLLAR.

	Mintage	AG-3	G-4	VG-8	F-12	VF-20	EF-40	AU-50
1793	35,334	$1,000.	$1,850.	$3,000.	$4,500.	$7,500.	$15,000.	$20,000.

HALF CENTS

Head Facing Right 1794-1797

1794 — Designer Robert Scot; weight 6.74 grams; composition: copper; approx. diameter 23.5 mm; edge: TWO HUNDRED FOR A DOLLAR.

1795 — Designer John Smith Gardner; weight 6.74 grams; composition: copper; approx. diameter 23.5 mm; edge: TWO HUNDRED FOR A DOLLAR.

1795-1797 (thin planchet) — Weight 5.44 grams; composition: copper; approx. diameter 23.5 mm; edge: plain (some 1797 are either lettered or gripped).

| | | Normal Head | | High Relief Head | | | |

	Mintage	AG-3	G-4	VG-8	F-12	VF-20	EF-40	AU-50
1794 Nml head .... }	81,600	$200.	$400.	$600.	$1,000.	$1,750.	$4,000.	$7,000.
1794 High relief head ...		225.	425.	650.	1,100.	1,900.	4,250.	7,500.

| | Pole to Cap | Punctuated Date | | No Pole to Cap | | | |

	AG-3	G-4	VG-8	F-12	VF-20	EF-40	AU-50
1795 All Kinds 139,690							
1795, Ltrd.edge, w pole ..	125.	350.	500.	800.	1,400.	3,200.	5,000.
1795, Ltrd.edge,Punc.Dt .	125.	350.	500.	800.	1,400.	3,200.	5,000.
1795, Plain Edge,Punc.Dt	110.	325.	475.	700.	1,300.	3,000.	4,800.
1795, Plain edge,no pole‡	110.	250.	450.	700.	1,200.	3,000.	6,000.
1796, With pole* .... } 1,390	5,000.	8,500.	12,500.	16,000.	24,000.	37,000.	60,000.
1796, No pole	10,000.	20,000.	30,000.	45,000.	70,000.	—	—

*The deceptive "Dr. Edwards" struck copy of this coin has a different head and larger letters.

  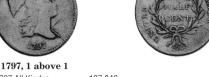

| | 1797, 1 above 1 | | | 1797 Low Head | | | |

	AG-3	G-4	VG-8	F-12	VF-20	EF-40	AU-50
1797 All Kinds‡ 127,840							
1797, 1 above 1, plain edge	150.	350.	475.	750.	1,400.	3,000.	4,800.
1797, Plain edge	200.	400.	525.	900.	1,750.	4,000.	5,000.
1797, Plain edge, low head	200.	400.	625.	1,300.	2,250.	5,500.	—
1797, Ltrd.edge	500.	1,200.	2,250.	4,750.	8,000.	24,000.	50,000.
1797, Gripped edge	6,500.	15,000.	40,000.	—	—	—	—

‡Many are struck on cut-down cents and a few are on planchets cut from Talbot, Allum & Lee tokens.

A modified reverse design was introduced during 1802 and used through 1808.

Designer Robert Scot: weight 5.44 grams; composition: copper; diameter 23.5 mm; plain edge.

AG-3 ABOUT GOOD — *Clear enough to identify.*
G-4 GOOD — *Bust outline clear, few details, date readable. Reverse lettering worn and incomplete.*
VG-8 VERY GOOD — *Some drapery shows. Date and legends complete.*
F-12 FINE — *Shoulder drapery and hair over brow worn smooth.*
VF-20 VERY FINE — *Only slight wear in above areas. Slight wear on reverse.*
EF-40 EXTREMELY FINE — *Light wear on highest parts of head and wreath.*
AU-50 ABOUT UNCIRCULATED — *Wear slight on the hair above forehead.*

| | | 1st Reverse
Style of 1800 | | 2nd Reverse
Style of 1803 | | |

	Mintage	AG-3	G-4	VG-8	F-12	VF-20	EF-40	AU-50
1800	202,908	$30.	$50.	$70.	$125.	$200.	$500.	$700.
1802, 2 /0, rev.of 1800	} 20,266	6,000.	16,000.	24,000.	35,000.	—	—	—
1802, 2 /0, 2nd. rev.		300.	600.	1,200.	2,800.	7,500.	18,000.	—
1803	} 92,000	25.	50.	70.	125.	250.	750.	1,000.
1803, widely spaced 3		25.	50.	70.	125.	250.	750.	1,000.

| Plain 4 | Crosslet 4 | Stemless Wreath | Stems to Wreath |

1804 All Kinds . . . 1,055,312							
1804, Plain 4, stems	30.	60.	90.	160.	275.	750.	1,500.
1804, Plain 4, stemless	25.	50.	65.	85.	150.	300.	500.
1804, Crosslet 4, stemless	25.	50.	65.	85.	150.	300.	500.
1804, Crosslet 4, stems	25.	50.	65.	85.	150.	300.	500.
1804, "Spiked chin"	30.	60.	75.	100.	175.	350.	575.

| 1804 "Spiked Chin" | Small 5 | Large 5 |

1805 All Kinds . . . 814,464							
1805, Med 5, stemless	25.	50.	65.	85.	150.	300.	500.
1805, Sm 5, stems	260.	650.	1,200.	2,500.	4,500.	9,000.	15,000.
1805, Lg 5, stems	25.	50.	65.	85.	150.	300.	500.

	Mintage	AG-3	G-4	VG-8	F-12	VF-20	EF-40	AU-50
		Small 6	**Large 6**				**1808, 8 over 7**	**Normal Date**
1806 All Kinds . .	356,000							
1806, Sm 6, stems		$50.	$200.	$350.	$550.	$1,000.	$2,200.	$4,500.
1806, Sm 6, stemless		25.	50.	65.	80.	125.	250.	500.
1806, Lg 6, stems		25.	50.	65.	80.	125.	250.	500.
1807	476,000	25.	50.	70.	85.	150.	400.	800.
1808, 8 over 7 . . }	400,000	60.	125.	250.	550.	1,100.	3,000.	7,500.
1808, NmlDt . . }		25.	50.	70.	85.	150.	400.	800.

CLASSIC HEAD TYPE 1809-1836

Designer John Reich. Standards same as previous issue.

G-4 GOOD—*LIBERTY only partly visible on hair band. Lettering, date, stars, worn but visible.*
VG-8 VERY GOOD—*LIBERTY entirely visible on hair band. Lower curls worn.*
F-12 FINE—*Only part wear on LIBERTY and hair at top worn in spots.*
VF-20 VERY FINE—*Lettering clear-cut. Hair only slightly worn.*
EF-40 EXTREMELY FINE—*Light wear on highest points of hair and leaves*
AU-50 ABOUT UNCIRCULATED—*Sharp hair detail with only a trace of wear on higher points.*
MS-60 UNCIRCULATED—*Typical brown to red surface. No trace of wear.*
MS-63 SELECT UNCIRCULATED—*Well-defined color, brown to red. No traces of wear.*

1809 Normal Date   **1809, 9 over inverted 9**   **1809 Small o Inside 0**

1811 Wide Date   **1811 Close Date**

	Mintage	G-4	VG-8	F-12	VF-20	EF-40	AU-50	MS-60	MS-63
1809 All Kinds	1,154,572								
1809, Sm o inside 0		$35.	$45.	$70.	$110.	$300.	$450.	$800.	$1,200.
1809, 9 over inverted 9		35.	60.	75.	100.	225.	600.	800.	1,500.
1809, NmlDt . . .		35.	45.	60.	80.	115.	200.	535.	750.
1810	215,000	35.	60.	100.	175.	425.	750.	1,600.	2,500.
1811 WdDt . . . . }	63,140	150.	350.	600.	1,400.	4,500.	6,000.	9,000.	10,000.
1811 ClDt . . . . . }		135.	300.	575.	1,300.	4,000.	4,000.	7,000.	8,000.
1811 Rev. of 1802. Unofficial restrike. *(Ex. Rare)*						—	—		
1825	63,000	35.	40.	60.	75.	150.	350.	750.	1,200.
1826	234,000	35.	40.	60.	75.	125.	250.	450.	600.

13 Stars   12 Stars

	Mintage	G-4	VG-8	F-12	VF-20	EF-40	AU-50	MS-60	MS-63
1828, 13 stars ..	} 606,000	$35.	$45.	$55.	$75.	$85.	$150.	$250.	$450.
1828, 12 stars ..		40.	50.	60.	85.	200.	300.	1,000.	1,500.
1829	487,000	35.	45.	55.	75.	125.	175.	300.	500.

Reverse
1831-1836

Reverse
1840-1857

Beginning in 1831 new coinage equipment and modified dies produced a raised rim on each side of these coins. Proofs and restrikes were made at the mint for sale to collectors. Restrikes are believed to have been struck c. 1858-61.

	Mintage	PF-40	PF-60	PF-63
1831, Original. (Beware of altered date)	2,200	$10,000.	$13,000.	$18,000.
1831, Restrike., Lg berries (Rev. of 1836)		—	5,000.	8,000.
1831, Res., Sm berries (Rev. of 1840-1857)		—	7,000.	13,000.

	Mintage	VG-8	F-12	VF-20	EF-40	AU-50	MS-60	PF-63
1832	51,000*	$40.	$55.	$65.	$85.	$150.	$350.	$4,500.
1833	103,000*	40.	55.	65.	85.	150.	325.	4,500.
1834	141,000*	40.	55.	65.	85.	150.	325.	4,500.
1835	398,000*	40.	55.	65.	85.	150.	325.	4,500.
1836, Original								7,500.
1836, Restrike. (Rev.of1840-57)								10,000.

*The figures given here are thought to be correct, although official mint records report these quantities for 1833-36 rather than 1832-35.

No half cents were struck in 1837. Because of the great need for small change, however, a large number of tokens similar in size to current large cents were issued privately by businessmen who needed them in commerce. A single half cent token was issued and is listed and illustrated below.

	G-4	VG-8	F-12	VF-20	EF-40	AU-50	MS-60
1837 Token (not a coin)	$30.	$40.	$50.	$85.	$165.	$275.	$500.

Brilliant red uncirculated half cents are worth more than prices shown.

Designer Christian Gobrecht; weight 5.44 grams; composition: copper; diameter 23 mm; plain edge.

VG-8 VERY GOOD—*Beads uniformly distinct. Hairlines show in spots.*
F-12 FINE—*Hairlines above ear worn. Beads sharp.*
VF-20 VERY FINE—*Lowest curl shows wear, hair otherwise distinct.*
EF-40 EXTREMELY FINE—*Light wear on highest points of hair and leaves.*
AU-50 ABOUT UNCIRCULATED—*Very slight trace of wear on hair above Liberty's ear*
MS-60 UNCIRCULATED—*No trace of wear. Lustre clear.*
MS-63 SELECT UNCIRCULATED—*No trace of wear.*
PF-63— *Nearly perfect.*

Both originals and restrikes use reverse of 1840-1857. Most originals have large berries and most restrikes have small berries in wreath.

	PF-63	PF-65
1840, Original	$5,000.	$7,500.
1840, Restrike	4,500.	7,000.
1841, Original	4,500.	7,000.
1841, Restrike	4,000.	6,500.
1842, Original	5,000.	7,500.
1842, Restrike	4,500.	7,000.
1843, Original	5,000.	7,000.
1843, Restrike	4,500.	7,000.
1844, Original	5,000.	7,500.
1844, Restrike	4,500.	7,000.

	PF-63	PF-65
1845, Original	$5,000.	$7,500.
1845, Restrike	4,500.	7,000.
1846, Original	5,000.	7,500.
1846, Restrike	4,500.	7,000.
1847, Original	5,500.	8,000.
1847, Restrike	4,000.	6,500.
1848, Original	5,500.	8,000.
1848, Restrike	4,500.	7,000.
1849, Original, SmDt .	5,000.	7,500.
1849, Restrike, SmDt .	5,500.	8,000.

Small Date   **Large Date**

Brilliant or red uncirculated half cents are worth more than prices shown.

	Mintage	VG-8	F-12	VF-20	EF-40	AU-50	MS-60	MS-63	PF-63
1849, LgDt . . .	39,864	$45.	$60.	$75.	$125.	$165.	$325.	$450.	—
1850	39,812	45.	60.	75.	130.	175.	375.	600.	4,500.
1851	147,672	40.	55.	65.	85.	135.	225.	400.	4,500.
1852 Orig									—
1852, Restrike									4,500.
1853	129,694	40.	55.	65.	85.	135.	225.	400.	—
1854	55,358	40.	55.	65.	85.	135.	225.	400.	4,500.
1855	56,500	40.	55.	65.	85.	135.	225.	400.	4,500.
1856	40,430	42.	60.	70.	95.	150.	250.	450.	4,500.
1857	35,180	60.	80.	100.	135.	200.	325.	500.	4,500.

BIBLIOGRAPHY
Breen, Walter, *Walter Breen's Encyclopedia of United States Half Cents 1793-1857.*
South Gate, California, 1983.
Cohen, Roger S., Jr. *American Half Cents—The "Little Half Sisters".* 2nd Edition, 1982.
Manley, Ronald P., *The Half Cent Die State Book. 1793-1857, United States, 1998.*

LARGE CENTS — 1793-1857

Cents and half cents were the first coins struck under the authority of the United States government. Coinage began in 1793 with laws specifying that the cent should weigh exactly twice as much as the half cent. Large cents were coined every year from 1793 to 1857 with the exception of 1815, when a lack of copper prevented production. All were coined at the Philadelphia Mint. Mintage records in some cases may be inaccurate, as many of the early pieces were struck later than the dates shown on the coins. Varieties listed are those most significant to collectors. Numerous other die varieties may be found because each of the early dies was individually made. Values of varieties not listed in this guide depend on collector interest, rarity and demand. Proof large cents were first made in 1817; all Proofs are rare, as they were not made available to the general public before the mid-1850s.

+ or – indicates change from previous year				TYPE COIN VALUES						
	G-4	F-12	EF-40	AU-50	MS-60	MS-63	MS-65	PF-60	PF-63	PF-65
Chain 1793 . . . . .5,250.+	10,000.+	30,000.+	50,000.+	80,000.+	95,000.	—			
Wreath 1793 . . . . .1,500.+	3,000.+	9,000.+	20,000.+	25,000.+	35,000.	67,000.+			
Liberty Cap 1793-1796 . . . . . . 200.	500.+	2,000.+	2,900.+	4,500.+	7,500.	24,000.+			
Draped Bust 1796-1807 . . . . . .40.	120.	750.+	1,250.	2,400.+	4,500.	16,000.+			
Classic Head 1808-1814 . . . . . .40.	200.	1,000.+	1,800.	2,800.+	8,000.	24,000.			
Coronet Head 1816-1839 . . . . .14.	26.+	100.+	200.+	300.+	500.+	1,400.+	—		
Braided Hair 1840-1857 . . . . . .13.	19.	50.	100.-	150.	250.-	900.	2,500.	4,500.	8,000.+

FLOWING HAIR, CHAIN TYPE REVERSE 1793

Designer Henry Voigt; weight 13.48 grams; composition: copper; approx. diameter 26-27 mm; edge: bars and slender vine with leaves.

AG-3 ABOUT GOOD — *Date and devices clear enough to identify.*
G-4 GOOD — *Lettering worn but readable. Bust has no detail.*
VG-8 VERY GOOD — *Date and lettering distinct, some details of head visible.*
F-12 FINE — *About half of hair, etc. details show.*
VF-20 VERY FINE — *Ear visible. Most of details can be seen.*
EF-40 EXTREMELY FINE — *Highest points of hair and back of temple show wear.*

Values shown for Fine and better copper coins are for those with attractive surfaces and color that are consistent with the amount of normal wear. Coins that are porous, corroded, or similarly defective are worth significantly lower prices.

Obverse	Ameri. Reverse	America Reverse

	AG-3	G-4	VG-8	F-12	VF-20	EF-40
1793 Chain 36,103						
1793, AMERI. in legend . . .	$2,200.	$6,000.	$8,000.	$12,000.	$24,000.	$40,000.
1793, AMERICA*	2,000.	5,250.	7,000.	10,000.	17,500.	30,000.

*Varieties with or without periods after date and LIBERTY.

LARGE CENTS

FLOWING HAIR, WREATH TYPE REVERSE 1793

The reverse of this type bears a "single-bow" wreath, as distinguished from the wreath tied with a double bow on the following type. A three-leaf sprig appears above the date on the obverse, and both sides have borders of small beads.

Introduction of this reverse answered criticism of the chain design, but the stronger modeling of the face and hair still failed to gain acceptance as representative of Liberty. After three months' production the design was abandoned in favor of the Liberty Cap type.

Instead of the normal sprig above the date, the rare "strawberry leaf" variety has a spray of trefoil leaves and a small blossom. The trefoils match those found on the normal wreath reverse. It is not clear why this variety was created. All known specimens are badly worn.

Designer Henry Voigt; weight 13.48 grams; composition: copper; approx. diameter 26-28 mm; edge: vine and bars, or lettered ONE HUNDRED FOR A DOLLAR followed by either a single or double leaf.

| | Wreath Type | | | | | Strawberry Leaf Var. | |

	Mintage	AG-3	G-4	VG-8	F-12	VF-20	EF-40	AU-50
1793 Wreath ...	63,353							
1793, Vine/bars edge		$450.	$1,500.	$1,750.	$3,000.	$5,000.	$9,000.	$20,000.
1793, Ltrd.edge		600.	1,600.	2,000.	3,500.	4,750.	10,000.	$20,000.
1793 Strawberry leaf				4 known				

LIBERTY CAP TYPE 1793-1796

Another major change was made in 1793 to satisfy continuing objections to the obverse portrait. This version appears to have been more successful, as it was continued into 1796. The 1793 pieces had beaded borders, but a border of denticles or "teeth" was adopted in 1794. A famous 1794 variety is the probably whimsical "starred" reverse, with a border of 94 tiny 5-pointed stars under the denticles.

Portrait variations listed below for 1794 are the result of several changes of die engravers. The so-called "Jefferson Head" of 1795 is now thought to be a sample for a proposed coinage contract by a private manufacturer, John Harper.

Planchets became too thin for edge lettering after the weight reduction ordered late in 1795. The variety with reeded edge was probably an experimental substitute, rejected in favor of a plain edge.

1793-1795 (thick planchet) — Designer Joseph Wright; weight 13.48 grams; composition: copper; approx. diameter 29 mm; edge: ONE HUNDRED FOR A DOLLAR followed by a single leaf.

1795-1796 (thin planchet) — Designer John Smith Gardner; weight 10.89 grams; composition: copper; approx. diameter 29 mm; plain edge.

1793 Vine and Bars edge	**Lettered edge 1793-1795**
Chain and Wreath type only	ONE HUNDRED FOR A DOLLAR

LARGE CENTS

1793-1794

Beaded Border, 1793 Only

"Head of 1793"
Head is in high
rounded relief

1794 Only   **1794-1796**

"Head of 1794"
Well defined hair,
hook on lowest curl

"Head of 1795"
Head in low relief,
no hook on lowest curl

1794 Starred Reverse

	Mintage	AG-3	G-4	VG-8	F-12	VF-20	EF-40	AU-50
1793, Lib. Cap	11,056	$1,500.	$3,000.	$5,000.	$8,000.	$20,000.	$40,000.	—
1794 All Kinds	918,521							
1794, "Head of 1793"		400.	1,000.	2,000.	3,000.	7,500.	17,500.	—
1794, "Head of 1794"		100.	250.	350.	550.	1,100.	2,750.	—
1794, "Head of 1795"		100.	250.	350.	500.	900.	2,500.	—
1794, Starred reverse		4,200.	8,500.	12,000.	25,000.	45,000.	—	—
1794, No fraction bar		100.	250.	400.	750.	1,500.	4,000.	—
1795, Ltrd.edge	37,000	125.	250.	400.	800.	1,500.	3,200.	—
1795, Plain edge	501,500	75.	200.	300.	500.	1,000.	2,000.	—
1795, Reeded edge		*(4 known)*						

1796-1807

Reeded Edge

"Jefferson Head"

This head was modified
slightly in 1798. See
page 82 for details.

1795 Jefferson Head (not a regular mint issue)								
Plain edge		3,750.	6,500.	12,000.	20,000.	45,000.		—
Lettered edge		*(3 known)*						
1796 Lib. Cap	109,825	125.	250.	425.	800.	1,700.	4,000.	—

[86]

LARGE CENTS
DRAPED BUST TYPE 1796-1807

Designer Robert Scot; weight 10.89 grams; composition: copper; approx. diameter 29 mm; plain edge.

AG-3 ABOUT GOOD—*Clear enough to identify.*
G-4 GOOD—*Lettering worn, but clear; date clear. Bust lacks details.*
VG-8 VERY GOOD—*Drapery partly visible. Less wear in date and lettering.*
F-12 FINE—*Hair over brow is smooth, some detail showing in other parts of hair.*
VF-20 VERY FINE—*Hairlines slightly worn. Hair over brow better defined.*
EF-40 EXTREMELY FINE—*Hair above forehead and left of eye outlined and detailed. Only slight wear on olive leaves.*

1794-1796	**1795-1798**	**1796-1807**

"Reverse of 1794" Note double leaf at top right; 14-16 leaves left, 16-18 leaves right.	"Reverse of 1795" Note single leaf at top right; 17-21 leaves left, 16-20 leaves right.	"Reverse of 1797" Note double leaf at top right; 16 leaves left, 19 leaves right.

LIHERTY
error

	Mintage	AG-3	G-4	VG-8	F-12	VF-20	EF-40
1796, Draped Bust ...	363,375						
1796, Reverse of 1794		$100.	$225.	$500.	$800.	$2,000.	$4,000.
1796, Reverse of 1795		80.	150.	275.	550.	1,300.	2,600.
1796, Reverse of 1797		75.	150.	275.	600.	1,350.	2,600.
1796, LIHERTY error		150.	275.	650.	1,200.	3,500.	6,500.
1796, Stemless reverse							

Gripped Edge

| | | **Stems** | | **Stemless** | | | |

		AG-3	G-4	VG-8	F-12	VF-20	EF-40
1797 All Kinds	897,510						
1797, Gripped edge, '96 rev. ...		35.	100.	200.	350.	750.	2,500.
1797, Plain edge, '96 rev.		42.	110.	210.	375.	825.	2,700.
1797, '97 rev., stems		30.	70.	150.	225.	500.	1,500.
1797, '97 rev., stemless		50.	125.	250.	500.	1,200.	4,000.

| Style 1 Hair | Style 2 Hair | 1798, 8 over 7 |

Style 1 hair appears on all 1796-97, many 1798 varieties and 1800 over 1798. Style 2 hair, used 1798-1807, is most easily recognized by the extra curl near the shoulder.

	Mintage	AG-3	G-4	VG-8	F-12	VF-20	EF-40
1798 All Kinds	1,841,745						
1798, 8 over 7		$50.	$125.	$250.	$500.	$1,600.	$4,000.
1798, Reverse of 1796		40.	90.	250.	500.	1,400.	5,000.
1798, 1st. hair style		25.	55.	100.	180.	475.	1,500.
1798, 2nd. hair style		22.	45.	80.	170.	400.	1,300.

| 1799, 9 over 8 | 1800 over 1798 | 1800, 80 over 79 |

		AG-3	G-4	VG-8	F-12	VF-20	EF-40
1799, 9/8*		1,000.	2,000.	3,500.	7,750.	20,000.	—
1799 NmIDt	Incl. above	750.	1,600.	3,200.	7,000.	17,000.	—
1800 All Kinds	2,822,175						
1800/1798 Style 1 hair		25.	60.	120.	250.	800.	3,200.
1800,80/79 Style 2 hair		25.	50.	100.	200.	450.	1,700.
1800, NmIDt		22.	45.	80.	175.	400.	1,400.

*Mintage for 1799 is included with the 1798 figure.

| Fraction 1/000 | Corrected Fraction | 1801 Reverse, 3 Errors |

Error-fraction dies appear on cents of 1801, 1802, and 1803, but all of these dies originated in 1801, possibly all by the same engraver.

LARGE CENTS

	Mintage	AG-3	G-4	VG-8	F-12	VF-20	EF-40
1801, All Kinds	1,362,837						
1801, Nml reverse		$20.	$40.	$70.	$140.	$325.	$950.
1801, 3 errors: 1/000,							
one stem & IINITED		55.	160.	300.	700.	1,500.	6,000.
1801, Fraction 1/000		20.	45.	75.	200.	400.	1,500.
1801, 1/100 over 1/000 ..		25.	60.	125.	250.	600.	1,750.
1802, All Kinds	3,435,100						
1802, Nml reverse		20.	40.	70.	150.	275.	750.
1802, Fraction 1/000		20.	50.	100.	200.	375.	1,300.
1802, Stemless wreath ..		20.	40.	70.	150.	275.	775.

Values shown for Fine and better copper coins are for those with attractive surfaces and color that are consistent with the amount of normal wear. Coins that are porous, corroded, or similarly defective are worth significantly lower prices.

1803 Small Date	**1803 Large Date**	**Small Fraction**	**Large Fraction**
Blunt 1	**Pointed 1**		

All small date varieties have a blunt 1 in date. Large dates have pointed 1 and noticeably larger 3.

		AG-3	G-4	VG-8	F-12	VF-20	EF-40
1803 All Kinds	3,131,691						
1803, SmDt, Sm. fract ...		20.	40.	65.	120.	275.	750.
1803, SmDt, Lg.fract		20.	40.	65.	120.	275.	750.
1803, LgDt, Sm.fract		2,200.	4,000.	7,500.	13,500.	20,000.	
1803, LgDt, Lg.fract		30.	70.	150.	300.	850.	2,500.
1803, 1/100 over 1/000 ..		20.	50.	90.	200.	425.	1,250.
1803, Stemless wreath ..		20.	50.	90.	200.	425.	1,250.

1804 With Normal or Broken Dies
(Broken die variety is illustrated)

Broken Dies

All genuine 1804 Cents have a crosslet 4 in the date and a large fraction. The 0 in the date is in line with the O in OF on the reverse of the coin. Values shown are for coins with normal or broken dies.

		AG-3	G-4	VG-8	F-12	VF-20	EF-40
1804	*96,500*	300.	600.	1,200.	2,600.	3,500.	8,000.

Restrike of 1804 Cent

1804 Unofficial restrike of 1860 (Uncirculated) .... $900.

A fake 1804 was manufactured from discarded mint dies. An altered 1803 die was used for the obverse and a die of the 1820 cent used for the reverse. They were struck c.1860 to satisfy the demand for this rare date. Known as the "restrike," it was a patchwork job and is easily distinguished from a genuine 1804 cent.

	Mintage	AG-3	G-4	VG-8	F-12	VF-20	EF-40
1805	941,116	$20.	$40.	$60.	$150.	$300.	$850.
1806	348,000	20.	45.	90.	200.	450.	1,500.

Small 1807, 7 over 6, blunt 1	**Lg. 1807, 7 over 6, pointed 1**	**"Comet" Variety**

1807 All Kinds 829,221						
1807, Sm 7/6,Blunt 1	1,100.	2,400.	4,000.	8,000.	16,000.	30,000.
1807, Lg 7/6	20.	40.	60.	140.	325.	900.
1807, Sm fraction	20.	40.	60.	160.	375.	1,100.
1807, Lg fraction	16.	40.	60.	175.	325.	850.
1807 "Comet" variety (die break behind head) .	23.	50.	90.	200.	450.	2,000.

CLASSIC HEAD TYPE 1808-1814

1808 to 1814 — This group does not compare in sharpness and quality to those struck before (1793-1807), nor to those struck after (1816 on). The copper used was "softer," having less metallic impurity. This impaired the wearing quality of the series. For this reason collectors find greater difficulty in obtaining these dates in choice condition.

Designer John Reich. Standards same as previous issue.

AG-3 ABOUT GOOD—*Details clear enough to identify.*
G-4 GOOD—*Legends, stars, date worn, but plain.*
VG-8 VERY GOOD—*LIBERTY all readable. Ear shows. Details worn but plain.*
F-12 FINE—*Hair on forehead and before ear nearly smooth. Ear and hair under ear sharp.*
VF-20 VERY FINE—*All hairlines show some detail. Leaves on reverse show slight wear.*
EF-40 EXTREMELY FINE—*All hairlines sharp. Very slight wear on high points.*

	Mintage	AG-3	G-4	VG-8	F-12	VF-20	EF-40
1808	1,007,000	$20.	$45.	$120.	$275.	$500.	$1,200.
1809	222,867	45.	110.	220.	425.	1,000.	2,500.

1810, 10 over 09	**Normal Date**	**1811, last 1 over 0**	**Normal Date**

		AG-3	G-4	VG-8	F-12	VF-20	EF-40
1810 All Kinds	1,458,500						
1810, 10/09		20.	45.	110.	225.	525.	1,300.
1810, NmlDt		20.	45.	80.	200.	500.	1,000.
1811, All Kinds	218,025						
1811, Last 1/0		30.	75.	125.	400.	1,250.	4,000.
1811, NmlDt		35.	90.	140.	350.	750.	1,600.

1812 Small date	**1812 Large date**	**1814 Plain 4**	**1814 Crosslet 4**

		AG-3	G-4	VG-8	F-12	VF-20	EF-40
1812, SmDt	} 1,075,500	18.	40.	75.	200.	500.	1,000.
1812, LgDt		18.	40.	75.	200.	500.	1,000.
1813	418,000	22.	50.	100.	220.	550.	1,350.
1814, Plain 4	} 357,830	18.	40.	75.	250.	500.	1,000.
1814, Crosslet 4		18.	40.	75.	250.	500.	1,000.

LARGE CENTS
CORONET TYPE 1816-1857

Designer Robert Scot; weight 10.89 grams; composition: copper; approx. diameter 28-29 mm; plain edge.

G-4 GOOD—*Head details partly visible. Even wear in date and legends.*
VG-8 VERY GOOD—*LIBERTY, date, stars, legends clear. Part of hair cord visible.*
F-12 FINE—*All hairlines show. Hair cords show uniformly.*
VF-20 VERY FINE—*Hair cords only slightly worn. Hairlines only partly worn, all well defined.*
EF-40 EXTREMELY FINE—*Both hair cords stand out sharply. All hairlines sharp.*
AU-50 ABOUT UNCIRCULATED—*Only traces of wear on the hair and the highest point on leaves and bow.*
MS-60 UNCIRCULATED—*Typical brown to red surface. No trace of wear.*
MS-63 UNCIRCULATED—*Some distracting contact marks or blemishes in prime focal areas. Luster may be impaired.*

MATRON HEAD 1816-1835

13 Stars   **15 Stars**

	Mintage	G-4	VG-8	F-12	VF-20	EF-40	AU-50	MS-60*	MS-63*
1816	2,820,982	$15.	$20.	$35.	$80.	$175.	$250.	$450.	$650.
1817, 13 stars ⎫		15.	20.	31.	65.	125.	200.	400.	500.
1817, 15 stars ⎭	3,948,400	17.	30.	45.	125.	450.	700.	2,250.	3,000.
1818	3,167,000	15.	20.	30.	60.	125.	200.	475.	600.

1819, 9 over 8   **1819 Large Date**   **1819 Small Date**

1819 All Kinds . .	2,671,000								
1819, 9/8		15.	21.	31.	80.	225.	300.	700.	1,000.
1819 LgDt		14.	19.	26.	60.	120.	250.	400.	650.
1819 SmDt		14.	19.	26.	60.	120.	250.	400.	650.

1820, 20 over 19   **1820 Large Date**   **1820 Small Date**
note 1 under 2   **note plain-topped 2**   **note curl-topped 2**

    *Red to bright red uncirculated large cents with attractive surfaces (not cleaned) command higher prices. Beware of slightly worn copper coins that have been cleaned and recolored to simulate uncirculated luster.

	Mintage	G-4	VG-8	F-12	VF-20	EF-40	AU-50	MS-60*	MS-63*
1820, All Kinds	..4,407,550								
1820, 20/19		$15.	$20.	$40.	$100.	$300.	$500.	$900.	$1,200.
1820, LgDt	....	14.	19.	25.	60.	140.	200.	300.	550.
1820, SmDt	....	14.	19.	25.	60.	140.	225.	350.	600.
1821	 389,000	25.	45.	110.	350.	1,200.	2,000.	6,000.	—
1822	2,072,339	14.	19.	40.	90.	250.	500.	900.	1,500.

1823, 3 over 2   **1823 Restrike**

		G-4	VG-8	F-12	VF-20	EF-40	AU-50	MS-60*	MS-63*
1823, 3/2	} 12,250	55.	100.	275.	650.	2,000.	3,500.	6,000.	—
1823 NrmlDt		60.	125.	300.	775.	2,750.	4,750.	7,500.	—
1823 Unofficial restrike, from broken ObvDie	....				.350.	450.	800.	1,000.	

The 1823 unofficial restrike was made at the same time and by the same people as the 1804 restrike copy (see page 84), using a discarded 1823 obverse and an 1813 reverse die. The dies are heavily rusted (producing lumps on the coin) and most examples have both dies cracked across.

1824, 4 over 2   **1826, 6 over 5**

		G-4	VG-8	F-12	VF-20	EF-40	AU-50	MS-60*	MS-63*
1824, 4/2	} 1,262,000	16.	30.	75.	250.	1,000.	2,000.	4,500.	—
1824, NmlDt ..		14.	20.	40.	150.	475.	800.	2,200.	3,500.
1825	1,461,100	14.	20.	28.	90.	300.	600.	1,800.	2,500.
1826, 6/5	} 1,517,425	20.	45.	100.	250.	850.	1,000.	2,500.	4,500.
1826, NmlDt ..		14.	19.	27.	85.	225.	400.	850.	1,250.
1827	2,357,732	14.	19.	27.	85.	200.	350.	700.	1,150.

This date-size appears on cents before 1828

This date-size appears on cents after 1828

		G-4	VG-8	F-12	VF-20	EF-40	AU-50	MS-60*
1828, Lg nar. date	} 2,260,624	14.	19.	30.	70.	175.	350.	1,100.
1828, Sm. WdDt		15.	22.	45.	110.	250.	475.	1,750.

*See footnote page 92.

LARGE CENTS

This large letter size appears on cents of 1808-1834.

Note individual letter size and proximity.

This medium letter size appears on cents of 1829-1837.

Note isolation of letters, esp. states.

	Mintage	G-4	VG-8	F-12	VF-20	EF-40	AU-50	MS-60*	MS-63*
1829, Lg Letters .	}1,414,500	$14.	$18.	$26.	$80.	$175.	$350.	$500.	$1,100.
1829, Med. Letters		15.	25.	100.	325.	400.	2,000.	—	
1830, Lg Letters .	}1,711,500	14.	18.	28.	65.	160.	275.	400.	750.
1830, Med. Letters		20.	35.	150.	400.	1,100.	3,000.	—	
1831, Lg Letters .	}3,359,260	14.	18.	26.	60.	125.	225.	350.	600.
1831, Med. Letters		14.	18.	26.	60.	150.	250.	400.	750.
1832, Lg Letters .	}2,362,000	14.	18.	26.	60.	125.	225.	350.	600.
1832, Med. Letters		14.	18.	26.	60.	125.	225.	350.	600.
1833	2,739,000	14.	18.	26.	60.	125.	225.	325.	550.

Large 8 and Stars   **Large 8, Small Stars**   **Small 8, Large Stars**

		G-4	VG-8	F-12	VF-20	EF-40	AU-50	MS-60	MS-63
1834 All Kinds . .	1,855,100								
1834 Lg 8,stars & rev.letters		14.	23.	70.	175.	500.	750.	2,000.	—
1834 Lg 8, stars,med.letters		150.	300.	450.	900.	2,750.	4,750.	—	—
1834 Lg 8, Sm stars,med.letters		14.	18.	26.	60.	125.	225.	350.	600.
1834,Sm 8, Lg stars,med.letters		14.	18.	26.	60.	125.	225.	350.	550.

Large 8 and Stars, Matron Head   **Small 8 and Stars, Matron Head**   **"Head of 1836" 1835-1837 Slim Bust**

		G-4	VG-8	F-12	VF-20	EF-40	AU-50	MS-60	MS-63
1835 All Kinds . .	3,878,400								
1835, Lg 8 & stars		14.	18.	26.	60.	200.	375.	700.	1,250.
1835, Sm 8 & stars		14.	18.	26.	60.	150.	250.	350.	650.
1835, "Head of 1836"		14.	18.	26.	50.	100.	200.	300.	500.
1836	2,111,000	14.	18.	26.	50.	100.	200.	300.	500.

*See footnote page 92.

Designer Christian Gobrecht; weight 10.89 grams; composition: copper; diameter 27.5 mm; plain edge.

G-4 GOOD — *Considerably worn. LIBERTY readable.*
VG-8 VERY GOOD — *Hairlines smooth but visible, outline of ear clearly defined.*
F-12 FINE — *Hairlines at top of head and behind ear worn but visible. Braid over brow plain, ear clear.*
VF-20 VERY FINE — *All details more sharp. Hair over brow shows only slight wear.*
EF-40 EXTREMELY FINE — *Hair above ear detailed, but slightly worn.*
AU-55-CHOICE ABOUT UNCIRCULATED — *Trace of wear on high points of hair above the ear and eye and on highest oints on leaves and bow*
MS-60 UNCIRCULATED — *Typical brown to red surface. No trace of wear.*
MS-63 UNCIRCULATED — *Some distracting contact marks or blemishes in prime focal areas. Luster may be impaired.*

1829-1837 Medium letters Note size and spacing of letters.	"Head of 1838" Beaded Cords note slim bust with beaded cords.	1837-1839 Small letters note size and spacing of letters.

	Mintage	G-4	VG-8	F-12	VF-20	EF-40	AU-50	MS-60*	MS-63*
1837 All Kinds	. .5,558,300								
1837, Pl.crd.,med.let	. . . . .	$14.	$19.	$25.	$45.	$100.	$200.	$300.	$500.
1837, Pl.crd.,Sm.let	. . . . . .	14.	19.	25.	45.	110.	225.	350.	550.
1837, Head of 1838	. . . . . .	14.	19.	25.	40.	90.	160.	275.	400.
1838	6,370,200	14.	19.	25.	40.	90.	150.	275.	375.

1839 over 1836 Note closed 9, plain cords.	Silly Head Note browlock at forehead.	Booby Head Note back tip of shoulder exposed.

1839 All Kinds	. .3,128,661								
1839, 9/6, plain cords	. . . . .	200.	400.	1,100.	2,200.	7,500.	9,000.	—	—
1839 Head 1838,beaded cords		14.	19.	20.	45.	100.	200.	300.	500.
1839, Silly Head	. . . .	15.	21.	30.	60.	150.	225.	800.	950.
1839, Booby Head	. . . . . .	14.	20.	30.	50.	100.	250.	600.	1,000.
1839, Petite Head	. . . .	14.	19.	26.	45.	110.	250.	375.	600.

The last two 1839 heads use a modified reverse that omits the line under CENT (see illustration on page 96).

---

* Red to bright red uncirculated large cents with attractive surfaces (not cleaned) command higher prices. Beware of slightly worn copper coins that have been cleaned and recolored to simulate uncirculated luster.

LARGE CENTS

1840 Large Date

1840 Small Date

Small Date over Large 18

	Mintage	G-4	VG-8	F-12	VF-20	EF-40	AU-50	MS-60*	MS-63*
1840 All Kinds	..2,462,700								
1840, LgDt	....	$13.	$17.	$20.	$28.	$70.	$140.	$275.	$500.
1840, SmDt	....	13.	17.	20.	28.	70.	140.	275.	500.
1840, SmDt,Lg 18	....	14.	18.	23.	40.	150.	350.	600.	1,000.
1841, SmDt	1,597,367	13.	17.	20.	30.	110.	220.	400.	750.

1842 Small Date

1842 Large Date

Small Letters 1839-1843

		G-4	VG-8	F-12	VF-20	EF-40	AU-50	MS-60*	MS-63*
1842, SmDt ..	} 2,383,390	13.	17.	19.	28.	80.	200.	350.	600.
1842, LgDt ..		13.	17.	19.	28.	80.	130.	250.	450.

"Head of 1840" Petite Head 1839-1843

"Head of 1844" Mature Head 1843-1857

Large Letters 1843-1857

		G-4	VG-8	F-12	VF-20	EF-40	AU-50	MS-60*	MS-63*
1843 All Kinds	..2,425,342								
1843, Petite,SmL	....	13.	17.	20.	27.	75.	125.	250.	400.
1843, Petite,LgL	....	15.	22.	40.	75.	200.	300.	750.	1,250.
1843, Mature,LgL	....	14.	18.	25.	40.	140.	250.	500.	900.
1844, NorDt ...	} 2,398,752	13.	17.	20.	30.	80.	140.	225.	450.
1844, /81 (error)		14.	21.	40.	85.	275.	450.	1,000.	2,000.
1845	3,894,804	13.	17.	20.	25.	65.	110.	200.	350.

*See footnote page 95.

LARGE CENTS

1846 Small Date
note squat date
with closed 6

1846 Medium Date
note medium height
with ball-top 6

1846 Tall Date
note vertically-stretched
date with open-mouthed 6

	Mintage	G-4	VG-8	F-12	VF-20	EF-40	AU-50	MS-60*	MS-63*
1846 All Kinds	4,120,800								
1846, SmDt		$13.	$17.	$19.	$25.	$60.	$110.	$200.	$325.
1846, MedDt		13.	17.	20.	25.	65.	120.	185.	400.
1846, TallDt		13.	18.	20.	35.	90.	150.	350.	750.
1847	} 6,183,669	13.	17.	19.	25.	60.	110.	200.	325.
1847, 7/sm 7		14.	19.	30.	50.	125.	375.	900.	1,500.

(1848 Small date is a rare contemporary counterfeit)

1848	6,415,799	13.	17.	19.	23.	60.	110.	200.	350.
1849	4,178,500	13.	17.	19.	25.	75.	125.	250.	400.
1850	4,426,844	13.	17.	19.	23.	55.	100.	150.	250.

1844, 44 over 81

1851, 51 over 81

1847, 7 over "Small" 7

These are not true overdates, but are some of the more spectacular of several date-punch blunders of the 1844-1854 period. The so-called "overdates" of 1844 and 1851 each have the date punched upside-down, then corrected normally.

1851, NmlDt	} 9,889,707	13.	17.	19.	23.	50.	100.	150.	250.
1851, /81 (error)		14.	18.	21.	45.	110.	175.	400.	700.
1852	5,063,094	13.	17.	19.	23.	50.	100.	150.	250.
1853	6,641,131	13.	17.	19.	23.	50.	100.	150.	250.
1854	4,236,156	13.	17.	19.	23.	50.	100.	150.	250.

*See footnote page 95.

| 1855 Upright 5's | 1855 Slanting 5's | 1855 Knob on ear |

Original sketches of engraver James B. Longacre's work reveal that slanting 5's were a peculiarity of his work. The figure punch for an upright 5 was probably the work of a craftsman.

	Mintage	G-4	VG-8	F-12	VF-20	EF-40	AU-50	MS-60*	MS-63*
1855, All Kinds	1,574,829								
1855, Upright 5's		$13.	$18.	$19.	$23.	$50.	$100.	$150.	$225.
1855, Slanting 5's		13.	18.	19.	23.	50.	100.	175.	275.
1855,Slanting 5's,knob on ear	13.	13.	19.	23.	35.	75.	150.	300.	500.
1856, Upright 5 }	2,690,463	13.	17.	19.	23.	50.	100.	150.	225.
1856, Slanting 5 }		13.	17.	19.	23.	50.	100.	150.	225.

| 1857 Large Date | 1857 Small Date |

| 1857, LgDt } | 333,546 | 40. | 50. | 60. | 70. | 90. | 175. | 300. | 500. |
| 1857, SmDt } | | 45. | 55. | 65. | 75. | 100. | 200. | 350. | 600. |

*See footnote page 95.

Passing of the Large Cent and Half Cent

By 1857 the cost of making and distributing copper coins had risen. Mint Director Snowden reported that they "barely paid expenses." Both cents and half cents had become unpopular; in fact, they hardly circulated outside of the larger cities. The practice of issuing subsidiary silver coins, which began in 1853, brought about a reform of the copper coinage. The half cent was abandoned and a smaller cent was introduced in 1857.

The law of 1857 brought important benefits to the citizens. By its terms Spanish coins were redeemed and melted at the mint in exchange for new small cents. The decimal system became popular and official thereafter, and the old method of reckoning in reals, medios, shillings, etc., was gradually given up, although the terms, "two bits" and "penny" are still commonly used. The new, convenient small cent won popular favor and soon became a useful instrument of retail trade and a boon to commerce.

For some unexplained reason a few experimental large cent pieces were made dated 1868.

BIBLIOGRAPHY

Breen, Walter. *Walter Breen's Encyclopedia of Early U.S. Cents 1793-1814.* Wolfeboro, NH, 2001.
Grellman, J.R. *Attribution Guide for United States Large Cents 1840-1857,* 3rd edition. Bloomington, MN, 2002.
Newcomb, H.R. *United States Copper Cents 1816-1857.* New York, 1944. (Reprinted 1983)
Noyes, William C. *United States Large Cents 1793-1814.* Bloomington, MN, 1991.
Noyes, William C. *United States Large Cents 1816-1839.* Bloomington, MN, 1991.
PENNY-WISE, official publication of Early American Coppers, Inc. (EAC)
Sheldon, Wm. H. *Penny Whimsy (1793-1814).* New York, 1958. (Reprinted 1965, 1976)
Wright, John D. *The Cent Book 1816-1839.* Bloomington, MN, 1992.

The Act of February 21, 1857 provided for the coinage of the new copper-nickel small cent. It also called for Spanish and Mexican coins and old copper cents and half cents in circulation to be called in and exchanged for U.S. silver coins and the new cents. The cent weighed 72 grains with a metallic composition of 88% copper and 12% nickel.

The 1856 Flying Eagle cent, a pattern, was made to show Congress how the new cent would look. Additional proof pieces were struck for sale to collectors. It is believed that between 1,500 and 2,500 pieces were struck in all. These have always been collected as regular issues because of their early widespread popularity. A few 1856 Eagle cents probably went into circulation during the Civil War.

Some 1858-dated cents have been altered into 1856. They are easy to spot because the shape of the 5 is different on the 1858 than it is on the 1856.

There are many varieties known for 1857 and 1858. The 1858 is found with 2 major variations. The "Large Letter" design shows the A and M in AMERICA joined, and the "Small Letter" design shows the A and M separated. Minor variations of the reverse designs of corn, wheat, cotton and tobacco appear on 1858 cents. The 1858, 8 over 7 variety can be identified by a small dot, or die defect, in the field above the first 8. During production, this die was ground down to a point where the 7 is no longer visible. These are not as desirable as coins with the 7 showing.

+ or – indicates change from previous year	TYPE COIN VALUES									
	G-4	F-12	EF-40	AU-50	MS-60	MS-63	MS-65	PF-60	PF-63	PF-65
Flying Eagle 1857-1858	20.00+	32.00+	130.00+	170.+	300.+	600.	3,500.	1,400.+	8,000.+	22,500.
Indian CN 1859	13.00+	20.00+	100.00+	185.+	225.+	450.	2,600.	600.+	1,500.+	5,000.+
Indian CN 1860-1864	8.00+	14.00+	35.00+	55.+	85.+	150.+	875.+	320.+	725.+	2,750.+
Indian 1864-1909	1.75+	2.50+	9.00+	18.+	30.+	50.+	150.+	120.+	200.+	400.+
Lincoln 1909-V.D.B	4.00+	4.50+	6.50+	8.	13.+	16.	50.	600.	1,500.	3,000.

FLYING EAGLE TYPE 1856-1858

Designer James B. Longacre; weight 4.67 grams; composition: .880 copper, .120 nickel; diameter 19 mm; plain edge. All coined at Philadelphia Mint.

G-4 GOOD—*All details worn, but readable.*
VG-8 VERY GOOD—*Feather details and eye are evident, but worn.*
F-12 FINE—*Eagle head details and feather tips sharp.*
VF-20 VERY FINE—*Feathers in right wing and tail show considerable detail.*
EF-40 EXTREMELY FINE—*Slight wear, all details sharp.*
AU-50 ABOUT UNCIRCULATED—*Slight wear on eagle's left wing and breast.*
MS-60 UNCIRCULATED—*No trace of wear. Light blemishes.*
MS-63 UNCIRCULATED—*Some distracting contact marks or blemishes in prime focal areas. Luster may be impaired.*
PF-63—*Nearly Perfect*

1858, 8 over 7

Large Letters

Small Letters

	Mintage	G-4	VG-8	F-12	VF-20	EF-40	AU-50	MS-60	MS-63	PF-63
1856 . . .	est. 2,000	$5,750.	$6,500.	$7,000.	$8,000.	$8,750.	$9,000.	$10,000.	$13,000.	$14,000.
1857 . . . *(485)*	7,450,000	20.	22.	32.	45.	130.	170.	300.	550.	8,000.
1858, LgL *(80)*	24,600,000	20.	22.	32.	45.	130.	170.	300.	550.	8,000.
1858, SmL *(200)*		20.	22.	32.	45.	130.	170.	300.	550.	8,000.
1858, 8/7(see picture)		65.	95.	190.	375.	750.	1,300.	3,000.	9,000.	

. . . .

INDIAN HEAD TYPE 1859-1909

The "Indian Head" cent first issued in 1859 is actually a representation of Liberty wearing an Indian headdress, not an actual Indian. The first year featured a Laurel wreath on the reverse. This was changed after one year to the Oak wreath with a small shield. Coins of 1859 and early 1860 show a pointed bust. Those made from late 1860 until 1864 have a more rounded bust. Prior to the issuance of 5 cent nickel pieces in 1866, these coins were commonly referred to as "nickels" or "nicks."

COPPER-NICKEL

Designer James B. Longacre; weight 4.67 grams; composition: .880 copper, .120 nickel; diameter 19 mm; plain edge. All coined at Philadelphia Mint.

G-4 GOOD—*No LIBERTY visible.*
VG-8 VERY GOOD—*At least three letters of LIBERTY readable on head band.*
F-12 FINE—*LIBERTY completely visible.*
VF-20 VERY FINE—*Slight but even wear on LIBERTY.*
EF-40 EXTREMELY FINE—*LIBERTY sharp. All other details sharp. Only slight wear on ribbon end.*
AU-50 ABOUT UNCIRCULATED—*Very slight trace of wear above the ear and the lowest curl of hair.*
MS-60 UNCIRCULATED—*No trace of wear. Light blemishes.*
MS-63 UNCIRCULATED—*Some distracting contact marks or blemishes in prime focal areas. Luster may be impaired.*

Without Shield at Top of Wreath
1859 Only

With Shield on Reverse
1860 to 1909

Variety 1 — Copper-nickel, Laurel Wreath Reverse 1859

Spotted, cleaned or discolored pieces are worth less than values shown.

	Mintage	G-4	VG-8	F-12	VF-20	EF-40	AU-50	MS-60	MS-63	PF-63
1859 .....*(800)*	36,400,000	$13.	$15.	$20.	$50.	$100.	$185.	$225.	$450.	$1,500.

Variety 2 — Copper-nickel, Oak Wreath with Shield 1860-1864

	Mintage	G-4	VG-8	F-12	VF-20	EF-40	AU-50	MS-60	MS-63	PF-63
1860 Pointed Bust ...	20,566,000	15.	17.	20.	35.	80.	135.	250.	425.	
1860 ...*(1,000)*		10.	12.	15.	19.	50.	80.	140.	200.	750.
1861 ...*(1,000)*	10,100,000	18.	30.	35.	45.	90.	150.	200.	250.	900.
1862 .....*(550)*	28,075,000	8.	11.	14.	20.	40.	60.	90.	150.	650.
1863 .....*(460)*	49,840,000	8.	11.	14.	19.	35.	55.	85.	150.	650.
1864 .....*(370)*	13,740,000	16.	21.	30.	40.	65.	80.	145.	185.	750.

Variety 3 — Bronze 1864-1909

During the Civil War, nearly all gold, silver and eventually the copper-nickel cent disappeared from circulation. In larger cities, thin copper cent-sized tokens began to be issued by merchants to fill the void left by the missing cents. The Government stepped in and with the act of April 22, 1864, issued its own thin bronze coin and made the issuance of the tokens illegal.

The obverse was redesigned near the end of 1864. A slightly sharper portrait included the designer's initial "L" for Longacre on the lower ribbon behind the neck. This design continued on until 1909 when the design was replaced with the Lincoln cent.

Indian Head Cent with "L"

If the coin is turned slightly (so Indian faces observer) the highlighted details of the "L" will appear to better advantage. The point of the bust is pointed on the variety with "L"; rounded without "L." The "L" is the last initial of the engraver, James B. Longacre.

SMALL CENTS

Designer James B. Longacre; weight 3.11 grams; composition: .950 copper, .050 tin and zinc; diameter 19 mm; plain edge; mints: Philadelphia, San Francisco.

Choice brilliant uncirculated and Proof small cents command higher prices. Spotted, cleaned or discolored pieces are worth less.

	Mintage	G-4	VG-8	F-12	VF-20	EF-40	AU-50	MS-60	MS-63	PF-63
1864, All Kinds	39,233,714									
1864, No. L *(150)*		7.00	$13.	$20.	$35.	$65.	$75.	$90.	$125.	$800.
1864, L must show *(20)*		55.00	75.	125.	160.	250.	325.	375.	600.	20,000.
1865* ...*(500+)*	35,429,286	8.00	12.	18.	25.	40.	60.	85.	125.	450.+
1866 ....*(725+)*	9,826,500	45.00	50.	65.	95.	170.	225.	250.	300.	450.
1867 ....*(625+)*	9,821,000	45.00	50.	75.	125.	200.	250.	270.	325.	450.
1868 ....*(600+)*	10,266,500	42.00	45.	65.	95.	160.	200.	235.	280.	450.
1869, over 9 ...		110.00	150.	250.	350.	500.	600.	650.	800.	
1869 ....*(600+)*	6,420,000	60.00	80.	200.	250.	350.	400.	450.	550.	600.
1870 ..*(1,000+)*	5,275,000	50.00	70.	175.	240.	325.	375.	425.	525.	550.
1871 ....*(960+)*	3,929,500	60.00	75.	250.	275.	350.	400.	450.	550.	600.
1872 ....*(950+)*	4,042,000	75.00	90.	280.	325.	425.	500.	550.	850.	900.

*One variety of 1865 appears to show traces of a 4 under the 5 in the date. On other varieties the tip of the 5 is either plain or curved. The 9 is doubled on some varieties of the 1869; on others it appears to be over an 8, although it is actually a doubled 9. None of these varieties is a true overdate. Varieties of 1870, 1871, 1872 and 1873 closed 3, have either a bold or shallow N in CENT.

Closed 3   **Open 3**

	Mintage	G-4	VG-8	F-12	VF-20	EF-40	AU-50	MS-60	MS-63	PF-63
1873 All Kinds ..	11,676,500									
1873, Cl 3 *(1,100+)*		20.00	30.	50.	100.	165.	200.	400.	500.	550.
1873, Doubled LIBERTY			300.	650.	1,100.	2,200.	4,000.	7,000.	12,500.	
1873, Op 3		18.00	27.	45.	80.	150.	175.	225.	300.	
1874 ....*(700+)*	14,187,500	15.00	18.	35.	45.	90.	125.	200.	225.	400.
1875 ....*(700+)*	13,528,000	15.00	18.	35.	45.	90.	125.	200.	225.	400.
1876 ..*(1,150+)*	7,944,000	30.00	35.	50.	75.	150.	200.	275.	350.	425.
1877 ....*(900+)*	852,500	550.00	700.	900.	1,200.	1,700.	2,000.	2,500.	3,500.	3,600.
1878 ...(2,350)	5,799,850	30.00	40.	55.	85.	200.	250.	300.	350.	400.
1879 ...(3,200)	16,231,200	7.00	11.	15.	35.	65.	75.	85.	100.	350.
1880 ...(3,955)	38,964,955	4.00	6.	7.	10.	25.	85.	100.	125.	300.
1881 ...(3,575)	39,211,575	4.00	5.	6.	9.	18.	28.	50.	85.	300.
1882 ...(3,100)	38,581,100	4.00	5.	6.	9.	18.	28.	50.	85.	300.
1883 ...(6,609)	45,598,109	4.00	5.	·6.	9.	18.	28.	50.	85.	300.
1884 ...(3,942)	23,261,742	4.50	6.	8.	12.	25.	35.	70.	100.	300.
1885 ...(3,790)	11,765,384	7.00	8.	13.	25.	60.	70.	100.	175.	300.
1886 ...(4,290)	17,654,290	5.00	7.	18.	50.	125.	150.	175.	200.	325.

On coins minted in 1859 to mid-1886, the last feather of the headdress points between I and C of AMERICA; on the second variety, from mid-1886 to 1909, it points between C and A.

	Mintage	G-4	VG-8	F-12	VF-20	EF-40	AU-50	MS-60	MS-63	PF-63
1886, Var II incl. above		6.00	11.	18.	70.	175.	200.	300.	450.	950.
1887 ...(2,960)	45,226,483	2.50	3.	22.	6.	16.	25.	50.	75.	300.

1888, last 8 over 7
A less prominent similar variety exists but is valued lower than the clear overdate.

	Mintage	G-4	VG-8	F-12	VF-20	EF-40	AU-50	MS-60	MS-63	PF-63
1888, over 7 ... }	37,494,414	900.00	1,200.	1,500.	3,000.	6,000.	15,000.	20,000.	25,000.	
1888 ...(4,582) }		2.50	3.	5.	7.	20.	25.	60.	125.	300.
1889 ...(3,336)	48,869,361	2.50	3.	4.	6.	12.	20.	50.	75.	300.

	Mintage	G-4	VG-8	F-12	VF-20	EF-40	AU-50	MS-60	MS-63	PF-63
1890 ...(2,740)	57,182,854	$2.50	$3.00	$3.50	$6.00	$12.	$25.	$45.	$75.	$300.
1891 ...(2,350)	47,072,350	2.50	3.00	3.50	6.00	12.	25.	45.	75.	300.
1892 ...(2,745)	37,649,832	2.50	3.00	3.50	6.00	12.	25.	45.	75.	300.
1893 ...(2,195)	46,642,195	2.50	3.00	3.50	6.00	12.	25.	45.	75.	300.
1894 ...(2,632)	16,752,132	4.00	5.00	9.00	12.00	40.	50.	75.	100.	300.
1894, DblDt		25.00	35.00	60.00	120.00	200.	300.	500.	850.	
1895 ...(2,062)	38,343,636	2.00	2.50	3.50	5.00	12.	23.	35.	60.	300.
1896 ...(1,862)	39,057,293	2.00	2.50	3.50	5.00	12.	23.	35.	60.	300.
1897 ...(1,938)	50,466,330	2.00	2.50	3.50	5.00	12.	23.	35.	60.	300.
1898 ...(1,795)	49,823,079	2.00	2.50	3.50	5.00	12.	23.	35.	60.	300.
1899 ...(2,031)	53,600,031	2.00	2.50	3.50	5.00	12.	23.	35.	60.	300.
1900 ...(2,262)	66,833,764	1.75	2.00	2.50	3.50	9.	18.	30.	50.	275.
1901 ...(1,985)	79,611,143	1.75	2.00	2.50	3.50	9.	18.	30.	50.	275.
1902 ...(2,018)	87,376,722	1.75	2.00	2.50	3.50	9.	18.	30.	50.	275.
1903 ...(1,790)	85,094,493	1.75	2.00	2.50	3.50	9.	18.	30.	50.	275.
1904 ...(1,817)	61,328,015	1.75	2.00	2.50	3.50	9.	18.	30.	50.	275.
1905 ...(2,152)	80,719,163	1.75	2.00	2.50	3.50	9.	18.	30.	50.	275.
1906 ...(1,725)	96,022,255	1.75	2.00	2.50	3.50	9.	18.	30.	50.	275.
1907 ...(1,475)	108,138,618	1.75	2.00	2.50	3.50	9.	18.	30.	50.	275.

**Location of mint mark S
on reverse of Indian cent
(1908 and 1909 only).**

	Mintage	G-4	VG-8	F-12	VF-20	EF-40	AU-50	MS-60	MS-63	PF-63
1908 ...(1,620)	32,327,987	1.75	2.00	2.50	3.50	9.	18.	30.	50.	300.
1908S	1,115,000	60.00	65.00	70.00	80.00	120.	200.	250.	300.	
1909 ...(2,175)	14,370,645	3.50	4.00	4.50	5.50	16.	21.	35.	55.	300.
1909S	309,000	300.00	350.00	375.00	400.00	450.	500.	600.	750.	

LINCOLN TYPE, WHEAT EARS REVERSE 1909-1958

Victor D. Brenner designed this cent which was issued to commemorate the hundredth anniversary of Lincoln's birth. The designer's initials V.D.B. appear on the reverse of a limited quantity of cents of 1909. The initials were restored, in 1918, to the obverse side on Lincoln's shoulder as illustrated on page 98. The Lincoln type was the first cent to have the motto IN GOD WE TRUST.

Matte proof coins were made for collectors from 1909 through 1916, and an exceptional specimen dated 1917 is also reported to exist.

Designer Victor D. Brenner; weight 3.11 grams; composition: .950 copper, .050 tin and zinc; diameter 19 mm; plain edge; mints: Philadelphia, Denver, San Francisco.

G-4 GOOD—Date worn but apparent. Lines in wheat heads missing. Full rims.
VG-8 VERY GOOD—Half of lines show in upper wheat heads.
F-12 FINE—Wheat lines worn but visible.
VF-20 VERY FINE—Cheek and jaw bones worn but separated. No worn spots on wheat heads.
EF-40 EXTREMELY FINE—Slight wear. All details sharp.
AU-50—Slight wear on Lincoln's cheek and jaw and on the wheat stalks.
MS-60 UNCIRCULATED—No trace of wear. Light blemishes or discoloration.
MS-63 SELECT UNCIRCULATED—No trace of wear. Slight blemishes. Red-Brown color.
MS-65 CHOICE UNCIRCULATED—No trace of wear. Barely noticeable blemishes. Nearly full red color.
PF-63—Nearly perfect.

SMALL CENTS

Location of designer's initials V.D.B. on 1909 reverse only.

No V.D.B. on reverse 1909-1958.

Location of mint mark.

Variety 1 — Bronze 1909-1942

Choice Brilliant Uncirculated cents command higher prices. Discolored (brown) or weakly struck pieces are worth less.

	Mintage	G-4	VG-8	F-12	VF-20	EF-40	AU-50	MS-60	MS-63
1909, V.D.B.	27,995,000	$4.00	$4.50	$5.00	$5.50	$6.50	$8.	$13.	$16.
1909, V.D.B.,Pf**	(1,194)								2,000.
1909S, V.D.B. . . .	484,000	460.00	550.00	620.00	700.00	750.00	850.	1,000.	1,300.
1909	72,702,618	1.50	1.75	2.00	2.50	3.50	8.	15.	20.
1909,Pf**	(2,352)								350.
1909S	1,825,000	60.00	65.00	80.00	120.00	175.00	200.	225.	275.
1909S, S over horiz. S		65.00	70.00	85.00	135.00	200.00	225.	250.	300.
1910 146,801,218		0.25	0.35	0.50	1.00	2.25	6.	15.	25.
1910,Pf**	(4,083)								300.
1910S	6,045,000	7.50	9.00	11.00	14.00	28.00	60.	80.	100.
1911 101,177,787		0.25	0.40	1.00	1.50	5.00	8.	20.	50.
1911,Pf**	(2,411)								325.
1911D	12,672,000	5.00	6.00	8.00	14.00	40.00	65.	90.	120.
1911S	4,026,000	17.00	18.00	20.00	24.00	45.00	80.	150.	250.
1912	68,153,060	1.25	1.50	2.00	5.00	9.00	18.	32.	45.
1912,Pf**	(2,172)								325.
1912D	10,411,000	6.00	6.25	8.00	20.00	50.00	75.	135.	200.
1912S	4,431,000	12.00	14.00	16.00	20.00	50.00	75.	125.	175.
1913	76,532,352	0.75	1.00	1.50	3.50	15.00	18.	30.	47.
1913,Pf**	(2,983)								350.
1913D	15,804,000	2.00	3.00	4.00	9.00	30.00	60.	90.	175.
1913S	6,101,000	7.00	8.00	9.00	14.00	35.00	70.	135.	240.
1914	75,238,432	0.50	0.75	1.50	4.00	14.00	30.	50.	62.
1914,Pf**	(1,415)								400.
1914D	1,193,000	120.00	160.00	220.00	280.00	525.00	900.	1,200.	2,200.
1914S	4,137,000	10.00	12.00	13.00	22.00	48.00	125.	250.	450.
1915	29,092,120	1.50	2.00	4.50	11.00	40.00	60.	85.	130.
1915,Pf**	(1,150)								550.
1915D	22,050,000	1.75	2.00	2.50	4.00	14.00	35.	70.	100.
1915S	4,833,000	6.00	7.00	8.00	12.00	40.00	130.	160.	235.
1916 131,833,677		0.20	0.25	0.35	1.00	3.00	8.	14.	30.
1916,Pf**	(600)								750.
1916D	35,956,000	0.50	0.60	1.25	2.25	9.00	20.	60.	110.
1916S	22,510,000	1.00	1.50	2.00	3.00	12.00	28.	75.	140.

Doubled Die Varieties of 1917 and 1936

1917, DblDieObv				125.00	275.00	500.00	750.	1,100.	1,800.
1917 196,429,785		0.20	0.25	0.30	1.00	3.00	8.	15.	30.
1917,**									—

*Beware of altered date or mint mark. No V.D.B. on shoulder of genuine 1914D cent.
**Matte Proof

SMALL CENTS

Designer's initials placed on Lincoln's shoulder next to rim, starting 1918.

	Mintage	G-4	VG-8	F-12	VF-20	EF-40	AU-50	MS-60	MS-63
1917D	55,120,000	$0.30	$0.40	$1.00	$2.50	$9.00	$22.	$65.	$135.
1917S	32,620,000	0.50	0.65	0.85	2.00	8.00	20.	70.	150.
1918	288,104,634	0.20	0.25	0.40	0.85	2.50	6.	14.	30.
1918D	47,830,000	0.30	0.50	1.00	2.00	8.50	18.	60.	120.
1918S	34,680,000	0.30	0.50	1.00	2.00	8.50	30.	70.	150.
1919	392,021,000	0.15	0.25	0.40	0.65	3.00	5.	12.	25.
1919D	57,154,000	0.25	0.30	0.45	1.30	5.00	30.	50.	100.
1919S	139,760,000	0.16	0.30	1.00	1.50	4.50	14.	38.	80.
1920	310,165,000	0.16	0.25	0.35	0.40	2.00	4.	13.	25.
1920D	49,280,000	0.25	0.35	0.60	1.50	8.00	25.	65.	110.
1920S	46,220,000	0.25	0.35	0.60	1.00	6.00	28.	90.	200.
1921	39,157,000	0.20	0.35	0.60	1.25	4.00	16.	42.	75.
1921S	15,274,000	1.00	1.40	1.75	3.75	18.00	60.	110.	190.
1922D	7,160,000	8.00	9.00	11.00	14.00	25.00	40.	80.	130.
1922 No D‡		400.00	500.00	650.00	800.00	1,650.00	3,000.	5,750.	20,000.
1922 Weak D		32.00	38.00	50.00	75.00	175.00	210.	350.	600.
1923	74,723,000	0.15	0.20	0.35	0.75	3.00	7.	15.	28.
1923S	8,700,000	2.00	2.50	4.00	6.50	25.00	70.	200.	400.
1924	75,178,000	0.15	0.20	0.35	0.60	3.50	9.	24.	50.
1924D	2,520,000	12.00	15.00	18.00	30.00	85.00	160.	275.	375.
1924S	11,696,000	1.00	1.25	1.75	3.00	14.00	60.	110.	225.
1925	139,949,000	0.15	0.25	0.35	0.50	2.00	6.	10.	23.
1925D	22,580,000	0.25	0.35	0.45	1.50	8.00	25.	60.	90.
1925S	26,380,000	0.20	0.25	0.35	1.00	8.00	20.	70.	150.
1926	157,088,000	0.15	0.20	0.30	0.45	1.50	4.	8.	17.
1926D	28,020,000	0.25	0.35	0.60	1.30	7.00	20.	60.	95.
1926S	4,550,000	2.25	3.00	5.00	6.50	15.00	55.	120.	250.
1927	144,440,000	0.15	0.20	0.30	0.55	1.50	4.	10.	18.
1927D	27,170,000	0.25	0.35	0.50	0.85	4.00	12.	50.	75.
1927S	14,276,000	0.65	0.80	1.40	2.50	10.00	25.	75.	135.
1928	134,116,000	0.15	0.20	0.30	0.55	1.50	3.	10.	18.
1928D	31,170,000	0.20	0.30	0.40	0.90	3.00	10.	30.	75.
1928S*	17,266,000	0.35	0.50	0.75	1.25	4.00	14.	65.	110.
1929	185,262,000	0.15	0.20	0.30	0.60	1.50	4.	8.	13.
1929D	41,730,000	0.15	0.25	0.35	0.70	3.00	6.	20.	37.
1929S	50,148,000	0.15	0.25	0.35	0.60	2.50	5.	14.	22.
1930	157,415,000	0.10	0.15	0.25	0.40	1.00	2.	6.	10.
1930D	40,100,000	0.15	0.20	0.30	0.45	2.50	4.	12.	27.
1930S	24,286,000	0.15	0.20	0.30	0.50	1.50	6.	10.	15.
1931	19,396,000	0.35	0.45	0.60	1.00	2.00	6.	20.	37.
1931D	4,480,000	2.75	3.00	3.75	4.50	9.00	30.	55.	85.
1931S	866,000	50.00	55.00	60.00	65.00	75.00	85.	90.	100.
1932	9,062,000	1.50	1.75	2.00	2.50	3.00	10.	20.	25.
1932D	10,500,000	0.70	0.90	1.20	1.75	2.50	7.	16.	30.
1933	14,360,000	0.75	0.90	1.25	1.50	3.00	9.	17.	30.
1933D	6,200,000	1.75	2.00	2.25	3.00	5.00	10.	22.	25.
1934	219,080,000	0.10	0.12	0.15	0.30	1.00	4.	8.	10.
1934D	28,446,000	0.15	0.25	0.30	0.45	2.00	5.	20.	25.
1935	245,388,000	0.10	0.12	0.15	0.20	0.50	1.	6.	8.
1935D	47,000,000	0.10	0.12	0.15	0.25	0.50	2.	8.	10.
1935S	38,702,000	0.10	0.15	0.25	0.50	2.00	5.	16.	20.

‡1922 cents with a weak or missing mintmark were made from extremely worn dies that originally struck normal 1922D cents. Three different die pairs were involved; two of them produced "weak D" coins. One die pair (#2, identified by a "strong reverse") is acknowledged as striking "No D" coins. Weak D cents are worth considerably less. Beware of removed mintmark.

*Large and small mint mark varieties, see page 73.

SMALL CENTS

	Mintage	VG-8	F-12	VF-20	EF-40	AU-50	MS-60	MS-63	PF-63
1936 . .(5,569)	309,637,569	0.10	0.15	0.25	0.50	1.50	3.00	8.00	200.
1936, DblDieObv.	—	—	55.00	90.00	100.00	250.00	1,000.00	
1936D	40,620,000	0.10	0.20	0.30	0.50	1.00	4.00	8.50	
1936S ......:	29,130,000	0.10	0.25	0.40	0.55	2.00	4.00	8.50	
1937 . .(9,320)	309,179,320	0.10	0.15	0.30	0.50	1.00	3.00	7.00	75.
1937D	50,430,000	0.10	0.15	0.25	0.40	1.00	3.00	9.00	
1937S	34,500,000	0.10	0.20	0.30	0.40	1.00	3.00	9.50	
1938 .(14,734)	156,696,734	0.10	0.15	0.20	0.30	1.00	2.00	8.00	60.
1938D	20,010,000	0.20	0.30	0.50	0.80	1.25	5.00	12.00	
1938S	15,180,000	0.35	0.45	0.55	0.75	1.10	4.00	10.00	
1939 .(13,520)	316,479,520	0.10	0.12	0.15	0.25	0.50	1.00	6.00	55.
1939D	15,160,000	0.45	0.55	0.65	0.85	1.25	5.00	11.00	
1939S	52,070,000	0.15	0.20	0.30	0.75	1.00	2.50	10.00	
1940 .(15,872)	586,825,872	0.10	0.12	0.15	0.40	0.60	2.00	6.00	45.
1940D	81,390,000	0.10	0.15	0.25	0.60	0.75	2.00	6.00	
1940S	112,940,000	0.10	0.12	0.15	0.50	1.00	1.75	6.25	
1941 .(21,100)	887,039,100	0.10	0.12	0.15	0.30	0.60	1.50	6.00	40.
1941D	128,700,000	0.10	0.12	0.15	0.50	1.00	3.00	9.00	
1941S‡	92,360,000	0.10	0.15	0.30	0.50	1.00	4.00	12.00	
1942 .(32,600)	657,828,600	0.10	0.12	0.15	0.20	0.50	0.75	5.00	42.
1942D	206,698,000	0.10	0.12	0.15	0.25	0.50	0.85	6.00	
1942S	85,590,000	0.15	0.25	0.30	0.85	1.25	5.50	17.00	

‡Large and small mint mark varieties, see page 67.

**1943D,
Boldly
Doubled
Mint Mark**

**1944D,
D over S**

Variety 2 — Zinc-coated Steel 1943, Only

Owing to a shortage of copper during the critical war year 1943, the Treasury Department resorted to the use of zinc-coated steel for our cents. No bronze cents were officially issued in 1943. A few specimens struck on bronze planchets by error are known to exist. Through a similar error, a few of the 1944 cents were struck on steel planchets.

1943 — Weight 2.70 grams; composition: steel, coated with zinc; diameter 19 mm; plain edge.

	Mintage	F-12	VF-20	EF-40	AU-50	MS-63	MS-65
1943	684,628,670	$0.25	$0.30	$0.40	$0.50	$2.00	$5.
1943D		0.25	0.35	0.45	0.75	2.75	7.
1943D Boldly ... ⎱ doubled mint mark ⎰	217,660,000	6.00	12.00	20.00	25.00	30.00	75.
1943S	191,550,000	0.35	0.50	0.60	1.00	4.00	13.

Variety 1 Resumed 1944-1958

Cartridge cases were salvaged for coinage of 1944 through 1946. Although the color was slightly different for uncirculated specimens, the coins proved satisfactory in every respect. The original alloy of 1864-1942 was resumed in 1947.

1944-1946 — Weight 3.11 grams; composition: .950 copper, .050 zinc; diameter 19 mm; plain edge.

	Mintage	VF-20	EF-40	AU-50	MS-63	MS-65
1944	1,435,400,000	0.10	0.20	0.35	0.75	2.
1944D .... ⎱ 1944D, D/S .... ⎰	430,578,000	0.10	0.20	0.35	0.75	2.
		125.00	175.00	250.00	*425.00	1,600.
1944S	282,760,000	0.10	0.20	0.35	0.75	6.
1945	1,040,515,000	0.10	0.20	0.35	0.75	2.
1945D	266,268,000	0.10	0.20	0.35	0.75	2.
1945S	181,770,000	0.10	0.20	0.35	0.75	6.

*Value for MS-60 is $200.. Two varieties exist, but only the one illustrated above is valued at the prices shown here, the other being less obvious and less valuable.

SMALL CENTS

	Mintage	VF-20	EF-40	AU-50	MS-63	MS-65	PF-65
1946	991,655,000	$0.10	$0.15	$0.35	$0.50	$2.00	
1946D	315,690,000	0.10	0.20	0.35	0.50	4.00	
1946S . . . . }	198,100,000	0.10	0.20	0.35	0.50	5.00	
1946S, S/D . . . . . }		25.00	75.00	125.00	225.00	500.00	
1947	190,555,000	0.10	0.20	0.40	0.80	3.00	
1947D	194,750,000	0.10	0.20	0.40	0.50	3.00	
1947S	99,000,000	0.15	0.25	0.50	0.75	6.00	
1948	317,570,000	0.10	0.20	0.35	0.75	2.00	
1948D	172,637,500	0.10	0.20	0.35	0.50	3.00	
1948S	81,735,000	0.15	0.30	0.35	0.80	6.00	
1949	217,775,000	0.10	0.20	0.35	1.00	4.00	
1949D	153,132,500	0.10	0.20	0.35	1.00	4.00	
1949S	64,290,000	0.20	0.30	0.35	2.00	6.00	
1950 . . .(51,386)	272,686,386	0.10	0.20	0.35	0.75	2.00	75.
1950D	334,950,000	0.10	0.20	0.35	0.50	2.00	
1950S	118,505,000	0.10	0.25	0.35	0.75	2.75	
1951 . . .(57,500)	284,633,500	0.10	0.25	0.35	0.60	2.75	80.
1951D	625,355,000	0.10	0.12	0.35	0.50	2.00	
1951S	136,010,000	0.15	0.25	0.50	1.00	3.00	
1952 . . .(81,980)	186,856,980	0.10	0.15	0.35	1.00	3.00	65.
1952D	746,130,000	0.10	0.15	0.25	0.50	3.00	
1952S	137,800,004	0.10	0.20	0.35	2.00	6.00	
1953 . .(128,800)	256,883,800	0.10	0.15	0.20	0.25	2.00	60.
1953D	700,515,000	0.10	0.15	0.20	0.25	2.00	
1953S	181,835,000	0.10	0.15	0.20	0.50	2.00	
1954 . .(233,300)	71,873,350	0.25	0.35	0.45	0.50	2.00	22.
1954D	251,552,500	0.10	0.12	0.20	0.25	1.00	
1954S	96,190,000	0.10	0.20	0.20	0.25	1.00	

1955 Doubled Die Error

The popular 1955 doubled die error coins were made from improperly prepared dies that show full-doubled outline of date and legend. Do not confuse
these with less valuable pieces showing only minor traces of doubling.
Counterfeits exist.

	Mintage	VF-20	EF-40	AU-50	MS-63	MS-65	PF-65
1955, DblDieObv. . . . . }	330,958,200	$900.00	$1,000.00	*$1,100.00	$2,400.00	$30,000.00	
1955 . . . . . (378,200) }		0.10	0.12	0.15	0.25	0.75	20.
1955D	563,257,500	0.10	0.10	0.15	0.25	0.50	
1955S	44,610,000	0.20	0.30	0.40	0.75	2.00	
1956 . . . . . .(669,384)	421,414,384	0.10	0.12	0.15	0.25	0.50	4.
1956D 1,098,201,100		0.10	0.12	0.15	0.25	0.50	
1957 . . . .(1,247,952)	283,787,952	0.10	0.12	0.15	0.25	0.50	4.
1957D 1,051,342,000		0.10	0.12	0.15	0.25	0.50	
1958 . . . . . .(875,652)	253,400,652	0.10	0.12	0.15	0.25	0.50	5.
1958 DblDieObv.	(Rare)					—	
1958D	800,953,300	0.10	0.12	0.15	0.25	0.50	

*Value for MS-60 Uncirculated is $1,250.

SMALL CENTS

LINCOLN TYPE, MEMORIAL REVERSE 1959 TO DATE

Frank Gasparro designed the Lincoln Memorial reverse which was introduced in 1959 on the 150th anniversary of Lincoln's birth.

Designer: Obv. V. D. Brenner, Rev. Frank Gasparro.1959-1962; weight 3.11 grams; composition: .950 copper, .050 tin and zinc; diameter 19 mm; plain edge. 1962-1982-composition changed to: .950 copper, .050 zinc. 1982-composition changed to: copper plated zinc. Core is 99.2% zinc, 0.8% copper, with a plating of pure copper. Total content is 97.5% zinc, 2.5% copper. Weight 2.5 grams. Both types issued in 1982. Mints: Philadelphia, Denver, San Francisco.

	Mintage		MS-63	MS-65	PF-65
1959	(1,149,291)	610,864,291	$0.20	$0.50	$3.00
1959D		1,279,760,000	0.20	0.50	

Small Date				**Large Date**	

	Mintage		MS-63	MS-65	PF-65
1960, LgDt	(1,691,602)	588,096,602	0.20	0.30	2.00
1960, SmDt			3.00	7.00	20.00
1960D, LgDt		1,580,884,000	0.20	0.30	1.50
1960D, SmDt			0.20	0.30	
1961	(3,028,244)	756,373,244	0.10	0.30	1.50
1961D		1,753,266,700	0.10	0.30	
1962	(3,218,019)	609,263,019	0.10	0.30	1.50
1962D		1,793,148,140	0.10	0.30	
1963	(3,075,645)	757,185,645	0.10	0.30	1.50
1963D		1,774,020,400	0.10	0.30	
1964	(3,950,762)	2,652,525,762	0.10	0.30	1.50
1964D		3,799,071,500	0.10	0.30	
1965		1,497,224,900	0.20	0.50	
1966		2,188,147,783	0.20	0.50	
1967		3,048,667,100	0.20	0.50	
1968		1,707,880,970	0.25	0.60	
1968D		2,886,269,600	0.10	0.40	
1968S	(3,041,506)	261,311,507	0.10	0.40	1.00

In 1969, the dies were modified to strengthen the design, and Lincoln's head was made slightly smaller. In 1973, dies were further modified and engraver's initials FG made larger. The initials were reduced slightly in 1974. During 1982 the dies were again modified and the bust, lettering and date made slightly smaller. One variety of the 1984 cent shows Lincoln's ear doubled. 1,579,324 cents dated 1974 were struck in aluminum as experimental pieces. None was placed in circulation and most were later destroyed. One was preserved for the National Collection in the Smithsonian Institution.

SMALL CENTS

| **1969S Doubled Die Error** | **Small Date (High 7)** | **Large Date (Low 7)** | **1971S Proof Doubled Die** |

	Mintage	MS-65	PF-65
1969	1,136,910,000	$0.70	
1969D	4,002,832,200	0.30	
1969S(2,934,631)			
	547,309,631	0.30	$1.00
1969S DblDieObv.		—	
1970	1,898,315,000	0.50	
1970D	2,891,438,900	0.20	
1970S (2,632,810)			
	693,192,814		
1970S, SmDt (high 7)		60.00	65.00
1970S, LgDt (low 7)		0.30	1.00
1970S DblDieObv.		—	
1971	1,919,490,000	0.80	
1971D	2,911,045,600	0.80	
1971S(3,220,733)			
	528,354,192	0.80	1.00

1972 Doubled Die Error

		MS-65	PF-65
1971S, DblDieObv.			650.00
1972, DblDieObv.		600.00	
1972	2,933,255,000	0.20	
1972D	2,665,071,400	0.25	
1972S(3,260,996)			
	380,200,104	0.30	1.00
1973	3,728,245,000	0.20	
1973D	3,549,576,588	0.20	
1973S(2,760,339)			
	319,937,634	0.30	1.00

	Mintage	MS-65	PF-65
1974	4,232,140,523	$0.20	
1974D	4,235,098,000	0.20	
1974S(2,612,568)			
412,039,228		0.30	$1.00
1975	5,451,476,142	0.20	
1975D	4,505,275,300	0.20	
1975S, Pf(2,845,450)			3.50
1976	4,674,292,426	0.20	
1976D	4,221,592,455	0.20	
1976S, Pf(4,149,730)		0.00	3.20
1977	4,469,930,000	0.20	
1977D	4,194,062,300	0.20	
1977S, Pf(3,251,152)			2.50
1978	5,558,605,000	0.20	
1978D	4,280,233,400	0.20	
1978S, Pf(3,127,781)		0.00	2.50
1979	6,018,515,000	0.20	
1979D	4,139,357,254	0.20	
1979S Pf(3,677,175)			
Filled S			4.00
Clear S			4.25
1980	7,414,705,000	0.20	
1980D	5,140,098,660	0.20	
1980S, Pf(3,554,806)			2.00
1981	7,491,750,000	0.20	
1981D	5,373,235,677	0.20	
1981S Pf(4,063,083)			
Filled S Pf			2.00
Clear S Pf			60.00
1982	10,712,525,000		
LgDt		0.20	
SmDt		0.30	
1982D	6,012,979,368		
LgDt		0.20	
1982S, Pf(3,857,479)			2.50

*Other slightly doubled varieties exist, but are worth less.

Copper Plated Zinc

Composition changed to copper plated zinc. Core is 99.2% zinc, 0.8% copper, with a plating of pure copper. Weight is 2.5 grams (approximately 20% lighter than the copper cents)

Large Date

Small Date

| 1982, LgDt ⎫ | Incl. above | 1.00 |
| 1982, SmDt ⎭ | | 1.25 |

| 1982D Lg.Dt ⎫ | Incl. above | .25 |
| 1982D Sm.Dt ⎭ | | .10 |

1983 Doubled Die Rev.

Doubled Ear Variety

	Mintage	MS-65	PF-65
1983, DblDieRev	.........$300.00		
1983	7,752,355,000	....0.20	
1983D	6,467,199,428	....0.20	
1983S, Pf	...(3,279,126)	....	$3.00
1984	8,151,079,000	....0.20	
1984, Doubled ear	........200.00		
1984D	5,569,238,906	....0.50	
1984S, Pf	...(3,065,110)	......—	4.00
1985	5,648,489,887	....0.20	
1985D	5,287,339,926	....0.20	
1985S, Pf	3,362,821	....	5.00
1986	4,491,395,493	....0.50	
1986D	4,442,866,698	....0.20	
1986S, Pf	...(3,010,497)	....	6.50
1987	4,682,466,931	....0.20	
1987D	4,879,389,514	....0.20	
1987S, Pf	...(4,227,728)	....	5.00
1988	6,092,810,000	....0.20	
1988D	5,253,740,443	....0.20	
1988S, Pf	...(3,262,948)	....	10.00
1989	7,261,535,000	....0.20	
1989D	...5,345,467,111	....0.20	
1989S, Pf	...(3,220,194)	....	10.00
1990	6,851,765,000	....0.20	
1990D	4,922,894,533	....0.20	
1990S, Pf	...(3,299,559)	....	6.00
1990, Pf w/o S	................3,000.00		
1991	5,165,940,000	....0.20	
1991D	4,158,446,076	....0.20	
1991S, Pf	...(2,867,787)	....	25.00
1992	4,648,905,000	....0.20	
1992D	4,448,673,300	....0.20	
1992 Close AM*	........200.00		
1992S, Pf	...(4,176,560)	....	4.00
1993	5,684,705,000	0.20	
1993D	...6,426,650,571	0.20	

	Mintage	MS-65	PF-65
1993S, Pf	(3,394,792)		$9.00
1994	6,500,850,000	$0.20	
1994D	...7,131,765,000	0.20	
1994S, Pf	(3,269,923)		8.00
1995	6,411,440,000	0.20	
1995, DblDieObv..		40.00	
1995D	...7,128,560,000	0.20	
1995S, Pf	(2,797,481)		9.00
1996	6,612,465,000	0.20	
1996D	...6,510,795,000	0.20	
1996S, Pf	(2,525,265)		4.50
1997	4,622,800,000	0.20	
1997D	...4,576,555,000	0.20	
1997S, Pf	(2,796,678)		10.00
1998	5,032,155,000	0.20	
1998 Wide AM*		30.00	
1998D	...5,225,353,500	0.20	
1998S Pf .	(2,086,507)		9.00
1999	5,237,600,000	0.20	
1999 Wide AM*		300.00	
1999D	...6,360,065,000	0.20	
1999S Pf .	(2,543,401)		5.00
2000	5,503,200,000	0.20	
2000 Wide AM*		40.00	
2000D	...8,774,220,000	0.20	
2000S Pf .	(3,082,483)		3.00
2001	4,959,600,000	0.20	
2001D	...5,374,990,000	0.20	
2001S Pf .	(2,294,043)		3.00
2002	3,260,800,000	0.20	
2002D	...4,028,055,000	0.20	
2002S Pf .	(2,277,720)		3.00
2003		0.20	
2003D ...		0.20	
2003S Pf .			3.00
2004		0.20	
2004D ...		0.20	
2004S Pf .			3.00

Some of the cents minted since 1994 show the faint trace of a mint mark and are believed to be the result of the letter having been removed from the master die during production of working dies for coinage. So-called "phantom" mint mark pieces were produced in Philadelphia but show traces of either a D or an S. Values for such pieces vary according to date and condition but are not significantly higher than for normal pieces.

*Varieties were made using Proof dies that have a wide space between AM in AMERICA. The letters nearly touch on other Uncirculated cents after 1993.

BIBLIOGRAPHY

Fivaz, Bill and Stanton, J.T. *The Cherrypickers' Guide to Rare Die Varieties.* Savannah, 1994.
Lange, David W. *The Complete Guide to Lincoln Cents.* Wolfeboro, N.H. 1996.
Snow, Richard. *Flying Eagle & Indian Cents.* Tucson, AZ, 1992.
Steve, Larry and Flynn, Kevin. *Flying Eagle and Indian Cent Die Varieties.* Jarretteville, MD, 1995.
Taylor, Sol. *The Standard Guide to Lincoln Cent.* Anaheim, CA, 1999.
Wexler, John and Flynn, Kevin. *The Authoritative Reference on Lincoln Cents.* Rancocas, NJ, 1996.

TWO-CENT PIECES — 1864-1873

The Act of April 22, 1864, which changed the weight and composition of the cent, included a provision for the bronze two cent piece. The weight was specified as 96 grains, the alloy being the same as for the cent.

The two cent piece is one of the short-lived issues of United States coinage. The motto "In God We Trust" appeared for the first time on the new coin due largely to the increased religious sentiment during the Civil War crisis.

There are two varieties for the first year of issue, 1864: the Small Motto, which is scarce, and the Large Motto. See illustrations below.

On the obverse the D in GOD is narrow on the Large Motto. The stem to the leaf shows plainly on the small motto variety. There is no stem on the Large Motto.

The first T in TRUST is very close to the ribbon crease at left on the Small Motto variety; there is a 1mm gap on the Large Motto variety.

It will be noted that the shield device is very similar to the nickel five cent piece introduced in 1866. Listed Proof mintages are estimates.

1864 Small Motto   **1864 Large Motto**

+ or – indicates change from previous year	TYPE COIN VALUES								
	G-4	F-12	EF-40	AU-50	MS-60	MS-63	MS-65	PF-60	PF-63	PF-65
1864-1873	15.+	22.+	40.+	60.	80.+	140.	425.+	310.+	450.+	875.+

Designer James B. Longacre; weight 6.22 grams; composition: .950 copper, .050 tin and zinc; diameter 23 mm; plain edge. All coined at Philadelphia Mint.

G-4 GOOD — *At least IN GOD visible.*
F-12 FINE — *Complete motto visible. WE weak.*
EF-40 EXTREMELY FINE — *WE is bold.*
AU-50 ABOUT UNCIRCULATED — *Leaf tips, arrow points and the word "WE" show trace of wear.*
MS-60 UNCIRCULATED — *No trace of wear. Light blemishes.*
MS-63 UNCIRCULATED — *Some distracting contact marks or blemishes in prime focal areas. Luster may be impaired.*
PF-63 — *Nearly Perfect*

Brilliant red choice Uncirculated and Proof coins command higher prices. Spotted, cleaned or discolored pieces are worth less.

	Mintage	G-4	F-12	VF-20	EF-40	AU-50	MS-60	MS-63	PF-63
1864, SmMotto	} 19,847,500	$100.	$200.	$325.	$500.	$600.	$725.	$1,000.	$15,000.
1864, LgMotto (100+)		15.	22.	28.	40.	60.	80.	140.	550.
1865* . . . .(500+)	13,640,000	15.	22.	28.	40.	60.	80.	140.	450.
1866 . . . .(725+)	3,177,000	15.	25.	30.	45.	60.	80.	140.	450.
1867 . . . .(625+)	} 2,938,750	15.	25.	30.	45.	60.	120.	175.	450.
1867, DblDie		—	—	150.	200.	250.	400.	600.	
1868 . . . .(600+)	2,803,750	16.	28.	35.	50.	80.	130.	200.	450.
1869 . . . .(600+)	1,546,500	17.	30.	40.	55.	100.	150.	200.	450.
1870 . . . . . .(1,000+)	861,250	18.	35.	45.	80.	125.	225.	250.	600.
1871 . . . .(960+)	721,250	23.	38.	55.	100.	150.	250.	325.	750.
1872 . . . .(950+)	65,000	225.	350.	525.	675.	750.	850.	1,200.	1,000.
1873,Cl 3.Pfs.only (Est. 600)		1,100.	1,200.	1,300.	1,400.				1,800.
1873, Op 3. Restrike (Est. 500)		900.	1,000.	1,200.	1,500.				2,200.

*One variety appears to show traces of a 4 under the 5 in the date. Other varieties show the tip of the 5 either plain or curved.

BIBLIOGRAPHY
Flynn, Kevin. *Getting Your Two Cents Worth*. Rancocas, NJ, 1994.
Kliman, Myron M. *The Two Cent Piece and Varieties*. South Laguna, CA, 1977.
Leone, Frank. *Longacre's Two Cent Piece Die Varieties & Errors*. College Point, NY, 1991.

SILVER THREE-CENT PIECES 1851-1873

This smallest of United States silver coins was authorized by Congress March 3, 1851. The first three-cent silver pieces had no lines bordering the six-pointed star. From 1854 through 1858 there were three lines, while issues of the last fifteen years show only two lines. Issues from 1854 through 1873 have an olive sprig over the III and a bundle of three arrows beneath. Nearly the entire production of non-Proof coins from 1863 to 1872 was melted in 1873.

+ or – indicates change from previous year	TYPE COIN VALUES									
	G-4	F-12	EF-40	AU-50	MS-60	MS-63	MS-65	PF-60	PF-63	PF-65
Variety 1 1851-1853	20.	28.	55.	120.	150.	260.	1,000.			
Variety 2 1854-1858	19.	30.	85.	170.	280.	625.	3,800.	1,000.	2,400.	7,500.
Variety 3 1859-1873	19.	28.	60.	110.	155.	275.	1,100.	250.	450.	1,400.

1851-1853 — Designer James B. Longacre; weight .80 gram; composition: .750 silver, .250 copper; diameter 14 mm; plain edge; mints: Philadelphia, New Orleans.

1854-1873 — Weight .75 gram; composition: .900 silver, .100 copper; diameter 14 mm; plain edge. All coined at Philadelphia Mint.

Mint mark location.
←

G-4 GOOD — Star worn smooth. Legend and date readable.
VG-8 VERY GOOD — Outline of shield defined. Legend and date clear.
F-12 FINE — Only star points worn smooth.
VF-20 VERY FINE — Only partial wear on star ridges.
EF-40 EXTREMELY FINE — Ridges on star points show.
AU-50 ABOUT UNCIRCULATED — Star shows trace of wear at each point. Center of shield may be weak.
MS-60 UNCIRCULATED — No trace of wear. Light blemishes.
MS-63 UNCIRCULATED — Some distracting contact marks or blemishes in prime focal areas. Luster may be impaired.

Variety 1 — 1851-1853

	Mintage	G-4	VG-8	F-12	VF-20	EF-40	AU-50	MS-60	MS-63	PF-63
1851 ..	5,447,400	$22.	$27.	$30.	$35.	$55.	$135.	$150.	$250.	—
1851O	720,000	25.	30.	35.	70.	135.	200.	325.	425.	
1852, 1 over inverted 2										
1852 ..	18,663,500	22.	27.	30.	35.	55.	135.	150.	250.	—
1853 ..	11,400,000	22.	27.	30.	35.	55.	135.	150.	250.	

Variety 2 1854-1858

Well-struck specimens command higher prices.

1854	671,000	24.	28.	32.	40.	95.	210.	325.	600.	12,000.
1855	139,000	27.	40.	50.	90.	165.	275.	500.	900.	4,500.
1856	1,458,000	22.	27.	32.	45.	90.	175.	280.	600.	4,000.
1857	1,042,000	22.	27.	32.	45.	90.	225.	300.	600.	3,500.
1858(300+)	1,604,000	22.	27.	32.	45.	90.	175.	280.	600.	2,500.

Variety 3 1859-1873

1862, 2 over 1

1859(800)	.365,000	20.	27.	30.	40.	60.	140.	160.	275.	450.
1860(1,000)	287,000	20.	27.	30.	40.	60.	140.	160.	275.	450.
1861(1,000)	498,000	20.	27.	30.	40.	60.	140.	160.	275.	450.
1862, 2/1	} 343,550	23.	29.	32.	45.	70.	150.	180.	375.	—
1862(550)		20.	27.	30.	40.	60.	140.	160.	275.	450.
1863, 3/2	} 21,460									1000.
1863(460)		275.	300.	325.	350.	375.	450.	600.	900.	550.
1864(470)	12,470	275.	300.	325.	325.	375.	450.	600.	900.	550.

SILVER THREE-CENT PIECES

	Mintage	F-12	VF-20	EF-40	AU-50	MS-60	MS-63	PF-63
1865 . . . . .(500)	8,500	$400.	$425.	$450.	$475.	$600.	$950.	$600.
1866 . . . .(725)	22,725	300.	325.	400.	450.	600.	900.	600.
1867 . . . .(625)	4,625	400.	425.	450.	475.	600.	900.	600.
1868 . . . . .(600)	4,100	400.	425.	450.	475.	600.	1,400.	600.
1869, 9/8 . . . . . . }	5,100							2,000.
1869 . . . . .(600) }		400.	425.	450.	475.	600.	900.	600.
1870 . . .(1,000)	4,000	400.	425.	450.	475.	600.	900.	650.
1871 . . . . .(960)	4,360	400.	425.	450.	475.	600.	900.	650.
1872 . . . . .(950)	1,950	425.	450.	475.	525.	700.	1,400.	650.
1873 . . . . .(600)	600	(Cl 3,PF only)		700.				1,100.

NICKEL THREE-CENT PIECES 1865-1889

The three-cent pieces struck in nickel composition were designed to replace the silver three-cent coins. Composition is 75% copper and 25% nickel. All were coined at Philadelphia and have plain edges.

+ or – indicates change from previous year		**TYPE COIN VALUES**							
	G-4	F-12	EF-40	AU-50	MS-60	MS-63	MS-65	PF-60	PF-63	PF-65
1865-1889 . . . . .13.	17.+	28.+	45.	85.	150.+	600.	175.+	325.+	500.

Designer James B. Longacre; weight 1.94 grams; composition: .750 copper, .250 nickel; diameter 17.9 mm; plain edge. All coined at Philadelphia Mint.

G-4 GOOD —*Date and legends complete though worn. III smooth.*
VG-8 VERY GOOD —*III is half worn. Rims complete.*
VF-20 VERY FINE —*Three-quarters of hair details show.*
EF-40 EXTREMELY FINE —*Slight, even wear.*
AU-50 ABOUT UNCIRCULATED —*Slight wear on hair curls, above the forehead, on the wreath and numeral III.*
MS-60 UNCIRCULATED —*No trace of wear. Light blemishes.*
MS-63 UNCIRCULATED —*Some distracting contact marks or blemishes in prime focal areas. Luster may be impaired.*

	Mintage	G-4	VG-8	VF-20	EF-40	AU-50	MS-60	MS-63	PF-63
1865 . . . .(500+)	11,382,000	$13.	$14.	$20.	$28.	$45.	$85.	$150.	$1,500.
1866 . . . .(725+)	4,801,000	13.	14.	20.	28.	45.	85.	150.	325.
1867 . . . .(625+)	3,915,000	13.	14.	20.	28.	45.	85.	150.	325.
1868 . . . .(600+)	3,252,000	13.	14.	20.	28.	45.	85.	150.	325.
1869 . . . .(600+)	1,604,000	13.	14.	20.	28.	50.	100.	175.	325.
1870 . . . . . .(1,000+)	1,335,000	13.	14.	20.	28.	50.	110.	175.	325.
1871 . . . .(960+)	604,000	13.	14.	20.	28.	50.	120.	175.	325.
1872 . . . .(950+)	862,000	13.	14.	20.	28.	50.	120.	175.	325.
1873, Cl 3 . . . .(1100+)	390,000	13.	14.	20.	28.	50.	130.	175.	325.
1873, Op 3	783,000	13.	14.	20.	28.	50.	120.	165.	
1874 . . . .(700+)	790,000	13.	14.	20.	28.	50.	120.	175.	325.
1875 . . . .(700+)	228,000	15.	17.	23.	35.	70.	150.	200.	325.
1876 . . . . . .(1,150+)	162,000	15.	17.	28.	38.	90.	175.	225.	325.
1877, Pfs only . .(510+)	510			1,000.	1,100.				1,500.
1878, Pfs only .(2,350)	2,350			450.	550.				750.
1879 . . . .(3,200)	41,200	50.	60.	80.	90.	125.	250.	400.	400.
1880 . . . .(3,955)	24,955	75.	85.	110.	130.	150.	275.	350.	400.
1881 . . . .(3,575)	1,080,575	13.	14.	20.	28.	45.	85.	175.	350.
1882 . . . .(3,100)	25,300	75.	80.	100.	120.	160.	275.	400.	425.
1883 . . . .(6,609)	10,609	135.	160.	225.	275.	300.	375.	750.	450.
1884 . . . .(3,942)	5,642	300.	325.	450.	500.	575.	800.	1,100.	500.
1885 . . . .(3,790)	4,790	375.	410.	535.	600.	575.	900.	1,100.	500.
1886, Pfs only .(4,290)	4,290			300.	350.				450.
1887 All Kinds } (2,960)	7,961	235.	275.	300.	325.	375.	475.	500.	450.
1887, 7/6 }				325.	375.				500.
1888 . . . .(4,582)	41,083	40.	45.	55.	70.	110.	250.	335.	350.
1889 . . . .(3,436)	21,561	65.	75.	90.	120.	130.	250.	375.	350.

TYPE COIN VALUES

+ or – indicates change from previous year	G-4	F-12	EF-40	AU-50	MS-60	MS-63	MS-65	PF-60	PF-63	PF-65
Shield-Rays 1866-1867	18.00	30.00	110.00	150.00	225.	400.	2,600.+	1,400.+	1,900.	3,500.
Shield-No Rays 1867-1883	14.00	18.00	35.00	50.00	100.	185.	625.	175.	300.	600.
Liberty Head-NC 1883	5.00	7.00	9.00	11.00	27.	45.	250.	200.	275.+	1,000.
Liberty Head-WC 1883-1912	2.00+	4.50+	26.00+	42.00+	65.	110.	500.	160.	225.+	500.
Buffalo Variety 1 1913	7.00	12.00+	20.00+	30.00+	40.+	55.+	150.+	600.	1,300.+	2,400.+
Buffalo Variety 2 1913-1938	.75	1.75+	2.50+	9.00+	15.+	30.+	40.+	550.	850.+	1,000.+
Jefferson Wartime 1942-1945	.60+	.70+	1.25+	2.50+	5.+	7.+	12.+	70.+	100.+	250.+

SHIELD TYPE 1866-1883

The shield type nickel was made possible by the Act of May 16, 1866. Its weight was set at 77-16/100 grains (5 grams) with the same composition as the nickel three-cent piece which was authorized in 1865, and a design similar to the two-cent coin. In 1866 the coin was designed with rays between the stars on the reverse. Some of the pieces minted in 1867 have the same details, but later the rays were eliminated creating two varieties for that year. There was no further change in the type until it was replaced by the Liberty head device in 1883. Only Proof pieces were struck in 1877 and 1878.

Designer James B. Longacre; weight 5 grams; composition: .750 copper, .250 nickel; diameter 20.5 mm; plain edge. All coined at Philadelphia Mint.

G-4 GOOD—*All letters in motto readable.*
VG-8 VERY GOOD—*Motto stands out clearly. Rims worn slightly but even. Part of shield lines visible.*
F-12 FINE—*Half of each olive leaf is smooth.*
EF-40 EXTREMELY FINE—*Leaf tips show slight wear. Cross over shield slightly worn.*
AU-50 ABOUT UNCIRCULATED—*Traces of light wear on only the high points of the design. Half of mint luster is present.*
MS-60 UNCIRCULATED—*No trace of wear. Light blemishes.*
MS-63 UNCIRCULATED—*Some distracting contact marks or blemishes in prime focal areas. Luster may be impaired.*
PF-63—*Nearly Perfect*

Variety 1

Rays Between Stars 1866-1867

1866 Repunched Date

Sharply struck uncirculated coins are valued higher than the prices shown here.

	Mintage	G-4	VG-8	F-12	EF-40	AU-50	MS-60	MS-63	PF-63
1866, Rays *(200+)*	14,742,500	$22.	$30.	$35.	$140.	$200.	$240.	$375.	$2,100.
1866, Repunched date		50.	70.	125.	250.	350.	550.	1,000.	
1867, Rays *(25+)*	2,019,000	28.	40.	50.	175.	250.	350.	450.	30,000.

Variety 2

Without Rays 1867-1883

Typical example of 1883, 3 over 2. Other varieties exist, as well as pieces with recut 3.

1867, No rays *(600+)*	28,890,500	15.	17.	20.	38.	60.	100.	175.	400.
1868 *(600+)*	28,817,000	15.	17.	20.	38.	60.	100.	175.	400.
1869 *(600+)*	16,395,000	15.	17.	20.	38.	60.	100.	175.	400.
1870 *(1000+)*	4,806,000	18.	20.	30.	60.	100.	150.	225.	400.
1871 *(960+)*	561,000	50.	60.	75.	180.	225.	325.	500.	450.
1872 *(950+)*	6,036,000	20.	23.	30.	60.	100.	165.	260.	400.
1873, Cl 3 *(1,100+)*	436,050	23.	30.	35.	125.	175.	300.	500.	400.
1873, Op 3 }	4,113,950	20.	23.	30.	60.	100.	165.	260.	
1873, Lg. over Sm 3 }								—	—

NICKEL FIVE-CENT PIECES

	Mintage	G-4	VG-8	F-12	EF-40	AU-50	MS-60	MS-63	PF-63
1874 . . . . *(700+)*	3,538,000	$20.	$27.	$45.	$70.	$100.	$165.	$275.	$400.
1875 . . . . *(700+)*	2,097,000	24.	30.	50.	90.	130.	200.	325.	500.
1876 . . . . . . *(1,150+)*	2,530,000	23.	30.	50.	90.	130.	200.		450.
1877, Pfs only *(510+)*	510				1,600.				2,300.
1878, Pfs only (2,350)	2,350				800.				1,000.
1879 . . . . . . (3,200)	} 29,100	300.	400.	500.	575.	600.	675.	750.	650.
1879, 9/8									700.
1880 . . . . . . (3,955)	19,955	375.	450.	550.	800.	1,500.	3,000.	6,000.	700.
1881 . . . . . . (3,575)	72,375	200.	250.	325.	475.	550.	650.	800.	500.
1882 . . . . . . (3,100)	11,476,000	15.	17.	20.	35.	60.	100.	170.	350.
1883 . . . . . . (5,419)	} 1,456,919	15.	19.	25.	45.	70.	125.	175.	350.
1883, 3/2		125.	175.	225.	450.	575.	675.	1,000.	

LIBERTY HEAD TYPE 1883-1912

In 1883 the type was changed to "Liberty Head." This type first appeared without the word CENTS on the coin, merely a large letter "V." Some of these "cent-less" coins were gold-plated and passed for five dollars. Later in that year the word CENTS was added to discourage the fraudulent practice.

Five 1913 Liberty Head nickels were originally owned by Col. E. H. R. Green (son of the famous Hetty Green). These have since been dispersed and are now held in various public and private collections. These were not a regular issue and were never placed in circulation.

Designer Charles E. Barber; weight 5 grams; composition: .750 copper, .250 nickel; diameter 21.2 mm; plain edge; mints: Philadelphia, Denver, San Francisco.

Sharply struck uncirculated coins are valued higher than the prices shown; dull or weakly struck pieces are worth less.

Variety 1 — Without CENTS 1883 Only

G-4 GOOD—No details in head. LIBERTY obliterated.
VG-8 VERY GOOD—At least 3 letters in LIBERTY readable.
F-12 FINE—All letters in LIBERTY show.
VF-20 VERY FINE—LIBERTY bold, including letter I.
EF-40 EXTREMELY FINE—LIBERTY sharp. Corn grains at bottom of wreath show, on reverse.
AU-50 ABOUT UNCIRCULATED—Traces of light wear on only the high points of the design. Half of mint luster is present.
MS-60 UNCIRCULATED—No trace of wear but can have many contact marks. Surface may be spotted, or luster faded.
MS-63 UNCIRCULATED—No trace of wear. Light blemishes.
PF-63—Nearly Perfect

	Mintage	G-4	VG-8	F-12	VF-20	EF-40	AU-50	MS-60	MS-63	PF-63
1883, w/o CENTS(5,219)	5,479,519	$5.	$6.	$7.	$8.	$9.	$11.	$27.	$45.	$275.

Variety 2 — With CENTS 1883-1913

Location of mint mark.
→

	Mintage	G-4	VG-8	F-12	VF-20	EF-40	AU-50	MS-60	MS-63	PF-63
1883, w/ CENTS .(6,783)	16,032,983	10.	12.	20.	30.	60.	80.	110.	150.	250.
1884 . . . .(3,942)	11,273,942	15.	20.	25.	35.	68.	95.	150.	225.	225.
1885 . . . .(3,790)	1,476,490	375.	450.	600.	700.	800.	1,000.	1,200.	1,500.	1,100.
1886 . . . .(4,290)	3,330,290	175.	250.	325.	400.	550.	650.	750.	900.	600.
1887 . . . .(2,960)	15,263,652	8.	12.	25.	32.	58.	80.	120.	175.	225.
1888 . . . .(4,582)	10,720,486	20.	28.	45.	75.	110.	150.	200.	250.	225.
1889 . . . .(3,336)	15,881,361	6.	10.	20.	30.	50.	80.	120.	150.	225.
1890 . . . .(2,740)	16,259,272	6.	10.	20.	30.	50.	90.	150.	200.	225.
1891 . . . .(2,350)	16,834,350	6.	10.	20.	30.	50.	80.	150.	175.	225.

NICKEL FIVE-CENT PIECES

	Mintage	G-4	VG-8	F-12	VF-20	EF-40	AU-50	MS-60	MS-63	PF-63
1892 (2,745)	11,699,642	$6.00	$9.00	$18.00	$24.	$55.	$100.	$125.	$150.	$225.
1893 (2,195)	13,370,195	6.00	9.00	18.00	24.	50.	90.	115.	150.	225.
1894 (2,632)	5,413,132	10.00	18.00	75.00	125.	180.	240.	275.	375.	225.
1895 (2,062)	9,979,884	4.00	5.00	20.00	30.	60.	100.	135.	180.	225.
1896 (1,862)	8,842,920	7.00	14.00	30.00	40.	60.	100.	135.	225.	225.
1897 (1,938)	20,428,735	3.00	4.00	10.00	18.	35.	60.	90.	150.	225.
1898 (1,795)	12,532,087	3.00	4.00	10.00	17.	33.	65.	140.	175.	225.
1899 (2,031)	26,029,031	2.00	2.50	7.50	14.	27.	50.	85.	125.	225.
1900 (2,262)	27,255,995	2.00	2.50	7.50	14.	28.	50.	85.	135.	225.
1901 (1,985)	26,480,213	2.00	2.50	4.50	10.	26.	50.	70.	125.	225.
1902 (2,018)	31,489,579	2.00	2.50	4.50	10.	26.	50.	70.	125.	225.
1903 (1,790)	28,006,725	2.00	2.50	4.50	10.	26.	50.	70.	125.	225.
1904 (1,817)	21,404,984	2.00	2.50	4.50	10.	26.	50.	70.	125.	225.
1905 (2,152)	29,827,276	2.00	2.50	4.50	10.	26.	50.	70.	125.	225.
1906 (1,725)	38,613,725	2.00	2.50	4.50	10.	26.	50.	70.	125.	225.
1907 (1,475)	39,214,800	2.00	2.50	4.50	10.	26.	50.	70.	125.	225.
1908 (1,620)	22,686,177	2.00	2.50	4.50	10.	26.	50.	70.	125.	225.
1909 (5,265)	11,590,526	2.50	3.00	4.75	11.	30.	55.	80.	135.	225.
1910 (3,298)	30,169,353	2.00	2.50	4.50	10.	26.	42.	65.	100.	225.
1911 (2,181)	39,559,372	2.00	2.50	4.50	10.	26.	42.	65.	100.	225.
1912 (2,220)	26,236,714	2.00	2.50	4.50	10.	26.	42.	65.	100.	225.
1912D	8,474,000	2.25	2.75	7.50	30.	55.	125.	275.	350.	
1912S	238,000	125.00	150.00	200.00	375.	650.	1,100.	1,250.	1,350.	
1913 Liberty head *(5 known)*									2,500,000.	

INDIAN HEAD or BUFFALO TYPE 1913-1938

These pieces are known as Buffalo, Bison or Indian Head nickels. In the first year of issue, 1913, there were two distinct varieties, the first showing the bison on a mound, and the second with the base redesigned to a thinner, straight line.

James E. Fraser designed this nickel employing three different Indians as models. His initial F is beneath the date. The bison was modeled after "Black Diamond" in the New York Central Park Zoo.

Matte Proof coins were made for collectors from 1913 to 1916. Specimen strikings of 1917 are reported.

Designer James Earle Fraser; weight 5 grams; composition: .750 copper, .250 nickel; diameter 21.2 mm; plain edge; mints: Philadelphia, Denver, San Francisco.

G-4 GOOD —*Legends and date readable. Horn worn off.*
VG-8 VERY GOOD —*Half horn shows.*
F-12 FINE —*Three-quarters of horn shows. Obv. rim intact.*
VF-20 VERY FINE —*Full horn shows. Indian's cheekbone worn.*
EF-40 EXTREMELY FINE —*Full horn. Slight wear on Indian's hair ribbon.*
AU-50 ABOUT UNCIRCULATED —*Traces of light wear on only the high points of the design. Half of mint luster is present.*
MS-60 UNCIRCULATED —*No trace of wear. Light blemishes.*
MS-63 UNCIRCULATED —*No trace of wear. Light blemishes.*
PF-63 —*Nearly Perfect*

Variety 1 — FIVE CENTS on Raised Ground

	Mintage	G-4	VG-8	F-12	VF-20	EF-40	AU-50	MS-60	MS-63	Matte PF-63
1913, Var. 1(1,520)	30,993,520	$8.	$10.	$12.	$14.	$20.	$30.	$40.	$55.	$1,300.
1913D, Var. 1	5,337,000	12.	15.	18.	24.	35.	50.	60.	70.	
1913S, Var. 1	2,105,000	35.	40.	45.	55.	70.	80.	100.	145.	

NICKEL FIVE-CENT PIECES
Variety 2 — FIVE CENTS in Recess

Mint mark below
FIVE CENTS.

1916 Doubled Die Obverse

1918D, 8 over 7

1913, Var. 2	Mintage	G-4	VG-8	F-12	VF-20	EF-40	AU-50	MS-60	MS-63	Matte PF-63
(1,514)	29,858,700	$8.00	$9.00	$10.00	$12.00	$18.	$25.	$30.	$60.	$900.
1913D, Var. 2	4,156,000	90.00	110.00	130.00	160.00	175.	200.	230.	300.	
1913S, Var. 2	1,209,000	250.00	300.00	350.00	375.00	425.	475.	525.	750.	
1914, 4/3 . . .				400.00	600.00	900.	2,000.			
1914 .(1,325)	20,665,738	15.00	17.00	20.00	22.00	30.	40.	50.	80.	850.
1914D	3,912,000	70.00	90.00	115.00	150.00	240.	280.	350.	450.	
1914S	3,470,000	20.00	30.00	40.00	50.00	75.	125.	170.	400.	
1915 .(1,050)	20,987,270	5.00	6.00	7.00	10.00	20.	40.	50.	75.	
1915D	7,569,000	15.00	20.00	30.00	50.00	100.	140.	250.	325.	
1915S	1,505,000	30.00	45.00	75.00	150.00	250.	400.	510.	750.	
1916 . . .(600)	63,498,066	4.00	5.00	6.00	7.00	9.	15.	40.	70.	1,500.
1916, DblDieObv.		1,800.	3,500.	6,500.	10,000.	12,800.	25,000.	45,000.	135,000.	
1916D	13,333,000	10.00	15.00	20.00	32.00	80.	110.	150.	250.	
1916S	11,860,000	6.00	10.00	15.00	30.00	70.	100.	175.	280.	
1917	51,424,019	4.00	5.00	6.00	7.00	13.	30.	50.	125.	—
1917D	9,910,000	15.00	20.00	35.00	70.00	125.	225.	300.	750.	
1917S	4,193,000	20.00	35.00	65.00	90.00	175.	300.	375.	1,250.	
1918	32,086,314	4.00	5.00	6.00	12.00	30.	45.	95.	300.	
1918D, 8/7 . } 8,362,000		1,000.	1,500.	2,700.	5000.	9,000.	12,000.	28,000.	60,000.	
1918D . . . . }		15.00	25.00	40.00	100.00	200.	325.	375.	1,200.	
1918S	4,882,000	12.00	25.00	42.00	90.00	175.	300.	500.	3,000.	
1919	60,868,000	1.50	2.00	2.50	6.00	12.	30.	45.	100.	
1919D‡	8,006,000	14.00	25.00	50.00	110.00	250.	350.	550.	1,500.	
1919S‡	7,521,000	8.00	20.00	40.00	100.00	250.	350.	500.	1,800.	
1920	63,093,000	1.50	2.00	2.50	5.00	12.	25.	50.	125.	
1920D‡	9,418,000	7.00	15.00	25.00	100.00	275.	325.	500.	1,800.	
1920S	9,689,000	4.00	7.00	20.00	90.00	175.	300.	500.	2,000.	
1921	10,663,000	3.00	4.00	6.00	20.00	50.	75.	100.	300.	
1921S	1,557,000	70.00	110.00	175.00	525.00	850.	1,200.	1,500.	2,200.	
1923	35,715,000	2.00	2.50	3.00	6.00	12.	30.	50.	150.	
1923S‡	6,142,000	6.00	8.00	18.00	125.00	275.	350.	450.	900.	
1924	21,620,000	1.50	2.00	5.00	10.00	18.	45.	65.	150.	
1924D	5,258,000	7.00	8.00	25.00	75.00	225.	300.	350.	1,000.	
1924S	1,437,000	15.00	30.00	100.00	475.00	1,250.	1,800.	2,400.	4,000.	
1925	35,565,100	3.00	3.50	4.00	8.00	15.	30.	40.	100.	
1925D‡	4,450,000	8.00	15.00	35.00	90.00	175.	250.	400.	750.	
1925S	6,256,000	5.00	10.00	18.00	85.00	175.	250.	450.	2,200.	
1926	44,693,000	1.00	1.50	2.50	4.00	10.	20.	35.	75.	
1926D‡	5,638,000	6.00	12.00	24.00	90.00	175.	275.	300.	550.	
1926S	970,000	18.00	30.00	75.00	450.00	900.	2,800.	4,200.	7,500.	
1927	37,981,000	1.00	1.25	2.50	4.00	10.	20.	30.	75.	
1927D	5,730,000	2.50	5.00	7.00	30.00	75.	125.	150.	300.	
1927S	3,430,000	1.50	3.00	5.00	32.00	85.	175.	500.	2,500.	
1928	23,411,000	1.00	1.25	2.50	5.00	10.	25.	30.	75.	
1928D	6,436,000	1.50	2.50	5.00	15.00	40.	45.	50.	100.	
1928S	6,936,000	2.00	2.25	3.00	12.00	27.	100.	250.	650.	

‡Uncirculated pieces with full sharp details are worth considerably more.

NICKEL FIVE-CENT PIECES

	Mintage	G-4	VG-8	F-12	VF-20	EF-40	AU-50	MS-60	MS-63	PF-63
1929	36,446,000	$1.00	$1.50	$2.50	$4.00	$10.00	$20.	$35.	$70.	
1929D	8,370,000	1.25	2.00	2.50	8.00	35.00	45.	60.	125.	
1929S	7,754,000	1.00	1.50	2.00	2.50	14.00	25.	50.	75.	
1930	22,849,000	1.00	1.50	2.50	4.00	10.00	20.	30.	70.	
1930S	5,435,000	1.00	1.50	2.50	3.00	12.00	30.	50.	110.	
1931S	1,200,000	15.00	16.00	18.00	20.00	22.00	40.	50.	75.	
1934	20,213,003	1.00	1.50	2.50	4.00	10.00	18.	50.	60.	
1934D*	7,480,000	1.00	1.50	2.50	5.00	15.00	40.	70.	100.	
1935	58,264,000	1.00	1.50	1.75	2.00	2.50	9.	20.	40.	
1935, DblDieRev		40.00	50.00	90.00	150.00	400.00	1,600.			
1935D	12,092,000	1.00	1.50	2.50	6.00	15.00	40.	60.	75.	
1935S	10,300,000	1.00	1.50	2.00	2.50	4.00	15.	50.	70.	
1936(4,420)	119,001,420	1.00	1.50	1.75	2.00	3.00	9.	15.	50.	1,200.
1936D	24,814,000	1.00	1.50	1.75	2.00	4.00	12.	35.	40.	
1936D, 3 1/2 legs		250.00	300.00	400.00	900.00	1000.00				
1936S	14,930,000	1.00	1.50	1.75	2.00	3.50	12.	35.	40.	
1937(5,769)	79,485,769	1.00	1.50	1.75	2.00	3.00	9.	15.	40.	1,000.

*Large and small mint mark varieties exist, see page 73.
Uncirculated pieces with full sharp details are worth considerably more.

1937D "3-Legged" Variety
A similar variety exists for 1936-D

1938 D over S

	Mintage	G-4	VG-8	F-12	VF-20	EF-40	AU-50	MS-60	MS-63	PF-63
1937D All Kinds	17,826,000	0.75	0.85	1.75	2.00	3.00	10.	30.	40.	
1937D, 3-Legged		350.00	500.00	600.00	650.00	700.00	1,000.	2,000.	5,000.	
1937S	5,635,000	0.75	0.85	1.75	2.00	3.50	10.	30.	40.	
1938D	} 7,020,000	2.00	2.50	3.00	3.25	3.75	9.	20.	30.	
1938D, D/S‡		5.00	7.50	10.00	15.00	18.00	30.	50.	75.	

‡Varieties exist.

JEFFERSON TYPE 1938 to Date

This obverse of this nickel was designed by Felix Schlag. He won an award of $1,000 in a competition with some 390 artists. His design established the definite public approval of portrait and pictorial themes rather than symbolic devices on our coinage.

Designer Felix Schlag; weight 5 grams; composition: 1938-1942, 1946- , .750 copper, .250 nickel; 1942-1945, .560 copper, .350 silver, .090 manganese; diameter 21.2 mm; plain edge; mints: Philadelphia, Denver, San Francisco. Net weight 1942-1945: .05626 oz. pure silver.

VG-8 VERY GOOD—*Second porch pillar from right nearly gone, other three still visible but weak.*
F-12 FINE—*Cheekbone worn flat. Hairlines and eyebrow faint. Second pillar weak, especially at bottom.*
VF-20 VERY FINE—*Second pillar plain and complete on both sides.*
EF-40 EXTREMELY FINE—*Cheekbone, hairlines, eyebrow slightly worn but well defined. Base of triangle above pillars visible but weak.*
AU-50 ABOUT UNCIRCULATED—*Traces of light wear on only the high points of the design. Half of mint luster is present.*
MS-65 CHOICE UNCIRCULATED—*No trace of wear. Barely noticeable blemishes.*
PF-65—*Nearly Perfect*

1939 Doubled Monticello and Five Cents

Uncirculated pieces with fully struck steps are valued higher.

NICKEL FIVE-CENT PIECES

	Mintage	VF-20	EF-40	AU-50	MS-60	MS-63	MS-65	PF-65
1938 ..(19,365) ..19,515,365		$0.50	$1.00	$1.50	$2.50	$3.50	$10.00	$125.00
1938D 5,376,000		1.50	2.00	3.00	4.00	7.00	12.00	125.00
1938S 4,105,000		2.50	3.00	3.50	4.00	7.00	12.00	
1939 ..(12,535) .120,627,535		0.25	0.50	0.75	1.50	2.50	4.00	125.00
1939 Doubled MONTICELLO and FIVE CENTS		60.00	75.00	125.00	150.00	300.00	600.	
1939D 3,514,000		6.00	12.00	25.00	50.00	70.00	90.00	
1939S 6,630,000		1.50	4.00	9.00	15.00	20.00	35.00	
1940 ..(14,158) .176,499,158		0.25	0.40	0.75	1.00	1.50	3.00	125.00
1940D 43,540,000		0.35	0.50	1.00	2.00	2.50	5.00	
1940S 39,690,000		0.35	0.50	1.00	2.25	3.00	5.50	
1941 ..(18,720) .203,283,720		0.20	0.30	0.50	0.75	1.50	5.00	125.00
1941D 53,432,000		0.25	0.40	1.50	2.50	3.50	5.00	
1941S‡ 43,445,000		0.30	0.50	1.50	3.00	4.00	6.00	
1942 ..(29,600) ..49,818,600		0.30	0.45	1.25	4.00	6.00	9.00	125.00
1942D ....} 1942D/horz. D .}	13,938,000	1.00 50.00	2.00 75.00	5.00 125.00	25.00 250.00	35.00 350.00	50.00 1,000.00	

‡Large and small mint mark varieties, see page 73.

Wartime Alloy Variety 1942-1945

On October 8, 1942, the wartime five-cent piece composed of copper (56%), silver (35%) and manganese (9%) was introduced to eliminate nickel, a critical war material. A larger mint mark was placed above the dome. Letter P (Philadelphia) was used for the first time, indicating the change of alloy.

Location of mint mark

1943 3 over 2

1943 Doubled Eye

	Mintage	VF-20	EF-40	AU-50	MS-60	MS-63	MS-65	PF-65
1942P .(27,600) ..57,900,600		1.00	1.50	3.00	7.00	10.00	15.00	250.
1942S 32,900,000		1.00	1.50	3.00	7.00	10.00	15.00	
1943P, 3/2 ...}		50.00	90.00	125.00	175.00	250.00	600.00	
1943P ....}	271,165,000	0.90	1.25	2.50	5.00	7.00	12.00	
1943P DblEye ⌡		30.00	50.00	75.00	100.00	150.00	350.00	
1943D 15,294,000		1.00	1.50	2.50	6.00	10.00	14.00	
1943S 104,060,000		0.90	1.25	2.50	5.00	7.00	12.00	
1944P 119,150,000		0.90	1.25	3.00	7.00	10.00	18.00	
1944D 32,309,000		0.90	1.25	3.00	6.00	10.00	17.00	
1944S 21,640,000		0.90	1.25	2.50	5.00	8.00	15.00	
1945P 119,408,100		0.90	1.25	2.50	5.00	7.00	17.00	
1945P DblDieRev.		20.00	30.00	50.00	75.00	125.00	300.00	
1945D 37,158,000		0.90	1.25	2.50	5.00	7.00	15.00	
1945S 58,939,000		0.90	1.25	2.50	5.00	7.00	15.00	

*1944 nickels without mint marks are counterfeits. Genuine pieces of other dates struck in nickel by error are known to exist.

Prewar composition and mint mark style resumed 1946-1967

	Mintage	VF-20	EF-40	AU-50	MS-60	MS-63	MS-65
1946 161,116,000		$0.25	$0.30	$0.35	$0.70	$2.00	$5.00
1946D 45,292,200		0.35	0.40	0.45	0.90	2.00	5.00
1946S 13,560,000		0.40	0.45	0.50	1.00	1.50	3.00
1947 95,000,000		0.25	0.30	0.35	0.70	1.40	3.00
1947D 37,822,000		0.30	0.35	0.40	0.80	1.50	3.00
1947S 24,720,000		0.40	0.45	0.50	1.00	1.50	3.00

NICKEL FIVE-CENT PIECES

	Mintage	MS--60	MS-63	MS-65	PF-65
1948	89,348,000	$1.00	$1.50	$3.00	
1948D	44,734,000	1.50	2.00	4.00	
1948S	11,300,000	1.50	2.00	4.00	
1949	60,652,000	2.50	4.00	7.00	
1949D	} 36,498,000	1.50	2.00	5.00	
1949D, D/S		150.00	200.00	350.00	
1949S	9,716,000	1.75	2.50	5.00	
1950 ...(51,386)	9,847,386	2.00	3.00	5.00	$60.00
1950D	2,630,030	8.50	10.00	15.00	
1951 ...(57,500)	28,609,500	3.00	4.00	8.00	55.00
1951D	20,460,000	4.00	5.00	9.00	
1951S	7,776,000	1.50	2.00	4.00	
1952 ....(81980)	64,069,980	1.00	1.50	3.00	40.00
1952D	30,638,000	3.50	5.00	8.00	
1952S	20,572,000	1.00	1.50	3.00	
1953 ..(128,800)	46,772,800	0.25	0.50	1.00	38.00
1953D	59,878,600	0.25	0.50	1.00	
1953S	19,210,900	0.75	1.00	1.50	

1954S,
S over D

1955D,
D over S*

	Mintage	MS--60	MS-63	MS-65	PF-65
1954 ..(233,300)	47,917,350	1.00	1.50	3.00	25.00
1954D	117,183,060	0.50	1.00	1.50	
1954S	} 29,384,000	1.75	2.00	3.00	
1954S, S/D		25.00	40.00	75.00	
1955 ..(378,200)	8,266,200	0.75	1.00	2.00	14.00
1955D	} 74,464,100	0.50	0.75	1.10	
1955D, D/S*		35.00	55.00	85.00	
1956 ..(669,384)	35,885,384	0.50	0.75	1.00	3.00
1956D	67,222,940	0.50	0.75	1.00	
1957 .(1,247,952)	39,655,952	0.50	0.75	1.00	3.00
1957D	136,828,900	0.50	0.70	1.00	
1958 ..(875,652)	17,963,652	0.60	0.80	1.50	4.00
1958D	168,249,120	0.40	0.50	1.00	
1959 .(1,149,291)	28,397,291	0.25	0.50	0.80	2.00
1959D	160,738,240	0.25	0.50	0.80	
1960 .(1,691,602)	57,107,602	0.25	0.50	0.80	1.50
1960D	192,582,180	0.25	0.50	0.80	
1961 .(3,028,144)	76,668,244	0.25	0.50	0.80	1.00
1961D	229,342,760	0.25	0.50	0.80	
1962 .(3,218,019)	100,602,019	0.25	0.50	0.80	1.00
1962D	280,195,720	0.25	0.50	0.80	
1963 .(3,075,645)	178,851,645	0.25	0.50	0.80	1.00
1963D	276,829,460	0.25	0.50	0.80	
1964 .(3,950,762)	1,028,622,762	0.25	0.50	0.80	1.00
1964D	1,787,297,160	0.25	0.50	0.80	
1965	136,131,380	0.25	0.50	0.80	
1966	156,208,283	0.25	0.50	0.80	—‡
1967	107,325,800	0.25	0.50	0.80	

*Varieties exist. Value is for that illustrated.
‡Two presentation pieces were given to the designer.

NICKEL FIVE-CENT PIECES
1968 to 2003

The designer's initials FS were added below the bust starting in 1966, and dies were further remodeled to strengthen the design in 1971, 1972, 1977 and 1982. Mint mark position was moved to the obverse starting in 1968.

Mintage	MS-63	MS-65	PF-65
1968D ...91,227,880	$0.25	$0.50	
1968S ...(3,041,506)			
........103,437,510	0.25	0.50	$1.00
1969D ..202,807,500	0.25	0.50	
1969S ...(2,934,631)			
........123,099,631	0.25	0.50	1.00
1970D ..515,485,380	0.25	0.50	
1970S ...(2,632,810)			
........241,464,814	0.25	0.50	1.00
1971 106,884,000	0.75	1.50	
1971D ..316,144,800	0.30	0.60	
1971 Pf w/o S*	—	—	1000.00
1971S, Pf .(3,220,733)	—	—	2.00
1972 202,036,000	0.25	0.50	
1972D ..351,694,600	0.25	0.50	
1972S, Pf .(3,260,996)	0.00	0.00	2.00
1973 384,396,000	0.25	0.50	
1973D ..261,405,000	0.25	0.50	
1973S, Pf .(2,760,339)	—	—	1.50
1974 601,752,000	0.25	0.50	
1974D ..277,373,000	0.25	0.50	
1974S, Pf .(2,612,568)	—	—	2.00
1975 181,772,000	0.50	1.00	
1975D ..401,875,300	0.25	0.50	
1975S, Pf .(2,845,450)	—	—	2.00
1976 367,124,000	0.45	0.90	
1976D ..563,964,147	0.45	0.90	
1976S, Pf .(4,149,730)	—	—	2.00
1977 585,376,000	0.25	0.50	
1977D ..297,313,422	0.50	1.00	
1977S, Pf .(3,251,152)	—	—	1.50
1978 391,308,000	0.25	0.50	
1978D ..313,092,780	0.25	0.50	
1978S, Pf .(3,127,781)	—	—	1.50
1979 463,188,000	0.25	0.50	
1979D ..325,867,672	0.25	0.50	**
1979S, Pf .(3,677,175)			
1979S, Pf, Filled S ...	—	—	1.50
1979S, Pf, Clear S ...	—	—	1.75
1980P ...593,004,000	0.25	0.50	
1980D ..502,323,448	0.25	0.50	
1980S, Pf .(3,554,806)	—	—	1.50
1981P ...657,504,000	0.25	0.50	
1981D ..364,801,843	0.25	0.50	
1981S, Pf .(4,063,083)	—	—	2.00
1982P ...292,355,000	2.50	4.50	
1982D ..373,726,544	1.75	3.00	

Mintage	MS-63	MS-65	PF-65
1982S, Pf .(3,857,479)	—	—	$3.00
1983P ...561,615,000	$1.50	$3.00	
1983D ..536,726,276	1.25	2.25	
1983S, Pf .(3,279,126)	—	—	3.00
1984P ...746,769,000	1.00	2.00	
1984D ..517,675,146	0.25	0.50	
1984S, Pf .(3,065,110)	—	—	5.00
1985P ...647,114,962	0.50	1.00	
1985D ..459,747,446	0.50	1.00	
1985S, Pf .(3,362,821)	—	—	4.00
1986P ...536,883,483	0.50	1.00	
1986D ..361,819,140	1.00	1.75	
1986S, Pf .(3,010,497)	—	—	7.00
1987P ...371,499,481	0.25	0.50	
1987D ..410,590,604	0.25	0.50	
1987S, Pf .(4,227,728)	—	—	3.00
1988P ...771,360,000	0.25	0.50	
1988D ..663,771,652	0.25	0.50	
1988S, Pf .(3,262,948)	—	—	6.50
1989P ...898,812,000	0.25	0.45	
1989D ..570,842,474	0.25	0.45	
1989S, Pf .(3,220,194)	—	—	5.00
1990P ...661,636,000	0.25	0.50	
1990D ..663,938,503	0.25	0.50	
1990S, Pf .(3,299,559)	—	—	5.00
1991P ...614,104,000	0.30	0.60	
1991D ..436,496,678	0.30	0.60	
1991S, Pf .(2,867,787)	—	—	5.00
1992P ...399,552,000	1.50	2.50	
1992D ..450,565,113	0.25	0.60	
1992S, Pf .(4,176,560)	—	—	4.00
1993P ...412,076,000	0.25	0.50	
1993D ..406,084,135	0.25	0.50	
1993S, Pf .(3,394,792)	—	—	4.00
1994P ...722,160,000	0.25	0.50	
1994P Special Unc.** .			
..........167,703	60.00	100.00	
1994D ..715,762,110	0.25	0.50	
1994S, Pf .(3,269,923)	—	—	3.00
1995P ...774,156,000	0.25	0.50	
1995D ..888,112,000	0.50	1.00	
1995S, Pf .(2,797,481)	—	—	5.00
1996P ...829,332,000	0.25	0.50	
1996D ..817,736,000	0.25	0.50	
1996S, Pf .(2,525,265)	0.00	0.00	3.00

*1971 Proof nickels without mint mark were made in error. See pages 73 and 75.
**Special "frosted" uncirculated pieces were included in the 1993 Thomas Jefferson commemorative dollar packaging (sold in 1994) and the 1997 Botanic Gardens Sets. They resemble Proof coins.

NICKEL FIVE-CENT PIECES

	Mintage	MS-63	MS-65	PF-65
1997P	470,972,000	$0.50	$1.00	
1997P Special Unc.	25,000	200.00	250.00	
1997D	466,640,000	1.00	2.00	
1997S Pf	(2,796,678)			$4.00
1998P	688,272,000	0.35	0.70	
1998D	635,360,000	0.35	0.70	
1998S Pf	(2,086,507)			4.00
1999P	1,212,000,000	0.25	0.50	
1999D	1,066,720,000	0.25	0.50	
1999S Pf	(2,543,401)			3.50
2000P	846,240,000	0.25	0.50	
2000D	1,509,520,000	0.25	0.50	
2000S Pf	(3,082,483)			2.00
2001P	675,704,000	0.25	0.50	
2001D	627,680,000	0.25	0.50	
2001S Pf	(2,294,043)			2.00
2002P	539,280,000	0.25	0.50	
2002D	(691,200,000) 691,200,000	0.25	0.50	
2002S Pf	(2,277,720)			2.00
2003 P		0.25	0.50	
2003 D		0.25	0.50	
2003S Pf				3.00

The "Peace Medal" nickel design for 2004 commemorates the bicentennials of the Louisiana Purchase and the Lewis and Clark expedition. The reverse side of the new nickel is a depiction of the original Jefferson Peace Medal designed in 1801. Lewis and Clark gave these medals as tokens to Native Americans they met during their journey. The second nickel design of 2004 features the keelboat that transported Lewis and Clark.

	MS-63	MS-65	PF-65
2004P Louisiana Purchase/Peace Medal	.25	.50	
2004D Louisiana Purchase/Peace Medal	.25	.50	
2004S Pf Louisiana Purchase/Peace Medal			3.00
2004P Lewis and Clark/Keelboat	.25	.50	
2004D Lewis and Clark/Keelboat	.25	.50	
2004S Pf Lewis and Clark/Keelboat			3.00

BIBLIOGRAPHY

Fletcher, Edward L., Jr. *The Shield Five Cent Series.* Ormond Beach, FL, 1994.
Lange, David W. *The Complete Guide to Buffalo Nickels.* Virginia Beach, VA, 2000.
Nagengast, Bernard. *The Jefferson Nickel Analyst.* Sidney, Ohio, 1979.
Peters, Gloria and Mahon, Cynthia. *The Complete Guide to Shield and Liberty Head Nickels.* Virginia Beach, VA, 1995.
Wescott, Michael. *The United States Nickel Five-Cent Piece.* Wolfeboro, NH, 1991.

The half-dime types present the same general characteristics as larger United States silver coins. Authorized by the Act of April 2, 1792, they were not coined until February, 1795, although some were dated 1794. At first the weight was 20.8 grains, and fineness 892.4. By the Act of January 18, 1837, the weight was slightly reduced to 20 5/8 grains and the fineness changed to .900. Finally the weight was reduced to 19.2 grains by the Act of February 21, 1853. Both half dimes and dimes offer many varieties in the early dates.

+ or – indicates change from previous year	**TYPE COIN VALUES**									
	G-4	F-12	EF-40	AU-50	MS-60	MS-63	MS-65	PF-60	PF-63	PF-65
Flowing Hair 1794-1795	800.+	1,350.+	3,500.+	6,000.+	9,000.+	12,500.+				
Drpd Bust, SE 1796-1797	850.+	1,600.+	5,000.+	7,800.+	12,500.+	25,000.+				
Drpd Bust, HE 1800-1805.....	600.+	1,200.+	3,500.+	7,000.+	8,500.+	13,000.+				
Cap Bust 1829-1837.............	25.+	50.+	130.+	200.-	300.	700.+	2,400.-			
Lib Seated-NS 1837-1838	35.+	65.+	200.+	400.+	700.+	900.	3,000.-			
Lib Seated-Stars 1838-1859 .	15.+	25.+	70.+	150.+	200.+	300.+	1,200.-	650.+	1,400.+	4,000.-
Lib. Seat-Arr. 1853-1855	15.+	20.+	60.+	125.+	200.+	300.-	1,750.-	4,000.	8,000.+	16,000.
Lib. Seat-Leg. 1860-1873	15.+	20.+	40.+	75.+	140.+	225.+	1,100.-		250.-	600.+	1,400.-

FLOWING HAIR TYPE 1794-1795

Designer Robert Scot; weight 1.35 grams; composition: .8924 silver, .1076 copper; approx. diameter 16.5 mm; reeded edge. All coined at Philadelphia Mint.

AG-3 ABOUT GOOD —*Details clear enough to identify.*
G-4 GOOD —*Eagle, wreath, bust outlined but lack details.*
VG-8 VERY GOOD —*Some details remain on face. All lettering readable.*
F-12 FINE —*Hair ends show. Hair at top smooth.*
VF-20 VERY FINE —*Hairlines at top show. Hair about ear defined.*
EF-40 EXTREMELY FINE —*Hair above forehead and at neck well defined but shows some wear.*
AU-50 ABOUT UNCIRCULATED —*Slight wear on high waves of hair, near ear and face, on the head and tip of eagle's wings.*
MS-60 UNCIRCULATED —*No trace of wear. Light blemishes.*
MS-63 UNCIRCULATED —*Some distracting marks or blemishes in prime focal areas. Luster may be impaired.*

	Mintage	AG-3	G-4	VG-8	F-12	VF-20	EF-40	AU-50	MS-60	MS-63
1794	} 86,416	$600.	$1,000.	$1,250.	$1,750.	$2,700.	$4,800.	$8,000.	$13,500.	$18,000.
1795		400.	800.	1,100.	1,350.	2,000.	3,500.	6,000.	9,000.	12,500.

DRAPED BUST TYPE, SMALL EAGLE REVERSE 1796-1797

Designer Robert Scot; weight 1.35 grams; composition: .8924 silver, .1076 copper; approx. diameter 16.5 mm; reeded edge. All coined at Philadelphia Mint.

AG-3 ABOUT GOOD —*Details clear enough to identify.*
G-4 GOOD —*Date, stars, LIBERTY readable. Bust outlined but no details.*
VG-8 VERY GOOD —*Some details show.*
F-12 FINE —*Hair and drapery lines worn, but visible.*
VF-20 VERY FINE —*Only left of drapery indistinct.*
EF-40 EXTREMELY FINE —*All hairlines show details.*
AU-50 ABOUT UNCIRCULATED —*Slight wear on bust, shoulder and hair; wear on head top of small eagle's wings.*
MS-60 UNCIRCULATED —*No trace of wear. Light blemishes.*
MS-63 UNCIRCULATED —*Some distracting marks or blemishes in prime focal areas. Luster may be impaired.*

	Mintage	AG-3	G-4	VG-8	F-12	VF-20	EF-40	AU-50	MS-60	MS-63
1796, 6/5		$600.	$1,000.	$1,250.	$1,950.	$4,000.	$7,000.	$12,500.	$22,000.	$32,000.
1796	} 10,230	550.	900.	1,200.	1,800.	3,000.	5,000.	8,000.	13,500.	25,000.
1796, LIKERTY		550.	950.	1,250.	1,800.	3,000.	5,000.	8,000.	14,500.	28,000.
1797, 15 stars		500.	850.	1,200.	1,600.	2,800.	5,000.	7,800.	12,500.	25,000.
1797, 16 stars	} 44,527	500.	850.	1,200.	1,600.	2,800.	5,000.	7,800.	12,500.	25,000.
1797, 13 stars		600.	850.	1,800.	2,500.	3,500.	7,500.	13,000.	29,000.	30,000.

HALF DIMES
DRAPED BUST TYPE, HERALDIC EAGLE REVERSE 1800-1805

1800 LIBEKTY

	Mintage	AG-3	G-4	VG-8	F-12	VF-20	EF-40	AU-50	MS-60	MS-63
1800	24,000	$300.	$600.	$750.	$1,200.	$1,800.	$3,500.	$7,000.	$8,500.	$13,000.
1800, LIBEKTY	16,000	300.	600.	750.	1,200.	1,800.	3,500.	7,000.	8,500.	13,000.
1801	27,760	350.	650.	850.	1,400.	2,000.	4,000.	7,500.	12,000.	18,000.
1802	3,060	8,000.	16,000.	22,500.	35,000.	60,000.	80,000.	—		
1803, Lg 8 }	37,850	350.	750.	900.	1,200.	1,800.	4,000.	7,000.	9,000.	15,000.
1803, Sm 8 }		400.	850.	1,000.	1,300.	2,200.	4,500.	7,500.	10,000.	16,000.
1805	15,600	400.	850.	1,000.	1,350.	2,250.	4,800.	12,000.	—	

CAPPED BUST TYPE 1829-1837

Designer William Kneass; weight 1.35 grams; composition: .8924 silver, .1076 copper; approx. diameter 15.5 mm; reeded edge. All coined at Philadelphia Mint.

G-4 GOOD—Bust outlined, no detail. Date and legend readable.
VG-8 VERY GOOD—Complete legend and date plain. At least 3 letters of LIBERTY show clearly.
F-12 FINE—All letters in LIBERTY show.
VF-20 VERY FINE—Full rims. Ear and shoulder clasp show plainly.
EF-40 EXTREMELY FINE—Ear very distinct, eyebrow and hair well defined.
AU-50 ABOUT UNCIRCULATED—Has traces of light wear on many of the high points. At least half of the mint luster is still present.
MS-60 UNCIRCULATED—No trace of wear. Light blemishes
MS-63 SELECT UNCIRCULATED—No trace of wear. Light blemishes. Attractive mint luster.

	Mintage	G-4	VG-8	F-12	VF-20	EF-40	AU-50	MS-60	MS-63
1829	1,230,000	$25.	$35.	$50.	$75.	$130.	$200.	$300.	$700.
1830	1,240,000	25.	35.	50.	75.	130.	200.	300.	700.
1831	1,242,700	25.	35.	50.	75.	130.	200.	300.	700.
1832	965,000	25.	35.	50.	75.	140.	225.	325.	750.
1833	1,370,000	25.	35.	50.	75.	130.	225.	300.	700.
1834 . . . . }	1,480,000	25.	35.	50.	75.	130.	200.	300.	700.
1834, 3/inverted 3 }		30.	40.	65.	120.	230.	450.	550.	950.
1835, All Kinds .	2,760,000								
1835, LgDt and 5c		25.	35.	50.	75.	130.	200.	300.	700.
1835, LgDt,Sm 5c		25.	35.	50.	75.	130.	200.	300.	700.
1835, SmDt,Lg 5c		25.	35.	50.	75.	130.	200.	300.	700.
1835, SmDt and 5c		25.	35.	50.	75.	130.	200.	300.	700.
1836, Sm 5C . . . }	1,900,000	25.	35.	50.	75.	130.	200.	300.	700.
1836, Lg 5C . . . }		25.	35.	50.	75.	130.	200.	300.	700.
1836, 3/inverted 3 }		30.	40.	65.	120.	230.	450.	550.	950.
1837, Sm 5c . . . }	871,000	30.	40.	65.	100.	175.	350.	800.	2,000.
1837, Lg 5c . . . }		25.	35.	50.	75.	130.	200.	300.	700.

LIBERTY SEATED TYPE 1837-1873
Variety 1 — No Stars on Obverse 1837-1838

Designer Christian Gobrecht; weight 1.34 grams; composition: .900 silver, .100 copper; diameter 15.5 mm; reeded edge; mints: Philadelphia, New Orleans.

G-4 GOOD—LIBERTY on shield smooth. Date and letters readable.
VG-8 VERY GOOD—At least 3 letters in LIBERTY are visible.
F-12 FINE—Entire LIBERTY visible, weak spots.
VF-20 VERY FINE—Entire LIBERTY strong and even.
EF-40 EXTREMELY FINE—LIBERTY and scroll edges distinct.
AU-50 ABOUT UNCIRCULATED—Has traces of light wear on many of the high points. At least half of the mint luster is still present.
MS-60 UNCIRCULATED—No trace of wear. Light blemishes.
MS-63 SELECT UNCIRCULATED—No trace of wear. Light blemishes. Attractive mint luster.

HALF DIMES

	Mintage	G-4	VG-8	F-12	VF-20	EF-40	AU-50	MS-60	MS-63
1837, SmDt ...	} 1,405,000	$35.	$45.	$65.	$125.	$200.	$450.	$850.	$1,100.
1837, LgDt		35.	45.	65.	125.	200.	400.	700.	900.
1838O, No stars	70,000	75.	125.	200.	400.	700.	1,000.	1,600.	7,000.

**No Drapery
from Elbow
1837-1840**

**Drapery
from Elbow
Starting 1840**

From 1838 through 1859 mint mark is located above bow on reverse. Large, medium or small mint mark varieties occur for several dates.

Variety 2 — Stars on Obverse 1838-1853

	Mintage	G-4	VG-8	F-12	VF-20	EF-40	AU-50	MS-60	MS-63
1838, NoDrap ..	} 2,225,000	15.	18.	25.	30.	70.	150.	250.	400.
1838, SmS		18.	28.	50.	90.	175.	350.	600.	1,000.
1839, NoDrap ..	1,069,150	15.	18.	25.	30.	70.	150.	250.	400.
1839O, NoDrap.	1,034,039	18.	20.	25.	32.	75.	160.	500.	1,800.
1840, NoDrap ..	1,034,000	15.	18.	25.	30.	70.	150.	250.	400.
1840O, NoDrap.	695,000	15.	18.	27.	35.	75.	225.	700.	2,000.
1840, Drapery ..	310,085	20.	35.	50.	100.	200.	350.	450.	800.
1840O, Drapery	240,000	30.	50.	100.	150.	400.	1,000.	2,800.	8,000.
1841	1,150,000	15.	18.	25.	30.	70.	150.	200.	300.
1841O	815,000	16.	20.	30.	45.	100.	275.	650.	1,500.
1842	815,000	15.	18.	25.	30.	70.	150.	200.	300.
1842O	350,000	28.	35.	60.	175.	500.	800.	1,200.	2,000.
1843	1,165,000	15.	18.	25.	30.	70.	150.	200.	300.
1844	430,000	15.	18.	25.	30.	70.	150.	200.	300.
1844O	220,000	75.	110.	180.	500.	1,000.	2,400.	5,000.	12,000.
1845	1,564,000	15.	18.	25.	30.	70.	150.	200.	300.
1846	27,000	200.	350.	600.	750.	2,000.	3,500.	9,000.	18,000.
1847	1,274,000	15.	18.	25.	30.	70.	150.	260.	500.
1848,Med. Date	} 668,000	15.	18.	25.	30.	70.	150.	200.	300.
1848,LgDt		20.	30.	40.	60.	125.	275.	550.	1,500.
1848O	600,000	18.	20.	30.	50.	100.	250.	400.	700.
1849, 9/6		20.	30.	35.	50.	100.	225.	400.	1,400.
1849, 9/8	} 1,309,000	25.	35.	45.	60.	120.	250.	600.	1,800.
1849, NmlDt ...		15.	18.	25.	30.	70.	150.	220.	500.
1849O	140,000	25.	35.	70.	200.	450.	1,000.	2,000.	4,000.
1850	955,000	15.	18.	25.	30.	70.	150.	200.	300.
1850O	690,000	18.	25.	30.	60.	100.	300.	750.	1,600.
1851	781,000	15.	18.	25.	30.	70.	150.	200.	300.
1851O	860,000	18.	20.	25.	40.	100.	225.	500.	800.
1852	1,000,500	15.	18.	25.	30.	70.	150.	200.	300.
1852O	260,000	25.	35.	60.	125.	250.	500.	850.	1,800.
1853, No arrows	135,000	30.	40.	60.	125.	225.	450.	750.	1,100.
1853O, No arrows	160,000	175.	250.	350.	600.	1,300.	2,500.	6,000.	12,000.

Variety 3 — Arrows at Date 1853-1855

As on the dimes, quarters and halves, arrows were placed at the sides of the date for a short period starting in 1853. They were placed there to denote the reduction of weight under the terms of the Act of February 21, 1853.

Weight 1.24 grams; composition: .900 silver, .100 copper; diameter 15.5 mm; reeded edge; mints: Philadelphia, New Orleans, San Francisco.

	Mintage	G-4	VG-8	F-12	VF-20	EF-40	AU-50	MS-60	MS63	PF-63
1853	13,210,020	$15.	$18.	$20.	$30.	$60.	$125.	$200.	$300.	
18530	2,200,000	17.	20.	30.	40.	70.	150.	275.	900.	
1854	5,740,000	15.	18.	20.	30.	60.	135.	225.	325.	
18540	1,560,000	17.	20.	30.	40.	70.	150.	275.	700.	
1855	1,750,000	15.	18.	20.	30.	60.	125.	200.	300.	$8,000.
18550	600,000	15.	20.	30.	50.	175.	200.	550.	1,100.	

Variety 2 Resumed 1856-1859
(Weight standard of 1853)

1858 Over Inverted Date

1856	4,880,000	15.	18.	20.	30.	60.	125.	175.	300.	5,000.
18560	1,100,000	15.	18.	20.	50.	100.	250.	550.	1,000.	
1857	7,280,000	15.	18.	20.	30.	60.	125.	175.	300.	4,000.
18570	1,380,000	15.	18.	22.	40.	65.	200.	350.	500.	
1858	3,500,000	15.	18.	20.	30.	60.	125.	175.	300.	1,800.
1858, Repunched high date		35.	50.	75.	110.	225.	350.	750.	1,600.	
1858,/inverted date		30.	45.	60.	90.	200.	300.	700.	1,400.	
18580	1,660,000	15.	18.	25.	45.	75.	150.	250.	400.	
18590	560,000	18.	20.	30.	45.	125.	200.	275.	350.	
1859	340,000	15.	18.	25.	40.	80.	125.	200.	400.	1,500.

A new die was utilized in 1859 at the Philadelphia Mint, in which the stars are hollow in the center and the arms of Liberty are slimmer.

During the years 1859 and 1860 interesting half dime patterns were made which do not bear our nation's identity. These are transitional pieces, not made for circulation, but struck at the time the inscription UNITED STATES OF AMERICA was being transferred from the reverse to the obverse.

	Mintage	F-12	MS-60	MS63	PF-63
1859,Obv of 59,rev. of 60	20	$20.	$25,000.		$25,000.
1860,Obv. Of 59,rev. of 60 (w/ stars)	.100	100.	3,750.	$3,750.	

Variety 4 — Legend on Obverse 1860-1873

HALF DIMES

Mint mark
below bow
1860-1869,
1872-1873.

Mint mark
above bow
1870-1872.

so-called
1861, 1 over 0

Mintage	G-4	VG-8	F-12	VF-20	EF-40	AU-50	MS-60	MS-63	PF-63
1860 Legend(1,000) .799,000	15.	18.	20.	25.	45.	75.	150.	225.	600.
1860O 1,060,000	15.	18.	20.	25.	45.	90.	200.	300.	
1861 .....(1,000)3,361,000	15.	18.	20.	25.	45.	75.	150.	225.	600.
1861, 1/0	30.	40.	60.	125.	250.	500.	600.	900.	
1862 ......(550)1,492,550	20.	25.	40.	50.	60.	100.	175.	250.	600.
1863 ......(460) ..18,460	150.	175.	225.	275.	450.	600.	700.	900.	750.
1863S 100,000	25.	35.	40.	50.	150.	300.	700.	1,000.	
1864 ......(470) ..48,470	300.	400.	450.	650.	900.	1,000.	1,100.	1,200.	750.
1864S 90,000	40.	50.	90.	125.	250.	400.	700.	1,400.	
1865 ......(500) ..13,500	250.	300.	400.	500.	600.	700.	800.	1,200.	750.
1865S 120,000	25.	35.	40.	60.	150.	500.	900.	1,800.	
1866 ......(725) ..10,725	300.	350.	400.	500.	600.	650.	750.	1,200.	650.
1866S 120,000	25.	35.	40.	60.	150.	350.	450.	900.	
1867 ......(625) ...8,625	400.	500.	600.	700.	800.	900.	1,000.	1,400.	750.
1867S 120,000	20.	30.	40.	60.	150.	300.	550.	1,100.	
1868 ......(600) ..89,200	50.	60.	100.	175.	300.	450.	650.	900.	750.
1868S 280,000	15.	18.	25.	30.	40.	125.	300.	600.	
1869 ......(600) .208,600	15.	18.	25.	30.	40.	150.	250.	300.	600.
1869S 230,000	15.	18.	25.	30.	40.	125.	300.	800.	
1870 .....(1,000) .536,000	15.	18.	20.	25.	40.	75.	140.	250.	600.
1870S ....(Unique)							253,000.		
1871 ......(960)1,873,960	15.	18.	20.	25.	40.	75.	140.	250.	600.
1871S 161,000	16.	20.	30.	60.	75.	175.	300.	500.	
1872 ......(950)2,947,950	15.	18.	20.	25.	40.	75.	140.	250.	600.
1872S, All Kinds 837,000									
1872S, mm. above bow	15.	18.	20.	25.	40.	75.	140.	250.	
1872S, mm. below bow	15.	18.	20.	25.	40.	75.	140.	250.	
1873, (Cl 3 only)(600)712,600	15.	18.	20.	25.	40.	75.	140.	250.	600.
1873S, (Cl 3 only) ..324,000	15.	18.	20.	25.	40.	75.	140.	250.	

BIBLIOGRAPHY

Blythe, Al. *The Complete Guide to Liberty Seated Half Dimes.* Virginia Beach, VA, 1992.
Breen, Walter. *United States Half Dimes: A Supplement.* New York, 1958.
Logan, Russell, and McClosky. *Federal Half Dimes 1792 – 1837.* Manchester, MI, 1998.
Newlin, H. P. *The Early Half-Dimes of the United States.* Philadelphia, 1883 (reprinted 1933).
Valentine, D. W. *The United States Half Dimes.* New York, 1931 (reprinted 1975).

DIMES — 1796 to Date

The designs of the dimes, first coined in 1796, follow closely those of the half dimes up through the Liberty seated type. The dimes in each instance weigh twice as much as the half dimes.

+ or – indicates change from previous year	TYPE COIN VALUES									
	G-4	F-12	EF-40	AU-50	MS-60	MS-63	MS-65	PF-60	PF-63	PF-65
Drpd Bust, SE 1796-1797 ...	1,200.+	2,200.+	5,000.+	7,000.+	10,000.+	18,000.+				
Drpd Bust, HE 1798-1807...	450.+	700.	1,800.+	2,500.	4,500.+	8,000.+				
Cap Bust lg. 1809-1828	25.+	50.+	375.+	600.	950.+	2,000.+	9,000.+			
Cap Bust sm. 1828-1837	25.+	35.+	250.+	325.-	750.+	1,400.+	6,500.+			
Lib Seated-NS 1837-1838...	30.+	75.+	500.+	700.-	1,000.	1,800.	6,000.-			
Lib. Seat-Stars 1838-1860..	15.+	25.+	45.+	40.-	275.	600.+	2,500.-	500.	1,200.	4,000.
Lib. Seat-Arr. 1853-1855	15.+	20.+	50.+	150.+	300.	675.-	2,750.-	4,000.+	12,000.+	30,000.+
Lib. Seat-Leg. 1860-1891 ...	13.+	18.+	30.+	75.+	150.+	250.+	850.-	250.-	600.+	1,300.-
Lib. Seat-Arr. 1873-1874 ...	15.+	25.+	125.	250.-	550.	900.	4,000.-	600.	1,200.+	5,000.+
Barber 1892-1916...............	1.75	4.	20.	55.+	90.	150.+	600.-	225.-	400.	1,200.-
Mercury 1916-1945	1.50+	.80	1.50	8.+	10.+	10.	24.-	125.+	180.+	400.
Roosevelt 1946-1964..........	.50-	.55-	.80	.85+	.90-	1.	1.25	1.20+	1.30+	1.50

DRAPED BUST TYPE, SMALL EAGLE REVERSE 1796-1797

Designer Robert Scot; weight 2.70 grams; composition: .8924 silver, .1076 copper; approx. diameter 19 mm; reeded edge. All coined at Philadelphia Mint.

AG-3 ABOUT GOOD—*Details clear enough to identify.*
G-4 GOOD—*Date readable. Bust outlined, but no detail.*
VG-8 VERY GOOD—*All but deepest drapery folds worn smooth. Hairlines nearly gone and curls lack detail.*
F-12 FINE—*All drapery lines visible. Hair partly worn.*
VF-20 VERY FINE—*Only left side of drapery is indistinct.*
EF-40 EXTREMELY FINE—*Hair well outlined and shows details.*
AU-50 ABOUT UNCIRCULATED—*Has traces of light wear on many of the high points. At least half of the mint luster is still present.*
MS-60 UNCIRCULATED—*No trace of wear. Light blemishes.*
MS-63 SELECT UNCIRCULATED—*Some distracting marks or blemishes in prime focal areas.*
Luster may be impaired.

1796   1797, 16 Stars

	Mintage	AG-3	G-4	VG-8	F-12	VF-20	EF-40	AU-50	MS-60	MS-63
1796	22,135	$600.	$1,200.	$1,800.	$2,200.	$3,200.	$5,000.	$7,000.	$10,000.	$18,000.
1797, 16 stars }	25,261	600.	1,200.	1,800.	2,300.	3,500.	6,000.	8,000.	11,000.	20,000.
1797, 13 stars		600.	1,200.	1,800.	2,300.	3,500.	6,000.	8,000.	11,000.	19,000.

DRAPED BUST TYPE, HERALDIC EAGLE REVERSE 1798-1807

		AG-3	G-4	VG-8	F-12	VF-20	EF-40	AU-50	MS-60	MS-63
1798 All Kinds	27,550									
1798/97, 16 stars on rev.		300.	600.	800.	950.	1,400.	2,500.	4,000.	6,000.	10,000.
1798/97,13 stars		700.	1,800.	2,500.	3,500.	6,000.	8,000.			
1798		300.	500.	600.	900.	1,200.	2,300.	3,000.	5,500.	10,000.
1798, Sm 8		350.	700.	1,000.	1,400.	2,000.	3,500.	5,000.	9,500.	15,000.
1800	21,760	300.	500.	600.	900.	1,300.	2,500.	3,500.	5,500.	9,000.

DIMES

	Mintage	AG-3	G-4	VG-8	F-12	VF-20	EF-40	AU-50	MS-60	MS-63
1801	34,640	$300.	$500.	$700.	$1,200.	$2,000.	$4,000.	$7,000.	$10,000.	$15,000.
1802	10,975	400.	800.	1,100.	1,500.	2,500.	5,500.	8,500.	18,000.	
1803	33,040	250.	500.	600.	850.	1,350.	3,500.	7,000.	10,000.	
1804 All Kinds .	8,265									
1804, 13 stars on rev.		600.	1,200.	1,800.	2,500.	4,200.	10,000.	27,000.	—	
1804, 14 stars on rev.		650.	1,300.	2,000.	3,000.	6,500.	17,000.	25,000.	35,000.	
1805, 4 ber. ... }	120,780	200.	450.	550.	700.	900.	1,800.	2,500.	4,500.	8,500.
1805, 5 ber. ... }		200.	450.	550.	700.	900.	2,200.	2,700.	6,000.	8,600.
1807	165,000	200.	450.	550.	700.	900.	1,800.	2,500.	4,500.	8,000.

CAPPED BUST TYPE 1809-1837

Designer John Reich; weight 2.70 grams; composition: .8924 silver, .1076 copper; approx. diameter 18.8 mm; reeded edge. All coined at Philadelphia Mint. Diameter c. 18.5 mm from 1828 to 1837.

AG-3 ABOUT GOOD—Details clear enough to identify.
G-4 GOOD—Date, letters and stars discernible. Bust outlined, no details.
VG-8 VERY GOOD—Legends and date plain. Minimum of 3 letters in LIBERTY.
F-12 FINE—Full LIBERTY. Ear and shoulder clasp visible. Part of rim shows both sides.
VF-20 VERY FINE—LIBERTY distinct. Full rim. Ear and clasp plain and distinct.
EF-40 EXTREMELY FINE—LIBERTY sharp. Ear distinct. Hair above eye well defined.
AU-50 ABOUT UNCIRCULATED—Traces of light wear on only the high points of the design. Half of mint luster is present.
MS-60 UNCIRCULATED—No trace of wear. Light blemishes.
MS-63 SELECT UNCIRCULATED—Some distracting marks or blemishes in prime focal areas. Luster may be impaired.

Variety 1 — Wide Border 1809-1828

	Mintage	G-4	VG-8	F-12	VF-20	EF-40	AU-50	MS-60	MS-63
1809	51,065	$110.	$175.	$300.	$500.	$1,000.	$1,600.	$3,900.	$5,000.
1811/9	65,180	75.	120.	250.	500.	950.	1,500.	3,200.	5,500.

1814 Small Date   1814 Large Date

	Mintage	G-4	VG-8	F-12	VF-20	EF-40	AU-50	MS-60	MS-63
1814, SmDt ..... }	421,500	$50.	$75.	$100.	$225.	$500.	$900.	$1,800.	$4,500.
1814, LgDt ...... }		30.	35.	50.	150.	400.	600.	1,000.	2,000.
1814, STATESOFAMERICA		55.	80.	120.	300.	550.	1,000.	2,000.	4,500.
1820, STATESOFAMERICA		30.	40.	75.	200.	500.	1,100.	2,000.	4,250.

DIMES

1820 Large 0

1821 Small Date

1821 Large Date

	Mintage	G-4	VG-8	F-12	VF-20	EF-40	AU-50	MS-60	MS-63
1820, Lg 0 ... }	942,587	$25.	$30.	$50.	$110.	$400.	$600.	$950.	$2,000.
1820, Sm 0 ...		25.	35.	55.	125.	425.	650.	1,000.	2,000.
1821, SmDt ... }	1,186,512	25.	35.	55.	150.	450.	750.	1,200.	2,700.
1821, LgDt ...		25.	35.	55.	125.	400.	650.	1,100.	2,100.
1822	100,000	400.	550.	900.	1,400.	2,600.	4,500.	9,000.	15,000.

1823, 3 over 2

Small E's

Large E's

		G-4	VG-8	F-12	VF-20	EF-40	AU-50	MS-60	MS-63
1823, 3/2 All Kinds 440,000									
1823, 3/2,Sm E's		25.	35.	55.	120.	400.	650.	1,200.	2,200.
1823, 3/2,Lg E's		25.	35.	55.	120.	400.	650.	1,200.	2,200.

1824, 4 over 2

Large Date

Small Date

		G-4	VG-8	F-12	VF-20	EF-40	AU-50	MS-60	MS-63
1824, 4/2 ..... }	510,000	30.	45.	100.	375.	625.	1,250.	2,000.	3,700.
1825		25.	35.	50.	110.	375.	700.	1,000.	2,400.
1827 1,215,000		25.	35.	50.	110.	375.	700.	1,000.	2,300.
1828 Both vars . 125,000									
1828,LgDt, curl base 2 ...		50.	80.	125.	300.	600.	1,000.	2,000.	3,500.

Variety 2 — Modified Design 1828-1837

New Mint equipment was used to make the small date 1828 dimes and subsequent issues. Unlike earlier coinage, these have beaded borders and a uniform diameter. Large date has curl base knob 2; small date has square base knob 2.

1829 Small 10c

Large 10c

1829 Curl base 2

1830, 30 over 29

	G-4	VG-8	F-12	VF-20	EF-40	AU-50	MS-60	MS-63
1828,SmDt, sq.base 2	$30.	$40.	$75.	$150.	$400.	$600.	$1,200.	$2,000.

DIMES

	Mintage	G-4	F-12	VF-20	EF-40	AU-50	MS-60	MS-63
1829 All Kinds 770,000								
1829, Curl base 2	$3,500.	$8,000.	$20,000.					
1829, Sm 10c		25.	40.	70.	$275.	$350.	$800.	$1,400.
1829, Medium 10c		25.	40.	70.	275.	350.	800.	1,500.
1829, Lg 10c		25.	50.	100.	300.	375.	900.	1,500.
1830 All Kinds 510,000								
1830, 30/29		35.	100.	200.	425.	600.	1,200.	2,500.
1830, Lg 10c		25.	35.	70.	250.	325.	750.	1,400.
1830, Sm 10c		25.	35.	70.	250.	325.	750.	1,400.
1831 771,350		25.	35.	70.	250.	325.	750.	1,400.
1832 522,500		25.	35.	70.	250.	325.	750.	1,400.
1833 .... } 485,000		25.	35.	70.	250.	325.	750.	1,400.
1833, Last 3 high . }		25.	35.	70.	250.	325.	750.	1,400.
1834, Sm 4 ..... } 635,000		25.	35.	70.	250.	325.	800.	1,500.
1834, Lg 4 ...... }		25.	35.	70.	250.	325.	750.	1,400.
1835 1,410,000		25.	35.	70.	250.	325.	750.	1,400.
1836 1,190,000		25.	35.	70.	250.	325.	750.	1,400.
1837 359,500		25.	35.	70.	250.	325.	750.	1,400.

LIBERTY SEATED TYPE 1837-1891
Variety 1 — No Stars on Obverse 1837-1838

Designer Christian Gobrecht; weight 2.67 grams; composition: .900 silver, .100 copper; diameter 17.9 mm; reeded edge; mints: Philadelphia, New Orleans.

No Drapery From Elbow
No Stars on Obverse

G-4 GOOD—*LIBERTY on shield smooth. Date and letters readable.*
F-12 FINE—*Entire LIBERTY visible, weak spots.*
VF-20 VERY FINE—*Entire LIBERTY strong and even.*
EF-40 EXTREMELY FINE—*LIBERTY and scroll edges distinct.*
AU-50—*Wear on Liberty's shoulder and hair high points; slight wear on breast, tail, and wing tips.*
MS-60 UNCIRCULATED—*No trace of wear. Light blemishes.*
MS-63 SELECT UNCIRCULATED—*Some distracting contact marks or blemishes in prime focal areas. Luster may be impaired.*

Mint marks on Liberty seated dimes are placed on the reverse within, or below, the wreath. Size of mint mark varies on many dates.

	Mintage	G-4	F-12	VF-20	EF-40	AU-50	MS-60	MS-63
1837, LgDt ...... } 682,500		30.	75.	260.	500.	700.	1,000.	1,800.
1837, SmDt ..... }		30.	75.	260.	500.	700.	1,000.	1,800.
1838O 406,034		40.	110.	350.	700.	1,200.	2,750.	6,000.

Variety 2 — Stars on Obverse 1838-1853

No Drapery from Elbow
Tilted Shield

1838 Small Stars   **1838 Large Stars**

	Mintage	G-4	F-12	VF-20	EF-40	AU-50	MS-60	MS-63
1838, SmS ..... }		20.	50.	80.	175.	400.	700.	1,300.
1838, LgS ..... } 1,992,500		15.	30.	35.	100.	250.	350.	800.
1838, PartDrap .		20.	50.	100.	180.	450.	850.	2,000.
1839 1,053,115		15.	30.	35.	100.	250.	350.	800.
1839O 1,323,000		18.	32.	40.	110.	275.	400.	1,200.
1840 981,500		15.	30.	35.	100.	250.	350.	800.
1840O 1,175,000		20.	35.	50.	125.	300.	900.	2,000.
1841 Pf, see page 131.								

DIMES

**Drapery from Elbow
Upright Shield**

	Mintage	G-4	F-12	VF-20	EF-40	AU-50	MS-60	MS-63
1840	377,500	$30.	$90.	$150.	$300.	$400.	$900.	$5,000.
1841*	1,622,500	15.	25.	30.	50.	125.	300.	600.
1841O	2,007,500	18.	30.	45.	75.	225.	900.	2,000.
1842	1,887,500	15.	25.	30.	45.	125.	360.	600.
1842O	2,020,000	17.	28.	60.	200.	1,200.	2,500.	6,000.
1843	1,370,000	15.	25.	30.	45.	125.	360.	800.
1843O	150,000	35.	100.	225.	600.	1,000.	2,500.	—
1844	72,500	200.	450.	700.	1,100.	1,650.	2,500.	6,500.
1845	1,755,000	15.	25.	30.	45.	125.	360.	750.
1845O	230,000	20.	55.	200.	500.	1,000.	2,500.	—
1846	31,300	75.	175.	350.	900.	2,000.	4,250.	9,000.
1847	245,000	18.	40.	60.	125.	325.	900.	2,500.
1848	451,500	18.	30.	45.	85.	150.	500.	850.
1849	839,000	15.	25.	35.	50.	125.	300.	900.
1849O	300,000	18.	40.	125.	300.	700.	2,200.	5,000.
1850	1,931,500	15.	25.	35.	50.	125.	275.	700.
1850O	510,000	18.	29.	75.	140.	400.	1,100.	2,500.
1851	1,026,500	15.	25.	35.	50.	125.	375.	800.
1851O	400,000	18.	35.	70.	160.	400.	2,000.	3,000.
1852	1,535,500	15.	25.	35.	50.	125.	360.	700.
1852O	430,000	20.	40.	125.	250.	350.	1,700.	3,000.
1853, No arrows	95,000	50.	110.	200.	300.	400.	800.	1,000.

*1841 Small stars, no drapery, upright shield. One Proof and one VF known.

Variety 3 — Arrows at Date 1853-1855

Weight 2.49 grams; composition: .900 silver, .100 copper; diameter 17.9 mm, reeded edge; mints: Philadelphia, New Orleans, San Francisco, Carson City.

**1853-1855
Arrows at Date**

**1856-1860
Small Date, Arrows Removed**

	Mintage	G-4	F-12	VF-20	EF-40	AU-50	MS-60	MS-63	PF-63
1853, w/ arrows	12,078,010	15.	20.	30.	50.	150.	300.	675.	
1853O	1,100,000	15.	20.	40.	100.	275.	1,000.	3,000.	
1854	4,470,000	15.	20.	30.	50.	150.	300.	675.	12,000.
1854O	1,770,000	15.	20.	35.	75.	175.	600.	1,300.	
1855	2,075,000	15.	20.	30.	50.	150.	350.	900.	12,000.

Variety 2 Resumed 1856-1860

	Mintage	G-4	F-12	VF-20	EF-40	AU-50	MS-60	MS-63	PF-63
1856, LgDt	} 5,780,000	15.	20.	30.	50.	150.	300.	700.	
1856, SmDt		15.	20.	30.	40.	125.	300.	700.	4,000.
1856O	1,180,000	15.	20.	30.	60.	250.	800.	1,500.	
1856S	70,000	100.	325.	500.	850.	1,400.	3,000.	—	

DIMES

	Mintage	G-4	F-12	VF-20	EF-40	AU-50	MS-60	MS-63	PF-63
1857	5,580,000	$15.	$18.	$25.	$40.	$125.	$300.	$625.	$4,000.
1857O	1,540,000	15.	20.	30.	60.	200.	425.	700.	
1858 . . . . .(300+)	1,540,000	15.	20.	25.	40.	125.	300.	700.	2,000.
1858O	290,000	20.	40.	85.	135.	300.	600.	1,000.	
1858S	60,000	90.	200.	400.	750.	1,300.	2,500.	12,000.	
1859 . . . . .(800)	430,000	15.	20.	30.	60.	125.	300.	700.	1,500.
1859O	480,000	16.	22.	50.	90.	250.	400.	800.	
1859S	60,000	100.	275.	425.	1,000.	2,000.	8,000.	—	
1860S	140,000	30.	55.	120.	275.	800.	2,000.	4,000.	

In 1859 an interesting dime pattern was made which does not bear our nation's identity. It is a "transitional" piece, not made for circulation, but struck at the time the inscription UNITED STATES OF AMERICA was being transferred from the reverse to the obverse.

1859, obverse of 1859 (with stars), reverse of 1860 . . . . 15,000.

Variety 4 — Legend on Obverse 1860-1873

	Mintage	G-4	F-12	VF-20	EF-40	AU-50	MS-60	MS-63	PF-63
1860 . . .(1,000)	607,000	15.	20.	30.	40.	125.	300.	700.	800.
1860O	40,000	300.	800.	1,400.	2,750.	4,500.	9,500.	—	
1861* . . .(1,000)	1,884,000	15.	20.	30.	40.	125.	225.	400.	800.
1861S	172,500	40.	100.	200.	400.	500.	1,400.	4,000.	
1862 . . . . .(550)	847,550	13.	18.	25.	30.	80.	200.	300.	700.
1862S	180,750	35.	62.	150.	250.	300.	1,400.	3,000.	
1863 . . . . .(460)	14,460	250.	500.	650.	725.	900.	1,200.	1,400.	800.
1863S	157,500	30.	50.	100.	175.	325.	1,000.	2,800.	
1864 . . . . .(470)	11,470	200.	400.	500.	800.	1,000.	1,200.	1,400.	800.
1864S	230,000	22.	40.	90.	125.	300.	900.	1,300.	
1865 . . . . .(500)	10,500	250.	550.	650.	750.	850.	1,100.	1,400.	850.
1865S	175,000	25.	50.	125.	225.	600.	2,000.	4,500.	
1866 . . . . .(725)	8,725	300.	550.	700.	800.	1,200.	1,300.	1,500.	800.
1866S	135,000	40.	70.	110.	225.	350.	1,000.	3,000.	
1867 . . . . .(625)	6,625	400.	700.	900.	1,100.	1,200.	1,400.	1,700.	950.
1867S	140,000	30.	70.	120.	225.	550.	1,200.	2,000.	
1868 . . . . .(600)	464,600	15.	25.	40.	70.	150.	300.	800.	600.
1868S	260,000	15.	35.	70.	125.	175.	400.	1,000.	
1869 . . . . .(600)	256,600	15.	30.	65.	100.	175.	400.	900.	600.
1869S	450,000	15.	20.	35.	65.	150.	400.	800.	
1870 . . .(1,000)	471,500	13.	18.	25.	50.	100.	200.	450.	600.
1870S	50,000	250.	400.	450.	550.	800.	1,850.	2,500.	
1871 . . . . .(960)	907,710	13.	18.	25.	40.	150.	300.	400.	600.
1871CC	20,100	1,000.	2,500.	4,000.	7,500.	10,000.	—		
1871S	320,000	20.	50.	75.	150.	300.	650.	1,500.	
1872 . . . . .(950)	2,396,450	13.	18.	25.	30.	75.	150.	250.	600.
1872CC	35,480	400.	1,100.	2,500.	5,000.	10,000.	—		
1872S	190,000	22.	75.	125.	225.	400.	1,200.	2,500.	
1873, Cl 3(1,100)	1,508,000	13.	18.	25.	35.	75.	150.	250.	600.
1873, Op 3	60,000	20.	45.	75.	125.	200.	550.	1,200.	
1873CC (Unique) . .12,400							632,500.		

*Dies modified slightly during 1861. First variety with only five vertical lines in top of shield is scarcer than the later variety.

DIMES

Variety 5 — Arrows at Date 1873-1874

In 1873 the dime was increased in weight to 2.50 grams. Arrows at date in 1873 and 1874 indicate this change.

Weight 2.50 grams; composition: .900 silver, .100 copper; diameter 17.9 mm; reeded edge; mints: Philadelphia, New Orleans, San Francisco, Carson City.

	Mintage	G-4	F-12	VF-20	EF-40	AU-50	MS-60	MS-63	PF-63
1873 . . . . .(800)	2,378,500	15.	25.	50.	125.	250.	550.	900.	1,200.
1873, DblDieObv		60.	200.	500.	1,000.				
1873CC	18,791	900.	3,250.	6,000.	10,000.	14,000.		—	
1873S	455,000	18.	35.	60.	175.	400.	1,000.	2,000.	
1874 . . . . .(700)	2,940,000	15.	25.	50.	125.	300.	600.	900.	1,200.
1874CC	10,817	2,500.	5,000.	9,000.	15,000.	23,000.		—	
1874S	240,000	22.	60.	100.	225.	500.	900.	2,000.	

Variety 4 Resumed 1875-1891

	Mintage	G-4	F-12	VF-20	EF-40	AU-50	MS-60	MS-63	PF-63
1875 . . . . .(700)	10,350,700	13.	15.	18.	27.	75.	150.	250.	500.
1875CC, Below bow									
All Kinds 4,645,000		15.	20.	30.	60.	100.	300.	500.	
1875CC, Above bow		13.	15.	25.	40.	75.	275.	450.	
1875S, Below bow									
All Kinds 9,070,000		13.	15.	20.	27.	75.	150.	250.	
1875S, Above bow		13.	15.	20.	37.	80.	150.	250.	
1876 . . .(1,150) 11,146,150		13.	15.	20.	27.	75.	150.	250.	500.
1876CC 8,270,000		13.	15.	20.	40.	80.	200.	400.	
1876S 10,420,000		13.	15.	20.	30.	75.	150.	250.	
1877 . . . . .(510) .7,310,510		13.	15.	20.	27.	75.	150.	250.	550.
1877CC 7,700,000		15.	18.	25.	40.	80.	200.	400.	
1877S 2,340,000		13.	15.	20.	30.	80.	150.	250.	
1878 . . . . .(800) .1,678,000		13.	15.	20.	27.	75.	150.	250.	500.
1878CC 200,000		50.	125.	200.	375.	550.	1,000.	1,600.	
1879 . . .(1,100) . . .15,100		200.	350.	450.	500.	600.	650.	700.	550.
1880 . . .(1,355) 37,355		150.	250.	350.	400.	500.	600.	700.	550.
1881 . . . . .(975) 24,975		150.	250.	350.	400.	500.	600.	700.	550.
1882 . . .(1,100) .3,911,100		13.	15.	18.	27.	75.	150.	250.	500.
1883 . . .(1,039) .7,675,712		13.	15.	18.	27.	75.	150.	250.	500.
1884 . . . . .(875) .3,366,380		13.	15.	18.	27.	75.	150.	250.	500.
1884S 564,969		20.	30.	50.	90.	300.	750.	1,200.	
1885 . . . . .(930) .2,533,427		13.	15.	18.	27.	75.	150.	250.	500.
1885S 43,690		400.	800.	1,400.	2,200.	3,750.	5,000.	7,000.	
1886 . . . . .(886) .6,377,570		13.	15.	18.	27.	75.	150.	250.	500.
1886S 206,524		25.	50.	75.	135.	200.	600.	1,200.	
1887 . . . . .(710) 11,283,939		13.	15.	18.	27.	75.	150.	250.	500.
1887S 4,454,450		13.	15.	18.	27.	75.	150.	250.	
1888 . . . . .(832) .5,496,487		13.	15.	18.	27.	75.	150.	250.	500.
1888S 1,720,000		13.	15.	18.	30.	100.	250.	750.	
1889 . . . . .(711) .7,380,711		13.	15.	18.	27.	75.	150.	250.	500.
1889S 972,678		15.	25.	50.	80.	150.	500.	900.	
1890 . . . . .(590) .9,911,541		13.	15.	18.	27.	75.	150.	250.	500.
1890S, Lg S 1,423,076		15.	23.	45.	75.	150.	350.	700.	
1890S, Sm S . . . .(Rare)		—	—						

DIMES

	Mintage	G-4	F-12	VF-20	EF-40	AU-50	MS-60	MS-63	PF-63
1891 . . . . .(600)	15,310,600	$13.	$15.	$18.	$27.	$75.	$150.	$250.	$600.
1891O	4,540,000	13.	15.	22.	45.	100.	200.	350.	
1891O, 0/0		50.	110.	150.	225.				
1891S	3,196,116	13.	15.	20.	30.	80.	175.	300.	

BARBER or LIBERTY HEAD TYPE 1892-1916

Designed by Charles E. Barber, Chief Engraver of the Mint, who also designed the 25- and 50-cent pieces. His initial B is at the truncation of the neck.

Designer Charles E. Barber; weight 2.50 grams; composition: .900 silver, .100 copper; diameter 17.9 mm; reeded edge; mints: Philadelphia, Denver, New Orleans, San Francisco. Net weight: .07234 oz. pure silver.

G-4 GOOD—Date and letters plain. LIBERTY is obliterated.
VG-8 VERY GOOD—At least 3 letters visible in LIBERTY.
F-12 FINE—All letters in LIBERTY visible, though some are weak.
VF-20 VERY FINE—All letters of LIBERTY evenly plain.
EF-40 EXTREMELY FINE—All letters in LIBERTY are sharp, distinct. Headband edges are distinct.
AU-50 ABOUT UNCIRCULATED—Slight traces of wear on the hair, cheekbone, leaf tips in wreath.
MS-60 UNCIRCULATED—No trace of wear. Light blemishes.
MS-63 SELECT UNCIRCULATED—Some distracting marks or blemishes in prime focal areas. Luster may be impaired.

Mint mark location is on the reverse below the wreath.

	Mintage	G-4	VG-8	F-12	VF-20	EF-40	AU-50	MS-60	MS-63	PF-63
1892 (1,245)	.12,121,245	$4.00	$6.00	$15.	$22.	$27.	$65.	$100.	$150.	$400.
1892O	.3,841,700	7.00	11.00	25.	40.	50.	75.	150.	275.	
1892S	.990,710	50.00	90.00	160.	190.	230.	250.	375.	750.	
1893, 3/2 . . .	} 3,340,732	125.00	135.00	150.	160.	180.	225.	700.	1,800.	850.
1893 . .(792)		7.00	10.00	17.	24.	36.	60.	150.	200.	400.
1893O	.1,760,000	25.00	35.00	100.	120.	150.	175.	300.	650.	
1893S	.2,491,401	9.00	18.00	25.	40.	55.	110.	275.	700.	
1894 . .(972)	.1,330,972	15.00	26.00	100.	125.	150.	175.	275.	500.	400.
1894O	.720,000	50.00	80.00	175.	225.	325.	600.	1,200.	2,500.	
1894S	.24									850,000.
1895 . .(880)	. . .690,880	65.00	125.00	300.	400.	500.	550.	700.	1,200.	550.
1895O	.440,000	300.00	400.00	750.	1,100.	2,000.	2,750.	6,000.	9,000.	
1895S	.1,120,000	35.00	45.00	125.	160.	200.	225.	500.	1,200.	
1896 . .(762)	.2,000,762	10.00	20.00	55.	65.	80.	100.	175.	500.	400.
1896O	.610,000	65.00	125.00	250.	325.	400.	600.	1,000.	2,400.	
1896S	.575,056	65.00	125.00	250.	300.	350.	450.	800.	1,500.	
1897 . .(731)	.10,869,264	2.00	3.00	6.	12.	25.	60.	125.	175.	400.
1897O	.666,000	55.00	100.00	250.	325.	400.	500.	900.	1,700.	
1897S	.1,342,844	12.00	25.00	100.	110.	125.	200.	400.	900.	
1898 . .(735)	.16,320,735	2.00	3.00	6.	10.	22.	60.	110.	150.	400.
1898O	.2,130,000	8.00	16.00	80.	100.	150.	200.	450.	1,200.	
1898S	.1,702,507	6.00	12.00	25.	35.	60.	120.	325.	1,200.	
1899 . .(846)	.19,580,846	2.00	3.00	6.	10.	22.	60.	110.	150.	400.
1899O	.2,650,000	6.00	15.00	65.	90.	135.	200.	400.	1,200.	
1899S	.1,867,493	6.00	12.00	20.	30.	40.	80.	300.	700.	
1900 . .(912)	.17,600,912	1.75	2.00	6.	10.	22.	60.	110.	150.	400.
1900O	.2,010,000	15.00	30.00	100.	125.	220.	325.	600.	1,000.	
1900S	.5,168,270	4.00	5.00	10.	15.	27.	65.	175.	400.	
1901 . .(813)	.18,860,478	2.00	3.00	6.	10.	22.	60.	110.	150.	400.
1901O	.5,620,000	3.00	4.25	12.	20.	50.	125.	450.	900.	

DIMES

	Mintage	G-4	VG-8	F-12	VF-20	EF-40	AU-50	MS-60	MS-63	PF-63
1901S	593,022	$70.00	$125.00	$350.	$400.	$500.	$650.	$1,000.	$1,700.	
1902 . .(777)	21,380,777	2.00	3.00	5.	7.	20.	55.	95.	150.	$400.
1902O	4,500,000	3.00	5.00	14.	24.	45.	100.	400.	1,000.	
1902S	2,070,000	5.00	15.00	50.	65.	100.	150.	400.	1,000.	
1903 . .(755)	19,500,755	2.00	3.00	5.	7.	20.	60.	95.	200.	400.
1903O	8,180,000	2.75	4.00	10.	15.	32.	80.	250.	600.	
1903S	613,300	60.00	125.00	350.	450.	750.	850.	1,200.	1,800.	
1904 . .(670)	14,601,027	2.00	3.50	6.	8.	20.	60.	100.	150.	400.
1904S	800,000	35.00	60.00	150.	200.	275.	450.	800.	1,500.	
1905 . .(727)	14,552,350	2.00	3.00	5.	7.	20.	60.	95.	150.	400.
1905O	} 3,400,000	3.00	7.00	30.	45.	60.	110.	275.	500.	
1905O Micr O *		12.00	25.00	80.	125.	200.	350.	850.		
1905S	6,855,199	2.50	4.50	8.	14.	35.	65.	250.	300.	
1906 . .(675)	19,958,406	2.00	2.50	4.	7.	20.	55.	90.	150.	400.
1906D	4,060,000	3.00	4.00	8.	14.	27.	65.	175.	375.	
1906O	2,610,000	4.00	10.00	45.	60.	80.	125.	200.	300.	
1906S	3,136,640	2.50	4.50	12.	22.	37.	85.	250.	500.	
1907 . .(575)	22,220,575	2.00	2.50	4.	7.	20.	60.	100.	150.	400.
1907D	4,080,000	2.25	4.00	9.	15.	35.	90.	300.	900.	
1907O	5,058,000	2.50	6.00	32.	45.	60.	70.	200.	400.	
1907S	3,178,470	2.50	4.50	12.	18.	45.	90.	400.	700.	
1908 . .(545)	10,600,545	2.00	2.50	4.	7.	20.	60.	95.	150.	400.
1908D	7,490,000	2.00	2.50	8.	11.	28.	60.	125.	300.	
1908O	1,789,000	5.00	12.00	45.	60.	80.	150.	300.	600.	
1908S	3,220,000	2.25	4.00	10.	16.	35.	150.	300.	700.	
1909 . .(991)	10,240,650	2.00	2.50	4.	7.	20.	60.	100.	150.	400.
1909D	954,000	6.00	15.00	65.	85.	135.	200.	500.	1,000.	
1909O	2,287,000	3.00	6.00	12.	22.	32.	90.	200.	500.	
1909S	1,000,000	6.00	15.00	75.	125.	175.	300.	550.	1,200.	
1910 . .(961)	11,520,551	2.00	2.50	4.	7.	20.	60.	100.	150.	400.
1910D	3,490,000	2.00	4.00	9.	16.	37.	85.	200.	450.	
1910S	1,240,000	4.00	8.00	50.	75.	100.	150.	400.	700.	
1911 . .(656)	18,870,543	2.00	2.50	4.	7.	20.	60.	100.	150.	400.
1911D	11,209,000	2.00	2.50	4.	7.	20.	60.	100.	150.	
1911S	3,520,000	2.00	3.50	9.	14.	35.	85.	200.	400.	
1912 . .(700)	19,350,000	2.00	2.50	4.	7.	20.	60.	100.	150.	400.
1912D	11,760,000	2.00	2.50	4.	7.	20.	60.	100.	150.	
1912S	3,420,000	2.25	4.00	9.	12.	30.	90.	175.	325.	
1913 . .(813)	19,760,622	2.00	2.50	4.	7.	20.	60.	100.	150.	400.
1913S	510,000	15.00	25.00	75.	125.	200.	300.	510.	750.	
1914 . .(655)	17,360,655	2.00	2.50	4.	7.	20.	60.	100.	150.	400.
1914D	11,908,000	2.00	2.50	4.	7.	20.	60.	100.	150.	
1914S	2,100,000	2.50	4.00	8.	15.	35.	75.	150.	350.	
1915 . .(450)	5,620,450	2.00	2.50	4.	7.	20.	60.	100.	150.	400.
1915S	960,000	5.00	9.00	32.	40.	60.	140.	300.	500.	
1916	18,490,000	2.00	2.50	4.	7.	20.	60.	100.	150.	
1916S	5,820,000	2.00	2.50	4.	7.	20.	60.	100.	150.	

*Normal and "microscopic" mint mark varieties, see page 73.

WINGED LIBERTY HEAD or "MERCURY" TYPE 1916-1945

Although this coin is commonly called the "Mercury Dime," the main device is in fact a representation of Liberty. The wings crowning her cap are intended to symbolize liberty of thought. The designer's monogram AW is right of neck.

Designer Adolph A. Weinman; weight 2.50 grams; composition: .900 silver, .100 copper; diameter 17.9 mm; reeded edge; mints: Philadelphia, Denver, San Francisco. Net weight: .07234 oz. pure silver.

DIMES

G-4 GOOD—*Letters and date clear. Lines and bands in fasces are obliterated.*
VG-8 VERY GOOD—*One-half of sticks discernible in fasces.*
F-12 FINE—*All sticks in fasces are defined. Diagonal bands worn nearly flat.*
VF-20 VERY FINE—*The two crossing diagonal bands must show.*
EF-40 EXTREMELY FINE—*Diagonal bands show only slight wear. Braids and hair before ear show clearly.*
AU-50—*ABOUT UNCIRCULATED*—*Slight trace of wear. Most mint luster is present.*
MS-63 SELECT UNCIRCULATED—*No trace of wear. Light blemishes. Attractive mint luster.*
MS-65—*CHOICE UNCIRCULATED*—*Only light scattered marks that are not distracting. Strong luster, good eye appeal.*

**Mint mark location is on reverse,
left of fasces.**

*Uncirculated values shown are for average pieces with minimum blemishes,
those with sharp strikes and split bands on reverse are worth much more.*

	Mintage	G-4	VG-8	F-12	VF-20	EF-40	AU-50	MS-63	MS-65
1916	. . . 22,180,080	$3.00	$4.00	$6.00	$8.	$10.	$24.	$45.	$100.
1916D	. . 264,000	750.00	1,100.00	1,800.00	2,750.	3,750.	6,000.	7,000.	18,500.
1916S	. . 10,450,000	4.00	6.00	9.00	11.	18.	25.	65.	200.
1917	. . . 55,230,000	2.00	2.50	3.00	6.	8.	12.	60.	150.
1917D	. . 9,402,000	4.50	6.00	11.00	20.	45.	95.	350.	1,200.
1917S	. . 27,330,000	2.00	3.00	5.00	7.	12.	27.	175.	500.
1918	. . . 26,680,000	2.50	4.00	6.00	12.	24.	40.	135.	435.
1918D	. . 22,674,800	3.00	4.00	5.00	11.	23.	50.	250.	600.
1918S	. . 19,300,000	3.00	3.50	5.00	8.	16.	40.	260.	675.
1919	. . . 35,740,000	2.50	3.00	4.00	6.	10.	30.	120.	325.
1919D	. . 9,939,000	5.00	6.00	12.00	25.	36.	75.	450.	1,500.
1919S	. . 8,850,000	3.50	4.00	8.00	15.	35.	75.	500.	1,000.
1920	. . . 59,030,000	1.75	2.00	4.00	6.	8.	14.	75.	250.
1920D	. . 19,171,000	3.00	3.50	4.75	8.	22.	50.	350.	775.
1920S	. . 13,820,000	3.00	4.00	5.00	8.	19.	40.	275.	1,300.
1921	. . . 1,230,000	40.00	60.00	100.00	275.	500.	750.	1,600.	3,400.
1921D	. . 1,080,000	55.00	100.00	150.00	335.	600.	900.	1,850.	3,000.
1923*	. . 50,130,000	2.00	3.00	4.00	5.	7.	15.	45.	125.
1923S	. . 6,440,000	3.00	4.00	7.00	12.	60.	100.	400.	1,200.
1924	. . . 24,010,000	1.75	3.00	4.00	6.	10.	25.	100.	200.
1924D	. . 6,810,000	3.00	4.00	7.00	15.	50.	100.	475.	1,200.
1924S	. . 7,120,000	3.00	4.00	5.00	9.	45.	100.	500.	1,200.
1925	. . . 25,610,000	1.75	3.00	3.75	5.	8.	20.	75.	200.
1925D	. . 5,117,000	4.00	5.00	12.00	40.	100.	200.	700.	1,800.
1925S	. . 5,850,000	3.00	4.00	7.00	12.	60.	100.	475.	1,500.
1926	. . . 32,160,000	1.50	2.00	2.50	4.	7.	15.	60.	250.
1926D	. . 6,828,000	2.75	3.75	5.00	8.	25.	55.	250.	600.
1926S	. . 1,520,000	7.00	9.00	20.00	50.	225.	400.	1,500.	3,000.
1927	. . . 28,080,000	1.50	2.00	3.00	4.	7.	12.	55.	135.
1927D	. . 4,812,000	4.00	5.00	6.00	20.	60.	90.	400.	1,300.
1927S	. . 4,770,000	3.00	3.50	5.00	8.	24.	50.	550.	1,500.
1928	. . . 19,480,000	1.50	2.00	3.00	5.	7.	17.	50.	130.
1928D	. . 4,161,000	4.00	5.00	8.00	18.	45.	80.	350.	900.
1928S‡	. 7,400,000	2.00	3.00	4.00	5.	15.	48.	250.	500.
1929	. . . 25,970,000	1.50	2.00	3.00	4.	6.	10.	35.	75.
1929D	. . 5,034,000	3.00	4.00	6.00	9.	15.	22.	38.	75.

* Coins dated 1923D are counterfeit.

‡ Large and small mint marks. See page 73.

	Mintage	G-4	VG-8	F-12	VF-20	EF-40	AU-50	MS-63	MS-65
1929S	4,730,000	$2.00	$3.00	$4.00	$5.00	$8.	$20.	$45.	$125.
1930*	6,770,000	1.75	2.00	3.00	5.00	8.	15.	50.	125.
1930S	1,843,000	3.00	4.00	5.00	7.00	15.	45.	110.	200.
1931	3,150,000	1.50	3.00	4.00	6.00	12.	20.	60.	150.
1931D	1,260,000	6.00	7.00	10.00	20.00	35.	50.	110.	225.
1931S	1,800,000	4.00	4.50	6.00	7.50	15.	35.	100.	250.

*Dimes dated 1930D are counterfeit.

	Mintage	F-12	VF-20	EF-40	MS-63	MS-65	PF-65
1934	24,080,000	1.20	1.50	3.50	30.	50.	
1934D ‡	6,772,000	1.70	2.25	7.50	60.	85.	
1935	58,830,000	1.20	1.50	2.00	15.	37.	
1935D	10,477,000	1.70	2.25	8.00	45.	80.	
1935S	15,840,000	1.20	1.50	4.00	30.	40.	
1936	.....(4,130) ..87,504,130	1.20	2.25	3.00	18.	30.	2,000.
1936D	16,132,000	1.70	3.00	5.00	30.	45.	
1936S	9,210,000	1.20	2.25	3.00	25.	35.	
1937	.....(5,756) ..56,865,756	1.20	1.50	2.25	15.	30.	800.
1937D	14,146,000	1.20	2.25	3.50	28.	45.	
1937S	9,740,000	1.20	2.25	3.00	28.	35.	
1938	.....(8,728) ..22,198,728	1.20	2.25	2.75	15.	25.	500.
1938D	5,537,000	2.00	2.75	3.00	20.	32.	
1938S	8,090,000	1.20	2.25	3.00	20.	32.	
1939	.....(9,321) ..67,749,321	1.20	1.50	2.50	12.	25.	450.
1939D	24,394,000	1.20	1.50	2.50	12.	25.	
1939S	10,540,000	1.50	2.00	3.00	25.	40.	
1940	.....(11,827) ..65,361,827	0.90	1.10	1.50	10.	24.	425.
1940D	21,198,000	0.90	1.10	1.50	14.	25.	
1940S	21,560,000	0.90	1.10	1.50	15.	25.	
1941	.....(16,557) ..175,106,557	0.90	1.10	1.50	12.	35.	400.
1941D	45,634,000	0.90	1.10	1.50	15.	25.	
1941S ‡	43,090,000	0.90	1.10	1.50	12.	30.	

1942, 2 over 1

1942D, 2 over 1

	Mintage	F-12	VF-20	EF-40	MS-63	MS-65	PF-65
1942, 2/1 .... }	205,432,329	600.00	700.00	800.00	4,000.	12,500.	
1942 .....(22,329)		0.80	1.00	1.50	10.	30.	400.
1942D, 2/1 .... }	60,740,000	600.00	700.00	800.00	3,750.	8,000.	
1942D		0.80	1.00	1.50	15.	30.	
1942S	49,300,000	0.80	1.00	1.50	15.	30.	
1943	191,710,000	0.80	1.00	1.50	12.	25.	
1943D	71,949,000	0.80	1.00	1.50	15.	30.	
1943S	60,400,000	0.80	1.00	1.50	15.	30.	
1944	231,410,000	0.80	1.00	1.50	12.	25.	
1944D	62,224,000	0.80	1.00	1.50	15.	30.	
1944S	49,490,000	0.80	1.00	1.50	15.	30.	
1945	159,130,000	0.80	1.00	1.50	10.	27.	
1945D	40,245,000	0.80	1.00	1.50	12.	30.	
1945S .... }	41,920,000	0.80	1.00	1.50	12.	30.	
1945S, Micro S ‡ ..		1.25	2.00	5.00	35.	90.	

‡Large and small mint mark varieties, see page 73.

ROOSEVELT TYPE 1946 to Date

John R. Sinnock (whose initials JS are at the truncation of the neck) designed this dime showing a portrait of Franklin D. Roosevelt. The design has heavier lettering and a more modernistic character than preceding types.

Mint mark on reverse 1946-1964. **Mint mark on obverse starting 1968.**

Silver Coinage — 1946-1964

Designer John R. Sinnock; weight 2.50 grams; composition: .900 silver, .100 copper; diameter 17.9 mm; reeded edge; mints: Philadelphia, Denver, San Francisco, West Point. Net weight: .07234 oz. pure silver.

EF-40 EXTREMELY FINE—*All lines of torch, flame and hair very plain.*
MS-63 SELECT UNCIRCULATED—*Some distracting contact marks or blemishes in prime focal areas.*
Luster may be impaired.
MS-65—CHOICE UNCIRCULATED—*Only light scattered marks that are not distracting.*
Strong luster, good eye appeal.
PF-65 —*Nearly Perfect.*

	Mintage	EF-40	MS-63	MS-65	PF-65
1946	255,250,000	$0.80	$1.75	$3.50	
1946D	61,043,500	0.80	1.35	4.00	
1946S	27,900,000	0.80	4.00	6.00	
1947	121,520,000	0.80	3.00	5.00	
1947D	46,835,000	0.80	5.00	7.00	
1947S	34,840,000	0.80	4.00	6.50	
1948	74,950,000	0.80	3.00	8.00	
1948D	52,841,000	0.80	3.00	8.00	
1948S	35,520,000	0.80	4.00	9.00	
1949	30,940,000	1.25	20.00	28.00	
1949D	26,034,000	1.00	7.50	14.00	
1949S	13,510,000	2.50	30.00	45.00	
1950 ......(51,386)	50,181,500	0.80	5.00	7.00	$35.00
1950D	46,803,000	0.80	4.00	6.50	
1950S	20,440,000	0.80	25.00	30.00	
1950S, S/D		75.00	250.00		
1951 ......(57,500)	103,937,602	0.80	1.25	3.00	30.00
1951D	56,529,000	0.80	1.50	3.00	
1951S	31,630,000	0.80	9.00	18.00	
1952 ......(81,980)	99,122,073	0.80	1.75	3.00	27.00
1952D	122,100,000	0.80	1.75	4.00	
1952S	44,419,500	0.80	4.50	10.00	
1953 .....(128,800)	53,618,920	0.80	1.50	4.00	27.00
1953D	136,433,000	0.80	2.00	3.00	
1953S	39,180,000	0.80	2.00	2.75	
1954 .....(233,300)	114,243,503	0.80	1.50	2.75	10.00
1954D	106,397,000	0.80	1.50	3.00	
1954S	22,860,000	0.80	1.50	3.00	
1955 .....(378,200)	12,828,381	0.80	1.50	4.00	9.00
1955D	13,959,000	0.80	1.50	3.00	
1955S	18,510,000	0.80	1.00	3.00	
1956 .....(669,384)	109,309,384	0.80	1.00	1.25	3.00
1956D	108,015,100	0.80	1.00	1.25	

DIMES

1960
Proof
Doubled
Die
Obverse

1964D
Doubled Die
Reverse

	Mintage	EF-40	MS-63	MS-65	PF-65
1957 . . . . . .(1,247,952) . . .161,407,952		$0.80	$1.00	$1.25	$2.50
1957D 113,354,330		0.80	1.25	2.00	
1958 . . . .(875,652) 32,785,652		0.80	1.00	1.25	3.00
1958D 136,564,600		0.80	1.00	1.25	
1959 . . . . . .(1,149,291) . . .86,929,291		0.80	1.00	1.25	1.50
1959D 164,919,790		0.80	1.00	1.25	
1960 . . . . . .(1,691,602) 72,081,602		0.80	1.00	1.25	1.50
1960, DblDieObv					300.00
1960D 200,160,400		0.80	1.00	1.25	
1961 . . . . . .(3,028,244) . . .96,758,244		0.80	1.00	1.25	1.50
1961D 209,146,550		0.80	1.00	1.25	
1962 . . . . . .(3,218,019) 75,668,019		0.80	1.00	1.25	1.50
1962D 334,948,380		0.80	1.00	1.25	
1963 . . . . . .(3,075,645) . .126,725,645		0.80	1.00	1.25	1.50
1963, Pf, DblDieRev					400.00
1963D 421,476,530		0.80	1.00	1.25	
1964* . . . . .(3,950,762) . .933,310,762		0.80	1.00	1.25	1.50
1964D* 1,357,517,180		0.80	1.00	1.25	
1964D, DblDieRev		50.00	250.00	300.00	

*Variations of 9 in date have either pointed or straight tail.

Clad Coinage — 1965 to date

Weight 2.27 grams; composition: outer layers of copper-nickel (.750 copper, .250 nickel) bonded to inner core of pure copper; diameter 17.9 mm; reeded edge. Silver Proofs: pre-1965 standards.

	Mintage	MS-65	PF-65		Mintage	MS-65	PF-65
1965 1,652,140,570		$0.45		1975S, Pf* . . . .(2,845,450)			1.25
1966 1,382,734,540		0.35		1976 568,760,000		0.40	
1967 2,244,007,320		0.30		1976D 695,222,774		0.40	
1968 424,470,400		0.25		1976S, Pf . . . . .(4,149,730)			1.00
1968D 480,748,280		0.25		1977 796,930,000		0.25	
1968S, Pf* . . . .(3,041,506)			$0.85	1977D 376,607,228		0.25	
1969 145,790,000		1.00		1977S, Pf . . . . .(3,251,152)			1.00
1969D 563,323,870		0.30		1978 663,980,000		0.25	
1969S, Pf . . . . .(2,934,631)			0.85	1978D 282,847,540		0.25	
1970 345,570,000		0.25		1978S, Pf . . . . .(3,127,781)			0.85
1970D 754,942,100		0.25		1979 315,440,000		0.25	
1970S, Pf* . . .(2,632,810)			0.85	1979D 390,921,184		0.25	
1971 162,690,000		0.50		1979S Pf . . . . .(3,677,175)			
1971D 377,914,240		0.40		Filled S			0.85
1971S, Pf . . . . .(3,220,733)			0.85	Clear S			1.50
1972 431,540,000		0.25		1980P 735,170,000		0.20	
1972D 330,290,000		0.25		1980D 719,354,321		0.20	
1972S, Pf . . . . .(3,260,996)			0.85	1980S, Pf . . . . .(3,554,806)			0.85
1973 315,670,000		0.25		1981P 676,650,000		0.20	
1973D 455,032,426		0.25		1981D 712,284,143		0.20	
1973S, Pf . . . . .(2,760,339)			0.85	1981S, Pf . . . . .(4,063,083)			0.85
1974 470,248,000		0.25		1982, (no mint mark)*		200.00	
1974D 571,083,000		0.25		1982P 519,475,000		3.00	
1974S, Pf . . . .(2,612,568)			1.00	1982D 542,713,584		1.50	
1975 585,673,900		0.30		1982S, Pf . . . . .(3,857,479)			1.50
1975D 313,705,300		0.25					

*1968, 1970, and 1975 Proof dimes without S mint mark were made in error. Some of the 1982 business strike dimes were also made without a mint mark. See page 73.

	Mintage	MS-65	PF-65		Mintage	MS-65	PF-65
1983P	647,025,000	$2.50		1994S, Silver Pf	(785,329)		$6.00
1983D	730,129,224	1.00		1995P	1,125,500,000	$0.25	
1983S, Pf*	(3,279,126)		$1.00	1995D	1,274,890,000	0.35	
1984P	856,669,000	0.30		1995S, Pf	(2,117,496)		17.50
1984D	704,803,976	0.50		1995S, Silver Pf	(679,985)		18.00
1984S, Pf	(3,065,110)		1.50	1996P	1,421,163,000	0.20	
1985P	705,200,962	0.50		1996D	1,400,300,000	0.20	
1985D	587,979,970	0.40		1996W ‡	1,457,000	15.00	
1985S, Pf	(3,362,821)		1.00	1996S, Pf	(1,750,244)		2.00
1986P	682,649,693	0.70		1996S, Silver Pf	(775,021)		6.50
1986D	473,326,970	0.60		1997P	991,640,000	0.20	
1986S, Pf	(3,010,497)		2.00	1997D	979,810,000	0.20	
1987P	762,709,481	0.20		1997S Pf	(2,055,000)		6.00
1987D	653,203,402	0.20		1997S Silver Pf	(741,678)		17.50
1987S, Pf	(4,227,728)		1.50	1998P	1,163,000,000	0.20	
1988P	1,030,550,000	0.20		1998D	1,172,250,000	0.20	
1988D	962,385,489	0.20		1998S Pf	(2,086,507)		2.00
1988S, Pf	(3,262,948)		2.00	1998S Silver Pf	(878,792)		6.00
1989P	1,298,400,000	0.20		1999P	2,164,000,000	0.20	
1989D	896,535,597	0.20		1999D	1,397,750,000	0.20	
1989S, Pf	(3,220,194)		2.50	1999S Pf	(2,543,401)		2.00
1990P	1,034,340,000	0.35		1999S Silver Pf	(800,000)		5.00
1990D	839,995,824	0.20		2000P	1,842,500,000	0.20	
1990S, Pf	(3,299,559)		1.75	2000D	1,818,700,000	0.20	
1991P	927,220,000	0.25		2000S Pf	(3,082,483)		1.00
1991D	601,241,114	0.25		2000S Silver Pf	(856,400)		3.50
1991S, Pf	(2,867,787)		2.50	2001P	1,369,590,000	0.20	
1992P	593,500,000	0.20		2001D	1,412,800,000	0.20	
1992D	616,273,932	0.20		2001S Pf	(2,294,043)		1.00
1992S, Pf	(2,858,981)		4.00	2001S Silver Pf	(889,697)		3.50
1992S, Silver Pf	1,317,579		5.00	2002P	1,187,500,000	0.20	
1993P	766,180,000	0.20		2002D	1,379,500,000	0.20	
1993D	750,110,166	0.20		2002S Pf	(2,277,720)		1.50
1993S, Pf	(2,633,439)		4.00	2002S Silver Pf	(888,826)		3.00
1993S, Silver Pf	(761,353)		6.00	2003P		0.20	
1994P	1,189,000,000	0.20		2003D		0.20	
1994D	1,303,268,110	0.20		2003S Pf			1.50
1994S, Pf	(2,484,594)		4.00	2003S Silver Pf			3.00
				2004P		0.20	
				2004D		0.20	
				2004S Pf			1.50
				2004S Silver Pf			3.00

*1983S Proof dimes without S mint mark were made in error. See page 75.
‡Issued in mint sets only.

BIBLIOGRAPHY

Ahwash, Kamal M. *Encyclopedia of United States Liberty Seated Dimes 1837-1891.* Kamal Press, 1977.
Davis, David; Logan, Russell; Lovejoy, Allen; McCloskey, John; Subjack, William.
  Early United States Dimes 1796-1837. Ypsilanti, Michigan, 1984.
Flynn, Kevin. *The Authoritive Reference on Roosevelt Dimes.* Brooklyn, NY, 2001
Greer, Brian, *The Complete Guide to Liberty Seated Dimes.* Virginia Beach, VA, 1992.
Kosoff, A. *United States Dimes from 1796.* New York, 1945.
Lange, David W. *The Complete Guide to Mercury Dimes.* Virginia Beach, VA 1993.
Lawrence, David, *The Complete Guide to Barber Dimes.* Virginia Beach, VA 1991.

TWENTY-CENT PIECES — 1875-1878

This short-lived coin was authorized by the Act of March 3, 1875. Soon after the appearance of the first twenty-cent pieces, people complained about the similarity in design and size to the quarter dollar. The eagle is very similar to that used on the Trade Dollar, but the edge of this coin is plain. Mint mark is positioned on the reverse below the eagle. Most of the 1876CC coins were melted at the mint and never released.

+ or – indicates change from previous year	TYPE COIN VALUES								
	G-4	F-12	EF-40	AU-50	MS-60	MS-63	MS-65	PF-60	PF-63	PF-65
1875-1878 ....100.+	120.+	175.+	300.	500.+	1,000	5,000.-	800.-	2,200+	8,500.+

Designer William Barber; weight 5 grams; composition: .900 silver, .100 copper; diameter 22 mm; plain edge; mints: Philadelphia, Carson City, San Francisco.

G-4 GOOD—*LIBERTY on shield obliterated. Letters and date legible.*
VG-8 VERY GOOD—*One or two letters in LIBERTY may show. Other details will be bold.*
F-12 FINE—*At least 3 letters of LIBERTY show.*
VF-20 VERY FINE—*LIBERTY completely readable, but partly weak.*
EF-40 EXTREMELY FINE—*LIBERTY sharp. Only slight wear on high points of the coin*
AU-50 ABOUT UNCIRCULATED—*Slight trace of wear on breast, headand knees.*
MS-60 UNCIRCULATED—*No trace of wear. Light blemishes.*
MS-63 SELECT UNCIRCULATED—*Some distracting blemishes in prime focal areas. Luster may be impaired.*

	Mintage	G-4	VG-8	F-12	VF-20	EF-40	AU-50	MS-60	MS-63	PF-63
1875 ...(2,790) ..39,700		$100.	$110.	$150.	$200.	$300.	$400.	$600.	$1,000.	$2,200.
1875CC 133,290		125.	150.	250.	300.	400.	550.	800.	1,800.	
1875S 1,155,000		100.	110.	120.	150.	175.	300.	500.	1,000.	
1876 ...(1,260) ..15,900		125.	150.	225.	300.	400.	500.	700.	1,200.	2,400.
1876CC 10,000								80,000.		
1877 .....(350) 350					2,000.	2,200.				3,500.
1878 .....(600) 600					1,800.	2,000.				3,200.

QUARTER DOLLARS — 1796 to Date

Authorized in 1792, this denomination was not issued until four years later. The first coinage, dated 1796, follows the pattern of the early half-dimes and dimes by the absence of a mark of value. In 1804 the value "25c" was added to the reverse. Figures were used until 1838 when the term "QUAR. DOL." appeared. It was not until 1892 that the value was spelled out entirely.

The first type weighed 104 grains which remained standard until modified to $103^1/_8$ grains by the Act of January 18, 1837. As with the dime and half dime, the weight was reduced and arrows placed at the date in 1853. Rays were placed in the field of the reverse during that year only.

The law of 1873 also affected the quarter, for the weight was slightly increased and arrows again placed at the date.

Proofs of some dates prior to 1856 are known to exist, and all are rare.

+ or – indicates change from previous year	TYPE COIN VALUES									
	G-4	F-12	EF-40	AU-50	MS-60	MS-63	MS-65	PF-60	PF-63	PF-65
Drpd Bust-SE 1796............5,000.+	12,000.+	22,000.+	28,000.+	40,000.+	55,000.+	—				
Drpd Bust-HE 1804-1807 ... 200.	400.	1,700.	2,800.+	4,500.	8,500.					
Lg. Bust 1815-1828 .... 50.	100.	625.	1,200.+	2,200.	3,500.-					
Sm. Bust 1831-1838............ 50.+	65.+	300.+	525.-	825.+	2,500.+	13,000.-				
Lib. Seated-NM 1838-1865.. 17.+	32.+	80.+	150.+	550.+	900.+	3,500.-	500.+	1,000.+	4,500.-	
Lib. Seat-A&R 1853 .... 17.+	30.+	150.	300.-	950.	2,000.-	15,000.-				
Lib. Seat-Arr. 1854-1855 .... 16.+	30.+	80.	200.-	500.	1,200.	7,000.-	6,000.	9,000.	2,500.+	
Lib. Seat-WM 1866-1891 .... 25.+	50.+	150.+	200.+	550.+	900.+	1,500.+	325.-	800.+	2,000.	
Lib. Seat-Arr. 1873-1874 .... 20.+	32.+	200.	400.	800.+	1,500.-	3,500.-	650.-	1,500.+	7,000.+	
Barber 1892-1916............... 5.+	18.	70.	110.	200.+	300.+	1,000.-	325.-	600.	1,700.	
Stand Lib. 1 1916-1917 ...... 22.+	50.+	80.+	175.+	225.+	300.+	900.+				
Stand Lib. 2 1917-1930 ...... 15.+	25.+	40.+	75.+	125.+	200.+	450.-				
Washington 1932-1964 ...... 1.50	3.+	3.	4.+	5.+	6.+	15.+	2.-	3.	5.	

QUARTER DOLLARS

DRAPED BUST TYPE, SMALL EAGLE REVERSE 1796

Designer Robert Scot; weight 6.74 grams; composition: .8924 silver, .1076 copper; approx. diameter 27.5 mm; reeded edge. All coined at Philadelphia.

AG-3 ABOUT GOOD—*Details clear enough to identify.*
G-4 GOOD—*Date readable. Bust outlined, but no detail.*
VG-8 VERY GOOD—*All but deepest drapery folds worn smooth. Hairlines nearly gone and curls lack detail.*
F-12 FINE—*All drapery lines visible. Hair partly worn.*
VF-20 VERY FINE—*Only left side of drapery is indistinct.*
EF-40 EXTREMELY FINE—*Hair well outlined and detailed.*
AU-50 ABOUT UNCIRCULATED— *Slight trace of wear on shoulder and highest waves of hair.*
MS-60 UNCIRCULATED—*No trace of wear. Light blemishes.*
MS-63 SELECT UNCIRCULATED—*Some distracting contact marks or blemishes in prime focal areas.*
  Luster may be impaired.

Mintage	AG-3	G-4	VG-8	F-12	VF-20	EF-40	AU-50	MS-60	MS-63
1796 . .6,146	$2,500.	$5,000.	$7,500.	$12,000.	$17,000.	$22,000.	$28,000.	$40,000.	$55,000.

DRAPED BUST TYPE, HERALDIC EAGLE REVERSE 1804-1807

	Mintage	AG-3	G-4	VG-8	F-12	VF-20	EF-40	AU-50	MS-60	MS-63
1804 6,738		800.	1,800.	2,400.	3,300.	4,500.	9,000.	17,000.	40,000.	—
1805 121,394		100.	200.	275.	400.	800.	1,700.	2,800.	4,600.	8,500.
1806, 6/5 . . . . } 206,124		110.	220.	300.	500.	1,000.	2,250.	3,500.	5,500.	16,000.
1806 . . . . . . }		100.	200.	275.	400.	800.	1,700.	2,800.	4,500.	8,500.
1807 . . . . . . }.220,643		100.	200.	275.	400.	800.	1,700.	2,800.	4,500.	8,500.

CAPPED BUST TYPE 1815-1838
Variety 1 — Large Size 1815-1828

Designer John Reich; weight 6.74 grams; composition: .8924 silver, .1076 copper; approx. diameter 27 mm; reeded edge. All coined at Philadelphia.

AG-3 ABOUT GOOD—*Details clear enough to identify.*
G-4 GOOD—*Date, letters and stars readable. Hair under headband smooth. Cap lines worn smooth.*
VG-8 VERY GOOD—*Rim well defined. Main details visible. Full LIBERTY on cap. Hair above eye nearly smooth.*
F-12 FINE—*All hairlines show but drapery has only part details. Shoulder clasp distinct.*
VF-20 VERY FINE—*All details show, but some wear. Clasp and ear sharp.*
EF-40 EXTREMELY FINE—*All details show distinctly. Hair well outlined.*
AU-50 ABOUT UNCIRCULATED—*Slight trace of wear on tips of curls and aove the eye, and on the wing and claw tips.*
MS-60 UNCIRCULATED—*No trace of wear. Light blemishes.*
MS-63 SELECT UNCIRCULATED—*Some distracting contact marks or blemishes in prime focal areas.*
  Luster may be impaired.

QUARTER DOLLARS

	Mintage	AG-3	G-4	VG-8	F-12	VF-20	EF-40	AU-50	MS-60	MS-63
1815	.89,235	$25.	$55.	$80.	$100.	$325.	$800.	$1,200.	$2,500.	$4,500.
1818, 8/5 . . }	361,174	25.	55.	80.	125.	350.	850.	1,300.	2,750.	4,600.
1818, NmlDt . }		25.	55.	75.	100.	300.	800.	1,200.	2,400.	4,500.
1819, Sm 9 . . }	144,000	25.	55.	75.	100.	300.	800.	1,200.	2,400.	4,500.
1819, Lg 9 . . . }		25.	55.	75.	100.	300.	800.	1,200.	2,400.	4,500.

1820 Small 0 **1820 Large 0** **1822, 25 over 50c**

1820, Sm 0 }	127,444	25.	55.	75.	100.	300.	800.	1,200.	2,400.	4,500.
1820, Lg 0 }		25.	55.	75.	100.	300.	800.	1,200.	2,400.	4,500.
1821	.216,851	25.	55.	75.	100.	300.	800.	1,200.	2,400.	4,500.
1822 All Kinds	.604,080	25.	60.	90.	135.	350.	850.	1,600.	3,000.	5,500.
1822, 25/50c		600.	1,600.	2,750.	4,000.	6,000.	9,500.	16,000.	20,000.	—
1823, 3/2	.17,800	4,500.	9,500.	14,500.	20,000.	25,000.	40,000.	55,000.		—

1825, 5 over 2 (wide date) **1825, 5 over 3 or 4 (close date)**

1824, 4/2 . . }		35.	80.	110.	225.	550.	1,500.	3,000.	6,000.	
1825, 5/2 . . }	168,000	35.	75.	100.	150.	400.	1,000.	1,500.	3,000.	5,000.
1825, 5/4 . . }		25.	50.	60.	100.	250.	625.	1,200.	2,200.	3,500.
1827,Original . . .	.4,000									100,000.
(Curl base 2 in 25c)										
1827,Restrike (Square base 2 in 25c)										50,000.
1828 All Kinds	102,000	25.	50.	60.	100.	250.	650.	1,300.	2,500.	5,000.
1828, 25/50c		60.	125.	250.	400.	850.	1,600.	3,000.	7,750.	—

Variety 2 — Reduced Size, No Motto on Reverse 1831-1838

Designer William Kneass; weight 6.74 grams; composition: .8924 silver, .1076 copper; diameter 24.3 mm; reeded edge. All coined at Philadelphia.

G-4 GOOD—*Bust well defined. Hair under headband smooth. Date, letters, stars readable. Scant rims.*
VG-8 VERY GOOD—*Details apparent but worn on high spots. Rims strong. Full LIBERTY.*
F-12 FINE—*All hairlines visible. Drapery partly worn. Shoulder clasp distinct.*
VF-20 VERY FINE—*Only top spots worn. Clasp sharp. Ear distinct.*
EF-40 EXTREMELY FINE—*Hair details and clasp are bold and clear.*
AU-50 ABOUT UNCIRCULATED—*Slight trace of wear on hair around the forehead an on the cheek and at the top and bottom tips of eagle's wings and left claw.*
MS-60 UNCIRCULATED—*No trace of wear. Light blemishes.*
MS-63 SELECT UNCIRCULATED—*Some distracting contact marks or blemishes in prime focal areas. Luster may be impaired.*

QUARTER DOLLARS

	Mintage	G-4	VG-8	F-12	VF-20	EF-40	AU-50	MS-60	MS-63
		Small Letters (1831)				**Large Letters**		**O/F in OF**	
1831, SmL	} 398,000	$50.	$55.	$65.	$95.	$300.	$525.	$825.	$2,500.
1831, LgL		50.	55.	65.	95.	300.	525.	825.	2,500.
1832	320,000	50.	55.	65.	95.	300.	525.	825.	2,500.
1833	156,000	55.	60.	75.	125.	350.	625.	1,400.	3,000.
1834	} 286,000	50.	55.	65.	95.	300.	525.	825.	2,500.
1834 O/F in OF ..		50.	55.	75.	125.	350.	600.	1,000.	3,000.
1835 1,952,000	1,952,000	50.	55.	65.	95.	300.	525.	825.	2,500.
1836	472,000	50.	55.	65.	95.	300.	525.	825.	3,000.
1837	252,400	50.	55.	65.	95.	300.	525.	825.	2,500.
1838	366,000	50.	55.	65.	95.	300.	525.	825.	2,500.

LIBERTY SEATED TYPE 1838-1891
Variety 1 — No Motto Above Eagle 1838-1853

Designer Christian Gobrecht; weight 6.68 grams; composition: .900 silver, .100 copper; diameter 24.3 mm; reeded edge; mints: Philadelphia, New Orleans.

G-4 GOOD—*Scant rim. LIBERTY on shield worn off. Date and letters readable.*
VG-8 VERY GOOD—*Rim fairly defined, at least 3 letters in LIBERTY evident.*
F-12 FINE—*LIBERTY complete, but partly weak.*
VF-20 VERY FINE—*LIBERTY strong.*
EF-40 EXTREMELY FINE—*Complete LIBERTY and edges of scroll. Clasp shows plainly.*
AU-50 ABOUT UNCIRCULATED—*Slight wear on Liberty's knees and breast and on the neck, wing toms, and claws.*
MS-60 UNCIRCULATED—*No trace of wear. Light blemishes.*
MS-63 SELECT UNCIRCULATED—*Some distracting contact marks or blemishes in prime focal areas. Luster may be impaired.*

No Drapery from Elbow   **Drapery from Elbow**

Mint mark location is on the reverse below the eagle.

	Mintage	G-4	VG-8	F-12	VF-20	EF-40	AU-50	MS-60	MS-63
1838, NoDrap	466,000	19.	25.	40.	75.	325.	500.	1,200.	4,000.
1839, NoDrap	491,146	19.	25.	40.	75.	325.	500.	1,200.	4,000.
1840O, NoDrap ...	382,200	22.	30.	45.	90.	375.	550.	1,300.	4,000.
1840, Drapery	188,127	22.	30.	45.	80.	175.	250.	900.	2,500.
1840O, Drapery ..	43,000	25.	37.	65.	100.	225.	450.	1,400.	2,750.
1841	120,000	45.	55.	100.	160.	225.	300.	900.	1,500.
1841O	452,000	20.	27.	42.	70.	165.	275.	800.	1,400.

Small Date   **Large Date**

	Mintage	G-4	VG-8	F-12	VF-20	EF-40	AU-50	MS-60	MS-63
1842,SmDt Pfs only								30,000.	
1842, LgDt	88,000	75.	100.	160.	250.	400.	600.	2,000.	3,000.

	Mintage	G-4	VG-8	F-12	VF-20	EF-40	AU-50	MS-60	MS-63
18420, SmDt ⎱	769,000	375.	500.	950.	1,600.	3,200.	7,000.		
18420, LgDt ⎰		21.	25.	45.	70.	175.	300.	1,500.	4,000.
1843	645,600	17.	20.	35.	40.	85.	150.	600.	900.
18430	968,000	21.	31.	55.	100.	235.	650.	1,700.	3,500.
1844	421,200	17.	20.	35.	45.	90.	150.	550.	900.
18440	740,000	19.	23.	45.	75.	200.	250.	1,100.	2,500.
1845	922,000	17.	20.	32.	45.	80.	150.	550.	1,000.
1846	510,000	17.	20.	35.	46.	90.	150.	550.	1,000.
1847	734,000	17.	20.	32.	45.	80.	150.	550.	1,000.
18470	368,000	25.	35.	70.	125.	235.	650.	2,000.	5,000.
1848	146,000	28.	38.	75.	125.	175.	275.	1,100.	2,800.
1849	340,000	20.	25.	50.	70.	150.	250.	800.	1,500.
18490 . . . . . ‡incl. below		350.	500.	850.	1,700.	3,200.	5,500.		
1850	190,800	25.	38.	60.	80.	150.	200.	800.	1,800.
18500	412,000	25.	38.	60.	80.	150.	400.	1,300.	2,700.
1851	160,000	33.	47.	75.	125.	175.	250.	850.	1,750.
18510	88,000	150.	250.	400.	600.	1,200.	2,500.	5,000.	
1852	177,060	35.	45.	75.	135.	200.	250.	750.	1,000.
18520	96,000	175.	250.	400.	650.	1,500.	3,250.	7,500.	15,000.
1853*,Recut Dt,no arrows or rays 44,200		225.	325.	475.	600.	1,000.	1,600.	2,800.	3,500.

‡Mintage for 18490 included with 18500.
*Beware of altered 1858, or removed arrows and rays.

Variety 2 — Arrows at Date, Rays Around Eagle 1853 Only

The reduction in weight is indicated by the arrows at the date. Rays were added on the reverse side in the field around the eagle. The arrows were retained through 1855, but the rays were omitted after 1853.

Weight 6.22 grams; composition: .900 silver, .100 copper; diameter 24.3 mm; reeded edge; mints: Philadelphia, New Orleans, San Francisco, Carson City.

1853, 3 over 4   18540, Huge O

		G-4	VG-8	F-12	VF-20	EF-40	AU-50	MS-60	MS-63
1853 . . . . . . ⎱	15,210,020	17.	20.	30.	50.	150.	300.	950.	2,000.
1853, 3/4 . . . ⎰		40.	70.	100.	200.	350.	600.	1,800.	5,500.
18530	1,332,000	20.	25.	40.	75.	225.	1,000.	2,700.	7,000.

Variety 3 — Arrows at Date, No Rays 1854-1855

		G-4	VG-8	F-12	VF-20	EF-40	AU-50	MS-60	MS-63
1854	12,380,000	16.	18.	32.	40.	80.	200.	500.	1,200.
18540 . . . . . ⎱	1,484,000	17.	20.	30.	50.	100.	200.	800.	1,800.
18540 Huge O ⎰		600.	1,000.	1,500.	2,750.	4,500.	10,000.	—	—
1855	2,857,000	16.	18.	32.	40.	80.	200.	550.	1,200.
18550	176,000	35.	50.	100.	250.	350.	750.	2,750.	7,000.
1855S	396,400	35.	50.	85.	140.	300.	700.	1,800.	5,000.

Variety 1 Resumed 1856-1865
(Weight Standard of 1853)

	Mintage	G-4	VG-8	F-12	VF-20	EF-40	AU-50	MS-60	MS-63	PF-63
1856	7,264,000	$17.	$20.	$32.	$40.	$60.	$150.	$400.	$700.	$4,250.
18560	968,000	17.	21.	35.	45.	100.	200.	1,100.	1,500.	

	Mintage	G-4	VG-8	F-12	VF-20	EF-40	AU-50	MS-60	MS-63	PF-63
1856S ...... }	286,000	$35.	$50.	$75.	$200.	$350.	$750.	$2,200.	$8,000.	
1856S, S/S ... }		40.	65.	130.	275.	600.	900.	2,400.	—	
1857 9,644,000		17.	20.	30.	40.	60.	150.	325.	650.	$3,500.
1857O 1,180,000		17.	20.	30.	40.	75.	250.	1,000.	2,000.	
1857S 82,000		60.	100.	180.	350.	600.	900.	2,500.	6,000.	
1858 ..(300+) 7,368,000		17.	20.	30.	40.	60.	150.	325.	650.	2,250.
1858O 520,000		17.	20.	35.	50.	125.	350.	1,400.	2,500.	
1858S 121,000		45.	75.	125.	275.	525.	1,000.	5,000.	—	
1859 ..(800) .1,344,000		17.	20.	30.	40.	60.	150.	325.	900.	1,250.
1859O 260,000		20.	25.	50.	65.	120.	350.	1,200.	2,500.	
1859S 80,000		80.	125.	200.	325.	1,000.	7,500.	—	—	
1860 ..(1,000) ...805,400		18.	20.	30.	40.	60.	150.	400.	700.	1,100.
1860O 388,000		18.	23.	35.	45.	75.	350.	1,100.	1,800.	
1860S 56,000		150.	235.	400.	825.	2,500.	4,000.	—	—	
1861 ..(1,000) ..4,854,600		17.	20.	30.	40.	60.	150.	400.	700.	1,100.
1861S 96,000		55.	90.	200.	320.	800.	1,800.	—	—	
1862 ...(550) ...932,550		17.	20.	30.	40.	60.	150.	400.	800.	1,100.
1862S 67,000		45.	65.	135.	235.	500.	900.	2,400.	6,000.	
1863 ...(460) ...192,060		25.	35.	60.	90.	150.	300.	625.	900.	1,100.
1864 ...(470) ...94,070		55.	65.	100.	150.	235.	400.	800.	1,200.	1,100.
1864S 20,000		250.	400.	625.	950.	1,800.	3,000.	—	—	
1865 ...(500) 59,300		55.	65.	120.	160.	250.	350.	700.	1,200.	1,100.
1865S 41,000		70.	100.	150.	375.	550.	1,000.	2,350.	3,300.	
1866 ....(Unique)										—

The 1866 Proof quarter, half and dollar without motto are not mentioned in the Director's Report, and were not issued for circulation.

Variety 4 Motto Above Eagle 1866-1873

The motto IN GOD WE TRUST was added to the reverse side in 1866. As on the half dollar and silver dollar, the motto has been retained since that time.

1866 ...(725)	17,525	275.	450.	500.	700.	1,000.	1,200.	1,800.	2,500.	900.
1866S	28,000	175.	275.	500.	800.	1,200.	1,800.	3,500.	5,000.	
1867 ...(625)	20,625	200.	250.	400.	500.	600.	800.	1,250.	4,000.	900.
1867S	48,000	175.	250.	350.	450.	700.	900.	4,000.	—	
1868 ...(600)	30,000	90.	125.	175.	250.	325.	500.	850.	1,400.	900.
1868S	96,000	75.	100.	125.	225.	500.	800.	2,600.	4,000.	
1869 ...(600)	16,600	250.	300.	400.	500.	700.	900.	1,500.	2,500.	900.
1869S	76,000	65.	100.	175.	250.	500.	1,000.	2,400.	4,000.	
1870 ..(1,000)	87,400	50.	60.	100.	150.	250.	400.	800.	1,200.	900.
1870CC	8,340	2,200.	3,500.	6,500.	10,000.	18,000.	25,000.	—	—	
1871 ...(960)	119,160	30.	40.	50.	100.	150.	300.	650.	1,000.	800.
1871CC	10,890	1,500.	2,500.	4,000.	12,000.	20,000.	—	—	—	
1871S	30,900	250.	350.	450.	600.	900.	1,500.	3,000.	4,000.	
1872 ...(950)	182,950	25.	35.	50.	100.	150.	200.	800.	1,600.	800.

QUARTER DOLLARS

	Mintage	G-4	VG-8	F-12	VF-20	EF-40	AU-50	MS-60	MS-63	PF-63
1872CC	22,850	$450.	$750.	$1,200.	$2,400.	$4,000.	$6,000.	$14,000.		
1872S	83,000	600.	800.	1,200.	1,600.	2,200.	3,200.	5,500.		
1873, Cl 3	(600) 40,600	100.	200.	300.	450.	650.	900.		2,200. $3,200.	$800.
1873, Op 3	172,000	25.	35.	55.	85.	150.	200.	550.	900.	
1873CC	4,000 (5 known)				—	—	—	185,000.		

Variety 5 — Arrows at Date 1873-1874

Arrows were placed at the date in the years 1873 and 1874 to denote the change of weight from 6.22 to 6.25 grams.

Weight 6.25 grams; composition: .900 silver, .100 copper; diameter 24.3 mm; reeded edge; mints: Philadelphia, San Francisco, Carson City, New Orleans.

	Mintage	G-4	VG-8	F-12	VF-20	EF-40	AU-50	MS-60	MS-63	PF-63
1873	(540) 1,271,700	20.	22.	32.	60.	200.	400.	800.	1,500.	1,500.
1873CC	12,462	1,500.	2,400.	4,800.	7,500.	12,500.	18,000.	35,000.	65,000.	
1873S	156,000	22.	30.	60.	95.	265.	500.	1,100.	2,200.	
1874	(700) 471,900	20.	22.	35.	65.	200.	425.	900.	1,600.	1,500.
1874S	392,000	20.	30.	60.	95.	265.	425.	900.	1,600.	

1877S, S over horizontal S

Variety 4 Resumed 1875-1891

	Mintage	G-4	VG-8	F-12	VF-20	EF-40	AU-50	MS-60	MS-63	PF-63
1875	(700) 4,293,500	17.	20.	30.	35.	55.	150.	250.	500.	600.
1875CC	140,000	60.	90.	150.	300.	500.	700.	1,700.	2,200.	
1875S	680,000	23.	37.	60.	100.	200.	300.	600.	1,100.	
1876	(1,150) 17,817,150	17.	20.	30.	35.	55.	150.	250.	500.	600.
1876CC *	4,944,000	25.	35.	45.	55.	90.	175.	450.	900.	
1876S	8,596,000	17.	20.	30.	35.	55.	150.	250.	500.	
1877	(510) 10,911,710	17.	20.	30.	35.	55.	150.	250.	500.	600.
1877CC	4,192,000	25.	35.	45.	55.	90.	175.	450.	800.	
1877S	8,996,000	17.	20.	30.	35.	55.	150.	250.	500.	
1877S, /horizontal S		—	—	75.	150.	250.	400.	800.	1,800.	
1878	(800) 2,260,800	17.	20.	30.	35.	55.	150.	250.	500.	600.
1878CC	996,000	25.	40.	50.	100.	150.	200.	600.	1,000.	
1878S	140,000	75.	150.	200.	275.	500.	650.	1,300.	2,100.	
1879	(1,100) 14,700	120.	140.	200.	225.	300.	350.	550.	750.	600.
1880	(1,355) 14,955	120.	140.	200.	225.	300.	350.	550.	750.	600.
1881	(975) 12,975	150.	175.	235.	275.	350.	450.	600.	800.	600.

*Variety with fine edge reeding is scarcer than that with normally spaced reeding.

QUARTER DOLLARS

	Mintage	G-4	VG-8	F-12	VF-20	EF-40	AU-50	MS-60	MS-63	PF-63
1882	.(1,100) . . .16,300	130.	160.	210.	265.	310.	400.	600.	800.	600.
1883	.(1,039) . . .15,439	135.	165.	210.	265.	310.	400.	600.	600.	600.
1884	. . .(875) 8,875	225.	250.	300.	350.	400.	500.	700.	900.	600.
1885	. . .(930) . . .14,530	125.	150.	220.	265.	310.	400.	600.	900.	600.
1886	. . .(886) 5,886	250.	350.	450.	550.	650.	750.	850.	1,200.	700.
1887	. . .(710) . . .10,710	200.	250.	325.	375.	450.	500.	650.	900.	600.
1888	. . .(832) . . .10,833	175.	225.	300.	400.	475.	550.	650.	800.	600.
1888S	1,216,000	17.	20.	30.	40.	60.	150.	250.	750.	
1889	. . .(711) . . .12,711	150.	175.	225.	275.	325.	400.	600.	800.	700.
1890	. . .(590) . . .80,590	50.	175.	95.	115.	175.	300.	500.	750.	600.
1891	. . .(600) 3,920,600	17.	55.	30.	40.	60.	150.	250.	500.	600.
1891O	6,800	125.	175.	300.	450.	800.	1,250.	3,000.	5,000.	
1891S	2,216,000	17.	20.	30.	40.	65.	150.	250.	500.	

—— BARBER or LIBERTY HEAD TYPE 1892-1916 ——

Like other silver coins of this type, the quarter dollars mintage from 1892 to 1916 were designed by Charles E. Barber. His initial B is found at the truncation of the neck of Liberty. There are two varieties of the 1892 reverse: 1) Eagle's wing covers only half of E in UNITED. 2) Eagle's wing covers most of E. Coins of the first variety reverse are somewhat scarcer than those of the second variety.

Designer Charles E. Barber; weight 6.25 grams; composition: .900 silver, .100 copper; diameter 24.3 mm; reeded edge; mints: Philadelphia, Denver, New Orleans, San Francisco. Net weight: .18084 oz. pure silver.

G-4 GOOD—*Date and legends readable. LIBERTY worn off headband.*
VG-8 VERY GOOD—*Minimum of 3 letters in LIBERTY readable.*
F-12 FINE—*LIBERTY completely readable but not sharp.*
VF-20 VERY FINE—*All letters in LIBERTY evenly plain.*
EF-40 EXTREMELY FINE—*LIBERTY bold, and its ribbon distinct.*
AU-50 ABOUT UNCIRCULATED—*Slight trace of wear above forehead, on the cheek and on the eagle's head wings and tail.*
MS-60 UNCIRCULATED—*No trace of wear. Light blemishes.*
MS-63 SELECT UNCIRCULATED—*Some distracting contact marks or blemishes in prime focal areas. Luster may be impaired.*
PF-63—*Reflective surfaces with only a few blemishes in secondary focal places. No major flaws.*

Mint mark location is on the reverse below the eagle.

	Mintage	G-4	VG-8	F-12	VF-20	EF-40	AU-50	MS-60	MS-63	PF-63
1892	. .(1,245) .8,237,245	$5.00	$8.	$20.	$35.	$70.	$125.	$200.	$300.	$600.
1892O	2,460,000	8.00	14.	35.	50.	90.	150.	300.	500.	
1892S	964,079	20.00	40.	70.	100.	150.	300.	500.	900.	
1893	. . .(792) .5,444,815	5.00	8.	25.	35.	75.	125.	200.	400.	600.
1893O	3,396,000	6.00	10.	25.	40.	80.	150.	300.	500.	
1893S	1,454,535	10.00	25.	50.	100.	150.	300.	500.	1,200.	
1894	. . .(972) .3,432,972	5.00	8.	30.	40.	85.	150.	250.	500.	600.
1894O	2,852,000	6.00	10.	35.	55.	90.	200.	350.	750.	
1894S	2,648,821	7.00	10.	35.	55.	90.	200.	350.	750.	
1895	. . .(880) .4,440,880	5.00	8.	30.	40.	75.	150.	250.	500.	600.
1895O	2,816,000	6.00	10.	35.	60.	100.	200.	400.	1,000.	
1895S	1,764,681	10.00	18.	45.	75.	100.	250.	400.	1,000.	
1896	. . .(762) .3,874,762	5.00	8.	25.	35.	75.	150.	250.	450.	600.
1896O	1,484,000	10.00	25.	90.	250.	400.	650.	900.	1,800.	
1896S	188,039	500.00	750.	1,200.	1,800.	3,000.	4,000.	5,000.	8,000.	
1897	. . .(731) .8,140,731	5.00	8.	20.	32.	70.	125.	200.	300.	600.
1897O	1,414,800	10.00	25.	80.	200.	375.	600.	800.	1,700.	

QUARTER DOLLARS

	Mintage	G-4	VG-8	F-12	VF-20	EF-40	AU-50	MS-60	MS-63	PF-63
1897S	542,229	25.00	60.	175.	250.	375.	600.	1,000.	1,600.	
1898	..(735) 11,100,735	5.00	7.	20.	35.	70.	125.	200.	300.	900.
1898O	1,868,000	8.00	18.	60.	125.	250.	375.	600.	1,500.	
1898S	1,020,592	7.00	15.	40.	50.	85.	200.	400.	1,400.	
1899	..(846) 12,624,846	5.00	7.	21.	32.	75.	125.	200.	300.	600.
1899O	2,644,000	8.00	13.	27.	45.	90.	250.	400.	900.	
1899S	708,000	12.00	25.	60.	80.	125.	250.	500.	1,200.	
1900	..(912) 10,016,912	5.00	7.	20.	32.	75.	150.	200.	300.	600.
1900O	3,416,000	8.00	20.	55.	100.	125.	350.	600.	900.	
1900S	1,858,585	7.00	12.	35.	50.	75.	125.	400.	1,000.	
1901	..(813) .8,892,813	7.00	10.	20.	35.	75.	125.	200.	300.	600.
1901O	1,612,000	30.00	50.	120.	225.	400.	700.	900.	2,000.	
1901S	72,664	4,000.00	6,500.	10,000.	13,000.	15,000.	18,000.	20,000.	35,000.	
1902	..(777) 12,197,744	6.00	8.	18.	30.	70.	125.	200.	300.	600.
1902O	4,748,000	7.00	14.	40.	75.	125.	200.	450.	1,500.	
1902S	1,524,612	10.00	15.	40.	75.	125.	225.	500.	1,000.	
1903	..(755) .9,670,064	5.50	8.	18.	30.	70.	125.	200.	500.	600.
1903O	3,500,000	7.00	10.	35.	50.	90.	250.	400.	1,400.	
1903S	1,036,000	12.00	18.	40.	60.	110.	250.	450.	900.	
1904	..(670) .9,588,813	5.50	7.	18.	30.	70.	125.	200.	300.	600.
1904O	2,456,000	7.00	12.	45.	75.	200.	400.	800.	1,500.	
1905	..(727) .4,968,250	6.50	9.	25.	30.	70.	125.	200.	400.	600.
1905O	1,230,000	12.00	25.	75.	150.	225.	350.	500.	1,300.	
1905S	1,884,000	8.00	12.	35.	55.	100.	200.	350.	1,200.	
1906	..(675) .3,656,435	6.00	8.	18.	32.	70.	125.	200.	300.	600.
1906D	3,280,000	6.00	9.	25.	40.	75.	150.	250.	500.	
1906O	2,056,000	6.00	9.	35.	50.	90.	200.	300.	600.	
1907	..(575) .7,192,575	5.00	8.	18.	32.	70.	125.	200.	300.	600.
1907D	2,484,000	5.00	8.	25.	45.	80.	175.	250.	800.	
1907O	4,560,000	5.00	8.	21.	32.	70.	150.	225.	500.	
1907S	1,360,000	6.00	10.	40.	55.	125.	250.	500.	1,000.	
1908	..(545) .4,232,545	5.00	7.	21.	32.	70.	125.	200.	400.	600.
1908D	5,788,000	5.00	7.	21.	32.	70.	125.	250.	500.	
1908O	6,244,000	5.00	7.	18.	30.	70.	125.	200.	350.	
1908S	784,000	15.00	30.	75.	125.	275.	450.	800.	1,400.	
1909	.(1,127) .9,268,650	5.00	7.	21.	30.	70.	110.	200.	300.	600.
1909D	5,114,000	6.00	8.	20.	35.	75.	150.	250.	400.	
1909O	712,000	15.00	30.	80.	175.	300.	500.	800.	1,800.	
1909S	1,348,000	6.00	8.	30.	50.	80.	200.	300.	800.	
1910	..(896) .2,244,551	6.00	8.	25.	35.	70.	150.	200.	350.	600.
1910D	1,500,000	6.00	9.	40.	60.	100.	250.	400.	1,000.	
1911	..(677) .3,720,543	5.00	8.	18.	30.	70.	125.	200.	300.	600.
1911D	933,600	6.00	15.	80.	200.	300.	500.	750.	1,400.	
1911S	988,000	6.00	8.	50.	70.	150.	275.	400.	800.	
1912	..(705) .4,400,700	5.50	8.	18.	32.	70.	125.	200.	300.	600.
1912S	708,000	6.00	9.	40.	60.	100.	225.	400.	1,000.	
1913	..(893) ..484,613	12.00	20.	65.	150.	400.	500.	1,000.	1,200.	750.
1913D	1,450,800	7.00	10.	30.	50.	85.	175.	300.	400.	
1913S	40,000	750.00	1,250.	2,500.	3,500.	4,500.	5,000.	6,000.	8,000.	
1914	..(610) .6,244,610	5.00	7.	18.	32.	70.	125.	200.	300.	750.
1914D	3,046,000	5.00	7.	18.	32.	70.	125.	200.	300.	
1914S	264,000	60.00	85.	150.	225.	400.	600.	900.	1,500.	
1915	..(450) .3,480,450	5.00	7.	18.	32.	70.	125.	200.	300.	750.
1915D	3,694,000	5.00	7.	18.	32.	70.	125.	200.	300.	
1915S	704,000	6.00	9.	25.	40.	80.	200.	300.	500.	
1916	1,788,000	5.00	7.	18.	32.	70.	125.	200.	300.	
1916D	6,540,800	5.00	7.	18.	32.	70.	125.	200.	300.	

This type quarter was designed by Hermon A. MacNeil. The left arm of Liberty is upraised uncovering a shield in the attitude of protection. Her right hand bears the olive branch of peace. MacNeil's initial M is located above and to the right of the date.

There was a modification in 1917 to cover Liberty's exposed breast. The reverse has a new arrangement of the stars and the eagle is higher.

In 1925 a depression was made in the pedestal on which Liberty stands and which bears the date. On the earlier issues the dates wore off easily because they were too high and were not protected by other features of the coin. The new "recessed" dates proved more durable as a result of this change.

No Proof coins of this type were officially issued, but specimen strikings of the first variety, dated 1917, are known to exist.

Designer Hermon A. MacNeil. Standards same as previous issue; mints: Philadelphia, Denver, San Francisco.

G-4 GOOD—Date and lettering readable. Top of date worn. Liberty's right leg and toes worn off. Left leg and drapery lines show much wear.

VG-8 VERY GOOD—Distinct date. Toes show faintly. Drapery lines visible above her left leg.

F-12 FINE—High curve of right leg flat from thigh to ankle. Left leg shows only slight wear. Drapery lines over right thigh seen only at sides of leg.

VF-20 VERY FINE—Garment line across right leg will be worn but show at sides.

EF-40 EXTREMELY FINE—Flattened only at high spots. Her toes are sharp. Drapery lines across right leg are evident.

AU-50 ABOUT UNCIRCULATED—AU-50 Slight trace of wear on head, knee cap, shield's center, and the highest point on the eagle's body.

MS-60 UNCIRCULATED—No trace of wear but can have many contact marks. Surface may be spotted, or luster faded.

MS-63 SELECT UNCIRCULATED—No trace of wear. Light blemishes. Attractive mint luster.

(Some modifications must be made for grading Variety 2)

Variety 1

Mint mark location is on   No Stars Below Eagle
obverse at left of date.

Uncirculated pieces with fully struck head of Liberty are worth more than double the prices listed below.

	Mintage	G-4	VG-8	F-12	VF-20	EF-40	AU-50	MS-60	MS-63
1916	52,000	$2,500.	$4,200.	$6,500.	$7,500.	$8,500.	$11,000.	$12,500.	$17,000.
1917, Variety 1	8,740,000	22.	35.	50.	60.	80.	175.	225.	300.
1917D, Variety 1	1,509,200	25.	35.	50.	65.	100.	175.	225.	350.
1917S, Variety 1	1,952,000	30.	40.	50.	75.	150.	200.	300.	400.

Variety 2	**Stars Below Eagle**		**1918S, 8 over 7**

	Mintage	G-4	VG-8	F-12	VF-20	EF-40	AU-50	MS-60	MS-63
1917, Variety 2	13,880,000	20.	25.	30.	35.	50.	85.	135.	225.
1917D, Variety 2	6,224,400	40.	45.	65.	75.	100.	140.	200.	300.
1917S, Variety 2	5,552,000	40.	50.	70.	75.	85.	120.	200.	300.
1918	14,240,000	15.	18.	30.	35.	50.	90.	135.	225.

QUARTER DOLLARS

	Mintage	G-4	VG-8	F-12	VF-20	EF-40	AU-50	MS-60	MS-63
1918D	7,380,000	$25.	$30.	$50.	$65.	$90.	$140.	$200.	$350.
1918S,		18.	20.	35.	40.	50.	90.	200.	300.
NmIDt	11,072,000								
1918S, 8/7		1,500.	1,750.	2,500.	3,200.	5,200.	9,000.	15,000.	30,000.
1919	11,324,000	35.	45.	55.	60.	75.	110.	150.	200.
1919D	1,944,000	75.	100.	175.	275.	400.	500.	700.	1,400.
1919S	1,836,000	75.	100.	175.	285.	500.	600.	750.	1,750.
1920	27,860,000	15.	20.	30.	35.	40.	75.	150.	225.
1920D	3,586,400	50.	55.	75.	100.	135.	190.	250.	800.
1920S	6,380,000	20.	25.	35.	40.	60.	100.	225.	800.
1921	1,916,000	160.	200.	300.	400.	475.	625.	800.	1,000.
1923	9,716,000	16.	20.	30.	35.	45.	75.	140.	225.
1923S	1,360,000	250.	350.	450.	600.	800.	900.	1,000.	1,200.
1924	10,920,000	17.	20.	25.	32.	40.	90.	125.	225.
1924D	3,112,000	50.	65.	90.	120.	175.	200.	250.	325.
1924S	2,860,000	26.	32.	40.	45.	95.	200.	275.	950.

Recessed Date Style 1925-1930

	Mintage	G-4	VG-8	F-12	VF-20	EF-40	AU-50	MS-60	MS-63
1925	12,280,000	3.	5.	7.	15.	35.	80.	125.	235.
1926	11,316,000	3.	5.	7.	15.	35.	75.	125.	235.
1926D	1,716,000	7.	10.	18.	35.	60.	100.	150.	235.
1926S	2,700,000	4.	6.	12.	25.	120.	225.	350.	800.
1927	11,912,000	3.	5.	7.	15.	35.	70.	120.	225.
1927D	976,000	15.	18.	25.	60.	130.	175.	250.	300.
1927S	396,000	25.	30.	75.	250.	1,000.	2,800.	3,750.	6,750.
1928	6,336,000	3.	5.	7.	15.	35.	75.	120.	225.
1928D	1,627,600	4.	7.	8.	20.	40.	90.	125.	225.
1928S*	2,644,000	4.	7.	8.	15.	35.	85.	125.	225.
1929	11,140,000	3.	5.	7.	15.	35.	70.	120.	225.
1929D	1,358,000	6.	7.	8.	16.	38.	85.	135.	225.
1929S	1,764,000	3.	6.	7.	15.	35.	85.	135.	225.
1930	5,632,000	3.	5.	7.	15.	35.	85.	135.	225.
1930S	1,556,000	4.	5.	8.	15.	35.	90.	135.	225.

*Large and small mint mark varieties, see page 73.

WASHINGTON TYPE 1932 to 1998

This type was intended to be a commemorative issue marking the two-hundredth anniversary of Washington's birth. John Flanagan, a New York sculptor, was the designer; his initials, JF, can be found at the base of Washington's neck. The mint mark is on the reverse below wreath, 1932 to 1964.

Weight 6.25 grams; composition: .900 silver, .100 copper; diameter 24.3 mm; reeded edge.

Net weight: .18084 oz. pure silver; mints: Philadelphia, Denver, San Francisco.

F-12 FINE—*Hairlines about ear are visible. Tiny feathers on eagle's breast are faintly visible.*
VF-20 VERY FINE—*Most hair details show. Wing feathers are clear.*
EF-40 EXTREMELY FINE—*Hairlines sharp. Wear spots confined to top of eagle's legs and center of breast.*
MS-60 UNCIRCULATED—*No trace of wear but can have many contact marks. Surface may be spotted, or luster faded.*
MS-63 SELECT UNCIRCULATED—*No trace of wear. Light blemishes. Attractive mint luster.*
MS-64 UNCIRCULATED—*Shows a few scattered contact marks. Good eye appeal and attractive luster.*
MS-65 CHOICE UNCIRCULATED—*Only light scattered contact marks that are not distracting. Strong luster, good eye appeal.*
PF-65—*Hardly any blemishes and no flaws*

1934 Doubled Die

QUARTER DOLLARS
Silver Coinage — 1932-1964

	Mintage	F-12	VF-20	EF-40	AU-50	MS-60	MS-63	MS-65
1932	5,404,000	$6.	$7.	$10.	$15.	$25.	$50.	$400.
1932D	436,800	125.	150.	225.	350.	1,000.	3,000.	24,000.
1932S	40,800,075	125.	140.	150.	175.	375.	1,250.	6,500.
1934, Light motto	} 31,912,052	4.	7.	10.	24.	50.	75.	250.
1934, Hvy. Motto		4.	6.	8.	12.	30.	50.	125.
1934, DblDie		75.	125.	175.	225.	350.	800.	3,200.
1934D	3,527,200	6.	10.	15.	80.	250.	325.	1,500.
1935	32,484,000	3.	4.	7.	9.	22.	35.	120.
1935D	5,780,000	6.	10.	20.	125.	250.	275.	900.
1935S	5,660,000	5.	7.	15.	35.	90.	125.	300.

**1937 Doubled
Die Obverse**

**1942D Doubled
Die Obverse**

**1943 Doubled
Die Obverse**

	Mintage	EF-40	AU-50	MS-60	MS-63	MS--65	PF-65
1936	(3,837) 41,303,837	$45.00	$40.	$20.	$30.	$90.	
1936D	5,374,000	45.00	250.	500.	700.	1,500.	1,800.
1936S	3,828,000	15.00	50.	120.	150.	400.	
1937	(5,542) 19,701,542	5.00	18.	30.	40.	100.	750.
1937, DblDieObv			300.	500.	800.		2,500.
1937D	7,189,600	15.00	30.	70.	90.	150.	—
1937S	1,652,000	20.00	100.	150.	200.	300.	
1938	(8,045) 9,480,045	15.00	40.	90.	100.	250.	450.
1938S	2,832,000	15.00	50.	90.	120.	225.	
1939	(8,795) 33,548,795	4.00	9.	15.	25.	60.	400.
1939D	7,092,000	9.00	20.	40.	50.	100.	
1939S	2,628,000	15.00	50.	90.	125.	300.	
1940	(11,246) 35,715,246	4.00	6.	15.	30.	75.	350.
1940D	2,797,600	18.00	75.	120.	150.	300.	
1940S	8,244,000	7.00	15.	25.	40.	70.	
1941	(15,287) 79,047,287	4.00	6.	8.	15.	50.	250.
1941D	16,714,800	5.00	9.	25.	60.	75.	
1941S *	16,080,000	5.00	8.	25.	45.	90.	
1942	(21,123) 102,117,123	3.00	4.	5.	9.	40.	250.
1942D	17,487,200	5.00	8.	15.	25.	50.	
1942D, DblDieObv		400.00	600.	1,000.	1,800.	—	
1942S	19,384,000	10.00	18.	65.	100.	250.	
1943	99,700,000	3.50	4.	5.	9.	50.	
1943 DblDieObv		225.00	350.	500.	800.	—	
1943D	16,095,600	7.00	12.	25.	35.	50.	
1943S	21,700,000	10.00	15.	30.	40.	60.	
1943S, DblDieObv		125.00	250.	500.	900.	3,000.	
1944	104,956,000	3.00	4.	5.	9.	40.	
1944D	14,600,800	6.00	9.	15.	20.	50.	
1944S	12,560,000	7.00	10.	15.	25.	45.	
1945	74,372,000	3.00	4.	5.	8.	50.	
1945D	12,341,600	8.00	12.	15.	30.	50.	
1945S	17,004,001	5.00	7.	10.	12.	40.	
1946	53,436,000	3.00	4.	5.	9.	45.	
1946D	9,072,800	3.00	4.	5.	9.	45.	
1946S	4,204,000	3.00	4.	5.	9.	45.	
1947	22,556,000	3.00	4.	5.	12.	45.	
1947D	15,338,400	3.00	4.	5.	12.	45.	
1947S	5,532,000	3.00	4.	5.	12.	45.	
1948	35,196,000	3.00	4.	5.	10.	45.	

*Large and small mint mark varieties, see page 73.

QUARTER DOLLARS

	Mintage	EF-40	AU-50	MS-60	MS-63	MS-65	PF-65
1948D	16,766,800	3.	4.	5.	9.	75.	
1948S	15,960,000	3.	4.	5.	9.	50.	
1949	9,312,000	10.	15.	40.	50.	75.	
1949D	10,068,400	4.	7.	12.	25.	50.	
1950 .....(51,386)	24,971,512	4.	5.	6.	9.	35.	60.00
1950D	21,075,600	4.	5.	6.	9.	35.	
1950D, D/S		100.	150.	250.	400.	1,500.	
1950S	10,284,004	4.	8.	12.	15.	60.	
1950S, S/D		150.	300.	400.	500.	900.	
1951 ....57,500)	43,505,602	4.	5.	6.	8.	30.	60.00
1951D	35,354,800	4.	5.	6.	8.	30.	
1951S	9,048,000	5.	7.	15.	30.	50.	
1952 ......(81,980)	38,862,073	3.	7.	10.	12.	20.	50.00
1952D	49,795,200	3.	4.	5.	10.	40.	
1952S	13,707,800	5.	6.	12.	25.	50.	
1953 ....(128,800)	18,664,920	3.	5.	7.	10.	40.	50.00
1953D	56,112,400	3.	4.	5.	8.	35.	
1953S	14,016,000	3.	4.	5.	7.	30.	
1954 ....(233,300)	54,645,503	3.	4.	5.	12.	30.	25.00
1954D	42,305,500	3.	4.	6.	10.	40.	
1954S	11,834,722	3.	4.	5.	7.	35.	
1955 .....(378,200)	18,558,381	3.	4.	5.	7.	25.	25.00
1955D	3,182,400	4.	5.	7.	10.	45.	
1956 ....(669,384)	44,813,384	3.	4.	5.	10.	20.	10.00
1956D	32,334,500	3.	4.	5.	7.	25.	
1957 ....(1,247,952)	47,779,952	3.	4.	5.	7.	25.	7.50
1957D	77,924,160	3.	4.	5.	8.	25.	
1958 .....(875,652)	7,235,652	3.	4.	5.	6.	20.	10.00
1958D	78,124,900	3.	4.	5.	6.	20.	
1959 ....(1,149,291)	25,533,291	3.	4.	5.	6.	20.	7.50
1959D	62,054,232	3.	4.	5.	6.	20.	
1960 ....(1,691,602)	30,855,602	3.	4.	5.	6.	15.	5.00
1960D	63,000,324	3.	4.	5.	6.	15.	
1961 ....(3,028,244)	40,064,244	3.	4.	5.	6.	15.	5.00
1961D	83,656,928	3.	4.	5.	6.	15.	
1962 ....(3,218,019)	39,374,019	3.	4.	5.	6.	15.	5.00
1962D	127,554,756	3.	4.	5.	6.	15.	
1963 ....(3,075,645)	77,391,645	3.	4.	5.	6.	15.	5.00
1963D	135,288,184	3.	4.	5.	6.	15.	
1964 ....(3,950,762)	564,341,347	3.	4.	5.	6.	15.	5.00
1964D	704,135,528	3.	4.	5.	6.	15.	

Clad Coinage — 1965 to Date

Proof coins from 1937 through 1972 were made from special dies with high relief and minor detail differences. Some of the circulation coins of 1956-1964 and 1969D-1972D were also made from reverse dies with these same features. A variety of the 1964D quarter occurs with the modified reverse normally found only on the clad coins.

Weight 5.67 grams; composition: outer layers of copper-nickel (.750 copper, .250 nickel) bonded to inner core of pure copper; diameter 24.3 mm; reeded edge. Silver Proofs 1992-1998; same as pre1965 standards.

 ◄— **Starting in 1968 mint mark is on obverse at right of ribbon.**

QUARTER DOLLARS

	Mintage	MS-63	MS-65	PF-65
1965	1,819,717,540	$1.00	$5.00	
1966	821,101,500	1.00	4.00	
1967	1,524,031,848	1.00	5.00	
1968	220,731,500	2.00	5.00	
1968D	101,534,000	1.00	4.00	
1968S, Pf	(3,041,506)			1.50
1969	176,212,000	3.00	5.00	
1969D	114,372,000	2.00	4.00	
1969S, Pf	(2,934,631)			1.50
1970	136,420,000	1.00	4.00	
1970D	417,341,364	1.00	4.00	
1970S, Pf	(2,632,810)			1.50

	Mintage	MS-63	MS-65	PF-65
1971	109,284,000	$1.00	$4.00	
1971D	258,634,428	1.00	2.00	
1971S, Pf	(3,220,733)			1.50
1972	215,048,000	1.00	3.00	
1972D	311,067,732	1.00	4.00	
1972S, Pf	(3,260,996)			1.50
1973	346,924,000	1.00	4.00	
1973D	232,977,400	1.00	5.00	
1973S, Pf	(2,760,339)			1.50
1974	801,456,000	1.00	4.00	
1974D	353,160,300	1.00	6.00	
1974S, Pf	(2,612,568)			1.50

Lightweight, thin quarters of 1970D were struck on metal intended for dimes.

BICENTENNIAL COINAGE DATED 1776-1976

In October of 1973, the Treasury announced an open contest for the selection of suitable designs for the Bicentennial reverses of the quarter, half dollar and dollar, with $5,000 to be awarded to each winner. Twelve semifinalists were chosen, and from these the symbolic entry of Jack L. Ahr was selected for the quarter reverse. It features a Colonial drummer facing left, with a victory torch encircled by thirteen stars at the upper left. Except for the dual dating, 1776-1976, the obverse remained unchanged. Only pieces with this dual dating were coined during 1975 and 1976. They were struck for general circulation and included in all the mint's offerings of Proof and uncirculated sets.

Designers John Flanagan and Jack L. Ahr. Silver issue: weight 5.75 grams; composition: outer layers of .800 silver, .200 copper bonded to inner core of .209 silver, .791 copper. Copper-nickel issue: weight 5.67 grams; composition: outer layers of .750 copper, .250 nickel bonded to inner core of pure copper. Diameter 24.3 mm; reeded edge. Net weight of silver issues: .0739 oz. pure silver.

	Mintage	MS-63	MS-65	PF-65
1776-1976, Copper-nickel clad	809,784,016	$1.00	$5.00	
1776-1976D, Copper-nickel clad	860,118,839	1.00	5.00	
1776-1976S, Copper-nickel clad	(7,059,099)			$1.00
1776-1976S, Silver clad	*11,000,000	3.00	6.00	
1776-1976S, SILVER CLAD	(*4,000,000)			6.50

*Approximate mintage. Several million were melted in 1982.

Eagle Reverse Resumed (Dies slightly modified to lower relief)

	Mintage	MS-63	MS-65	PF-65
1977	468,556,000	$1.00	$5.00	
1977D	256,524,978	1.00	3.00	
1977S, Pf	(3,251,152)			1.50
1978	521,452,000	1.00	5.00	
1978D	287,373,152	1.00	5.00	
1978S, Pf	(3,127,781)			1.50
1979	515,708,000	1.00	5.00	
1979D	489,789,780	1.00	3.00	

	Mintage	MS-63	MS-65	PF-65
1979S PF	(3,677,175)			
Filled S				$1.50
Clear S				3.00
1980P	635,832,000	$1.00	5.00	
1980D	518,327,487	1.00	4.00	
1980S, Pf	(3,554,806)			1.50
1981P	601,716,000	1.00	5.00	
1981D	575,722,833	1.00	3.00	

QUARTER DOLLARS

	Mintage	MS-63	MS-65	PF-65		Mintage	MS-63	MS-65	PF-65
1981S, Pf	. .(4,063,083)			$2.	1992P	384,764,000	$0.75	$10.	
1982P	500,931,000	$3.00	$15.		1992D	389,777,107	0.75	5.	
1982D	480,042,788	1.50	10.		1992S, Pf	. . . .(2,858,981)			$3.
1982S, Pf	. .(3,857,479)			2.	1992S,Silver Pf(1,317,579)				5.
1983P	673,535,000	7.00	40.		1993P	639,276,000	0.75	6.	
1983D	617,806,446	3.00	20.		1993D	645,476,128	0.75	6.	
1983S, Pf	. .(3,279,126)			3.	1993S, Pf	. . . .(2,633,439)			4.
1984P	676,545,000	1.00	5.		1993S,Silver Pf	.(761,353)			8.
1984D	546,483,064	1.00	5.		1994P	825,600,000	0.50	10.	
1984S, Pf	. .(3,065,110)			3.	1994D	880,034,110	0.50	5.	
1985P	775,818,962	1.00	8.		1994S, Pf	. . . .(2,484,594)			4.
1985D	519,962,888	1.00	5.		1994S,Silver Pf	(785,329)			12.
1985S, Pf	. .(3,362,821)			2.	1995P	1,004,336,000	0.75	6.	
1986P	551,199,333	3.00	5.		1995D	1,103,216,000	0.75	5.	
1986D	504,298,660	3.00	10.		1995S, Pf	. . . .(2,117,496)			15.
1986S, Pf	. .(3,010,497)			4.	1995S,Silver Pf	.(679,985)			15.
1987P	582,499,481	0.50	5.		1996P	925,040,000	0.50	4.	
1987D	655,594,696	0.50	3.		1996D	906,868,000	0.50	4.	
1987S, Pf	. .(4,227,728)			3.	1996S, Pf	. . . .(1,750,244)			5.
1988P	562,052,000	1.00	6.		1996S,Silver Pf	.(775,021)			10.
1988D	596,810,688	0.50	5.		1997P	595,740,000	0.50	4.	
1988S, Pf	. .(3,262,948)			2.	1997D	599,680,000	0.50	4.	
1989P	512,868,000	0.75	6.		1997S Pf	. . . .(2,055,000)			10.
1989D	896,535,597	0.75	3.		1997S,Silver Pf	.(741,678)			18.
1989S, Pf	. .(3,220,194)			2.	1998P	896,268,000	0.50	3.	
1990P	613,792,000	0.75	5.		1998D	821,000,000	0.50	3.	
1990D	927,638,181	0.75	3.		1998S Pf	. . . .(2,086,507)			10.
1990S, Pf	. .(3,299,559)			6.	1998S Silver Pf	.(878,792)			10.
1991P	570,968,000	0.75	6.						
1991D	630,966,693	0.75	5.						
1991S, Pf	. .(2,867,787)			3.					

STATEHOOD QUARTER DOLLARS
1999-2008

The United States Mint 50 State Quarters Program begun in 1999 will produce a series of 50 quarter dollar coins with special designs honoring each state. Five different designs will be issued each year during the period 1999-2009. States are being commemorated in the order of their entrance into statehood.

These are all legal tender coins of standard weight and composition. The obverse side depicting President George Washington has been modified slightly to include some of the wording previously used on the reverse. The modification was authorized by special legislation, and carried out by Mint Sculptor-Engraver William Cousins, whose initials have been added to the truncation of Washington's neck adjacent to those of the original designer, John Flanagan.

Each state theme is being proposed, and approved, by the governor of the state. Final designs will be created by mint personnel.

Circulation coins are made at the Philadelphia and Denver mints. Proof coins are made in San Francisco.

Weight 5.67 grams; composition: outer layers of copper-nickel (.750 copper, .250 nickel) bonded to inner core of pure copper; diameter 24.3 mm reeded edge. Silver Proof: pre-1965 standards

	Mintage	AU-50	MS-63	MS-65	PF-65
1999P Delaware	373,400,000	$0.50	$1.25	$3.00	
1999D Delaware	401,424,000	0.50	1.25	3.00	
1999S Delaware Pf	(3,713,359)				$5.00
1999S Delaware Silver Pf	(800,000)				10.00
1999P Pennsylvania	349,000,000	0.50	1.50	4.00	
1999D Pennsylvania	358,332,000	0.50	1.25	3.00	
1999S Pennsylvania Pf	(3,713,359)				5.00
1999S Pennsylvania Silver Pf	(800,000)				10.00
1999P New Jersey	363,200,000	0.40	0.75	1.50	
1999D New Jersey	299,028,000	0.45	1.00	3.00	
1999S New Jersey Pf	(3,713,359)				5.00
1999S New Jersey Silver Pf	(800,000)				10.00
1999P Georgia	451,188,000	0.40	0.75	1.25	
1999D Georgia	488,744,000	0.40	0.75	1.25	
1999S Georgia Pf	(3,713,359)				5.00
1999S Georgia Silver Pf	(800,000)				10.00
1999P Connecticut	688,744,000	0.35	0.60	1.00	
1999D Connecticut	657,880,000	0.35	0.60	1.00	
1999S Connecticut Pf	(3,713,359)				5.00
1999S Connecticut Silver Pf	(800,000)				10.00

	Mintage	AU-50	MS-63	MS-65	PF-65
2000P Massachusetts	628,600,000	0.35	0.60	1.00	
2000D Massachusetts	535,184,000	0.35	0.60	1.00	
2000S Massachusetts Pf	(4,020,083)				5.00
2000S Massachusetts Silver Pf	(856,400)				8.00
2000P Maryland	678,200,000	0.35	0.60	1.00	
2000D Maryland	556,532,000	0.35	0.60	1.00	
2000S Maryland Pf	(4,020,083)				5.00
2000S Maryland Silver Pf	(856,400)				8.00
2000P South Carolina	742,576,000	0.35	0.60	1.00	
2000D South Carolina	566,208,000	0.35	0.60	1.00	
2000S South Carolina Pf	(4,020,083)				5.00
2000S South Carolina Silver Pf	(856,400)				8.00
2000P New Hampshire	673,040,000	0.35	0.50	1.00	
2000D New Hampshire	495,976,000	0.35	0.50	1.00	
2000S New Hampshire Pf	(4,020,083)				5.00
2000S New Hampshire Silver Pf	(856,400)				8.00
2000P Virginia	943,000,000	0.35	0.50	1.00	
2000D Virginia	651,616,000	0.35	0.50	1.00	
2000S Virginia Pf	(4,020,083)				5.00
2000S Virginia Silver Pf	(856,400)				8.00

QUARTER DOLLARS

	Mintage	AU-50	MS-63	MS-65	PF-65
2001P New York	655,400,000	$0.35	$0.50	$1.00	
2001D New York	619,640,000	0.35	0.50	1.00	
2001S New York Pf	(3,093,274)				$5.00
2001S New York Silver Pf	(889,697)				8.00
2001P North Carolina	627,600,000	0.35	0.50	1.00	
2001D North Carolina	427,876,000	0.35	0.50	1.00	
2001S North Carolina Pf	(3,093,274)				5.00
2001S North Carolina Silver Pf	(889,697)				8.00
2001P Rhode Island	423,000,000	0.35	0.50	1.00	
2001D Rhode Island	447,100,000	0.35	0.50	1.00	
2001S Rhode Island Pf	(3,093,274)				5.00
2001S Rhode Island Silver Pf	(889,697)				8.00
2001P Vermont	423,400,000	0.75	1.00	1.25	
2001D Vermont	459,404,000	0.75	1.00	1.25	
2001S Vermont Pf	(3,093,274)				5.00
2001S Vermont Silver Pf	(889,697)				8.00
2001P Kentucky	353,000,000	0.75	1.00	1.25	
2001D Kentucky	370,564,000	0.75	1.00	1.25	
2001S Kentucky Pf	(3,093,274)				5.00
2001S Kentucky Silver Pf	(889,697)				8.00
2002P Tennessee	361,600,000	1.20	1.90	2.20	
2002D Tennessee	286,468,000	0.70	1.40	2.00	
2002S Tennessee Pf	(3,039,320)				5.00
2002S Tennessee Silver Pf	(888,826)				8.00
2002P Ohio	217,200,000	0.35	0.70	1.35	
2002D Ohio	414,832,000	0.35	0.70	1.35	
2002S Ohio Pf	(3,039,320)			5.00	
2002S Ohio Silver Pf	(888,826)				8.00
2002P Louisiana	362,000,000	0.35	0.70	1.35	
2002D Louisiana	402,204,000	0.35	0.70	1.35	
2002S Louisiana Pf	(3,039,320)				5.00
2002S Louisiana Silver Pf	(888,826)				8.00
2002P Indiana	362,600,000	0.35	0.50	1.00	
2002D Indiana	327,200,000	0.35	0.50	1.00	
2002S Indiana Pf	(3,039,320)				5.00
2002S Indiana Silver Pf	(888,826)				8.00
2002P Mississippi	290,000,000	0.40	0.85	1.45	
2002D Mississippi	289,600,000	0.35	0.50	1.00	
2002S Mississippi Pf	(3,039,320)				5.00
2002S Mississippi Silver Pf	(888,826)				8.00

QUARTER DOLLARS

	Mintage	AU-50	MS-63	MS-65	PF-65
2003P Illinois	225,800,000	$0.50	$0.75	$1.50	
2003D Illinois	237,400,000	0.35	0.50	1.00	
2003S Illinois Pf					$5.00
2003S Illinois Silver Pf					8.00
2003P Alabama	225,000,000	0.40	0.65	1.30	
2003D Alabama	232,400,000	0.35	0.50	1.00	
2003S Alabama Pf					5.00
2003S Alabama Silver Pf					8.00
2003P Maine	217,400,000	0.35	0.50	1.00	
2003D Maine	231,900,000	0.35	0.50	1.00	
2003S Maine Pf					5.00
2003S Maine Silver Pf					8.00
2003P Missouri	225,000,000	0.35	0.50	1.00	
2003D Missouri	228,200,000	0.35	0.50	1.00	
2003S Missouri Pf					5.00
2003S Missouri Silver Pf					8.00
2003P Arkansas		0.35	0.65	1.30	
2003D Arkansas		0.35	0.65	1.30	
2003S Arkansas Pf					5.00
2003S Arkansas Silver Pf					8.00

	Mintage	AU-50	MS-63	MS-65	PF-65
2004P Michigan		0.35	0.60	1.25	
2004D Michigan		0.35	0.60	1.25	
2004S Michigan Pf					5.00
2004S Michigan Silver Pf					8.00
2004P Florida		0.35	0.60	1.25	
2004D Florida		0.35	0.60	1.25	
2004S Florida Pf					5.00
2004S Florida Silver Pf					8.00
2004P Texas		0.35	0.60	1.25	
2004D Texas		0.35	0.60	1.25	
2004S Texas Pf					5.00
2004S Texas Silver Pf					8.00
2004P Iowa		0.35	0.60	1.25	
2004D Iowa		0.35	0.60	1.25	
2004S Iowa Pf					5.00
2004S Iowa Silver Pf					8.00
2004P Wisconsin		0.35	0.60	1.25	
2004D Wisconsin		0.35	0.60	1.25	
2004S Wisconsin Pf					5.00
2004S Wisconsin Silver Pf					8.00

	Mintage	AU-50	MS-63	MS-65	PF-65
2005 California					
2005 Minnesota					
2005 Oregon					
2005 Kansas					
2005 West Virginia					
2006 Nevada					
2006 Nebraska					
2006 Colorado					
2006 North Dakota					
2006 South Dakota					
2007 Montana					
2007 Washington					
2007 Idaho					
2007 Wyoming					
2007 Utah					
2008 Oklahoma					
2008 New Mexico					
2008 Arizona					
2008 Alaska					
2008 Hawaii					

Some Statehood quarters were accidentally made with disoriented dies and are valued higher than ordinary pieces. Normal United States coins have dies oriented in "coin alignment," where the reverse appears upside down when the coin is rotated from right to left. Values for the rotated die quarters vary according to the amount of shifting. The most valuable are those that are shifted 180 degrees so that both sides appear upright when the coin is turned over (medal alignment).

BIBLIOGRAPHY

Bressett, Kenneth. *The Official Whitman Statehood Quarters Collector's Handbook.* New York, N.Y. 2000.
Briggs, Larry. *The Comprehensive Encyclopedia of United States Seated Quarters.* Lima, Ohio, 1991.
Browning, A. W. *The Early Quarter Dollars of the United States 1796-1838.* New York, 1925.
    (Reprinted 1992)
Cline, J. H. *Standing Liberty Quarters.* 3rd edition, 1996.
Duphorne, R. *The Early Quarter Dollars of The United States.* 1975.
Fivaz, Bill and Stanton, J.T. *The Cherrypickers' Guide to Rare Die Varieties.* Savannah, 1991.
Haseltine, J. W. *Type Table of United States Dollars, Half Dollars and Quarter Dollars.* Philadelphia,
    1881 (reprinted 1927, 1968).
Kelman, Keith N. *Standing Liberty Quarters.* N.H., 1976.
Lawrence, David. *The Complete Guide to Barber Quarters.* Virginia Beach, VA, 1989.

HALF DOLLARS
1794 to Date

The half dollar, authorized by the Act of April 2, 1792, was not minted until December, 1794. The early types of this series have been extensively collected by die varieties, of which many exist for most dates. Valuations given below are in each case for the most common variety; scarcer ones as listed by Overton (see bibliography) generally command higher prices.

The weight of the half dollar was 208 grains and its fineness .8924 when first issued. This standard was not changed until 1837 when the law of January 18, 1837 specified 206¼ grains, .900 fine. This fineness continued in use until 1965.

Arrows at the date in 1853 indicate the reduction of weight to 192 grains, in conformity with the Act of February 21, 1853. During that year only, rays were added to the field on the reverse side to identify the lighter coins. Arrows remained in 1854 and 1855.

The 1866 Proof quarter, half and dollar without motto are not mentioned in the Director's Report, and were not issued for circulation.

In 1873 the weight was raised by law to 192.9 grains and arrows were again placed at the date, to be removed in 1875.

+ or – indicates change from previous year	TYPE COIN VALUES								
	G-5	F-12	EF-40	AU-50	MS-60	MS-63	MS-65	PF-60	PF-63	PF-65
Flowing Hair 1794-1795	550.00+	1,000.	5,250.+	7,000.		23,000.+	50,000.+	175,000.+		
Drpd. Bust, SE 1796-1797 ..	12,000.+	20,000.+	50,000.+	75,000.+		75,000.-	1,000,000.	1,000,000.		
Drpd. Bust, HE 1801-1807 ...	140.00	225.00-	800.+	2,500.+	5,500.+	12,500.+	1,000,000.+			
Cap Bust Type 1807-1836 ...	38.00+	55.00+	100.+	250.00+	525.	1,400.	6,500.-			
Cap Bust, RE 1836-1839	40.00+	70.00+	160.+	340.00-	800.	2,000.	12,000. -			
Lib. Seated-NM 1839-1866 .	18.00+	35.00+	100.+	180.00+	475.+	800.-	4,500.+	550.+	1200.+	5,500.
Lib. Seated-A&R 1853	20.00+	40.00+	250.+	600.00+	1,500.+	3,000.-	18,050.-			
Lib .Seat-Arr. 1854-1855.....	20.00+	42.00+	110.+	250.00	700.+	1,500.	7,500.-	7,000.	12,000.	25,000.
Lib. Seat-WM 1866-1891	18.00+	38.00+	80.+	180.00+	425.+	1,000.+	2,800.-	450.-	800.-	2,600.+
Lib. Seat-Arr. 1873-1874.....	25.00+	55.00+	250.+	380.00+	950.+	2,000.	2,000.	850.-	2,000.	9,500.+
Barber 1892-1915	10.00+	25.00	100.-	250.00-	400.+	700.-	2,500.-	400.-	700.–	2,750.+
Lib. Walking 1916-1947	4.00+	4.50+	7.+	12.00-	28.-	40.	100.-	250.-	350.+	950.+
Franklin 1948-1963	2.50-	3.00-	4.	4.50+	5.	9.+	50.+	5.-	10.+	25.+
Kennedy 1964 Silver	2.50	3.00+	4.+	4.50+	5.+	5.+	8.+	3.	5.	9.+

FLOWING HAIR TYPE 1794-1795

Designer Robert Scot; weight 13.48 grams; composition: .8924 silver, .1076 copper; approx. diameter 32.5 mm; edge: FIFTY CENTS OR HALF A DOLLAR with decorations between words.

AG-3 ABOUT GOOD—*Clear enough to identify.*
G-4 GOOD—*Date and letters sufficient to be readable. Main devices outlined, but lack details.*
VG-8 VERY GOOD—*Major details discernible. Letters well formed but worn.*
F-12 FINE—*Hair ends distinguishable. Top hairlines show, but otherwise worn smooth.*
VF-20 VERY FINE—*Hair in center shows some detail. Other details more bold.*
EF-40 EXTREMELY FINE—*Hair above head and down neck detailed, with slight wear.*
AU-50 ABOUT UNCIRCULATED—*All hair shows with slight wear on the bust and top edges of eagle's wings, head, and breast.*

2 Leaves under Wings

	Mintage	AG-3	G-4	VG-8	F-12	VF-20	EF-40	AU-50
1794	23,464	$1,000.	$1,800.	$2,800.	$4,000.	$7,000.	$15,000.	$37,500.

HALF DOLLARS

	Mintage	AG-3	G-4	VG-8	F-12	VF-20	EF-40	AU-50
1795 All Kinds 299,680		$275.	$550.	$750.	$1,000.	$2,200.	$5,250.	$7,000.
1795, Recut date		275.	550.	750.	1,000.	2,500.	5,750.	8,000.
1795,3 leaves under each wing		525.	1,000.	1,800.	3,200.	5,500.	12,000.	18,000.

Varieties of 1795 are known with final S in STATES over D, with A in STATES over E, and with Y in LIBERTY over a star. All are scarce. Some 1795 half dollars were weight-adjusted by inserting a silver plug in the center of the blank planchet before striking the coin.

DRAPED BUST TYPE, SMALL EAGLE REVERSE 1796-1797

Designer Robert Scot; weight 13.48 grams; composition: .8924 silver, .1076 copper; approx. diameter 32.5 mm; edge: FIFTY CENTS OR HALF A DOLLAR with decorations between words.

AG-3 ABOUT GOOD—*Clear enough to identify.*
G-4 GOOD—*Date and letters sufficient to be readable. Main devices outlined, but lack details.*
VG-8 VERY GOOD—*Major details discernible. Letters well formed but worn.*
F-12 FINE—*Hair ends distinguishable. Top hairlines show, but otherwise smooth worn.*
VF-20 VERY FINE—*Right side of drapery slightly worn. Left side to curls is smooth.*
EF-40 EXTREMELY FINE—*All lines in drapery on bust will show distinctly around to hair curls.*
AU-50 ABOUT UNCIRCULATED—*Slight trace of wear on cheek, hair, and shoulder.*

1796, 15 Stars   **1796, 16 Stars**

	Mintage	AG-3	G-4	VG-8	F-12	VF-20	EF-40	AU-50
1796, 15 stars . .		$8,000.	$12,000.	$14,000.	$20,000.	$28,000.	$50,000.	$75,000.
1796, 16 stars . . } 3,918		9,000.	13,500.	15,000.	22,000.	32,000.	50,000.	90,000.
1797, 15 stars . .		8,000.	12,000.	14,000.	20,000.	28,000.	50,000.	75,000.

DRAPED BUST TYPE, HERALDIC EAGLE REVERSE
1801-1807

	Mintage	G-4	VG-8	F-12	VF-20	EF-40	AU-50	MS-60
1801 30,289		$300.	$500.	$800.	$1,800.	$3,500.	$12,500.	$30,000.
1802 29,890		250.	400.	650.	1,200.	3,500.	12,000.	32,000.
1803, Sm 3 . . } 188,234		150.	225.	325.	550.	1,300.	3,800.	7,500.
1803, Lg 3 . .		140.	180.	250.	475.	900.	2,500.	8,000.

| 1805, 5 over 4 | | 1806, 6 over 5 | | | | |

	Mintage	G-4	VG-8	F-12	VF-20	EF-40	AU-50	MS-60
1805, 5/4 ···· }	211,722	$200.	$300.	$600.	$800.	$2,100.	$5,000.	$22,000.
1805, NmlDt		150.	175.	250.	425.	1,000.	2,500.	7,000.

Knobbed Top 6, Small Stars   **Branch Stem through Claw**

Pointed Top 6   **Branch Stem Not Through Claw**

	G-4	VG-8	F-12	VF-20	EF-40	AU-50	MS-60
1806 All Kinds ..839,576							
1806, 6/5	160.	180.	250.	425.	1,000.	2,500.	6,000.
1806, 6/inverted 6	175.	275.	600.	900.	2,000.	5,500.	10,000.
1806,Knobbed 6,LgS ..	150.	165.	225.	400.	800.	2,500.	5,500.
(traces of overdate) .							
1806,Knobbed 6,SmS ..	150.	165.	225.	400.	800.	2,500.	5,500.
1806,Knobbed 6, ...	16,000.	20,000.	32,000.	50,000.	75,000.		
Stem not through claw							
1806,Pointed 6, ...	150.	175.	240.	400.	800.	2,500.	5,500.
stem through claw* .							
1806,Pointed 6, ...	150.	175.	240.	400.	800.	2,500.	5,500.
stem not through claw							
1807 301,076	150.	175.	240.	400.	800.	2,500.	5,500.

*One variety shows E in STATES over A.

CAPPED BUST TYPE, Lettered Edge 1807-1836

John Reich designed this capped head concept of Liberty. The head of Liberty facing left was used on all U.S. silver coin denominations for the next thirty years. Reich was the first artist to consistently include the denomination on our gold and silver coins. A German immigrant, John Reich became an engraver for the Mint, and served from 1807 to 1817, after having been freed from a bond of servitude by a Mint official.

Designer John Reich; weight 13.48 grams; composition: .8924 silver, .1076 copper; approx. diameter 32.5 mm; edge varieties, 1807-1814: FIFTY CENTS OR HALF A DOLLAR; 1814-1831: star added between DOLLAR and FIFTY; 1832-1836: vertical lines added between words.

G-4 GOOD—Date and letters readable. Bust worn smooth with outline distinct.
VG-8 VERY GOOD—LIBERTY visible but faint. Legends distinguishable.
    Clasp at shoulder visible. Curl above it nearly smooth.
F-12 FINE—Clasp and adjacent curl clearly outlined with slight details.
VF-20 VERY FINE—Clasp at shoulder clear. Curl has wear on highest point. Hair over brow distinguishable.
EF-40 EXTREMELY FINE—Clasp and adjacent curl fairly sharp. Brow and hair above distinct. Curls well defined.
AU-50 ABOUT UNCIRCULATED—Trace of wear on hair over eye, and over ear.
MS-60 UNCIRCULATED—No trace of wear. Light blemishes. May have slide marks from storage handling.
MS-63 SELECT UNCIRCULATED—Some distracting contact marks or blemishes in prime focal areas.
    Luster may be impaired.

HALF DOLLARS

First style (Variety 1) 1807-1808

1807 Small Stars	1807 Large Stars	1807, 50 over 20

	Mintage	G-4	F-12	VF-20	EF-40	AU-50	MS-60	MS-63
1807, All Kinds	.750,500							
1807, SmS		$60.	$200.	$375.	$800.	$2,500.	$4,500.	$11,000.
1807, LgS		55.	180.	350.	700.	2,200.	4,250.	10,500.
1807, Same, 50/20		50.	140.	260.	475.	2,100.	4,000.	8,000.
1807 "Bearded" Liberty		350.	750.	1,250.	2,600.	7,500.	13,000.	—
1808, 8/7	}1,368,600	50.	100.	175.	350.	1,000.	2,000.	5,000.
1808		45.	65.	100.	275.	650.	1,500.	3,000.

Remodeled Portrait and Eagle 1809-1836

1809 Experimental edge, xxxx between words.	1809 Experimental edge, IIIII between words.

HALF DOLLARS

	Mintage	G-4	F-12	VF-20	EF-40	AU-50	MS-60	MS-63
1809 All Kinds	1,405,810							
1809, Nml edge		$45.	$65.	$100.	$225.	$550.	$1,400.	$3,000.
1809, XXXX edge		45.	65.	120.	250.	800.	1,800.	4,500.
1809, IIIIII edge		45.	65.	120.	250.	800.	1,800.	4,500.
1810	1,276,276	45.	65.	100.	225.	550.	1,300.	3,000.

"Punctuated" Date 18.11

1811 Small 8

1811 Large 8

1812, 2 over 1, Small 8

1812, 2 over 1, Large 8

	Mintage	G-4	F-12	VF-20	EF-40	AU-50	MS-60	MS-63
1811 All Kinds	1,203,644							
1811,(18.11) 11/10		50.	80.	140.	325.	700.	1,600.	7,500.
1811, Sm 8		40.	60.	90.	175.	425.	1,000.	2,000.
1811, Lg 8		40.	60.	90.	175.	425.	1,000.	2,000.
1812, All Kinds	1,628,059							
1812, 2/1, Sm 8		45.	90.	175.	300.	700.	2,200.	5,000.
1812, 2/1, Lg 8		1,400.	3,500.	5,500.	9,000.	12,000.	22,000.	—
1812		50.	60.	100.	175.	375.	900.	2,000.
1812 Single leaf below wing		700.	1,100.	2,200.	3,500.	6,000.	10,000.	—

1813, 50 C. over UNI

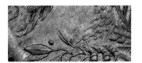

Single leaf below wing

1814, 4 over 3

1814 E over A in STATES

	Mintage	G-4	F-12	VF-20	EF-40	AU-50	MS-60	MS-63
1813	} 1,241,903	40.	60.	90.	165.	375.	1,000.	2,500.
1813, 50C/UNI		50.	90.	150.	250.	650.	1,600.	5,000.
1814, All Kinds	1,039,075							
1814, 4/3		50.	100.	160.	325.	850.	1,800.	5,500.
1814, E/A in STATES		45.	65.	100.	250.	700.	1,300.	4,200.
1814		40.	60.	80.	200.	450.	1,000.	2,200.
1814 Single leaf below wing		50.	85.	150.	425.	1,200.	2,000.	3,500.

1817, 7 over 3 | **1817, 7 over 4** | **1817 Punctuated Date**

	Mintage	G-4	F-12	VF-20	EF-40	AU-50	MS-60	MS-63
1815, 5/2	47,150	$750.	$1,500.	$2,000.	$3,200.	$5,000.	$10,000.	$20,000.
1817, All Kinds	1,215,567							
1817, 7/3		80.	225.	375.	750.	1,600.	3,500.	8,500.
1817, 7/4	40,000.	100,000.	140,000.	180,000.	225,000.			
1817, Dated 1817		40.	65.	100.	180.	425.	1,000.	2,000.
1817		40.	60.	75.	160.	400.	1,000.	2,000.
1817 Single leaf below wing		45.	85.	120.	350.	850.	1,800.	3,000.

1818, 1st 8 Small, 2nd 8 over 7

1818, 1st 8 Large, 2nd 8 over 7

1819 Small 9 over 8

1819 Large 9 over 8

1818, All Kinds	1,960,322						
1818, 8/7, Sm 8	40.	65.	90.	175.	700.	1,300.	5,000.
1818, 8/7 Lg 8	40.	65.	90.	175.	700.	1,300.	5,000.
1818	40.	60.	80.	150.	350.	900.	1,800.
1819, All Kinds	2,208,000						
1819, Sm 9/8	40.	60.	80.	175.	500.	1,200.	3,500.
1819, Lg 9/8	40.	60.	80.	175.	500.	1,200.	3,500.
1819	40.	60.	80.	150.	350.	900.	2,500.

**1820, 20 over 19
Square Base 2**

**1820, 20 over 19
Curl Base 2**

**Curl Base, No Knob 2,
Small Date**

1820, All Kinds	751,122						
1820, 20/19, Sq 2	50.	75.	160.	350.	800.	1,500.	3,500.
1820, 20/19, Curl 2	50.	75.	160.	350.	800.	1,500.	3,500.
1820, Curl base 2, SmDt.	45.	70.	110.	250.	600.	1,100.	3,000.

**Square Base, Knob 2,
Large Date**

**Square Base, No Knob 2,
Large Date**

	Mintage	G-4	F-12	VF-20	EF-40	AU-50	MS-60	MS-63
1820,Sq.base knb 2,LgDt.		$45.	$70.	$110.	$250.	$600.	$1,100.	$3,000.
1820,Sq.base no knb 2,LgDt		45.	70.	110.	250.	600.	1,100.	3,000.
1820 No serifs on E's		250.	375.	600.	850.	2,250.	5,000.	8,500.
1821	1,305,797	40.	60.	80.	150.	500.	1,000.	2,200.
1822	1,559,573	45.	65.	100.	150.	350.	550.	1,800.
1822, 2 over 1		50.	90.	140.	250.	600.	1,400.	2,000.

1823 Broken 3

1823 Patched 3

1823 Ugly 3

1823 All Kinds	1,694,200						
1823	40.	55.	70.	125.	325.	650.	1,500.
1823, Broken 3	50.	90.	140.	325.	650.	1,200.	2,800.
1823, Patched 3	45.	80.	110.	225.	550.	1,100.	2,400.
1823, Ugly 3	40.	60.	80.	160.	400.	850.	2,200.

**"Various Dates"
(probably 4 over
2 over 0)**

1824, 4 over 1

1824, 4 over 4

1824, 4 over 4

**4 over 4 varieties are easily mistaken for the
scarcer 4 over 1 variety. Notice the distance
between the 2's and 4's in the illustrations.**

1824, All Kinds	3,504,954						
1824	40.	60.	70.	110.	275.	575.	1,400.
1824, over various dates	40.	60.	70.	120.	275.	575.	1,400.
1824, 4/1	40.	60.	70.	110.	275.	575.	1,400.
1824, 4/4 (2 var.)	40.	60.	70.	120.	325.	700.	1,500.
1825	2,943,166	40.	60.	70.	110.	250.	525.	1,500.
1826	4,004,180	40.	60.	70.	110.	250.	525.	1,500.
1827, All Kinds	5,493,400						
1827, 7/6	40.	60.	80.	160.	375.	900.	1,800.
1827, Sq. base 2	40.	60.	70.	110.	250.	525.	1,500.
1827, Curl base 2	40.	60.	70.	110.	275.	550.	1,500.

1828 Curl Base, Knob 2

1828 Square Base 2, Large 8's

1828 Square Base 2, Small 8's

1828 Large Letters

1828 Small Letters

	Mintage	G-4	F-12	VF-20	EF-40	AU-50	MS-60	MS-63
1828, All Kinds	3,075,200							
1828, Curl base no knob 2		$40.	$60.	$70.	$110.	$275.	$550.	$1,400.
1828, Curl base knob 2		45.	65.	75.	140.	300.	700.	1,400.
1828, Sq. base, Lg. 8's		40.	55.	65.	100.	250.	525.	1,400.
1828, Sq. base 2, Sm8's, LgL		40.	55.	65.	100.	250.	525.	1,400.
1828, Sq base 2, Sm.8's&let.		40.	60.	80.	140.	325.	800.	1,800.
1829, 9/7 ...		45.	65.	85.	150.	350.	800.	2,500.
1829	3,712,156	40.	55.	65.	100.	250.	525.	1,400.
1829 LgL ...		50.	60.	70.	120.	325.	900.	1,800.

1830 Small 0

1832 Large Letters Reverse

Raised segment lines to right, 1830. Raised segment lines to left, 1830-1831.

Adopted edge 1830-1836.

		G-4	F-12	VF-20	EF-40	AU-50	MS-60	MS-63
1830, Sm 0 ...		38.	55.	65.	100.	250.	525.	1,400.
1830, Lg 0	4,764,800	38.	55.	65.	100.	250.	525.	1,400.
1830 LgL		1,200.	2,500.	3,500.	4,500.	9,000.	—	
1831 5,873,660		38.	55.	65.	100.	250.	525.	1,400.
1832	4,797,000	38.	55.	65.	100.	250.	525.	1,400.
1832, LgL		38.	55.	65.	100.	275.	550.	1,500.
1833 5,206,000		38.	55.	65.	100.	250.	525.	1,400.

1834 Large Date   1834 Small Date

1834 Lg. Letters Reverse 1834 Sm. Letters Reverse 1836, 50 over 00

**Proofs of 1833, 1834 and 1835 with crushed edge lettering use the same reverse
die as the 1836 with beaded border reverse. All are very rare.**

Portrait Modified Slightly 1834-1836

	Mintage	G-4	F-12	VF-20	EF-40	AU-50	MS-60	MS-63
1834, All Kinds	6,412,004							
1834, LgDt & letter.		$38.	$55.	$65.	$110.	$250.	$525.	$1,400.
1834, LgDt.,Sm Letter.		38.	55.	65.	110.	250.	525.	1,400.
1834,SmDt,Stars, Letter.		38.	55.	65.	110.	250.	525.	1,400.
1835	5,352,006	38.	55.	65.	110.	250.	525.	1,400.
1836		38.	55.	65.	110.	250.	525.	1,400.
1836/1336	6,545,000	45.	60.	85.	125.	275.	650.	1,400.
1836, 50/00		55.	85.	125.	200.	525.	1,400.	3,500.
1836 Beaded border on rev.		40.	65.	100.	200.	450.	900.	1,750.

Variety 2 — Reeded Edge, Reverse "50 CENTS" 1836-1837

Designer Christian Gobrecht; weight 13.36 grams; composition: .900 silver, .100 copper; diameter 30 mm; reeded edge; mints: Philadelphia.

G-4 GOOD—*LIBERTY discernible on headband.*
VG-8 VERY GOOD—*Minimum of 3 letters in LIBERTY must be clear.*
F-12 FINE—*LIBERTY complete.*
VF-20 VERY FINE—*LIBERTY is sharp. Shoulder clasp is clear.*
EF-40 EXTREMELY FINE—*LIBERTY sharp and strong. Hair details show.*
AU-50 ABOUT UNCIRCULATED—*Slight trace of wear on cap, c heek, and hair above the forehead, claws, wing tops, and the head*
MS-60 UNCIRCULATED—*No trace of wear. Light blemishes.*
MS-63 SELECT UNCIRCULATED—*Some distracting contact marks or blemishes in prime focal areas. Luster may be impaired.*

	Mintage	G-4	VG-8	F-12	VF-20	EF-40	AU-50	MS-60	MS-63
1836	1,200	$650.	$850.	$1,100.	$1,400.	$2,200.	$4,000.	$9,500.	$16,000.
1837	3,629,820	40.	50.	75.	110.	160.	340.	800.	2,000.

HALF DOLLARS

Variety 3 — Reeded Edge, Reverse "HALF DOL." 1838-1839

The 1838O was the first branch mint half dollar, though not mentioned in the Director's report. The New Orleans chief coiner stated that only 20 were struck. In 1838-39 the mint mark appears on the obverse; thereafter, through 1915, all mint marks are placed on the reverse.

	Mintage	G-4	VG-8	F-12	VF-20	EF-40	AU-50	MS-60	MS-63
1838	3,546,000	$50.	$60.	$70.	$100.	$185.	$350.	$800.	$2,000.
1838O	(20)						75,000.	80,000.	100,000.	250,000.
1839	1,392,976	50.	60.	70.	100.	185.	350.	900.	2,100.
1839,Small Letter Reverse					—	—			
1839O	178,976	140.	175.	275.	400.	700.	1,200.	3,000.	6,000.

LIBERTY SEATED TYPE 1839-1891

Variety 1 — No Motto Above Eagle 1839-1853

Designer Christian Gobrecht; weight 13.36 grams; composition: .900 silver, .100 copper; diameter 30.6 mm; reeded edge; mints: Philadelphia, New Orleans.

G-4 GOOD —*Scant rim. LIBERTY on shield worn off. Date and letters readable.*
VG-8 VERY GOOD —*Rim fairly defined. At least 3 letters in LIBERTY are evident.*
F-12 FINE —*LIBERTY complete, but weak.*
VF-20 VERY FINE —*LIBERTY mostly sharp.*
EF-40 EXTREMELY FINE —*LIBERTY entirely sharp. Scroll edges and clasp distinct.*
AU-50 ABOUT UNCIRCULATED —*Slight trace of wear on Liberty's breast and knees, head, claws and wing tops of eagle.*
MS-60 UNCIRCULATED —*No trace of wear. Light blemishes.*
MS-63 SELECT UNCIRCULATED —*Some distracting contact marks or blemishes in prime focal areas. Luster may be impaired.*

1839 NoDrap from elbow	40.	60.	125.	300.	700.	1,600.	4,800.

HALF DOLLARS

Modified obverse, drapery from elbow. Small letters in legend 1839-1841.

Drapery from Elbow Starting 1839	Small Letters in Legend 1839-41	1840 (only) with Medium Letters and Large Eagle

	Mintage	G-4	VG-8	F-12	VF-20	EF-40	AU-50	MS-60	MS-63
1839, Drpy Frm elbow	1,972,400	$23.	$30.	$45.	$70.	$125.	$160.	$500.	$1,500.
1840, SmL	1,435,008	20.	35.	50.	80.	135.	185.	600.	1,000.
1840, MedL*	} 855,100	100.	160.	225.	300.	575.	1,000.	2,900.	5,500.
1840O		20.	30.	45.	60.	110.	175.	500.	1,500.
1841	310,000	30.	42.	85.	140.	250.	350.	1,200.	1,900.
1841O	401,000	18.	26.	40.	60.	125.	180.	700.	1,200.
1842, SmDt, SmL ...				—	—				
1842O, SmDt, SmL ..	203,000	525.	825.	1,300.	2,100.	4,250.	6,500.	13,000.	25,000.

*Struck at the New Orleans Mint from a reverse die of the previous style without mint mark.

Modified reverse with large letters in legend 1842-1853.

Small Date

Medium Date	Large Letter Reverse	1844O Double Date

1842, SmDt .... } 2,012,764	25.	40.	55.	80.	150.	250.	1,000.	2,500.
1842, Med. Dt	18.	30.	45.	60.	110.	200.	650.	1,200.
1842O, Med. Dt 754,000	19.	26.	38.	55.	110.	250.	850.	3,500.
1843 3,844,000	18.	25.	35.	45.	100.	200.	475.	900.
1843O 2,268,000	18.	25.	35.	45.	100.	200.	675.	1,200.
1844 1,766,000	18.	25.	35.	45.	100.	200.	475.	900.
1844O .... } 2,005,000	18.	25.	35.	45.	100.	200.	800.	1,800.
1844O, DblDt	400.	600.	1,000.	1,400.	2,500.	5,000.	9,000.	—
1845 589,000	20.	30.	50.	60.	150.	250.	750.	2,000.
1845O .... } 2,094,000	18.	25.	35.	45.	100.	175.	675.	900.
1845O, NoDrap‡	30.	45.	60.	90.	275.	250.	1,000.	4,000.

‡Drapery missing because of excessive die polishing.

In 1846 the date size was again enlarged. The 1846 medium date is approximately the size of the 1842 medium date shown. Tall date is similar to 1853. See illustrations of cents on page 91.

	Mintage	G-4	VG-8	F-12	VF-20	EF-40	AU-50	MS-60	MS-63
1846, Med. Dt.	2,210,000	$18.	$25.	$40.	$50.	$100.	$175.	$575.	$1,350.
All Kinds									
1846, Tall Dt		20.	25.	40.	50.	120.	250.	750.	1,400.
1846,/ horizontal 6(err)		100.	175.	275.	400.	575.	1,200.	3,250.	9,000.
1846O, MedDt	2,304,000	20.	25.	40.	50.	110.	200.	800.	1,800.
1846O,Tall Dt		125.	225.	325.	500.	1,000.	1,800.	5,500.	
1847, 7/6	1,156,000	1,800.	2,500.	3,200.	4,500.	6,500.	8,000.	16,000.	
1847, NmlDt		18.	25.	40.	50.	100.	175.	500.	800.
1847O	2,584,000	18.	25.	40.	50.	110.	185.	600.	1,800.
1848	580,000	30.	40.	60.	100.	200.	425.	1,000.	1,500.
1848O	3,180,000	20.	25.	40.	50.	100.	190.	750.	1,800.
1849	1,252,000	20.	25.	40.	50.	125.	285.	775.	1,500.
1849O	2,310,000	20.	25.	40.	50.	100.	200.	750.	2,000.
1850	227,000	175.	225.	300.	425.	675.	725.	1,600.	3,000.
1850O	2,456,000	20.	25.	40.	50.	100.	180.	600.	850.
1851	200,750	200.	300.	400.	500.	750.	800.	1,600.	2,400.
1851O	402,000	20.	25.	40.	50.	150.	200.	675.	1,000.
1852	77,130	275.	400.	550.	700.	950.	1,200.	1,800.	2,000.
1852O	144,000	45.	75.	125.	200.	450.	725.	2,200.	6,000.
1853O			150,000.	175,000.	250,000.				

Variety 2 — Arrows at Date, Rays Around Eagle 1853 Only

Weight 12.44 grams; composition: .900 silver, .100 copper; diameter 30.6 mm; reeded edge; mints: Philadelphia, New Orleans, San Francisco, Carson City.

		G-4	VG-8	F-12	VF-20	EF-40	AU-50	MS-60	MS-63
1853	3,532,708	20.	25.	40.	100.	250.	600.	1,500.	3,000.
1853O All Kinds	1,328,000	20.	27.	45.	120.	275.	675.	2,500.	4,500.

Variety 3 — Arrows at Date, No Rays 1854-1855

		G-4	VG-8	F-12	VF-20	EF-40	AU-50	MS-60	MS-63
1854	2,982,000	20.	27.	42.	65.	110.	250.	700.	1,500.
1854O	5,240,000	20.	27.	42.	65.	110.	250.	700.	1,500.
1855, /1854	759,500	50.	75.	150.	250.	390.	600.	2,000.	3,000.
1855, NmlDt		20.	27.	42.	65.	110.	250.	700.	1,750.
1855O	3,688,000	20.	27.	42.	65.	110.	250.	700.	1,500.
1855S	129,950	300.	425.	800.	1,400.	3,200.	5,500.	12,500.	—

Variety 1 Design Resumed 1856-1866
(weight standard of 1853)

		G-4	VG-8	F-12	VF-20	EF-40	AU-50	MS-60	MS-63
1856	938,000	18.	22.	38.	50.	100.	200.	500.	950.
1856O	2,658,000	18.	22.	38.	50.	100.	200.	500.	950.
1856S	211,000	35.	55.	90.	200.	450.	900.	3,500.	—
1857	1,988,000	18.	22.	38.	50.	100.	200.	500.	950.
1857O	818,000	18.	23.	40.	55.	110.	250.	850.	2,600.
1857S	158,000	45.	75.	140.	225.	450.	1,000.	3,500.	—

	Mintage	G-4	VG-8	F-12	VF-20	EF-40	AU-50	MS-60	MS-63	PF-63
1858 ..(300+)	.4,226,000	$18.	$22.	$38.	$50.	$100.	$200.	$450.	$900.	$2,500.
1858O	7,294,000	18.	22.	38.	50.	100.	200.	450.	900.	
1858S	476,000	22.	27.	40.	90.	180.	300.	950.	3,500.	
1859 ...(800)	..748,000	18.	22.	38.	50.	100.	250.	475.	1,000.	1,300.
1859O	..2,834,000	18.	22.	38.	50.	100.	225.	450.	1,000.	
1859S	566,000	21.	25.	40.	60.	135.	250.	950.	2,750.	
1860 .(1,000)	..303,700	21.	25.	38.	50.	100.	250.	725.	1,000.	1,200.
1860O	1,290,000	20.	25.	38.	50.	100.	200.	450.	1,000.	
1860S	472,000	21.	25.	38.	50.	90.	200.	700.	2,750.	
1861 .(1,000)	.2,888,400	18.	22.	38.	50.	90.	200.	500.	900.	1,200.
1861O	2,532,633	18.	22.	38.	50.	90.	200.	500.	900.	
1861O Cracked obv.*	...	65.	90.	165.	250.	325.	500.	1,200.	2,000.	

* Crack from nose to border, same obverse die used for Confederate half dollars.

The 1861O quantity includes 330,000 struck under the United States government, 1,240,000 for the State of Louisiana after it seceded from the Union, and 962,633 after Louisiana joined the Confederate States of America. As all these 1861O coins were struck from U.S. dies, it is impossible to distinguish one from another. They should not be confused with the very rare Confederate half dollar of 1861 which has a distinctive reverse.

	Mintage	G-4	VG-8	F-12	VF-20	EF-40	AU-50	MS-60	MS-63	PF-63
1861S	939,500	18.	22.	38.	50.	90.	200.	500.	900.	
1862 ...(550)	..253,550	25.	35.	50.	110.	200.	250.	625.	1,000.	1,200.
1862S	1,352,000	18.	22.	38.	50.	90.	200.	500.	900.	
1863 ..(460)	..503,660	22.	25.	40.	55.	100.	220.	500.	1,150.	1,200.
1863S	916,000	22.	25.	40.	55.	100.	220.	500.	1,150.	
1864 ...(470)	..379,570	28.	40.	55.	90.	135.	250.	500.	1,150.	1,200.
1864S	658,000	20.	25.	40.	55.	100.	225.	600.	2,500.	
1865 ...(500)	..511,900	21.	25.	40.	50.	125.	250.	700.	1,200.	1,200.
1865S	675,000	20.	25.	40.	55.	100.	225.	650.	1,500.	
1866S, No motto	.60,000	80.	110.	200.	350.	725.	1,400.	4,750.	7,000.	
1866	....									
		(Unique-see similar 1866 quarter and dollar)								

**Variety 4 —
"In God We Trust"
Above Eagle
1866-1873
1875-1891**

	Mintage	G-4	VG-8	F-12	VF-20	EF-40	AU-50	MS-60	MS-63	PF-63
1866 ...(725)	..745,625	18.	22.	38.	50.	90.	180.	475.	1,100.	800.
1866S	994,000	18.	22.	38.	50.	90.	200.	575.	1,500.	
1867 ...(625)	..449,925	20.	40.	60.	80.	160.	225.	525.	1,200.	800.
1867S	1,196,000	18.	22.	38.	50.	90.	180.	550.	1,800.	
1868 ...(600)	..418,200	30.	40.	65.	150.	225.	275.	600.	1,200.	800.
1868S	1,160,000	18.	22.	38.	50.	100.	200.	600.	1,600.	
1869 ...(600)	..795,900	19.	23.	40.	55.	125.	200.	525.	1,100.	800.
1869S	656,000	19.	23.	40.	55.	125.	200.	800.	2,500.	
1870 .(1,000)	..634,900	18.	22.	38.	50.	100.	180.	425.	1,000.	800.
1870CC	54,617	700.	1,000.	1,800.	4,000.	11,000.	20,000.	—	—	
1870S	1,004,000	18.	22.	38.	50.	100.	200.	700.	2,200.	
1871 ...(960)	1,204,560	18.	22.	38.	50.	100.	200.	475.	1,100.	800.
1871CC	153,950	150.	250.	450.	800.	1,800.	3,000.	10,000.	40,000.	
1871S	2,178,000	18.	22.	40.	50.	100.	200.	650.	1,200.	

HALF DOLLARS

	Mintage	G-4	VG-8	F-12	VF-20	EF-40	AU-50	MS-60	MS-63	PF-63
1872 ...(950)	.881,550	$18.	$22.	$40.	$50.	$100.	$200.	$475.	$1,400.	$800.
1872CC	.257,000	60.	100.	225.	400.	900.	1,400.	4,000.	25,000.	
1872S	.580,000	23.	40.	60.	100.	150.	275.	1,100.	2,200.	
1873, Cl 3 (600)	.587,600	23.	40.	60.	100.	150.	225.	600.	1,100.	800.
1873, Op 3	.214,200	2,500.	3,000.	3,500.	4,500.	6,500.	8,000.	18,000.	—	
1873CC	.122,500	140.	250.	350.	600.	1,350.	2,800.	8,500.	50,000.	
1873S No arrows	.5,000				*Unknown in any collection.*					

Variety 5 — Arrows at Date 1873-1874

Arrows were placed at the date to denote a change in weight from 12.44 to 12.50 grams.

Weight 12.50 grams; composition: .900 silver, .100 copper; diameter 30.6 mm; reeded edge; mints: Philadelphia, Carson City, San Francisco.

1873 ...(550)	.1,815,700	25.	40.	55.	100.	250.	360.	950.	2,000.	2,000.
1873CC	.214,560	125.	225.	350.	900.	1,800.	2,400.	6,000.	15,000.	
1873S	.228,000	50.	75.	125.	250.	425.	700.	2,500.	6,000.	
1874 ...(700)	.2,360,300	25.	40.	55.	100.	250.	360.	950.	2,000.	2,000.
1874CC	.59,000	300.	500.	800.	1,300.	2,000.	3,500.	10,000.	18,000.	
1874S	.394,000	32.	42.	80.	200.	350.	650.	1,700.	3,750.	

Variety 4 Resumed 1875-1891

1875 ...(700)	6,027,500	18.	22.	38.	50.	90.	180.	500.	700.	800.
1875CC	1,008,000	24.	40.	65.	75.	150.	250.	650.	1,350.	
1875S	3,200,000	18.	22.	38.	50.	90.	180.	500.	700.	
1876 ..(1,150)	8,419,150	18.	22.	38.	50.	90.	180.	500.	700.	800.
1876CC	1,956,000	18.	22.	38.	50.	100.	200.	650.	1,350.	
1876S	4,528,000	18.	22.	38.	50.	90.	180.	500.	700.	
1877 ....(510)	8,304,510	18.	22.	38.	50.	90.	180.	500.	700.	800.
1877 7/6			100.	325.	650.	1,000.				
1877CC	1,420,000	22.	30.	50.	70.	135.	250.	700.	900.	
1877S	5,356,000	18.	22.	38.	50.	90.	180.	500.	700.	
1878 ....(800)	1,378,400	18.	22.	38.	50.	90.	180.	500.	700.	800.
1878CC	62,000	300.	425.	750.	1,100.	2,750.	3,000.	6,500.	20,000.	
1878S	12,000	10,000.	12,000.	16,000.	22,000.	26,000.	32,000.	42,000.	90,000.	
1879 ..(1,100)	.5,900	225.	275.	350.	400.	475.	600.	800.	1,000.	800.
1880 ..(1,355)	.9,755	225.	275.	350.	400.	475.	600.	800.	1,000.	800.
1881 ....(975)	.10,975	225.	275.	350.	400.	475.	600.	800.	1,000.	800.
1882 ..(1,100)	.5,500	250.	300.	400.	450.	500.	650.	850.	1,000.	800.
1883 ..(1,039)	.9,039	200.	250.	300.	375.	425.	500.	800.	1,000.	800.
1884 ....(875)	.5,275	300.	350.	400.	500.	600.	750.	900.	1,100.	800.
1885 ....(930)	.6,130	300.	350.	400.	500.	600.	750.	900.	1,150.	800.
1886 ....(886)	.5,886	300.	350.	400.	500.	600.	700.	900.	1,200.	800.
1887 ....(710)	.5,710	300.	350.	400.	500.	600.	600.	800.	1,200.	800.
1888 ....(832)	.12,833	250.	300.	350.	400.	450.	550.	750.	1,000.	800.
1889 ....(711)	.12,711	250.	300.	350.	400.	450.	550.	750.	1,000.	800.
1890 ....(590)	.12,590	250.	300.	350.	400.	450.	550.	750.	1,000.	800.
1891 ....(600)	.200,600	40.	60.	90.	110.	150.	200.	550.	750.	800.

HALF DOLLARS
BARBER or LIBERTY HEAD TYPE 1892-1915

Like the dime and quarter dollar, this type was designed by Charles E. Barber, whose initial B is at the truncation of the neck.

Designer Charles E. Barber; weight 12.50 grams; composition: .900 silver, .100 copper; diameter 30.6 mm; reeded edge; mints: Philadelphia, Denver, New Orleans, San Francisco.

G-4 GOOD—*Date and legends readable. LIBERTY worn off headband.*
VG-8 VERY GOOD—*Minimum of 3 letters readable in LIBERTY.*
F-12 FINE—*LIBERTY completely readable, but not sharp.*
VF-20 VERY FINE—*All letters in LIBERTY evenly plain.*
EF-40 EXTREMELY FINE—*LIBERTY bold, and its ribbon distinct.*
AU-50 ABOUT UNCIRCULATED—*Slight trace of wear above forehead, leaf tips, and cheek. Also on the head, tail and wing tips of eagle.*
MS-60 UNCIRCULATED—*No trace of wear. Light blemishes.*
MS-63 SELECT UNCIRCULATED—*Some distracting contact marks or blemishes in prime focal areas. Luster may be impaired.*
PF-63—*Reflective surfaces with only a few blemishes in secondary focal places. No major flaws.*

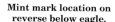

Mint mark location on reverse below eagle.

	Mintage	G-4	VG-8	F-12	VF-20	EF-40	AU-50	MS-60	MS-63	PF-63
1892 .(1,245)	.935,245	$25.	$32.	$60.	$90.	$250.	$275.	$450.	$750.	$800.
1892O	.390,000	175.	250.	350.	425.	500.	550.	900.	1,600.	
1892O, Micro O*	1,200.	2,000.	2,750.	3,250.	4,750.	7,500.	12,000.			
1892S	1,029,028	200.	300.	350.	400.	500.	600.	900.	2,000.	
1893 ...(792)	1,826,792	16.	25.	55.	100.	200.	300.	600.	1,000.	800.
1893O	1,389,000	25.	50.	80.	160.	300.	400.	625.	1,200.	
1893S	740,000	120.	160.	220.	350.	500.	600.	1,200.	2,500.	
1894 ...(972)	1,148,972	20.	40.	90.	130.	225.	350.	500.	800.	800.
1894O	2,138,000	15.	25.	70.	120.	250.	300.	500.	900.	
1894S	4,048,690	13.	20.	50.	100.	200.	300.	450.	1,200.	
1895 ...(880)	1,835,218	12.	15.	45.	80.	100.	300.	550.	900.	800.
1895O	1,766,000	15.	20.	60.	110.	230.	350.	550.	1,300.	
1895S	1,108,086	20.	30.	80.	120.	260.	350.	550.	1,250.	
1896 ...(762)	.950,762	18.	25.	60.	110.	240.	300.	550.	850.	800.
1896O	924,000	25.	35.	120.	160.	350.	600.	1,300.	3,000.	
1896S	1,140,948	70.	100.	135.	225.	375.	500.	1,200.	3,000.	
1897 ...(731)	2,480,731	11.	12.	35.	80.	135.	300.	450.	750.	800.
1897O	632,000	60.	120.	350.	700.	850.	1,100.	1,500.	2,800.	
1897S	933,900	125.	160.	275.	425.	700.	900.	1,300.	3,000.	
1898 ...(735)	2,956,735	10.	12.	30.	75.	140.	300.	400.	750.	800.
1898O	874,000	20.	35.	150.	220.	400.	500.	950.	2,750.	
1898S	2,358,550	13.	20.	45.	90.	225.	325.	800.	3,000.	
1899 ...(846)	5,538,846	10.	12.	30.	75.	150.	300.	400.	750.	800.
1899O	1,724,000	12.	18.	50.	100.	225.	325.	600.	1,100.	
1899S	1,686,411	12.	18.	50.	90.	220.	300.	575.	2,200.	
1900 ...(912)	4,762,912	10.	12.	25.	75.	130.	300.	400.	750.	700.
1900O	2,744,000	11.	14.	40.	90.	250.	350.	700.	2,900.	
1900S	2,560,322	11.	14.	40.	90.	185.	280.	575.	1,800.	
1901 ...(813)	4,268,813	10.	12.	25.	70.	125.	300.	400.	700.	700.
1901O	1,124,000	12.	20.	60.	120.	300.	425.	1,300.	4,000.	
1901S	847,044	20.	40.	120.	250.	600.	850.	1,600.	4,200.	
1902 ...(777)	4,922,777	10.	12.	25.	70.	125.	300.	400.	700.	700.
1902O	2,526,000	12.	18.	45.	90.	200.	300.	700.	1,900.	

*Normal and "microscopic" mint mark varieties, see page 73.

HALF DOLLARS

	Mintage	G-4	VG-8	F-12	VF-20	EF-40	AU-50	MS-60	MS-63	PF-63
1902S	1,460,670	$12.	$20.	$60.	$110.	$250.	$350.	$600.	$1,750.	
1903	...(755) .2,278,755	10.	12.	25.	80.	160.	300.	450.	1,000.	$700.
1903O	2,100,000	10.	15.	50.	90.	200.	325.	600.	1,300.	
1903S	1,920,772	10.	15.	50.	90.	220.	350.	600.	1,500.	
1904	...(670) .2,992,670	10.	12.	25.	65.	140.	280.	400.	1,000.	700.
1904O	1,117,600	15.	20.	60.	140.	320.	450.	1,200.	2,500.	
1904S	553,038	20.	40.	180.	400.	700.	1,300.	2,500.	7,500.	
1905	...(727) ..662,727	15.	20.	50.	100.	250.	300.	550.	1,250.	700.
1905O	505,000	15.	25.	90.	150.	250.	350.	675.	1,500.	
1905S	2,494,000	12.	15.	40.	90.	200.	325.	600.	1,700.	
1906	...(675) .2,638,675	10.	12.	25.	65.	125.	250.	400.	700.	700.
1906D	4,028,000	10.	12.	30.	80.	160.	250.	400.	700.	
1906O	2,446,000	10.	12.	40.	80.	180.	280.	600.	1,000.	
1906S	1,740,154	10.	15.	50.	90.	220.	300.	550.	1,000.	
1907	...(575) .2,598,575	10.	12.	25.	65.	125.	250.	400.	700.	700.
1907D	3,856,000	10.	12.	30.	75.	150.	270.	400.	700.	
1907O	3,946,600	10.	12.	30.	75.	150.	300.	450.	750.	
1907S	1,250,000	14.	20.	75.	130.	350.	600.	900.	3,500.	
1908	...(545) .1,354,545	10.	12.	25.	65.	125.	250.	400.	700.	700.
1908D	3,280,000	10.	12.	25.	65.	125.	250.	400.	700.	
1908O	5,360,000	10.	12.	25.	65.	135.	300.	450.	850.	
1908S	1,644,828	10.	15.	50.	90.	220.	350.	700.	2,200.	
1909	...(950) .2,368,650	10.	12.	25.	65.	125.	250.	400.	700.	700.
1909O	925,400	15.	20.	50.	110.	275.	500.	700.	1,500.	
1909S	1,764,000	10.	12.	30.	80.	200.	300.	600.	1,000.	
1910	.(1,005) ..418,551	12.	15.	75.	130.	275.	300.	700.	1,000.	700.
1910S	1,948,000	10.	12.	30.	90.	175.	275.	550.	700.	
1911	...(682) .1,406,543	10.	12.	25.	65.	125.	250.	400.	700.	700.
1911D	695,080	10.	14.	35.	85.	185.	275.	500.	800.	
1911S	1,272,000	10.	13.	30.	85.	175.	300.	550.	1,100.	
1912	...(700) .1,550,700	10.	12.	25.	65.	125.	250.	425.	700.	700.
1912D	2,300,800	10.	12.	25.	65.	125.	250.	425.	700.	
1912S	1,370,000	10.	12.	25.	75.	165.	300.	450.	900.	
1913	...(768) ..188,627	25.	35.	140.	225.	400.	650.	1,000.	1,500.	1,000.
1913D	534,000	10.	14.	35.	90.	200.	260.	450.	800.	
1913S	604,000	10.	15.	45.	90.	200.	300.	600.	1,000.	
1914	...(610) ..124,610	35.	50.	200.	350.	550.	750.	1,000.	1,500.	1,300.
1914S	992,000	10.	12.	30.	75.	200.	300.	500.	900.	
1915	...(450) ..138,450	28.	40.	120.	250.	400.	675.	1,000.	2,200.	1,200.
1915D	1,170,400	10.	12.	25.	70.	125.	275.	450.	700.	
1915S	1,604,000	10.	12.	25.	70.	125.	275.	450.	700.	

LIBERTY WALKING TYPE 1916-1947

This type was designed by A. A. Weinman whose monogram AAW appears under the tip of the wing feathers. On the 1916 coins and some of the 1917 coins the mint mark is located on the obverse below the motto.

Designer Adolph A. Weinman; weight 12.50 grams; composition: .900 silver, .100 copper; diameter 30.6 mm; reeded edge; mints: Philadelphia, Denver, San Francisco. Net weight: .36169 oz. pure silver.

G-4 GOOD—Rims are defined. Motto IN GOD WE TRUST readable.
VG-8 VERY GOOD—Motto is distinct. About half of skirt lines at left are clear.
F-12 FINE—All skirt lines evident, but worn in spots. Details in sandal below motto are clear.
VF-20 VERY FINE—Skirt lines sharp including leg area. Little wear on breast and right arm.
EF-40 EXTREMELY FINE—All skirt lines bold.
AU-50 ABOUT UNCIRCULATED—Slight trace of wear on head, knee and breast tips also on the claws and head.
MS-60 UNCIRCULATED—No trace of wear. Light blemishes.
MS-63 SELECT UNCIRCULATED—Some distracting contact marks or blemishes in prime focal areas. Luster may be impaired.
PF-65—Choice Brilliant surfaces with no noticeable blemishes or flaws. May have a few scattered barely noticeable marks or hairlines.

HALF DOLLARS

Locations of mint mark.

Choice uncirculated, well-struck specimens are worth more than values listed.

	Mintage	G-4	VG-8	F-12	VF-20	EF-40	AU-50	MS-60	MS-63	PF-65
1916	608,000	$30.	$35.	$60.	$130.	$175.	$225.	$300.	$400.	
1916D, (Obv.)	1,014,400	28.	32.	45.	90.	160.	225.	325.	550.	
1916S (Obv.)	508,000	100.	110.	165.	350.	600.	750.	1,000.	2,000.	
1917	12,292,000	5.	7.	10.	20.	40.	65.	150.	185.	
1917D, (Obv.)	765,400	15.	20.	50.	100.	175.	250.	535.	1,000.	
1917D, (Rev.)	1,940,000	12.	18.	30.	90.	225.	500.	800.	1,700.	
1917S, (Obv.)	952,000	20.	30.	60.	285.	750.	1,200.	2,200.	4,500.	
1917S, (Rev.)	5,554,000	6.	8.	15.	30.	50.	150.	350.	1,800.	
1918	6,634,000	7.	10.	18.	50.	150.	250.	550.	1,000.	
1918D	3,853,040	7.	10.	25.	60.	190.	350.	1,000.	2,500.	
1918S	10,282,000	6.	7.	15.	30.	60.	150.	500.	2,000.	
1919	962,000	18.	22.	45.	160.	500.	700.	1,100.	3,000.	
1919D	1,165,000	14.	18.	45.	175.	600.	1,000.	3,600.	12,000.	
1919S	1,552,000	14.	18.	35.	160.	725.	1,500.	2,700.	6,200.	
1920	6,372,000	6.	7.	13.	25.	60.	125.	325.	650.	
1920D	1,551,000	10.	12.	30.	140.	375.	800.	1,300.	4,000.	
1920S	4,624,000	6.	8.	16.	50.	200.	400.	750.	2,800.	
1921	246,000	120.	160.	250.	650.	1,500.	2,500.	3,500.	5,000.	
1921D	208,000	185.	225.	325.	775.	2,250.	3,000.	3,500.	6,000.	
1921S	548,000	30.	35.	125.	650.	4,500.	7,000.	10,000.	22,000.	
1923S	2,178,000	9.	14.	22.	75.	250.	1,400.	2,200.	3,800.	
1927S	2,392,000	6.	7.	14.	35.	110.	350.	850.	2,000.	
1928S ‡	1,940,000	7.	8.	15.	50.	130.	350.	850.	2,200.	
1929D	1,001,200	7.	8.	14.	25.	60.	250.	350.	650.	
1929S	1,902,000	7.	8.	13.	25.	85.	200.	350.	800.	
1933S	1,786,000	7.	8.	11.	15.	50.	225.	550.	1,100.	
1934	6,964,000	4.	5.	6.	7.	12.	30.	85.	100.	
1934D ‡	2,361,000	4.	6.	7.	10.	30.	85.	150.	210.	
1934S	3,652,000	4.	5.	6.	7.	30.	100.	350.	800.	
1935	9,162,000	4.	5.	6.	7.	10.	25.	45.	75.	
1935D	3,003,800	4.	6.	7.	8.	28.	60.	135.	220.	
1935S	3,854,000	4.	5.	6.	7.	25.	100.	250.	425.	
1936 .(3,901)	12,617,901	4.	5.	6.	7.	9.	25.	60.	75.	$5,500.
1936D	4,252,400	4.	5.	6.	7.	20.	50.	100.	120.	
1936S	3,884,000	4.	5.	6.	7.	20.	60.	135.	175.	
1937 .(5,728)	9,527,728	4.	5.	6.	7.	10.	25.	40.	65.	1,600.
1937D	1,676,000	7.	8.	9.	12.	30.	110.	225.	275.	
1937S	2,090,000	6.	7.	8.	10.	20.	60.	175.	225.	
1938 .(8,152)	4,118,152	4.	5.	6.	8.	12.	40.	75.	135.	1,200.
1938D	491,600	50.	60.	65.	70.	115.	250.	500.	600.	

‡ Large and small mint mark varieties, see page 73. Pieces dated 1928D are counterfeit.

HALF DOLLARS

	Mintage	F-12	VF-20	EF-40	AU-50	MS-60	MS-63	PF-65
1939 . . . .(8,808)	.6,820,808	$4.50	$6.	$8.	$25.	$45.	$65.	$1,100.
1939D 4,267,800		5.00	7.	10.	25.	45.	80.	
1939S 2,552,000		7.00	9.	16.	60.	125.	150.	
1940 . . .(11,279)	.9,167,279	4.50	5.	7.	15.	30.	55.	1,000.
1940S 4,550,000		4.50	5.	7.	20.	45.	70.	
1941* . .(15,412)	24,207,412	4.50	5.	7.	12.	38.	50.	*950.
1941D 11,248,400		4.50	5.	9.	18.	40.	65.	
1941S 8,098,000		4.50	5.	8.	30.	75.	100.	
1942 . . .(21,120)	47,839,120	4.50	5.	7.	12.	40.	60.	1,000.
1942D 10,973,800		4.50	5.	7.	18.	35.	75.	
1942S ‡ 12,708,000		4.50	5.	7.	18.	40.	60.	
1943 53,190,000		4.50	5.	7.	12.	35.	40.	
1943D 11,346,000		4.50	5.	7.	20.	50.	70.	
1943S 13,450,000		4.50	5.	7.	20.	45.	50.	
1944 28,206,000		4.50	5.	7.	12.	35.	42.	
1944D 9,769,000		4.50	5.	7.	18.	28.	55.	
1944S 8,904,000		4.50	5.	7.	18.	40.	55.	
1945 31,502,000		4.50	5.	7.	12.	35.	40.	
1945D 9,966,800		4.50	5.	7.	15.	35.	50.	
1945S 10,156,000		4.50	5.	7.	15.	40.	50.	
1946 12,118,000		4.50	5.	7.	12.	40.	50.	
1946, DblDieRev		15.00	35.	55.	100.	250.	400.	
1946D 2,151,000		6.00	10.	14.	20.	40.	55.	
1946S 3,724,000		4.50	5.	7.	18.	40.	50.	
1947 4,094,000		4.50	5.	7.	18.	40.	50.	
1947D 3,900,600		4.50	5.	7.	22.	45.	60.	

*Proofs struck with or without designer's initials.

‡Large and small mint mark varieties exist, see page 73.

FRANKLIN-LIBERTY BELL TYPE 1948-1963

The Benjamin Franklin half dollar and the Roosevelt dime were both designed by John R. Sinnock whose initials appear below the shoulder. The Liberty Bell is similar to that used by Sinnock on the 1926 Sesquicentennial commemorative half dollar modeled from a sketch by John Frederick Lewis.

Designer John R. Sinnock; weight 12.50 grams; composition: .900 silver, .100 copper; diameter 30.6 mm; reeded edge; mints: Philadelphia, Denver, San Francisco. Net weight: .36169 oz. pure silver.

VF-20 VERY FINE—At least half of the lower and upper incused lines on the rim of the bell must show.

EF-40 EXTREMELY FINE—Wear spots appear at top of end curls and hair back of ears. On reverse, Liberty Bell will show wear at top and on lettering.

MS-63 SELECT UNCIRCULATED—Some distracting contact marks or blemishes in prime focal areas. Luster may be impaired.

MS-65 CHOICE UNCIRCULATED—Only light scattered contact marks that are not distracting. Strong luster, good eye appeal.

PF-65—Choice Brilliant surfaces with no noticeable blemishes or flaws. May have a few scatered barely noticeable marks or hairlines.

Mint mark location.

Choice, well-struck uncirculated halves command higher prices.

HALF DOLLARS

	Mintage	VF-20	EF-40	MS-60	MS-63	MS-65	PF-65
1948	3,006,814	$5.00	$7.00	$18.	$22.	$85.	
1948D	4,028,600	3.50	5.00	12.	20.	160.	
1949	5,614,000	5.00	8.00	40.	55.	175.	
1949D	4,120,600	5.00	10.00	40.	60.	850.	
1949S	3,744,000	5.00	18.00	60.	90.	150.	
1950	(51,386)	7,793,509	3.50	5.00	30.	35.	125.	$475.
1950D	8,031,600	3.50	4.00	25.	35.	500.	
1951	(57,500)	16,859,602	3.50	4.00	14.	20.	75.	380.
1951D	9,475,200	4.00	6.00	27.	38.	275.	
1951S	13,696,000	4.00	5.00	25.	35.	110.	
1952	(81,980)	21,274,073	3.50	4.00	12.	20.	85.	225.
1952D	25,395,600	3.50	4.00	9.	15.	250.	
1952S	5,526,000	5.00	8.00	40.	50.	110.	
1953	(128,800)	2,796,920	4.00	7.00	16.	30.	250.	140.
1953D	20,900,400	3.50	6.00	12.	15.	120.	
1953S	4,148,000	3.50	6.00	25.	30.	90.	
1954	(233,300)	13,421,502	3.50	4.00	8.	12.	85.	100.
1954D	25,445,580	3.50	4.00	8.	15.	150.	
1954S	4,993,400	3.50	4.00	8.	15.	60.	
1955	(378,200)	2,876,381	7.00	8.00	15.	20.	55.	90.
1956	(669,384)	4,701,384	3.50	5.00	8.	15.	50.	45.
1957	(1,247,952)	6,361,952	3.50	5.00	7.	12.	50.	30.
1957D	19,966,850	3.50	4.00	8.	12.	50.	
1958	(875,652)	4,917,652	3.50	4.50	7.	15.	60.	35.
1958D	23,962,412	3.50	4.00	6.	10.	55.	
1959	(1,149,291)	7,349,291	3.50	4.50	6.	12.	125.	30.
1959D	13,053,750	3.50	4.00	6.	12.	150.	
1960	(1,691,602)	7,715,602	3.50	4.50	6.	12.	160.	30.
1960D	18,215,812	3.50	4.00	6.	10.	500.	

**1961 Proof
Doubled Die**

	Mintage	VF-20	EF-40	MS-60	MS-63	MS-65	PF-65
1961	(3,028,244)	11,318,244	3.50	4.50	6.	10.	175.	40.
1961 DblDie Pf							1,250.
1961D	20,276,442	3.50	4.00	5.	10.	250.	
1962	(3,218,019)	12,932,019	3.50	4.00	5.	10.	200.	25.
1962D	35,473,281	3.50	4.00	5.	9.	275.	
1963	(3,075,645)	25,239,645	3.50	4.00	5.	10.	80.	30.
1963D	67,069,292	3.50	4.00	5.	9.	80.	

KENNEDY TYPE 1964 to Date

Gilroy Roberts, Chief Engraver of the Mint in 1963, designed the obverse of this coin. His stylized initials are on the truncation of the forceful bust of President John F. Kennedy. The reverse, which uses the presidential coat of arms for the motif, is the work of the next Chief Engraver, Frank Gasparro, who was appointed in February 1965. A few of the pieces dated 1971D and 1977D were struck in silver clad by error.

Designers Gilroy Roberts and Frank Gasparro. 1964–: Standards same as previous issue; 1965-1970: weight 11.50 grams; composition: outer layers of .800 silver, .200 copper bonded to inner core of .209 silver, .791 copper; 1971: weight 11.34 grams; composition: outer layers of copper-nickel (.750 copper, .250 nickel) bonded to inner core of pure copper; diameter 30.6 mm; reeded edge. Net weight: 1964 .36169 oz. pure silver. 1965-1970 .1479 oz. pure silver, mints: Philadelphia, Denver, San Francisco.

1964 Mint mark location

1968 Mint mark location

Silver Coinage 1964

	Mintage	MS-63	PF-65
1964	.277,254,766	$5.00	
1964	(3,950,762)		$9.00

	Mintage	MS-63	PF-65
1964 Heavily accented hair incl. above			$20.00
1964D	.156,205,446	$5.00	

Silver Clad Coinage 1965-1970

	Mintage	MS-63	PF-65
1965	.65,879,366	3.00	
1966	.108,984,932	3.00	
1967	.295,046,978	3.00	
1968D	.246,951,930	3.00	
1968S, Pf	.(3,041,506)		4.00

Issued only in mint sets.

	Mintage	MS-63	PF-65
1969D	.129,881,800	3.00	
1969S, Pf	.(2,934,631)		4.00
1970D	.*2,150,000	16.00	
1970S, Pf	.(2,632,810)		10.00

Copper-Nickel Clad Coinage

Design was slightly modified several times between 1971 and present.

1974D Doubled Die Obverse

(Note prominent doubling of RUS.)

	Mintage	MS-63	PF-65
1971	.155,164,000	$1.50	
1971D	.302,097,424	1.50	
1971S, Pf	.(3,220,733)		$3.00
1972	.153,180,000	2.00	
1972D	.141,890,000	2.00	
1972S, Pf	.(3,260,996)		3.00
1973	.64,964,000	2.00	

	Mintage	MS-63	PF-65
1973D	.83,171,400	$1.50	
1973S, Pf	.(2,760,339)		$2.50
1974	.201,596,000	1.50	
1974D	.79,066,300	1.50	
1974D, DblDieObv		150.00	
1974S, Pf	.(2,612,568)		2.50

HALF DOLLARS

BICENTENNIAL COINAGE DATED 1776-1976

In an open contest for the selection of suitable designs for the special Bicentennial reverses of the quarter, half dollar and dollar, Seth G. Huntington's winning entry was featured on the half dollar. It shows Independence Hall in Philadelphia as the center device. The obverse was unchanged except for the dual dating 1776-1976. They were the only coins struck during 1975 and 1976 and were used for general circulation as well as being included in proof and uncirculated sets.

Designers Gilroy Roberts and Seth Huntington. Silver clad: weight 11.50 grams; composition: outer layers of .800 silver, .200 copper bonded to inner core of .209 silver, .791 copper; copper-nickel clad: weight 11.34 grams; composition: outer layers of copper-nickel (.750 copper, .250 nickel) bonded to inner core of pure copper; diameter 30.6 mm; reeded edge. Net weight: silver clad coinage .14792 oz. pure silver.

	Mintage	MS-63	PF-65
1776-1976, Copper-nickel clad	234,308,000	$1.50	
1776-1976D, Copper-nickel clad	287,565,248	1.50	
1776-1976S, Copper-nickel clad	(7,059,099)		$2.00
1776-1976S, Silver clad	*11,000,000	4.00	5.00
1776-1976 Silver Clad	*(4,000,000)	5.00	

*Approximate mintage, many were melted in 1982.

Eagle Reverse Resumed

	Mintage	MS-63	PF-65		Mintage	MS-63	PF-65
1977	43,598,000	$1.50		1984P	26,029,000	$2.00	
1977D	31,449,106	1.50		1984D	26,262,158	2.00	
1977S, Pf	(3,251,152)		$2.50	1984S, Pf	(3,065,110)		$5.00
1978	14,350,000	1.75		1985P	18,706,962	3.00	
1978D	13,765,799	3.00		1985D	19,814,034	3.50	
1978S, Pf	(3,127,781)		2.50	1985S, Pf	(3,362,821)		4.00
1979	68,312,000	1.50		1986P	13,107,633	7.00	
1979D	15,815,422	1.50		1986D	15,336,145	6.00	
1979S, Pf, Filled S			2.50	1986S, Pf	(3,010,497)		10.00
1979S, Pf, Clear S			15.00	1987P	*2,890,758	4.00	
1980P	44,134,000	1.25		1987D	*2,890,758	4.00	
1980D	33,456,449	1.25		1987S, Pf	(4,227,728)		4.00
1980S, Pf	(3,554,806)		2.50	1988P	13,626,000	4.00	
1981P	29,544,000	2.00		1988D	12,000,096	3.00	
1981D	27,839,533	1.25		1988S, Pf	(3,262,948)		6.00
1981S, Pf	(4,063,083)		2.50	1989P	24,542,000	2.50	
1982P	10,819,000	4.00		1989D	23,000,216	2.00	
1982D	13,140,102	4.00		1989S, Pf	(3,220,194)		5.00
1982S, Pf	(3,857,479)		2.50	1990P	22,278,000	2.50	
1983P	34,139,000	4.50		1990D	20,096,242	3.00	
1983D	32,472,244	4.50		1990S, Pf	(3,299,559)		5.00
1983S, Pf	(3,279,126)		3.50				

*Not issued for circulation; included with uncirculated and souvenir sets

Mintage	MS-63	PF-65
1991P 14,874,000	$3.00	
1991D 15,054,678	4.00	
1991S, Pf ...(2,867,787)		$12.00
1992P 17,628,000	1.50	
1992D 17,000,106	3.00	
1992S, Pf ...(2,858,981)		8.00
1992S,		
Silver Pf ..(1,317,579)		12.00
1993P 15,510,000	2.00	
1993D 15,000,006	3.00	
1993S, Pf ...(2,633,439)		14.00
1993S,		
Silver Pf ....(761,353)		22.00
1994P 23,718,000	2.00	
1994D 23,828,110	2.00	
1994S, Pf ...(2,484,594)		8.00
1994S,		
Silver Pf ....(785,329)		30.00
1995P 26,496,000	2.00	
1995D 26,288,000	2.00	
1995S, Pf ...(2,117,496)		27.00
1995S,		
Silver Pf ....(679,985)		100.00
1996P 24,442,000	2.00	
1996D 24,744,000	2.00	
1996S, Pf ...(1,750,244)		9.00
1996S,		
Silver Pf ....(775,021)		45.00
1997P 20,882,000	2.00	
1997D 19,876,000	2.00	
1997S Pf ...(2,055,000)		22.00
1997S		
Silver Pf ....(741,678)		90.00

Mintage	MS-63	PF-65
1998P 15,646,000	$1.75	
1998D 15,064,000	1.75	
1998S Pf ...(2,086,507)		$13.50
1998S		
Silver Pf 878,792		27.50
1998S Silver Matte Finish		260.00
1999P 8,900,000	1.50	
1999D 10,682,000	1.50	
1999S Pf ...(2,543,401)		12.00
1999S		
Silver Pf ....(800,000)		30.00
2000P 22,600,000	1.50	
2000D 19,466,000	1.50	
2000S Pf ...(3,082,483)		7.00
2000S		
Silver Pf ....(856,400)		10.00
2001P 21,200,000	10.00	
2001D 19,504,000	2.00	
2001S Pf ...(2,294,043)		10.00
2001S		
Silver Pf ....(889,697)		15.00
2002P 3,100,000	2.00	
2002D 2,500,000	2.00	
2002S Pf ...(2,277,720)		7.00
2002S		
Silver Pf ....(761,600)		12.00
2003P	1.00	
2003D	1.00	
2003S Pf		7.00
2003S Silver Pf		12.00
2004P	1.00	
2004D	1.00	
2004S Pf		7.00
2004S Silver Pf		12.00

BIBLIOGRAPHY

Fox, Bruce. *The Complete Guide to Walking Liberty Half Dollars.* Virginia Beach, VA, 1993.

Lawrence, David. *The Complete Guide to Barber Halves.* Virginia Beach, VA, 1991.

Overton, Al C. *Early Half Dollar Die Varieties 1794-1836.* Colorado Springs, 1967. Third Edition, 1990, edited by Donald Parsley.

Peterson, Glenn R. *The Ultimate Guide to Attributing Bust Half Dollars.* Rocky River, OH, 2000.

Wiley, Randy and Bugert, Bill. *The Complete Guide to Liberty Seated Half Dollars.* Virginia Beach, VA, 1993.

SILVER DOLLARS — 1794 to Date

The silver dollar was authorized by Congress April 2, 1792. Weight and fineness were specified at 416 grains and 892.4 fine. The first issues appeared in 1794 and until 1804 all silver dollars had the value stamped on the edge: HUNDRED CENTS, ONE DOLLAR OR UNIT. After a lapse in coinage of the silver dollar during the period 1804 to 1835, coins were made with either plain or reeded edges and the value was placed on the reverse side.

The weight was changed by the law of January 18, 1837 to 412$\frac{1}{2}$ grains, fineness .900. The coinage was discontinued by the Act of February 12, 1873 and reauthorized by the Act of February 28, 1878. The dollar was again discontinued after 1935, and since then only copper-nickel pieces have been coined for circulation. See bullion coins on page 347

ORIGIN OF THE DOLLAR

The word *dollar* evolves from German *thaler*, the name given to the first large-sized European silver coin. Designed as a substitute for the gold *florin*, the coin originated in the Tyrol in 1484. So popular did these large silver coins become during the 16th century that many other countries struck similar pieces, giving them names derived from "thaler". In the Netherlands the coin was called *rijksdaalder*, in Denmark *rigsdaler*, in Italy *tallero*, in Poland *talar*, in France *jocandale*, in Russia *jefimok*. All these names are abbreviations of "joachimsthaler." Until the discovery of the great silver deposits in Mexican and South American mines, the mint with the greatest output of large silver coins was that of Joachimsthal in the Bohemian Erzgebirge.

The Spanish dollar, or piece-of-eight, was widely used and familiar to everyone in the English-American colonies. It was only natural therefore that the word "dollar" was adopted officially as the standard monetary unit of the United States by Congress on July 6, 1785. The Continental Dollar of 1776 is described on page 39.

+ or − indicates change from previous year					**TYPE COIN VALUES**					
	G-4	F-12	EF-40	AU-50	MS-60	MS-63	MS-65	PF-60	PF-63	PF-65
Flowing Hair 1794-1795	1,000.+	3,000.+	10,000.+	15,000.+	37,500.+					
Drpd Bust, SE 1795-1798	1,000.+	2,400.+	7,500.+	9,500.+	30,000.+					
Drpd Bust, HE 1798-1804	750.+	1,300.+	3,600.+	6,000.+	15,000.					
Lib Seat-NM 1840-1866	165.+	225.+	375.+	600.+	1,100.+	3,000.+	15,000.-	1,300.+	2,900.+	12,000.
Lib. Seat-WM 1866-1873	165.+	210.+	375.+	600.+	950.-	2,800.-	22,000.-	1,300.+	3,000.	11,000.+
U.S. Trade Dol 1873-1883	70.+	120.+	150.+	250.	425.-	1,400.+	7,500.-	750.-	2,500.	5,500.-
Morgan Dol 1878-1921	9.	12.+	16.+	18.+	21.+	28.+	90.	750.+	1,800.-	5,000.-
Peace Dol 1921-1935	9.+	11.+	12.+	13.+	16.	28.+	120.+	10,000.	15,000.	35,000.

FLOWING HAIR TYPE 1794-1795

Varieties listed are those most significant to collectors, but numerous minor variations may be found because each of the early dies was individually made. Blanks were weighed before the dollars were struck and overweight pieces were filed to remove excess silver. Coins showing old "adjustment marks" may be worth less than values shown here. Some Flowing Hair type dollars of 1794 and 1795 were weight-adjusted by inserting a small (8mm) silver plug in the center of the blank planchet before striking the coin. Values of variations not listed in this guide depend on collector interest and demand.

Values shown here for uncirculated pieces are for well struck, attractive coins with a minimum of surface marks.

Designer Robert Scot; weight 26.96 grams; composition: .8924 silver, .1076 copper; approx. diameter 39-40 mm; edge: HUNDRED CENTS ONE DOLLAR OR UNIT with decorations between words.

AG-3 ABOUT GOOD—*Clear enough to identify.*
G-4 GOOD—*Date and letters readable. Main devices outlined, but lack details.*
VG-8 VERY GOOD—*Major details discernible. Letters well formed but worn.*
F-12 FINE—*Hair ends distinguishable. Top hairlines show, but otherwise worn smooth.*
VF-20 VERY FINE—*Hair in center shows some detail. Other details more bold.*
EF-40 EXTREMELY FINE—*Hair well defined but will show some wear.*
AU-50 ABOUT UNCIRCULATED—*Slight trace of wear on tips of highest curls and breast feathers are usually weak.*
MS-60 UNCIRCULATED—*No trace of wear. Light blemishes.*

SILVER DOLLARS

Mintage	AG-3	G-4	VG-8	F-12	VF-20	EF-40	AU-50	MS-60
1794 . . .1,758	$15,000.	$25,000.	$35,000.	$45,000.	$75,000.	$140,000.	$220,000.	$350,000.

Two Leaves Beneath Each Wing		**Three Leaves Beneath Each Wing**		**Silver Plug 1795**

	Mintage	AG-3	G-4	VG-8	F-12	VF-20	EF-40	AU-50	MS-60
1795 2 Leaves	}	700.	1,100.	1,700.	3,000.	5,250.	11,000.	16,500.	42,500.
1795, 3 Leaves	} 160,295	650.	1,000.	1,500.	3,000.	5,000.	10,000.	15,000.	37,500.
1795, Slvr plug	}	900.	1,500.	2,500.	4,500.	8,750.	14,500.	20,000.	80,000.

DRAPED BUST TYPE, SMALL EAGLE REVERSE 1795-1798

AG-3 ABOUT GOOD—*Clear enough to identify.*
G-4 GOOD—*Bust outlined, no detail. Date readable, some leaves evident.*
VG-8 VERY GOOD—*Drapery worn except deepest folds. Hairlines smooth.*
F-12 FINE—*All drapery lines distinguishable. Hairlines near cheek and neck show some detail.*
VF-20 VERY FINE—*Left side of drapery worn smooth.*
EF-40 EXTREMELY FINE—*Drapery shows distinctly. Hair well outlined and detailed.*
AU-50 ABOUT UNCIRCULATED—*Slight trace of wear on the bust shoulder and hair left of forehead and also on the breast and top edges of wings.*
MS-60 UNCIRCULATED—*No trace of wear. Light blemishes.*

		AG-3	G-4	VG-8	F-12	VF-20	EF-40	AU-50	MS-60
1795,Off-Center bust	} 42,738	700.	1,000.	1,350.	2,400.	3,750.	7,500.	9,500.	30,000.
1795, Centered bust		650.	1,000.	1,350.	2,400.	3,750.	7,500.	9,500.	30,000.

Small Date	Large Date

Small Letters					Large Letters		
Mintage	**AG-3**	**G-4**	**VG-8**	**F-12**	**VF-20**	**EF-40**	**AU-50**	**MS-60**
1796, All Kinds 79,920								
1796 SmDt Sm Letter (3 Var.)$750.	$1,200.	$1,500.	$2,600.	$4,250.	$8,500.	$12,000.	$38,000.
1796,SmDt,Lg Letter ..... 650.	1,000.	1,400.	2,500.	4,000.	8,000.	10,000.	35,000.
1796,LgDt,Sm Letter ..... 650.	1,000.	1,400.	2,500.	4,000.	8,000.	10,000.	35,000.
1797, All kinds 7,776								
1797,10 stars l.,6 right ... 650.	1,000.	1,400.	2,500.	4,000.	8,000.	10,000.	35,000.
1797,9 stars l.,7 r, Lg Letter 600.	1,000.	1,400.	2,500.	4,000.	8,000.	10,000.	35,000.
1797, 9 stars l., 7 r. ,Sm Letter 800.	1,400.	2,400.	3,300.	6,000.	11,500.	20,000.	70,000.
1798, All kinds ...327,536								
1798, 15 stars on obv. .... 950.	1,300.	1,850.	2,750.	4,600.	9,500.	14,000.	42,500.
1798, 13 stars on obv. .... 850.	1,200.	1,650.	2,500.	4,250.	8,000.	11,000.	38,750.

HERALDIC EAGLE REVERSE 1798-1804

G-4 GOOD—*Letters and date readable. E PLURIBUS UNUM illegible.*
VG-8 VERY GOOD—*Motto partially readable. Only deepest drapery details visible. All other lines smooth.*
F-12 FINE—*All drapery lines distinguishable. Hairlines near cheek and neck show some detail.*
VF-20 VERY FINE—*Left side of drapery worn smooth.*
EF-40 EXTREMELY FINE—*Drapery is distinct. Hair well detailed.*
AU-50 ABOUT UNCIRCULATED—*AU-50 Slight trace of wear on the bust shoulder and hair left of forehead and also on the breast and top edges of wings.*
MS-60 UNCIRCULATED—*No trace of wear. Light blemishes.*

The two earliest reverse dies of 1798 have five vertical lines in the stripes in the shield. All dollar dies thereafter have four vertical lines.

**4 vertical lines
in shield**

	G-4	**VG-8**	**F-12**	**VF-20**	**EF-40**	**AU-50**	**MS-60**
1798 Knob 9, 5 vertical lines	$750.	$900.	$1,350.	$2,300.	$3,750.	$6,250.	$15,000.
1798 Knob 9, 4 vertical lines	750.	900.	1,350.	2,300.	3,750.	6,250.	
1798 Knob 9,10 arrows	750.	900.	1,600.	2,400.	3,900.	6,500.	—
1798 Pointed 9, ClDt	750.	900.	1,350.	2,300.	3,750.	6,250.	15,000.
1798 Pointed 9, WdDt	750.	900.	1,350.	2,300.	3,750.	6,250.	15,000.

1799 over 98, Stars 7 and 6 **Stars 8 and 5**

	Mintage	G-4	VG-8	F-12	VF-20	EF-40	AU-50	MS-60
1798 Pointed 9, 5 vertical lines		750.	900.	1,400.	2,300.	3,800.	6,500.	17,000.
1798 Pointed 9,10 arrows		750.	900.	1,300.	2,200.	3,600.	6,000.	15,000.
1798 Pointed 9, 4 berries		750.	900.	1,300.	2,200.	3,700.	6,500.	16,500.
1799 All Kinds	423,515							
1799,9/8 rev.W/ 15 stars		800.	1,000.	1,400.	2,400.	3,800.	6,500.	16,000.
1799,9/8 rev.W/ 13 stars		800.	1,000.	1,300.	2,300.	3,750.	6,500.	16,000.
1799,Irr. Dt.15-star rev		750.	900.	1,300.	2,200.	3,700.	6,200.	15,000.
1799,Irr. Dt.13-star rev		750.	900.	1,300.	2,200.	3,800.	6,500.	15,000.
1799, NmlDt		750.	900.	1,300.	2,300.	3,800.	6,200.	15,000.
1799,Stars-8 left, 5 right		750.	900.	1,500.	2,500.	4,000.	7,000	18,000.
1800, All Kinds	220,920							
1800, Very wide Dt,low8		750.	900.	1,400.	2,300.	4,000.	6,200.	15,000.
1800, "Dotted date" from die breaks		750.	900.	1,400.	2,300.	4,000.	6,200.	
1800, Only 12 arrows		750.	900.	1,400.	2,300.	3,700.	6,000.	15,000.
1800, Nml dies		750.	900.	1,400.	2,300.	3,800.	6,200.	15,000.
1800, AMERICAI		750.	900.	1,400.	2,300.	3,800.	6,500.	16,000.
1801	54,454	750.	900.	1,400.	2,300.	4,250.	7,500.	24,000.
1801 Proof restrike (rev. struck from first die of 1804 dollar).								100,000.

1802 over 1 **Small 3** **Large 3**

1802, All Kinds	41,650							
1802, 2/1,narrow date		800.	1,000.	1,500.	2,500.	4,250.	7,000.	19,000.
1802, 2/1, Wide Dt		800.	1,000.	1,500.	2,500.	4,250.	7,000.	19,000.
1802,Narrow NmlDt		750.	950.	1,400.	2,400.	3,800.	6,400.	15,250.
1802,Wide NmlDt		800.	1,000.	1,500.	2,500.	3,800.	6,400.	15,250.
1802,Prooff restrike								85,000.
1803, Sm 3 ⎫		800.	1,000.	1,500.	2,500.	3,800.	7,000.	15,250.
1803, Lg 3 ⎬ 85,634		800.	1,000.	1,500.	2,500.	3,800.	7,000.	15,250.
1803, Proof restrike								95,000.

FIRST REVERSE

SECOND REVERSE

Note position of words STATES OF with relation to clouds.

1804 First reverse, Original (Childs specimen sold for $4,140,000 in 1999.)
1804 Second reverse, Restrike (Adams specimen sold for $874,000 in 2001.)
1804 Second reverse, Restrike with plain edge. Unique in Smithsonian.

The 1804 dollar is one of the most publicized rarities in the entire series of United States coins. There are specimens known as originals (first reverse), of which eight are known, and restrikes (second reverse), of which seven are known, one of which has a plain edge.

Numismatists have found that the 1804 "original" dollars were struck at the Mint in the 1834-35 period, for use in presentation Proof sets. The first known specimen, a Proof, was obtained from a mint officer by Mr. Stickney on May 9, 1843, in exchange for an "Immune Columbia" piece in gold. Later, in 1859, the pieces known as restrikes and electrotypes were made at the Mint to supply the needs of collectors who wanted specimens of these dollars.

Evidence that these pieces were struck during the later period is based on the fact that the 1804 dollars differ from issues of 1803 or earlier and conform more closely to those struck after 1836, their edges or borders having beaded segments and raised rim, not elongated denticles such as are found on the earlier dates.

Although the mint records state that 19,570 dollars were coined in 1804, in no place does it mention that they were dated 1804. It was the practice in those days to use old dies as long as they were serviceable with no regard in the annual reports for the dating of the coins. It is probable that the 1804 total for dollars actually covered coins that were dated 1803.

BIBLIOGRAPHY

Bolender, M. H. *The United States Early Silver Dollars from 1794 to 1803.* 3rd edition. Iola, WI, 1982. (Reprinted 1987)

Bowers, Q. David. *The Rare Silver Dollars Dated 1804.* Wolfeboro, NH, 1999.

Bowers, Q. David. *Silver Dollars and Trade Dollars of the United States: A Complete Encyclopedia.* Wolfeboro, NH, 1993.

Haseltine, J. W. *Type Table of United States Dollars, Half Dollars and Quarter Dollars.* Philadelphia, 1881 (reprinted 1927, 1968).

Newman, Eric P. and Bressett, Kenneth E. *The Fantastic 1804 Dollar.* Racine, WI, 1962.

SILVER DOLLARS

GOBRECHT DOLLARS — 1836-1839

Suspension of silver dollar coinage was lifted in 1831, but it was not until 1835 that steps were taken to resume coinage. Late in that year the mint director R.M. Patterson, ordered engraver Christian Gobrecht to prepare a pair of dies based on designs by Thomas Sully and Titian Peale. The first obverse die, dated 1836, bore the seated figure of Liberty on the obverse with the inscription C. GOBRECHT F. (F. is an abbreviation for the Latin word *Fecit* or "made it") in the field above the date. On the reverse was a large eagle flying left surrounded by twenty-six stars and the legend UNITED STATES OF AMERICA • ONE DOLLAR •. It is not known if coins from these dies were struck at that time. A new obverse die with Gobrecht's name on the base of Liberty was prepared, and in December 1836, 1,000 coins were struck for circulation. These coins weighed 416 grains, which was the standard enacted in 1792.

In early 1837 the weight was lowered to 412$\frac{1}{2}$ grains and pieces were struck in March, 1837, using the dies of 1836. Dies were oriented in a medal fashion (top to top when rotated) to distinguish them from those struck in December 1836. Dollars issued for circulation in 1836, 1837, and 1839 are found with different die alignments. The "original" issue of December 1836 has the nomal "coin" orientation (reverse upright when coin is turned on a horizontal axis) with the eagle flying upward.

From the late 1850s to the 1870s the Mint continued to strike Gobrecht dollars to satisfy collector demands. Mules, which had mismatched designs or edge devices, were made in that period and are rare. Restrikes and mules are seldom seen in worn condition.

Original 1836 die orientation   **Die alignment of original**
Using either "coin" or "medal" turn.   **issues dated 1838 and 1839.**

Gobrecht dollars, both original issues and restrikes, were made in either coin turn orientation ↑↓ (I and III), or medal turn orientation ↑↑ (II and IV), and were struck in four basic die alignments.

Die Alignment I: ↑↓, head of Liberty opposite DO of DOLLAR, eagle flying upward.
Die Alignment II: ↑↑, head of Liberty opposite ES of STATES, eagle flying upward.
Die Alignment III: ↑↓, head of Liberty opposite N of ONE, eagle flying level.
Die Alignment IV: ↑↑, head of Liberty opposite F of OF, eagle flying level.

Rotated dies are common for original issue and restrike Gobrecht dollars. The 600 coins produced for circulation in March 1837 had dies that rotated from die alignment II to die alignment IV during the striking.

	VF-20	EF-40	AU-50	PF-60
1836 C. GOBRECHT F. in field above date. Eagle flying left amid stars. Plain edge. Die alignment I, ↑↓. Pattern				$27,500.
1836 C. GOBRECHT F. on base. Rev. as above. Plain edge, die alignment I, ↑↓. Circulation issue. 1,000 struck	$6,500.	$10,000.	$14,000.	16,500.
1836 As above. Plain edge. Die alignment II - die alignment. IV, ↑↑. Circulation issue struck in 1837. 600 struck	6,500.	10,000.	14,000.	16,500.

	VF-20	EF-40	AU-50	PF-60
1838 Similar obv., designer's name omitted, stars added around border. Rev. Eagle flying in plain field. Reeded edge. Die alignment IV, ↑↑. (Pattern)	11,000.	16,000.	18,000	25,000.
1839 As above. Reeded edge. Die alignment IV, ↑↑ Circulation issue. 300 struck	10,000.	15,000.	17,000.	22,000.

RESTRIKES

Restrikes were produced from the late 1850s to the 1870s, and are not official coins. They were all oriented in either die alignment III (coin turn), or die alignment IV (medal turn), with eagle flying level, and almost all were struck from a cracked reverse die.

1836 Name below base. Eagle in plain field. Plain edge.	75,000.
1836 Name on base. Reeded edge	100,000.
1838 Designer's name omitted. Plain edge	45,000.
1839 Designer's name omitted. Plain edge	30,000.

SILVER DOLLARS
— LIBERTY SEATED TYPE — HERALDIC EAGLE 1840-1873 —

Starting in 1840 silver dollars were issued for general circulation, but by spring 1853 the silver content of such pieces was worth more than the face value, and later issues were not seen in circulation but were used mainly in export trade. This situation continued through the late 1860s. The seated figure of Liberty device was adopted for the obverse, but the flying eagle design was rejected in favor of the more familiar form with olive branch and arrows used for the other silver denominations.

The 1866 proof quarter, half and dollar without motto are not mentioned in the Director's Report, and were not issued for circulation.

Mint mark location is on the reverse below eagle.

Designer Christian Gobrecht; weight 26.73 grams; composition: .900 silver, .100 copper; diameter 38.1 mm; reeded edge; mints: Philadelphia, New Orleans, Carson City, San Francisco. Net weight: .77344 oz. pure silver.

VG-8 VERY GOOD—Any 3 letters of LIBERTY at least two-thirds complete.
F-12 FINE—All 7 letters of LIBERTY visible though weak.
VF-20 VERY FINE—LIBERTY is strong but its ribbon shows slight wear.
EF-40 EXTREMELY FINE—Horizontal lines of shield complete. Eagle's eye plain.
AU-50 ABOUT UNCIRCULATED—Traces of light wear on only the high points of the design. Half of mint luster is present.
MS-60 UNCIRCULATED—No trace of wear. Light marks or blemishes.
PF-60—Surface may have several contact marks, hairlines or light rubs. Luster may be dull and eye appeal lacking.
PF-63—Reflective surfaces with only a few blemishes in secondary focal places. No major flaws.

	Mintage	VG-8	F-12	VF-20	EF-40	AU-50	MS-60	PF-60	PF-63
1840	61,005	$190.	$240.	$300.	$450.	$775.	$2,250.	$12,500.	$30,000.
1841	173,000	185.	225.	280.	400.	650.	1,650.	12,500.	3,000.
1842	184,618	185.	225.	280.	400.	625.	1,150.	12,500.	32,000.
1843	165,100	185.	225.	280.	400.	650.	1,400.	12,500.	32,000.
1844	20,000	200.	275.	375.	525.	1,150.	2,900.	10,250.	39,000.
1845	24,500	235.	275.	375.	550.	1,350.	6,750.	13,000.	35,000.
1846	110,600	185.	225.	280.	425.	625.	1,450.	10,250.	30,000.
1846O	59,000	200.	250.	300.	500.	950.	3,000.		
1847	140,750	185.	225.	280.	400.	650.	1,100.	13,000.	26,500.
1848	15,000	325.	425.	600.	775.	1,375.	3,200.	13,000.	33,000.
1849	62,600	185.	225.	280.	425.	800.	1,800.	12,500.	39,000.
1850	7,500	450.	575.	850.	1,250.	2,500.	5,300.	12,500.	33,000.
1850O	40,000	250.	375.	625.	1,200.	3,000.	8,000.		
1851,Orgl, Hgh Dt	1,300	5,000.	9,000.	11,000.	13,000.	19,000.	30,000.	24,000.	35,000.
1851,Restrk,Dt cntrd								21,000.	34,000.
1851O									
1852 Original	1,100	4,000.	8,000.	10,000.	12,000.	20,000.	27,500.	30,000.	44,000.
1852, Restrike								12,500.	30,000.
1853	46,110	210.	275.	375.	600.	1,200.	2,400.	16,000.	32,000.
1854	33,140	1,200.	1,800.	2,500.	3,750.	5,500.	14,000.	10,500.	19,500.
1855	26,000	1,000.	1,300.	2,000.	3,100.	4,500.	7,500.	11,000.	20,000.
1856	63,500	375.	400.	550.	1,100.	1,800.	3,800.	5,500.	14,500.
1857	94,000	375.	400.	550.	1,100.	1,500.	2,700.	5,000.	9,500.
1858 Estimated (300+)		2,800.	3,200.	4,500.	5,250.	5,600.		7,000.	10,000.

[189]

SILVER DOLLARS

	Mintage	VG-8	F-12	VF-20	EF-40	AU-50	MS-60	MS-63	PF-63
1859 . . . .(800)	.256,500	$225.	$325.	$425.	$550.	$650.	$1,600.	$5,250.	$3,500.
1859O	.360,000	185.	225.	275.	380.	600.	950.	3,000.	
1859S	.20,000	300.	425.	550.	1,350.	3,400.	9,500.		
1860 . .(1,330)	.218,930	250.	300.	425.	500.	625.	1,000.	3,000.	3,500.
1860O	.515,000	185.	225.	275.	380.	600.	1,000.	3,000.	
1861 . .(1,000)	.78,500	600.	725.	875.	1,000.	2,000.	3,000.	5,250.	3,500.
1862 . . . .(550)	.12,090	475.	700.	800.	950.	2,000.	3,000.	5,250.	3,500.
1863 . . . .(460)	.27,660	325.	365.	450.	600.	1,100.	2,500.	5,000.	3,250.
1864 . . . .(470)	.31,170	225.	300.	450.	550.	1,100.	2,500.	5,400.	3,250.
1865 . . . .(500)	.47,000	200.	275.	435.	525.	1,100.	2,500.	5,200.	3,250.
1866 NO MOTTO	. .(725)								
1866	.49,625	225.	300.	425.	500.	900.	1,700.	3,450.	3,000.
1867 . . . .(625)	.47,525	200.	275.	400.	475.	850.	1,700.	3,600.	3,000.

	Mintage	VG-8	F-12	VF-20	EF-40	AU-50	MS-60	MS-63	PF-63
1868 . . . .(600)	.162,700	185.	235.	350.	450.	850.	1,700.	6,000.	3,000.
1869 . . . .(600)	.424,300	200.	235.	300.	425.	700.	1,700.	4,000.	3,000.
1870 . .(1,000)	.416,000	185.	225.	275.	400.	625.	1,300.	3,100.	3,000.
1870CC	.11,758	350.	525.	750.	1,450.	3,500.	10,000.	23,000.	
1870S		75,000.	100,000.	200,000.	300,000.	600,000.			1,000,000.
1871 . . . .(960)	1,074,760	185.	225.	275.	400.	625.	1,100.	3,000.	3,200.
1871CC 1,376		2,200.	3,200.	5,000.	9,400.	25,000.	50,000.		
1872 . . . .(950)	1,106,450	185.	210.	275.	375.	650.	1,100.	3,000.	3,000.
1872CC 3,150		1,200.	1,900.	3,000.	4,300.	9,750.	21,000.	40,000.	
1872S 9,000		275.	400.	550.	1,100.	2,500.	8,500.	30,000.	
1873 . . . .(600)	.293,600	190.	235.	285.	375.	650.	3,000.	3,000.	
1873CC 2,300		4,500.	6,250.	9,000.	16,000.	30,000.	75,000.	125,000.	
1873S 700				Unknown in any collection.					

TRADE DOLLARS 1873-1885

This coin was issued for circulation in the Orient to compete with dollar-size coins of other countries. Many pieces that circulated in the Orient were counterstamped with Oriental characters, known as "chop marks." They were legal tender in the U.S., but when silver prices declined, Congress repealed the provision and authorized the Treasury to limit coinage to export demand. In 1887, the Treasury to redeemed all Trade dollars that were not mutilated. The law authorizing Trade dollars was repealed in February, 1887.

Modifications to the Trade dollar design are distinguished as follows:

Reverse 1: Berry under eagle's left talon; arrowhead ends over 0. Used on all coins from all mints in 1873 and 1874, and occasionally in 1875 and 1876.

Reverse 2: Without extra berry under talon; arrowhead ends over 2. Used occasionally at all mints from 1875 through 1876, and on all coins from all mints 1877 through 1885.

Obverse 1: Ends of scroll point to left; extended hand has only three fingers. Used on all coins at all mints 1873 through 1876.

Obverse 2: Ends of scroll point downward; hand has four fingers. Used in combination with Reverse 2 on one variety of 1876S, and on all coins at all mints from 1877 through 1885.

TRADE DOLLARS 1873 - 1885

Designer William Barber; weight 27.22 grams; composition: .900 silver, .100 copper; diameter 38.1mm; reeded edge; mints: Philadelphia, Carson City, San Francisco. Net weight: .7874 oz. pure silver.

VG-8 VERY GOOD — *About half of mottoes IN GOD WE TRUST and E PLURIBUS UNUM will show. Rim on both sides well defined.*
F-12 FINE — *Mottoes and LIBERTY readable but worn.*
EF-40 EXTREMELY FINE — *Mottoes and LIBERTY are sharp. Only slight wear on rims.*
AU-50 ABOUT UNCIRCULATED — *Slight trace of wear on Liberty's left breast and left knee and hair above ear. Also on the eagle's head, knee, and wing tips.*
MS-60 UNCIRCULATED — *No trace of wear. Light blemishes.*
MS-63 SELECT UNCIRCULATED — *Some distracting contact marks or blemishes in prime focal areas. Luster may be impaired.*
PF-63 — *Reflective surfaces with only a few blemishes in secondary focal places. No major flaws.*

**1875S
S over CC
Mint mark location on reverse
above letter "D"
in dollar.**

	Mintage	VG-8	F-12	EF-40	AU-50	MS-60	MS-63	PF-63
1873 . . . .(865)	.397,500	$100.	$175.	$200.	$300.	$650.		$2,500.
1873CC	.124,500	150.	200.	500.	1,000.	2,500.	6,000.	
1873S	.703,000	100.	125.	225.	375.	900.	2,000.	
1874 . . . .(700)	.987,800	100.	125.	200.	300.	450.	1,400.	2,500.
1874CC	1,373,200	100.	200.	275.	400.	1,000.	2,200.	
1874S	2,549,000	100.	125.	150.	250.	425.	1,400.	
1875 . . . .(700)	.218,900	150.	300.	500.	800.	1,750.	2,750.	2,750.
1875 Rev. 2		150.	300.	475.	750.	1,650.	2,500.	
1875CC	1,573,700	100.	120.	250.	300.	800.	2,800.	
1875CC Rev. 2		100.	175.	275.	350.	1,250.	2,500.	
1875S	4,487,000	100.	125.	150.	250.	425.	1,400.	
1875S Rev. 2		100.	125.	175.	275.	500.	1,600.	
1875S, S/CC		200.	300.	725.	1,100.	2,500.	7,500.	
1876 . . . . . .(1,150)	.456,150	100.	130.	175.	275.	500.	1,500.	2,500.
1876 Rev. 2		100.	125.	150.	250.	450.	1,400.	
1876CC Rev. 1 . . .		150.	200.	400.	1,000.	3,000.	9,500.	
1876CC	.509,000	125.	175.	350.	900.	2,300.	7,000.	
1876S	5,227,000	100.	130.	175.	275.	450.	1,600.	
1876S Rev. 2		100.	125.	150.	250.	425.	1,400.	
1876S Obv. 2/Rev. 2		125.	150.	200.	300.	600.	1,750.	
1877 . . . .(510)	3,039,710	100.	125.	150.	250.	500.	1,500.	2,500.
1877CC	.534,000	140.	200.	475.	600.	1,100.	2,500.	
1877S	9,519,000	100.	125.	150.	250.	450.	1,500.	
1878 . . . .(900)				1,000.				2,500.
1878CC	.*97,000	400.	600.	1,700.	3,000.	8,000.	15,000.	
1878S	4,162,000	100.	125.	150.	250.	450.	1,500.	
1879 . . . . .(1,541)				1,000.				2,500.
1880 . . . . .(1,987)				1,000.				2,500.
1881 . . . . . .(960)				1,100.				2,500.
1882 . . . . .(1,097)				1,000.				2,500.
1883 . . . .(979)				1,100.				2,500.
1884 . . . .(10)								250,000.
1885 . . . .(5)								920,000.

*44,148 Trade dollars were melted on July 19, 1878. Many of these may have been 1878CC.

SILVER DOLLARS
LIBERTY HEAD OR MORGAN TYPE 1878-1921

The coinage law of 1873 made no provision for the standard silver dollar. During the lapse in coinage of this denomination the gold dollar became the unit coin, and the trade dollar was used for our commercial transactions with the Orient.

Resumption of coinage of the silver dollar was authorized by the Act of February 28, 1878, known as the Bland-Allison Act. The weight (412$\frac{1}{2}$ grains) and fineness (.900) were to conform with the Act of January 18, 1837.

George T. Morgan, formerly a pupil of Wyon in the Royal Mint in London, designed the new dollar. His initial M is found at the truncation of the neck, at the last tress. It also appears on the reverse on the left-hand loop of the ribbon.

Coinage of the silver dollar was suspended after 1904 when demand was low and the bullion supply became exhausted. Under provisions of the Pittman Act of 1918, 270,232,722 silver dollars were melted and later, in 1921, coinage of the silver dollar was resumed. The Morgan design, with some slight refinements, was employed until the new Peace design was adopted later in that year.

Varieties listed are those most significant to collectors. Numerous other variations exist. Values are shown for the most common pieces. Prices of variations not listed in this guide depend on collector interest and demand.

Sharply struck, "proof-like" coins have a highly reflective surface and are very scarce, usually commanding substantial premiums.

Mint mark location is on reverse below wreath.

BIBLIOGRAPHY

Bowers, Q. David. *Silver Dollars and Trade Dollars of the United States: A Complete Encyclopedia.* Wolfeboro, NH, 1993.
Bowers, Q. David. *The Official RED BOOK™ of Morgan Silver Dollars: A Complete History and Price Guide.* Atlanta, GA, 2004.
Fey, Michael S., and Jeff Oxman. *The Top 100 Morgan Dollar Varieties.* Morris Planes, NJ, 1997.
Highfill, John W. *The Comprehensive U.S. Silver Dollar Encyclopedia.* Broken Arrow, OK, 1992.
Van Allen, Leroy C. and Mallis, A. George. *Comprehensive Catalogue and Encyclopedia of U.S. Morgan and Peace Silver Dollars.* New York. 1997.
Willem, John M. *The United States Trade Dollar.* Second edition, Racine, Wis., 1965.

Designer George T. Morgan; weight 26.73 grams; composition: .900 silver, .100 copper; diameter 38.1 mm; reeded edge; mints: Philadelphia, New Orleans, Carson City, Denver, San Francisco. Net weight: .77344 oz. pure silver.

First Reverse
8 Tail Feathers, 1878 Philadelphia Only

Second Reverse **Third Reverse**

Parallel top arrow feather, concave breast. **Slanted top arrow feather, convex breast.** **1878 doubled tail feathers**

SILVER DOLLARS

VF-20 VERY FINE — *Two-thirds of hairlines from top of forehead to ear must show. Ear well defined. Feathers on eagle's breast worn.*
EF-40 EXTREMELY FINE — *All hairlines strong and ear bold. Eagle's feathers all plain but slight wear on breas and wing tips.*
AU-50 ABOUT UNCIRCULATED — *Slight trace of wear on the bust shoulder and hair left of forehead and also on the breast and top edges of wings.*
MS-60 UNCIRCULATED — *No trace of wear. Has full mint luster but may be noticeably marred by scuff marks or bag abrasions.*
MS-63 SELECT UNCIRCULATED — *No trace of wear, full mint luster, few noticeable surface marks.*
MS-64 UNCIRCULATED — *Shows a few scattered contact marks. Good eye appeal and attractive luster.*
MS-65 CHOICE UNCIRCULATED — *Only light scattered contact marks that are not distracting. Strong luster, good eye appeal.*
PF-63 ATTRACTIVE PROOF — *Reflective surfaces with only a few blemishes in secondary focal places. No major flaws.*

	Mintage	VF-20	EF-40	AU-50	MS-60	MS-63	MS-64	MS-65	PF-63
1878, 8 Feathers (500)	750,000	$21.	$24.	$40.	$110.	$150.	$400.	$1,200.	$2,300.
1878, 7 Feathers (250)	9,759,550								
1878, Clear double Feathers		22.	28.	50.	110.	250.	400.	3,300.	
1878, 7 Feathers, 2nd rev.		20.	23.	35.	60.	110.	300.	1,700.	
1878,7 Feathers, 3rd rev.		21.	23.	35.	70.	130.	400.	2,700.	7,000.
1878CC	2,212,000	75.	80.	100.	190.	225.	500.	1,350.	
1878S	9,774,000	22.	25.	35.	50.	60.	90.	275.	
1879 (1,100)	14,807,100	15.	18.	20.	30.	60.	125.	1,000.	2,000.
1879CC, CC / CC	756,000	135.	350.	875.	1,850.	4,250.	6,500.		
1879CC,Clear CC	2,887,000	150.	500.	1,000.	2,000.	5,000.	7,500.	19,000.	
1879O		15.	18.	22.	75.	160.	425.	3,250.	
1879S, Second Rev.	9,110,000	17.	23.	35.	90.	375.	1,250.	7,000.	
1879S, Third Rev.		17.	20.	22.	32.	45.	60.	125.	
1880, 80/79*	12,601,355	18.	23.	40.	80.	300.	500.		
1880 (1,355)		17.	20.	23.	30.	55.	125.	750.	2,400.

1880CC, 80 over 79‡

1880CC, 8 over high 7*

1880CC, 8 over low 7

	Mintage	VF-20	EF-40	AU-50	MS-60	MS-63	MS-64	MS-65	PF-63
1880CC, All Kinds	591,000								
1880CC, 80/79, 2nd rev.‡		150.	200.	275.	400.	500.	1,500.	2,500.	
1880CC,8/7,2nd rev.		150.	200.	275.	400.	475.	900.	2,300.	
1880CC,8/high 7,3rd rev.*		140.	190.	225.	340.	425.	625.	1,000.	
1880CC,8/low 7,3rd rev.		140.	190.	275.	400.	450.	625.	1,000.	
1880CC,Third reverse		160.	225.	300.	450.	500.	700.	1,000.	
1880O, 8/7*	5,305,000	18.	25.	34.	75.	400.	1,900.		
1880O		16.	18.	22.	65.	300.	1,600.	21,000.	
1880S, 8/7*	8,900,000	17.	20.	28.	44.	50.	75.		
1880S, 0/9		18.	21.	29.	45.	50.	75.		
1880S		15.	18.	20.	30.	38.	50.	90.	
1881 (984)	9,163,984	16.	18.	20.	30.	55.	135.	800.	1,800.
1881CC	296,000	250.	300.	350.	400.	475.	525.	700.	
1881O	5,708,000	16.	18.	20.	30.	45.	130.	1,600.	
1881S	12,760,000	16.	18.	20.	30.	45.	6.	115.	
1882 (1,100)	11,101,100	16.	18.	20.	30.	45.	55.	430.	1,800.
1882CC	1,133,000	100.	110.	120.	200.	225.	300.	500.	
1882O	6,090,000	16.	18.	20.	28.	42.	70.	800.	
1882O, O/S*		22.	28.	55.	175.	950.	2,750.	25,000.	

*Several die varieties. Values shown are for the most common.
‡7 and 9 show within the 80, no tip below second 8.

Proof Morgan Dollars where indicated in mintage record (quantity shown in parenthesis) are valued approximately as follows:

Proof-60 $850.00   Proof-65 $5,200

	Mintage	VF-20	EF-40	AU-50	MS-60	MS-63	MS-64	MS-65	PF-63
1882S	9,250,000	$16.	$18.	$20.	$35.	$45.	$60.	$125.	
1883 (1,039)	12,291,039	16.	18.	20.	30.	45.	60.	170.	$1,800.
1883CC	1,204,000	100.	110.	115.	180.	200.	275.	400.	
1883O	8,725,000	16.	18.	20.	30.	45.	60.	125.	
1883S	6,250,000	18.	34.	175.	475.	2,000.	3,800.	18,000.	
1884 (875)	14,070,875	16.	18.	20.	30.	45.	60.	300.	1,800.
1884CC	1,136,000	100.	110.	120.	185.	200.	240.	400.	
1884O	9,730,000	16.	18.	20.	30.	45.	60.	125.	
1884S	3,200,000	17.	40.	250.	3,500.	23,000.	100,000.	180,000.	
1885 (930)	17,787,930	16.	18.	20.	30.	45.	60.	125.	1,800.
1885CC	228,000	300.	340.	400.	450.	500.	600.	1,000.	
1885O	9,185,000	16.	18.	20.	30.	45.	60.	125.	
1885S	1,497,000	20.	30.	85.	175.	275.	525.	1,900.	
1886 (886)	19,963,886	16.	18.	20.	30.	45.	60.	125.	1,800.
1886O	10,710,000	17.	20.	100.	500.	3,200.	7,500.	200,000.	
1886S	750,000	50.	75.	100.	250.	375.	575.	3,000.	
1887, 7/6 } (710)	20,290,710	25.	45.	100.	275.	700.	1,000.	4,500.	
1887		16.	18.	20.	30.	45.	60.	125.	1,800.
1887O, 7/6 }	11,550,000	30.	60.	140.	375.	2,500.	10,000.	25,000.	
1887O		17.	20.	30.	60.	125.	375.	4,000.	
1887S	1,771,000	20.	25.	45.	100.	250.	600.	3,500.	
1888 (832)	19,183,932	16.	18.	20.	30.	45.	60.	200.	1,800.
1888O	12,150,000	16.	18.	20.	30.	45.	60.	400.	
1888O, Double Die Obverse		75.	125.	320.	1,500.	—			

**1888O
Doubled Die
Obverse
Lips especially
prominent.
"Hot Lips"
variety**

**1901 Doubled Die Reverse
Note Tail Feathers**

	Mintage	VF-20	EF-40	AU-50	MS-60	MS-63	MS-64	MS-65	PF-63
1888S	657,000	75.	85.	100.	250.	375.	500.	3,500.	
1889 (811)	21,726,811	16.	18.	20.	30.	45.	60.	125.	1,800.
1889CC	350,000	1,500.	3,000.	5,000.	15,000.	25,000.	47,000.	280,000.	
1889O	11,875,000	17.	20.	40.	150.	375.	650.	5,000.	
1889S	700,000	45.	55.	70.	275.	375.	500.	1,800.	
1890 (590)	16,802,590	16.	18.	26.	30.	55.	125.	2,200.	1,900.
1890CC	2,309,041	75.	100.	135.	350.	650.	1,600.	6,500.	
1890O	10,701,000	16.	22.	30.	60.	100.	250.	1,500.	
1890S	8,230,373	16.	18.	25.	60.	100.	225.	1,000.	
1891 (650)	8,694,206	16.	18.	25.	60.	135.	500.	6,500.	1,900.
1891CC	1,618,000	90.	95.	140.	350.	600.	1,000.	4,000.	
1891O	7,954,529	16.	20.	40.	140.	325.	700.	9,000.	
1891S	5,296,000	18.	20.	25.	65.	125.	250.	1,200.	
1892 (1,245)	1,037,245	25.	35.	75.	150.	375.	750.	4,000.	1,900.
1892CC	1,352,000	125.	250.	325.	675.	1,100.	1,800.	6,500.	
1892O	2,744,000	20.	30.	65.	175.	280.	600.	4,500.	
1892S	1,200,000	50.	175.	1,700.	25,000.	55,000.	85,000.	150,000.	

For Proof-60 and Proof-65 Morgan dollar prices see page 193.

SILVER DOLLARS

	Mintage	VF-20	EF-40	AU-50	MS-60	MS-63	MS-64	MS-65	PF-63
1893 ...(792)	...378,792	$125.	$200.	$250.	$500.	$1,000.	$1,500.	$6,500.	$2,200.
1893CC	677,000	350.	1,000.	1,250.	2,500.	5,000.	9,000.	45,000.	
1893O	300,000	150.	250.	650.	1,500.	6,000.	18,000.		
1893S*	100,000	4,000.	7,000.	18,000.	55,000.	90,000.	225,000.	400,000.	
1894 ...(972)	...110,972	800.	850.	1,500.	2,000.	4,500.	6,000.	20,000.	35,000.
1894O	1,723,000	40.	60.	175.	600.	3,200.	6,500.	40,000.	
1894S	1,260,000	65.	120.	300.	500.	850.	1,500.	5,000.	
1895, Pf‡ (880)	12,880	‡ 22,000.	‡25,000.	‡27,500.	‡35,000.	‡40,000.	‡45,000.	‡35,000.	
1895O	450,000	175.	275.	900.	12,000.	35,000.	60,000.	175,000.	
1895S	400,000	275.	475.	1,000.	1,800.	4,200.	6,500.	18,000.	
1896 ...(762)	...9,976,762	16.	18.	20.	30.	45.	60.	125.	1,800.
1896O	4,900,000	18.	20.	200.	850.	7,000.	40,000.	150,000.	
1896S	5,000,000	50.	160.	450.	1,000.	2,000.	2,500.	15,000.	
1897 ...(731)	...2,822,731	16.	18.	20.	30.	45.	60.	125.	1,800.
1897O	4,004,000	18.	22.	125.	600.	4,500.	15,000.	45,000.	
1897S	5,825,000	16.	18.	25.	60.	100.	160.	600.	
1898 ...(735)	...5,884,735	16.	18.	20.	30.	45.	60.	250.	1,800.
1898O	4,440,000	16.	18.	20.	30.	45.	60.	125.	
1898S	4,102,000	25.	30.	75.	250.	425.	650.	2,200.	
1899 ...(846)	...330,846	45.	60.	75.	110.	225.	300.	700.	1,800.
1899O	12,290,000	16.	18.	20.	30.	45.	60.	125.	
1899S	2,562,000	25.	45.	100.	300.	350.	600.	2,000.	
1900 ...(912)	...8,830,912	16.	18.	20.	30.	45.	60.	200.	1,800.
1900O ......} 1900O, O/CC⁺ }	12,590,000	16. / 35.	18. / 50.	20. / 125.	30. / 225.	45. / 600.	60. / 850.	225. / 2,000.	
1900S	3,540,000	22.	35.	80.	240.	300.	450.	1,400.	
1901* ..(813)	...6,962,813	35.	65.	325.	1,700.	16,500.	40,000.	150,000.	3,000.
1901, Double Die Reverse		200.	600.	2,000.	4,000.	—			
1901O	13,320,000	16.	18.	20.	30.	45.	60.	185.	
1901S	2,284,000	35.	50.	200.	350.	650.	850.	3,500.	
1902 ...(777)	...7,994,777	16.	18.	25.	45.	90.	125.	500.	1,800.
1902O	8,636,000	16.	18.	20.	30.	45.	60.	125.	
1902S	1,530,000	100.	120.	200.	300.	500.	800.	2,800.	
1903 ...(755)	...4,652,755	40.	50.	60.	75.	80.	85.	240.	1,800.
1903O	4,450,000	200.	300.	375.	425.	450.	500.	750.	
1903S	1,241,000	100.	300.	1,400.	3,200.	4,800.	5,500.	7,500.	
1904 ...(650)	...2,788,650	20.	30.	40.	80.	300.	500.	4,000.	1,900.
1904O	3,720,000	16.	18.	20.	30.	45.	60.	125.	
1904S	2,304,000	60.	225.	600.	1,000.	2,000.	2,500.	6,500.	
1921	44,690,000	14.	16.	18.	21.	28.	40.	120.	—
1921D	20,345,000	15.	17.	19.	35.	55.	125.	300.	
1921S	21,695,000	15.	17.	19.	25.	62.	160.	1,500.	

*Authentication is recommended. Beware of altered mint mark.
‡Beware of removed mint mark. Values are for Proofs; business strikes are not known to exist.
+Several die varieties.
For Proof-60 and Proof-65 Morgan dollar prices see page 193.

PEACE TYPE 1921-1935

The dollar issued from 1921 to 1935 was a commemorative peace coin, which might easily have been a half dollar. The Peace dollar, in fact, was issued without congressional sanction, under the terms of the Pittman Act, which referred to the bullion and in no way affected the design.

Anthony De Francisci, a medalist, designed this dollar. His monogram is located in the field of the coin under the neck of Liberty.

The new Peace dollar was placed in circulation January 3, 1922. 1,006,473 pieces were struck in December, 1921.

The high relief of the 1921 design was found impractical for coinage and was slightly modified in 1922 after 35,401 coins were made and most of them melted at the mint. The rare matte and satin finish proof specimens of 1922 are of both the high relief style of 1921, as well as of the normal relief.

SILVER DOLLARS

Legislation dated August 3, 1964 authorized the coinage of 45 million silver dollars, and 316,076 dollars of the Peace design dated 1964 were struck at the Denver mint in 1965. Plans for completing this coinage were subsequently abandoned and all of these coins were melted. None were preserved or released for circulation.

Designer Anthony De Francisci; weight 26.73 grams; composition: .900 silver, .100 copper; diameter 38.1 mm; reeded edge; mints: Philadelphia, Denver, San Francisco. Net weight: .77344 oz. pure silver.

Mint mark location is on reverse below ONE.

VF-20 VERY FINE—*Hair over eye well worn. Some strands over ear well defined. Some eagle feathers on top and outside edge of right wing will show.*

EF-40 EXTREMELY FINE—*Hairlines over brow and ear are strong though slightly worn. Outside wing feathers at right and those at top are visible but faint.*

AU-50 ABOUT UNCIRCULATED—*Slight trace of wear. Most of mint luster is present although marred by contact marks.*

MS-60 UNCIRCULATED—*No trace of wear. Has full mint luster but may be noticeably marred by stains, surface marks or bag abrasions.*

MS-63—*Some distracting contact marks or blemishes in prime focal areas. Luster may be impaired.*

MS-64 UNCIRCULATED—*Shows a few scattered contact marks. Good eye appeal and attractive luster.*

MS-65—**CHOICE UNCIRCULATED**—*Only light scattered contact marks that are not distracting. Strong luster, good eye appeal.*

	Mintage	VF-20	EF-40	AU-50	MS-60	MS-63	MS-64	MS-65	Matte PF-65
1921, high relief ..	1,006,473	$75.	$85.	$120.	$200.	$325.	$600.	$2,500.	$35,000.
1922, high relief ..	35,401			—					35,000.
1922, Nml relief ...	51,737,000	11.	12.	13.	16.	30.	40.	140.	35,000.
1922D	15,063,000	11.	12.	13.	25.	50.	75.	400.	
1922S	17,475,000	11.	12.	13.	23.	60.	275.	2,000.	
1923	30,800,000	11.	12.	13.	16.	30.	40.	140.	
1923D	6,811,000	11.	12.	18.	55.	120.	250.	1,000.	
1923S	19,020,000	11.	12.	14.	25.	65.	200.	6,000.	
1924	11,811,000	12.	12.	14.	16.	28.	45.	125.	
1924S	1,728,000	20.	30.	60.	190.	425.	1,000.	7,500.	
1925	10,198,000	12.	12.	14.	16.	30.	45.	120.	
1925S	1,610,000	14.	16.	32.	65.	135.	500.	20,000.	
1926	1,939,000	12.	14.	17.	32.	60.	85.	325.	
1926D	2,348,700	12.	15.	28.	60.	130.	250.	600.	
1926S	6,980,000	12.	14.	18.	40.	75.	220.	800.	
1927	848,000	20.	30.	45.	70.	130.	250.	2,000.	
1927D	1,268,900	20.	25.	75.	145.	275.	600.	5,000.	
1927S	866,000	20.	25.	65.	135.	300.	700.	10,000.	
1928	360,649	300.	350.	375.	425.	550.	750.	4,500.	
1928S	1,632,000	22.	30.	55.	140.	500.	1,500.	20,000.	
1934	954,057	18.	22.	40.	90.	175.	275.	900.	
1934D*	1,569,500	18.	22.	40.	95.	260.	500.	1,600.	
1934S	1,011,000	60.	150.	475.	1,600.	2,800.	4,200.	6,500.	
1935	1,576,000	13.	17.	30.	65.	100.	150.	600.	
1935S‡	1,964,000	15.	22.	90.	210.	320.	500.	1,100.	

*Large and small mint mark varieties, see page 73.

‡Varieties exist with either 3 or 4 rays below ONE, and are of equal value.

Honoring both President Dwight D. Eisenhower and the first landing of man on the moon, this design is the work of Chief Engraver Frank Gasparro, whose initials are on the truncation and below the eagle. The reverse is an adaptation of the official Apollo 11 insignia. Collectors' coins were struck in 40% silver composition, and the circulation issue in copper-nickel.

Since 1971, the dies for the Eisenhower dollar have been modified several times by changing the relief, strengthening the design and making the world above the eagle more clearly defined.

Low relief (variety I) dies, with flattened world and three islands off Florida, were used for all copper-nickel issues of 1971, uncirculated silver of 1971, and most copper-nickel coins of 1972.

High relief (variety II) dies, with round world and weak or indistinct islands, were used for all proofs of 1971, all silver issues of 1972, and the reverse of some exceptional and scarce Philadelphia copper-nickel coins of 1972.

Improved high relief reverse dies (variety III), were used for late 1972 Philadelphia copper-nickel coins and for all subsequent issues. Modified high relief dies were also used on all issues beginning in 1973.

A few 1974D and 1977D dollars in silver clad composition were made in error.

Designer Frank Gasparro. Silver issue: weight 24.59 grams; composition: outer layers of .800 silver, .200 copper bonded to inner core of .209 silver, .791 copper. Copper-nickel issue: weight 22.68 grams; composition: outer layers of .750 copper, .250 nickel bonded to inner core of pure copper. Diameter 38.1 mm; reeded edge; mints: Philadelphia, Denver, San Francisco. Net weight of silver issues: .3161 oz. pure silver.

Mint mark location is above the date.

	Mintage	EF-40	MS-63	PF-65
1971, Copper-nickel clad	47,799,000	$1.50	$4.00	
1971D, Copper-nickel clad	68,587,424	1.50	2.50	
1971S, Silver clad ....(4,265,234)	6,868,530		6.50	$7.00
1972, Copper-nickel clad, variety I	} 75,890,000	2.00	4.00	
1972, Copper-nickel clad, variety II		5.00	50.00	
1972, Copper-nickel clad, variety III		2.00	4.00	
1972D, Copper-nickel clad	92,548,511	1.50	2.50	
1972S, Silver clad ....(1,811,631)	2,193,056		7.00	7.00
1973, Copper-nickel clad	*2,000,056		12.00	
1973D, Copper-nickel clad	*2,000,000		12.00	
1973S, Copper-nickel clad .....(2,760,339)				10.00
1973S, Silver clad ....(1,013,646)	1,883,140		8.50	30.00
1974, Copper-nickel clad	27,366,000	1.50	3.00	
1974D, Copper-nickel clad	45,517,000	1.50	3.00	
1974S, Copper-nickel clad .....(2,612,568)				7.00
1974S, Silver clad ....(1,306,579)	1,900,156		6.00	7.00

*1,769,258 of each sold only in sets and not released for circulation. Unissued coins destroyed at mint.

EISENHOWER DOLLARS
BICENTENNIAL COINAGE DATED 1776-1976

The national significance of the Bicentennial of the United States was highlighted with the adoption of new reverse designs for the quarter, half dollar and dollar. Nearly a thousand entries were submitted after the Treasury announced in October of 1973 that an open contest was to be held for the selection of the new designs. After the field was narrowed down to twelve semifinalists, the judges chose the rendition of the Liberty Bell superimposed on the moon to appear on the dollar coins. This design is the work of Dennis R. Williams.

The obverse remained unchanged except for the dual date 1776-1976, which appeared on all dollars made during 1975 and 1976. These dual-dated coins were included in the various offerings of proof and uncirculated coins made by the mint. They were also struck for general circulation. The lettering was modified early in 1975 to produce a more attractive design.

Designers Frank Gasparro and Dennis R. Williams. Silver issue: weight 24.59 grams; composition: outer layers of .800 silver, .200 copper bonded to inner core of .209 silver, .791 copper. Copper-nickel issue: weight 22.68 grams; composition: outer layers of .750 copper, .250 nickel bonded to inner core of pure copper. Diameter 38.1 mm; reeded edge; mints: Philadelphia, Denver, San Francisco. Net weight of silver issues: .3161 oz. pure silver.

Variety 1: Design in low relief, bold lettering on reverse.
Variety 2: Sharp design, delicate lettering on reverse.

	Mintage	EF-40	MS-63	PF-65
1776-1976, Copper-nickel clad, variety 1 ...	4,019,000	$1.50	$6.00	
1776-1976, Copper-nickel clad, variety 2 ...	113,318,000	1.50	3.00	
1776-1976D,Copper-nickel clad, variety 1 ..	21,048,710	1.50	3.50	
1776-1976D,Copper-nickel clad, variety 2 ..	82,179,564	1.50	3.00	
1776-1976S,Copper-nickel clad, variety 1 ...	(2,845,450)			$10.
1776-1976S,Copper-nickel clad, variety 2 ...	(4,149,730)			7.
1776-1976S,Silver clad variety 1	*11,000,000		14.00	
1776-1976S,Silver clad variety 1	*(4,000,000)			18.
1776-1976, Silver clad, variety 2				—

*Approximate mintage.

EAGLE REVERSE RESUMED

	Mintage	EF-40	MS-63	PF-65
1977, Copper-nickel clad	12,596,000	1.50	4.00	
1977D, Copper-nickel clad	32,983,006	1.50	3.00	
1977S, Copper-nickel clad	(3,251,152)			7.
1978, Copper-nickel clad	25,702,000	1.50	2.50	
1978D, Copper-nickel clad	33,012,890	1.50	3.00	
1978S, Copper-nickel clad	(3,127,781)			9.

BIBLIOGRAPHY
Wexler, Crawford, and Flynn. *The Authoritative Reference on Eisenhower Dollars.* Rancocas, NJ, 1998.

Intended to honor this pioneer in women's rights, legislation dated October 10, 1978, provided for the issuance of the Susan B. Anthony dollar coin. Both obverse and reverse designs were the work of Chief Engraver of the U.S. Mint, Frank Gasparro, whose initials FG are located below the portrait and the eagle.

Placement of Susan B. Anthony's likeness on the dollar represented the first time that a woman, other than a model or mythical figure, has appeared on a circulating U.S. coin. The reverse design is the same as that used on the Eisenhower dollar. Mint marks P, D or S appear on the obverse, slightly above Anthony's right shoulder.

The size of this coin caused it to be confused with the quarter and half dollar, and it failed to gain widespread public acceptance. No coins were made for circulation from 1981 to 1998. In 1999 additional pieces were made to meet the needs of vending machines.

Designer Frank Gasparro; weight 8.1 grams; composition: outer layers of copper-nickel (.750 copper, .250 nickel) bonded to inner core of pure copper; diameter 26.5 mm; reeded edge; mints: Philadelphia, Denver, San Francisco.

1979S Filled S (Type I)	1979S Clear S (Type II rounded) 1981S First S (Type I, rounded)	1981S Clear S (Type II, flat)

1979 Narrow Rim (Far Date)

1979 Wide Rim (Near Date)

	Mintage	MS-63	PF-65		Mintage	MS-63	PF-65
1979P*	360,222,000			1980S	20,422,000	$2.00	
Narrow rim	....	$2.		1980S, Proof	..(3,554,806)		$10.00
Wide rim	....	11.		1981P ‡	3,000,000	6.00	
1979D	288,015,744	2.		1981D ‡	3,250,000	6.00	
1979S	109,576,000	2.		1981S ‡	3,492,000	6.00	
Proof, Filled S	....		$10.	1981S, Proof	..(4,063,083)		8.50
Proof, Clear S	....		100.	1981S, Proof, Clear S	.....		225.00
1980P	27,610,000	2.		1999P	29,592,000	2.50	
1980D	41,628,708	2.		1999P Proof	....		10.00
				1999D	11,776,000	2.50	

*The obverse design was modified in 1979 to widen the border rim. Late issues of 1979P and subsequent issues have the wide rim. Dies for the 1999 coins were further modified to strengthen details on the reverse.

‡Issued only in Mint sets.

SACAGAWEA DOLLARS 2000 –

The design of this coin was selected in national competition from among 120 submissions that were considered by a panel appointed by Treasury Secretary Robert Rubin. The adopted motif depicts Sacagawea, a young Native American Shoshone as conceived by artist Glenna Goodacre. On her back she carries Jean Baptiste, her infant son. The reverse shows an eagle in flight designed by mint engraver Thomas D. Rogers, Sr.

The composition exemplifies the spirit of Liberty, Peace, and Freedom shown by Sacagawea in her conduct as interpreter and guide to explorers Meriwether Louis and William Clark during their famed journey westward from the great northern plains to the Pacific.

These coins have a distinctive golden color and a plain edge to distinguish them from other denominations or coins of a similar size. The change in composition and appearance was mandated under the United States Dollar Coin Act of 1997.

Several distinctive finishes can be identified on the Sacagawea dollars as a result of the mint attempting to adjust the dies, blanks, strikes or finishing to produce coins with minimum spotting and a better surface color. One group of 5,000 pieces, dated 2000, with a special finish were presented to sculptor Glenna Goodacre in payment for the obverse design. Unexplained error coins made from mismatched dies (a 50-state quarter obverse combined with a Sacagawea dollar reverse) are extremely rare.

Designers: Obv. Glenna Goodacre; Rev. Thomas D. Rogers, Sr.; weight 8.1 grams; composition: pure copper core with outer layers of manganese brass. The alloy contains .770 copper, .120 zinc, .070 manganese, and .040 nickel; diameter 26.5 mm; plain edge; mints: Philadelphia, Denver, San Francisco; 22-karat gold numismatic specimens dated 2000W were struck at West Point in 1999.

	Mintage	MS-63	PF-65
2000P	.767,140,000	$2.	
2000D	.518,916,000	2.	
2000S Proof	(3,082,483)		$10.
2001P	.62,468,000	2.	
2001D	.70,939,500	2.	
2001S Proof	(2,294,043)		35.
2002P	.3,865,610	3.	
2002D	.3,732,000	3.	
2002S Proof	(2,319,766)		25.
2003P		3.	
2003D		3.	
2003S Proof			9.
2004P		3.	
2004D		3.	
2004S Proof			9.

SPECIAL MILLENNIUM SET

	UNC
2000D Sacagawea dollar, 2000(W) Silver Eagle dollar, Series 1999 $1 Federal Reserve note	$125.

GOLD

Gold has served as money or established the monetary value of currencies longer than any other material. The use of gold coins was widespread in Europe by the fourth century B.C.

The earliest coins circulated in the United States were foreign coins, mostly silver and gold, brought from Europe. The Coinage Act in 1792 established an independent monetary system with the dollar as the basic United States monetary unit containing 24¾ grains of fine gold, based on the world price of $19.39 a troy ounce (480 grains). Congress changed the gold specification in 1834 and again in 1837, when it set the dollar price of gold at $20.67 an ounce.

In 1934, United States citizens were prohibited from holding monetary gold in this country; this was extended in 1961 to gold held abroad as well. The dollar price was set at $35 per ounce in 1934. Use of gold in international trade was further restricted as the price rose. The government revalued it at $38 per ounce in 1972, then $42.22 in 1973. It has fluctuated widely over the past few years. All restrictions on holding gold were removed on December 31, 1974.

GOLD DOLLARS 1849-1889

Coinage of the gold dollar was authorized by the Act of March 3, 1849. The weight was 25.8 grains, fineness .900. The first type, struck until 1854, is known as the Liberty Head or small-sized type (type 1).

In 1854 the dollar coins were made larger in diameter and thinner. The design was changed to a feather headdress on a female, generally referred to as the Indian Head or large-sized type. In 1856 the type was changed slightly by enlarging the size of the head.

+ or – indicates change from previous year	**TYPE COIN VALUES**									
	F-12	VF-20	EF-40	AU-50	MS-60	MS-63	MS-65	PF-60	PF-63	PF-65
Liberty Type 1 1849-1854	110.+	135.-	195.+	225.+	320.+	1,200.+	5,000.+			
Indian Type 2 1854-1856	180.+	325.+	425.+	650.+	3,400.+	14,500.-	*35,000.-*	75,000.	150,000.	250,000.
Indian Type 3 1856-1889	110.+	135.-	175.	210.+	300.	1,000.+	1,800.	2,500.+	4,500.+	8,000.-

> Values of common gold coins have been based on the current bullion price of gold, $425 per oz., and may vary with the prevailing spot price. The weight and content is stated in the introduction to each series, and may be used to recalculate bullion value.

LIBERTY HEAD TYPE 1849-1854

Designer James B. Longacre; weight 1.672 grams; composition: .900 gold, .100 copper; diameter 13 mm; reeded edge; mints: Philadelphia, Charlotte, Dahlonega, New Orleans, San Francisco. Net weight: .04837 oz. pure gold.

VF-20 VERY FINE — *LIBERTY* on headband complete and readable. Knobs on coronet are defined.

EF-40 EXTREMELY FINE — *Slight wear on Liberty's hair.* Knobs on coronet sharp.

AU-50 ABOUT UNCIRCULATED — *Trace of wear on head band. Nearly full luster.*

AU-55-CHOICE ABOUT UNCIRCULATED — Evidence of friction on design high points.

MS-60 UNCIRCULATED — No trace of wear. Light marks and blemishes.

MS-63 SELECT UNCIRCULATED — Some distracting contact marks or blemishes in prime focal areas. Luster may be impaired.

Type 1
With closed or open wreath.

Mint mark is below wreath.

	Mintage	VF-20	EF-40	AU-50	AU-55	MS-60	MS-63
1849 Open wreath-All Kinds*	688,567	$150.	$200.	$235.	$250.	$340.	$1,750.
1849 Small Head, no L		165.	250.	275.	300.	600.	2,250.
1849 Closed wreath *(ends closer to numeral)*	150.	200.	235.	250.	340.	1,500.
1849C Closed wreath . . . . . . } 11,634		1,200.	1,500.	2,500.	4,500.	10,500.	19,000.
1849C Open wreath *(Ex. Rare)* }		200,000.	325,000.	—	—	—	—
1849D Open wreath	21,588	1,200.	1,500.	2,100.	3,250.	5,250.	13,500.
1849O Open wreath	215,000	165.	250.	375.	600.	1,100.	3,000.
1850	481,953	145.	195.	245.	320.	1,200.	
1850C	6,966	1,200.	1,500.	2,750.	5,000.	9,000.	27,500.
1850D	8,382	1,250.	1,600.	3,000.	5,500.	10,500.	28,000.
1850O	14,000	265.	400.	850.	1,350.	3,500.	6,500.

GOLD DOLLARS

	Mintage	VF-20	EF-40	AU-50	AU-55	MS-60	MS-63
1851	3,317,671	$145.	$195.	$225.	$245.	$320.	$1,200.
1851C	41,267	1,200.	1,500.	2,000.	2,250.	3,500.	6,500.
1851D	9,882	1,250.	1,600.	2,100.	2,750.	6,000.	14,500.
1851O	290,000	165.	210.	300.	400.	850.	2,650.
1852	2,045,351	145.	195.	225.	245.	320.	1,200.
1852C	9,434	1,200.	1,500.	2,000.	2,600.	4,750.	12,500.
1852D	6,360	1,250.	1,600.	2,750.	3,750.	8,500.	25,000.
1852O	140,000	165.	225.	400.	750.	1,600.	6,250.
1853	4,076,051	145.	195.	225.	245.	320.	1,200.
1853C	11,515	1,200.	1,500.	2,100.	2,750.	5,750.	13,500.
1853D	6,583	1,250.	1,600.	2,750.	4,000.	9,000.	30,000.
1853O	290,000	165.	200.	275.	375.	700.	2,600.
1854	855,502	145.	195.	225.	245.	320.	1,200.
1854D	2,935	1,650.	2,250.	5,750.	7,000.	12,000.	35,000.
1854S	14,632	325.	450.	850.	1,150.	2,500.	6,500.

INDIAN HEAD TYPE, Small Head 1854-1856

Standards same as previous issue. Diameter changed to 15 mm.

Type 2

VF-20 VERY FINE —Feather curl tips outlined but details worn.
EF-40 EXTREMELY FINE —Slight wear on tips of feather curls on head dress.
AU-50 ABOUT UNCIRCULATED —Trace of wear on feathers, nearly full luster.
AU-55-CHOICE ABOUT UNCIRCULATED —Evidence of friction on design high points. Most of mint luster remains.
MS-60 UNCIRCULATED —No trace of wear. Light marks and blemishes.
MS-63 SELECT UNCIRCULATED —Some distracting contact marks or blemishes in prime focal areas. Luster may be impaired.

	Mintage	VF-20	EF-40	AU-50	AU-55	MS-60	MS-63	PF-63
1854	783,943	$325.	$425.	$650.	$1,050.	$3,400.	$14,500.	$165,000.
1855	758,269	325.	425.	650.	1,050.	3,400.	14,500.	150,000.
1855C	9,803	1,500.	3,250.	6,750.	11,500.	22,500.		
1855D	1,811	4,500.	9,000.	21,500.	26,500.	47,500.	95,000.	
1855O	55,000	500.	725.	1,550.	2,600.	6,750.	22,500.	
1856S	24,600	950.	1,350.	2,300.	3,100.	7,750.	27,500.	

INDIAN HEAD TYPE, Large Head 1856-1889

Type 3

VF-20 VERY FINE —Curled feathers have slight detail. Details worn smooth at eyebrow, hair below headdress and behind ear and bottom curl.
EF-40 EXTREMELY FINE —Slight wear above and to right of eye and on top of curled feathers.
AU-50 ABOUT UNCIRCULATED —Trace of wear on feathers, nearly full luster.
AU-55-CHOICE ABOUT UNCIRCULATED —Evidence of friction on design high points. Most of mint luster remains.
MS-60 UNCIRCULATED —No trace of wear. Light marks and blemishes.
MS-63 SELECT UNCIRCULATED —Some distracting contact marks or blemishes in prime focal areas. Luster may be impaired.
PF-63 ATTTRACTIVE PROOF — Reflective surfaces with only a few blemishes in secondary focal places. No major flaws.

	Mintage	VF-20	EF-40	AU-50	AU-55	MS-60	MS-63	PF-63
1856, Upright 5	1,762,936	150.	195.	235.	300.	525.	1,100.	
1856, Slant 5		135.	175.	210.	235.	300.	1,000.	20,000.
1856D	1,460	3,800.	5,750.	8,000.	11,500.	30,000.	75,000.	
1857	774,789	135.	175.	210.	235.	300.	1,000.	12,500.
1857C	13,280	1,000.	1,500.	3,500.	5,500.	12,500.	29,000.	
1857D	3,533	1,100.	2,000.	4,000.	5,000.	10,000.	32,000.	
1857S	10,000	500.	600.	1,100.	1,800.	6,000.	20,000.	
1858	117,995	135.	175.	210.	235.	300.	1,000.	7,500.
1858D	3,477	1,150.	1,600.	2,850.	4,500.	10,000.	25,000.	
1858S	10,000	350.	550.	1,300.	1,750.	5,750.	16,500.	
1859 ....(80)	168,324	135.	175.	210.	235.	325.	1,100.	6,500.
1859C	5,235	1,200.	1,750.	3,750.	6,750.	15,000.	32,500.	
1859D	4,952	1,200.	1,750.	2,850.	5,250.	11,000.	26,000.	
1859S	15,000	250.	600.	1,600.	2,250.	5,800.	17,000.	
1860 ....(154)	36,668	145.	200.	225.	250.	450.	1,100.	5,000.
1860D	1,566	2,750.	4,000.	7,250.	12,000.	25,000.	55,000.	

	Mintage	VF-20	EF-40	AU-50	AU-55	MS-60	MS-63	PF-63
1860S	.13,000	$285.	$450.	$750.	$1,100.	$2,500.	$7,000.	
1861	..(349)..527,499	145.	200.	225.	250.	450.	1,100.	5,000.
1861D		7,500.	11,500.	21,500.	26,500.	36,500.	75,000.	
1862	..(35).1,361,390	145.	200.	225.	250.	450.	1,100.	5,500.
1863	..(50)...6,250	550.	1,100.	2,250.	3,250.	4,500.	8,500.	6,000.
1864	..(50)...5,950	350.	475.	750.	950.	1,250.	3,000.	7,500.
1865	..(25)...3,725	375.	600.	850.	1,050.	1,750.	3,750.	7,500.
1866	..(30)...7,130	350.	500.	725.	850.	1,150.	2,250.	7,000.
1867	..(50)...5,250	400.	525.	750.	900.	1,250.	2,250.	5,500.
1868	..(25)..10,525	275.	400.	550.	600.	1,100.	2,250.	6,500.
1869	..(25)...5,925	350.	475.	750.	850.	1,250.	2,250.	6,500.
1870	..(35)...6,335	300.	400.	650.	750.	1,150.	2,250.	6,000.
1870S	..3,000	475.	800.	1,250.	1,600.	2,850.	7,500.	
1871	..(30)...3,930	300.	400.	650.	750.	1,150.	2,250.	6,000.
1872	..(30)...3,530	300.	400.	650.	750.	1,150.	2,250.	6,500.
1873, Cl 3	.(25)...1,825	400.	750.	1,100.	1,350.	1,850.	4,500.	14,500.
1873, Open 3	...123,300	145.	200.	225.	250.	450.	1,100.	
1874	..(20).198,820	145.	200.	225.	250.	450.	1,100.	8,500.
1875	..(20).....420	2,250.	3,850.	5,250.	5,750.	7,500.	9,500.	15,000.
1876	..(45)...3,245	275.	325.	500.	575.	750.	1,350.	5,000.
1877	..(20)...3,920	275.	325.	500.	575.	750.	1,350.	6,500.
1878	..(20)...3,020	275.	325.	500.	575.	750.	1,350.	5,000.
1879	..(30)...3,030	175.	275.	375.	500.	650.	1,300.	5,000.
1880	..(36)...1,636	175.	275.	375.	425.	600.	1,250.	5,000.
1881	..(87)...7,707	175.	275.	375.	425.	600.	1,250.	5,000.
1882	...(125)..5,125	175.	275.	375.	425.	600.	1,250.	4,500.
1883	...(207)..11,007	175.	275.	375.	425.	600.	1,250.	4,500.
1884	.(1,006)...6,236	175.	275.	375.	425.	600.	1,250.	4,500.
1885	.(1,105)..12,261	175.	275.	375.	425.	600.	1,250.	4,500.
1886	.(1,016)...6,016	175.	275.	375.	425.	600.	1,250.	4,500.
1887	.(1,043)...8,543	175.	275.	375.	425.	600.	1,250.	4,500.
1888	.(1,079)..16,580	175.	275.	375.	425.	600.	1,250.	4,500.
1889	.(1,779)...30,729	165.	265.	350.	400.	575.	1,200.	4,500.

BIBLIOGRAPHY

Akers, David W., *Gold Dollars* (and other gold denominations). Englewood, Ohio, 1975-1982.
Bowers, Q. David, *United States Gold Coins. An Illustrated History.* Wolfeboro, NH, 1982.
Breen, Walter, *Major Varieties of U.S. Gold Dollars* (and other gold denominations). Chicago, 1964.

—— QUARTER EAGLES ($2.50 GOLD PIECES)—1796-1929 ——

Authorized by the Act of April 2, 1792, they weighed 67.5 grains, 916 2/3 fine until the weight was changed to 64.5 grains, fineness 899.225, by the Act of June 28, 1834. The Act of January 18, 1837 established fineness at .900. Most dates before 1834 are rare. The first issue was struck in 1796, most of which had no stars on the obverse.

Proofs of some dates prior to 1855 are known to exist, and all are rare.

+ or − indicates change from previous year	TYPE COIN VALUES									
	F-12	VF-20	EF-40	AU-50	MS-60	MS-63	MS-65	PF-60	PF-63	PF-65
Cap Bust Right-NS 1796	22,500.+	35,000.+	65,000.+	77,500.+	165,000.+	220,000.	110,000.			
Cap Bust Right 1796-1807	5,000.+	7,000.+	8,250.+	12,000.+	22,500.+	40,000.+				
Cap Bust Left-Lg. 1808	22,500.+	30,000.+	39,500.+	65,000.+	87,500.+	125,000.				
Cap Bust Left-Sm. 1821-1827	5,500.+	7,250.+	8,500.+	11,500.+	22,000.+	27,500.			75,000.	
Cap Bust Left-Sm. 1829-1834	4,800.+	6,250.+	7,750.+	10,500.+	14,500.+	18,000.				40,000
Classic Head 1834-1839	250.+	325.+	475.+	700.+	2,150.+	5,500.-			27,500.	
Lib Coronet 1840-1907	120.	160.+	190.+	210.+	285.	750.+	5,000.	5,000.+	5,000.	13,000
Indian Head 1908-1929	120.	160.	175.	200.+	285.+	1,100.+		2,600.	6,750.+	14,000

QUARTER EAGLES ($2.50 GOLD PIECES)
CAPPED BUST TO RIGHT 1796-1807

Designer Robert Scot; weight 4.37 grams; composition: .9167 gold, .0833 silver and copper; approx. diameter 20 mm; reeded edge.

F-12 FINE—*Hair worn smooth on high spots. E PLURIBUS UNUM weak but readable.*
VF-20 VERY FINE—*Some wear on high spots.*
EF-40 EXTREMELY FINE—*Only slight wear on hair and cheek.*
AU-50 ABOUT UNCIRCULATED—*Trace of wear on cap, hair, cheek and drapery.*
AU-55-CHOICE ABOUT UNCIRCULATED—*Evidence of friction on design high points. Most of mint luster remains.*
MS-60 UNCIRCULATED—*No trace of wear. Light blemishes.*

No Stars on Obverse 1796 Only

Stars on Obverse 1796-1807

	Mintage	F-12	VF-20	EF-40	AU-50	AU-55	MS-60
1796, No stars on obv.	963	$22,500.	$35,000.	$65,000.	$77,500.	$87,500.	$165,000.
1796, Stars on obv.	432	21,000.	32,000.	55,000.	72,500.	85,000.	130,000.
1797	427	16,000.	19,500.	28,000.	47,500.	60,000.	110,000.
1798	1,094	6,500.	9,500.	12,500.	26,500.	34,000.	57,500.
1802, 2/1	3,035	5,500.	7,500.	9,000.	13,000.	16,000.	25,000.
1804, 13-Star reverse ..... } 3,327		27,500.	37,500.	75,000.	140,000.	175,000.	
1804, 14-Star reverse		5,500.	7,500.	9,000.	13,000.	16,000.	25,000.
1805	1,781	5,250.	7,250.	8,500.	12,500.	15,000.	25,000.
1806, 6/4, stars 8L, 5R	1,136	5,250.	7,250.	8,500.	12,500.	15,000.	25,000.
1806, 6/5, stars 7L, 6R	480	9,000.	13,500.	18,500.	35,000.	50,000.	85,000.
1807	6,812	5,000.	7,000.	8,250.	12,000.	14,000.	22,500.

CAPPED BUST TO LEFT, Large Size 1808

Designer John Reich. Standards same as previous issue.

F-12 FINE—*E PLURIBUS UNUM on reverse, and LIBERTY on headband readable but weak.*
VF-20 VERY FINE—*Motto and LIBERTY clear.*
EF-40 EXTREMELY FINE—*All details of hair are plain.*
AU-50 ABOUT UNCIRCULATED—*Trace of wear above eye, on top of cap, cheek and hair.*
AU-55-CHOICE ABOUT UNCIRCULATED—*Evidence of friction on design high points. Most of mint luster remains.*
MS-60 UNCIRCULATED—*No trace of wear. Light blemishes.*

1808	2,710	$22,500.	$30,000.	$39,500.	$65,000.	$75,000.	$87,500.

CAPPED HEAD TO LEFT 1821-1834

Those dated 1829 through 1834 are smaller in diameter than the 1821-1827 pieces. They also have smaller letters, dates and stars.

Standards same as previous issue. Diameter changed to approximately 18.5 mm.

1821	6,448	$5,500.	$7,250.	$8,500.	$11,500.	$13,500.	$25,000.
1824, 4/1	2,600	5,500.	7,250.	8,500.	11,500.	13,500.	22,000.
1825	4,434	5,500.	7,250.	8,500.	11,500.	13,500.	22,000.
1826, 6/5	760	7,500.	9,500.	11,500.	13,500.	20,000.	37,500.
1827	2,800	5,500.	7,250.	8,500.	11,500.	13,500.	22,000.

QUARTER EAGLES ($2.50 GOLD PIECES)
Reduced Size 1829-1834

	Mintage	F-12	VF-20	EF-40	AU-50	AU-55	MS-60
1829	3,403	$4,800.	$6,250.	$7,750.	$10,500.	$12,500.	$14,500.
1830	4,540	4,800.	6,250.	7,750.	10,500.	12,500.	14,500.
1831	4,520	4,800.	6,250.	7,750.	10,500.	12,500.	14,500.
1832	4,400	4,800.	6,250.	7,750.	10,500.	12,500.	14,500.
1833	4,160	4,800.	6,250.	7,750.	10,500.	12,500.	14,500.
1834, (Motto)	4,000	9,000.	12,500.	18,500.	32,500.	37,500.	45,000.

CLASSIC HEAD TYPE, No Motto on Reverse 1834-1839

In 1834 the quarter eagle was redesigned. A ribbon binding the hair, bearing the word LIBERTY, replaces the Liberty cap. The motto was omitted from the reverse. In 1840 a coronet and smaller head were designed to conform in appearance with that of the larger gold coins.

Designer William Kneass; weight 4.18 grams; composition: .8992 gold, .1008 silver and copper changed to .900 gold in 1837; diameter 18.2 mm; reeded edge; mints: Philadelphia, Charlotte, Dahlonega, New Orleans.

F-12 FINE—LIBERTY *readable and complete. Curl under ear outlined but no detail.*
VF-20 VERY FINE—LIBERTY *plain. Hair curl has detail.*
EF-40 EXTREMELY FINE—*Small amount of wear on top of hair and below L in* LIBERTY*. Wear evident on wing.*
AU-50 ABOUT UNCIRCULATED—*Trace of wear on coronet and hair above ear.*
AU-55-CHOICE ABOUT UNCIRCULATED—*Evidence of friction on design high points. Most of mint luster remains.*
MS-60 UNCIRCULATED—*No trace of wear. Light blemishes.*
MS-63 SELECT UNCIRCULATED—*Some distracting contact marks or blemishes in prime focal areas. Luster may be impaired.*

Mint mark location.

	Mintage	F-12	VF-20	EF-40	AU-50	AU-55	MS-60	MS-63
1834, No motto . . .	112,234	$250.	$325.	$475.	$700.	$1,000.	$2,150.	$5,500.
1835	131,402	250.	325.	475.	700.	1,000.	2,350.	7,500.
1836, Script 8	} 547,986	250.	325.	475.	700.	1,000.	2,150.	5,500.
1836, Block 8		250.	325.	475.	700.	1,000.	2,150.	5,500.
1837	45,080	250.	325.	475.	800.	1,100.	3,000.	10,000.
1838	47,030	250.	325.	475.	750.	1,100.	2,350.	7,500.
1838C	7,880	1,200.	1,650.	3,000.	6,750.	10,000.	26,000.	38,500.
1839	27,021	275.	425.	750.	1,750.	2,750.	5,750.	15,000.
1839C	18,140	1,200.	1,500.	2,500.	4,000.	7,500.	22,000.	38,500.
1839D	13,674	1,200.	1,500.	3,000.	6,000.	9,000.	24,000.	45,000.
1839O	17,781	500.	650.	1,150.	1,850.	2,850.	6,500.	21,500.

1839, So-called "9 over 8" varieties for P, C and D mints are made from defective punches.

Mint mark location.

Designer Christian Gobrecht; weight 4.18 grams; composition: .900 gold, .100 copper; diameter 18 mm; reeded edge; mints: Philadelphia, Charlotte, Dahlonega, New Orleans, San Francisco; Net weight: .12094 oz. pure gold.

	Mintage	VF-20	EF-40	AU-50	AU-55	MS-60	MS-63
1840	18,859	$300.	$800.	$3,500.	$3,950.	$7,000.	$15,000.
1840C	12,822	1,250.	2,000.	5,000.	7,500.	16,000.	37,500.
1840D	3,532	2,950.	8,000.	16,000.	22,500.	35,000.	
1840O	33,580	350.	850.	2,200.	2,850.	10,000.	25,000.
1841, Proofs Only	55,000.	85,000.	100,000.	125,000.	150,000.	
1841C	10,281	1,150.	1,850.	3,500.	6,000.	20,000.	
1841D	4,164	2,050.	3,750.	9,500.	14,500.	26,000.	47,500.
1842	2,823	1,100.	3,000.	7,200.	13,500.	22,000.	
1842C	6,729	1,500.	3,250.	8,500.	11,500.	26,000.	
1842D	4,643	1,800.	3,600.	10,000.	16,000.	30,000.	
1842O	19,800	500.	1,300.	2,750.	5,500.	15,000.	32,500.
1843	100,546	175.	250.	450.	650.	2,000.	3,500.
1843C, SmDt, crosslet 4	2,988	2,400.	5,000.	8,500.	12,000.	23,000.	
1843C, LgDt.,plain 4	23,076	1,200.	1,750.	3,500.	5,750.	8,750.	21,500.
1843D, SmDt., crosslet 4	36,209	1,250.	2,000.	3,150.	4,500.	9,000.	35,000.
1843O, SmDt.,crosslet 4	288,002	225.	300.	500.	750.	2,200.	8,500.
1843O, LgDt.,plain 4	76,000	300.	700.	1,600.	3,250.	7,500.	
1844	6,784	475.	850.	2,150.	4,000.	7,500.	
1844C	11,622	1,200.	2,000.	6,250.	9,000.	20,000.	45,000.
1844D	17,332	1,200.	2,000.	3,000.	4,250.	9,000.	27,500.
1845	91,051	250.	325.	525.	750.	1,400.	4,500.
1845D	19,460	1,200.	2,000.	3,250.	5,250.	13,500.	35,000.
1845O	4,000	1,200.	2,400.	6,000.	8,000.	18,000.	52,500.
1846	21,598	300.	700.	1,350.	2,000.	6,500.	22,000.
1846C	4,808	1,450.	2,500.	9,000.	11,500.	20,000.	30,000.
1846D	19,303	1,200.	2,000.	3,250.	5,250.	12,000.	26,000.
1846O	62,000	300.	500.	1,150.	1,850.	5,500.	19,500.
1847	29,814	240.	375.	850.	1,400.	4,000.	10,000.
1847C	23,226	1,200.	2,000.	2,600.	4,250.	7,000.	17,500.
1847D	15,784	1,200.	2,000.	2,850.	5,250.	10,000.	23,500.
1847O	124,000	275.	450.	1,050.	2,150.	5,000.	16,500.

CAL. Above Eagle on Reverse

California Gold Quarter Eagle

In 1848 about two hundred and thirty ounces of gold were sent to Secretary of War Marcy by Col. R. B. Mason, Military Governor of California. The gold was turned over to the mint and made into quarter eagles. The distinguishing mark "CAL." was punched above the eagle on the reverse side, while the coins were in the die. Several specimens with prooflike surface are known.

	Mintage	VF-20	EF-40	AU-50	AU-55	MS-60	MS-63
1848	7,497	$550.	$1,100.	$2,000.	$2,750.	$6,500.	$16,500.
1848, CAL. above eagle	1,389	13,500.	27,500.	32,500.	37,500.	55,000.	65,000.
1848C	16,788	1,200.	2,000.	2,900.	4,850.	14,000.	32,500.
1848D	13,771	1,200.	2,000.	2,900.	5,000.	11,000.	32,500.
1849	23,294	265.	500.	1,000.	1,550.	3,200.	7,500.
1849C	10,220	1,200.	2,000.	5,000.	9,000.	22,500.	42,500.
1849D	10,945	1,200.	2,000.	4,000.	8,000.	18,000.	
1850	252,923	175.	200.	325.	550.	1,200.	3,750.
1850C	9,148	1,200.	2,000.	3,500.	6,500.	19,000.	35,000.
1850D	12,148	1,200.	2,000.	3,500.	6,500.	16,000.	35,000.
1850O	84,000	265.	450.	1,450.	2,150.	4,850.	14,500.
1851	1,372,748	175.	200.	235.	300.	375.	1,750.

QUARTER EAGLES ($2.50 GOLD PIECES)

	Mintage	VF-20	EF-40	AU-50	AU-55	MS-60	MS-63	PF-63
1851C	14,923	$1,200.	$2,000.	$4,500.	$7,000.	$14,000.	$35,000.	
1851D	11,264	1,200.	2,000.	3,750.	6,500.	13,000.	35,000.	
1851O	148,000	200.	400.	975.	2,250.	5,000.	12,500.	
1852	1,159,681	175.	200.	235.	300.	375.	1,750.	
1852C	9,772	1,200.	2,000.	4,000.	8,000.	17,500.	35,000.	
1852D	4,078	1,600.	2,850.	7,500.	11,000.	22,500.	42,500.	
1852O	140,000	225.	325.	1,000.	1,450.	5,250.	13,500.	
1853	1,404,668	175.	200.	235.	300.	375.	1,750.	
1853D	3,178	1,600.	3,000.	5,250.	7,500.	18,000.	42,500.	
1854	596,258	175.	200.	235.	300.	375.	1,750.	
1854C	7,295	1,350.	2,500.	5,500.	8,500.	18,000.		
1854D	1,760	3,250.	7,500.	14,000.	19,000.	32,500.	75,000.	
1854O	153,000	200.	300.	600.	800.	1,750.	7,500.	
1854S	246	65,000.	95,000.	175,000.	—	—		
1855	235,480	175.	200.	235.	300.	375.	2,350.	
1855C	3,677	1,750.	3,500.	7,000.	12,500.	30,000.	47,500.	
1855D	1,123	4,250.	8,000.	17,000.	25,000.	42,000.		
1856	384,240	170.	200.	235.	275.	350.	2,000.	$50,000.
1856C	7,913	1,250.	2,400.	4,750.	7,500.	15,000.	35,000.	
1856D	874	7,500.	13,500.	24,000.	32,500.	57,500.		
1856O	21,100	275.	750.	1,500.	2,750.	8,000.		
1856S	72,120	225.	400.	1,250.	1,850.	6,000.	12,500.	
1857	214,130	170.	200.	235.	275.	350.	2,000.	37,500.
1857D	2,364	1,450.	3,000.	4,000.	7,000.	14,000.	28,500.	
1857O	34,000	200.	350.	1,400.	2,150.	5,250.	14,500.	
1857S	69,200	200.	400.	1,350.	2,250.	6,500.	15,000.	
1858	47,377	175.	235.	450.	575.	1,400.	3,250.	27,500.
1858C	9,056	1,200.	2,000.	3,250.	4,250.	8,500.	35,000.	

A modified reverse design (smaller letters and arrowheads) was used on Philadelphia issues from 1859 through 1907, and on San Francisco issues of 1877 through 1879. A few Philadelphia Mint pieces were made in 1859, 1860 and 1861 with the old large letters reverse design.

Old Reverse　　　　**New Reverse**

	Mintage	VF-20	EF-40	AU-50	AU-55	MS-60	MS-63	PF-63
1859 Old rev		225.	450.	900.	1,250.	3,750.	8,500.	
1859 New rev(80)	39,444	185.	250.	500.	750.	1,300.	3,250.	20,000.
1859D	2,244	2,000.	3,250.	5,500.	8,500.	24,000.		
1859S	15,200	450.	1,100.	2,500.	3,500.	8,000.	18,500.	
1860 Old rev		2,100.	3,450.	5,500.	7,500.	11,000.	18,500.	
1860 New rev(112)	22,675	175.	235.	450.	575.	1,100.	2,500.	16,500.
1860C	7,469	1,350.	2,150.	4,200.	7,500.	22,500.	45,000.	
1860S	35,600	275.	650.	1,300.	2,150.	4,250.	13,500.	
1861 Old rev		500.	1,100.	2,100.	3,250.	5,000.	11,000.	
1861 New rev(90)	1,283,878	160.	190.	210.	225.	400.	950.	15,000.
1861S	24,000	400.	1,000.	3,500.	5,000.	8,500.		
1862, 2/1	} 98,543	1,000.	1,950.	4,000.	5,500.	9,000.		
1862 ....(35)		185.	275.	500.	750.	1,500.	3,750.	15,000.
1862S	8,000	1,000.	2,200.	4,500.	7,500.	18,500.		
1863, Pfs only(30)	30							45,000.
1863S	10,800	750.	1,600.	4,500.	7,500.	17,500.	32,500.	
1864 ....(50)	2,874	5,500.	12,500.	24,000.	30,000.	40,000.		15,000.
1865 ....(25)	1,545	4,250.	10,000.	22,000.	27,500.	37,000.	45,000.	15,000.
1865S	23,376	300.	675.	1,400.	2,250.	5,500.	13,500.	
1866 ....(30)	3,110	1,250.	3,500.	6,500.	10,000.	16,000.	27,500.	12,000.
1866S	38,960	375.	850.	1,800.	3,500.	8,500.	22,500.	

QUARTER EAGLES ($2.50 GOLD PIECES)

	Mintage	VF-20	EF-40	AU-50	AU-55	MS-60	MS-63	PF-63
1867	(50) ...3,250	$375.	$750.	$1,500.	$2,250.	$4,500.	$8,500.	$12,000.
1867S	28,000	375.	800.	1,750.	2,750.	5,500.	16,500.	
1868	(25) ...3,625	225.	450.	750.	900.	3,000.	8,750.	13,500.
1868S	34,000	225.	500.	1,100.	1,750.	5,250.	12,500.	
1869	(25) ...4,345	225.	375.	800.	1,250.	3,250.	8,750.	10,500.
1869S	29,500	300.	550.	1,200.	1,750.	5,150.	12,500.	
1870	(35) ...4,555	235.	375.	750.	1,250.	3,500.	9,500.	10,500.
1870S	16,000	235.	450.	1,000.	1,850.	5,250.	14,500.	
1871	(30) ...5,350	225.	400.	650.	1,100.	2,500.	4,500.	10,500.
1871S	22,000	200.	325.	650.	1,000.	2,500.	4,750.	
1872	(30) ...3,030	400.	800.	1,500.	2,500.	5,750.	12,500.	10,500.
1872S	18,000	225.	400.	1,000.	1,750.	4,750.	12,500.	
1873, Cl 3	..(25) ..55,225	175.	200.	300.	375.	750.	1,500.	10,500.
1873, Open 3	122,800	160.	190.	200.	225.	285.	1,500.	
1873S	27,000	230.	450.	1,100.	1,500.	2,750.	7,500.	
1874	(20) ...3,940	275.	400.	800.	1,100.	2,600.	6,500.	12,500.
1875	(20) 420	3,750.	5,500.	8,500.	10,500.	18,000.	24,000.	17,500.
1875S	11,600	200.	400.	750.	1,100.	4,250.	9,500.	
1876	(45) ...4,221	250.	650.	1,100.	2,100.	3,600.	8,500.	9,500.
1876S	5,000	250.	600.	1,100.	1,750.	4,000.	9,500.	
1877	(20) ...1,652	375.	700.	1,000.	1,350.	3,000.	8,500.	9,500.
1877S	35,400	175.	200.	225.	300.	700.	2,500.	
1878	(20) .286,260	170.	195.	215.	255.	375.	850.	9,500.
1878S	178,000	170.	195.	215.	255.	475.	2,250.	
1879	(30) ..88,990	170.	195.	215.	255.	375.	1,500.	9,500.
1879S	43,500	185.	275.	600.	1,150.	2,200.	5,500.	
1880	(36) ...2,996	250.	350.	650.	850.	1,400.	3,250.	9,500.
1881	(51) 691	1,750.	3,000.	4,500.	5,500.	9,500.	25,000.	9,500.
1882	(67) ...4,067	250.	350.	500.	650.	850.	2,800.	6,500.
1883	(82) ...2,002	250.	375.	850.	1,250.	2,350.	6,000.	6,500.
1884	(73) ...2,023	250.	375.	750.	800.	1,750.	3,250.	6,500.
1885	(87) 887	1,000.	1,750.	2,750.	3,250.	4,750.	8,500.	6,500.
1886	(88) ...4,088	235.	300.	525.	750.	1,350.	2,750.	6,500.
1887	(122) ..6,282	235.	275.	400.	450.	1,100.	2,650.	6,500.
1888	(97) ..16,098	175.	225.	275.	325.	500.	950.	6,500.
1889	(48) ..17,648	175.	225.	275.	325.	500.	950.	6,500.
1890	(93) ...8,813	185.	225.	300.	350.	600.	1,000.	6,500.
1891	(80) ..11,040	180.	250.	300.	350.	475.	1,100.	6,500.
1892	(105) ...2,545	200.	300.	425.	450.	900.	2,750.	5,500.
1893	(106) ..30,106	165.	200.	250.	300.	425.	950.	5,500.
1894	(122) ...4,122	185.	250.	375.	450.	750.	1,850.	5,500.
1895	(119) ..6,119	165.	200.	250.	300.	375.	1,000.	5,500.
1896	(132) ..19,202	160.	200.	210.	300.	325.	850.	5,500.
1897	(136) ..29,904	160.	200.	210.	300.	325.	775.	5,500.
1898	(165) ..24,165	160.	200.	210.	300.	325.	775.	5,500.
1899	(150) ..27,350	160.	200.	210.	300.	325.	775.	5,500.
1900	(205) ..67,205	160.	190.	210.	225.	285.	750.	5,000.
1901	(223) ..91,323	160.	190.	210.	225.	285.	750.	5,000.
1902	(193) .133,733	160.	190.	210.	225.	285.	750.	5,000.
1903	(197) .201,257	160.	190.	210.	225.	285.	750.	5,000.
1904	(170) .160,960	160.	190.	210.	225.	285.	750.	5,000.
1905*	....(144) .217,944	160.	190.	210.	225.	285.	750.	5,000.
1906	(160) .176,490	160.	190.	210.	225.	285.	750.	5,000.
1907	(154) .336,448	160.	190.	210.	225.	285.	750.	5,000.

*Pieces dated 1905S are counterfeit.

Values of common gold coins have been based on the current bullion
price of gold and vary with the prevailing spot price.

QUARTER EAGLES ($2.50 GOLD PIECES)
INDIAN HEAD TYPE 1908-1929

The new type represents a departure from all preceding coin types in the United States series. Bela Lyon Pratt was the designer of this and the similar half eagle piece. The coin has no raised edge and the main devices and legends are incuse.

Designer Bela Lyon Pratt; weight 4.18 grams; composition: .900 gold, .100 copper; diameter 18 mm; reeded edge; mints: Philadelphia, Denver. Net weight: .12094 oz. pure gold.

VF-20 VERY FINE — Hair cord knot distinct. Feathers at top of head clear. Cheekbone worn.
EF-40 EXTREMELY FINE — Cheekbone, war bonnet and headband feathers slightly worn.
AU-50 ABOUT UNCIRCULATED — Trace of wear on cheekbone and headdress.
MS-60 UNCIRCULATED — No trace of wear. Light blemishes.
MS-63 SELECT UNCIRCULATED — Some distracting contact marks or blemishes in prime focal areas. Luster may be impaired.
MS-64 UNCIRCULATED — Shows a few scattered contact marks. Good eye appeal and attractive luster.
PF-63 ATTRACTIVE PROOF — Reflective surfaces with only a few blemishes in secondary focal places. No major flaws.

Mint mark location is on reverse left of arrows.

	Mintage	VF-20	EF-40	AU-50	MS-60	MS-63	MS-64	Matte PF-63
1908 .....(236)..565,057		$160.	$175.	$200.	$325.	$1,500.	$1,850.	$6,750.
1909 .....(139)..441,899		160.	175.	200.	325.	1,900.	2,600.	7,500.
1910 .....(682)..492,682		160.	175.	200.	325.	1,950.	3,000.	7,500.
1911 .....(191)..704,191		160.	175.	200.	325.	1,450.	2,250.	6,750.
1911D* 55,680		1,400.	2,500.	3,500.	6,000.	22,500.	27,500.	
1912 .....(197)..616,197		160.	175.	200.	325.	2,400.	3,200.	6,750.
1913 .....(165)..722,165		160.	175.	200.	300.	1,450.	2,250.	6,750.
1914 .....(117)..240,117		160.	200.	250.	500.	5,500.	9,250.	6,750.
1914D 448,000		160.	175.	210.	325.	1,950.	4,750.	
1915 .....(100)..606,100		160.	175.	200.	300.	1,450.	2,250.	7,500.
1925D 578,000		160.	175.	200.	285.	1,100.	1,350.	
1926 446,000		160.	175.	200.	285.	1,100.	1,350.	
1927 388,000		160.	175.	200.	285.	1,100.	1,350.	
1928 416,000		160.	175.	200.	285.	1,100.	1,350.	
1929 532,000		160.	175.	200.	285.	1,100.	1,350.	

*Values for coins with bold mint mark; weak D pieces are worth less. Beware of counterfeits.

THREE DOLLAR GOLD PIECES—1854-1889

The three dollar gold piece was authorized by the Act of February 21, 1853. The coin was first struck in 1854. It was never popular and saw very little circulation.

The coin weighs 77.4 grains, .900 fine. The head on the obverse represents an Indian princess with hair tightly curling over the neck, head crowned with a circle of feathers, the band of which is inscribed LIBERTY. A wreath of tobacco, wheat, corn and cotton occupies the field of the reverse, with the denomination and date within it.

Restrikes of some years were made at the Mint; particularly Proofs of 1865 and 1873.

In the year 1854 only, the word DOLLARS is in much smaller letters than in years 1855 through 1889. The 1856 proof has DOLLARS in large letters cut over the same word in small letters.

+ or – indicates change from previous year	TYPE COIN VALUES								
		F-12	VF-20	EF-40	AU-50	MS-60	MS-63	MS-65	PF-60	PF-63	PF-65
Indian Head 1854-1889 ...		450.+	650.+	900.+	1,250.+	2,500.+	5,500.+	12,500.+	5,000.+	11,500.+	21,000.-

Designer James B. Longacre, weight 5.015 grams; composition: .900 gold, .100 copper; diameter 20.5 mm; reeded edge; mints: Philadelphia, Dahlonega, New Orleans, San Francisco. Net weight: .14512 oz. pure gold.

THREE DOLLAR GOLD PIECES

Mint mark location is on reverse below wreath.

VF-20 VERY FINE—*Eyebrow, hair about forehead and ear and bottom curl are worn smooth. Curled feather-ends have faint details showing.*

EF-40 EXTREMELY FINE—*Light wear above and to right of eye. and on top of curled feathers.*

AU-50 ABOUT UNCIRCULATED—*Trace of wear on top of curled feathers in hair above and to right of eye.*

AU-55-CHOICE ABOUT UNCIRCULATED—*Evidence of friction on design high points. Most of mint luster remains.*

MS-60 UNCIRCULATED—*No trace of wear. Light blemishes.*

MS-63 SELECT UNCIRCULATED—*Some distracting contact marks or blemishes in prime focal areas. Luster may be impaired.*

MS-60 UNCIRCULATED—*No trace of wear. Light blemishes.*

PF-63 ATTRACTIVE PROOF— *Reflective surfaces with only a few blemishes in secondary focal places. No major flaws.*

	Mintage	VF-20	EF-40	AU-50	AU-55	MS-60	MS-63	PF-63
1854	138,618	$650.	$900.	$1,300.	$1,750.	$2,750.	$6,000.	$65,000.
1854D	1,120	9,500.	18,500.	30,000.	45,000.	100,000.		
1854O	24,000	1,500.	3,000.	6,000.	9,500.	22,500.		
1855	50,555	650.	900.	1,300.	1,750.	3,000.	6,250.	45,000.
1855S	6,600	1,150.	2,750.	6,500.	8,500.	22,000.	85,000.	
1856	26,010	700.	1,000.	1,400.	1,800.	2,850.	6,500.	35,000.
1856S‡	34,500	750.	1,250.	2,500.	4,500.	9,500.	22,500.	
1857	20,891	650.	900.	1,300.	1,800.	3,000.	9,000.	20,000.
1857S	14,000	1,000.	2,600.	6,000.	8,000.	16,000.	35,000.	
1858	2,133	950.	1,500.	2,500.	3,500.	7,000.	16,500.	20,000.
1859	(80) 15,638	675.	900.	1,300.	1,750.	2,750.	6,250.	17,500.
1860	(119) 7,155	750.	1,000.	1,400.	1,800.	2,750.	6,750.	13,500.
1860S	7,000	900.	2,250.	5,750.	9,500.	18,500.		
1861	(113) 6,072	750.	1,150.	1,650.	2,150.	3,250.	9,500.	13,500.
1862	(35) 5,785	750.	1,150.	1,650.	2,150.	3,250.	9,500.	13,500.
1863	(39) 5,039	750.	1,150.	1,650.	2,150.	3,250.	9,500.	13,500.
1864	(50) 2,680	850.	1,250.	1,850.	2,750.	3,750.	9,500.	13,500.
1865	(25) 1,165	1,500.	2,750.	5,250.	6,250.	11,500.	23,500.	17,500.
1866	(30) 4,030	850.	1,050.	1,550.	2,250.	3,250.	9,500.	15,000.
1867	(50) 2,650	850.	1,050.	1,550.	2,250.	3,250.	9,500.	15,000.
1868*	(25) 4,875	850.	1,050.	1,550.	2,250.	3,250.	9,000.	15,000.
1869*	(25) 2,525	850.	1,050.	1,750.	2,300.	3,950.	11,500.	15,000.
1870	(35) 3,535	850.	1,150.	1,850.	2,400.	4,250.	12,500.	15,000.
1870S	(Unique) 1		3,000,000.					
1871	(30) 1,330	750.	1,050.	1,750.	2,150.	3,500.	9,500.	15,000.
1872	(30) 2,030	750.	1,050.	1,750.	2,150.	3,500.	9,500.	15,000.
1873,Open 3 (Orig)	(25)	25		6,250.	9,500.			30,000.
1873,Closed 3		3,500.	5,000.	8,500.	11,500.	22,500.	37,500.	27,500.
1874	(20) 41,820	650.	900.	1,250.	1,700.	2,500.	5,500.	20,000.
1875, Pfs only	(20) 20			45,000.				95,000.
1876, Pfs only	(45) 45			14,000.				30,000.
1877	(20) 1,488	1,350.	3,250.	6,500.	8,500.	14,000.	35,000.	20,000.
1878*	(20) 82,324	650.	900.	1,250.	1,700.	2,500.	5,500.	20,000.
1879	(30) 3,030	750.	1,000.	1,350.	1,850.	2,750.	5,750.	15,000.
1880	(36) 1,036	800.	1,500.	2,250.	2,750.	3,250.	6,250.	15,000.
1881	(54) 554	1,350.	2,500.	4,500.	5,500.	6,750.	11,500.	15,000.
1882	(76) 1,576	900.	1,250.	1,950.	2,350.	3,250.	6,750.	11,500.
1883	(89) 989	950.	1,450.	2,150.	2,650.	3,750.	7,500.	11,500.
1884	(106) 1,106	950.	1,450.	2,150.	2,650.	3,750.	7,500.	11,500.
1885	(109) 910	950.	1,450.	2,150.	2,650.	3,750.	7,500.	11,500.
1886	(142) 1,142	950.	1,450.	2,150.	2,650.	3,750.	7,500.	11,500.
1887	(160) 6,160	650.	900.	1,500.	1,800.	2,750.	5,750.	11,500.
1888	(291) 5,291	650.	900.	1,250.	1,700.	2,500.	5,500.	11,500.
1889	(129) 2,429	650.	900.	1,250.	1,700.	2,500.	5,500.	11,500.

‡Small and medium S varieties exist.

* Varieties showing traces of possible overdating include: 1868/7, 1869/8 and 1878/7.

FOUR DOLLAR GOLD OR "STELLA"

These pattern coins were first suggested by the Hon. John A. Kasson, then U.S. Minister to Austria; and it was through the efforts of Dr. W. W. Hubbell, who patented the goloid metal used in making the goloid metric dollars, that we have these beautiful and interesting pieces.

There are two distinct types in both years of issue. Charles E. Barber designed the flowing hair type, and George T. Morgan the coiled hair. They were struck as patterns in gold, aluminum, copper and white metal. Only those struck in gold are listed. Mintage figures are estimates. The exact numbers are unknown.

	Mintage	EF-40	AU-50	PF-60	PF-63	PF-64	PF-65
1879, Flowing hair	(425)	$55,000.	$65,000.	$75,000.	$95,000.	$115,000.	$135,000.
1879, Coiled hair	(25)			200,000.	240,000.	275,000.	325,000.
1880, Flowing hair	(25)			100,000.	135,000.	165,000.	220,000.
1880, Coiled hair	(20)			325,000.	400,000.	485,000.	600,000.

HALF EAGLES ($5.00 GOLD PIECES)

The half eagle was the first gold coin actually struck for the United States. The $5.00 piece was authorized to be coined by the Act of April 2, 1792, and the first type weighed 135 grains, 916 2/3 fine. The Act of June 28, 1834 changed the weight to 129 grains, 899.225 fine. Fineness became .900 by the Act of January 18, 1837.

There are many varieties among the early dates caused by changes in the number of stars, style of eagle, overdates, and differences in the size of figures in the dates. Those dated prior to 1807 do not bear any mark of value. The 1822 half eagle is considered the most valuable regular issue coin of the entire United States series. Proofs of some dates prior to 1855 are known to exist, and all are rare. Commemorative and bullion $5 coins have been made at West Point since 1986 and 1994 respectively, thus this is the only U.S. denomination made at each of the eight mints.

+ or − indicates change from previous year	TYPE COIN VALUES									
	F-12	VF-20	EF-40	AU-50	MS-60	MS-63	MS-65	PF-60	PF-63	PF-65
Cap Bust-Sm. Eag. 1795-1798	10,500.+	15,500.+	19,500.+	26,000.+	42,000.+	130,000.+	250,000.			
Cap Bust-Lg. Eag. 1795-1807	2,500.+	3,500.+	4,500.+	5,000.+	8,000.+	15,000.+	80,000.			
Cap Draped Bust 1807-1812	2,500.+	3,500.+	4,500.+	5,500.+	8,000.+	15,000.+	85,000.			
Cap Head 1813-1834	2,500.+	3,250.+	4,800.+	5,750.+	8,500.+	16,000.+	80,000.			
Classic Head 1834-1838	225.	500.+	500.+	750.	2,600.+	7,000.+	45,000.+			
Lib Coronet-NM 1839-1866	150.+	175.+	225.+	325.+	1,100.-	7,250.+	26,000.+	8,000.+	20,000.+	65,000.+
Lib Coronet 1866-1908	130.+	155.-	165.-	180.+	235.+	750.+	3,000.	3,500.+	10,000.+	22,000.-
Indian Head 1908-1929	150.+	185.+	220.	250.-	350.+	1,750.+	12,000.	4,000.+	10,000.+	24,000.

HALF EAGLES ($5.00 GOLD PIECES)
CAPPED BUST TO RIGHT, SMALL EAGLE 1795-1798

This type was struck from mid-1795 to early 1798, when the small eagle reverse was changed to the large or "heraldic" eagle. Note that the 1795 and 1797 dates exist for both types, but the heraldic reverses of these dates were in 1798 using serviceable 1795 and 1797 dies.

Designer Robert Scot; weight 8.75 grams; composition: .9167 gold, .0833 silver and copper; approx. diameter 25 mm; reeded edge.

F-12 FINE—*Hair worn smooth but with distinct outline. For heraldic type, E PLURIBUS UNUM is faint but readable.*
VF-20 VERY FINE—*Slight to noticeable wear on high spots such as hair, turban, eagle's head and wings.*
EF-40 EXTREMELY FINE—*Slight wear on hair and highest part of cheek.*
AU-50 ABOUT UNCIRCULATED—*Trace of wear on cap, hair, cheek and drapery.*
MS-60 UNCIRCULATED—*No trace of wear. Light blemishes.*
MS-63 SELECT UNCIRCULATED—*Some distracting contact marks or blemishes in prime focal areas. Luster may be impaired.*

	Mintage	F-12	VF-20	EF-40	AU-50	AU-55	MS-60	MS-63
1795 Small eagle*	8,707	$10,500.	$15,500.	$19,500.	$26,000.	$32,500.	$42,500.	$130,000.

*One variety has the final S in STATES punched over an erroneous D.

1796, 6 over 5		**1797, 15 Stars**		**1797, 16 Stars**				
1796, 6/5	6,196	12,500.	16,500.	22,500.	29,000.	34,000.	57,000.	165,000.
1797, 15 stars	} 3,609	15,000.	20,000.	32,500.	55,000.	85,000.	135,000.	
1797, 16 stars		13,000.	17,500.	27,500.	50,000.	75,000.	120,000.	
1798, Small eagle	*(7 known)*	—	125,000.	250,000.	350,000.	—		

CAPPED BUST TO RIGHT, HERALDIC EAGLE 1795-1807

	Mintage	F-12	VF-20	EF-40	AU-50	AU-55	MS-60	MS-63
1795, Heraldic eagle*		$10,000.	$15,000.	$22,500.	$42,500.	$57,500.	$85,000.	$165,000.
1797, 7/5*		10,000.	12,500.	20,000.	50,000.	70,000.	110,000.	
1797, 16 star obverse* *(Unique)*								
1797, 15 star obverse* *(Unique)*								
1798, Small 8		2,500.	3,750.	5,500.	9,000.	13,000.	20,000.	
1798, Lg.8,13 star rev	} 24,867	2,250.	3,500.	5,000.	8,500.	12,000.		
1798, Lg.8,14 star rev		3,000.	4,500.	7,500.	17,000.	22,500.	32,000.	
1799	7,451	2,500.	3,500.	4,500.	8,000.	13,000.	18,000.	38,000.

*These four pieces are thought to have been struck in 1798 and included in the mintage figure for that year.

HALF EAGLES ($5.00 GOLD PIECES)

1802 over 1

1803 over 2

Small 8 over Large 8

	Mintage	F-12	VF-20	EF-40	AU-50	AU-55	MS-60	MS-63
1800	37,628	$2,500.	$3,500.	$4,500.	$5,500.	$6,000.	$8,000.	$15,000.
1802, 2/1	53,176	2,500.	3,500.	4,500.	5,500.	6,000.	8,000.	15,000.
1803, 3/2	33,506	2,500.	3,500.	4,500.	5,500.	6,000.	8,000.	15,000.
1804, Small 8 . . . } 30,475		2,500.	3,500.	4,500.	5,500.	6,000.	8,000.	15,000.
1804,Sm 8/Lg 8 }		2,500.	3,500.	4,500.	5,500.	6,000.	8,000.	15,000.
1805	33,183	2,500.	3,500.	4,500.	5,500.	6,000.	8,000.	15,000.

Pointed 6, Stars 8 and 5   Round Top 6, Stars 7 and 6

1806, Pointed top 6 . . 9,676	2,750.	3,750.	4,750.	5,600.	6,500.	9,500.	17,000.
1806, Round top 6 . .54,417	2,500.	3,500.	4,500.	5,500.	6,000.	8,000.	15,000.
1807 32,488	2,500.	3,500.	4,500.	5,500.	6,000.	8,000.	15,000.

CAPPED BUST TO LEFT 1807-1812

Designer John Reich. Standards same as previous issue.

F-12 FINE —*LIBERTY readable but partly weak.*
VF-20 VERY FINE —*Headband edges slightly worn. LIBERTY is bold.*
EF-40 EXTREMELY FINE —*Slight wear on highest portions of hair. 80% of major curls are plain.*
AU-50 ABOUT UNCIRCULATED — *Trace of wear above eye, on top of cap, cheek and hair.*
AU-55-CHOICE ABOUT UNCIRCULATED —*Evidence of friction on design high points. Most of mint luster remains.*
MS-60 UNCIRCULATED —*No trace of wear. Light blemishes.*
MS-63 SELECT UNCIRCULATED —*Some distracting contact marks or blemishes in prime focal areas. Luster may be impaired.*

	Mintage	F-12	VF-20	EF-40	AU-50	AU-55	MS-60	MS-63
1807	51,605	$2,500.	$3,500.	$4,500.	$5,500.	$6,000.	$8,000.	$15,000.

1808, 8 over 7   Normal Date   1809, 9 over 8

HALF EAGLES ($5.00 GOLD PIECES)

	Mintage	F-12	VF-20	EF-40	AU-50	AU-55	MS-60	MS-63
1808, 8/7 ⎫		$2,750.	$3,750.	$4,750.	$6,500.	$8,000.	$12,000.	$25,000.
1808 ⎬ 55,578		2,500.	3,500.	4,500.	5,500.	6,000.	8,000.	15,000.
1809, 9/8	33,875	2,500.	3,500.	4,500.	5,500.	6,000.	8,000.	15,000.

Small Date	**Large Date**	**Large 5**	**Tall 5**

	Mintage	F-12	VF-20	EF-40	AU-50	AU-55	MS-60	MS-63
1810 All Kinds	100,287							
1810, Small Date, Small 5		6,000.	22,000.	35,000.	50,000.	65,000.		
1810, Small Date, Tall 5		2,500.	3,750.	4,750.	6,000.	6,250.	9,000.	20,000.
1810, Large Date, Small 5		12,000.	18,000.	28,000.	45,000.	50,000.	80,000.	
1810, Large Date, Large 5		2,500.	3,500.	4,500.	5,500.	6,000.	8,000.	15,000.
1811, Small 5 ⎫		2,500.	3,500.	4,500.	5,500.	6,000.	8,000.	15,000.
1811, Tall 5 ⎬ 99,581		2,500.	3,500.	4,500.	5,500.	6,000.	8,000.	15,000.
1812	58,087	2,500.	3,500.	4,500.	5,500.	6,000.	8,000.	15,000.

CAPPED HEAD TO LEFT (large diameter) 1813-1829

	Mintage	F-12	VF-20	EF-40	AU-50	AU-55	MS-60	MS-63
1813	95,428	$2,500.	$3,800.	$4,800.	$5,750.	$6,750.	$8,500.	$16,000.
1814, 4/3	15,454	3,000.	4,000.	5,000.	6,000.	7,000.	9,000.	25,000.
1815	635			70,000.	100,000.	125,000.	150,000.	200,000.
1818, All Kinds	48,588							
1818,		3,000.	4,000.	5,000.	6,000.	6,750.	9,000.	25,000.
1818, STATESOF one word		3,250.	4,250.	5,250.	6,500.	7,000.	12,000.	28,000.
1818, 5D/50		—	4,750.	5,750.	8,500.	10,000.	18,000.	30,000.
1819 ⎫				35,000.	45,000.	55,000.	60,000.	
1819, 5D/50 ⎬ 51,723			—	25,000.	35,000.	40,000.	50,000.	75,000.

Curved Base 2	**Square Base 2**	**Small Letters**	**Large Letters**

	Mintage	F-12	VF-20	EF-40	AU-50	AU-55	MS-60	MS-63
1820 All Kinds	263,806							
1820,Curved-base 2,Sm. Letter		3,500.	5,000.	6,500.	7,500.	8,500.	12,000.	24,000.
1820,Curved-base 2,Lg. Letter		3,500.	5,000.	6,500.	7,500.	8,500.	12,000.	24,000.
1820,Square-base 2		3,500.	5,000.	6,500.	7,500.	8,500.	12,000.	24,000.
1821	34,641	10,000.	15,000.	20,000.	28,000.	35,000.	50,000.	125,000.

| 1825, 5 over 1 | 1825, 5 over 4 |

	Mintage	F-12	VF-20	EF-40	AU-50	AU-55	MS-60	MS-63
1822 *(3 known)* ...	17,796		—	*$3,000,000.+*	—			
1823	14,485	$2,500.	$3,250.	5,000.	$6,750.	$9,500.	$16,500.	$28,000.
1824	17,340	5,250.	9,500.	16,000.	24,000.	30,000.	36,000.	55,000.
1825, 5/1 .... } 1825, 5/4 *(2 known)* }	29,060	6,000.	9,500.	12,500. 300,000.	18,500.	30,000.	36,000.	55,000.
1826	18,069	4,500.	8,500.	12,000.	18,000.	26,000.	34,000.	48,000.
1827	24,913	7,500.	12,000.	18,000.	24,000.	30,000.	38,000.	65,000.

Large Date

	Mintage	F-12	VF-20	EF-40	AU-50	AU-55	MS-60	MS-63
1828, 8/7 .... } 1828 .... }	28,029	12,000.	24,000.	32,000.	42,000.	55,000.	110,000.	225,000.
		10,000.	16,000.	24,000.	36,000.	50,000.	80,000.	125,000.
1829, Large Date ..	57,442						200,000.	

CAPPED HEAD TO LEFT (reduced diameter) 1829-1834

The half eagles dated 1829 (small date) through 1834 are smaller in diameter than the earlier pieces. They also have smaller letters, dates and stars.

Standards as before. Modified design by William Kneass. Diameter 23.8 mm.

| 1829 Small Date | 1830 Large 5D | 1830 Small 5D | 1832 13 Stars
Square Base 2 |

	Mintage	F-12	VF-20	EF-40	AU-50	AU-55	MS-60	MS-63
1829 Small Date ...incl. above		$50,000.	$95,000.	$150,000.	$200,000.	$240,000.	$300,000.	
1830 Sm or Lg 5 D .	126,351	$15,000.	18,000.	24,000.	28,000.	32,000.	42,000.	58,000.
1831 Sm or Lg 5 D .	140,594	15,000.	18,000.	24,000.	28,000.	32,000.	42,000.	60,000.

1832,Curved-base 2,
  12 stars *(6 known)* }
1832,Sq-base 2, ...
  13 stars }
	157,487		—
			15,000.
				120,000.
				18,000.
					165,000.
					24,000.
						—
						28,000.
							32,000.	42,000.	60,000.

HALF EAGLES ($5.00 GOLD PIECES)

	Mintage	F-12	VF-20	EF-40	AU-50	AU-55	MS-60	MS-63
1833 Large Date	}193,630	$15,000.	$18,000.	$24,000.	$28,000.	$32,000.	$42,000.	$60,000.
1833 Small Date		15,000.	18,000.	24,000.	28,000.	32,000.	42,000.	60,000.

Plain 4   Crosslet 4

	Mintage							
1834 Plain 4	}50,141	15,000.	18,000.	24,000.	28,000.	32,000.	42,000.	60,000.
1834 Crosslet 4 ..		15,000.	18,000.	24,000.	28,000.	32,000.	42,000.	60,000.

CLASSIC HEAD TYPE 1834-1838

As on the quarter eagle of 1834, the motto E PLURIBUS UNUM was omitted from the new, reduced size half eagle in 1834, to distinguish the old coins which had become worth more than face value.

Designer William Kneass; weight 8.36 grams; composition: .8992 gold, .1008 silver and copper, changed to .900 gold in 1837; diameter 22.5 mm; reeded edge; mints: Philadelphia, Charlotte, Dahlonega.

Mint mark above date. See page 205.

	Mintage						
1834 Plain 4 ‡	}657,460	325.	500.	750.	1150.	2,600.	7,000.
1834 Crosslet 4		1,600.	3,000.	5,500.	8,000.	15,000.	42,000.
1835 ‡	371,534	325.	500.	750.	1,150.	2,750.	9,000.
1836	553,147	325.	500.	750.	1,150.	2,750.	9,000.
1837‡	207,121	350.	600.	850.	1,250.	3,500.	13,000.
1838	286,588	350.	500.	750.	1,150.	3,200.	11,000.
1838C	17,179	2,400.	4,200.	11,000.	18,000.	34,000.	85,000.
1838D	20,583	2,200.	4,500.	7,500.	11,500.	22,500.	42,000.

‡Varieties have either script 8 or block style 8 in date.

CORONET TYPE, No Motto Above Eagle 1839-1866

Designer Christian Gobrecht; weight 8.359 grams; composition: .900 gold, .100 copper; diameter (1839-40) 22.5 mm. (1840-1866) 21.6 mm; reeded edge; mints: Philadelphia, Charlotte, Dahlonega, New Orleans, San Francisco. Net weight: .24187 oz. pure gold.

VF-20 VERY FINE —*LIBERTY bold. Major lines show in neckhair.*
EF-40 EXTREMELY FINE —*Neck hair details clear. Slight wear on top and lower part of coronet, and hair.*
AU-50 ABOUT UNCIRCULATED —*Trace of wear on coronet and hair above eye.*
AU-55-CHOICE ABOUT UNCIRCULATED —*Evidence of friction on design high points. Most of mint luster remains.*
MS-60 UNCIRCULATED —*No trace of wear. Light blemishes.*
MS-63 SELECT UNCIRCULATED —*Some distracting contact marks or blemishes in prime focal areas. Luster may be impaired.*
PF-63 —*Attractive reflective surfaces with only a few blemishes in secondary focal places. No major flaws.*

Mint mark above date 1839 only, below eagle 1840-1908.

	Mintage	VF-20	EF-40	AU-50	AU-55	MS-60	MS-63	PF-63
1839	118,143	$275.	$475.	$1,200.	$1,500.	$3,800.	$18,000.	
1839C	17,205	2,200.	3,400.	6,500.	10,000.	22,000.	50,000.	
1839D	18,939	2,200.	3,200.	5,500.	9,000.	18,000.		
1840 *	137,382	250.	400.	1,250.	2,000.	3,750.	12,000.	
1840C *	18,992	2,000.	3,500.	7,500.	12,500.	24,000.	55,000.	
1840D *	22,896	2,000.	3,500.	7,500.	10,000.	16,000.	45,000.	
1840 O *	40,120	450.	1,000.	1,750.	2,750.	8,000.	26,000.	
1841	15,833	400.	950.	1,500.	2,200.	5,000.	10,000.	
1841C	21,467	1,500.	1,900.	3,250.	6,750.	20,000.	42,000.	
1841D	29,392	1,500.	2,000.	4,500.	6,750.	15,000.	30,000.	
1841O	50							

*Scarce varieties of the 1840 coins have the fine edge reeding and wide rims of the 1839 issues.

HALF EAGLES ($5.00 GOLD PIECES)

1847

	Mintage	VF-20	EF-40	AU-50	AU-55	MS-60	MS-63	PF-63
1842 Small Letter } 1842 Large Letter }	27,578	$375. 750.	$1,200. 1,800.	$3,500. 6,000.	$6,000. 8,000.	$12,000. 16,000.		
1842C Small Date .. } 1842C Large Date .. }	27,432	8,500. 1,500.	20,000. 2,000.	38,000. 3,600.	65,000. 6,000.	90,000. 18,000.	36,000.	
1842D Small Date .. } 1842D Large Date .. }	59,608	1,500. 2,600.	2,000. 5,500.	3,500. 14,000.	5,500. 22,000.	14,000. 40,000.	34,000.	
1842O	16,400	1,000.	3,400.	11,000.	16,000.	24,000.		
1843	611,205	175.	225.	325.	500.	1,600.	9,000.	
1843C	44,277	1,500.	2,200.	4,800.	7,000.	16,000.	35,000.	
1843D	98,452	1,500.	2,200.	3,500.	5,500.	10,000.	26,000.	
1843O Small Letter ..	19,075	700.	1,750.	2,800.	5,000.	24,000.	32,000.	
1843O Large Letter ..	82,000	300.	1,400.	2,600.	4,250.	12,500.	28,000.	
1844	340,330	185.	250.	375.	525.	1,750.	7,500.	
1844C	23,631	1,750.	2,750.	7,000.	11,000.	22,000.	36,000.	
1844D	88,982	1,750.	2,200.	3,500.	5,500.	11,000.	32,000.	
1844O	364,600	275.	400.	800.	1,350.	4,500.	13,500.	
1845	417,099	185.	250.	375.	525.	1,750.	9,500.	
1845D	90,629	1,750.	2,200.	3,500.	5,000.	11,000.	25,000.	
1845O	41,000	450.	900.	3,500.	6,500.	12,500.	26,000.	
1846 Large Date .. } 1846 Small Date .. }	395,942	185. 185.	275. 275.	600. 400.	1,200. 650.	3,500. 3,000.		
1846C	12,995	1,500.	3,200.	6,750.	10,500.	21,000.	55,000.	
1846D 1846D High 2nd D/D }	80,294	1,750. 1,750.	2,200. 2,200.	3,800. 3,500.	5,500. 5,000.	13,500. 11,000.	26,000.	
1846O	58,000	400.	1,100.	3,800.	6,000.	12,000.	25,000.	
1847	915,981	200.	250.	350.	475.	1,500.	8,000.	
1847 Top of extra very low 7 at border		240.	285.	600.	1,100.	2,500.	9,500.	
1847C	84,151	1,750.	2,200.	3,500.	5,500.	12,000.	26,000.	
1847D	64,405	1,750.	2,200.	3,200.	5,000.	8,500.	17,500.	
1847O	12,000	2,200.	6,000.	12,000.	18,000.	28,000.		
1848	260,775	240.	285.	450.	650.	1,500.	10,500.	
1848C	64,472	1,750.	2,200.	3,200.	6,500.	18,000.	48,000.	
1848D	47,465	1,750.	2,200.	3,200.	6,000.	14,000.	36,000.	
1849	133,070	185.	250.	700.	1,200.	2,800.		
1849C	64,823	1,750.	2,200.	3,200.	5,500.	13,000.	32,000.	
1849D	39,036	1,750.	2,200.	3,200.	6,500.	15,000.	38,000.	
1850	64,491	300.	650.	1,200.	1,800.	3,650.	15,000.	
1850C	63,591	1,750.	2,200.	3,200.	6,000.	13,000.	26,000.	
1850D	43,984	1,750.	2,200.	3,200.	6,500.	28,000.		
1851	377,505	200.	250.	350.	475.	2,800.	9,500.	
1851C	49,176	1,750.	2,200.	3,400.	6,500.	15,000.	48,000.	
1851D	62,710	1,750.	2,200.	3,800.	7,000.	13,000.	32,000.	
1851O	41,000	600.	1,300.	3,500.	6,500.	13,000.	20,000.	
1852	573,901	200.	250.	325.	450.	1,200.	8,000.	
1852C	72,574	1,750.	2,200.	3,200.	5,000.	7,500.	24,000.	
1852D	91,584	1,750.	2,200.	3,600.	5,000.	12,000.	28,000.	
1853	305,770	200.	250.	350.	475.	1,500.	8,500.	
1853C	65,571	1,750.	2,200.	3,200.	4,800.	7,500.	26,000.	

Column group headers: **1842 Large Date** / **Large Letters** / **Small Letters** / **Extra 7 at border**

[217]

	Mintage	VF-20	EF-40	AU-50	AU-55	MS-60	MS-63	PF-63
1853D	89,678	$1,750.	$2,200.	$3,200.	$4,400.	$8,500.	$24,000.	
1854	160,675	200.	250.	500.	1,000.	2,000.	8,500.	
1854C	39,283	1,750.	2,200.	3,800.	6,500.	14,000.	42,000.	
1854D	56,413	1,750.	2,200.	3,200.	5,000.	10,500.	28,000.	
1854O	46,000	325.	600.	1,500.	2,400.	7,500.	22,000.	
1854S	268			—	1,000,000.	—		
1855	117,098	200.	250.	350.	600.	1,600.	8,500.	—
1855C	39,788	1,750.	2,200.	3,800.	6,000.	16,000.	36,000.	
1855D	22,432	1,750.	2,200.	3,800.	6,000.	18,000.	42,000.	
1855O	11,100	750.	2,100.	4,500.	6,500.	18,000.		
1855S	61,000	400.	1,400.	3,000.	5,000.	13,500.		
1856	197,990	200.	250.	350.	600.	2,000.	12,000.	—
1856C	28,457	1,750.	2,200.	3,800.	6,500.	18,000.		.
1856D	19,786	1,750.	2,200.	3,800.	6,500.	11,500.	35,000.	
1856O	10,000	750.	1,850.	5,000.	7,500.	13,000.		
1856S	105,100	325.	750.	1,350.	2,450.	7,500.	28,000.	
1857	98,188	200.	250.	350.	475.	1,600.	8,500.	—
1857C	31,360	1,750.	2,200.	3,800.	5,250.	9,000.	32,000.	
1857D	17,046	1,750.	2,200.	3,800.	6,500.	12,500.	36,000.	
1857O	13,000	750.	1,600.	4,500.	6,500.	12,500.	48,000.	
1857S	87,000	325.	750.	1,500.	2,750.	10,000.	18,000.	
1858	15,136	250.	500.	800.	1,500.	3,500.	10,500.	—
1858C	38,856	1,750.	2,200.	3,800.	6,000.	12,500.	36,000.	
1858D	15,362	1,750.	2,200.	3,800.	6,000.	12,500.	38,000.	
1858S	18,600	950.	2,750.	7,500.	11,000.			
1859	(80) 16,814	300.	500.	850.	1,600.	6,000.	12,000.	35,000.
1859C	31,847	1,750.	2,200.	3,800.	6,500.	16,000.	42,000.	
1859D	10,366	1,750.	2,200.	3,600.	6,000.	13,000.	38,000.	
1859S	13,220	1,600.	3,750.	6,500.	10,500.	26,000.		
1860	(62) 19,825	250.	550.	1,000.	1,600.	3,500.	15,000.	30,000.
1860C	14,813	1,750.	2,750.	4,250.	8,250.	13,000.	28,000.	
1860D	14,635	1,750.	2,750.	4,250.	8,500.	16,500.	45,000.	
1860S	21,200	1,200.	2,400.	6,000.	8,500.	24,000.		
1861	(66) 688,150	200.	250.	375.	450.	1,100.	7,250.	30,000.
1861C	6,879	2,200.	4,500.	8,500.	13,000.	28,000.	95,000.	
1861D	1,597	6,000.	9,500.	20,000.	28,000.	45,000.	125,000.	
1861S	18,000	1,250.	4,000.	7,500.	11,500.			
1862	(35) 4,465	750.	1,750.	3,500.	5,500.	18,000.		30,000.
1862S	9,500	3,000.	6,000.	16,000.	25,000.	50,000.		
1863	(30) 2,472	1,200.	3,600.	7,500.	12,500.	25,000.		30,000.
1863S	17,000	1,500.	4,500.	12,500.	17,500.	32,500.		
1864	(50) 4,220	700.	1,800.	3,500.	7,500.	13,000.		20,000.
1864S	3,888	6,500.	12,500.	32,000.		—		
1865	(25) 1,295	1,500.	3,750.	9,500.	14,000.	20,000.		25,000.
1865S	27,612	1,500.	2,750.	6,000.	9,000.	19,000.		
1866S	9,000	1,750.	4,000.	12,500.	17,500.			

Variety 2 — Motto Above Eagle 1866-1908

Designer Christian Gobrecht; weight 8.359 grams; composition: .900 gold, .100 copper; diameter 21.6 mm; reeded edge; mints: Philadelphia, Carson City, Denver, New Orleans, San Francisco. Net weight: .24187 oz. pure gold.

VF-20 VERY FINE —*Half of hairlines above coronet missing. Hair curls under ear evident, but worn. Motto and its ribbon sharp.*

EF-40 EXTREMELY FINE —*Small amount of wear on top of hair and below L in LIBERTY. Wear evident on wing tips and neck of eagle.*

AU-50 ABOUT UNCIRCULATED —*Trace of wear on tip of coronet and hair above eye.*

AU-55-CHOICE ABOUT UNCIRCULATED —*Evidence of friction on design high points. Most of mint luster remains.*

MS-60 UNCIRCULATED —*No trace of wear. Light blemishes.*

MS-63 SELECT UNCIRCULATED —*Some distracting con tact marks or blemishes in prime focal areas. Luster may be impaired.*

PF-63 ATTRACTIVE PROOF — *Reflective surfaces with only a few blemishes in secondary focal places. No major flaws.*

	Mintage	VF-20	EF-40	AU-50	AU-55	MS-60	MS-63	PF-63
1866 . . . . .(30) 6,730		$800.	$1,350.	$3,250.	$5,250.	$14,000.		$20,000.
1866S 34,920		950.	2,750.	8,500.	12,000.			
1867 . . . . .(50) 6,920		450.	1,300.	3,250.	5,250.	12,000.		18,000.
1867S 29,000		1,250.	3,000.	12,500.	17,000.			
1868 . . . . .(25) 5,725		550.	1,000.	3,250.	6,000.	12,500.		22,000.
1868S 52,000		425.	1,500.	3,750.	6,000.	18,500.		
1869 . . . . .(25) 1,785		850.	1,850.	4,000.	6,000.	14,000.		22,000.
1869S 31,000		600.	1,800.	4,500.	8,000.	22,500.		
1870 . . . . .(35) 4,035		750.	1,800.	3,250.	5,750.	15,000.		22,000.
1870CC 7,675		6,000.	16,500.	30,000.	35,000.	75,000.		
1870S 17,000		1,000.	2,200.	8,000.	12,000.	25,000.		
1871 . . . . .(30) 3,230		750.	1,500.	3,250.	6,000.	14,000.		22,000.
1871CC 20,770		1,500.	4,500.	14,000.	20,000.	55,000.	95,000.	
1871S 25,000		450.	1,100.	3,600.	7,500.	15,000.		
1872 . . . . .(30) 1,690		750.	1,500.	3,000.	5,000.	12,000.	19,500.	22,000.
1872CC 16,980		1,250.	6,000.	20,000.	30,000.			
1872S 36,400		500.	800.	3,000.	7,000.	14,000.		
1873, Cl 3 . .(25) }112,505		165.	200.	400.	550.	1,200.	6,750.	22,000.
1873, Open 3		165.	200.	300.	350.	800.	4,250.	
1873CC 7,416		3,000.	12,500.	28,000.	38,000.	60,000.		
1873S 31,000		650.	950.	3,750.	6,250.	20,000.		
1874 . . . . .(20) 3,508		500.	1,150.	2,250.	3,750.	12,500.	22,500.	24,000.
1874CC 21,198		1,000.	2,500.	10,000.	15,000.	32,500.		
1874S 16,000		850.	1,750.	4,750.	7,500.			
1875 . . . . .(20) 220		38,000.	47,500.	65,000.	80,000.			75,000.
1875CC 11,828		1,750.	3,750.	12,000.	20,000.	45,000.		
1875S 9,000		800.	2,200.	6,000.	9,000.	20,000.		
1876 . . . . .(45) 1,477		800.	2,000.	3,500.	7,000.	10,000.	16,000.	15,000.
1876CC 6,887		1,500.	4,250.	12,000.	15,000.	38,000.		
1876S 4,000		1,300.	3,500.	8,500.	11,000.			20,000.
1877 . . . . .(20) 1,152		800.	2,100.	3,500.	5,250.	13,500.		
1877CC 8,680		1,200.	3,500.	8,500.	13,000.	42,000.		
1877S 26,700		300.	600.	1,750.	4,000.	8,750.		
1878 . . . . .(20) . . .131,740		170.	185.	200.	225.	425.	1,950.	20,000.
1878CC 9,054		3,750.	10,000.	20,000.	28,000.			
1878S 144,700		180.	195.	215.	400.	850.	4,500.	
1879 . . . . .(30) . . .301,950		180.	195.	215.	250.	375.	1,750.	18,000.
1879CC 17,281		600.	1,500.	3,250.	6,500.	19,500.		
1879S 426,200		175.	195.	200.	265.	950.	3,500.	
1880 . . . . .(36) . .3,166,436		165.	175.	185.	200.	235.	1,100.	14,000.
1880CC 51,017		400.	750.	1,650.	4,500.	10,500.		
1880S 1,348,900		165.	175.	185.	200.	235.	950.	
1881, 1/0 . . . . . }5,708,802		285.	575.	750.	950.	1,250.	6,500.	
1881 . . . . . .(42)		165.	175.	185.	200.	235.	750.	14,000.
1881 CC 13,886		500.	1,750.	6,000.	9,500.	21,500.	55,000.	
1881S 969,000		165.	175.	185.	200.	235.	900.	
1882 . . . . .(48) . .2,514,568		165.	175.	185.	200.	235.	850.	14,000.
1882 CC 82,817		325.	500.	750.	1,950.	7,500.		

HALF EAGLES ($5.00 GOLD PIECES)

	Mintage	VF-20	EF-40	AU-50	AU-55	MS-60	MS-63	PF-63
1882S	.969,000	$165.	$175.	$185.	$200.	$235.	$950.	
1883 ......(61)	...233,461	165.	175.	185.	200.	265.	1,400.	14,000.
1883 CC	...12,598	400.	1,000.	3,250.	6,500.	15,000.		
1883S	...83,200	165.	185.	225.	285.	900.	3,250.	
1884 ......(48)	...191,078	165.	185.	225.	285.	750.	2,750.	14,000.
1884 CC	...16,402	550.	1,050.	2,750.	4,750.	15,000.		
1884S	...177,000	165.	175.	185.	225.	325.	1,750.	
1885 ......(66)	...601,506	165.	175.	185.	200.	235.	850.	14,000.
1885S	.1,211,500	165.	175.	185.	200.	235.	800.	
1886 ......(72)	...388,432	165.	175.	185.	200.	245.	1,050.	14,000.
1886S	.3,268,000	165.	175.	185.	200.	235.	800.	
1887 Pfs only(87)	87							55,000.
1887S	.1,912,000	165.	175.	185.	200.	235.	800.	
1888 ......(95)	18,296	185.	225.	275.	325.	500.	1,850.	11,000.
1888S	...293,900	175.	225.	375.	675.	1,150.	4,750.	
1889 ......(45)	7,565	225.	325.	525.	675.	1,050.	2,850.	14,000.
1890 ......(88)	4,328	300.	500.	700.	950.	1,950.	7,250.	14,000.
1890CC	...53,800	250.	325.	550.	625.	1,050.	4,850.	
1891 ......(53)	...61,413	165.	185.	215.	265.	475.	1,750.	12,000.
1891CC	...208,000	235.	325.	450.	515.	750.	3,450.	
1892 ......(92)	...753,572	165.	175.	185.	200.	235.	1,100.	12,000.
1892CC	...82,968	235.	345.	475.	775.	1,650.	7,500.	
1892O	...10,000	475.	850.	1,275.	1,800.	3,000.	11,000.	
1892S	...298,400	165.	175.	200.	400.	575.	3,500.	
1893 ......(77)	..1,528,197	165.	175.	185.	200.	235.	800.	12,000.
1893CC	...60,000	275.	350.	650.	800.	1,600.	7,500.	
1893O	...110,000	200.	250.	375.	475.	1,100.	6,500.	
1893S	...224,000	165.	175.	200.	20.	300.	1,100.	
1894 ......(75)	...957,955	165.	175.	185.	200.	235.	800.	12,000.
1894O	...16,600	200.	275.	425.	700.	1,250.	5,800.	
1894S	...55,900	225.	300.	525.	950.	2,800.	8,500.	
1895 ......(81)	..1,345,936	165.	175.	185.	200.	235.	800.	10,000.
1895S	...112,000	200.	300.	500.	850.	2,800.	6,800.	
1896 ......(103)	...59,063	165.	175.	185.	210.	235.	1,000.	10,000.
1896S	...155,400	200.	250.	400.	600.	1,250.	6,500.	
1897 ......(83)	...867,883	155.	165.	180.	200.	235.	800.	10,000.
1897S	...354,000	185.	200.	300.	450.	850.	5,500.	
1898 ......(75)	...633,495	165.	175.	185.	200.	235.	800.	10,000.
1898S	.1,397,400	165.	175.	185.	200.	250.	1,000.	
1899 ......(99)	.1,710,729	165.	175.	185.	200.	235.	800.	10,000.
1899S	.1,545,000	165.	175.	185.	200.	235.	850.	
1900 ......(230)	.1,405,730	165.	175.	185.	200.	235.	800.	10,000.
1900S	...329,000	165.	175.	185.	210.	240.	850.	
1901 ......(140)	...616,040	165.	175.	185.	200.	235.	800.	10,000.
1901S, 1/0	} 3,648,000	165.	185.	225.	275.	325.	850.	
1901S		165.	175.	185.	200.	235.	800.	
1902 ......(162)	...172,562	165.	175.	185.	200.	235.	800.	10,000.
1902S	...939,000	165.	175.	185.	200.	235.	800.	
1903 ......(154)	...227,024	165.	175.	185.	200.	235.	800.	10,000.
1903S	.1,855,000	165.	175.	185.	200.	235.	800.	
1904 ......(136)	...392,136	165.	175.	185.	200.	235.	800.	10,000.
1904S	...97,000	190.	210.	300.	450.	850.	3,400.	
1905 ......(108)	...302,308	165.	175.	185.	200.	235.	800.	10,000.
1905S	...880,700	165.	175.	225.	300.	500.	1,650.	

Values of common gold coins have been based on the current bullion price of gold and may vary with the prevailing spot price.

HALF EAGLES ($5.00 GOLD PIECES)

	Mintage	VF-20	EF-40	AU-50	AU-55	MS-60	MS-63	PF-63
1906 .....(85) 348,820		$165.	$175.	$185.	$200.	$235.	$800.	$10,000.
1906D 320,000		165.	175.	185.	200.	235.	800.	
1906S 598,000		165.	175.	185.	210.	275.	1,100.	
1907 .....(92) 626,192		165.	175.	185.	200.	235.	800.	10,000.
1907D 888,000		165.	175.	185.	200.	235.	800.	
1908 421,874		165.	175.	185.	200.	235.	800.	

INDIAN HEAD TYPE 1908-1929

This type conforms to the quarter eagle of the same date. The sunken (incuse) designs and lettering make these two series unique in our United States coinage.

Designer Bela Lyon Pratt; weight 8.359 grams; composition: .900 gold, .100 copper; diameter 21.6 mm; reeded edge; mints: Philadelphia, Denver, New Orleans, San Francisco. Net weight: .24187 oz. pure gold.

Mint mark location.

VF-20 VERY FINE—*Noticeable wear on large middle feathers and tip of eagle's wing.*
EF-40 EXTREMELY FINE—*Cheekbone, war bonnet and headband feathers slightly worn.*
  Feathers on eagle's upper wing show considerable wear.
AU-50 ABOUT UNCIRCULATED—*Trace of wear on cheekbone and headdress.*
AU-55 CHOICE ABOUT UNCIRCULATED—*Evidence of friction on design high points. Most of mint luster remains.*
MS-60 UNCIRCULATED—*No trace of wear. Light blemishes.*
MS-63 SELECT UNCIRCULATED—*Some distracting con tact marks or blemishes in prime focal areas.*
  Luster may be impaired.
PF-63—*Attractive reflective surfaces with only a few blemishes in secondary focal places. No major flaws.*

Scarcer coins with well-struck mint marks command higher prices.

	Mintage	VF-20	EF-40	AU-50	AU-55	MS-60	MS-63	Matte PF-63
1908 .....(167) 578,012		$185.	$220.	$250.	$275.	$350.	$1,750.	$10,000.
1908D 148,000		185.	220.	250.	275.	350.	1,750.	
1908S 82,000		250.	400.	575.	750.	1,350.	2,800.	
1909 .....(78) 627,138		185.	220.	250.	275.	350.	1,750.	12,000.
1909D 3,423,560		185.	220.	250.	275.	350.	1,750.	
1909O* 34,200		1,500.	2,000.	2,500.	5,000.	11,000.	52,000.	
1909S 297,200		235.	275.	350.	425.	1,500.	11,000.	
1910 .....(250) 604,250		185.	220.	250.	275.	350.	1,750.	12,000.
1910D 193,600		185.	220.	250.	275.	400.	2,000.	
1910S 770,200		225.	275.	350.	550.	1,250.	6,000.	
1911 .....(139) 915,139		185.	220.	250.	275.	350.	1,750.	11,000.
1911D 72,500		375.	525.	650.	1,000.	3,750.	32,000.	
1911S 1,416,000		225.	275.	350.	550.	700.	2,800.	
1912 .....(144) 790,144		185.	220.	250.	275.	350.	1,750.	11,000.
1912S 392,000		215.	265.	350.	550.	1,750.	13,000.	
1913 .....(99) 916,000		185.	220.	250.	275.	350.	1,750.	11,000.
1913S 408,000		225.	275.	350.	650.	1,500.	13,500.	
1914 .....(125) 247,125		185.	220.	250.	275.	350.	1,750.	11,000.
1914D 247,000		185.	220.	250.	275.	350.	2,800.	
1914S 263,000		225.	265.	325.	550.	1,400.	13,000.	
1915 ‡ ....(75) 588,075		185.	220.	250.	275.	350.	1,750.	15,000.
1915S 164,000		225.	300.	500.	725.	2,000.	15,000.	
1916S 240,000		210.	240.	375.	425.	600.	2,800.	
1929 662,000		5,000.	5,500.	6,000.	6,500.	8,000.	9,500.	

*Beware spurious "O" mint mark.
‡Pieces dated 1915D are counterfeit.

EAGLES ($10. GOLD PIECES) — 1795-1933

Coinage authority including specified weights and fineness of the eagle conforms to that of the half eagle. The small eagle reverse was used until 1797 when the large, heraldic eagle replaced it. The early dates have variations in the number of stars, the rarest date being 1798. Many of these early pieces show file scratches from the Mint's practice of adjusting weight. No eagles were struck dated 1805 to 1837. Proofs of some dates prior to 1855 are known to exist, and all are rare.

+ or – indicates change from previous year				TYPE COIN VALUES						
	F-12	VF-20	EF-40	AU-50	MS-60	MS-63	MS-65	PF-60	PF-63	PF-65
Cap Bust-Sm. Eag. 1795-1797	15,000.+	18,500.+	28,000.+	36,000.+	62,000.+	135,000.+	135,000.-			
Cap Bust-Lg. Eag. 1797-1804.	6,000.+	7,500.+	9,500.+	12,500.+	19,000.+	32,000.+	140,000.+			
Lib Coronet-NM 1838-1866....	250.+	275.+	325.+	550.	3,500.	12,500.-	52,000.	10,500.+	35,000.+	80,000.+
Lib Coronet 1866-1907..........	210.+	235.+	250.+	275.+	300.	900.+	4,000.+	4,000.+	11,000.	30,000.+
Indian Head-NM 1907-1908....	270.-	280.-	400.	425.-	600.+	2,500.+	6,000.-			
Indian Head 1908-1933	260.	325.	400.+	420.+	550.+	900.+	3,600.+	5,000.+	15,000.+	35,000.+

CAPPED BUST TO RIGHT, SMALL EAGLE 1795-1797

Designer Robert Scott; weight 17.50 grams; composition: .9167 gold, .0833 silver and copper; approx. diameter 33 mm; reeded edge.

F-12 FINE — *Details on turban and head obliterated.*
VF-20 VERY FINE — *Neck hair lines and details under turban and over forehead are worn but distinguishable.*
EF-40 EXTREMELY FINE — *Definite wear on hair to left of eye and strand of hair across and around turban, also on eagle's wing tips.*

AU-50 ABOUT UNCIRCULATED — *Trace of wear on cap, hair, cheek and drapery*
AU-55 CHOICE ABOUT UNCIRCULATED — *Evidence of friction on design high points. Most of mint luster remains.*
MS-60 UNCIRCULATED — *No trace of wear. Light blemishes.*
MS-63 SELECT UNCIRCULATED — *Some distracting con act marks or blemishes in prime focal areas. Luster may be impaired.*

	Mintage	F-12	VF-20	EF-40	AU-50	AU-55	MS-60	MS-63
1795,13 leaves below eagle	} 5,583	$15,000.	$18,500.	$28,000.	$36,000.	$42,000.	$62,000.	$135,000.
1795, 9 leaves below eagle		26,000.	42,000.	55,000.	80,000.	100,000.	185,000.	
1796	4,146	16,000.	20,000.	32,000.	38,000.	46,000.	72,000.	185,000.
1797 Small eagle	3,615	22,000.	28,000.	38,000.	65,000.	82,000.	155,000.	

CAPPED BUST TO RIGHT, HERALDIC EAGLE 1797-1804

	Mintage	F-12	VF-20	EF-40	AU-50	AU-55	MS-60	MS-63
1797, Large eagle 10,940		$6,000.	$8,200.	$12,000.	$18,000.	$22,000.	$32,000.	$58,000.
1798, 8/7, 9 stars left, 4 right 900		13,000.	22,000.	32,000.	46,000.	62,000.	95,000.	225,000.
1798 8/7, 7 stars left, 6 right 842		26,000.	42,000.	63,000.	120,000.	145,000.	210,000.	
1799 SmObv. Stars ...	} 37,449	6,500.	7,500.	9,500.	12,500.	15,000.	19,000.	32,000.
1799 LgObv. Stars ...		6,500.	7,500.	9,500.	12,500.	15,000.	19,000.	32,000.
1800	5,999	6,500.	7,500.	10,000.	13,000.	16,000.	24,000.	55,000.

EAGLES ($10. GOLD PIECES)

	Mintage	F-12	VF-20	EF-40	AU-50	AU-55	MS-60	MS-63
1801	44,344	$6,500.	$7,500.	$9,500.	$12,500.	$15,000.	$19,000.	$32,000.
1803,SmRev. stars	} 15,017	6,500.	7,500.	10,000.	13,000.	16,000.	22,000.	42,000.
1803,LgRev. stars		6,500.	7,500.	10,000.	13,000.	16,000.	22,000.	42,000.
1804	3,757	7,500.	8,500.	15,000.	21,000.	26,000.	34,000.	95,000.
1804 Plain 4, Proof, restrike *(4 known)*								750,000.

CORONET TYPE, No Motto Above Eagle 1838-1866

In 1838 the weight and diameter of the eagle were reduced and the obverse and reverse were redesigned. Liberty now faces left and the word LIBERTY is placed on the coronet. A more natural appearing eagle is used on the reverse. The value, TEN D., is shown for the first time on this denomination.

Designer Christian Gobrecht; weight 16.718 grams; composition: .900 gold, .100 copper, diameter 27 mm; reeded edge; mints: Philadelphia, New Orleans, San Francisco. Net weight: .48375 oz. pure gold.

Mint mark location on reverse below eagle.

VF-20 VERY FINE—*Hairlines above coronet partly worn. Curls under ear worn but defined.*
EF-40 EXTREMELY FINE—*Small amount of wear on top of hair and below L in LIBERTY. Wear evident on wing tips and neck of eagle.*
AU-50 ABOUT UNCIRCULATED—*Trace of wear on tip of coronet and hair above eye.*
AU-55-CHOICE ABOUT UNCIRCULATED—*Evidence of friction on design high points. Most of mint luster remains.*
MS-60 UNCIRCULATED—*No trace of wear. Light blemishes.*
MS-63 SELECT UNCIRCULATED—*Some distracting contact marks or blemishes in prime focal areas. Luster may be impaired.*
PF-63—*Attractive reflective surfaces with only a few blemishes in secondary focal places. No major flaws.*

	Mintage	VF-20	EF-40	AU-50	AU-55	MS-60	MS-63	PF-63
1838	7,200	$1,200.	$3,000.	$6,000.	$9,500.	$32,000.	$75,000.	
1839 Large Letter	25,801	1,000.	2,000.	5,000.	9,000.	26,000.	55,000.	

The Liberty head style of 1838 and 1839 (large letters) differs from that used for subsequent issues.

	Mintage	VF-20	EF-40	AU-50	AU-55	MS-60	MS-63	PF-63
1839 Small Letter	12,447	1,600.	3,500.	6,000.	9,500.	32,000.	80,000.	
1840	47,338	350.	600.	1,500.	2,800.	10,000.		
1841	63,131	300.	525.	1,250.	2,250.	7,500.	26,000.	
18410	2,500	2,300.	4,500.	11,000.	18,500.			
1842 Small Date	18,623	300.	500.	1,800.	3,000.	10,000.	23,000.	
1842 Large Date	62,884	300.	550.	1,800.	3,000.	10,000.	23,000.	
18420	27,400	450.	700.	2,800.	7,500.	24,000.	42,000.	
1843	75,462	300.	550.	1,800.	3,000.	12,500.		
18430	175,162	400.	600.	1,500.	3,750.	12,000.		
1844	6,361	1,300.	2,500.	5,500.	8,000.	17,000.	38,000.	
18440	118,700	400.	600.	1,800.	3,500.	16,000.		
1845	26,153	500.	900.	2,250.	3,250.	14,500.		
18450	47,500	450.	850.	2,000.	3,500.	16,000.		
1846	20,095	700.	1,150.	5,000.	9,500.	22,000.		

EAGLES ($10. GOLD PIECES)

	Mintage	VF-20	EF-40	AU-50	AU-55	MS-60	MS-63	PF-63
1846O	} 81,780	$450.	$850.	$4,000.	$6,500.	$16,500.		
1846O 6 / 5		600.	1,000.	3,500.	7,000.			
1847	862,258	275.	325.	550.	800.	3,500.	18,500.	
1847O	571,500	325.	425.	625.	1,200.	5,500.	17,500.	
1848	145,484	325.	425.	700.	1,200.	5,000.	23,000.	
1848O	35,850	550.	1,200.	3,600.	7,500.	13,000.	28,000.	
1849	653,618	300.	375.	625.	950.	3,600.	12,500.	
1849O	23,900	850.	1,800.	5,250.	8,000.	19,000.		
1850 Large Date	} 291,451	300.	375.	600.	900.	4,000.	16,000.	
1850 Small Date		350.	900.	2,200.	3,800.	9,000.	28,000.	
1850O	57,500	500.	1,000.	2,500.	5,500.	15,000.		
1851	176,328	300.	400.	900.	1,250.	4,500.	24,000.	
1851O	263,000	400.	600.	1,250.	3,000.	6,500.	26,000.	
1852	263,106	300.	385.	550.	1,050.	4,500.		
1852O	18,000	750.	1,200.	3,600.	8,000.	22,000.		

**1853,
3 over 2**

	Mintage	VF-20	EF-40	AU-50	AU-55	MS-60	MS-63	PF-63
1853, 3/2	} 201,253	550.	750.	1,500.	3,500.			
1853		300.	385.	550.	900.	3,800.	15,000.	
1853O	51,000	400.	500.	1,000.	2,500.	14,000.		
1854	54,250	300.	400.	700.	1,250.	6,000.	22,000.	
1854O,Lg or SmDt	52,500	400.	750.	1,500.	3,000.	10,000.		
1854S	123,826	325.	500.	1,250.	2,000.	10,000.		
1855	121,701	300.	375.	600.	1,000.	4,000.	18,500.	
1855O	18,000	650.	1,500.	5,500.	8,500.	20,000.		
1855S	9,000	1,300.	2,500.	6,000.	8,500.			
1856	60,490	300.	375.	600.	1,050.	4,200.	12,500.	
1856O	14,500	750.	1,000.	4,000.	7,000.	15,000.		
1856S	68,000	325.	600.	1,250.	2,500.	9,000.	25,000.	
1857	16,606	450.	850.	2,000.	3,800.	12,500.		
1857O	5,500	1,200.	2,000.	3,500.	6,000.	18,500.		
1857S	26,000	450.	1,100.	2,500.	4,500.	11,000.	17,000.	
1858*	2,521	5,000.	8,500.	13,000.	17,000.	40,000.		
1858O	20,000	400.	750.	1,750.	3,500.	10,000.	28,000.	
1858S	11,800	1,750.	3,500.	6,000.	12,000.			
1859 (80)	16,093	375.	700.	1,200.	2,500.	8,500.	15,000.	55,000.
1859O	2,300	3,750.	7,500.	15,000.	20,000.			
1859S	7,000	2,000.	4,500.	13,000.	18,500.			
1860 (50)	15,105	400.	800.	1,600.	2,750.	8,500.	20,000.	40,000.
1860O	11,100	600.	1,200.	2,000.	4,250.	14,500.		
1860S	5,000	3,000.	6,000.	14,500.	24,000.			
1861 (69)	113,233	300.	350.	600.	850.	3,500.	15,000.	35,000.
1861S	15,500	1,500.	3,000.	7,000.	12,000.	30,000.		
1862 (35)	10,995	500.	1,000.	2,200.	3,000.	12,500.		35,000.
1862S	12,500	1,600.	3,000.	6,000.	10,000.			
1863 (30)	1,248	4,000.	7,500.	17,000.	24,000.	45,000.	75,000.	37,500.
1863S	10,000	1,750.	3,750.	9,000.	13,000.	26,000.		
1864 (50)	3,580	1,700.	3,250.	7,000.	10,000.	17,500.		37,500.
1864S	2,500	5,000.	13,500.	27,000.	35,000.			

Beware removed mint mark.

	Mintage	VF-20	EF-40	AU-50	AU-55	MS-60	MS-63	PF-63
1865 .....(25) 4,005		$1,700.	$3,500.	$7,000.	$9,000.	$36,000.	$65,000.	$37,500.
1865S .... } 16,700		4,000.	8,500.	15,000.	20,000.	45,000.		
1865S,865/Inverted 186 }		3,000.	7,000.	12,000.	18,000.			
1866S 8,500		2,750.	5,000.	12,000.	17,000.	45,000.		

Variety 2 — Motto Above Eagle 1866-1907

Standards as before. Mints: Philadelphia, Carson City, Denver, New Orleans, San Francisco.

VF-20 VERY FINE—*Half of hairlines over coronet visible. Curls under ear worn but defined. IN GOD WE TRUST and its ribbon are sharp.*
EF-40 EXTREMELY FINE—*Small amount of wear on top of hair and below L in LIBERTY. Wear evident on wing tips and neck of eagle.*
AU-50 ABOUT UNCIRCULATED—*Trace of wear on hair above eye and on coronet.*
AU-55-CHOICE ABOUT UNCIRCULATED—*Evidence of friction on design high points. Most of mint luster remains.*
MS-60 UNCIRCULATED—*No trace of wear. Light blemishes.*
MS-63 SELECT UNCIRCULATED—*Some distracting contact marks or blemishes in prime focal areas. Luster may be impaired.*
PF-63—*Attractive reflective surfaces with only a few blemishes in secondary focal places. No major flaws.*

Mint mark location is on the reverse below the eagle.

	Mintage	VF-20	EF-40	AU-50	AU-55	MS-60	MS-63	PF-63
1866 .....(30) 3,780		900.	2,000.	4,250.	9,000.	21,000.		30,000.
1866S 11,500		1,500.	3,500.	7,000.	11,000.			
1867 .....(50) 3,140		1,500.	3,000.	5,000.	8,000.	27,000.		30,000.
1867S 9,000		2,500.	6,000.	8,500.	17,500.			
1868 .....(25) 10,655		550.	800.	2,000.	3,500.			30,000.
1868S 13,500		1,250.	2,250.	4,500.	6,750.			
1869 .....(25) 1,855		1,500.	3,000.	6,000.	14,000.	28,000.		30,000.
1869S 6,430		1,500.	2,600.	6,000.	14,000.	26,000.		
1870 .....(35) 4,025		800.	250.	2,750.	6,500.	16,500.		30,000.
1870CC 5,908		12,500.	26,000.	48,000.	75,000.			
1870S 8,000		1,200.	2,500.	6,500.	12,500.	28,000.		
1871 .....(30) 1,820		1,300.	2,500.	4,250.	8,500.	18,000.		32,500.
1871CC 8,085		3,000.	6,000.	20,000.	24,000.	60,000.		
1871S 16,500		1,200.	2,200.	6,000.	10,000.			
1872 .....(30) 1,650		2,200.	3,800.	9,500.	10,500.	18,000.		30,000.
1872CC 4,600		3,500.	11,000.	22,500.	32,500.			
1872S 17,300		600.	1,150.	2,250.	5,250.	18,000.		
1873 .....(25) 825		4,000.	8,500.	16,000.	19,500.	40,000.		35,000.
1873CC 4,543		7,500.	15,000.	30,000.	45,000.			
1873S 12,000		1,000.	250.	4,500.	8,000.	21,000.		
1874 .....(20) 53,160		275.	320.	400.	475.	2,000.	8,500.	32,500.
1874CC 16,767		1,000.	2,750.	8,500.	12,000.			
1874S 10,000		1,000.	3,000.	7,500.	12,000.			
1875 .....(20) 120		40,000.	55,000.	80,000.	100,000.			120,000.
1875CC 7,715		4,800.	10,000.	20,000.	32,000.	70,000.	95,000.	
1876 .....(45) 732		3,000.	7,500.	15,000.	20,000.			30,000.
1876CC 4,696		3,000.	6,750.	20,000.	28,000.			
1876S 5,000		1,250.	2,500.	6,000.	9,500.			
1877 .....(20) 817		2,500.	5,000.	9,500.	11,500.	26,000.		32,500.
1877CC 3,332		2,500.	5,000.	14,000.	19,000.			
1877S 17,000		450.	650.	2,000.	3,400.	20,000.		
1878 .....(20) 73,800		265.	285.	325.	425.	950.	4,500.	25,000.

EAGLES ($10. GOLD PIECES)

	Mintage	VF-20	EF-40	AU-50	AU-55	MS-60	MS-63	PF-63
1878CC	3,244	$4,500.	$9,500.	$20,000.	$28,000.			
1878S	26,100	375.	650.	1,850.	3,000.	$10,500.	$24,000.	
1879 ....(30)	384,770	240.	260.	325.	400.	650.	3,500.	$25,000.
1879CC	1,762	8,500.	14,000.	26,000.	31,000.			
1879O	1,500	2,200.	4,250.	10,000.	15,000.	32,000.		
1879S	224,000	235.	250.	275.	450.	900.	5,500.	
1880 ....(36)	1,644,876	235.	250.	275.	285.	310.	2,400.	20,000.
1880CC	11,190	500.	750.	1,600.	4,000.	13,500.		
1880O	9,200	400.	675.	1,400.	2,250.	8,500.		
1880S	506,250	235.	250.	285.	325.	375.	3,000.	
1881 ....(40)	3,877,260	235.	250.	275.	285.	310.	1,100.	2,000.
1881CC	24,015	400.	700.	1,150.	1,250.	6,500.		
1881O	8,350	375.	650.	1,200.	2,100.	8,000.		
1881S	970,000	235.	250.	275.	285.	365.	3,800.	
1882 ....(40)	2,324,480	235.	250.	275.	285.	310.	1,000.	20,000.
1882CC	6,764	700.	1,200.	2,800.	7,000.	13,000.		
1882O	10,820	350.	550.	1,200.	2,100.	7,000.	16,500.	
1882S	132,000	235.	250.	275.	285.	400.	3,000.	
1883 ....(40)	208,740	235.	250.	275.	285.	310.	2,000.	20,000.
1883CC	12,000	450.	650.	2,250.	4,250.	12,500.		
1883O	800	4,000.	7,500.	12,500.	15,000.	35,000.		
1883S	38,000	235.	260.	300.	450.	900.	9,500.	
1884 ....(45)	76,905	235.	250.	275.	300.	675.	3,750.	20,000.
1884CC	9,925	650.	1,000.	2,500.	4,500.	12,000.	32,000.	
1884S	124,250	235.	250.	275.	300.	550.	4,250.	
1885 ....(65)	253,527	235.	250.	275.	285.	375.	3,500.	17,000.
1885S	228,000	235.	250.	275.	285.	365.	3,800.	
1886 ....(60)	236,160	235.	250.	275.	285.	310.	2,250.	17,000.
1886S	826,000	235.	250.	275.	285.	315.	1,250.	
1887 ....(80)	53,680	235.	250.	285.	425.	800.	3,500.	17,000.
1887S	817,000	235.	250.	275.	285.	310.	2,250.	
1888 ....(75)	132,996	235.	250.	300.	400.	650.	3,800.	17,000.
1888O	21,335	245.	250.	275.	425.	575.	5,500.	
1888S	648,700	235.	250.	275.	285.	310.	2,800.	
1889 ....(45)	4,485	325.	450.	850.	1,500.	2,800.	6,000.	17,000.
1889S	425,400	235.	250.	275.	285.	310.	1,850.	
1890 ....(63)	58,043	235.	250.	300.	325.	850.	4,000.	15,000.
1890CC	17,500	375.	500.	750.	1,000.	2,200.	13,000.	
1891 ....(48)	91,868	235.	250.	275.	285.	300.	3,000.	15,000.
1891CC	103,732	350.	425.	525.	575.	750.	4,500.	
1892 ....(72)	797,552	235.	250.	275.	285.	300.	1,450.	15,000.
1892CC	40,000	350.	425.	650.	1,150.	3,600.	8,500.	
1892O	28,688	245.	265.	290.	310.	450.	6,000.	
1892S	115,500	235.	250.	275.	285.	300.	3,000.	
1893 ....(55)	1,840,895	235.	250.	275.	285.	300.	900.	15,000.
1893CC	14,000	410.	625.	1,300.	2,500.	2,800.		
1893O	17,000	245.	285.	350.	400.	650.	5,500.	
1893S	141,350	235.	250.	275.	285.	300.	3,750.	
1894 ....(43)	2,470,778	235.	250.	275.	285.	300.	900.	15,000.
1894O	107,500	235.	250.	385.	575.	1,050.	4,750.	
1894S	25,000	275.	350.	650.	850.	3,000.		
1895 ....(56)	567,826	235.	250.	275.	285.	300.	925.	15,000.
1895O	98,000	245.	265.	300.	375.	500.	3,500.	
1895S	49,000	300.	350.	650.	1,000.	2,350.	9,500.	
1896 ....(78)	76,348	235.	250.	275.	280.	300.	1,600.	15,000.
1896S	123,750	235.	300.	475.	525.	2,200.	8,500.	
1897 ....(69)	1,000,159	235.	250.	275.	280.	300.	900.	15,000.

EAGLES ($10. GOLD PIECES)

	Mintage	VF-20	EF-40	AU-50	AU-55	MS-60	MS-63	PF-63
18970	42,500	$245.	$285.	$350.	$385.	$750.	$3,500.	
1897S	234,750	235.	275.	325.	385.	675.	3,000.	
1898 ....(67)	812,197	235.	250.	275.	280.	300.	1,250.	$15,000.
1898S	473,600	235.	250.	275.	280.	350.	3,000.	
1899 ....(86)	1,262,305	235.	250.	275.	280.	300.	900.	12,000.
18990	37,047	245.	260.	300.	350.	600.	3,750.	
1899S	841,000	235.	250.	275.	280.	300.	2,000.	
1900 ....(120)	293,960	235.	250.	275.	280.	300.	900.	12,000.
1900S	81,000	240.	255.	285.	290.	750.	3,500.	
1901 ....(85)	1,718,825	235.	250.	275.	280.	300.	900.	12,000.
19010	72,041	245.	260.	300.	325.	400.	2,500.	
1901S	2,812,750	235.	250.	275.	280.	300.	900.	
1902 ....(113)	82,513	235.	250.	275.	280.	300.	900.	12,000.
1902S	469,500	235.	250.	275.	280.	300.	900.	
1903 ....(96)	125,926	235.	250.	275.	280.	300.	900.	12,000.
19030	112,771	245.	260.	300.	325.	400.	2,500.	
1903S	538,000	235.	250.	275.	280.	300.	900.	
1904 ....(108)	162,038	235.	250.	275.	280.	300.	900.	12,000.
19040	108,950	245.	255.	285.	300.	400.	2,500.	
1905 ....(86)	201,078	235.	250.	275.	280.	300.	1,000.	12,000.
1905S	369,250	240.	260.	285.	300.	1,000.	3,500.	
1906 ....(77)	165,497	235.	250.	275.	280.	300.	1,250.	12,000.
1906D	981,000	235.	250.	275.	280.	300.	900.	
19060	86,895	245.	260.	300.	320.	400.	2,500.	
1906S	457,000	240.	255.	285.	290.	385.	2,500.	
1907 ....(74)	1,203,973	235.	250.	275.	280.	300.	900.	12,000.
1907D	1,030,000	235.	250.	275.	280.	300.	1,050.	
1907S	210,500	235.	250.	275.	280.	300.	2,500.	

Values of common gold coins have been based on the current bullion price of gold and may vary with the prevailing spot price.

INDIAN HEAD TYPE 1907-1933

Augustus Saint-Gaudens, considered by many the greatest of modern sculptors, introduced a new high standard of art in United States coins evidenced by his eagle and double eagle types of 1907. The obverse of the eagle shows the head of Liberty crowned with an Indian war bonnet while an impressively majestic eagle dominates the reverse side. A departure from older standards is found on the edge of the piece, where 46 raised stars are arranged signifying the states of the Union, instead of a lettered or reeded edge (48 stars 1912 and later).

The first of these coins struck had no motto IN GOD WE TRUST as did the later issues starting in 1908. President Theodore Roosevelt personally objected to the use of the Deity's name on coins. The motto was restored to the coins by an Act of Congress in 1908.

Designer Augustus Saint-Gaudens. Standards same as previous issue. Edge 1907-1911: 46 raised stars; 1912-1933: 48 raised stars. Net weight: .48375 oz. pure gold; mints: Philadelphia, Denver, San Francisco.

VF-20 VERY FINE—*Bonnet feathers worn near band. Hair high points show wear.*
EF-40 EXTREMELY FINE—*Slight wear on cheekbone and headdress feathers.*
   Eagle's eye and left wing will show slight wear.
AU-50 ABOUT UNCIRCULATED—*Trace of wear on hair above eye and on forehead.*
AU-55-CHOICE ABOUT UNCIRCULATED—*Evidence of friction on design high points. Most of mint luster remains.*
MS-60 UNCIRCULATED—*No trace of wear. Light blemishes.*
MS-63 SELECT UNCIRCULATED—*Some distracting contact marks or blemishes in prime focal areas.*
   Luster may be impaired.
PF-63 ATTRACTIVE PROOF—*Reflective surfaces with only a few blemishes in secondary focal places.*
   No major flaws.

EAGLES ($10. GOLD PIECES)
Variety 1 — No Motto on Reverse 1907-1908

No Motto

Mint mark location is above left tip of branch on 1908-D no motto, and at left of arrow points thereafter.

Choice uncirculated (MS-65) coins are rare and worth substantial premiums.

	Mintage	VF-20	EF-40	AU-50	AU-55	MS-60	MS-63	PF-63
1907 Wire rim, periods 500			$11,000.	$13,000.	$16,000.	$19,000.	$26,000.	
1907, Rounded rim, periods before and after •E•PLURIBUS•UNUM•42 *			25,000.	30,000.	32,000.	38,000.	62,000.	
1907 No periods 239,406		360.	400.	425.	450.	600.	2,500.	
1908 No motto 33,500		280.	425.	475.	500.	950.	4,000.	
1908D No motto 210,000		380.	400.	425.	500.	775.	5,750.	

*20,000 minted and all but 42 were melted at the Mint.

Variety 2 — Motto on Reverse 1908-1933

With Motto
IN GOD WE TRUST

								Matte PF-63
1908 . . . .(116)	341,486	350.	400.	420.	450.	550.	1,750.	15,000.
1908D	836,500	360.	400.	460.	500.	750.	6,500.	
1908S	59,850	450.	475.	650.	1,000.	2,100.	8,500.	
1909 . . . .(74)	184,863	325.	400.	420.	450.	550.	2,000.	16,000.
1909D	121,540	350.	425.	435.	465.	950.	3,250.	
1909S	292,350	350.	400.	420.	450.	700.	3,500.	
1910 . . . .(204)	318,704	325.	400.	420.	450.	550.	1,200.	16,000.
1910D	2,356,640	325.	400.	420.	450.	550.	1,000.	
1910S	811,000	350.	425.	435.	465.	750.	5,500.	
1911 . . . .(95)	505,595	325.	400.	420.	450.	550.	1,200.	15,000.
1911D	30,100	475.	650.	950.	1,600.	4,200.	15,000.	
1911S	51,000	400.	525.	625.	850.	1,250.	6,500.	
1912 . . . .(83)	405,083	325.	400.	420.	450.	550.	1,200.	15,000.
1912S	300,000	375.	410.	435.	465.	900.	4,750.	
1913 . . . .(71)	442,071	325.	400.	420.	450.	550.	1,000.	15,000.
1913S	66,000	450.	650.	850.	1,600.	4,250.	22,500.	
1914 . . . .(50)	151,050	400.	420.	450.	550.	1,750.	16,000.	
1914D	343,500	325.	400.	420.	450.	550.	1,750.	
1914S	208,000	325.	400.	420.	450.	550.	1,750.	
1915 . . . .(75)	351,075	350.	410.	435.	465.	600.	5,000.	

	Mintage	VF-20	EF-40	AU-50	AU-55	MS-60	MS-63	Matte PF-63
1915S	59,000	$400.	$650.	$800.	$1,350.	$3,200.	$8,500.	
1916S	138,500	350.	425.	455.	465.	750.	3,750.	
1920S	126,500	6,500.	8,500.	10,000.	13,500.	16,500.	52,500.	
1926	1,014,000	325.	400.	420.	450.	550.	900.	
1930S	96,000	6,500.	7,000.	8,000.	9,500.	12,500.	19,500.	
1932	4,463,000	325.	400.	420.	450.	550.	900.	
1933	312,500					100,000.	190,000.	

DOUBLE EAGLES ($20. GOLD PIECES) — 1849-1933

This largest denomination of all regular United States issues was authorized to be coined by the Act of March 3, 1849. Its weight was 516 grains, .900 fine. The 1849 double eagle is a unique pattern and reposes in the Smithsonian. The 1861 reverse design by Anthony C. Paquet was withdrawn soon after striking. Very few specimens are known.

+ or – indicates change from previous year	**TYPE COIN VALUES**									
	F-12	VF-20	EF-40	AU-50	MS-60	MS-63	MS-65	PF-60	PF-63	PF-65
Lib Coronet-NM 1849-1866	.550.+	650.+	700.+	750.	1,200.-	6,000.-	*10,000.-*	25,000.-	47,500.+	*160,000.-*
Lib *(Twenty D.)* 1866-1876	.475.+	525.+	535.+	550.-	825.+	9,750.+	*75,000.-*	15,000.+	35,000.+	*150,000.+*
Lib 1877-1907	.450.+	500.+	505.+	525.+	560.+	900.+	*4,800.+*	9,000.+	19,500.+	*60,000.+*
Saint-Gaudens-RN, HR 1907	3,500.+	4,400.+	7,500.+	9,000.+	12,000.+	20,000.+	*34,000.-*	15,000.+	30,000.+	*50,000.+*
Saint-Gaudens 1907-1933	.450.+	475.+	520.+	535.+	575.+	700.+	*1,400.+*	9,000.+	20,000.+	*46,000.+*

Designer James B. Longacre; weight 33.436 grams; composition: .900 gold, .100 copper; diameter 34 mm; reeded edge; mints: Philadelphia, Carson City, Denver, New Orleans, San Francisco. Net weight: .96750 oz. pure gold.

VF-20 VERY FINE — *LIBERTY is bold. Prongs on crown defined. Lower half worn flat. Hair worn about ear.*
EF-40 EXTREMELY FINE — *Trace of wear on rounded prongs of crown and down hair curls. Minor bag marks.*
AU-50 ABOUT UNCIRCULATED — *Trace of wear on hair over eye and on coronet.*
AU-55 CHOICE ABOUT UNCIRCULATED — *Evidence of friction on design high points. Most of mint luster remains.*
MS-60 UNCIRCULATED — *No trace of wear. Light blemishes.*
MS-63 SELECT UNCIRCULATED — *Some distracting contact marks or blemishes in prime focal areas.*
   Luster may be impaired.
PF-63 — *Attractive reflective surfaces with only a few blemishes in secondary focal places. No major flaws*

Mint mark location is below the eagle.   1853, 3 over 2

Without Motto on Reverse 1849-1866

	Mintage	VF-20	EF-40	AU-50	AU-55	MS-60	MS-63	PF-63
1849 . .*(Pattern)*	1			Smithsonian collection				
1850	1,170,261	$675.	$1,050.	$2,400.	$2,800.	$5,500.	$40,000.	
1850O	141,000	800.	1,300.	6,000.	9,000.	30,000.		
1851	2,087,155	650.	725.	900.	1,250.	2,750.	18,000.	
1851O	315,000	700.	850.	1,600.	3,250.	15,000.	50,000.	
1852	2,053,026	650.	750.	900.	1,250.	3,000.	12,500.	
1852O	190,000	700.	850.	1,750.	2,900.	13,500.	45,000.	
1853 3/2	} 1,261,326	700.	1,200.	3,000.	6,500.	35,000.		
1853		650.	725.	900.	1,400.	4,000.	20,000.	

	Mintage	VF-20	EF-40	AU-50	AU-55	MS-60	MS-63	PF-63
1853O	71,000	$675.	$1,000.	$2,300.	$4,500.	$25,000.		
1854 Small Date	} 757,899	650.	725.	900.	1,500.	5,250.	19,000.	
1854 Large Date		650.	850.	2,000.	3,000.	12,500.		
1854O	3,250	25,000.	50,000.	100,000.	110,000.	175,000.		
1854S	141,468	675.	775.	1,200.	1,500.	3,400.	11,000.	
1855	364,666	650.	725.	1,050.	1,600.	7,250.	30,000.	
1855O	8,000	2,200.	5,250.	16,500.	22,500.	67,500.		
1855S	879,675	650.	700.	950.	1,500.	5,200.	10,000.	
1856	329,878	675.	750.	1,000.	2,000.	7,800.	20,000.	
1856O	2,250	35,000.	67,500.	105,000.	125,000.	195,000.		
1856S	1,189,750	650.	725.	1,000.	1,350.	4,250.	9,000.	
1857	439,375	650.	725.	800.	1,000.	3,000.	25,500.	
1857O	30,000	950.	1,550.	3,600.	7,000.	20,000.	102,500.	
1857S	970,500	650.	700.	825.	1,000.	3,000.	6,000.	
1858	211,714	725.	875.	1,075.	1,400.	4,350.	32,500.	
1858O	35,250	1,200.	1,800.	4,250.	6,500.	24,000.		
1858S	846,710	650.	725.	875.	1,500.	7,000.	40,000.	
1859 .....(80)	43,677	900.	1,900.	3,600.	7,000.	27,500.		65,000.
1859O	9,100	3,000.	6,000.	13,500.	25,000.	75,000.		
1859S	636,445	650.	700.	900.	1,250.	4,400.		
1860 .....(59)	577,729	650.	700.	850.	1,100.	3,500.	17,000.	55,000.
1860O	6,600	2,900.	5,400.	13,500.	22,500.	80,000.		
1860S	544,950	650.	700.	875.	1,500.	5,200.	18,500.	
1861 .....(66)	2,976,519	625.	700.	750.	1,000.	1,200.	8,350.	55,000.
1861O	17,741	2,200.	3,600.	10,500.	20,000.	80,000.		
1861S	768,000	650.	725.	1,500.	2,250.	7,500.	25,000.	

1861S Normal Obverse

1861S Paquet Reverse

	Mintage	VF-20	EF-40	AU-50	AU-55	MS-60	MS-63	PF-63
1861, Paquet rev. (Tall letters)						1,000,000.		
1861S, Paquet rev. (Tall letters)		10,000.	20,000.	32,500.	37,500.	57,500.		
1862 .....(35)	92,168	750.	1,200.	2,400.	5,000.	14,000.	30,000.	47,500.
1862S	854,173	625.	750.	1,450.	2,800.	9,500.	35,000.	
1863 .....(30)	142,820	650.	800.	1,550.	3,500.	15,000.	32,500.	47,500.
1863S	966,570	650.	775.	1,250.	2,000.	5,750.	25,000.	
1864 .....(50)	204,285	700.	900.	1,450.	3,000.	12,500.		47,500.
1864S	793,660	625.	700.	1,500.	2,250.	5,750.	20,000.	
1865 .....(25)	351,200	650.	725.	925.	1,500.	5,500.	19,500.	47,500.
1865S	1,042,500	650.	725.	925.	1,600.	3,600.	6,250.	
1866S	Est.120,000	1,500.	2,500.	10,000.	11,000.	31,000.		

DOUBLE EAGLES ($20. GOLD PIECES)
Motto Above Eagle, Value TWENTY D. 1866-1876

	Mintage	VF-20	EF-40	AU-50	AU-55	MS-60	MS-63	PF-63
1866 . . . . . .(30)	698,775	$600.	$700.	$1,100.	$1,600.	$4,350.	$25,000.	$35,000.
1866S	842,250	550.	600.	1,100.	2,000.	14,000.		
(*see preceding page*)								
1867 . . . . . .(50)	251,065	550.	575.	775.	950.	2,000.	18,000.	35,000.
1867S	920,750	550.	625.	1,300.	2,500.	15,000.		
1868 . . . . . .(25)	98,600	750.	1,000.	1,650.	3,000.	8,800.	35,000.	35,000.
1868S	837,500	550.	650.	1,100.	1,750.	7,750.		
1869 . . . . . .(25)	175,155	600.	800.	1,050.	2,000.	5,500.	18,500.	35,000.
1869S	686,750	525.	550.	950.	1,500.	4,750.	27,000.	
1870 . . . . . .(35)	155,185	600.	825.	1,400.	2,500.	8,250.		35,000.
1870CC	3,789	77,500.	105,000.	185,000.	195,000.	250,000.		
1870S	982,000	550.	575.	800.	1,250.	4,750.	26,000.	
1871 . . . . . .(30)	80,150	600.	825.	1,400.	1,750.	3,650.	23,500.	35,000.
1871CC	17,387	3,350.	5,750.	12,500.	17,500.	37,500.		
1871S	928,000	550.	575.	650.	950.	3,300.	19,500.	
1872 . . . . . .(30)	251,880	550.	600.	650.	1,000.	2,400.	22,500.	35,000.
1872CC	26,900	1,700.	2,150.	4,900.	7,500.	25,000.		
1872S	780,000	550.	575.	625.	1,000.	2,600.	22,000.	
1873 Cl 3 ..(25) ⎫...1,709,825		575.	650.	875.	1,000.	2,200.		35,000.
1873 Open 3 ...⎭...1,709,825		550.	575.	600.	625.	850.	10,000.	
1873CC Closed 3 22,410		1,600.	2,500.	5,000.	8,000.	25,000.		
1873S Closed 3 .⎫...1,040,600		525.	550.	575.	625.	1,400.	19,000.	
1873S Open 3 ..⎭...1,040,600		625.	675.	750.	2,000.	5,500.		
1874 . . . . . .(20) 366,800		525.	535.	550.	600.	1,000.	17,500.	35,000.
1874CC	115,085	1,000.	1,350.	2,150.	2,500.	6,750.		
1874S	1,214,000	525.	535.	550.	600.	1,200.	22,500.	
1875 . . . . . .(20)	295,740	525.	535.	550.	575.	850.	9,750.	60,000.
1875CC	111,151	950.	1,150.	1,400.	1,550.	2,000.	15,750.	
1875S	1,230,000	525.	535.	550.	570.	850.	14,500.	
1876 . . . . . .(45)	583,905	525.	535.	550.	570.	825.	10,250.	*35,000.
1876CC	138,441	950.	1,150.	1,450.	1,800.	3,600.	30,000.	
1876S	1,597,000	525.	535.	550.	570.	825.	10,250.	

*A transitional Proof pattern also exists dated 1876 but of the type of 1877.

Value spelled TWENTY DOLLARS, 1877-1907

DOUBLE EAGLES ($20. GOLD PIECES)

	Mintage	VF-20	EF-40	AU-50	AU-55	MS-60	MS-63	PF-63
1877 . . . . (20)	397,670	$500.	$505.	$525.	$535.	$600.	$4,700.	$28,000.
1877CC	42,565	1,100.	1,400.	1,850.	3,500.	14,500.		
1877S 1,735,000		500.	505.	525.	535.	600.	11,000.	
1878 . . . . . . (20)	543,645	500.	505.	525.	535.	600.	4,750.	31,000.
1878CC	13,180	1,750.	2,450.	4,000.	6,000.	23,000.		
1878S 1,739,000		500.	505.	525.	530.	650.	19,250.	
1879 . . . . . . (30)	207,630	500.	505.	525.	550.	900.	11,250.	32,500.
1879CC	10,708	1,800.	2,650.	5,100.	7,500.	22,000.		
1879O	2,325	3,850.	6,000.	13,250.	20,000.	61,000.	94,000.	
1879S 1,223,800		500.	505.	525.	550.	1,200.		
1880 . . . . . . (36)	51,456	500.	505.	525.	675.	2,700.	15,500.	30,000.
1880S	836,000	500.	505.	525.	550.	875.	14,000.	
1881 . . . . . . (61)	2,260	4,000.	6,000.	12,000.	16,000.	39,000.		30,000.
1881S	727,000	500.	505.	525.	550.	800.	15,500.	
1882 . . . . . . (59)	630	7,000.	14,000.	25,000.	30,000.	55,000.	120,000.	30,000.
1882CC	39,140	1,050.	1,200.	1,700.	2,500.	5,500.		
1882S 1,125,000		500.	505.	525.	530.	600.	14,000.	
1883 Pfs only (92)	92							50,000.
1883CC	59,962	1,000.	1,200.	1,450.	1,750.	3,500.	20,000.	
1883S 1,189,000		500.	505.	525.	530.	600.	7,500.	
1884 Pfs only (71)	71							50,000.
1884CC	81,139	975.	1,150.	1,450.	1,650.	2,300.	12,000.	
1884S	916,000	500.	505.	525.	530.	590.	6,200.	
1885 . . . . . . (77)	828	6,000.	7,500.	10,000.	13,000.	27,000.	51,000.	25,000.
1885CC	9,450	1,900.	2,700.	4,800.	5,750.	10,000.	52,500.	
1885S	683,500	500.	505.	525.	530.	590.	6,250.	
1886 . . . . . . (106)	1,106	7,250.	10,000.	27,000.	30,000.	41,000.	67,500.	22,500.
1887 Pfs only (121)	121							32,500.
1887S	283,000	500.	505.	525.	530.	600.	12,750.	
1888 . . . . . (105)	226,266	500.	505.	525.	530.	600.	4,250.	20,000.
1888S	859,600	500.	505.	525.	530.	600.	5,000.	
1889 . . . . . . (41)	44,111	500.	505.	550.	560.	650.	10,000.	21,000.
1889CC	30,945	1,100.	1,300.	1,900.	2,050.	2,750.	13,250.	
1889S	774,700	500.	505.	525.	530.	600.	6,000.	
1890 . . . . . . (55)	75,995	500.	505.	525.	530.	600.	4,600.	19,500.
1890CC	91,209	1,000.	1,075.	1,250.	1,400.	2,050.	24,000.	
1890S	802,750	500.	505.	525.	530.	600.	7,600.	
1891 . . . . . . (52)	1,442	3,000.	4,500.	8,000.	11,000.	27,000.		20,000.
1891CC	5,000	3,100.	4,750.	7,000.	8,000.	13,250.	37,000.	
1891S 1,288,125		500.	505.	525.	530.	560.	3,000.	
1892 . . . . . . (93)	4,523	1,050.	1,450.	2,300.	2,500.	5,000.	16,250.	19,500.
1892CC	27,265	1,050.	1,275.	1,750.	1,900.	2,750.	22,500.	
1892S	930,150	500.	505.	525.	530.	560.	3,700.	
1893 . . . . . . (59)	344,339	500.	505.	525.	530.	560.	2,200.	20,000.
1893CC	18,402	1,250.	1,600.	1,800.	2,000.	2,500.	12,750.	
1893S	996,175	500.	505.	525.	530.	560.	3,500.	
1894 . . . . . . (50) 1,368,990		500.	505.	525.	530.	560.	1,250.	19,500.
1894S 1,048,550		500.	505.	525.	530.	560.	2,200.	
1895 . . . . . . (51) 1,114,656		500.	505.	525.	530.	560.	1,100.	19,500.
1895S 1,143,500		500.	505.	525.	530.	560.	2,200.	
1896 . . . . . . (128)	792,663	500.	505.	525.	530.	560.	1,500.	19,500.
1896S 1,403,925		500.	505.	525.	530.	560.	2,000.	
1897 . . . . . . (86) 1,383,261		500.	505.	525.	530.	560.	1,100.	20,000.
1897S 1,470,250		500.	505.	525.	530.	560.	1,250.	
1898 . . . . . . (75)	170,470	500.	505.	540.	545.	600.	4,400.	19,500.
1898S 2,575,175		500.	505.	525.	530.	560.	1,050.	
1899 . . . . . . (84) 1,669,384		500.	505.	525.	530.	560.	900.	19,500.
1899S 2,010,300		$500.	$505.	$525.	$530.	$560.	$1,700.	

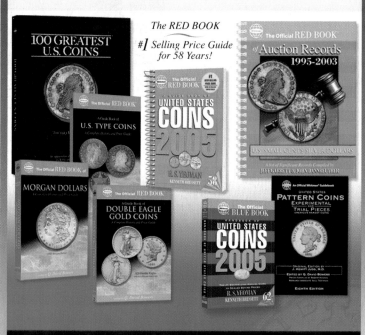

DOUBLE EAGLES ($20. GOLD PIECES)

	Mintage	VF-20	EF-40	AU-50	AU-55	MS-60	MS-63	PF-63
1900 . . . . .(124) . .1,874,584		$500.	$505.	$525.	$530.	$560.	$900.	$19,500.
1900S 2,459,500		500.	505.	525.	530.	560.	2,100.	
1901 . . . . . .(96) 111,526		500.	505.	525.	530.	560.	900.	19,500.
1901S 1,596,000		500.	505.	525.	530.	560.	3,500.	
1902 . . . . .(114) 31,254		500.	505.	575.	600.	825.	9,500.	19,500.
1902S 1,753,625		500.	505.	525.	530.	560.	3,500.	
1903 . . . . .(158) 287,428		500.	505.	525.	530.	560.	900.	19,500.
1903S 954,000		500.	505.	525.	530.	560.	1,500.	
1904 . . . . . .(98) . .6,256,797		500.	505.	525.	530.	560.	900.	19,500.
1904S 5,134,175		500.	505.	525.	530.	560.	900.	
1905 . . . . . .(92) 59,011		500.	505.	525.	575.	875.	12,750.	19,500.
1905S 1,813,000		500.	505.	525.	530.	570.	3,500.	
1906 . . . . . .(94) 69,690		500.	505.	525.	530.	560.	6,000.	19,500.
1906D 620,250		500.	505.	525.	530.	560.	1,750.	
1906S 2,065,750		500.	505.	525.	530.	560.	2,100.	
1907 . . . . . .(78) . .1,451,864		500.	505.	525.	530.	560.	900.	19,500.
1907D 842,250		500.	505.	525.	530.	560.	1,700.	
1907S 2,165,800		500.	505.	525.	530.	560.	2,100.	

Values of common gold coins are based on the current bullion price of gold and may vary with the prevailing spot price.

SAINT-GAUDENS TYPE 1907-1933

The $20 gold piece designed by Augustus Saint-Gaudens is considered to be the most beautiful United States coin. The first coins issued were 11,250 high relief pieces struck for general circulation. The relief is much higher than later issues and the date 1907 is in Roman numerals. A few of the Proof coins were made using the lettered edge collar from the extremely high relief version. These can be distinguished by a pronounced bottom left serif on the N in UNUM, and other minor differences. High-relief Proofs are trial or experimental pieces. Flat-relief double eagles were issued later in 1907 with Arabic numerals, and continued through 1933.

The field of the rare extremely high relief experimental pieces is excessively concave and connects directly with the edge without any border, giving it a sharp knifelike appearance; Liberty's skirt shows two folds on the side of her right leg; the Capitol building in the background at left is very small; the sun, on the reverse side, has 14 rays, as opposed to the regular high relief coins that have only 13 rays extending from the sun.

The Proof finish of 1908 and 1911-1915 coins was originally referred to as "Sand Blast Proof" by the Mint. Proof coins minted in 1909 and 1910 have a different finish that is described as "Satin Proof."

Designer Augustus Saint-Gaudens. Standards same as previous issue. Mints: Philadelphia, Denver, San Francisco. Edge: E PLURIBUS UNUM with words divided by stars. One specimen of the high relief variety with plain edge is known.

VF-20 VERY FINE—Minor wear on legs and toes. Eagle's left wing and breast feathers worn.

EF-40 EXTREMELY FINE—Drapery lines on chest visible. Wear on left breast, knee and below.
   Eagle's feathers on breast and right wing are bold.

AU-50 ABOUT UNCIRCULATED—Trace of wear on nose, breast and knee. Wear visible on eagle's wings.

MS-60 UNCIRCULATED—No trace of wear. Light marks or blemishes.

See page 6-7 for information on investment grade coins.

Extremely High Relief Patterns of 1907

Proof

1907 EX. high relief, plain edge *(Unique)* . . . . —
1907 EX. high relief, lettered edge . . . . .2003 Goldberg Auction: $1,150,000

DOUBLE EAGLES ($20.00 GOLD PIECES)

	Mintage	VF-20	EF-40	AU-50	AU-55	MS-60	MS-63
1907 High relief, Roman numerals (MCMVII), wire rim	12,367	$6,000.	$7,500.	$9,000.	$9,500.	$12,000.	$20,000.
1907 Same, flat rim		6,000.	7,500.	9,000.	9,500.	12,000.	20,000.

With No Motto IN GOD WE TRUST, 1907-1908

Arabic Numerals

No Motto

1907 Arabic numerals ..	361,667	$510.	$520.	$535.	$545.	$575.	$975.
1908	4,271,551	510.	520.	535.	545.	575.	700.
1908D	663,750	510.	520.	535.	545.	575.	950.

Mint mark location is on obverse above date.

With Motto IN GOD WE TRUST, 1908-1933

							Matte PF-63
1908 ....(101) ..156,359	$510.	$520.	$535.	$545.	$585.	$1,400.	$19,500.
1908D 349,500	510.	520.	535.	545.	585.	1,050.	
1908S 22,000	800.	1,100.	1,650.	2,250.	4,250.	11,750.	

Double eagles from 1907 to 1911 have 46 stars on the obverse and 48 stars from 1912 to 1933.

1909, 9 over 8

	Mintage	VF-20	EF-40	AU-50	AU-55	MS-60	MS-63	Matte PF-63
1909, 9/8	} 161,282	$520.	$570.	$650.	$725.	$1,150.	$6,000.	
1909 ......(67)		510.	520.	600.	665.	575.	3,500.	$20,000.
1909D	52,500	510.	520.	750.	800.	1,200.	7,000.	
1909S	2,774,925	510.	520.	535.	545.	575.	765.	
1910 ......(167)	482,167	510.	520.	535.	545.	575.	725.	19,500.
1910D	429,000	510.	520.	535.	545.	575.	725.	
1910S	2,128,250	510.	520.	535.	545.	575.	900.	
1911 ......(100)	197,350	510.	520.	535.	550.	590.	1,900.	19,500.
1911D	846,500	510.	520.	535.	545.	575.	740.	
1911S	775,750	510.	520.	535.	545.	575.	750.	
1912 ......(74)	149,824	510.	520.	535.	545.	580.	1,350.	19,500.
1913 ......(58)	168,838	510.	520.	535.	545.	580.	2,850.	19,500.
1913D	393,500	510.	520.	535.	545.	580.	875.	
1913S	34,000	510.	520.	535.	545.	1,200.	3,700.	
1914 ......(70)	95,320	510.	520.	535.	545.	580.	1,700.	19,500.
1914D	453,000	510.	520.	535.	545.	575.	760.	
1914S	1,498,000	510.	520.	535.	545.	575.	725.	
1915 ......(50)	152,050	510.	520.	550.	560.	635.	2,150.	19,500.
1915S	567,500	510.	520.	535.	545.	575.	725.	
1916S	796,000	510.	520.	535.	555.	635.	900.	
1920	228,250	510.	520.	535.	545.	575.	825.	
1920S	558,000	7,500.	10,000.	14,000.	16,000.	24,500.	50,000.	
1921	528,500	10,000.	15,000.	19,000.	25,000.	37,000.	115,000.	
1922	1,375,500	510.	520.	535.	545.	575.	700.	
1922S	2,658,000	550.	600.	800.	805.	825.	2,350.	
1923	566,000	510.	520.	535.	545.	575.	700.	
1923D	1,702,250	510.	520.	535.	545.	575.	750.	
1924	4,323,500	510.	520.	535.	545.	575.	700.	
1924D	3,049,500	800.	1,000.	1,450.	1,500.	1,800.	6,600.	
1924S	2,927,500	800.	1,000.	1,450.	1,650.	2,450.	6,350.	
1925	2,831,750	510.	520.	535.	545.	575.	700.	
1925D	2,938,500	900.	1,200.	2,050.	2,200.	3,150.	8,850.	
1925S	3,776,500	1,000.	1,250.	1,800.	3,000.	5,500.	19,250.	
1926	816,750	510.	520.	535.	545.	575.	700.	
1926D	481,000	1,500.	2,000.	3,300.	4,500.	8,250.	22,000.	
1926S	2,041,500	850.	1,050.	1,550.	1,600.	1,750.	4,200.	
1927	2,946,750	510.	520.	535.	545.	575.	700.	
1927D	180,000			250,000.	275,000.	325,000.	500,000.	
1927S	3,107,000			6,500.	8,000.	12,000.	51,000.	
1928	8,816,000	510.	520.	535.	545.	575.	700.	
1929	1,779,750			8,200.	8,600.	10,250.	20,000.	
1930S	74,000			19,750.	21,000.	24,000.	47,500.	
1931	2,938,250			11,250.	13,500.	18,500.	28,500.	
1931D	106,500			11,750.	15,000.	25,500.	32,500.	
1932	1,101,750			14,000.	15,000.	19,000.	26,500.	
1933	445,500	*2002 Auction $7,590,020*		...*(Unique)*				

COMMEMORATIVE COINS

Commemorative coins have been popular since the days of the Greeks and Romans. In the beginning they served to record and honor important events and in the absence of newspapers they proved highly useful in passing along news of the day.

Many modern nations have issued commemorative coins and such pieces are highly esteemed by collectors. No nation has surpassed our own country when it comes to commemorative coins and in this we have reason to be proud.

The unique position occupied by commemoratives in United States coinage is largely due to the fact that with few exceptions all commemorative coins have a real historical significance. The progress and advance of people in the New World are presented in an interesting and instructive manner on the commemorative issues. Such a record of facts artistically presented on our gold and silver memorial issues appeals strongly to the collector who favors the historical side of numismatics. It is the historical features of the commemoratives, in fact, that create interest among many people who would otherwise have little interest in coins.

Commemorative issues are considered for coinage by two committees of Congress — The Committee on Banking, Housing and Urban Affairs, and the Committee on Banking and Financial Services of the House, as well as the Citizens Commemorative Coin Advisory Committee. Congress is guided to a great extent by the reports of these committees when passing upon bills authorizing commemorative coins.

These special coins are usually issued either to commemorate events or to help pay for monuments or celebrations that commemorate historical persons, places or things. The commemorative coins are offered in most instances by a commission in charge of the event to be commemorated, and sold at a price in advance of the face value of the piece. All are of the standard weight and fineness of traditional gold, silver, or clad coins, and all are legal tender.

Commemorative coins are popularly collected either by major types or in sets with mint mark varieties. In many years no special commemorative coins were issued. Some regular coins such as the Lincoln cent of 1909, Washington quarter of 1932, 1999-2009, and Bicentennial issues of 1976 are also commemorative in nature.

Display set of 1915-S Panama Pacific International expedition commemorative coins in glass fronted copper frame as some were originally sold. Contains the silver half dollar plus gold dollar, $2.50, and two varieties of $50.

Unless otherwise stated, the coinage figures given represent the total outstanding mintage. In many cases, larger quantities were minted but were not all sold. The unsold coins were usually returned to the mint and melted, although some were placed in circulation at face value.

Note: The commemorative coins listed on pages 240-287 are arranged alphabetically within denomination. The gold is listed alphabetically without regard to denomination. The modern commemorative coin section on page 261 and beyond is arranged chronologically.

COMMEMORATIVE COINS

High quality brilliant uncirculated commemoratives (MS-65) are worth far more than uncirculated (MS-60) pieces, which are often dull, cleaned, or blemished by contact marks.

A limited number of Proof strikings or presentation pieces were made for some of the 1892-1954 issues. All are very rare and valuable.

PRICE PERFORMANCE

Few people would ever guess, or even believe, that this country once issued an official half dollar bearing the portrait of P. T. Barnum, the famous con man who is credited with the saying "There's a sucker born every minute." He had nothing to do with the coins, which were made in 1936 long after his death, but the exceptional honor and the fact that the 50c coins were sold to the public for $2.00 each would have made him smile about bilking the public one last time.

Barnum did not have the last laugh in this matter. Those people who were fortunate enough to buy one of the original coins in 1936, and save it in perfect condition, find that today their treasure is worth over $300.00! Only 25,000 of the pieces were made, and at the time they were not very popular even with the few people who ever heard about them.

The Bridgeport commemorative half dollar with P. T. Barnum's portrait is but one of many different designs that have been used on special coins made for collectors since 1892. During that time commemorative coins have been issued to celebrate the founding of cities, mark expositions, honor famous citizens and presidents, and even to promote the Olympic contests in recent years. These coins are not normally placed in circulation, and are usually distributed by some agency at a price over face value with the surplus going to fund the event being celebrated. All commemorative coins made since 1982 have been distributed through the Mint with proceeds going directly to the government, and from there, to the various sponsoring organizations.

It has mostly been in recent years that the general public has learned about commemorative coins. They have long been popular with coin collectors who enjoy the artistry and history associated with them, as well as the tremendous profit that they have made from owning these rare pieces. Very few of them ever reached circulation because they were all originally sold above face value, and because they are all so rare. Most of the early issues were of the half dollar denomination, and were usually made in quantities of less than 20,000 pieces. This is miniscule when compared to the regular half dollar pieces which are made by the millions each year, and still rarely seen in circulation.

At the beginning of 1988 prices of commemoratives in MS-65 condition had risen so high that most collectors had to content themselves with pieces in lower grades. Investors continued to apply pressure to the high quality pieces and drive prices even higher, while the collector community went after coins in grades from About Uncirculated to MS-63. For several months the pressure from both influences caused prices to rise very rapidly for all issues and grades of commemoratives without even taking the price adjustment breather that usually goes along with such activity.

By 1990 prices dropped to the point where several of the commemoratives began to look like bargains once again. Many of the MS-65 pieces held firm at price levels above the $3,000.00 mark, but others were still available at under $500.00 even for coins of similar mintage. Coins in MS-63 or MS-64 were priced at but a fraction of the MS-65 pieces which would seem to make them reasonably priced because the demand for these pieces is universal, and not simply keyed to grade, rarity or speculator pressure.

Historically, the entire series of commemorative coins has frequently undergone a roller coaster cycle of price adjustments. These cycles have usually been of short duration, lasting from months to years, with prices always recovering and eventually exceeding previous levels.

COMMEMORATIVE SILVER
Isabella Quarter, Alabama, Albany
ISABELLA QUARTER DOLLAR

In 1893 the Board of Lady Managers of the Columbian Exposition petitioned for a souvenir quarter dollar. Authority was granted March 3, 1893. The coin known as the Isabella quarter was designed by C. E. Barber. These souvenir quarters were sold for $1.00. The obverse has the crowned bust of Queen Isabella of Spain. The kneeling female on the reverse with distaff and spindle is emblematic of women's industry.

	Mintage	AU-50	MS-60	MS-63	MS-65
1893 Columbian Exposition, Chicago ..24,214		$425.	$600.	$700.	$2,700.

ALABAMA CENTENNIAL

The Alabama half dollars were authorized in 1920 for the centennial, which was celebrated in 1919, but they were not struck until 1921. The coins, designed by Laura Gardin Fraser, were offered first during President Harding's visit to Birmingham, October 26, 1921. The St. Andrews cross, an emblem on the state flag, appears on a part of the issue between the figures 2 x 2 indicating the twenty-second state of the Union. The obverse has busts of William Wyatt Bibb, first governor of Alabama, and T. E. Kilby, governor at the time of the centennial. This is the first instance of the use of a living person's portrait on a United States coin.

2 x 2 in Field

	AU-50	MS-60	MS-63	MS-65
1921, Alabama Centennial, with 2X2 in field of obverse 6,006	$190.	$325.	$550.	$2,250.
1921, Alabama Centennial, no 2X2 59,038	125.	200.	425.	2,300.

ALBANY, NEW YORK CHARTER

The 250th anniversary of the granting of a charter to the city of Albany was the occasion for a commemorative half dollar. The reverse design shows Governor Dongan, Peter Schuyler and Robert Livingston. The obverse depicts a beaver gnawing on a maple branch. Gertrude K. Lathrop of Albany was the designer.

	AU-50	MS-60	MS-63	MS-65
1936 Albany, New York 17,671	$210.	$225.	$245.	$325.

COMMEMORATIVE SILVER
Antietam, Arkansas
BATTLE OF ANTIETAM

A souvenir half dollar was designed by William Marks Simpson and struck in 1937 to commemorate the seventy-fifth anniversary of the famous Civil War battle to thwart Lee's invasion of Maryland. The opposing generals McClellan and Lee are featured on the obverse while the Burnside Bridge, an important tactical objective, is shown on the reverse. The Battle of Antietam, on September 17, 1862, was one of the bloodiest single-day battles of the war with total losses of about 25,000 men.

	Mintage	AU-50	MS-60	MS-63	MS-65
1937 Battle of Antietam	18,028	$425.	$450.	$470.	$700.

ARKANSAS CENTENNIAL

This souvenir issue marked the one hundredth anniversary of the admission of Arkansas into the Union. Edward Everett Burr designed the piece and models were prepared by Emily Bates of Arkansas. Although 1936 was the centennial year the first of several issues was brought out in 1935 from all three mints. The 1937 and 1938 issues

were the same as those of 1935 except for the dates. They were sold by the distributors at $8.75 per set of three coins. The reverse shows accolated heads of an Indian chief of 1836 and an American girl of 1936. During 1936 a second design was authorized by Congress. Senator Joseph T. Robinson consented to have his portrait placed on the reverse side of the coins which were struck at the Philadelphia Mint. (See listing on page 254).

	Mintage		MS-60	MS-63	MS-65
1935 Arkansas Centennial	13,012				
1935D Same type D mint	5,505	Set	$210.	$235.	$750.
1935S Same type S mint	5,506				
1936 Arkansas Centennial, same as 1935-date 1936 on rev	9,660				
1936D Same type D mint	9,660	Set	210.	235.	775.
1936S Same type S mint	9,662				
1937 Arkansas Centennial (same as 1935)	5,505				
1937D Same type D mint	5,505	Set	250.	310.	925.
1937S Same type S mint	5,506				
1938 Arkansas Centennial (same as 1935)	3,156				
1938D Same type D mint	3,155	Set	335.	425.	1,725.
1938S Same type S mint	3,156				
1939 Arkansas Centennial (same as 1935)	2,104				
1939D Same type D mint	2,104	Set	625.	825.	3,000.
1939S Same type S mint	2,105				
Single, type coin			$57.50	70.	80.	250.

COMMEMORATIVE SILVER
Bay Bridge, Boone
BAY BRIDGE SAN FRANCISCO - OAKLAND

The opening of the San Francisco Bay Bridge was the occasion for a special souvenir fifty-cent piece. The designs were the work of Jacques Schnier, a San Francisco artist. A California grizzly bear dominates the obverse. The famous landmark bridge is shown on the reverse. The coins were struck at the San Francisco Mint in November 1936. The bear depicted was a composite of animals in local zoos.

	Mintage	AU-50	MS-60	MS-63	MS-65
1936S San Francisco Oakland Bay Bridge 71,424		$95.	$115.	$125.	$260.

DANIEL BOONE BICENTENNIAL

Date added in field.

This coin type, which was minted for five years, was first struck in 1934 to commemorate the two hundredth anniversary of the famous frontiersman's birth. The change of date to 1935 for the second year's coinage brought about the addition of the commemorative date 1934 above the words PIONEER YEAR. Coinage covered several years similar to the schedule for the Texas issues. The models for this coin were prepared by Augustus Lukeman. The obverse bears a portrait of Daniel Boone. The reverse shows Boone with Chief Black Fish.

	Mintage	AU-50	MS-60	MS-63	MS-65
1934 Daniel Boone Bicentennial ...10,007		$65.	$70.	$80.	$170.
1935 Same Type 10,010					
1935D Same Type D mint 5,005		Set	225.	285.	565.
1935S Same Type S mint 5,005					
1935 Daniel Boone same as 1934 same 1934 on reverse 10,008					
1935D Same Type D mint 2,003		Set	620.	750.	1,900.
1935S Same Type S mint 2,004					
1936 Daniel Boone (same as above) 12,012					
1936D Same Type D mint 5,005		Set	225.	275.	565.
1936S Same Type S mint 5,006					
1937 Daniel Boone (same as above) .9,810					
1937D Same Type D mint 2,506		Set	590.	675.	1,175.
1937S Same Type S mint 2,506					
1938 Daniel Boone (same as above) .2,100					
1938D Same Type D mint 2,100		Set	800.	980.	1,625.
1938S Same Type S mint 2,100					
Single, type coin		65.	70.	80.	170.

BRIDGEPORT, CONNECTICUT CENTENNIAL

In commemoration of the one hundredth anniversary of the incorporation of the city of Bridgeport a special fifty-cent piece was authorized May 15, 1936. Henry Kreis designed this coin. The head of P. T. Barnum, Bridgeport's best known citizen, occupies the obverse. An ultra-modernistic eagle dominates the reverse.

	Mintage	AU-50	MS-60	MS-63	MS-65
1936 Bridgeport, Conn., Centennial	25,015	$115.	$125.	$135.	$235.

CALIFORNIA DIAMOND JUBILEE

The California half dollar was designed by Jo Mora, a noted California sculptor. The obverse bears a kneeling figure of a Forty Niner. The reverse shows a walking grizzly bear, the state emblem. The celebration for which these coins were struck marked the seventy-fifth anniversary of the admission of California into the Union.

1925S California Diamond Jubilee	86,394	$115.	$125.	$180.	$1,000.

CARVER-WASHINGTON

Designed by Isaac Scott Hathaway, this coin portrays the conjoined busts of two prominent black Americans. Booker T. Washington was a lecturer, educator, and principal of Tuskegee Institute. He urged training to advance independence and efficiency for his race. George Washington Carver was an agricultural chemist who worked to improve the economy of the south. He spent part of his life teaching crop improvement and new uses for soybeans, peanuts, sweet potatoes and cotton waste. Money obtained from the sale of these commemoratives was to be used "to oppose the spread of communism among Negroes in the interest of national defense."

1951 Carver-Washington	110,018			
1951D Same Type D mint	10,004	Set	$85.	$95.	$525.
1951S Same Type S mint	10,004			

COMMEMORATIVE SILVER
Carver-Washington, Cincinnati, Cleveland

	Mintage	AU-50	MS-60	MS-63	MS-65
1952 Same Type as 1951 ...2,006,292					
1952D Same Type D mint 8,006		Set	$85.	$110.	$360.
1952S Same Type S mint 8,006					
1953 Same Type as 1951 8,003					
1953D Same Type D mint 8,003		Set	85.	110.	525.
1953S Same Type S mint 108,020					
1954 Same Type as 1951 12,006					
1954D Same Type D mint 12,006		Set	85.	100.	400.
1954S Same Type S mint 122,024					
Single, type coin		$13.	14.	18.	50.

CINCINNATI MUSIC CENTER

Although the head of Stephen Foster, "America's Troubadour," dominates the obverse of this special issue, the anniversary celebrated bears no relation to him. The coins, designed by Constance Ortmayer of Washington, D. C., were supposedly struck to commemorate the fiftieth anniversary in 1936 of Cincinnati as a center of music. The coins were struck at the three mints and were sold only in sets at $7.75, the highest initial cost of a new type.

	Mintage	AU-50	MS-60	MS-63	MS-65
1936 Cincinnati Music Center 5,005					
1936D Same Type D 5,005		Set	$700.	$750.	$2,300.
1936S Same Type S 5,006					
Single, type coin		$190.	210.	230.	600.

CLEVELAND GREAT LAKES EXPOSITION

A special coinage of fifty-cent pieces was authorized in commemoration of the centennial celebration of Cleveland, Ohio on the occasion of the Great Lakes Exposition held there in 1936. The designs were prepared by Brenda Putnam. Although half the coinage was struck in 1937 all were dated 1936. The obverse has a bust of Moses Cleaveland

and the reverse displays a map of the Great Lakes region with a compass pointed at Cleveland. Nine Great Lakes cities are marked by stars.

	Mintage	AU-50	MS-60	MS-63	MS-65
1936 Cleveland, ...50,030		$65.	$70.	$75.	$210.
Great Lakes Exposition					

COMMEMORATIVE SILVER
Columbia, South Carolina, Columbian, Connecticut

— COLUMBIA, SOUTH CAROLINA SESQUICENTENNIAL —

Souvenir half dollars were authorized to help finance the extensive celebrations marking the sesquicentennial of the founding of Columbia in 1786. A. Wolfe Davidson designed the coin which was struck at all three mints and sold in sets. The obverse bears the figure of Justice with sword and scales. At the left is the Capitol of 1786 and at the right the Capitol of 1936. A palmetto tree, the state emblem, is the reverse device.

	Mintage	AU-50	MS-60	MS-63	MS-65
1936 Columbia, S.C., Sesquicentennial	.9,007 ⎫				
1936D Same Type D mint ....8,009 ⎬		Set	$525.	$560.	$800.
1936S Same Type S mint ....8,007 ⎭					
Single, type coin		$155.	175.	190.	275.

——— COLUMBIAN EXPOSITION HALF DOLLAR ———

The first United States commemorative coin was the Columbian half dollar designed by Olin Lewis Warner. C.E. Barber engraved the obverse showing the bust of Columbus; and G. T. Morgan engraved the reverse having a representation of Columbus' flagship the *Santa Maria* above two hemispheres. The coins were sold for $1.00 each at the World's

Columbian Exposition in Chicago during 1893. A great many remained unsold and a substantial quantity was later released for circulation at face value. Approximately 100 brilliant Proofs were struck for each date.

1892 Columbian Exp. Chicago 950,000	$18.	$30.	$75.	$725.
1893 Same Type 1,550,405	16.	30.	75.	875.

——————— CONNECTICUT TERCENTENARY ———————

In commemoration of the three hundredth anniversary of the founding of the Colony of Connecticut, a souvenir half dollar was struck. Henry Kreis designed the coin. The famous "Charter Oak" is the main device on the reverse. According to tradition the Royal Charter was secreted in the tree during the reign of James II who wished to revoke it. The Charter was produced after the king's overthrow in 1688 and the Colony continued under its protection.

1935 Connecticut Tercentenary 25,018	$160.	$190.	$210.	$550.

COMMEMORATIVE SILVER
Delaware, Elgin, Gettysburg
DELAWARE TERCENTENARY

The three hundredth anniversary of the landing of the Swedes in Delaware was the occasion for a souvenir issue of half dollars. The colonists landed on a spot which is now Wilmington and established a church which is the oldest Protestant church still used for worship. Their ship *Kalmar Nyckel* is shown on the reverse of the coin and the Old Swedes Church is on the obverse. Designs were chosen from a competition that was won by Carl L. Schmitz. This coin was authorized in 1936, struck in 1937 and dated 1938 on the reverse and 1936 on the obverse. The anniversary was celebrated in 1938 both in Sweden and America. A two kronor coin was issued in Sweden to commemorate the same event.

	Mintage	AU-50	MS-60	MS-63	MS-65
1936 Delaware Tercentenary 20,993		$210.	$240.	$250.	$350.

ELGIN, ILLINOIS CENTENNIAL

The one hundredth anniversary of the founding of Elgin was marked by a special issue of half dollars in 1936. The proceeds were devoted to financing a Pioneer Memorial statue, which is depicted on the reverse of the coin. The year 1673 bears no relation to the event but refers to the year in which Joliet and Marquette entered Illinois Territory. The designs were prepared by Trygve Rovelstad who also designed the Memorial, which was not dedicated until 2001.

1936 Elgin, Illinois, Centennial 20,015	$160.	$175.	$185.	$225.

BATTLE OF GETTYSBURG

On June 16, 1936 Congress authorized a coinage of fifty-cent pieces in commemoration of the 1863 Battle of Gettysburg. The models were prepared by Frank Vittor, a Pittsburgh sculptor. Portraits of a Union and a Confederate veteran are shown on the obverse. Two shields representing the Union and Confederate armies separated by a double-bladed fasces are on the reverse.

1936 Battle of Gettysburg 26,928	$275.	$310.	$340.	$635.

COMMEMORATIVE SILVER
Grant, Hawaiian, Hudson

GRANT MEMORIAL

This coin was struck during 1922 as a centenary souvenir of Ulysses S. Grant's birth. A star which appeared on the first issues was later removed, creating a second variety. The star has no particular significance. Laura Gardin Fraser designed both the Grant half dollar and gold dollar. The reverse shows the frame house in Point Pleasant, Ohio, where Grant was born April 27, 1822.

Star in obverse field
(Fake stars usually have flattened spot on reverse.)

	Mintage	AU-50	MS-60	MS-63	MS-65
1922, Grant Memorial. Star in obv. field	4,256	$650.	$1,250.	$1,500.	$7,000.
1922, Same, no star	67,405	75.	90.	150.	775.

HAWAIIAN SESQUICENTENNIAL

This small issue was struck to commemorate the 150th anniversary of the arrival on the Hawaiian Islands of Captain James Cook in 1778. The design was sketched by Juliette May Fraser of Honolulu and executed by Chester Beach. Captain Cook is shown on the obverse and a native chief on the reverse. The coins were distributed in 1928 and sold for $2.00 each, the highest initial sale price up to that time.

1928 Hawaiian Sesquicentennial 9,958	$1,100.	$1,400.	$1,850.	$5,000.
1928 Hawaiian Sesquicentennial sandblast Proof presentation piece ...50				24,000.

HUDSON, NEW YORK SESQUICENTENNIAL

This souvenir half dollar marked the one hundred and fiftieth anniversary of the founding of Hudson, New York, which was named after the explorer Hendrik Hudson. The designs by Chester Beach show Hudson's flagship the *Half Moon* on the obverse and the seal of the City of Hudson on the reverse. Details of the seal include representations of Neptune with trident on a spouting whale and a mermaid blowing a conch shell.

1935 Hudson, N.Y. Sesquicentennial ...10,008	$435.	$500.	$525.	$1,350.

COMMEMORATIVE SILVER
Huguenot, Illinois, Iowa
HUGUENOT-WALLOON TERCENTENARY

Settling of the Huguenots and Walloons in the New World was the occasion commemorated by this issue. New Netherland, now New York, was founded in 1624 by a group of Dutch colonists. The persons represented on the obverse were not directly concerned with the occasion, however. They are Admiral Coligny and William the Silent. The reverse shows the vessel *Nieuw Nederland*. G. T. Morgan prepared the models for this coin.

	Mintage	AU-50	MS-60	MS-63	MS-65
1924 Huguenot-Walloon Tercentenary	142,080	$100.	$120.	$155.	$480.

ILLINOIS CENTENNIAL

The obverse was designed by G. T. Morgan and the reverse by J. R. Sinnock. The obverse shows the head of Lincoln taken from the statue by Andrew O'Connor in Springfield, Illinois. The reverse is based on the Illinois State Seal. This coin was authorized to commemorate the one hundredth anniversary of the admission of Illinois into the Union, the first souvenir piece for such an event.

1918 Illinois Centennial	100,058	$80.	$110.	$120.	$450.

IOWA CENTENNIAL

This half dollar, commemorating the one hundredth anniversary of Iowa's statehood, was designed by Adam Pietz of Philadelphia. The reverse shows the Iowa state seal, and the obverse has the first stone capitol building at Iowa City. This issue was sold first to the residents of Iowa and only a small remainder to others. Nearly all of the issue was disposed of within several months, except for some that were held back by the state for sale at future anniversary dates.

1946 Iowa Centennial	100,057	$65.	$72.	$80.	$115.

COMMEMORATIVE SILVER
Lexington, Long Island, Lynchburg
LEXINGTON-CONCORD SESQUICENTENNIAL

The two famous battles fought in 1775 are commemorated on this coin. A statue of the familiar Minute Man is depicted on the obverse, and the Old Belfry at Lexington is the reverse device. Chester Beach designed the coin. The famous statue by Daniel Chester French located in Concord was used for the design.

	Mintage	AU-50	MS-60	MS-63	MS-65
1925 Lexington-Concord Sesquicentennial 162,013		$65.	$75.	$110.	$590.

LONG ISLAND TERCENTENARY

This souvenir issue was authorized to commemorate the three hundredth anniversary of the first white settlement on Long Island which was at Jamaica Bay by Dutch colonists. The design was prepared by Howard Kenneth Weinman, son of the sculptor A. A. Weinman who designed the regular Liberty walking type half dollar. Accolated heads depicting a Dutch settler and an Indian are shown on the obverse, while a Dutch sailing vessel is the reverse device. This was the first issue for which a date was specified (1936) irrespective of the year minted or issued, as a safeguard against extending the coinage over a period of years.

1936 Long Island Tercentenary 81,826		$60.	$67.	$80.	$370.

LYNCHBURG, VIRGINIA SESQUICENTENNIAL

The issuance of a charter to the city of Lynchburg in 1786 was commemorated in 1936 by a special coinage of half dollars. The models for the coin were prepared by Charles Keck. The obverse bears a portrait of Senator Carter Glass, a native of Lynchburg and former Secretary of the Treasury, who objected to the idea of using portraits of living men on coins. Despite his mild protests, his likeness was incorporated on the coin. The reverse shows Liberty standing, with the old Lynchburg courthouse in the background.

1936 Lynchburg, Va., ...20,013 Sesquicentennial		$150.	$170.	$185.	$275.

COMMEMORATIVE SILVER
Maine, Maryland, Missouri
MAINE CENTENNIAL

Congress authorized the Maine Centennial half dollar May 10, 1920, to be sold at the Centennial celebration at Portland. They were received too late for this event and were sold by the state Treasurer for many years. Anthony de Francisci modeled this coin according to specifications furnished him. The obverse device is the arms of the state of Maine; the latin word DIRIGO means: I direct.

	Mintage	AU-50	MS-60	MS-63	MS-65
1920 Maine Centennial	50,028	$90.	$115.	$155.	$525.

MARYLAND TERCENTENARY

The three hundredth anniversary of the founding of the Maryland Colony by Cecil Calvert (known as Lord Baltimore) was the occasion for this special coin. The profits from the sale of this issue were used to finance the celebration in Baltimore during 1934. Hans Schuler designed the coin which shows the facing head of Lord Baltimore on the obverse and the arms of Maryland on the reverse, reminiscent of the Maryland colonial pieces.

1934 Maryland Tercentenary	25,015	$115.	$130.	$170.	$300.

MISSOURI CENTENNIAL

The one hundredth anniversary of the admission of Missouri to the Union was celebrated at Sedalia during August 1921. To mark the occasion Congress authorized the coinage of a fifty-cent piece. Robert Aitken designed the piece that shows the bust of a frontiersman on the obverse, and another frontiersman and Indian on the reverse. The first coins struck show 2★4 incused, indicating that Missouri was the twenty-fourth star in the flag. The type without this marking was struck later, but was the first to be sold.

2 ★ 4 in field

1921, Missouri Centennial 2★4 in field	5,000	$415.	$500.	$940.	$5,100.
1921, Missouri Centennia, no 2★4	15,428	250.	425.	775.	5,200.

COMMEMORATIVE SILVER
Monroe, New Rochelle, Norfolk

MONROE DOCTRINE CENTENNIAL

The motion picture industry promoted this issue in conjunction with a motion picture exposition in June 1923. The obverse shows the heads of James Monroe and John Quincy Adams who were identified with the Monroe Doctrine. The Western Hemisphere is portrayed on the reverse by two female figures. Chester Beach prepared the models for this coin.

	Mintage	AU-50	MS-60	MS-63	MS-65
1923S Monroe Doctrine Centennial	.274,077	$30.	$49.	$150.	$2,500.

NEW ROCHELLE, NEW YORK

To observe the founding of New Rochelle in 1688 by French Huguenots, a special half dollar was issued in 1938. The title to the land that the Huguenots purchased from John Pell provided that a fattened calf be given away every year on June 20th. This is represented by a calf and figure of John Pell on the obverse of the coin. The fleur-de-lis, which is shown on the reverse, is adopted from the Seal of the city. Both sides of the coin were designed by Gertrude K. Lathrop.

		AU-50	MS-60	MS-63	MS-65
1938 New Rochelle, N.Y.	15,266	$260.	$275.	$280.	$400.

NORFOLK, VIRGINIA BICENTENNIAL

To provide funds for the celebration of Norfolk's anniversary of its growth from a township in 1682 to a royal borough in 1736, Congress first passed a law for the striking of medals. The proponents, however, being dissatisfied finally succeeded in winning authority for half dollars commemorating the 300th anniversary of the original Norfolk land grant and the 200th anniversary of the establishment of the borough. William Marks Simpson and his wife Marjorie Emory Simpson designed the piece. The obverse shows the Seal of the City of Norfolk with a three-masted ship as the central device. The reverse features the Royal Mace of Norfolk presented by Lieutenant Governor Dinwiddie in 1753.

		AU-50	MS-60	MS-63	MS-65
1936 Norfolk, Va. Bicentennial	16,936	$350.	$360.	$375.	$425.

COMMEMORATIVE SILVER
Oregon, Panama-Pacific
OREGON TRAIL MEMORIAL

This memorial coin was struck in commemoration of the Oregon trail and in memory of the pioneers, many of whom lie buried along fhe famous 2,000 mile highway of history. James Earle Fraser and his wife, Laura Gardin Fraser, prepared the designs. The original issue was struck at Philadelphia and San Francisco in 1926.

Coinage was resumed in 1928 (released in 1933), 1933, 1934, and 1936 to 1939. The 1933 half dollar was the first commemorative coin struck at the Denver Mint.

		Mintage	AU-50	MS-60	MS-63	MS-65
1926	Oregon Trail Memorial	47,955	$100.	$110.	$120.	$245.
1926S	Same Type S mint	83,055	100.	110.	120.	245.
1928	Oregon Trail Memorial (same as 1926)	6,028	150.	160.	175.	310.
1933D	Oregon Trail Memorial(same), D mint	5,008	220.	240.	260.	525.
1934D	Oregon Trail Memorial (same), D mint	7,006	135.	150.	160.	290.
1936	Oregon Trail Memorial (same as 1926)	10,006	100.	115.	125.	250.
1936S	Same type S mint	5,006	120.	130.	160.	310.
1937D	Oregon Trail Memorial, D mint	12,008	120.	130.	150.	250.
1938	Oregon Trail Mem. (same as 1926)	6,006				
1938D	Same Type D mint	6,005	Set	520.	615.	775.
1938S	Same Type S mint	6,006				
1939	Oregon Trail Mem. (same as 1926)	3,004				
1939D	Same Type D mint	3,004	Set	1,150.	1,250.	2,000.
1939S	Same Type S mint	3,005				
	Single, type coin		100.	110.	120.	245.

PANAMA-PACIFIC EXPOSITION

This half dollar was designed by C. E. Barber (obv.) and George T. Morgan. The exposition held in San Francisco in 1915 celebrated the opening of the Panama Canal. The coins were struck at the San Francisco Mint and were sold at $1.00 each during the exposition. A representation of Columbia with the golden gate in the back-

ground is the principal feature of the obverse. The Panama-Pacific coins have the distinction of being the first commemorative coins to carry the motto IN GOD WE TRUST which appears above the eagle.

	Mintage	AU-50	MS-60	MS-63	MS-65
1915S Panama-Pacific Exposition	27,134	$310.	$355.	$650.	$2,400.

PILGRIM TERCENTENARY

To commemorate the landing of the Pilgrims at Plymouth, Massachusetts in 1620, Congress authorized a special half dollar May 12, 1920. Cyrus E. Dallin, a Boston sculptor, executed the designs furnished him by the Commission. His initial D is placed below Bradford's elbow. The obverse has a portrait of Governor Bradford. The reverse shows the "Mayflower." The first issue had no date on the obverse. The coins struck in 1921 show that date in addition to 1620-1920. There was a large coinage of both issues and not all were sold. A total of 128,000 were returned to the mint and melted.

	Mintage	AU-50	MS-60	MS-63	MS-65
1920 Pilgrim Tercentenary 152,112		$60.	$70.	$90.	$425.

→ **With 1921 Date Added in Field on Obverse.**

	Mintage	AU-50	MS-60	MS-63	MS-65
1921 Same type 20,053		$110.	$125.	$150.	$575.

PROVIDENCE, RHODE ISLAND TERCENTENARY

The three hundredth anniversary of Roger Williams' founding of Providence was the occasion for this special half dollar in 1936. The designs were the work of Arthur Graham Carey and John Howard Benson. The obverse shows Roger Williams in a canoe being welcomed by an Indian. The reverse has the anchor of Hope with a shield and mantling in the background. Although the founding of Providence was being celebrated, no mention of the city is to be found on the coin.

1936 Rhode Island Tercentenary .20,013 ⎫				
1936D Same Type D mint ....15,010 ⎬ Set	$220.	$250.	$675.	
1936S Same Type S mint ....15,011 ⎭				
Single, type coin	$65.	70.	85.	215.

COMMEMORATIVE SILVER
Roanoke, Robinson, San Diego
ROANOKE ISLAND, NORTH CAROLINA

A celebration was held in Old Fort Raleigh in 1937 to commemorate the 350th anniversary of Sir Walter Raleigh's "Lost Colony" and the birth of Virginia Dare, the first white child born in British North America. A special half dollar for the occasion was designed by William Marks Simpson of Baltimore. The obverse bears a portrait of Sir Walter Raleigh and the reverse has a figure representing Ellinor Dare holding the child Virginia Dare.

	Mintage	AU-50	MS-60	MS-63	MS-65
1937 Roanoke Island, N.C.	29,030	$170.	$200.	$215.	$220.

ROBINSON-ARKANSAS CENTENNIAL

A new reverse design for the Arkansas Centennial coin was authorized by the Act of June 26, 1936. Senator Joseph T. Robinson, still living at the time, his portrait was used, is the subject for the new issue engraved by Henry Kreis. The obverse, designed by Everett Burr, was unchanged. The law specified a change in the reverse, because of the fact that the obverse side is that which bears the date. From a numismatic viewpoint, however, the side which has the portrait is usually considered the obverse. Thus in this instance, the side with the eagle device is often considered the reverse.

1936 Arkansas Centennial (Robinson)	25,265	$95.	$100.	$115.	$300.

SAN DIEGO-CALIFORNIA-PACIFIC EXPOSITION

Congress approved the coinage of souvenir half dollars for the exposition on May 3, 1935. Robert Aitken designed the coin which was struck at the San Francisco Mint. The same type with date 1936 was struck at the Denver Mint, under authority of the special Recoinage Act of May 6, 1936, which specified that 180,000 pieces could be recoined with the date 1936 irrespective of the year of issue. The obverse displays a seated female with spear and a bear in the left background. The reverse shows the observation tower and the State of California building at the Exposition.

1935S San Diego, California-Pacific Exp. .	70,132	$55.	$85.	$90.	$130.
1936D D mint (same as 1935)	30,092	60.	95.	100.	150.

Sesquicentennial, Old Spanish Trail, Stone Mountain
— **SESQUICENTENNIAL OF AMERICAN INDEPENDENCE** —

The one hundred and fiftieth anniversary of the signing of the Declaration of Independence was the occasion for an International Fair held in Philadelphia in 1926. To help raise funds for financing the fair, special issues of half dollars and quarter-eagles were authorized by Congress. For the first time a portrait of a president appeared on a coin struck during his lifetime. Presidents Coolidge and Washington are depicted on the obverse of the half dollar. The reverse bears an accurate model of the Liberty Bell. John R. Sinnock, Chief Engraver of the United States Mint, modeled the sesquicentennial coins from designs by John Frederick Lewis. The dies were in very low relief causing much loss of detail.

	Mintage	AU-50	MS-60	MS-63	MS-65
1926 Sesquicentennial of American Independence	141,120	$60.	$80.	$160.	$5,000.

===== **OLD SPANISH TRAIL** =====

This coin commemorated the four hundredth anniversary of the overland trek of the Cabeza de Vaca Expedition through the gulf states in 1535. L. W. Hoffecker designed the coin, and models were prepared by Edmund J. Senn. The explorer's name literally translated means "head of a cow;" therefore this device was chosen for the obverse. The reverse bears a yucca tree and a map showing the Old Spanish Trail.

1935 Old Spanish Trail	10,008	$775.	$875.	$900.	$1,200.

===== **STONE MOUNTAIN MEMORIAL** =====

The models for this coin were prepared by Gutzon Borglum. The first coins were struck at Philadelphia January 21, 1925, General Thomas "Stonewall" Jackson's birthday. Generals Robert E. Lee and Jackson, mounted, are shown on the obverse. The funds received from the sale of this large issue of half dollars were devoted to the expense of carving figures of Confederate leaders and soldiers on Stone Mountain in Georgia. The carving was completed and dedicated in 1970. Some of these coins were privately counterstamped on the reverse with letters and numbers by individual state sales agencies. These are generally valued much higher than normal coins.

1925 Stone Mountain Memorial	1,314,709	$40.	$60.	$75.	$210.

TEXAS CENTENNIAL

This issue commemorated the independence of Texas in 1836. The first of several dates was offered in 1934. The later dates were struck at all three mints. The models were prepared by Pompeo Coppini. The reverse shows the kneeling figure of winged Victory, and on each side, medallions with portraits of General Sam Houston and Stephen Austin, founders of the Republic and State of Texas. The large five-pointed star behind the eagle on the obverse carries out the "Lone Star" tradition.

	Mintage	AU-50	MS-60	MS-63	MS-65
1934 Texas Centennial 61,463		$90.	$100.	$115.	$160.
1935 Texas Centennial (same as 1934) 9,996					
1935D Same Type D Mint 10,007		Set	290.	325.	520.
1935S Same Type S Mint 10,008					
1936 Texas Centennial (same as 1934) 8,911					
1936D Same Type D Mint 9,039		Set	290.	325.	500.
1936S Same Type S Mint 9,055					
1937 Texas Centennial (same as 1934) 6,571					
1937D Same Type D Mint 6,605		Set	290.	325.	520.
1937S Same Type S Mint 6,637					
1938 Texas Centennial (same as 1934) 3,780					
1938D Same Type D Mint 3,775		Set	620.	725.	1,400.
1938S Same Type S Mint 3,814					
Single, type coin		—	100.	115.	160.

FORT VANCOUVER CENTENNIAL

Dr. John McLoughlin, shown on the obverse of this coin, built Fort Vancouver (Washington) on the Columbia River in 1825. The sale of the coins at $1.00 each helped to finance the pageant staged for the celebration. Laura Gardin Fraser prepared the models for this coin which was minted in San Francisco. The S mint mark was omitted. The reverse has a pioneer settler in buckskin suit with a musket in his hands. Fort Vancouver is in the background.

1925 Fort Vancouver Centennial 14,994	$230.	$300.	$375.	$1,350.

COMMEMORATIVE SILVER
Vermont, B. T. Washington
VERMONT SESQUICENTENNIAL

This souvenir issue commemorates the 150th Anniversary of the Battle of Bennington and the Independence of Vermont. Authorized in 1925, it was not coined until 1927. The models were prepared by Charles Keck. The obverse shows the head of Ira Allen, founder of Vermont. The reverse bears a catamount on a pedestal.

	Mintage	AU-50	MS-60	MS-63	MS-65
1927 Vermont Sesquicentennial (Bennington) 28,142		$150.	$170.	$180.	$800.

BOOKER T. WASHINGTON MEMORIAL

This commemorative coin was issued to perpetuate the ideals and teachings of Booker T. Washington and to construct memorials to his memory. Issued from all mints, it received wide distribution from the start. The reverse has the legend FROM SLAVE CABIN TO HALL OF FAME. His log cabin birthplace is shown beneath. This coin was designed by Isaac Scott Hathaway, as was the Carver-Washington half dollar issued under the same authority.

		AU-50	MS-60	MS-65
1946 Booker T. Washington .*1,000,546 1946D Same Type D Mint . . . . . .200,113 1946S Same Type S Mint . . . . . .500,279 }	Set	$50.	$70.	$150.
1947 Same Type as 1946 . . . . . .100,017 1947D Same Type D Mint . . . . . .100,017 1947S Same Type S Mint . . . . . .100,017 }	Set	70.	82.	250.
1948 Same Type as 1946 . . . . .8,005 1948D Same Type D Mint . . . . .8,005 1948S Same Type S Mint . . . . .8,005 }	Set	135.	145.	190.
1949 Same Type as 1946 . . . . .6,004 1949D Same Type D Mint . . . . .6,004 1949S Sam Typ S Mint . . . . .6,004 }	Set	210.	220.	320.
1950 Same Type as 1946 . . . . .6,004 1950D Same Type D Mint . . . . .6,004 1950S Same Type S Mint . . . . . .512,091 }	Set	120.	130.	175.
1951 Same Type as 1946 . . . . . .510,082 1951D Same Type D Mint . . . . .7,004 1951S Same Type S Mint . . . . .7,004 }	Set	110.	130.	185.
Single, type coin	$12.	15.	17.	50.

*Minted; quantity melted unknown.

COMMEMORATIVE SILVER
Wisconsin, York County, Lafayette Dollar
WISCONSIN TERRITORIAL CENTENNIAL

The one hundredth anniversary of the Wisconsin Territorial government was the occasion for this issue. The original design was made by David Parsons, a University of Wisconsin student. Benjamin Hawkins, a New York artist, made changes to conform with technical requirements. The reverse has the Territorial Seal, which includes a forearm holding a pickaxe over a mound of lead ore, and the inscription 4th DAY OF JULY ANNO DOMINI 1836. The obverse shows a badger on a log, the state emblem, and arrows representing the Black Hawk War of the 1830s.

	Mintage	AU-50	MS-60	MS-63	MS-65
1936 Wisconsin Centennial	25,015	$155.	$165.	$180.	$275.

YORK COUNTY, MAINE TERCENTENARY

A souvenir half dollar was authorized by Congress upon the three hundredth anniversary of the founding of York County, Maine. Brown's Garrison on the Saco River was the site of a town that was settled in 1636. The designs were made by Walter H. Rich of Portland. The obverse design shows a stockade, and the reverse has an adaptation of the York County seal.

1936 York County, Maine Tercentenary	25,015	$150.	$165.	$170.	$200.

LAFAYETTE DOLLAR

The heads of Washington and Lafayette appear on this issue, which was the first commemorative coin of one dollar denomination, and the first authorized United States coin to bear a portrait of one of our presidents. The dies were prepared by C. E. Barber. The statue on the reverse is similar to the monument of General Lafayette that was erected in Paris as a gift of the American people. The coins were sold by the Lafayette Memorial Commission for $2.00 each.

1900 Lafayette Dollar	36,026	$350.	$600.	$1,500.	$8,500.

COMMEMORATIVE GOLD
Grant, Lewis & Clark, Louisiana Purchase, McKinley
GRANT MEMORIAL GOLD DOLLARS

Like the half-dollar commemorative coins, the gold dollars were first issued with a star which was removed for the later issues. The designs by Laura Gardin Fraser are the same as for the half-dollar coinage.

	Mintage	AU-50	MS-60	MS-63	MS-65
1922 Grant Memorial Dollar with star 5,016		$1,100.	$1,275.	$1,800.	$3,750.
1922 Grant Memorial Dollar no star 5,000		1,050.	1,150.	1,800.	3,750.

LEWIS AND CLARK EXPOSITION

The Lewis and Clark Centennial Exposition was held in Portland, Oregon in 1905. A souvenir issue of gold dollars was struck to mark the event with the dates 1904 and 1905. The two famous explorers are represented on either side of the coin which was designed by C. E. Barber. A bronze memorial of the Indian guide, Sacagawea, who assisted in the famous expedition, was erected in Portland, Oregon and financed by the sale of these coins.

1904 Lewis and Clark Dollar 10,025		$525.	$775.	$1,900.	$10,000.
1905 Lewis and Clark Dollar 10,041		525.	850.	2,500.	16,500.

LOUISIANA PURCHASE EXPOSITION

The first souvenir gold coins were authorized for the Louisiana Purchase Exposition held in St. Louis in 1904. There are two varieties of gold dollars — one with the head of Jefferson who was president when the Louisiana Territory was purchased from France; and the other President William McKinley who sanctioned the Exposition. The reverse is the same for each variety. The designs were by C. E. Barber.

*1903 Louisiana Purchase Jefferson Dollar 17,500		$340.	$450.	$650.	$3,000.
*1903 Louisiana Purchase McKinley Dollar 17,500		300.	400.	650.	3,000.

*Proofs exist of each type.

McKINLEY MEMORIAL GOLD DOLLAR

The sale of the McKinley dollars aided in paying for a memorial building at Niles, Ohio, the martyred president's birthplace. The obverse showing a profile of McKinley was designed by C. E. Barber; the reverse with the memorial building was designed by G. T. Morgan.

McKinley, Panama-Pacific

	Mintage	AU-50	MS-60	MS-63	MS-65
1916 McKinley Memorial Dollar	15,000	$270.	$350.	$550.	$2,700.
1917 McKinley Memorial Dollar	5,000	350.	500.	1,100.	3,750.

PANAMA-PACIFIC INTERNATIONAL EXPOSITION

Charles Keck designed the gold dollar, the obverse of which has the head of a man representing a Panama Canal laborer. Two dolphins encircle ONE DOLLAR on the reverse.

The quarter eagle was the work of Charles E. Barber and George T. Morgan. The obverse shows Columbia with a caduceus in her left hand seated on a hippocampus typifying the use of the Panama Canal. An American eagle with raised wings is shown on the reverse.

The fifty-dollar gold piece was designed by Robert Aitken and was issued in both round and octagonal form. The obverse bears a helmeted head of Minerva; the owl, symbol of wisdom, is on the reverse. The octagonal issue has eight dolphins in the angles on both sides. Other devices are smaller on the octagonal variety.

	Mintage	AU-50	MS-60	MS-63	MS-65
1915S Panama-Pacific Exposition Dollar	15,000	$315.	$365.	$525.	$2,750.
1915S Panama-Pacific Exposition $2.50	6,749	1,150.	1,400.	2,900.	5,250.

	Mintage	AU-50	MS-60	MS-63	MS-65
1915S Panama-Pacific $50.00 Round	483	26,000.	33,000.	49,000.	105,000.

MODERN COMMEMORATIVE GOLD
Panama-Pacific, United States Sesquicentennial

	Mintage	AU-50	MS-60	MS-63	MS-65
1915S Panama-Pacific $50.00 Octagonal	645	$25,000.	$30,000.	$44,000.	$95,000.

— SESQUICENTENNIAL OF AMERICAN INDEPENDENCE —

The obverse of this special gold quarter eagle has a standing female figure symbolic of Liberty, holding in one hand a scroll representing the Declaration of Independence and in the other the Torch of Freedom. The reverse bears a representation of Independence Hall in Philadelphia. The coin was designed by John R. Sinnock.

	Mintage				
1926 U.S. Sesquicentennial $2.50 46,019		$270.	$300.	$550.	$3,750.

════ MODERN COMMEMORATIVES — Washington ════
──────── GEORGE WASHINGTON ────────

This coin, the first commemorative half dollar issued since 1954, commemorated the 250th anniversary of the birth of George Washington. It was also the first 90% silver coin produced by the U.S. Mint since 1964. Designed by Elizabeth Jones, Chief Sculptor and Engraver of the United States, the obverse features George Washington astride a horse. The reverse depicts the eastern facade of Mount Vernon. The Uncirculated version was struck at Denver and the Proof at San Francisco.

	Mintage	MS-65	PF-65
1982D George Washington-250th Anniversary 2,210,458		$6.00	
1982S Same Proof . . . .(4,894,044)			$5.50

Los Angeles Olympiad

LOS ANGELES XXIII OLYMPIAD

Three distinctive coins were issued to commemorate the 1984 Los Angeles Summer Olympic Games. The silver dollar dated 1983 was designed by Elizabeth Jones, Chief Engraver of the Mint. On the obverse is a representation of the traditional Greek discus thrower inspired by the ancient work of the sculptor Myron. The reverse depicts the head and upper body of an American eagle.

	Mintage	MS-65	PF-65
1983P Discus Thrower Silver Dollar	.294,543	$12.	
1983D Same Type D Mint	.174,014	12.	
1983S Same Type S Mint . . . . (1,577,025)	174,014	12.	$13.

The 1984 Olympic silver dollar was designed by Robert Graham, an American sculptor who created the sculpture placed at the entrance to the Los Angeles Memorial Coliseum. The obverse depicts Graham's sculpture with the Coliseum in the background. The reverse features an American eagle.

		MS-65	PF-65
1984P Olympic Coliseum Silver Dollar	217,954	$14.	
1984D Same Type D Mint	116,675	21.	
1984S Same Type S Mint . . . .(1,801,210)	116,675	20.	$13.

Mintage of a commemorative gold coin for the 1984 Olympics was the first U.S. gold piece issued in over 50 years. The weight, size and fineness are the same as the last ten dollar coin issued in 1933. It is the first coin ever to bear the W mint mark for West Point.

The obverse depicts two runners bearing the Olympic torch aloft, and was designed by John Mercanti from a concept by James Peed, an artist at the Mint. The eagle on the reverse is modeled after the Great Seal.

	Mintage	MS-65	PF-65
1984P Olympic Gold Eagle	(33,309)	$300.	
1984D Olympic Gold Eagle	(34,533)		320.
1984S Olympic Gold Eagl	(48,551)	250.	
1984W Olympic Gold Eagle	(381,085) 75,886	$240.	260.

STATUE OF LIBERTY

The first copper-nickel clad half dollar commemorative depicts this country's heritage as a nation of immigrants. The obverse, designed by Edgar Steever, pictures a ship of immigrants steaming into New York harbor, with the Statue of Liberty greeting them in the foreground and the New York skyline in the distance. The reverse, designed by Sherl Joseph Winter, has a scene of an immigrant family with their belongings on the threshold of America. Weight and composition are the same as that of regular issue clad half dollars.

	Mintage	MS-65	PF-65
1986D, Statue of Liberty Half Dollar	928,008	$6.50	
1986S, Same type S mint Proof	(6,925,627)		$6.75

Designed by Mint artist John Mercanti, this .900 fine silver dollar commemorates Ellis Island as the "Gateway to America." The obverse features a classic pose of Liberty in the foreground, with the Ellis Island Immigration Center standing behind her. On the reverse is a depiction of Liberty's torch, along with the words "Give me your tired, your poor, your huddled masses yearning to breathe free." Matthew Peloso assisted in the model work on the reverse.

	Mintage	MS-65	PF-65
1986P Statue of Liberty Silver Dollar	723,635	$11.50	
1986S Same Type S Mint Proof	(6,414,638)		$17.50

The commemorative half eagle is also the first of this denomination to be minted in over fifty years. Standards for weight and size are the same as previous half eagle gold coins. The design is the creation of the Mint's chief engraver, Elizabeth Jones. The obverse features a compelling close-up view of Liberty's face

in sharp relief with the inscription 1986 LIBERTY. An eagle in flight adorns the reverse. All were minted at West Point and bear the W mint mark.

1986W Statue of Liberty Gold $5.00	(404,013)	95,248	140.00	140.00

CONSTITUTION BICENTENNIAL

The silver dollar commemorating the 200th anniversary of the United States Constitution was designed by Patricia Lewis Verani using standard weight, size and fineness. A quill pen, a sheaf of parchment and the words WE THE PEOPLE are depicted on the obverse. The reverse portrays a cross section of Americans from various periods representing contrasting lifestyles.

1987P U.S. Constitution Silver Dollar	451,629	$14.00	
1987S Same Type S Mint Proof	(2,747,116)		$14.00

A modernistic design by Marcel Jovine was selected for the $5 gold coin of standard weight, size and fineness commemorating the bicentennial of the United States Consitution. The obverse portrays a stylized eagle holding a massive quill pen. Another large quill pen is featured on the reverse. To the left are nine stars signifying the first colonies that ratified the Constitution. Four stars to the right represent the remaining original states. Both uncirculated and Proof versions were minted at West Point.

1987W U.S. Constitution Gold $5.00	(651,659)	214,225	$140.00	$140.00

OLYMPIAD 1988

The 1988 Olympic silver dollar commemorates the U.S. participation in the Seoul Olympiad. Its size and weight are identical to other silver dollars. Design of the obverse is by Patricia Lewis Verani. The reverse is by Mint Sculptor Engraver Sherl Joseph Winter.

	Mintage	MS-65	PF-65
1988D Olympic Silver Dollar 191,368		$14.00	
1988S Same Type S Mint Proof . . . .(1,359,366)			$14.00

The 1988 $5.00 gold Olympic coin was designed by Elizabeth Jones, Chief Sculptor and Engraver of the U.S. Mint. The obverse features Nike, goddess of Victory, wearing a crown of olive leaves. The reverse features Marcel Jovine's stylized Olympic flame, evoking the spectacle of the Games and the renewal of the Olympic spirit every four years.

1988W Olympic Gold $5.00 . . . .(281,465)	62,913	$140.00	$140.00

CONGRESS BICENTENNIAL

The obverse is designed by sculptor Patricia L. Verani and features a detailed bust of the Statue of Freedom. The reverse, designed by William Woodward offers a full view of the Capitol Building accented by a wreath of stars. The clad composition is approximately 92% copper, 8% nickel.

1989D Congress Bicentennial Half Dollar 163,753	$8.50	
1989S Same Type S Mint Proof . . . .(767,897)		$8.50

Designed by muralist William Woodward, the obverse of the dollar features the Statue of Freedom which towers atop the Capitol dome. The reverse shows the Mace of the House of Representatives which resides in the House Chamber whenever the House is in session. The Mace's staff is topped by an eagle astride a world globe. A scarce variety of the 1989D dollar shows the dies rotated 360° rather than the normal "coin turn" of 180°.

	Mintage	MS-65	PF-65
1989D Congress Silver Dollar	135,203	$17.	
1989S Same Type S Mint Proof	(762,198)		$21.

The Capitol Dome is depicted on the obverse of the $5.00 gold coin and is the work of Mint Engraver John Mercanti. The reverse features a majestic eagle atop the canopy overlooking the Old Senate Chamber.

1989W Congress Gold $5.00	(164,690)	46,899	150.	150.

EISENHOWER CENTENNIAL

The unusual design on this coin features the profile of President Eisenhower facing right, which is superimposed over his own left-facing profile as a five-star general. It is the creation of Mint Engraver John Mercanti. The reverse shows the Eisenhower home at Gettysburg, a National Historic Site, and was designed by Marcel Jovine. The coin was issued to celebrate the 100th anniversary of the birth of the 34th president.

1990W Eisenhower Silver Dollar	241,669	$17.	
1990P Same Type P Mint Proof	(1,144,461)		$23.

MODERN COMMEMORATIVES
Mount Rushmore
MOUNT RUSHMORE GOLDEN ANNIVERSARY

The 50th anniversary of the Mount Rushmore National Memorial was commemorated on three coins. Surcharges from the sale of these pieces were divided between the Treasury Department and the Mount Rushmore National Memorial Society of Black Hills, South Dakota, with money going to finance restoration work on the national landmark. The obverse of the copper-nickel half dollar was designed by New Jersey artist Marcel Jovine, and features a view of the famous carving by Gutzon Borglum. The reverse designed by Mint Sculptor-Engraver James Ferrell shows an American bison with the words GOLDEN ANNIVERSARY.

	Mintage	MS-65	PF-65
1991D Mount Rushmore Half Dollar	172,754	$19.	
1991S Same Type S Mint Proof	(753,257)		$19.

The Mount Rushmore Golden Anniversary silver dollar obverse was designed by Marika Somogyi. It displays the traditional portraits of Presidents George Washington, Thomas Jefferson, Theodore Roosevelt and Abraham Lincoln as sculptured on the mountain by Gutzon Borglum, who earlier had modeled the figures shown on the Stone Mountain Commemorative coin. The reverse which was designed by former Chief Sculptor-Engraver of the Mint, Frank Gasparro, features a small outline map of the United States with the great seal above.

	Mintage	MS-65	PF-65
1991P Mount Rushmore Silver Dollar	133,139	35.	
1991S Same Type S Mint Proof	(738,419)		40.

The $5.00 gold coin commemorating the 50th anniversary of the Mount Rushmore National Memorial features an American eagle flying above the monument with LIBERTY and the date in the field. The obverse was designed by Mint Sculptor-Engraver John Mercanti, and the reverse was designed by Rhode Island artist Robert Lamb, and engraved by Mint Sculptor-Engraver William Cousins. The size, weight and fineness is the same as for all other half eagle coins.

MODERN COMMEMORATIVES
Mount Rushmore, Korean War, U.S.O.

	Mintage	MS-65	PF-65
1991W Mount Rushmore Gold $5.00 ....(111,991)	31,959	$185.	$160.

KOREAN WAR MEMORIAL

The 38th anniversary of the end of the Korean War was the occasion for striking this coin which honors the end of the conflict and those who served in combat. The design has been criticized as being cluttered, and the occasion no more than a fund raising opportunity for the creation of a national monument in Washington. The obverse, designed by Sculptor-Engraver of the U.S. Mint, John Mercanti, features an Army Infantryman in full gear. On the reverse is an outline map of Korea with North and South divided at the 38th parallel, designed by Mint Sculptor-Engraver James Ferrell.

1991D Korean War Silver Dollar 213,049	$16.	
1991P Same Type P Mint Proof ....(618,488)		$18.

UNITED SERVICE ORGANIZATIONS

A special commemorative silver dollar was struck to honor the 50th anniversary of United Service Organizations. The group was founded in 1941 to supply social, recreational, welfare and spiritual facilities to armed services personnel. Surcharges on sales of the coins were divided equally between the USO and the Department of the Treasury. The coins were launched on Flag Day, June 14, using designs selected in a limited competition between Mint staff and five outside invited artists. The obverse uses a banner inscribed USO designed by Rhode Island artist Robert Lamb. On the reverse is a globe with an eagle on top, and is the work of Mint Sculptor-Engraver John Mercanti.

	Mintage	MS-65	PF-65
1991D USO Silver Dollar 124,958		$17.00	
1991S Same Type S Mint Proof ....(321,275)			$18.00

XXV OLYMPIAD 1992

The XXV Olympiad held Winter Olympic games in Albertville and Savoie, France, and Summer Olympic games in Barcelona, Spain. United States commemorative coins were issued to honor the participation of American athletes and finance the training of the athletes. Competitive designs were selected from 1,107 entries.

The clad half dollar obverse designed by Mint Sculptor-Engraver William Cousins depicts a gymnast in motion. The reverse, by Steven M. Bieda, has the inscription "Citius, Altius, Fortius" (the Olympic motto: Faster, Higher, Stronger) with an olive branch crossing the Olympic torch.

1992P Olympic Clad Half Dollar 161,619		$8.50	
1992S Same Type S Mint Proof ....(519,699)			$8.50

The 1992 Olympic silver dollar obverse is a rendering by John R. Deecken of a pitcher firing a ball to home plate. The reverse, by sculptor Marcel Jovine, combines the Olympic rings, olive branches, stars and stripes, with a bold USA. Uncirculated dollars minted at Denver have the phrase XXV OLYMPIAD impressed four times around the edge, alternately inverted, on a reeded background.

MODERN COMMEMORATIVES
Olympiad, White House

	Mintage	MS-65	PF-65
1992D Olympic Silver Dollar	187,552	$25.	
1992S Same Type S Mint Proof	(504,505)		$28.

The obverse of the 1992 Olympic $5 gold was designed by James Sharpe, and modeled by T. James Ferrell. It depicts a sprinter in a burst of speed. The reverse, by James Peed, unites two impressive symbols, the Olympic rings and the American bald eagle. Size and fineness of these coins is the same as for other United States commemorative issues.

1992W Olympic Gold $5.00	27,732	(77,313)	$160.	$145.

White House 200th Anniversary

The obverse of this coin, designed by Mint Sculptor Edgar Z. Steever IV, depicts the north portico of the White House. The reverse, by Mint Sculptor Chester Y. Martin, features a bust of James Hoban, the original architect, and the main entrance he designed.

	Mintage	MS-65	PF-65
1992D White House Silver Dollar	123,803	$35.	
1992W Same Type W Mint Proof	(375,849)		$40.

Columbus
Christopher Columbus Quincentenary

The copper-nickel half dollar, designed by Mint Sculptor T. James Ferrell, depicts Columbus landing in the New World on the obverse, and his three ships on the reverse.

	Mintage	MS-65	PF-65
1992D Columbus Half Dollar	135,718	$12.	
1992S Same Type S Mint Proof	(390,255)		$12.

Mint Sculptor John Mercanti designed this silver dollar obverse which features a full-length figure of Columbus beside a globe, with his ships above. The reverse, by Mint Sculptor Thomas D. Rogers, Sr., is a split image of the *Santa Maria* and the U.S. space shuttle *Discovery*.

	Mintage	MS-65	PF-65
1992D Columbus Silver Dollar	106,949	$30.	
1992P Same Type P Mint Proof	(385,241)		$40.

The five dollar gold coin obverse, designed by Mint Sculptor T. James Ferrell, bears a portrait of Columbus facing a map of the New World. The reverse, by Mint Sculptor Thomas D. Rogers, Sr., shows the Crest of the Admiral of the Ocean Sea.

	Mintage		MS-65	PF-65
1992W Columbus Gold $5.00	(79,730)	24,329	$200.	$165.

The silver half dollar in this series depicts James Madison penning the Bill of Rights. It was designed by Mint Sculptor T. James Ferrell. The reverse, by Dean McMullen, displays the torch of freedom. 9,656 of the Uncirculated version were privately marked on the edge with a serial number and the initials of the Madison Foundation and the American Numismatic Association.

	Mintage	MS-65	PF-65
1993W Bill of Rights Silver Half Dollar	173,224	$20.	
1993S Same Type S Mint Proof	(559,758)		$18.

A portrait of James Madison is shown on the obverse of this silver dollar designed by William Krawczewicz. Dean McMullen designed the reverse which shows Montpelier, the Virginia home of James and Dolley Madison.

	Mintage	MS-65	PF-65
1993D Bill of Rights Silver Dollar	98,383	$20.	
1993S Same Type S Mint Proof	(534,001)		$22.

The obverse of the five dollar gold coin was designed by Scott R. Blazek. It features Madison studying the Bill of Rights. On the reverse, by Joseph D. Peña, is a quotation by Madison, accented by an eagle, torch and laurel branch.

	Mintage		MS-65	PF-65
1993W Bill of Rights Gold $5.00	(78,651)	23,266	$200.	$180.

Each of the three coins in this series is dated 1991-1995, and commemorate the 50th anniversary of U.S. involvement in World War II, which lasted from 1941 to 1945. Pieces were coined and issued in 1993. The obverse of the clad half dollar was designed by George Klauba. It depicts the faces of three members of the service superimposed upon the "V" for victory symbol. The reverse, by Bill J. Leftwich, portrays a Pacific island battle scene.

	Mintage	MS-65	PF-65
(1993) 1991-1995P World War II			
Clad Half Dollar . . . .(290,343)	192,968	$35.	$37.

U.S. Mint Sculptor/Engraver Thomas D. Rogers, Sr. designed the silver dollar showing an American soldier on the beach at Normandy. The reverse depicts the shoulder sleeve insignia of Supreme Headquarters Allied Expeditionary Force, with a quotation from Dwight D. Eisenhower.

(1993) 1991-1995D World War II		
Silver Dollar 94,708	$28.	
(1993) Same Type W Mint Proof . . . .(322,422)		$40.

Both Proof and uncirculated versions of the $5 gold coin were struck at the West Point mint. The obverse, designed by Charles J. Madsen, depicts an American serviceman with rifle raised in victory. The reverse, by Edward Southworth Fisher, features a "V" for victory in the center with Morse code for the letter superimposed.

(1993) 1991-1995W World War II			
Gold $5.00 . . . .(65,461)	23,089	$200.	$180.

The 1994 World Cup Tournament was the culmination of soccer games among 141 nations. The United States was selected to host the XV FIFA World Cup play-off, and three commemorative coins were issued to celebrate the event. Each of the coins employs a shared design on the reverse.

The obverse of the clad half dollar depicts a soccer player in action. It was designed by Richard T. LaRoche. The reverse, designed by Dean McMullen, features the official World Cup USA 1994 logo flanked by laurel branches.

	Mintage	MS-65	PF-65
1994D World Cup Tournament Clad Half Dollar 52,836		$10.	
1994P Same Type P Mint Proof . . . .(122,412)			$10.

The obverse of the silver dollar coin features two competing players converging on a soccer ball. It was designed by Dean McMullen who also executed the reverse design, the official logo which is used on all of the World Cup coins.

	Mintage	MS-65	PF-65
1994D World Cup Tournament Silver Dollar 81,698		$28.	
1994S Same Type S Mint Proof . . . .(576,978)			$32.

Both Proof and uncirculated versions of the $5.00 gold coin were struck at the West Point mint. The obverse, designed by William J. Krawczewicz, depicts the modernistic gold World Cup Trophy. The reverse was designed by Dean McMullen and shows the same logo used on other World Cup coins.

	Mintage	MS-65	PF-65
1994W World Cup Tournament			
Gold $5.00 . . . .(89,619) 22,464		$180.	$160.

THOMAS JEFFERSON
250th Anniversary Birth of Thomas Jefferson

	Mintage	MS-65	PF-65
1993 (1994) P Thomas Jefferson Silver Dollar 266,927		$26.	
1993 (1994) S Same Type S Mint Proof . . . .(332,891)			$32.

VIETNAM VETERANS MEMORIAL
10th Anniversary of Vietnam Veterans Memorial in Washington, D.C.

1994W Vietnam Veterans Memorial Silver Dollar 57,317	$90.	
1994P Same Type P Mint Proof . . . .(226,262)		$100.

U.S. POWs
Tribute to American Prisoners of War

1994W U.S. POW Silver Dollar 54,790	$90.	
1994P Same Type P Mint Proof . . . .(220,100)		$70.

MODERN COMMEMORATIVES
Women Veterans, U.S. Capitol , Civil War Battlefields

WOMEN VETERANS
All Women, Past and Present, Who Served in the Armed Forces

	Mintage	MS-65	PF-65
1994W Women Veterans Silver Dollar 53,054		$50.	
1994P Same Type P Mint Proof ....(213,201)			$40.

U.S. CAPITOL
The Bicentennial of the U.S. Capitol

1994D U.S. Capitol Silver Dollar 68,352		$24.	
1994S Same Type S Mint Proof ....(279,416)			$25.

CIVIL WAR BATTLEFIELDS
Preservation of Historic Battlefields

1995S Civil War Battlefield Preservation Clad Half Dollar ..119,510		$45.	
1995S Same Type S Mint Proof ....(330,099)			$45.

	Mintage	MS-65	PF-65
1995P Civil War Battlefield Preservation Silver Dollar	45,866	$70.	
1995S Same Type S Mint Proof	(55,246)		$85.

1995W Civil War Battlefield Preservation Gold $5.00	12,735	$500.	
1995W Same Type W Mint Proof	(55,246)		$375.

CENTENNIAL OLYMPIC GAMES
Atlanta, Georgia Olympic Games

1995S Olympic Games. Basketball Clad Half Dollar	171,001	$23.	
1995S Same Type S Mint Proof	(169,655)		$17.
1995S Olympic Games. Baseball Clad Half Dollar	164,605	23.	
1995S Same Type S Mint Proof	(118,087)		16.
1996S Olympic Games. Swimming Clad Half Dollar	49,533	140.	
1996S Same Type S Mint Proof	(114,315)		40.
1996S Olympic Games. Soccer Clad Half Dollar	52,836	85.	
1996S Same Type S Mint Proof	(122,412)		100.

	Mintage	MS-65	PF-65
1995D Olympic Games. Gymnastics Silver Dollar	42,497	$85.	
1995P Same Type P Mint Proof	(182,676)		$40.
1995D Olympic Games. Paralympics Silver Dollar	28,649	95.	
1995P Same Type P Mint Proof	(138,337)		40.
1995D Olympic Games. Track and Field Silver Dollar	24,796	90.	
1995P Same Type P Mint Proof	(136,935)		40.
1995D Olympic Games. Cycling Silver Dollar	19,662	135.	
1995P Same Type P Mint Proof	(118,795)		37.
1996D Olympic Games. Tennis Silver Dollar	15,983	240.	
1996P Same Type P Mint Proof	(92,016)		85.
1996D Olympic Games. Paralympics Silver Dollar	14,497	325.	
1996P Same Type P Mint Proof	(84,280)		85.
1996D Olympic Games. Rowing Silver Dollar	16,258	275.	
1996P Same Type P Mint Proof	(151,890)		75.
1996D Olympic Games. High Jump Silver Dollar	15,697	315.	
1996P Same Type P Mint Proof	(124,502)		50.

	Mintage	MS-65	PF-65
1995W Olympic Games. Torch Runner Gold $5.00	14,675	$275.	
1995W Same Type W Mint Proof	(57,442)		$225.
1995W Olympic Games. Stadium Gold $5.00	10,579	365.	
1995W Same Type W Mint Proof	(43,124)		260.
1996W Olympic Games. Flag Bearer Gold $5.00	9,174	375.	
1996W Same Type W Mint Proof	(32,886)		300.
1996W Olympic Games. Cauldron Gold $5.00	9,210	400.	
1996W Same Type W Mint Proof	(38,555)		315.

SPECIAL OLYMPICS GAMES

	Mintage	MS-65	PF-65
1995W Shriver Silver Dollar	89,301	$24.	
1995P Same Type P Mint Proof	(351,764)		$21.

NATIONAL COMMUNITY SERVICE

1996S Community Service Silver Dollar	23,468	$250.	
1996S Same Type S Mint Proof	(100,787)		$95.

SMITHSONIAN INSTITUTION 150TH ANNIVERSARY

1996D Smithsonian Silver Dollar	30,593	$135.	
1996P Same Type P Mint Proof	(126,616)		$60.

	Mintage	MS-65	PF-65
1996W Smithsonian Gold $5.00 21,840		$350.	
1996W Same Type W Mint Proof . . . . (8,948)			$600.

BOTANIC GARDENS

	Mintage	MS-65	PF-65
1997P Botanic Gardens Silver Dollar 57,272		$45.	
1997P Same Type P Mint Proof . . . .(264,528)			$45.

JACKIE ROBINSON

	Mintage	MS-65	PF-65
1997S Jackie Robinson Silver Dollar 30,180		$70.	
1997S Same Type S Mint Proof . . . .(110,002)			$70.

	Mintage	MS-65	PF-65
1997W Jackie Robinson Gold $5.00 5,174		$2,000.	
1997W Same Type W Mint Proof . . . .(24,072)			$500.

FRANKLIN D. ROOSEVELT

	Mintage	MS-65	PF-65
1997W Franklin D. Roosevelt Gold $5.00 11,805		$300.	
1997W Same Type W Mint Proof . . . .(29,233)			$290.

NATIONAL LAW ENFORCEMENT
OFFICERS MEMORIAL

1997P Law Enforcement Silver Dollar 28,575		$170.	
1997P Same Type P Mint Proof . . . .(110,428)			$150.

ROBERT F. KENNEDY

1998S Robert F. Kennedy Silver Dollar 106,422		$33.	
1998S Same Type S Mint Proof . . . .(99,020)			$43.

BLACK REVOLUTIONARY WAR PATRIOTS

	Mintage	MS-65	PF-65
1998S Black Patriots Silver Dollar	.37,210	$120.	
1998S Same Type S Mint Proof	(75,070)		$110.

DOLLEY MADISON COMMEMORATIVE

1999P Dolley Madison Silver Dollar	.89,100	$45.	
1999P Same Type P Mint Proof	(224,400)		$50.

GEORGE WASHINGTON COMMEMORATIVE GOLD

1999W George Washington Gold $5.00	.22,511	$290.	
1999W Same Type W Mint Proof	(41,693)		$290.

YELLOWSTONE NATIONAL PARK

	Mintage	MS-65	PF-65
1999P Yellowstone Silver Dollar	62,000	$52.	
1999P Same Type P Mint Proof	(144,900)		$52.

LIBRARY OF CONGRESS BICENTENNIAL

2000P Library of Congress Silver Dollar	$40.	
2000P Same Type P Mint Proof		$42.
2000W Library of Congress bimetallic $10.00 Gold & Platinum	1,250.	
2000W Same Type W Mint Proof		600.

LEIF ERICSON MILLENNIUM

2000P Leif Ericson Silver Dollar	28,100	$85.
2000P Same Type P Mint Proof	(142,900)	$60.

MODERN COMMEMORATIVES
AMERICAN BUFFALO COMMEMORATIVE

	Mintage	MS-65	PF-65
2001D Buffalo / Indian Silver Dollar 227,131		$135.	
2001P Same Type P Mint Proof ....(272,869)			$135.

CAPITOL VISITOR CENTER

2001P Visitor Center, clad Half Dollar ....99,157 $14.
2001P Same Type P Mint Proof ....(77,962) $18.

2001P Visitor Center Silver Dollar ....35,380 $42.
2001P Same Type P Mint Proof ....(143,793) $44.

2001W Visitor Center $5.00 ....6,761 $650.
2001W Same Type W Mint Proof ....(27,652) $310.

MODERN COMMEMORATIVES
SALT LAKE OLYMPIC GAMES

	Mintage	MS-65	PF-65
2002P Salt Lake Olympic Silver Dollar 35,287		$38.00	
2002P Same Type P Mint Proof . . . .(142,813)			$38.00

2002W Salt Lake Olympic $5.00 5,727		315.00	
2002W Same Type W Mint Proof . . . .(8,882)			280.00

WEST POINT BICENTENNIAL

2002W West Point Bicentennial Silver Dollar 101,236		$36.00	
2002W Same Type W Mint Proof . . . .(282,743)			$38.00

FIRST FLIGHT CENTENNIAL

2003P First Flight Clad Half-Dollar		$10.75	
2003P Same Type P Mint Proof			$13.50
2003P First Flight Silver Dollar		33.00	
2003P Same Type P Mint Proof			37.00
2003W First Flight $10.00		365.00	
2003W Same Type W Mint Proof			375.00

THOMAS A. EDISON

2004P Thomas A. Edison Silver Dollar		$33.00	
2004P Same Type P Mint Proof			$37.00

Date	Price
1983 and 1984 Proof dollars	$24.
1983 and 1984 6 coin set. One 1983 and one 1984 uncirculated and Proof dollar.	
One Uncirculated & one Proof gold $10.00*.	600.
1983 Collector set. 1983 PDS uncirculated dollars.	35.
1984 Collector set. 1984 PDS uncirculated dollars.	50.
1983 and 1984 gold and silver uncirculated set. One 1983 and one 1984	
uncirculated dollar and one 1984 uncirculated gold $10.00.	290.
1983 and 1984 gold and silver Proof set. One 1983 and one 1984 Proof dollar	
and one 1984 Proof $10.00*.	290.

1986 STATUE OF LIBERTY

1986 2 coin set: Proof silver dollar and clad half dollar.	23.
1986 3 coin set: Proof silver dollar, clad half dollar and gold $5.00.	160.
1986 2 coin set: uncirculated silver dollar and clad half dollar.	23.
1986 3 coin set: uncirculated silver dollar, clad half dollar and gold $5.00.	160.
1986 6 coin set: 1 each of Proof and uncirculated.*	335.

1987 CONSTITUTION

1987 2 coin set: uncirculated silver dollar and gold $5.00.	150.
1987 2 coin set: Proof silver dollar and gold $5.00.	150.
1987 4 coin set: 1 each of Proof and uncirculated.*	300.

1988 OLYMPIAD

1988 2 coin set: uncirculated silver dollar and gold $5.00.	150.
1988 2 coin set: Proof silver dollar and gold $5.00.	150.
1988 4 coin set: 1 each of Proof and uncirculated.*	300.

1989 CONGRESS

1989 2 coin set: Proof silver dollar and clad half dollar.	24.
1989 3 coin set: Proof silver dollar, clad half dollar and gold $5.00.	160.
1989 2 coin set: uncirculated silver dollar and clad half dollar.	24.
1989 3 coin set: uncirculated silver dollar, clad half dollar and gold $5.00.	175.
1989 6 coin set: 1 each of Proof and uncirculated.*	336.

*Packaged in cherrywood box.

GOVERNMENT COMMEMORATIVE SETS

1991 MOUNT RUSHMORE

Date	Price
1991 2 coin set: uncirculated half dollar and dollar.	$50.
1991 2 coin set: Proof half dollar and silver dollar.	58.
1991 3 coin set: uncirculated half dollar, silver dollar and gold $5.00.	225.
1991 3 coin set: Proof half dollar, silver dollar and gold $5.00.	200.
1991 6 coin set: 1 each of Proof and uncirculated.*	450.

1992 XXV OLYMPIAD

1992 2 coin set: uncirculated half dollar and dollar.	30.
1992 2 coin set: Proof half dollar and dollar	34.
1992 3 coin set: uncirculated half dollar, dollar and gold $5.00	200.
1992 3 coin set: Proof half dollar, dollar and gold $5.00	180.
1992 6 coin set: 1 each of Proof and uncirculated.*	360.

1992 COLUMBUS

1992 2 coin set: uncirculated half dollar and dollar.	36.
1992 2 coin set: Proof half dollar and silver dollar.	50.
1992 3 coin set: uncirculated half dollar, silver dollar and gold $5.00.	250.
1992 3 coin set: Proof half dollar, silver dollar and gold $5.00.	215.
1992 6 coin set: 1 each of Proof and uncirculated.*	450.

1993 BILL OF RIGHTS

1993 2 coin set: uncirculated half dollar and dollar.	32.
1993 2 coin set: Proof half dollar and silver dollar.	34.
1993 3 coin set: uncirculated half dollar, silver dollar and gold $5.00.	245.
1993 3 coin set: Proof half dollar, silver dollar and gold $5.00.	210.
1993 6 coin set: 1 each of Proof and uncirculated.*	450.
1993 "Young Collector" set: silver half dollar.	18.
1993 "Educational" set: silver half dollar and Madison medal.	13.

1993 THOMAS JEFFERSON

1993 3 piece set: Jefferson dollar, 1994 nickel and $2.00 note (issued in 1994)	85.

1993 WORLD WAR II

1993 2 coin set: uncirculated half dollar and dollar.	56.
1993 2 coin set: Proof half dollar and silver dollar.	60.
1993 3 coin set: uncirculated half dollar, silver dollar and gold $5.00.	250.
1993 3 coin set: Proof half dollar, silver dollar and gold $5.00.	250.
1993 6 coin set: 1 each of Proof and uncirculated.*	500.
1993 "Young Collector" set: clad half dollar.	18.
1993 "Victory" set: silver half dollar, French franc.	18.

1994 WORLD CUP SOCCER

1994 2 coin set: uncirculated half dollar and dollar.	35.
1994 2 coin set: Proof half dollar and silver dollar.	38.
1994 3 coin set: uncirculated half dollar, silver dollar and gold $5.00.	224.
1994 3 coin set: Proof half dollar, silver dollar and gold $5.00.	190.
1994 6 coin set: 1 each of Proof and uncirculated.*	400.
1994 "Young Collector" set: uncirculated clad half dollar.	12.
1994 "Special Edition" set: Proof clad half dollar and silver dollar.	26.

1994 U.S. VETERANS

1994 3 coin set: Uncirculated POW, Vietnam and Women dollar	225.
1994 3 coin set: Proof POW, Vietnam and Women dollar	200.

Packaged in cherrywood box.

1995 SPECIAL OLYMPICS

Date	Price
1995 2 coin set: Proof Schriver dollar, 1995-S Kennedy .50¢	$100.

1995 CIVIL WAR BATTLEFIELD PRESERVATION

1995 2 coin set: uncirculated half dollar and dollar ....90.
1995 2 coin set: Proof half dollar and silver dollar ....110.
1995 3 coin set: uncirculated half dollar, dollar and gold $5.00 ....600.
1995 3 coin set: Proof half dollar, dollar and gold $5.00 ....475.
1995 6 coin set: 1 each of Proof and uncirculated.* ....1,000.
1995 "Young Collector" set: uncirculated half dollar ....25.
1995 2 coin "Union Set": half dollar and dollar ....60.
1995 3 coin "Union Set": half dollar, dollar and gold $5.00 ....350.

1995-96 CENTENNIAL OLYMPIC GAMES

1995 4 coin set #1: uncirculated .50¢ Basketball,
   $1.00 Gymnast, $1.00 Paralympics, $5.00 Torch ....550.
1995 4 coin set #2: Proof .50¢ Basketball, $1.00 Gymnast,
   $1.00 Paralympics, $5.00 Torch ....335.
1995 2 coin set #1: Proof $1.00 Gymnast, $1.00 Paralympics ....75.
1995 "Young Collector" set: uncirculated Basketball half dollar ....18.
1995-96 16 coin set: 1 each all uncirculated coins.* ....1,400.
1995-96 16 coin set: 1 each all Proof coins.* ....1,450.
1995-96 32 coin set: 1 each all uncirculated and Proof coins.* ....5,000.

1996 NATIONAL COMMUNITY SERVICE

1996 Proof silver dollar and Saint-Gaudens stamp ....100.

1996 SMITHSONIAN INSTITUTION 150TH ANNIVERSARY

1996 2 coin set: Proof dollar and gold $5.00 ....400.
1996 4 coin set: 1 each of Proof and uncirculated. * ....1,000.
1996 "Young Collector" set: Proof silver dollar ....60.

1997 BOTANIC GARDENS

1997 Dollar, Jefferson nickel and $1.00 note .... 245.

1997 JACKIE ROBINSON

1997 2 coin set: Proof dollar and $5.00 gold ....500.
1997 4 coin set: 1 each of Proof and uncirculated ....2,500.
1997 3 piece legacy set: Baseball card, pin and $5.00 gold ....500.

1997 NATIONAL LAW ENFORCEMENT OFFICERS MEMORIAL

1997 Insignia set: dollar, lapel pin and patch ....10.

1998 ROBERT F. KENNEDY

1998 2 coin set: RFK dollar and JFK silver half dollar ....385.
1998 2 coin set: RFK dollar, Proof and uncirculated ....75.

1998 BLACK REVOLUTIONARY WAR PATRIOTS

1998 2 coin set: uncirculated and Proof dollar ....210.
1998 "Young Collector" set: uncirculated dollar ....120.
1998 Coin and 4 stamps set ....120.

Packaged in cherrywood box.

GOVERNMENT COMMEMORATIVE SETS

1999 DOLLEY MADISON COMMEMORATIVE

Date   **Price**

1999 2 coin set: Proof and uncirculated dollars . . . .$100.

1999 GEORGE WASHINGTON

1999 2 coin set: 1 each Proof and uncirculated $5.00 gold . . . . .600.

1999 YELLOWSTONE NATIONAL PARK

1999 2 coin set: 1 each Proof and uncirculated dollars . . . .   100.

2000 LEIF ERICSON MILLENNIUM

2000 2 coin set: Proof $1.00 and Islandic 1,000 kronur . . . . .100.

2001 AMERICAN BUFFALO

2001 2 coin set: Proof and uncirculated dollars . . . . .270.
2001 coinage and currency set . . . . .160.

2001 CAPITOL VISITOR CENTER

2001 3 coin Proof set . . . . .350.

2002 SALT LAKE OLYMPIC GAMES

2002 2 coin Proof set . . . . .320.
2002 4 coin Proof and uncirculated set . . . . .675.

BIBLIOGRAPHY

Bowers, Q. David. *Commemorative Coins of the United States: a Complete Encyclopedia.* Wolfeboro, N.H., 1991.
Bullowa, David M. *The Commemorative Coinage of the United States 1892-1938.* New York, 1938.
Mosher, Stuart. *The Commemorative Coinage of the United States 1892-1938.* New York, 1940.
Slabaugh, Arlie. *United States Commemorative Coinage.* Racine, 1975.
Swiatek, Anthony and Breen, Walter. *The Encyclopedia of United States Silver and Gold Commemorative Coins 1892-1954.* New York, 1981.
Taxay, Don. *An Illustrated History of U.S. Commemorative Coinage.* New York, 1967.

PRIVATE OR TERRITORIAL GOLD COINS

The words "private gold," used with reference to coins struck outside of the United States Mint, is a general term. In the sense that no state or territory had authority to coin money, private gold simply refers to those interesting necessity pieces of various shapes, denominations and degrees of intrinsic worth that were circulated in isolated areas of our country by individuals, assayers, bankers, etc. Some will use the words "territorial" and "state" to cover certain issues because they were coined and circulated in a territory or state. While the state of California properly sanctioned the ingots stamped by F. D. Kohler as state assayer, in no instance were any of the gold pieces struck by authority of any of the territorial governments.

The stamped $50 and other gold coins, sometimes called "ingots," but in coin form, were made by Augustus Humbert, the United States Assayer of Gold, but were not receivable at face value for government payments, despite the fact that Humbert was an officual agent. However, such pieces circulated widely in commerce.

Private coins were circulated in most instances because of a shortage of regular coinage. In the western states particularly, money became so scarce that the very commodity that the pioneers had come so far to acquire was converted into a local medium of exchange.

Ephraim Brasher's New York doubloon of 1787 is also a private American gold issue and is described on page 50.

BIBLIOGRAPHY

Adams, Edgar H. *Private Gold Coinage of California 1849-1855.* Brooklyn, N.Y., 1913.
Adams, Edgar H. *Official Premium Lists of Private and Territorial Gold Coins.* Brooklyn, N.Y., 1909.
Bowers, Q. David. *The History of United States Coinage as Illustrated by the Garrett Collection.* Los Angeles, Cal., 1979.
Bowers, Q. David. *A California Gold Rush History Featuring Treasure from the S.S. Central America.* Wolfeboro, NH, 2001.
Breen, Walter and Gillio, Ronald. *California Pioneer Fractional Gold.* Santa Barbara, Cal., 1983.
Clifford, Henry H. *Pioneer Gold Coinage in the West- 1848-1861.* Reprint from "The Westerners Brand Book- Book Nine." Los Angeles Corral, 1961.
Doering, David. *California Fractional Gold.* Seal Beach, Cal., 1982.
Griffin, Clarence. *The Bechtlers and Bechtler Coinage and Gold Mining in North Carolina 1814-1830.* Spindale, N.C., 1929.
Kagin Donald H. *Private Gold Coins and Patterns of the United States.* New York, 1981.
Lee, Kenneth W. *California Gold — Dollars, Half Dollars, Quarter Dollars.* Santa Ana, Cal., 1979.
Owens, Dan. *California Coiners and Assayers.* Wolfeboro, NH; and New York City, 2000.
Seymour, Dexter C. *The 1830 Coinage of Templeton Reid.* American Numismatic Society Museum Notes No. 22. New York, 1977.

TEMPLETON REID
Georgia 1830

The first private gold coinage under the Constitution was struck by Templeton Reid, a jeweler and gunsmith, in Milledgeville, Georgia in July, 1830. To be closer to the mines, he moved to Gainesville where most of his coins were made. Although weights were accurate, Reid's assays were not and his coins were slightly short of claimed value. Accordingly, he was severely attacked in the newspapers and soon lost the public's confidence. He closed his mint before the end of October, 1830 and his output amounted only to about 1,600 coins. Denominations struck were $2.50, $5.00 and $10.00.

1830 $2.50	V.Fine	$45,000.
1830 $5.00	V.Fine	135,000

1830 TEN DOLLARS . . . .**V.Good** $150,000.
(No Date) TEN DOLLARS . . . .**V.Good** 110,000.

TEMPLETON REID
"California Gold 1849"

The enigmatic later issues of Templeton Reid were probably made from California gold. Reid, who never went to California, was then a cotton gin maker in Columbus, Georgia, where he died in 1851. The coins were in denominations of ten and twenty-five dollars. Struck copies of both exist in various metals.

The only specimen known of the $25.00 piece was stolen from the Cabinet of the U.S. Mint on August 16, 1858. It was never recovered.

1849 TEN DOLLAR CALIFORNIA GOLD (Smithsonian Collection) . . . . *(Unique)*
1849 TWENTY-FIVE DOLLARS CALIFORNIA GOLD . . . . *(Unknown)*

THE BECHTLERS
Rutherford County, N. C. 1830-1852

A skilled German metallurgist, Christopher Bechtler, assisted by his son August, and nephew, Christopher, Jr., operated a private mint in Rutherford, North Carolina. Rutherford County, along with other areas in the Piedmont region of North Carolina and Georgia, were the principal sources of the nation's gold supply from 1790 until the California gold strikes in 1848.

The coins minted by the Bechtlers were only three denominations, but they covered a wide variety of weights and sizes. Rotated dies are common throughout the series. In 1831, the Bechtlers produced the first gold dollar in the United States. The United States Mint struck its first circulating gold dollar in 1849. Bechtler coins were well accepted by the public and circulated widely in the Southeast.

The inscription "August 1, 1834" on several varieties of $5.00 pieces has a special significance. The Secretary of the Treasury recommended to the Mint Director that gold coins of the reduced weight bear the authorization date. This was not done on federal gold coinage, but Christopher Bechtler evidently acted on the recommendation to avoid difficulty with Treasury authorities.

	VF-20	EF-40	AU-50	UNC
ONE DOLLAR N. CAROLINA, 30 gr.. . . . .$1,800.	$3,100.	$4,800.	$12,000.
ONE DOLLAR N. CAROLINA, 28 gr,. centered, no star . . .3,000.	4,000.	7,750.	15,000.
ONE DOLLAR N. CAROLINA, 28 gr. high, no star . . . . . . .6,750.	9,500.	15,000.	24,000.

ONE DOLLAR CAROLINA, 28 gr. N reversed . . . . .1,500.	2,300.	3,400.	6,250.
$2.50 CAROLINA, 67 gr. 21 carats . . . . .4,700.	8,500.	10,000.	18,000.

$2.50 CAROLINA, 70 gr. 20 carats . . . . .4,750.	8,500.	10,000.	18,500.
$2.50 GEORGIA, 64 gr. 22 carats . . . . .4,750.	8,750.	10,500.	19,000.
$2.50 GEORGIA, 64 gr. 22 carats — even 22 . . . . .6,250.	9,500.	12,500.	27,500.

$2.50 NORTH CAROLINA, 75 gr. 20 carats.

RUTHERFORD in a circle. Border of lg. beads . . . . . .11,000.	16,000.	24,000.	37,500.
$2.50 NORTH CAROLINA, without 75 G . . . . .11,000.	15,500.	23,000.	36,500.

$2.50 NORTH CAROLINA, without 75 G,
  CAROLINA above 250 instead of gold . . . .   *(Unique)*

$2.50 NORTH CAROLINA, 20 carats on obv.
  75 gr. on rev. Border finely serrated . . . .   —   —   —

5 DOLLARS NORTH CAROLINA, 150 gr. 20 carats . . . . . .9,000.	13,500.	22,500.	42,500.
5 DOLLARS. Same as last variety without 150 G.	—	—	

THE BECHTLERS

	VF-20	EF-40	AU-50	UNC
5 DOLLARS CAROLINA, RUTHERFORD, 140 G 20 carats. AUGUST 1, 1834.				
Plain edge ....$5,000.	$7,500.	$10,000.	$20,000.	
Reeded edge ....9,000.	15,000.	27,500.	35,000.	
5 DOLLARS BECHTLER without star and C.	—			
5 DOLLARS CAROLINA,134 gr. 21 carats, with star .....4,750.	7,250.	9,000.	16,500.	
5 DOLLARS CAROLINA,134 gr. 21 carats, no star, ...	—	—		

(Obverse of A. Bechtler as shown below)

5 DOLLARS GEORGIA, RUTHERFORD,				
128 gr. 22 carats ....5,500.	7,750.	11,000.	2,100.	
Similar. Colon before 22 and after 128 G	—	—		
....				
5 DOLLARS GEORGIA, RUTHERFORD				
128 gr. 22 carats ....5,500.	7,750.	11,000.	21,000.	
5 DOLLARS CAROLINA, RUTHERFORD				
140 gr. 20 carats. AUGUST 1, 1834 ....5,250.	7,500.	10,000.	20,000.	
Similar. 20 distant from carats ....6,500.	10,000.	15,000.	22,000.	

AUGUST BECHTLER

	VF-20	EF-40	AU-50	UNC
1 DOLLAR CAROLINA, 27 gr. 21 carats ....$1,100.	$1,650.	$2,500.	$4,250.
5 DOLLARS CAROLINA, 134 gr. 21 carats ....5,000.	6,500.	9,500.	22,500.

	VF-20	EF-40	AU-50	UNC
5 DOLLARS CAROLINA, 128 gr. 22 carats	$9,000.	$12,000.	$17,000.	$27,000.
5 DOLLARS CAROLINA, 141 gr. 20 carats	7,500.	11,000.	15,000.	26,000.

(Restrikes in "Proof" using original dies were made about 1920.)

NORRIS, GREGG & NORRIS
San Francisco 1849

Collectors consider this piece the first of the California private gold coins. A newspaper account dated May 31, 1849, described a five-dollar gold coin, struck at Benicia City, though with the imprint San Francisco. It mentioned the private stamp of Norris, Gregg and Norris. The initials N. G. and N. were not identified until 1902 when the coins of Augustus Humbert were sold.

	F-12	VF-20	EF-40	AU-50	UNC
1849 HALF EAGLE — Plain edge	$3,500.	$5,250.	$8,500.	$12,000.	$24,000.
1849 HALF EAGLE — Reeded edge	3,500.	5,250.	8,500.	12,000.	24,000.
1850 HALF EAGLE with STOCKTON beneath date					(Unique)

MOFFAT & CO.
San Francisco 1849-1853

The firm of Moffat and Company was perhaps the most important of the California private coiner. The assay office they conducted was semi-official in character. The successors to this firm, Curtis, Perry and Ward, later established the United States Branch mint of San Francisco.

In June or July, 1849, Moffat & Co. began to issue small rectangular pieces of gold owing to lack of coin in the locality, in values from $9.43 to $264. The $9.43, $14.25 and $16.00 varieties are the only types known today.

The unique specimens of the $9.43 and $14.25 ingots are in the National Coin Collection in the Smithsonian.

$9.43 Ingot *(Unique)* .... —
$14.25 Ingot *(Unique)* .... —
$16.00 Ingot .... $35,000.

The dies for the $10.00 piece were cut by a Bavarian, Albert Kuner. The words MOFFAT & CO. appear on the coronet of Liberty instead of the word LIBERTY as in regular United States issues.

	F-12	VF-20	EF-40	AU-50	UNC
1849 FIVE DOL. (All varieties)	$1,200.	$1,800.	$3,200.	$5,200.	$11,500.
1850 FIVE DOL (All varieties)	1,200.	1,900.	3,300.	5,500.	12,500.
1849 TEN DOL.	2,600.	3,700.	8,200.	14,000.	25,000.
1849 TEN D	2,600.	3,900.	9,000.	16,000.	30,000.

United States Assay Office
AUGUSTUS HUMBERT
U. S. Assayer 1851

Augustus Humbert, a New York watchcase maker, was appointed United States Assayer, and he placed his name and the government stamp on the ingots of gold issued by Moffat & Co. The assay office, a provisional government mint, was a temporary expedient to accommodate the Californians until the establishment of a permanent branch mint.

The fifty-dollar gold piece was accepted as legal tender on a par with standard U.S. gold coins and was known variously as a slug, quintuple eagle or five-eagle piece. It was officially termed an ingot.

LETTERED EDGE VARIETIES

	F-12	VF-20	EF-40	AU-50	UNC
1851 50 D C 880 THOUS., no 50 on reverse. Sunk in edge: AUGUSTUS HUMBERT UNITED STATES ASSAYER OF GOLD CALIFORNIA 1851	$9,000.	$13,500.	$20,000.	$29,000.	$45,000.

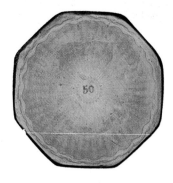

	F-12	VF-20	EF-40	AU-50	UNC
1851 50 D C Similar to last variety, but 50 on reverse	$11,000.	$18,500.	$27,500.	$42,000.	$57,000.
1851 Similar to last variety, but 887 THOUS	10,000.	16,000.	24,000.	36,000.	52,500.
1851 50 D C 887 THOUS., no 50 on reverse	—	—	—	—	—

REEDED EDGE VARIETIES

 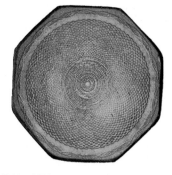

	F-12	VF-20	EF-40	AU-50	UNC
1851 FIFTY DOLLS 880 THOUS. "Target" reverse	$7,000.	$9,500.	$15,000.	$23,000.	$40,000.
1851 FIFTY DOLLS 887 THOUS. "Target" reverse	7,000.	9,500.	15,000.	23,000.	40,000.
1852 FIFTY DOLLS 887 THOUS.	7,000.	9,500.	16,000.	24,000.	42,000.

A unique Proof specimen of the 1851 with 887 THOUS. was sold at the Garrett II auction in 1980 for $500,000.

The withdrawal of the discredited private coins of $5.00, $10.00 and $20.00 denominations as a result of the new U.S. Assay operations caused a new turn of affairs for Californians. Fractional currency coins of almost every nation were pressed into service by the Californians, but the supply was too small to help to any extent. Moffat & Co. proceeded in January 1852 to issue a new ten-dollar piece bearing the stamp MOFFAT & CO.

		Close Date	**Wide Date**				
			F-12	**VF-20**	**EF-40**	**AU-50**	**UNC**
1852 TEN D. MOFFAT & CO. (Close Date)	. . . .	$2,750.	$4,400.	$8,500.	$20,000.	$45,000.
1852 TEN D. MOFFAT & CO. (Wide Date)	. . . .	2,750.	4,400.	8,500.	20,000.	45,000.

		F-12	**VF-20**	**EF-40**	**AU-50**	**UNC**
1852 TEN DOLS. 1852, 2 over 1	. . . .	1,800.	3,200.	5,750.	9,500.	$18,000.
1852 TEN DOLS.	. . . .	1,600.	2,500.	4,250.	7,500.	$15,000.

| | | **F-12** | **VF-20** | **EF-40** | **AU-50** | **UNC** |
| 1852 TWENTY DOLS. 1852, 2 over 1 | . . . . | 4,000. | 6,750. | 12,000. | 23,000. | 55,000. |

The firm of Moffat & Co. was dissolved in 1852 and a newly reorganized company known as the United States Assay Office of Gold, took over the contract. Principals were Curtis, Perry and Ward.

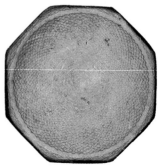

	F-12	VF-20	EF-40	AU-50	UNC
1852 FIFTY DOLLS. 887 THOUS.	$7,000.	$9,500.	$15,000.	$23,000.	$40,000.
1852 FIFTY DOLLS. 900 THOUS.	7,000.	1,000.	16,000.	24,000.	42,000.

1852 TEN DOLS 884 THOUS.	1,400.	2,200.	3,500.	6,500.	14,000.

1853 TEN D. 884 THOUS.	5,000.	9,000.	17,500.	25,000.	55,000.
1853 TEN D. 900 THOUS.	3,200.	4,750.	7,750.	12,000.	18,000.

	F-12	VF-20	EF-40	AU-50	UNC
1853 TWENTY D. 884 THOUS.	$6,000.	$10,000.	$15,000.	$22,500.	$35,000.

1853 TWENTY D. 900 THOUS.	1,600.	2,200.	3,800.	5,750.	10,500.

U. S. ASSAY — MOFFAT

The last Moffat issue was a 1853 twenty dollar piece that is very similar to the U.S. double eagle of that period. It was struck after the retirement of John L. Moffat from the Assay Office.

	F-12	VF-20	EF-40	AU-50	UNC
1853 TWENTY D.	$3,000.	$4,000.	$6,000.	$9,000.	$20,000.

J. H. BOWIE

Joseph H. Bowie joined his cousins in San Francisco in 1849 and possibly produced a limited coinage of gold pieces. A trial piece of the dollar denomination is known in copper, but may never have reached the coinage stage. Little is known about the company or reason for issuing these pieces.

J. H. BOWIE

1849 1 DOLLAR (copper). . . . . —
1849 5 DOLLARS. . . . . —

CINCINNATI MINING & TRADING CO.

The origin and location of this company are unknown.

	EF-40	UNC
1849 FIVE DOLLARS	*(Unique)*	
1849 TEN DOLLARS	$275,000.	—

(Beware of spurious specimens cast in base metal with word TRACING in place of TRADING.)

— MASSACHUSETTS AND CALIFORNIA COMPANY —
San Francisco 1849

This company was believed to have been organized in Northampton, Mass. in May, 1849.

	F-12	EF-40
1849 FIVE D.	$75,000.	$150,000.

MINERS' BANK
San Francisco 1849

The institution of Wright & Co., exchange brokers located in Portsmouth Square, San Francisco, was known as the Miners' Bank.

A ten dollar piece was issued in the autumn of 1849, but the coins were not readily accepted because they were worth less than face value. The firm was dissolved on January 14, 1850. Unlike most California issues, the gold in these coins was alloyed with copper.

Plain border   **Crimped border**

	VF-20	EF-40	AU-50	UNC
(1849) TEN. D, plain border.	$10,000.	$17,000.	$25,000.	$50,000.
(1849) TEN. D., crimped border	11,000.	19,000.	27,000.	54,000.

J. S. ORMSBY
Sacramento 1849

The initials J. S. O., which appear on certain issues of California privately coined gold pieces, represent the firm of J. S. Ormsby & Co. They struck both five and ten dollar denominations, all undated.

VF-20

(1849) 5 DOLLS. Plain edge *(Possibly Unique)*	—
(1849) 5 DOLLS. Reeded edge *(Unique-Smithsonian Collection)*	—
(1849) 10 DOLLS. *(4 known)*	$170,000.

PACIFIC COMPANY
San Francisco 1849

The origin of the Pacific Co. is very uncertain. All data regarding the firm is based on conjecture.

Edgar H. Adams wrote that he believed that the coins bearing the stamp of the Pacific Company were produced by the coining firm of Broderick and Kohler. The coins were probably handstruck, with the aid of a sledgehammer.

1849 1 DOLLAR *(Unique)* ...... *(2 known)*
1849 5 DOLLARS
   E. Fine .... $200,000.

1849 10 DOLLARS
   A. Unc. .... $250,000.

F. D. KOHLER
California State Assayer 1850

The State Assay Office was authorized April 12, 1850. Governor Burnett appointed F. D. Kohler that year, who thereupon sold his assaying business to Baldwin & Co. He served at both the San Francisco and Sacramento Offices. The State Assay Offices were discontinued at the time the U. S. Assay Office was established Feb. 1, 1851.

Ingots issued ranged from $36.55 to $150.00 An Ex. F. specimen sold in the Garrett Sale, 1980 for $200,000.

$36.55 Sacramento	—
$37.31 San Francisco	—
$40.07 San Francisco	—
$45.34 San Francisco	—
$50.00 San Francisco	—
$54.09 San Francisco	—

Note: A $40.07 ingot was stolen from the Mint Cabinet in 1858 and never recovered.

DUBOSQ & COMPANY
San Francisco 1850

Theodore Dubosq, a Philadelphia jeweler, took melting and coining machinery to San Francisco in 1849.

	VF-40
1850 FIVE D.	$70,000.
1850 TEN D.	.75,000.

BALDWIN & COMPANY
San Francisco 1850

George C. Baldwin and Thomas S. Holman were in the jewelry business in San Francisco and were known as Baldwin & Co. They were the successors to F. D. Kohler & Co., taking over its machinery and other equipment in May, 1850.

	F-12	VF-20	EF-40	AU-50	UNC
1850 FIVE DOLLAR	$4,500.	$8,000.	$16,000.	$20,000.	$29,000.
1850 TEN DOLLARS — Horseman type	.22,500.	42,000.	57,500.	85,000.	125,000.

1851 TEN D.	.7,000.	13,500.	25,000.	37,500.	75,000.

BALDWIN & COMPANY

The Baldwin & Co. $20.00 piece was the first of that denomination issued in California. Baldwin coins were believed to have contained about 2 percent copper alloy.

	EF-40	UNC
1851 TWENTY D.	$150,000.	—

SHULTZ & COMPANY
San Francisco 1851

The firm located in back of Baldwin's establishment operated a brass foundry beginning in 1851. Judge G. W. Shultz and William T. Garratt were partners in the enterprise.

	F-12	VF-20	EF-40	AU-50
1851 FIVE D	$18,500.	$38,000.	$48,000.	$65,000.

DUNBAR & COMPANY
San Francisco 1851

Edward E. Dunbar operated the California Bank in San Francisco. Dunbar later returned to New York and organized the famous Continental Bank Note Co.

	EF-40
1851 FIVE D	$140,000.

WASS, MOLITOR & COMPANY
San Francisco 1852-1855

The gold smelting and assaying plant of Wass, Molitor & Co. was operated by two Hungarian patriots, Count S. C. Wass and A. P. Molitor. They maintained an excellent laboratory and complete apparatus for analysis and coinage of gold.

The company struck five, ten, twenty and fifty dollar coins. In 1852 they produced a ten dollar piece similar in design to the five dollar denomination. The difference is in the reverse legend which reads: S.M.V. (Standard Mint Value) CALIFORNIA GOLD TEN D.

No pieces were coined in 1853 or 1854, but they brought out the twenty dollar and fifty dollar pieces in 1855. A considerable number of the fifty dollar coins were made. There was a ten dollar piece issued in 1855 also, with the Liberty head and small close date.

Large Head, Pointed Bust

	F-12	VF-20	EF-40	AU-50	UNC
1852 FIVE DOLLARS. Small Head with rounded bust	$2,800.	$5,750.	$12,000.	$17,000.	$37,500.
1852 FIVE DOLLARS. Large Head with pointed bust	2,750.	5,500.	10,500.	15,500.	33,000.

Large Head　　　　　**Small Head**

Small Date　　　　　**1855**

1852 TEN D. Large Head	2,000.	3,250.	5,500.	10,000.	16,000.
1852 TEN D. Small Head	4,750.	6,250.	14,000.	20,000.	40,000.
1852 TEN D. Small Closed Date	8,000.	15,000.	28,000.	60,000.	
1855 TEN D.	10,000.	16,000.	22,000.	30,000.	55,000.

	Large Head		**Small Head**		
	F-12	VF-20	EF-40	AU-50	UNC
1855 TWENTY DOLLAR Large Head	—	—	$15,000.	—	—
1855 TWENTY DOLLAR Small Head	$9,000.	$18,000.	28,000.	$45,000.	$75,000.

1855 50 DOLLARS	17,500.	23,000.	33,000.	55,000.	130,000.

KELLOGG & COMPANY
San Francisco 1854-1855

John G. Kellogg went to San Francisco October 12, 1849, from Auburn, New York. At first he was employed by Moffat and Company, and remained with that organization when control passed to Curtis, Perry and Ward. When the United States Assay Office was discontinued December 14, 1853, Mr. Kellogg became associated with G. F. Richter, who had been an assayer in the government assay office. These two set up business as Kellogg & Richter December 19, 1853.

When the U. S. Assay Office ceased operations a period ensued during which no private firm was striking gold. The new San Francisco branch mint did not produce coins for some months after Curtis & Perry took the contract for the government (Ward having died). The lack of coin was again keenly felt by businessmen who petitioned Kellogg & Richter to "supply the vacuum" by issuing private coin. Their plea was soon answered, for on February 9, 1854, Kellogg & Co. placed their first twenty-dollar piece in circulation.

The firm dissolved late in 1854 and reorganized as Kellogg & Humbert. The latter partner was Augustus Humbert, for some time identified as U.S. Assayer of Gold in California. Regardless of the fact that the branch mint was then producing coins, Kellogg & Humbert issued $20.00 coins in 1855 in a quantity greater than before.

	F-12	VF-20	EF-40	AU-50	UNC
1854 TWENTY D. . . . .$1,750.		$2,500.	$4,300.	$5,750.	$14,000.

The 1855 twenty-dollar piece is similar to that dated 1854. The letters on the reverse side are larger and the arrows longer on one 1854 variety. There are several die varieties of both issues.

1855 TWENTY D. . . . . .1,750.		2,500.	4,500.	6,250.	16,000.

In 1855 Ferdinand Grüner cut the dies for a round format $50.00 gold coin for Kellogg & Co., but coinage seems to have been limited to presentation pieces. Only 10 to 12 pieces are known to exist. A "commemorative restrike" was made in 2001 using transfer dies made from the original and gold recovered from the S.S. Central America. These pieces have the inscription S. S. CENTRAL AMERICA GOLD, C.H.S. on the reverse ribbon.

	Proof
1855 FIFTY DOLLS.	$200,000.

OREGON EXCHANGE COMPANY
Oregon City, 1849
THE BEAVER COINS OF OREGON

Upon the discovery of gold in California there was a great exodus of settlers who joined in the hunt for the precious metal. Soon returning gold seekers offered their gold dust, which became the accepted medium of exchange. As in other western areas of that time, the uncertain qualities of the gold and weighing devices tended to irk the tradespeople, and petitions were made to the legislature for a standard gold coin issue.

On February 16, 1849, the legislature passed an act providing for a mint and specified five- and ten-dollar gold coins without alloy. Oregon City, the largest city in the territory with a population of about 1,000, was designated as the location for the mint. At the time this act was passed, Oregon had been brought into the United States as a territory by act of Congress. When the new governor arrived March second, he declared the coinage act unconstitutional.

The public-spirited people, however, continued to work for a convenient medium of exchange and soon took matters into their own hands by starting a private mint. Eight men of affairs whose names were Kilborne, Magruder, Taylor, Abernethy, Willson, Rector, Campbell and Smith set up the Oregon Exchange Company.

The coins struck were of virgin gold as specified in the original act. Ten-dollar dies were made later, and were of finer design and workmanship.

		F-12	VF-20	EF-40	AU-50	UNC
1849 5 D	(6,000 minted)	$14,000.	$24,000.	$36,000.	$55,000.	—

1849 TEN D	(2,850 minted)	32,000.	57,500.	85,000.	125,000.	—

MORMON GOLD PIECES
Salt Lake City, Utah 1849-1860

The first name given to the organized Mormon Territory was the "State of Deseret," the last word meaning "honey bee." The beehive, which is shown on the reverse of the five-dollar 1860 piece, was a favorite device of the followers of Joseph Smith and Brigham Young. The clasped hands appear on most Mormon coins and exemplify strength in unity. "Holiness to the Lord" was an inscription frequently used.

MORMON GOLD PIECES

Brigham Young was the instigator of the coinage system and personally supervised the mint which was housed in a little adobe building in Salt Lake City. The mint was inaugurated late in 1849 as a public convenience.

	F-12	VF-20	EF-40	AU-50	UNC
1849 TWO AND HALF DOLLARS	$7,500.	$11,500.	$17,500.	$26,000.	$42,500.
1849 FIVE DOLLARS	5,750.	10,000.	14,000.	20,000.	35,000.

	F-12	VF-20	EF-40
1849 TEN DOLLARS	$120,000.	$150,000.	$180,000.

	F-12	VF-20	EF-40
1849 TWENTY DOLLARS	$40,000.	$65,000.	$95,000.

The Mormon twenty-dollar piece was the first of that denomination to be coined in this country.

1850 FIVE DOLLARS

Fine	$6,000.
V. Fine	10,500.
Ex. Fine	15,000.
A. Unc.	22,000.
Unc.	40,000.

MORMON GOLD PIECES

1860 5D

Fine	$10,000.
V. Fine	20,000.
Ex. Fine	27,500.
A. Unc.	35,000.
Unc.	45,000.

COLORADO GOLD PIECES
Clark, Gruber & Co. — Denver 1860-1861

Clark, Gruber and Co. was a well-known private minting firm in Denver, Colorado, in the early sixties.

	F-12	VF-20	EF-40	AU-50	UNC
1860 2½ D	$1,300.	$1,900.	$3,250.	$4,400.	$11,000.
1860 5D	1,600.	2,400.	3,600.	4,750.	12,000.

1860 TEN D	5,000.	7,000.	11,500.	16,000.	27,000.
1860 TWENTY D	29,000.	45,000.	75,000.	110,000.	—

The $2.50 and five-dollar pieces of 1861 follow closely the designs of the 1860 issues. The main difference is found in the legends. The reverse side now has CLARK GRUBER & CO. DENVER. PIKES PEAK is on the coronet of Liberty.

1861 2½ D	1,300.	1,900.	3,500.	6,000.	12,500.
1861 FIVE D	1,600.	2,500.	3,900.	6,500.	22,500.
1861 TEN D	1,650.	2,600.	4,000.	7,250.	18,000.

COLORADO GOLD PIECES

	F-12	VF-20	EF-40	AU-50	UNC
1861 TWENTY D	$6,250.	$11,500.	$25,000.	$40,000.	$95,000.

JOHN PARSONS & COMPANY
Tarryall Mines — Colorado 1861

Very little is known regarding the mint of John Parsons and Co., although it is reasonably certain that it operated in the South Park section of Park County Colorado near the original town of Tarryall, in the summer of 1861.

PIKES PEAK GOLD

	VF-20
(1861) Undated 2 ½ D	$125,000.
(1861) Undated FIVE D	150,000.

J. J. CONWAY & COMPANY
Georgia Gulch, Colorado, 1861

Records show that the Conway Mint operated for a short while in 1861. As in all gold mining areas the value of gold dust caused disagreement among the merchants and the miners. The firm of J. J. Conway & Co. solved this difficulty by bringing out its gold pieces in August 1861.

	VF-20
(1861) Undated 2 ½ DOLL'S	$75,000.
(1861) Undated FIVE DOLLARS	125,000.

(1861) Undated
   TEN DOLLARS . . . .—

CALIFORNIA SMALL DENOMINATION GOLD

There was a scarcity of small coins during the California gold rush and starting in 1852, quarter, half and dollar pieces were privately minted from native gold to alleviate the shortage. The need and acceptability of these pieces declined after 1856 and they then became popular as souvenirs. Private coinage became illegal with passage of the Act of 1864, but production continued until 1882 before the law was enforced.

The designs of the early issues were similar to those of the larger territorials. Later issues showed greater variety, had lower intrinsic value, and were often struck from highly polished dies giving Prooflike surfaces. In contrast to the tokens, which lack the denomination and were often back dated, California small denomination gold was mostly made in the year indicated (1852-1882). Authentic pieces have CENTS, DOLLAR, or an abbreviation thereof on the reverse.

Many thousand pieces still exist; of these nearly 500 different varieties have been identified, many of them very rare. Although some of the early pieces are machine made with reeded edges, most are hand struck and have crude designs and incomplete features. Many bear the maker's initials: D, DN, GL, DERIB, N, NR, L, H, G, GG, FD, or DERI. Major types are listed below; values are for the commonest varieties of each type. The tokens are generally much less valuable. Modern restrikes and replicas (which often have a bear in the design) have no numismatic value.

Values are only for genuine coins with the denomination on the reverse
expressed as: CENTS, DOL, DOLL., or DOLLAR.

QUARTER DOLLAR — OCTAGONAL

	EF-40	AU-50	MS-60
Large Liberty Head:			
Value and date in wreath	$135.	$210.	$300.
Value and date in beaded circle	140.	235.	350.
Value and CAL in wreath	125.	165.	250.
Small Liberty Head:			
Value and date in wreath	125.	165.	250.
Value and date in beaded circle	130.	175.	260.
Value in shield, date in wreath	130.	175.	275.
Value and CAL in wreath	130.	185.	350.
Large Indian Head:			
Value in wreath	180.	250.	375.
Value and CAL in wreath	145.	220.	350.
Small Indian Head:			
Value in wreath	175.	235.	425.
Value and CAL in wreath	400.	500.	750.
Washington Head 1872:			
Value and CAL in wreath	425.	650.	1,000.

CALIFORNIA SMALL DENOMINATION GOLD
QUARTER DOLLAR — ROUND

	EF-40	AU-50	MS-60
Large Liberty Head:			
Value and date in wreath	$135.	$220.	$300.
Value and CAL in wreath	125.	180.	275.
25 CENTS in wreath		*Rare*	
Small Liberty Head:			
Value and date in wreath	135.	220.	325.
Value in shield, date in wreath	135.	240.	425.
Value and CAL in wreath	135.	220.	275.
Large Indian Head:			
Value in wreath	300.	425.	650.
Value and CAL in wreath	250.	350.	525.
Small Indian Head:			
Value in wreath	135.	225.	400.
Value and CAL in wreath	275.	400.	650.
Washington Head 1872:			
Value and CAL in wreath	475.	700.	1,000.

HALF DOLLAR — OCTAGONAL

Large Liberty Head:			
Value and date in wreath	175.	275.	450.
Value and date in beaded circle	115.	160.	300.
Value and CAL in wreath	160.	300.	450.
Legend surrounds wreath	300.	475.	700.
Small Liberty Head:			
Value and date in wreath	145.	250.	425.
Value and CAL in wreath	125.	230.	335.
Small eagle with rays	800.	1,050.	1,800.
Large eagle with raised wings	800.	1,050.	1,800.
Large Indian Head:			
Value in wreath	160.	300.	450.
Value and CAL in wreath	140.	275.	425.
Small Indian Head:			
Value in wreath	185.	325.	500.
Value and CAL in wreath	350.	4,750.	650.

HALF DOLLAR — ROUND

Liberty Head:			
Value and date in wreath	135.	200.	335.
Value and CAL in wreath	150.	250.	400.
CALIFORNIA GOLD around wreath	160.	250.	425.
Eagle with shield			
Large Indian Head:			
Value in wreath	145.	220.	360.
Value and CAL in wreath	125.	200.	300.
Small Indian Head:			
Value in wreath	160.	250.	400.
Value and CAL in wreath	140.	220.	335.
Arms of California 1853			

DOLLAR — OCTAGONAL

Liberty Head:			
Value and date in wreath	325.	475.	800.
Value in beaded circle	350.	500.	850.
Legend around wreath	350.	550.	1,000.
Large eagle	1,550.	2,400.	3,750.
Large Indian Head:			
Value and date in wreath	450.	750.	1,250.
Value in wreath	500.	800.	1,400.
Small Indian Head:			
Value and CAL in wreath	500.	800.	1,400.

DOLLAR — ROUND

	EF-40	AU-50	MS-60
Liberty Head:			
Value and date in wreath	$1,100.	$1,500.	$2,600.
Date beneath head	1,600.	2,200.	3,500.
Indian Head:			
Date beneath head	1,350.	1,900.	3,300.

=== CALIFORNIA GOLD INGOT BARS ===

During the Gold Rush era, gold coins, ingots, and "dust" were sent by steamship from San Francisco to other ports, most importantly to New York City and London, where the gold was sold or, in some instances, sent to mints for conversion into coins. The typical procedure in the mid-1850s was to send the gold by steamship from San Francisco to Panama, where it was sent across 48 miles of land on the Panama Railroad, then loaded aboard another ship at the town of Aspinwall on the Atlantic side. On September 12, 1857, the *S.S. Central America,* en route from Aspinwall to New York City with over 475 passengers, over 100 crew members, and an estimated $1.6 million in gold (in an era in which pure gold was valued at $20.67 per ounce) was lost at sea. Miraculously, over 150 people, including all but one of the women and children, were rescued by passing ships. The *S.S. Central America* went to the bottom of the Atlantic Ocean off the Carolina coast.

In the 1980s a group of researchers in Ohio formed the Columbus-America Discovery Group and secured financing to search for the long-lost ship. After much study and many explorations, the wreck of the *S.S. Central America* was discovered 7,200 feet below the surface. Tommy Thompson, Bob Evans, and others from C-ADG used the robotic *Nemo,* a sophisticated device weighing several tons, to photograph the wreck and to carefully bring to the surface many artifacts. A king's ransom in gold ingots was found along with over 7,500 coins, the last mostly consisting of Mint State 1857-S double eagles.

The over 500 gold ingots furnished a unique opportunity to study specimens that, after conservation, were essentially in the same condition as they were in 1857. These bore the imprints of five different California assayers who operated seven offices. With few exceptions, each ingot bears individual stamps indicating its maker, a serial number, the weight in ounces, the fineness (expressed in thousandths, such as 784 indicating 784/1000th pure gold), and the 1857 value in dollars. The smallest bar found was issued by Blake & Co., weighed 4.95 ounces, was 795 fine, and was stamped with a value of $81.34. The largest ingot, dubbed the "Eureka" bar, bore the imprint of Kellogg & Humbert, and was stamped with a weight of 933.94 ounces, 903 fine, and a value of $17,433.57.

Blake & Co., Sacramento, California: From December 28, 1855, to May 1858, Blake & Co. was operated by Gorham Blake and W.R. Waters. • 34 ingots recovered. Serial numbers in the 5,100 and 5,200 series. Lowest weight and value: 4.95 ounces, $81.34. Highest weight and value: 157.40 ounces, $2,655.05. These bars have beveled or "dressed" edges and may have seen limited use in California commerce.

Harris, Marchand & Co., Sacramento and Marysville: Founded in Sacramento in 1855 by Harvey Harris and Desiré Marchand, with Charles L. Farrington as the "& Co." The Marysville office was opened in January 1856. Serial numbers in the 6,000 series are attributed to Sacramento, comprising 36 bars, and a single bar in the 7,000 series (7095) is attributed to Marysville. The Marchand bars each have a circular coin-style counterstamp on the face. Lowest weight and value (Sacramento): 9.87 ounces, $158.53. Highest weight and value (Sacramento): 295.20 ounces, $5,351.73. • Unique Marysville bar: 174.04 ounces, $3,389.06.

Henry Hentsch, San Francisco: Henstch, a Swiss, was an entrepreneur involved in banking, real estate, assaying, and other ventures. In February 1856, he opened an assay office as an annex to his bank. It is likely that many of his ingots were exported to Europe, where he had extensive banking connections. • 33 ingots recovered. Lowest weight and value: 12.52 ounces, $251.82. Highest weight and value: 238.84 ounces, $4,458.35.

Justh & Hunter, San Francisco and Marysville: Emanuel Justh, a Hungarian, was a lithographer in San Francisco in the early 1850s. In 1854-5 he worked as assistant assayer at the San Francisco Mint. Solomon Hillen Hunter came to California from Baltimore. The Justh & Hunter partnership was announced in May 1855. • Although study is continuing, the 60 ingots in the 4,000 series are tentatively attributed to San Francisco, and the 26 ingots in the 9,000 series are attributed to Marysville. • Lowest weight and value (San Francisco): 5.24 ounces, $92.18. Highest weight and value (San Francisco): 866.19 ounces, $15,971.93. • Lowest weight and value (Marysville): 19.34 ounces, $356.21. Highest weight and value (Marysville): 464.65 ounces, $8,759.90.

Kellogg & Humbert, San Francisco: John Glover Kellogg and Augustus Humbert, two of the most famous names in the minting of California gold coins, formed the partnership of Kellogg & Humbert in spring 1855. The firm was one of the most active of all California assayers during the mid-1850s. • 346 ingots recovered, constituting the majority of those found. • Lowest weight and value: 5.71 ounces, $101.03. Highest weight and value: 933.94 ounces, $17,433.57.

A selection of gold ingots from the S.S. *Central America* treasure (with an 1857-S $20 double eagle shown for scale, near lower left). • 1: In background: Harris, Marchand & Co., Marysville office, serial number 7095, 174.04 ounces, 942 fine, $3,389.06 (all values as stamped in 1857) • 2: Standing, back left: Henry Hentsch, San Francisco, serial number 3120, 61.93 ounces, 886 fine, $1,134.26 • 3: Next to preceding, vertical: Kellogg & Humbert, San Francisco, serial number 215, 944 fine, $1,045.96 • Next to preceding, small and near center: Blake & Co., Sacramento, 19.30 ounces, 946 fine, $297.42 • In front of preceding: Another Blake & Co. ingot, rectangular "Twix Bar" shape, serial number 5216, 915 fine, $266.12 • To right of both Blake ingots: Justh & Hunter, Marysville office, serial number 9440, 41.79 ounces, $761.07 • Far right: Justh & Hunter, San Francisco office, serial number 4243, 51.98 ounces, 916 fine, $984.27 • Lower right foreground: Harris, Marchand & Co., Sacramento office, serial number 6514, 35.33 ounces, 807 fine, $589.38 • Lower right, near $20: Harris, Marchand & Co., Sacramento office, serial number 6486, 12.64 ounces, 950 fine, $245.00.

CIVIL WAR TOKENS — 1861-1864

Civil War Tokens are generally divided into two groups: tradesmen's tokens, and anonymously issued pieces with political or patriotic themes. They came into existence only because of the scarcity of government coins and disappeared as soon as the bronze coins of 1864 met the public demand for small copper change.

From the outset of the Civil War, government cents were insufficient in number, widely hoarded and worth a premium over all other currencies. As a result of this scarcity of cent pieces, private copper coins were issued by many individuals. Their wide circulation was made possible by the scarcity of copper-nickel cents and the public dislike of fractional paper money.

The tradesmen's tokens were issued by various firms to provide change and advertise the dealers' wares. They usually bore an implied or an explicit promise of redemption in goods or money. The second type was simply unauthorized substitutes for government coins, produced at a profit by private manufacturers and put into general circulation through various agencies.

These tokens are of great variety in composition and design. A number were more or less faithful imitations of the copper-nickel cent. A few of this type have the word "NOT" in very small letters above the words "ONE CENT."

Many pieces, especially of the tradesmen token type, were individual in device and size, representing any caprice of design or slogan that appealed to the maker. Some were political or patriotic in character, carrying the likeness of some military leader such as McClellan or bearing such inscriptions as "Millions for contractors, not one cent for the widows." An estimated 50,000,000 or more of these pieces were issued. Approximately 10,000 different varieties have been recorded.

The legal status of the Civil War Tokens was uncertain. Mint Director Pollock thought they were illegal; however, there was no law prohibiting the issue of tradesmen's tokens or of private coins not in imitation of United States coins. A law was passed April 22, 1864 prohibiting the issue of any one or two-cent coins, tokens, or devices for use as money, and on June 8 another law was passed which abolished private coinage of every kind.

Values shown are for the most common tokens in each category. Uncirculated pieces are valued much higher.

	F-12	VF-20	EF-40	UNC
Copper or Brass Tokens	$10.	$12.	$16.	$38.
Nickel or German Silver Tokens	30.	45.	65.	115.
White Metal Tokens	32.	50.	70.	125.
Copper-Nickel Tokens	43.	60.	85.	150.
Silver Tokens	100.	170.	225.	450.

BIBLIOGRAPHY

Fuld, George and Melvin. *U.S. Civil War Store Cards.* Lawrence, MA, 1975.

CONFEDERATE STATES OF AMERICA
CONFEDERATE 1861 HALF DOLLAR

The half dollar struck by the Confederacy was unknown to collectors until 1879. A specimen of the coin and the Confederate die were found in the possession of Dr. B. F. Taylor of New Orleans. Mr. E. Mason, Jr. of Philadelphia purchased Dr. Taylor's specimen and the reverse die and later sold them to J. W. Scott and Company of New York.

CONFEDERATE STATES OF AMERICA
1861

Five hundred genuine 1861 half dollars from the New Orleans mint were acquired by J. W. Scott and Company. The reverses were smoothed off and then restamped with the Confederate die. These are known as restrikes, and usually have slightly flattened obverses.

According to records only four originals were struck. These were made on a hand press. Original silver half dollar planchets were used, as well as the original obverse die. One of the coins was given to the Secretary of the Confederacy Memminger who passed it on to President Jefferson Davis for his approval. Another was given to Prof. J. L. Riddell of the University of Louisiana. Dr. E. Ames of New Orleans received a third specimen, the last being kept by Chief Coiner B. F. Taylor, who sold it later as mentioned above.

Lack of bullion prevented the Confederate government from proceeding with any coinage plans that might have been made.

J. W. Scott struck some tokens in white metal using the Confederate reverse die and a special die bearing the inscription:

4 ORIGINALS STRUCK BY ORDER OF C. S. A. IN NEW ORLEANS 1861
******* REV. SAME AS U.S. (FROM ORIGINAL DIE SCOTT)

	Confederate Reverse		Scott Obverse	
	Mintage	VF-20	EF-40	UNC
1861 HALF DOL. *(Ex. Rare)* Stacks Auction 2003 $632,500.	4	—	—	—
1861 HALF DOL. Restrike	500	$4,700.	5,500.	$7,500.
1861 Scott Token obverse. Confederate reverse	500	1,750.	2,200.	3,200.

THE CONFEDERATE CENT

An order to make cents for the Confederacy was placed with Mr. Robert Lovett Jr., an engraver and die-sinker of Philadelphia, through a jewelry firm of that city. Fearing arrest by the United States government for giving assistance to the enemy, Mr. Lovett decided against delivering the coins to the Confederate government and hid the coins in his cellar.

The original dies were later purchased by Capt. John W. Haseltine who made restrikes from the dies. In 1960 the dies were copied and additional pieces made by Robert Bashlow. These show die cracks and rust marks that distinguish them from earlier copies. They have very little numismatic value.

1861 Cent original (copper-nickel)	**Unc.**	12	$34,000.
1861 Cent restrike (copper)	**Proof**	55	7,500.
1861 Cent restrike (gold)	**Proof**	7	28,000.
1861 Cent restrike (silver)	**Proof**	12	8,750.

LESHER REFERENDUM DOLLARS

Coined by Joseph Lesher of Victor, Colorado, in 1900 and 1901, these private tokens were used in trade to some extent, and stocked by various merchants who redeemed them in goods. Coins were numbered and a blank space left at bottom of 1901 issues, in which were stamped names of businessmen who bought them. All are quite rare; many varieties are extremely rare. Composition is .950 fine silver alloyed with copper.

	EF-40	AU-50	UNC
1900 First type, no business name	$1,750.	$2,400.	$4,000.
1900 A.B. Bumstead, with or without scrolls	1,050.	1,400.	2,400.
1900 Bank type	10,500.	13,500.	—
1901 Imprint type, no name	1,150.	1,750.	2,750.
1901 Imprint type, with name (as listed below)			
Boyd Park	1,300.	1,800.	2,850.
Slusher	1,550.	2,100.	3,100.
Mullen	2,600.	4,500.	6,500.
Cohen, Klein	4,000.	5,750.	—
Alexander	5,000.	7,000.	—
White	9,000.	12,000.	—
Goodspeeds, Nelson	9,000.	12,000.	—
A.W. Clark		27,400.	—

FEUCHTWANGER TOKENS

Dr. Lewis Feuchtwanger produced a metal that was really a variety of German silver consisting of nickel, copper and some zinc. He suggested as early as 1837 to Congress that his metal be substituted for copper, and made one-cent and three-cent trial pieces that circulated freely during the coin shortage of 1836-1844.

	F-12	EF-40	AU-50	UNC
1837 One Cent, Eagle	$80.	$200.	$300.	$450.
1837 Three-Cent, N.Y. Coat of Arms	300.	1,000.	1,800.	3,500.
1837 Three-Cent, Eagle	600.	2,250.	3,600.	6,250.
1864 Three-Cent, Eagle	500.	1,800.	3,250.	5,500.

We are indebted to the following contributors who initially helped bring the first Hard Times token special section together in the 1978 *Guide Book*: Edward Janis, Gil Steinberg, Joseph Levine, and Paul Koppenhaver. Larry Johnson revised the text and updated the valuations to reflect today's token prices.

"The issues commonly called Hard Times tokens mark a period of peculiar interest in the Numismatic history of the United States. They form a group by themselves as distinct as the Colonial Series so-called, or the State Issues which followed the Revolution. Unlike those, they had no semblance of authority behind them, and they combine, therefore, the character of Political pieces with the catch-words of party cries; of Satirical pieces with sarcastic allusions to the sentiments or speeches of the leaders of opposing parties; and in some degree also of Necessity pieces, in a time when, to use one of the phrases of the day, 'money was a cash article,' hard to get for daily needs; and though the dearth of a circulating medium, was not quite so great as it occasionally seems to have been over the border, when even buttons were made to do duty, not alone as is jestingly said, for the contribution-box, yet currency was difficult to obtain for the small change of petty expenses." This quotation is the introduction to Lyman Haynes Low's *Hard Times Tokens*, second edition reference published in 1906. Low's token numbering system of the 183 types of Hard Times token known to him has been expanded to nearly 500 different types identified in Russell Rulau's *Standard Catalog of United States Tokens*, 1700-1900.

Prior to Andrew Jackson's election as President of the United States in 1829, the Second Bank of the United States operated under a 20-year charter which granted it complete control over the currency system of the United States. Jackson disliked this bank not only for economic reasons, but also because of political considerations. In 1832 Jackson vetoed a bill rechartering the bank, preferring instead to order the transfer of government deposits to state banks, many of which were owned by political cronies.

This action unfortunately also took away some stability from an already shaky economy and created a growing climate of mistrust. Jackson's economic policies contributed to a nation-wide financial collapse. By 1837 hundreds of banks and large businesses had closed; the nation was gripped by a severe depression. Specie payments (disbursements in gold and silver) were suspended on May 10th, 1837, in an attempt to stop the outflow of scarce reserves. Even the small change needed for everyday necessities was hoarded, and large cent sized tokens quickly appeared as substitutes for coins to fill this compelling need, circulating freely at the value of one cent. The economic principle of Gresham's Law (bad money drives the good from circulation) was again proven to be reliable.

The primary attraction of Hard Times tokens is the wide variety of styles and themes used to reflect the passions of the day. Many are satirical pieces produced by Jackson's political enemies to lampoon the president's economic policies. Some voice anti-slavery sentiments. Legends on these pieces often made use of popular slogans, such as the most famous battle cry of the United States naval battle with Tripoli, MILLIONS FOR DEFENSE- NOT ONE CENT FOR TRIBUTE. Most are store cards used to promote various enterprises. It must be noted that a token could be produced for as little as a half cent each, which could result in a nice profit when used in place of a cent when making change. It is estimated that 10-20 million tokens were produced during this era. Many common varieties can be found in inexpensive lower grades at most coin shows, while some are quite rare and elusive. The collecting challenge is to find choice examples in any grade; outstanding examples in both color and strike will command large premiums. Many large coin collections also contain examples of Hard Times tokens because of their important role in our monetary history.

This special section is intended to be an introduction to the series, once described by Neil Carothers as "Quaint and curious relics of our currency history." Store card/political mules, as well as those pieces dedicated entirely to advertising, are omitted because of space limitations. Interested collectors are encouraged to obtain a reprint of Low's reference book as well as the new *Standard Catalog* to gain a better appreciation and understanding of this fascinating series.

	VF-20	EF-40	AU-50
L1, HT1. Andrew Jackson			
Copper.	$5,000.	$8,000.	—

	VF-20	EF-40	AU-50
L5, HT7. Jackson, small head			
Brass.	$400.	$700.	$900.

L3, HT5. Jackson President
   Brass. . . . . . . $250. $600. $700.

L57, HT76. Van Buren, facing left
   Brass. . . . . . $2,500. $3,500. $4,500.

L4, HT6. Jackson Pres. of U.S.
   Brass. . . . . $200. $400. $600.

L162, HT77. Van Buren, right
   Copper. . . . . . . $350. $500. $750.

	VF-20	EF-40	AU-50

L56, HT75. Van Buren, left
  Copper $90. $180. $400.

	VF-20	EF-40	AU-50

L7. HT15. Whig Victory
  Copper....... $2,000. $3,000. 3,500.

L13, HT26. William Seward
  Brass ....$200. $300. $450.
L14, HT27. Glory & Pride
  Brass ....$350. $550. $900.

L66. HT24. Agriculture
  Copper........ $175. $300. $500.

L16, HT30. Gulian Verplanck
  Brass.......... $150. $250. $400.

L54. HT81. Women & Sister
  Copper........ $100. $250. $400.

L6, HT14. Wings of New York
  Brass.......... $350. $550. $800.

L49.. HT73. Half Cent 1837
  Copper .... $85. $150. $275.

	VF-20	EF-40	AU-50
L55, HT63. Loco Foco 1838			
Copper	$40.	$75.	$200.

L37, HT61. Benton Mint Drop
Copper . . . . $25. $60. $175.

	VF-20	EF-40	AU-50
L8. HT9. My Victory/Jackson			
Copper	$20	$55.	$125.

L12, HT25. A Plain System
Copper . . . . $30. $75. $135.

L18, HT32. Executive Experiment
Copper . . . . $20. $40. $75.

L51, HT70. Roman Firmness
Copper . . . . $20. $40. $80.

	VF-20	EF-40	AU-50
L40, HT65. Head/May Tenth			
Copper. . . . . $20.		$75.	$120.
L47, HT66. Phoenix/May Tenth			
Copper. . . . . $20.		$40.	$75.

	VF	EF	AU
L21, HT35. Not One Cent. .			
Copper. . . . . $125.		$300.	$400.
L31, HT46. Not One Cent, Motto			
Copper. . . . . $20.		$40.	$75.

L45, HT56. Phoenix/Not One Cent
    Copper. . . . . $25. $50. $125.

L63, HT21. Ship/No Lighting
    Copper. . . . . $20. $85. $150.

	VF-20	EF-40	AU-50
L44, HT69. Ship/Jackson			
Copper. . . . . $20.		$50.	$100.

	VF-20	EF-40	AU-50
L60, HT18. Ship/Lighting. .			
Copper.	$20.	$50.	$100.

	VF-20	EF-40	AU-50
L59, HT17. Ship/Wreath Boarder			
Copper.	$20.	$50.	$100.

L58, HT16. Ship/Star Boarder			
Copper.	$20.	$45.	$90.

L65, HT23. Ship/Liberty Head			
Copper.	$75.	$150.	$210.

BIBLIOGRAPHY

Tutou, Russell. *Standard Catalog of the United States Tokens 1700-1900,* Iola , Wisconsin, 1997.

COINS AND TOKENS OF HAWAII

There are only five official coins that were issued by the Kingdom of Hawaii. These include the 1847 cent issued by King Kamehameha III and the 1883 silver dimes, quarters, halves and dollars of King Kalakaua I which bear his portrait. The 1883 eighth dollar is a pattern, while the 1881 five cent piece was an unofficial issue. After Hawaii became a U.S. Territory in 1900, the legal tender status of these coins was removed and most were withdrawn and melted. Owing to a lack of small change on the islands, the early tokens were widely accepted and circulated freely.

One Cent 1847   Ten Cents 1883

	Mintage	F-12	VF-20	EF-40	MS-60	MS-63	PF
1847 Cent	100,000	$250.	$325.	$500.	$900.	$2,000.	
1881 Five Cents		3,000.	4,000.	6,500.	10,000.	16,000.	—
1883 Ten Cents (26)	250,000	55.	90.	225.	1,000.	2,000.	8,000.
1883 Eighth Dollar (12 1/2 c) (20)							35,000.
1883 Quarter Dollar (26)	500,000	55.	75.	100.	200.	350.	9,000.
1883 Half Dollar (26)	700,000	90.	125.	225.	1,000.	2,000.	11,000.
1883 Dollar (26)	500,000	275.	375.	650.	3,750.	9,000.	15,000.

HAWAIIAN TOKENS

Thomas Hobron Token 1879   Haiku Plantation 1882

Wailuku Plantation 1871   Wailuku Plantation 1880

	F-12	VF-20	EF-40
Waterhouse Token 1860. Title of Kamehameha IV	$750.	$1,400.	$3,000.
Wailuku Plantation Token, 12 1/2 (cents) 1871	350.	600.	1,300.
Wailuku Plantation Token, 1 Real 1880	350.	600.	1,250.
Wailuku Plantation Token, Half Real 1871 and 1880	750.	1,300.	1,800.
Thomas Hobron Token, 12 1/2 (cents) 1879	275.	400.	700.
Haiku Plantation Token, One Real 1882	350.	500.	800.

	F-12	VF-20	EF-40	AU-50
Grove Ranch Plantation Token, 12 1/2 (cents) 1886	$650.	$800.	$1,400.	
Grove Ranch Plantation Token, 12 1/2 (cents) 1887	800.	1,250.	2,000.	
Kahului Railroad Token, 10 cents 1891	550.	900.	1,500.	2,500.
Kahului Railroad Token, 15 cents 1891	550.	900.	1,500.	2,500.
Kahului Railroad Token, 20 cent 1891	550.	900.	1,500.	2,500.
Kahului Railroad Token, 25 cents 1891	550.	900.	1,500.	2,500.
Kahului Railroad Token, 35 cents1891	550.	900.	1,500.	2,500.
Kahului Railroad Token, 75 cents 1891	550.	900.	1,500.	2,500.

ALASKA RURAL REHABILITATION CORPORATION
TOKENS OF 1935

These tokens were issued by the U. S. Government for the use of the colonists of the Matanuska Valley Colonization Project to supply them with much needed Federal aid. They were redeemable only at the ARRC stores. The "Bingles," as they were called, were in use only about six months during 1935-1936 after which they were redeemed for regular U. S. money and destroyed. They were issued on a basis of family dependents. Each token is the size of the corresponding U. S. coin with the exception of the one cent piece which is octagonal. The design is the same on both sides of each denomination.

Aluminum

	Mintage	EF-40	UNC		Mintage	EF-40	UNC
1c	5,000	$25.	$60.	25c	3,000	$35.	$70.
5c	5,000	25.	60.	50c	2,500	50.	110.
10c	10	25.	60.	$1.00	2,500	75.	170.

Brass

	Mintage	EF-40	UNC		Mintage	EF-40	UNC
$5.00	1,000	100.	210.	$10.00	1,000	150.	240.

UNITED STATES COINAGE FOR THE PHILIPPINES

The Philippine Islands were acquired by the United States in 1899 as part of a treaty with Spain ending the Spanish-American War of the previous year. A military government was replaced with a civil administration in 1901, and one of its first tasks was to sponsor a new coinage that was compatible with the old Spanish issues, yet was also legally exchangeable for American money at the rate of two Philippine pesos to the U.S. dollar.

The resulting coins were introduced in 1903 and bear the identities of both the Philippines (Filipinas in Spanish) and the United States of America. Following Spanish custom, the peso was divided into 100 centavos. A dollar-size coin valued at one peso was the principal issue in this series, but silver fractions were also minted in values of 50, 20 and 10 centavos. Minor coins included the copper-nickel five-cent piece, as well as one-centavo and half-centavo coins of bronze.

A rise in the price of silver forced the reduction of the fineness and weight for each silver denomination beginning in 1907, and subsequent issues are smaller in diameter. The smaller size of the new silver issues led to confusion between the silver 20-centavo piece and the copper-nickel five-centavo piece resulting in a mis-matching of dies for these two denominations in 1918 and again in 1928. A solution was found by reducing the diameter of the five-centavo piece beginning in 1930.

In 1935 the Commonwealth of the Philippines was established by an act of Congress, and a three-piece set of commemorative coins was issued the following year to mark this transition. Despite the popularity of United States commemoratives at that time, these sets sold poorly, and thousands remained within the Philippine Treasury at the onset of World War II. The commonwealth arms was adapted to all circulating issues beginning in 1937.

The advance on the Philippines by Japanese forces in 1942 prompted removal of much of the Treasury's bullion to the United States. More than 15 million pesos worth of silver remained, mostly in the form of one-peso pieces of 1907-1912 and the ill-fated 1936 commemoratives. These coins were hastily crated and dumped into Manila's Caballo Bay to prevent their capture. Partially recovered after the war, these coins were badly corroded from their exposure to salt water, adding further to the scarcity of high grade pre-war silver coins.

The Philippines became an independent republic on July 4, 1946, ending a historic and colorful chapter in U.S. history and numismatics.

═══ PHILIPPINES UNDER SOVEREIGNTY OF THE U.S. ═══
─── Bronze Coinage ───
Half Centavo

	Mintage	VF-20	EF-40	MS-60	MS-63
1903	12,084,000	$1.00	$2.25	$15.	$20.
1903 Proof	(2,558)			40.	60.
1904	5,654,000	1.25	3.00	20.	30.
1904 Proof	(1,355)			40.	75.
1905 Proof only	(471)		75.00	125.	200.
1906 Proof only	(500)		50.00	90.	150.
1908 Proof only	(500)		50.00	90.	150.

PHILIPPINES UNDER SOVEREIGNTY OF THE U.S.

Philippine coins dated from 1903 to 1919 were struck at the Philadelphia and San Francisco Mints. Those dated after 1920 were made in Manila. During World War II coins of 1944 and 1945 were made at Philadelphia, Denver and San Francisco.

Price Contributors to the Philippine Listings
Lyman Allen, Gary G. Allison, Raymond Czahor

Bronze Coinage

One Centavo

	Mintage	VF-20	EF-40	MS-60	MS-63
1903	10,790,000	$1.00	$2.50	$15.	$25.
1903 Proof	(2,558)			35.	60.
1904	17,040,400	1.00	3.00	18.	25.
1904 Proof	(1,355)			30.	70.
1905	10,000,000	1.50	3.00	25.	40.
1905 Proof	(471)		75.00	125.	200.
1906 Proof only	(500)		50.00	90.	150.
1908 Proof only	(500)		50.00	90.	150.
1908S	2,187,000	5.00	12.00	50.	75.
1909S	1,737,612	15.00	25.00	80.	125.
1910S	2,700,000	5.00	10.00	60.	100.
1911S	4,803,000	3.00	6.00	40.	95.
1912S	3,001,000	5.00	10.00	60.	110.
1913S	5,000,000	2.00	6.00	40.	50.
1914S	5,000,500	2.00	6.00	40.	50.
1915S	2,500,000	40.00	90.00	400.	600.
1916S	4,330,000	10.00	25.00	100.	150.
1917S	7,070,000	4.00	10.00	35.	65.
1918S	1,160,000	3.00	6.00	45.	80.
1918S Large S		125.00	250.00	900.	1,500.
1919S	454,000	2.00	6.00	45.	70.
1920S	2,500,000	12.00	20.00	180.	250.
1920	3,552,259	2.00	9.00	45.	80.
1921	7,282,673	2.00	7.00	45.	70.
1922	3,519,100	2.00	6.00	45.	60.
1925M	9,325,000	2.00	6.00	35.	50.
1926M	9,000,000	2.00	6.00	35.	50.
1927M	9,270,000	1.50	5.00	35.	45.
1928M	9,150,000	1.50	5.00	35.	40.
1929M	5,657,161	3.00	9.00	40.	60.
1930M	5,577,000	1.50	4.00	25.	50.
1931M	5,659,355	1.50	5.00	25.	40.
1932M	4,000,000	3.00	8.00	40.	60.
1933M	8,392,692	1.50	4.00	25.	40.
1934M	3,179,000	1.50	4.00	30.	45.
1936M	17,455,463	1.00	4.00	30.	40.

PHILIPPINES UNDER SOVEREIGNTY OF THE U.S.
Copper-Nickel Coinage

Large Size Five Centavos
1903-28

Reduced Size Five Centavos
1930-35

	Mintage	VF-20	EF-40	MS-60	MS-63
1903	8,910,000	$1.00	$3.	$20.	$30.
1903 Proof	(2,558)			35.	75.
1904	1,075,000	2.00	4.	25.	35.
1904 Proof	(1,075)			40.	100.
1905 Proof only	(471)		75.	125.	200.
1906 Proof only	(500)		60.	110.	175.
1908 Proof only	(500)		60.	110.	175.
1916S	300,000	50.00	75.	500.	750.
1917S	2,300,000	4.00	12.	100.	150.
1918S	2,780,000	3.00	10.	75.	150.
1918S Mule. Small date reverse of 20 Centavos		400.00	1,000.	3,000.	5,000.
1919S	1,220,000	6.00	15.	100.	175.
1920	1,421,078	8.00	15.	125.	175.
1921	2,131,529	6.00	13.	100.	190.
1925M	1,000,000	15.00	40.	125.	200.
1926M	1,200,000	7.00	15.	75.	125.
1927M	1,000,000	6.00	12.	50.	75.
1928M	1,000,000	6.00	12.	50.	75.
1930M	2,905,182	2.50	5.	45.	65.
1931M	3,476,790	2.50	5.	50.	75.
1932M	3,955,861	2.00	4.	40.	65.
1934M	2,153,729	3.00	8.	75.	110.
1935M	2,754,000	2.50	5.	65.	90.

Silver Coinage

Large Size Ten Centavos
1903-06

Reduced Size Ten Centavos
1907-35

1903	5,102,658	3.00	5.	30.	50.
1903 Proof	(2,558)			40.	80.
1903S	1,200,000	15.00	35.	250.	425.
1904	10,000	18.00	35.	100.	125.
1904 Proof	(1,355)			65.	120.
1904S	5,040,000	2.50	5.	35.	60.
1905 Proof only	(471)		85.	140.	225.
1906 Proof only	(500)		75.	120.	175.

PHILIPPINES UNDER SOVEREIGNTY OF THE U.S.

	Mintage	VF-20	EF-40	MS-60	MS-63
1907	1,500,781	$3.00	$5.00	$45.	$70.
1907S	4,930,000	2.25	3.50	35.	60.
1908 Proof only	(500)		60.00	90.	175.
1908S	3,363,911	2.00	5.00	45.	65.
1909S	312,199	30.00	60.00	300.	475.
1911S	1,000,505	3.00	8.00	50.	100.
1912S	1,010,000	4.00	9.00	75.	150.
1913S	1,360,693	4.00	9.00	60.	75.
1914S	1,180,000	5.00	10.00	125.	225.
1915S	450,000	15.00	40.00	250.	450.
1917S	5,991,148	2.00	3.00	35.	60.
1918S	8,420,000	1.50	2.50	25.	40.
1919S	1,630,000	2.00	4.00	45.	75.
1920	520,000	5.00	12.00	75.	140.
1921	3,863,038	1.50	2.50	21.	40.
1929M	1,000,000	1.50	2.50	20.	40.
1935M	1,280,000	1.50	2.50	20.	30.

Large Size Twenty Centavos 1903-06	Reduced Size Twenty Centavos 1907-29

	Mintage	VF-20	EF-40	MS-60	MS-63
1903	5,350,231	3.50	5.00	40.	75.
1903 Proof	(2,558)			65.	110.
1903S	150,080	20.00	60.00	300.	475.
1904	10,000	30.00	45.00	90.	150.
1904 Proof	(1,355)			90.	150.
1904S	2,060,000	4.00	7.00	60.	110.
1905 Proof only	(471)		110.00	200.	300.
1905S	420,000	12.00	20.00	150.	200.
1906 Proof only	(500)		100.00	150.	225.
1907	1,250,651	4.00	16.00	80.	125.
1907S	3,165,000	3.00	5.00	60.	75.
1908 Proof only	(500)		80.00	135.	225.
1908S	1,535,000	3.00	5.00	50.	75.
1909S	450,000	15.00	45.00	250.	500.
1910S	500,259	15.00	45.00	325.	550.
1911S	505,000	12.00	30.00	200.	300.
1912S	750,000	8.00	20.00	175.	250.
1913S	948,565	6.00	15.00	140.	200.
1914S	795,000	4.00	15.00	125.	200.
1915S	655,000	12.00	45.00	275.	450.
1916S	1,435,000	6.00	15.00	90.	150.
1917S	3,150,655	3.00	5.00	35.	60.
1918S	5,560,000	3.00	4.00	35.	50.
1919S	850,000	5.00	6.00	50.	80.
1920	1,045,415	5.00	10.00	100.	150.
1921	1,842,631	3.00	4.00	40.	65.
1928M Mule. Large date reverse of 5 Centavos	100,000	15.00	50.00	400.	700.
1929M	1,970,000	3.00	4.00	21.	50.

PHILIPPINES UNDER SOVEREIGNTY OF THE U.S.

Large Size Fifty Centavos **1903-06**

	Mintage	VF-20	EF-40	MS-60	MS-63
1903	3,099,061	$8.00	$14.	$60.	$110.
1903 Proof	(2,558)			75.	150.
1903S			*(rare)*		
1904	10,000	35.00	45.	100.	185.
1904 Proof	(1,355)			100.	180.
1904S	216,000	10.00	20.	100.	140.
1905 Proof only	(471)		125.	225.	375.
1905S	852,000	15.00	35.	250.	550.
1906 Proof only	(500)		125.	200.	350.

Reduced Size Fifty Centavos **1907-21**

1907	1,200,625	8.00	20.	90.	175.
1907S	2,112,000	5.00	12.	75.	125.
1908 Proof only	(500)			200.	350.
1908S	1,601,000	6.00	12.	120.	350.
1909S	528,000	10.00	30.	50.	325.
1917S	674,369	8.00	25.	120.	225.
1918S	2,202,000	4.50	8.	50.	100.
1919S	1,200,000	5.00	9.	85.	135.
1920	420,000	4.50	8.	35.	75.
1921	2,316,763	3.00	4.	25.	55.

Large Size One Peso **1903-06**

PHILIPPINES UNDER SOVEREIGNTY OF THE U.S.

	Mintage	VF-20	EF-40	MS-60	MS-63
1903	2,788,901	$18.00	$30.00	$150.00	$250.00
1903 Proof	(2,558)			175.00	300.00
1903S	11,361,000	16.00	20.00	120.00	180.00
1904	11,355	75.00	110.00	200.00	300.00
1904 Proof	(1,355)			200.00	350.00
1904S	6,600,000	16.00	25.00	125.00	200.00
1905 Proof only	(471)		250.00	400.00	800.00
1905S	6,056,000	20.00	45.00	200.00	400.00
1906 Proof only	(500)		250.00	400.00	600.00
1906S	201,000	1,200.00	2,500.00	6,500.00	11,000.00

Reduced Size One Peso
1907-12

1907S	10,278,000	5.00	10.00	75.00	110.00
1908 Proof only	(500)			400.00	500.00
1908S	20,954,944	5.00	10.00	60.00	100.00
1909S	7,578,000	6.00	12.00	65.00	110.00
1910S	3,153,559	8.00	25.00	125.00	225.00
1911S	463,000	20.00	40.00	600.00	1,000.00
1912S	680,000	20.00	800.00	600.00	1,250.00

═══ COMMONWEALTH ISSUES OF THE PHILIPPINES ═══
──────────── Bronze Coinage ────────────

One Centavo

1937M	15,790,492	1.00	2.00	10.00	16.00
1938M	10,000,000	0.75	2.00	8.00	12.00
1939M	6,500,000	1.00	2.00	10.00	20.00
1940M	4,000,000	0.75	1.50	8.00	12.00
1941M	5,000,000	1.00	2.00	10.00	25.00
1944S	58,000,000	0.10	0.25	1.00	1.50

COMMONWEALTH ISSUES OF THE PHILIPPINES

Copper-Nickel Coinage

Five Centavos

	Mintage	VF-20	EF-40	MS-60	MS-63
1937M	2,493,872	$3.50	$6.00	$35.	$50.00
1938M	*4,000,000*	1.00	2.50	20.	30.00
1941M	*2,750,000*	3.00	6.00	30.	50.00

Copper-Nickel-Zinc Alloy

1944	21,198,000	0.20	0.30	1.25	2.50
1944S	14,040,000	0.20	0.30	1.00	1.50
1945S	72,796,000	0.20	0.25	0.75	1.50

Silver Coinage

Ten Centavos

1937M	3,500,000	1.25	3.00	20.00	25.00
1938M	*3,750,000*	1.00	2.00	12.00	15.00
1941M	*2,500,000*	1.25	2.50	15.00	22.00
1944D	31,592,000	0.30	0.50	1.25	2.00
1945D	137,208,000	0.25	0.50	1.00	1.75

Twenty Centavos

1937M	2,665,000	2.00	3.00	20.00	35.00
1938M	*3,000,000*	1.50	2.00	9.00	15.00
1941M	*1,500,000*	2.00	2.75	11.00	20.00
1944D	28,596,000	0.50	0.75	1.75	3.00
1944D, D/S }	82,804,000	10.00	20.00	45.00	80.00
1945D		0.30	0.50	1.25	2.50

COMMONWEALTH ISSUES OF THE PHILIPPINES
Silver Coinage

Fifty Centavos

	Mintage	VF-20	EF-40	MS-60	MS-63
1944S	19,187,000	$1.00	$2.00	$4.50	$6.00
1945S	18,120,000	1.00	2.00	4.50	6.00

PHILIPPINE COMMEMORATIVE ISSUES
Establishment of the Commonwealth

Silver Fifty Centavos

1936M	20,000	27.00	45.00	70.00	85.00

Silver Pesos

Bust of Murphy and Quezon

1936M	10,000	50.00	65.00	140.00	175.00

Bust of Roosevelt and Quezon

	Mintage	VF-20	EF-40	MS-60	MS-63
1936M	10,000	$50.	$65.	$140.	$175.

BIBLIOGRAPHY
Allen, Lyman L., *U.S. Philippine Coins,* Lyman Allen Numismatic Services, Oakland Park, FL, 1998.
Shafer, Neil, *United States Territorial Coinage for The Philippine Islands,* Whitman Publishing
Company, 1961.

CHECKING YOUR COINS FOR AUTHENTICITY

Coin collectors occasionally encounter counterfeit coins, or coins that have been altered or changed so that they appear to be something other than what they really are. Any coin that does not seem to fit the description of similar pieces listed in this catalog should be looked upon with suspicion. Experienced coin dealers can usually tell quickly if a coin is genuine or not, and would never knowingly sell spurious coins to a collector. Coins found in circulation or bought from a non-professional source should be examined carefully.

The risk of purchasing a spurious coin can be minimized through the use of common sense and an elementary knowledge of the techniques used by counterfeiters. It is well to keep in mind that the more popular a coin is among collectors and the public, the more likely it is that counterfeits and replicas will abound. Generally, collector coins valued at under $100 are rarely replicated because of the high cost of making such items. The same is true of counterfeits that are made to deceive the public. In modern times few counterfeit coins have been made because it is more profitable for the fakers to print paper money.

REPLICAS: Reproductions of famous and historical coins have been distributed for decades by marketing firms and souvenir vendors. These pieces are often tucked away by the original recipients as curios, and later are found in old furniture by others who believe they have discovered objects of great value. Most replicas are poorly made by the casting method, and are virtually worthless. They can sometimes be identified by a seam that runs around the edge of the piece where the two halves of the casting mold were joined together. Genuine specimens of extremely rare or valuable coins are almost never found in unlikely places.

COUNTERFEITS: For many centuries counterfeiters have produced base metal forgeries of gold and silver coins to deceive the public in the normal course of trade. These pieces are usually crudely made and easily detected by close examination. Crudely cast counterfeit copies of older coins are the most prevalent. These can usually be detected by the casting bubbles or pimples that can be seen with low power magnification. Pieces struck from hand made dies are more deceptive, but the engravings do not match those of genuine mint products.

More recently, as coin collecting has gained popularity and rare coin prices have risen, "numismatic" counterfeits have become more common. The majority of these are die-struck gold coin counterfeits that have been mass produced overseas since 1950. Forgeries exist of most U.S. gold coins dated between 1870 and 1933, as well as all issues of the gold dollar and three dollar gold piece. Most of these are very well made, as they were intended to pass the close scrutiny of collectors. Few gold coins of earlier dates have been counterfeited, but false 1799 $10 gold pieces and 1811 $5 coins have been made. Gold coins in less than extremely fine condition are seldom counterfeited.

Silver dollars dated 1804, Lafayette dollars, several of the low-mintage commemorative half dollars and the 1795 half dimes have been forged in quantity. Minor-coin forgeries made in recent years are the 1909-S V.D.B., 1914-D and 1955 doubled die Lincoln cents, as well as 1877 Indian Head cents, 1856 Flying Eagle cents and, on a much smaller scale, a variety of dates of half cents and large cents. Nineteenth century copies of colonial coins are also sometimes encountered. In this catalog a star has been placed adjacent to the colonial coins where deceptive copies exist.

ALTERATIONS: Coins are occasionally altered by adding, removing or changing a design feature (such as a mint mark or date digit) or by polishing, sandblasting, acid etching, toning or plating the surface of a genuine piece. Changes of this sort are usually done to deceive collectors. Among U.S. gold coins, only the 1927-D double eagle is commonly found with an added mint mark. On $2.50 and $5.00 gold coins, 1839 to 1856, New Orleans "O" mint marks have been altered to "C" (for Charlotte, N.C.) in a few instances.

Over a century ago $5.00 gold pieces were imitated by gold plating 1883 Liberty five cent coins without the word CENTS on the reverse. Other coins commonly created fraudulently through alteration include the 1799 large cent,1909-S, 1909-S V.D.B., 1914-D, 1922 "plain" and 1943 "copper" cents. The 1913 Liberty nickel has been extensively replicated by altering 1910 and 1912 nickels. Scarce, high-grade Denver and San Francisco mint Buffalo nickels of the 1920's, 1916-D and 1942 over 1941 dimes, 1918 over 1917-S and 1932-D and S quarters and 1804 silver dollars have all been made by altering genuine coins of other dates or mints.

DETECTION: The best way to detect counterfeit coins is to compare suspected pieces with others of the same issue. Carefully check size, color, luster, weight, edge devices and design details. Replicas generally have less detail than their genuine counterparts when studied under magnification. Modern struck counterfeits made to deceive collectors are an exception to this rule. Any questionable gold coin should be referred to an expert for verification.

Cast forgeries are usually poorly made and of incorrect weight. Base metal is often used in place of gold or silver, and the coins are light weight and often incorrect in color and luster. Deceptive cast pieces have been made using real metal content and modern dental techniques, but these too usually vary in quality and color.

Detection of alterations sometimes involves comparative examination of the suspected areas of a coin (usually mint marks and date digits) at magnification ranging from 10x to 40x. Coins of exceptional rarity or value should never be purchased without a written guarantee of authenticity.

Professional authentication of rare coins for a fee is available with the services offered by commercial grading services, and by some independent coin dealers.

MISSTRUCK COINS AND ERROR PIECES

With the production of millions of coins each year, it is natural that a few abnormal pieces escape inspection and are inadvertently released for circulation, usually in original bags or rolls of new coins. These are not considered regular issues because they were not made intentionally. They are all eagerly sought by collectors for the information they shed on minting techniques, and as a variation from normal date and mint series collecting.

Nearly every misstruck or error coin is unique in some way, and prices may vary from coin to coin. They may all be classified in general groups related to the kind of error or manufacturing malfunction involved. Collectors value these pieces according to the scarcity of each kind of error for each type of coin. Non-collectors usually view them as curios, and often believe that they must be worth much more than normal coins because they look so strange. In reality, the value assigned to various types of errors by collectors and dealers reflects both supply and demand, and is based on recurring transactions between willing buyers and sellers.

The following listings show current average values for the most frequently encountered kinds of error coins. In each case the values shown are for coins that are unmarred by serious marks or scratches, and in uncirculated condition for modern issues, and extremely fine condition for obsolete types. Exceptions are valued higher or lower. Error coins of rare date issues generally do not command a premium beyond their normal values. In most cases each of these coins is unique in some respect and must be valued according to its individual appearance, quality, and eye appeal.

There are many other kinds of errors and misstruck coins beyond those listed in this catalog. Some are more valuable, and others less valuable then the most popular pieces that are listed here as examples of what this interesting field contains. The pieces illustrated are general examples of the types described.

Early in 2002 the mints changed their production methods to a new system designed to eliminate deformed planchets, off-center strikes and similar errors. They also changed the delivery system of bulk coin, and no longer shipped loose coins in sewn bags to be counted and wrapped by banks or counting rooms where error coins were often found and sold to collectors. Under the new system, coins are packaged in large quantities and go directly to automated counters that filter out deformed coins. The result has been that very few error coins have entered the market since late 2002, and almost none after that date. The values shown in these listings are for pre-2002 coins, those dated after that, with but a few exceptions are valued considerably higher.

For additional details and information about these coins the following books are recommended:

Margolis, Arnold. *The Error Coin Encyclopedia.* Second Edition, 1993.
Herbert, Alan. *Official Price Guide to Minting Varieties and Errors.* New York, 1991.
Fivaz, Bill and Stanton, J.T. *The Cherrypickers' Guide to Rare Die Varieties.* Third Edition. Savannah, 1994.

The coins discussed in this section must not be confused with others that have been mutilated or damaged after leaving the mint. Examples of such pieces include coins that have been scratched, hammered, engraved, impressed, acid etched, or plated by individuals to simulate something other than a normal coin. Those pieces have no numismatic value, and can only be considered as altered coins not suitable for a collection.

1. CLIPPED PLANCHET: An incomplete coin, missing 10-25% of the metal.

Incomplete planchets result from accidents when the steel rods used to punch out blanks from the metal strip overlap a portion of the strip already punched. There are curved, straight, ragged, incomplete and elliptical clips. Values may be greater or less depending on the nature and size of the clip. Coins with more than one clip usually command higher values.

2. MULTIPLE STRIKE: Coin has additional image from being struck again off center. Value increases with number of strikes. These minting errors occur when a finished coin goes back into the press and is struck again with the same dies. The presence or absence of a date will also affect values.

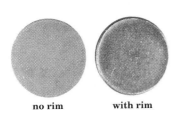

no rim   **with rim**

3. BLANK or PLANCHET: A blank of metal intended for coinage but not struck with dies. In the process of preparing blanks for coinage the pieces are first punched from a strip of metal and then milled to upset the rim. In most instances first process pieces (blanks without upset rim) are slightly more valuable than the finished planchets. Values shown are for the most common pieces.

4. DEFECTIVE DIE: Coin shows raised metal from a large die crack, or small rim break. Coins that show evidence of light die cracks, polishing or very minor die damage are generally of little or no value. Prices shown here are for coins with very noticeable raised die crack lines, or those where the die breaks away producing an unstruck area known as a cud.

5. OFF CENTER: Coin has been struck out of collar and incorrectly centered with part of the design missing. Values are for coins with approximately 10-20% of design missing from obsolete type coins; 20-60% missing from modern coins. These are misstruck coins that were made when the planchet did not enter the coinage press properly. Coins that are only struck slightly off center, with none of the design missing, are called Broadstrikes (see category 6). Those with nearly all of the impression missing are generally worth more, but those with a readable date and mint are the most valuable.

6. BROADSTRIKE: A coin that was struck outside of the retaining collar. When coins are struck without being contained in the collar die they spread out larger than a normal piece. All denominations have a plain edge.

7. LAMINATION: A flaw with a fragment of metal peeled off the coin's surface. This defect occurs when a foreign substance such as gas oxides or dirt becomes trapped in the strip as it is rolled out to the proper thickness. Lamination flaws may be missing or still attached to the coin's surface. Minor flaws may only decrease a coin's value, while a clad coin that is missing the full surface of one or both sides is worth more than the values listed here.

8. BROCKAGE: Mirror image of the design impressed on the opposite side of the same coin. These errors are caused when a struck coin remains on either die after striking, and impresses its image into the next blank planchet as it is struck, leaving a negative or mirror image. Off-center and partial brockage coins are worth less than those with a full impression. Coins with negative impressions on both sides are usually mutilated pieces made outside the mint by pressing coins together.

9. WRONG PLANCHET: A coin struck on a planchet intended for another denomination or of the wrong metal. Examples of these are cents struck on dime planchets, nickels on cent planchets, or quarters on dime planchets. Values vary depending on the type of error involved. Those struck on coins of a different denomination that were previously struck normally, are of much greater value.

The Kennedy 50¢ struck on an Anthony $1 planchet is very rare. Coins struck over other coins of a different denomination are usually valued three to five times higher than these prices. Values for 50-State quarter errors vary with each type and state, and are generally much higher than for other quarters. Coins made from mis-matched dies (Statehood quarter obverse combined with Sacagawea dollar reverse) are extremely rare.

np = not possible

UNITED STATES PATTERN PIECES

United States patterns are a fascinating part of numismatics that encompass a myriad of designs and experimental pieces made by the Mint in an effort to improve our nation's coinage. They provide students and collectors a chronology of the recurrent efforts of engravers and artists to present their work for approval. Throughout the 200-plus years of federal coinage production, concepts meant to improve various aspects of our circulating coins have been proposed, and incorporated into representative patterns. Such changes have been prompted by an outcry for higher aesthetics, an call for a more convenient denomination, or a need to overcome striking deficiencies. The pattern, bearing its particular proposed design or innovation, provides a tangible example for Mint and Treasury Department officials or members of Congress to evaluate. If adopted, the pattern becomes a familiar regular issue; those that were rejected have become part of our country's numismatic history.

The patterns listed and illustrated in this section are representative of the much larger group of pieces traditionally included in this area by collectors. Such pieces generally include die and hub trails, off-metal proofs of regular issues, and various combinations of dies that were sometimes struck at a later date. Certain well-known members of this extended pattern family historically have been included with regular issues in many numismatic reference books. The gold Stellas of 1879 and 1880; certain Gobrecht dollars of 1836, 1838 and 1839; and the Flying Eagle cents of 1856 are such examples. No official mintage figures of patterns and related pieces were recorded in most instances, and the number extant of each can usually only be estimated from auction appearances, and from those found in museum holdings and important private collections. Although most of these pieces are very rare, the over 2000 distinct varieties make them unexpectedly collectible.

Unlike regular coin issues that were emitted through the usual channels of commerce, and proofs of regular issues that were struck expressly for sale to collectors, patterns were not intended to be sold. Yet as a matter of Mint policy in accordance with certain previously established restrictions, innumerable patterns were sold and traded to collectors, disseminated to government officials, and made available to numismatic societies. Not until mid-1887 did the Mint develop stringent regulations prohibiting their sale and distribution. In the succeeding decades the Mint relaxed this policy on occasions, and several patterns were placed in the national collection at the Smithsonian Institution, given to Mint and Treasury officials, or otherwise escaped destruction. The number of patterns that were released from the Mint fell dramatically after the 1887 regulations were imposed.

The private possession of patterns has not been without its controversy. Most significant was the 1910 seizure by government agents of a parcel containing some twenty-three "pattern pieces" belong to John W. Haseltine, a leading Philadelphia coin dealer. The government asserted that the patterns were removed from the Mint without authority, and that they remained the property of the United States. Haseltine's attorney successfully used the Mint's pre-1887 policies in his defense, and recovered the patterns a year after their confiscation. This set precedent for ownership, at least for the patterns minted prior to 1887, as all of the pieces in question predated that year.

Among the grandest impressions ever produced at our Mint are the two varieties of pattern fifty-dollar gold pieces of 1877. Officiation titled Half Unions, these large patterns were created to satisfy banking and mercantile interest, but never adopted. Specimens were struck in copper, and one of each in gold. Both of the gold pieces were purchased around 1908 by a prominent numismatist, reportedly for a staggering $10,000 apiece. Now preserved in the Smithsonian Institution, these Half Unions are regarded as national treasures.

Special credit is due to the following individuals for contributing to this feature: Marc Crane, Robert Hughes, Andy Lustig, and Eddie Wilson. The following source is recommended for additional information, descriptions and complete listings: *United States Pattern Coins and Experimental Trial Pieces: America's Rarest Coins,* Ed. Q. David Bowers; also http://www. harrybassfoundation.org; and http://uspatterns.com.

J-52

J-67

	PF-60	PF-63	PF-65
1836 Two Cents (J-52) This proposal for a two cent coin is one of the earliest collectible patterns. Designs by Christian Gobrecht and Franklin Peale	$2,500.	$3,750.	$6,500.
1836 Gold Dollar (J-67) Gobrecht styled the first gold dollar pattern after the familiar Mexican "cap and rays" design, then legal tender in this country.	12,500.	17,500.	25,500.

J-73

J-119

	PF-60	PF-63	PF-65
1838 Half Dollar (J-73) Christian Gobrecht likely designed this proposed, but rejected, successor to the long-running capped bust half dollar design.	$3,500.	$5,500.	$9,500.
1850 Cent (J119) The first attempt by the mint to reduce the size of the copper cent by creating a holed silver-copper cent.	2,000.	2,750.	3,750.

J-125

J-145

	PF-60	PF-63	PF-65
1850 Trime (J-125) A year before the first three cent piece was issued, these attractive patterns revived the earlier "cap and rays" dollar design.	$1,500.	$2,150.	$4,500.
1852 Gold Dollar (J-145) Various pattern ring dollars were produced after 1849. This is the most attractive design, and the most commonly found.	9,500.	12,500.	19,500.

J-164

J-177

	PF-60	PF-63	PF-65
1854 Cent (J-164) The Mint considered making reduced weight cents before adopting the small copper-nickel cent in 1856. Liberty Head and Eagle types	$2,000.	$2,500.	$4,500.
1856 Half Cent (J-177) Before producing copper-nickel small size cents in 1856, the Mint experimented with that alloy using half cent dies.	2,500.	3,500.	6,500.

J-235

	PF-60	PF-63	PF-65
1859 Half Dollar (J235) Design for a new half dollar by Anthony C. Paquet.	$1,750.	$2,500.	$4,500.

J-305   J-329

	PF-60	PF-63	PF-65
1863 Washington Two Cent Piece (J-305) Before introduction of the two cent coin, two basic designs were considered. If the Washington design had been adopted, it would have been the first to depict a historical figure	$1,750.	$2,500.	$3,500.
1863 Postage Currency Dime (J-329) A shortage of silver coins prompted the Mint to consider redeeming fractional currency with a reduced-weight silver coin. Various experiment alloys and weights were used for these patterns.	2,250.	3,000.	5,000.

J-407   J-435

	PF-60	PF-63	PF-65
1865 Bimetallic Two Cent Piece (J-407) This experimental piece is the first "clad" coin. It consists of an irregular and streaky layer of silver fused to layer of copper. The experiment was considered an unmitigated disaster	$3,500.	$8,500.	$15,000.
1865 Seated Dollar, With Motto (J-435) "In God We Trust" first appeared on circulating silver coinage in 1866. This transitional pattern proceeded it.	15,000.	25,000.	50,000.

J-486

1866 Lincoln Five Cents (J-486) A number of pattern nickels were produced in 1866 including one depicting the recently assassinated President.

PF-60	PF-63	PF-65
$4,500.	$7,500.	$15,000.

J-561

1867 Aluminum Five Cents (J-561) Aluminum was considered because, unlike nickel, the coins would have contained five cents worth of metal.

PF-60	PF-63	PF-65
$2,500.	$3,500.	$5,000.

J-727

1869-70. Standard Silver Coin (J-727) This lightweight piece was proposed as a way of controlling the silver hoarding that followed the Civil War.

PF-60	PF-63	PF-65
$1,500.	$2,000.	$2,750.

J-1195   *J-1235*

1872 Amazonian Quarter (J-1195) Many of the most popular patterns have been given colorful nicknames by collectors in appreciation of their artistry.

PF-60	PF-63	PF-65
$17,500.	$35,000.	$55,000.

1872 Amazonian Gold $3 (J-1235) contained in the mint's only uniform gold set using the same design from the gold dollar to the double eagle.

—	—	800,000

J-1281

1873 Bailly Trade Dollar (J-1281) Several different pattern Trade Dollars were produced in 1873 prior to selecting the seated design by William Barber.

	PF-60	PF-63	PF-65
	$2,750.	$4,500.	$7,500.

J-1373

1874 Bickford Eagle (J-1373) An effort to standardize international trade and a monetary union, this pattern was denominated in six world currencies (gold)

	PF-60	PF-63	PF-65
		$200,000.	$350,000.

J-1392

1875 Sailor Head Twenty Cents (J-1392) William Barber's "Sailor Head" is one of the most elegant of several rejected designs for a twenty cent coin.

	PF-60	PF-63	PF-65
	$2,700.	$5,000.	$8,500.

J-1512   J-1528

1877 Morgan Half Dollar (J-1512) Before his famous Morgan dollar design was adopted, the designer George Morgan's "Liberty Head" appeared a year earlier on patterns of other denominations. This 1877 pattern half dollar pairs the well know obverse with a dramatic "Defiant Eagle" reverse.

PF-60	PF-63	PF-65
$15,000.	$27,000.	$50,000.

1877 50 cent (J-1528) One of William Barber's to compare with the Morgan example.

$16,000.	$27,000.	$42,500.

J-1549

1877 Half Union (J-1549) This famous $50 pattern by William Barber would have been the highest denomination ever issued by the U.S. Mint. The gold impression is unique, but copper specimens, sometimes gilt, occasionally come to the market. Varieties exist with a somewhat larger or smaller head (copper).

PF-60	PF-63	PF-65
$95,000.	$140,000.	$225,000.

J-1590

1879 Quarter - dollar (J-1590) The Washlady design. Charles Barber's first attempt at a uniform silver design.

7,500.	12,500.	22,500.

J-1609

	PF-60	PF-63	PF-65
1879 $1 (J-1609) The Schoolgirl design.	$22,000.	$42,500.	$80,000.

J-1617

	PF-60	PF-63	PF-65
1879 Metric Dollar (J-1617) In 1878-1880, an ill-fated attempt to settle the rivalry between silver and gold resulted in a small size pattern dollars containing both metals. The alloy is visually indistinguishable from silver.	$2,000.	$3,000.	$4,500.

J-1669

J-1698

	PF-60	PF-63	PF-65
1881 1, 3 and 5 cent (J-1669) The Mint's last attempt at a uniform set of minor coins struck in nickel.	$1,600.	$2,550.	$4,450.
1882 Quarter-Dollar (J-1698) The Shield Earring design. George Morgan's attempt at a uniform silver design.	15,000.	22,500.	40,000.

J-1761

1891 Barber Quarter (J-1761) Charles Barber prepared various pattern dimes, quarters and half dollars in 1891. The piece illustrated is similar to the adopted design. Only one coin in this series is known outside of the Smithsonian collection. (silver)

—   —   150,000.

J-1770

1896 Shield Nickel (J-1770) At the request of the House of Representatives, the Mint struck experimental cents and nickels with similar designs.

PF-60	PF-63	PF-65
$1,500.	$2,250.	$3,750.

J-1905

1907 Indian Head Double Eagle (J-1905) Designed by Augustus Saint-Gaudens, this pattern is unique and extremely valuable. A variation of the reverse of this beautiful design was eventually used on the twenty dollar gold coins of 1907-1933. (gold)

PF-60	PF-63	PF-65
—	$2,000,000.	—

J-1797

J-2063

1916 Walking Liberty Half Dollar (J-1797) Various pattern Mercury dimes, Standing Liberty quarters and Walking Liberty half dollars were struck, all dated 1916. All are extremely rare, but a few found their way into circulation. (silver)

PF-60	PF-63	PF-65
$40,000.	$65,000.	$125,000.

1942 Experimental Cent (J-2063) Before settling on the zinc-coated steel composition used for the Lincoln cents of 1943, the Mint considered various alternative compositions including plastics. Most were struck by outside contractors using specially prepared dies provided by the Mint. (light tan plastic)

1,000.	1,500.	2,500.

BULLION VALUE OF SILVER COINS

Silver Price Per Ounce.	Wartime Nickel .05626 oz.	Dime .07234 oz.	Quarter .18084 oz.	Half Dollar .36169 oz.	Silver Clad Half Dollar .14792 oz.	Silver Dollar .77344 oz.
$3.00	$.17	$.22	$.58	$1.09	$.45	$2.32
3.50	.20	.25	.63	1.27	.52	2.71
4.00	.23	.29	.72	1.45	.59	3.10
4.50	.25	.32	.81	1.63	.66	3.48
5.00	.28	.36	.90	1.81	.74	3.87
5.50	.31	.40	1.00	1.99	.81	4.26
6.00	.34	.44	1.09	2.17	.89	4.64
6.50	.36	.47	1.18	2.35	.96	5.03
7.00	.40	.51	1.27	2.53	1.04	5.42
7.50	.42	.55	1.36	2.72	1.11	5.80
8.00	.45	.58	1.45	2.90	1.19	6.19
8.50	.48	.62	1.54	3.08	1.26	6.58
9.00	.50	.65	1.63	3.26	1.33	6.96

BULLION VALUE OF GOLD COINS

Gold Price Per Ounce	$5.00 Liberty Head 1839-1908 Indian Head 1908-1929 .24187 oz.	$10.00 Liberty Head 1838-1907 Indian Head 1907-1933 .48375 oz.	$20.00 1849-1933 .96750 oz.
$ 200.00	$ 48.37	$ 96.75	$ 193.50
225.00	54.42	108.85	217.69
250.00	60.47	120.94	241.88
275.00	66.52	133.03	266.07
300.00	72.50	145.13	290.25
325.00	78.60	157.22	314.44
350.00	84.65	169.31	338.63
375.00	90.70	181.40	362.81
400.00	96.75	193.50	387.00
425.00	102.80	205.60	411.19
450.00	108.84	217.69	435.38
475.00	114.89	229.78	459.56
500.00	120.94	241.87	483.75

The U.S. bullion coins first issued in 1986 are unlike the older regular issues. They contain the following amounts of pure metal: Silver $1, 1 oz.; Gold $50, 1 oz.; $25, $1/2$ oz.; $10, $1/4$ oz.; $5, $1/10$ oz

UNITED STATES BULLION COINS
Silver

The silver eagle is a one ounce bullion coin with a face value of one dollar. The obverse has Adolph A. Weinman's Walking Liberty design used on the half dollar coins from 1916 through 1947. His initials are on the hem of the gown. The reverse design is a rendition of a heraldic eagle by John Mercanti.

Designers: Adolph A. Weinman (obverse), John Mercanti (reverse); composition 99.93% silver, .07% copper; weight 31.101 grams; diameter 40.6mm; net weight one oz. fine silver; reeded edge; mints: Philadelphia, San Francisco and West Point.

	Mintage	UNC	Proof		Mintage	UNC	Proof
$1 1986	5,393,005	$19.00		$1 1996	3,603,386	30.00	
$1 1986S	(1,446,778)		32.00	$1 1996P	(473,021)		50.00
$1 1987	11,442,335	12.00		$1 1997	4,295,004	12.00	
$1 1987S	(904,732)		32.00	$1 1997P	(429,682)		95.00
$1 1988	5,004,646	12.00		$1 1998	4,847,549	12.00	
$1 1988S	(557,370)		85.00	$1 1998P	(452,319)		40.00
$1 1989	5,203,327	12.00		$1 1999	7,408,640	12.00	
$1 1989S	(617,694)		32.00	$1 1999P	(549,769)		70.00
$1 1990	5,840,210	13.00		$1 2000(W)	9,239,132	12.00	
$1 1990S	(695,510)		32.00	$1 2000P			40.00
$1 1991	7,191,066	12.00		$1 2001(W)	9,001,711	12.00	
$1 1991S	(511,925)		62.00	$1 2001P			35.00
$1 1992	5,540,068	12.00		$1 2002(W)		11.00	
$1 1992S	(498,654)		40.00	$1 2002W			35.00
$1 1993	6,763,762	12.00		$1 2003W		10.00	35.00
$1 1993P	(403,625)		125.00	$1 2003P			
$1 1994	4,227,319	12.00		$1 2004W		10.00	35.00
$1 1994P	(372,168)		115.00	$1 2004P			
$1 1995	4,762,051	12.00					
$1 1995P	(395,400)		100.00				
$1 1995W	(30,125)		2,300.00				

UNITED STATES BULLION COINS

The gold American Eagle bullion coins are made in four denominations that contain 1 oz., $\frac{1}{2}$ oz., $\frac{1}{4}$ oz. and $\frac{1}{10}$ oz. of gold. The obverse features a modified rendition of the Augustus Saint-Gaudens design used on U.S. twenty dollar gold pieces from 1907 until 1933. The reverse displays a "family of eagles" motif designed by Mrs. Miley Busiek and engraved by Sherl J. Winter.

Uncirculated American Eagles, unlike their Proof counterparts, are not sold directly to the general public, but to a series of authorized buyers. These buyers obtain the uncirculated bullion coins from the Mint based on the current spot price of the metal plus a small premium. The coins are then sold to secondary distributors for sale to other dealers and the general public. These coins have legal-tender status only for their stated dollar face value.

UNITED STATES BULLION COIN SETS

	Proof
1987 Gold Set. $50.00, 25.00	$1,250.
1988 Gold Set. $50.00, 25.00, 10.00, 5.00	1,200.
1989 Gold Set. $50.00, 25.00, 10.00, 5.00	1,200.
1990 Gold Set. $50.00, 25.00, 10.00, 5.00	1,200.
1991 Gold Set. $50.00, 25.00, 10.00, 5.00	1,200.
1992 Gold Set. $50.00, 25.00, 10.00, 5.00	1,200.
1993 Gold Set. $50.00, 25.00, 10.00, 5.00	1,200.
1993 Bicentennial Gold Set. $25.00, 10.00, 5.00, $1 Silver Eagle and medal	600.
1994 Gold Set. $50.00, 25.00, 10.00, 5.00	1,200.
1995 Gold Set. $50.00, 25.00, 10.00, 5.00	1,200.
1995 Anniversary Gold Set. $50.00, 25.00, 10.00, 5.00, and $1 Silver Eagle	3,500.
1996 Gold Set. $50.00, 25.00, 10.00, 5.00	1,200.
1997 Gold Set. $50.00, 25.00, 10.00, 5.00	1,200.
1997 Impressions of Liberty Set. $100 platinum, $50 gold, $1 silver	1,700.
1998 Gold Set. $50.00, 25.00, 10.00, 5.00	1,200.
1999 Gold Set. $50.00, 25.00, 10.00, 5.00	1,200.
2000 Gold Set. $50.00, 25.00, 10.00, 5.00	1,300.
2001 Gold Set. $50.00, 25.00, 10.00, 5.00	1,200.
2002 Gold Set. $50.00, 25.00, 10.00, 5.00	1,200.
2003 Gold Set. $50.00, 25.00, 10.00, 5.00	1,200.
2004 Gold Set. $50.00, 25.00, 10.00, 5.00	1,200.

Designers: Augustus Saint-Gaudens (obverse), Miley Busiek (reverse); composition, 91.67% gold, 3% silver, 5.33% copper; reeded edge; mints: Philadelphia, West Point. $5 diameter 16.5mm; weight 3.393 grams; net weight 1/10 oz. fine gold.

TENTH-OUNCE GOLD $5.00

	Mintage	UNC	Proof
$5 MCMLXXXVI (1986)	912,609	$55.	
$5 MCMLXXXVII (1987)	580,266	55.	
$5 MCMLXXXVIII (1988)	159,500	190.	
$5 MCMLXXXVIII (1988)P	(143,881)		$80.
$5 MCMLXXXIX (1989)	264,790	90.	
$5 MCMLXXXIX (1989)P	(84,924)		80.
$5 MCMXC (1990)	210,210	70.	
$5 MCMXC (1990)P	(99,349)		80.
$5 MCMXCI (1991)	165,200	115.	
$5 MCMXCI (1991)P	(70,334)		80.
$5 1992	209,300	60.	
$5 1992P	(64,902)		90.
$5 1993	210,709	65.	
$5 1993P	(58,649)		80.
$5 1994	206,380	60.	
$5 1994W	(62,100)		75.
$5 1995	223,025	55.	
$5 1995W	(48,675)		75.
$5 1996	401,964	55.	
$5 1996W	(57,449)		90.
$5 1997	528,266	55.	
$5 1997W	(35,164)		100.
$5 1998	1,344,520	55.	
$5 1998W	(39,706)		75.
$5 1999	2,750,338	55.	
$5 1999W	(19,919)		75.
$5 1999W, UNC made from unpolished Proof dies		400.	
$5 2000	569,153	55.	
$5 2000W			90.
$5 2001	269,147	55.	
$5 2001W			90.
$5 2002		55.	
$5 2002W			80.
$5 2003		55.	
$5 2003W			80.
$5 2004		55.	
$5 2004W			80.

Designers: Augustus Saint-Gaudens (obverse), Miley Busiek (reverse); composition, 91.67% gold, 3% silver, 5.33% copper; reeded edge; mints: Philadelphia, West Point. $10 diameter 22mm; weight 8.483 grams; net weight 1/4 oz. fine gold.

QUARTER-OUNCE GOLD $10.00

	Mintage	UNC	Proof
$10 MCMLXXXVI (1986)	726,031	$150.	
$10 MCMLXXXVII (1987)	269,255	150.	
$10 MCMLXXXVIII (1988)	49,000	160.	
$10 MCMLXXXVIII (1988)P	(98,028)		$160.
$10 MCMLXXXIX (1989)	81,789	135.	
$10 MCMLXXXIX (1989)P	(53,593)		160.
$10 MCMXC (1990)	41,000	150.	
$10 MCMXC (1990)P	(62,674)		160.
$10 MCMXCI (1991)	36,100	260.	
$10 MCMXCI (1991)P	(50,840)		160.
$10 1992	59,546	135.	
$10 1992P	(42,290)		160.
$10 1993	71,864	135.	
$10 1993P	(46,271)		160.
$10 1994	72,650	135.	
$10 1994W	(47,600)		160.
$10 1995	83,752	135.	
$10 1995W	(46,825)		160.
$10 1996	60,318	135.	
$10 1996W	(37,755)		160.
$10 1997	108,805	135.	
$10 1997W	(29,984)		160.
$10 1998	309,829	135.	
$10 1998W	(29,731)		160.
$10 1999	564,232	135.	
$10 1999W	(34,410)		160.
$10 1999W, UNC made from unpolished Proof dies		450.	
$10 2000	128,964	135.	
$10 2000W			160.
$10 2001	71,280	135.	
$10 2001W			160.
$10 2002		135.	
$10 2002W			150.
$10 2003		140.	
$10 2003W			150.
$10 2004		140.	
$10 2004W			150.

Designers: Augustus Saint-Gaudens (obverse), Miley Busiek (reverse); composition, 91.67% gold, 3% silver, 5.33% copper; reeded edge; mints: Philadelphia, West Point. $25 diameter 27mm; weight 16.966 grams; net weight 1/2 oz. fine gold.

HALF-OUNCE GOLD $25.00

	Mintage	UNC	Proof
$25 MCMLXXXVI (1986)	.599,566	$275.	
$25 MCMLXXXVII (1987)	.131,255	290.	
$25 MCMLXXXVII (1987)P	.(143,398)		$325.
$25 MCMLXXXVIII (1988)	.45,000	325.	
$25 MCMLXXXVIII (1988)P	.(76,528)		325.
$25 MCMLXXXIX (1989)	.44,829	450.	
$25 MCMLXXXIX (1989)P	.(44,264)		325.
$25 MCMXC (1990)	.31,000	425.	
$25 MCMXC (1990)P	.(51,636)		325.
$25 MCMXCI (1991)	.24,100	700.	
$25 MCMXCI (1991)P	.(53,125)		325
$25 1992	.54,404	290.	
$25 1992P	.(40,982)		325.
$25 1993	.73,324	270.	
$25 1993P	.(43,319)		325.
$25 1994	.62,400	260.	
$25 1994W	.(44,100)		325.
$25 1995	.53,474	260.	
$25 1995W	.(46,200)		325.
$25 1996	.39,287	270.	
$25 1996W	.(34,769)		325.
$25 1997	.79,605	260.	
$25 1997W	.(26,801)		325.
$25 1998	.169,029	250.	
$25 1998W	.(25,550)		325.
$25 1999	.263,013	250.	
$25 1999W	.(30,452)		325.
$25 2000	.79,287	250.	
$25 2000W			325.
$25 2001	.48,047	260.	
$25 2001W			325.
$25 2002		250.	
$25 2002W			325.
$25 2003		250.	
$25 2003W			325.
$25 2004		250.	
$25 2004W			325.

Designers: Augustus Saint-Gaudens (obverse), Miley Busiek (reverse); composition, 91.67% gold, 3% silver, 5.33% copper; reeded edge; mints: Philadelphia, West Point. $50 diameter 32.7mm; weight 33.931 grams; net weight one oz. fine gold.

ONE OUNCE GOLD $50.00

	Mintage	UNC	Proof
$50 MCMLXXXVI (1986)	1,362,650	$500.	
$50 MCMLXXXVI (1986)W	(446,290)		$610.
$50 MCMLXXXVII (1987)	1,045,500	500.	
$50 MCMLXXXVII (1987)W	(147,498)		610.
$50 MCMLXXXVIII (1988)	465,000	500.	
$50 MCMLXXXVIII (1988)W	(87,133)		610.
$50 MCMLXXXIX (1989)	415,790	500.	
$50 MCMLXXXIX (1989)W	(53,960)		610.
$50 MCMXC (1990)	373,210	500.	
$50 MCMXC (1990)W	(62,401)		610.
$50 MCMXCI (1991)	243,100	500.	
$50 MCMXCI (1991)W	(50,411)		610.
$50 1992	275,000	500.	
$50 1992W	(44,835)		610.
$50 1993	480,192	500.	
$50 1993W	(34,389)		610.
$50 1994	221,633	500.	
$50 1994W	(46,300)		610.
$50 1995	200,636	500.	
$50 1995W	(48,075)		610.
$50 1996	189,148	500.	
$50 1996W	(36,086)		610.
$50 1997	664,508	500.	
$50 1997W	(27,803)		610.
$50 1998	1,468,530	500.	
$50 1998W	(26,047)		610.
$50 1999	1,505,026	500.	
$50 1999W	(31,446)		610.
$50 2000	433,319	500.	
$50 2000W			610.
$50 2001	143,605	500.	
$50 2001W			610.
$50 2002		500.	
$50 2002W			610.
$50 2003		500.	
$50 2003W			610.
$50 2004		500.	
$50 2004W			610.

═══ UNITED STATES BULLION PLATINUM COINS ═══

American Eagle platinum coins are made in four denominations that are different from the similar gold coins. The one ounce coin is designated $100.00 and contains one ounce of pure platinum. Fractional denominations containing 1/2 ounce, 1/4 ounce or 1/10 ounce, are called $50, $25 and $10 respectively. Each of the platinum proof coins features a different design on the reverse.

Designers: John M. Mercanti (obverse), Thomas D. Rogers, Sr. (original reverse); composition, 99.95% platinum; reeded edge; mints: Philadelphia, West Point. $100 diameter 32.70mm; weight 1.0005 oz.

───── ONE OUNCE PLATINUM $100.00 ─────

	Mintage	UNC	PF
1997	56,000	$1,200.	
1997W	(16,000)		$1,250.
1998	133,002	1,200.	
1998W	(26,047)		1,250.
1999	56,707	1,200.	
1999W	(12,351)		1,250.
2000	10,003	1,200.	
2000W			1,250.
2001	14,070	1,200.	
2001W			1,250.
2002		1,200.	
2002W			1,250.
2003		1,200.	
2003W			1,300.
2004		1,200.	
2004W			1,300.

VISTAS OF LIBERTY DESIGNS ON REVERSE OF PROOF COINS

1998

1999

2000

2001

2002

─── **HALF-OUNCE PLATINUM $50.00** ───

Designers: John M. Mercanti (obverse), Thomas D. Rogers, Sr. (original reverse); composition, 99.95% platinum; reeded edge; mints: Philadelphia, West Point. $50 diameter 27mm; weight 0.5003 oz.

	Mintage	UNC	Proof
1997	20,500	$600.	
1997W	(14,637)		$625.
1998	32,415	600.	
1998W	(13,919)		625.
1999	32,309	600.	
1999W	(11,098)		625.
2000	18,892	600.	
2000W			625.
2001	12,815	625.	
2001W			625.
2002		600.	
2002W			625.
2003		600.	
2003W			675.
2004		600.	
2004W			675.

─── **QUARTER-OUNCE PLATINUM $25.00** ───

Designers: John M. Mercanti (obverse), Thomas D. Rogers, Sr. (original reverse); composition, 99.95% platinum; reeded edge; mints: Philadelphia, West Point. $25 diameter 22mm; weight 0.2501 oz.

	Mintage	UNC	Proof
1997	27,100	$310.	
1997W	(18,726)		$325.
1998	38,887	310.	
1998W	(14,203)		325.
1999	39,734	310.	
1999W	(13,524)		325.
2000	20,054	310.	
2000W			325.
2001	21,815	325.	
2001W			325.
2002		325.	
2002W			350.
2003		310.	
2003W			400.
2004		310.	
2004W			400.

UNITED STATES BULLION PLATINUM COINS
TENTH-OUNCE PLATINUM $10.00

Designers: John M. Mercanti (obverse), Thomas D. Rogers, Sr. (original reverse); composition, 99.95% platinum; reeded edge; mints: Philadelphia, West Point. $10 diameter 16.50mm; weight 0.10005 oz.

	Mintage	UNC	Proof
1997	70,250	$130.	
1997W	(37,260)		$140.
1998	39,525	150.	
1998W	(19,919)		140.
1999	55,955	130.	
1999W	(19,123)		140.
2000	34,027	130.	
2000W			140.
2001	52,017	130.	
2001W		140.	
2002		150.	
2002W			150.
2003		140.	
2003W			160.
2004		140.	
2004W			160.

UNITED STATES BULLION COIN SET

1997 Platinum Set. $100.00, 50.00, 25.00, 10.00	$2,700.
1998 Platinum Set. $100.00, 50.00, 25.00, 10.00	2,500.
1999 Platinum Set. $100.00, 50.00, 25.00, 10.00	2,400.
2000 Platinum Set. $100.00, 50.00, 25.00, 10.00	2,600.
2001 Platinum Set. $100.00, 50.00, 25.00, 10.00	2,600.
2002 Platinum Set. $100.00, 50.00, 25.00, 10.00	2,300.
2003 Platinum Set. $100.00, 50.00, 25.00, 10.00	2,300.
2004 Platinum Set. $100.00, 50.00, 25.00, 10.00	2,300.

THE GUIDE BOOK AS A COLLECTIBLE

A Guide Book of United States Coins has long held the record for being the longest running annual retail coin price guide. It has now passed its fiftieth anniversary, and collectors seem to be almost as interested in assembling sets of old *Red Books* as of old coins. The reason for this popularity seems to be that collectors have a penchant for completing sets of many things. The demand for old editions of the *Red Book* that are still in existence has created a solid market for them.

Those who save old editions of the *Red Book* seem to do so for many reasons. Some maintain a reference library of all kinds of coin publications. To them having one of each edition is essential, because that is the way old books are collected. Others are speculators who believe that the value of old editions will go up as interest and demand increases. The great majority of people who save old *Red Books* do so to maintain a record of coin prices going back further than any other source.

Following price trends in old *Red Books* is a good indicator of how well coins of any date or denomination are doing in comparison to each other. The price information published in this book each year is an average of what the entire market is paying for each coin. As such it is a valuable benchmark showing how prices have gone up or down over the years. It is information like this that often gives investors an edge in predicting what the future may hold.

Old *Red Books* are also a handy source of information about collecting trends. They show graphically how grading has changed over the years, what new coins have been discovered and added to the listings and which areas are growing in popularity. Studying these old books can be educational as well as nostalgic. It's great fun to see what your favorite coins sold for 15, 25 or more years ago. It can also be a bit frustrating to realize what might have been if we had only bought the right coins at the right time in years past.

Many collectors have asked about the quantities printed of each edition. Unfortunately that information has never been published, and now even the manufacturer has no records of how many were made. The original author, R.S. Yeoman, told inquirers that the first press run on November 1946 was for 9,000 copies. In February 1947 an additional 9,000 copies were printed to satisfy the unexpected demand.

There was a slight difference between the first and second printing. The wording in the first printing, at the bottom of page 135 reads, "which probably accounts for the scarcity of *this date*," That line was changed to "...the scarcity of *1903-0*" in the second printing.

The second edition had a press run of 22,000. The printing of each edition thereafter gradually increased, with the highest number ever being reached with the 18th edition, dated 1965. In that year, at the top of a booming coin market, a whopping 1,200,000 copies were produced. Since that time the numbers have decreased in proportion to the market, but still maintain a record of being the world's largest selling coin publication each year.

In some years a very limited number of *Red Books* were made for use by price contributors. Those were interleaved with blank pages. No more than 50 copies were ever made for any one year. Perhaps fewer than 20 were made in the first few years. Three of these still exist for the first edition, and one of the second edition. They are valued at $1,500 each. Those made in the 1960s sell for around $50 each today.

There are other unusual *Red Books* that command exceptional prices. One of the most popular is the special edition that was made for, and distributed only to, people who attended the 1986 ANA banquet in Milwaukee. Only 500 of those were printed with a special commemorative cover. Copies have sold for $75 to $100 each and are always in demand.

Error books are also popular with collectors. The most common is one with double stamped printing on the cover. The second most frequently seen are those with the cover put on upside down. Probably the best known of the error books is the 1963, 16th edition with a missing page. For some uncanny reason page 239 is duplicated in some of those books, and page 237 is missing. The error was corrected on most of the printing.

Those who collect old *Red Books* find them in the strangest places; everywhere from flea markets to Hospital libraries. Garage sales are the most fruitful source. I have heard many stories of collectors finding first or second editions in a garage sale for 10¢ or 25¢. Others come from book stores at 50¢ or $1, but if you want to collect these books seriously you will probably have to look for them in numismatic book auctions. There you will compete with others, and probably have to pay prices close to those shown in the accompanying chart.

The terminology used to describe book condition differs from that utilized in grading coins. A "very fine" book is one that is nearly new, with minimal signs of use. Early editions of the *Red Book* are rarely if ever found in anything approaching "New" condition. Exceptionally well-preserved older editions command a substantial premium and are in great demand. Nice used copies that are still clean and in good shape, but slightly worn from use, are also desirable. Perhaps the gilt stamping on the front cover and spine is a bit indistinct; someone may have added their name, or made notes, inside. Only the early editions are worth a premium in badly worn condition.

VALUATION GUIDE FOR PAST ISSUES OF THE GUIDE BOOK

Year/Edition	Issue Price	VG	F	VF	New
1947-1st, 1st printing	$1.50	$300.00	$500.00	$750.00	
1947-1st, 2nd printing	1.50	250.00	400.00	650.00	
1948-2nd	1.50	75.00	125.00	175.00	
1949-3rd	1.50	75.00	125.00	175.00	
1951/52-4th	1.50	50.00	100.00	150.00	
1952/53-5th	1.50	125.00	250.00	350.00	
1953/54-6th	1.50	40.00	50.00	75.00	150.00
1954/55-7th	1.75	40.00	50.00	75.00	150.00
1955-8th	1.75	25.00	35.00	60.00	100.00
1956-9th	1.75	25.00	30.00	50.00	85.00
1957-10th	1.75	20.00	30.00	40.00	65.00
1958-11th	1.75		10.00	15.00	35.00
1959-12th	1.75		15.00	25.00	35.00
1960-13th	1.75		6.00	8.00	18.00
1961-14th	1.75		4.00	6.00	15.00
1962-15th	1.75		4.00	5.00	8.00
1963-16th	1.75		4.00	5.00	8.00
1964-17th	1.75		4.00	5.00	7.00
1965-18th	1.75		3.00	4.00	6.00
1966-19th	1.75		3.00	4.00	6.00
1967-20th	1.75		3.00	5.00	8.00
1968-21st	2.00		3.00	5.00	10.00
1969-22nd	2.00		3.00	5.00	10.00
1970-23rd	2.50		3.00	6.00	11.00
1971-24th	2.50		3.00	4.00	6.00
1972-25th	2.50		6.00	9.00	12.00
1973-26th	2.50		4.00	5.00	7.00
1974-27th	2.50		2.00	4.00	6.00
1975-28th	3.00			4.00	5.00
1976-29th	3.95			4.00	5.00
1977-30th	3.95			4.00	6.00
1978-31st	3.95			4.00	5.00
1979-32nd	3.95			4.00	6.00
1980-33rd	3.95		7.00	10.00	19.00
1981-34th	4.95			2.00	5.00
1982-35th	4.95			2.00	5.00

VALUATION GUIDE FOR PAST ISSUES OF THE GUIDE BOOK

Year/Edition	Issue Price	VG	F	VF	New
1983-36th	5.95	2.00	5.00		
1984-37th	5.95			2.00	5.00
1985-38th	5.95			2.00	5.00
1986-39th	5.95			2.50	5.00
1987-40th, special A.N.A. cover			10.00	50.00	275.00
1987-40th	6.95			3.00	6.00
1988-41st	6.95			3.00	5.00
1989-42nd	6.95			3.00	8.00
1990-43rd	7.95			2.00	7.00
1991-44th	8.95			2.00	5.00
1992-45th	8.95			2.00	6.00
1992-45th, special A.N.A. cover		5.00	20.00	150.00	
1993-46th, hard bound	9.95			2.25	7.00
1993-46th, soft bound	6.95			1.00	5.00
1994-47th, hard bound	9.95			1.00	4.00
1994-47th, soft bound	7.95			1.00	4.00
1995-48th, hard bound	10.95			1.00	4.00
1995-48th, soft bound	7.95	800.00	800.00	1.00	3.00
1996-49th, hard bound	10.95				4.00
1996-49th, soft bound	7.95				3.00
1997-50th, hard bound	11.95				5.00
1997-50th, coilbound	8.95				5.00
1997-50th, special anniv. cover	24.95			20.00	120.00
1998-51st, hard board	11.95				3.00
1998-51st, soft bound	8.95				2.00
1999-52nd hard bound	11.95				2.00
1999-52nd coilbound	8.95				2.00
2000-53rd hard bound	12.95				2.00
2000-53rd coilbound	8.95				2.00
2001-54th hard bound	13.95				2.00
2001-54th coilbound	9.95				2.00
2002-55th hard bound	14.95				2.00
2002-55th coilbound	10.95				2.00
2002-A.N.A. special edition	100.			20.00	125.00
2002 S.S. Central America			25.00	150.00	
2003-56th hard bound	15.95				
2003-56th coilbound	11.95				
2003-56th soft bound	11.95				
2004-57th hard bound	15.95				
2004-57th coilbound	12.95				
2004-57th soft bound	11.95				
2005-57th hard bound	15.95				
2005-57th coilbound	12.95				
2005-57th soft bound	11.95				

COINS FROM TREASURES AND HOARDS
A KEY TO UNDERSTANDING RARITY AND VALUE
by Q. David Bowers

ELEMENTS OF RARITY

In many instances the mintage of a coin can be a determinant of its present-day rarity and value. However, across American numismatics there are many important exceptions, some very dramatic. Some of these situations are well known, others less so. On the following pages I discuss famous hoards, finds, and treasures as well as some that are not so well known.

PERPLEXING SILVER DOLLARS

As an introduction and example, if you peruse through this issue of the *Guide Book* you will find *many* listings of Morgan silver dollars 1878-1921 where the mintage figure does not seem to correlate with a coin's price. As examples, among such coins the 1901, of which 6,962,813 were made for circulation, an MS-65 coin is valued at $150,000. In the same series the 1884-CC, of which only 1,136,000 were struck, is listed at $400., or only a tiny fraction of the value of a 1901.

Why the difference? The explanation is that nearly all of the 6,962,000 dollars of 1901 were either placed into circulation at the time, and became worn, or were melted generations ago. Very few were saved by collectors, and today MS-65 coins are extreme rarities. On the other hand, of the 1,126,000 1885-CC silver dollars minted, relatively few went into circulation. Vast quantities were sealed in 1,000-coin cloth bags and put into government storage. Generations later, as coin collecting became popular, thousands were paid out by the Treasury Department. Years later, in the early 1960s, when silver metal rose in value, there was a "run" on long-stored silver dollars, and it was learned in March 1964 that 962,638 1884-CC dollars, amounting to 84.7% of the original mintage, were still in the hands of the Treasury Department!

With this information the prices become understandable. Even though the 1901 had a high mintage, few were saved, and although worn coins are common, gem MS-65 coins are rarities. In contrast, nearly all of the low-mintage 1885-CC dollars were stored by the government, and today most of them still exist, including in MS-65 grade.

There are many other situations in which mintages are not particularly relevant to the availability and price of coins today. Often a special circumstance will lead to certain coins being saved in especially large quantities, later dramatically affecting the availability and value of such pieces.

Here are some of them:

EXCITEMENT OF A NEW DESIGN

In the panorama of American coinage some new designs have captured the fancy of the public that saved them in large quantities when they were released. In many other instances new designs were ignored, and coins slipped into circulation unnoticed.

In 1909 much publicity was given to the new Lincoln portrait to be used on the one-cent piece, replacing the familiar Indian Head motif. On the reverse in tiny letters were the initials, V.D.B., of the coin's designer, Victor David Brenner. The occasion was the 100th anniversary of Lincoln's birth. Coinage commenced at the Philadelphia and San Francisco mints. In total, 27,995,000 1909 V.D.B. cents were struck and 484,000 of the 1909-S V.D.B.

On August 2, 1909, the new cents were released to the public. A mad scramble ensued, and, soon, banks had to ration the number paid out to any single individual, this being particularly true in the East. Interest in the West was less intense, and fewer coins were saved. A controversy arose as to the V.D.B. initials, and some newspaper notices complained that as Brenner had been paid for his work, there was no point in giving his initials a prominent place on the coins, (never mind that artists' initials had been used on other coins for a long time. As examples, the M initial of George T. Morgan appeared on both the obverse and reverse of silver dollars from 1878 onward, Chief Engraver Charles E. Barber was memorialized by a B on the neck of Miss Liberty on dimes, quarters, and half dollars from 1892 onward, and the recent (1907 onward) double eagles bore the monogram of Augustus Saint-Gaudens prominently on the obverse. The offending V.D.B. initials were removed, and later 1909 and 1909-S cents were made without this feature.

Word spread that the cents with V.D.B. would be rare, and even more were saved. Today, the 1909 V.D.B. cents are readily available in Mint State. The 1909-S V.D.B., of lower mintage and of which far fewer were saved, lists for $1,300. in MS-63.

A few years later at the Denver Mint, 1,193,000 1914-D cents were struck. Not much attention was paid to them, and today examples are rare, an MS-63 listing for $2,200. Years later only 866,000 1931-S cents were made. However, at this time there was a strong and growing interest in the numismatic hobby, and the low mintage figure was widely publicized, and although the mintage of the 1931-S is lower than for the 1914-D, an MS-63 1931-S is valued at just $100.

──────── **OTHER POPULAR FIRST-YEAR COINS** ────────

Among other United States coins struck since 1792, these first-year-of issue varieties were saved in large numbers and are especially plentiful today (a partial list):

• **1943 Zinc-coated steel cent.** The novel appearance of this coin resulted in many being saved as curiosities.

• **1883 Liberty Head nickel without CENTS.** The Mint expressed the value of this new design simply as V, without mention of CENTS, not particularly unusual, as three-cent pieces of the era were simply denominated as III. Certain people gold-plated the new nickels and pass them off as $5 gold coins of similar diameter. Soon, the Mint added CENTS. News accounts were printed that the "mistake" coins without CENTS would be recalled and would become very rare. So many were saved that today this variety is the most plentiful in Mint State of any Liberty Head nickel in the entire series from 1883 to 1913.

• **1913 Buffalo nickel.** These were saved in large quantities, and today there are more Mint State coins of this year in existence than for any other issue of the next 15 years.

• **1837 Liberty Seated, No Stars half dime.** Several thousand or more were saved, a large number for a half dime of the era. Apparently, they were attractive curiosities at the time, the same being true of the dimes of this year. The cameo-like appearance seems to have made them attractive curiosities, the same being true of the dimes of this year.

• **1837 Liberty Seated, No Stars dime.** Somewhat over a thousand were saved, a large number for a dime of the era.

• **1916 "Mercury" dime.** Quantities were saved of the 1916 and 1916-S, the first year of issue. . However, for some reason the low-mintage 1916-D was generally overlooked and today is very rare in Mint State.

• **1932 Washington quarter.** At the Philadelphia Mint 5,504,000 were minted, and it likely that several hundred thousand were saved, making them plentiful today. The 1932-D quarter was struck to the extent of

436,800, but for some reason was overlooked by the public, with the result that Mint State coins are rare today. On the other hand, of the 408,000 1932-S quarters struck, thousands were saved. Today, Mint State 1932-S quarters are at least 10 to 20 times more available than are equivalent examples of the higher-mintage 1932-D.

• **1999 onward, statehood quarters.** Beginning in 1999, five different quarter dollar designs were produced each year, with motifs observing the states in the order that they joined the Union. These coins were highly publicized, and many were, and still are, saved as souvenirs.

• **1964 Kennedy half dollar.** The popularity of the assassinated president was such that although hundreds of millions were minted, it is likely that most were saved as souvenirs. This was also the last year of the 90% silver content half dollar, further increasing its popularity.

• **2000 Sacagawea "golden dollar."** These coins, intended to be a popular substitute for paper dollars and to last much longer in circulation, were launched with much fanfare in 2000, and more than just a few were saved by the public. However, the coin did not catch on for general use in commerce.

• **MCMVII (1907) High Relief gold $20.** Although only 12,367 were minted, at least 6,000 survive today, mostly in Mint State. Released in December 1907, the coin, by famous sculptor Augustus Saint-Gaudens, created a sensation, and soon the coins were selling for $30 each. Today, Mint State coins are plentiful, but as the demand for them is extremely strong, choice specimens sell for strong prices.

• **1892 and 1893 World's Columbian Exposition commemorative half dollars.** These, the first commemorative half dollars, were widely publicized, and hundreds of thousands were saved. Today they are very common.

COINS FEW PEOPLE NOTICED

In contrast to the above, most coins of new designs attracted no particular notice, and examples were not saved in unusual quantities. In sharp contrast to the ultra-popular Kennedy half dollar of 1964, its predecessor design, the Franklin half dollar launched in 1948, generated very little interest, and even numismatist generally ignored them—perhaps preferring the old Liberty Walking design that had been a favorite for a long time.

Although a long list could be made, here are some first-year-of-issue coins that were *not* noticed in their own time. Consequently, specimens range from scarce to rare in Mint State today:

• **1793 cent and half cent.** As popular as these may be today, in 1793 there was no known instance in which a numismatist or museum deliberately saved pieces as souvenirs.

• **1794-1795 half dime, half dollar, and silver dollar.** The Flowing Hair coins, highly desired today, seem to have attracted little notice in their time, and again there is no record of any having been deliberately saved.

• **1807 and related Capped Bust coinages.** The Capped Bust and related coins of John Reich, assistant engraver at the Mint, were first used in 1807 on the silver half dollar and gold $5, later on certain other denominations. Today these are extremely popular with collectors, but in their time they were not noticed, and few were saved in Mint State.

• **1839 Liberty Seated half dollar.** Today, examples are very elusive, particularly the very first version without drapery at the elbow. The variety attracted no notice when it was first issued, nor did the with-drapery issue that followed it. (should you explain that varieties, in general, were not attracting attention or was this an anomaly?)

• **1840 Liberty Seated dollar.** Specimens are very scarce in Mint State today and are virtually unknown in gem preservation.

• **1892 Barber dime, quarter, and half dollar.** In 1892 the new Liberty Head design by Charles E. Barber replaced the long-lived Liberty Seated motif. The new coins received bad press notices, this unattributed item published in an 1892 newspaper, being representative: "During the week which closed last Saturday some of the new coins issued by the United States government crept into circulation and were commented on by beholders from different points of view.... On one side there appears a spread-eagle and on the other the profile of a head surmounted by the legend: 'In God We Trust.' The eagle is a meager and ill-fed specimen of our noble bird and the profile is that of a goddess of liberty, though it looks like the head of the ignoble Emperor Vitellius with a goiter. To be extremely frank, these new coins are not artistic. Even this mild statement is unduly flattering to the designers.... The nation has poor luck in getting up designs for coins. The reason is not apparent unless it be that sufficient inducements are not offered to bring our really good designers into competition...." Another factor detracting from public interest was the wide attention besides, public attention was focused on the forthcoming commemorative half dollars of the World's Columbian Exposition. Not many were saved.

• **1938 Jefferson nickel.** Although the numismatic hobby was dynamic at the time, the new nickel design attracted little notice, and no unusual quantities were saved. The market was still reeling from the burst bubble of the 1935-1936 commemorative craze, and there was little incentive in saving coins for investment.

─────────── **THE 1962-1964 TREASURY RELEASE** ───────────

The Bland-Allison Act of February 28, 1878, a political boondoggle passed to accommodate silver-mining interests in the West, mandated that the Treasury Department buy millions of ounces of silver each year and convert it to silver dollars. At the time the world price of silver bullion was dropping, and there were economic difficulties in the mining states. From 1878 to 1904 and again in 1921, silver dollars of the Morgan design were minted under this legislation and subsequent acts, to the extent of 656,989,387 pieces. From 1921 to 1935 silver dollars of the Peace design were produced in the amount of 190,577,279 pieces.

Although silver dollars were used in commerce in certain areas of the West, by and large paper currency served the needs of trade and exchange. As these hundreds of millions of newly-minted dollars were not needed, most were put up in 1,000-coin canvas bags and stored in Treasury vaults. In 1918, under terms of the Pittman Act, 270,232,722 Morgan dollars were melted. At the time, the market for silver was temporarily strong, and there was a call for bullion to ship to India. No accounting was kept of the dates and mints involved in the destruction. Just the quantities were recorded (this procedure being typical when the Treasury melted old coins). . However, hundreds of millions remained.

Now and again there was a call for pieces for circulation, especially in the West, and in the East and Midwest there was a modest demand for pieces for use as holiday and other gifts. and in such instances many were paid out. The earlier example of the high-mintage 1901 dollar being rare in Mint State, as most were circulated, is reflective of this. Others coins were stored, such as the aforementioned low-mintage 1884-CC, of which 84.7% were still in the hands of the Treasury as late as 1964! At this time the Treasury decided to hold back bags that were marked as having Carson City dollars, although in records of storage no account was made of them earlier.

Beginning in a significant way in the 1950s, silver dollars became very popular with numismatist. The rarest of all Morgan silver dollars by 1962 was considered to be the 1903-O. In the *Guide Book* an Uncirculated coin listed for $1,500, the highest price for any variety. Experts estimated that fewer than a dozen Mint State coins existed in all of numismatics. It was presumed that most had been melted in 1918 under the Pittman Act.

Then this:

In November 1962, during the normal payout of silver dollars as gifts for the holiday season, some long-sealed bags of coins were taken from a vault in the Philadelphia Mint that had remained under seal since 1929. It was soon found that brilliant 1903-O dollars were among these! A treasure hunt ensued, and hundreds of thousands of these former rarities were found. The rush was on!

From then until March 1964, hundreds of millions of Morgan and Peace dollars were emptied from government and bank storage. At one time a long line of people, some with wheelbarrows, formed outside of the Treasury Building in Washington, DC, to obtain bags of dollars. Finally, only about three million coins remained, mostly the aforementioned Carson City issues, which the Treasury decided to hold back. These were later sold at strong premiums in a series of auctions held by the General Services Administration.

In the meantime Morgan and Peace dollars became very large and important sections of the coin hobby, as they remain today. However, as can be seen, the combined elements of some coins having been melted in 1918, others having been placed into circulation generations ago, and still others existing in Mint State from long-stored hoards, results in silver dollar prices bearing little relation to mintage figures in many instances.

OTHER FAMOUS HOARDS

While the great Treasury release of 1962-1964 is the most famous of all hoards, quite a few others have attracted interest and attention over the years. Here are some of them:

• **Castine Hoard of Early Silver Coins (discovered in the 1840s):** From November 1840 through April 1841 Captain Stephen Grindle and his son Samuel unearthed many silver coins on their farm on the Bagaduce River about six miles from the harbor of Castine, Maine. The number of pieces found was not recorded, but is believed to have been between 500 and 2,000, buried in 1690 (the latest date observed) or soon afterward. Most pieces were foreign silver coins, but dozens of Massachusetts Pine Tree shillings and related silver coins were found. This hoard stands today as one of the most famous in American history.

• **Bank of New York Hoard (1856):** Circa 1856 a keg containing several thousand 1787 Fugio copper cents was found at the Bank of New York at 44 Wall Street. Each was in Mint State, most with brown toning. For many years these were given out as souvenirs and keepsakes to clients. By 1948, when numismatist Damon G. Douglas examined them, there were 1,641 remaining. Today, many remain at the bank and are appreciated for their history and value.

• **Nichols Find of Copper Cents (by 1859):** In the annals of American numismatics one of the most famous hoards is the so-called Nichols Find, consisting of 1796 and 1797 copper cents, Mint State, perhaps about 1,000 totally. These were distributed in the late 1859s by David Nichols. By 1863 all were gone, by which time they were worth $3 to $4 each, or less than a thousandth of their present day value.

• **Randall Hoard of Copper Cents (1860s):** Sometime soon after the Civil War, a wooden keg filled with as-new copper cents was located in the South, said to have been beneath an old railroad platform in Georgia. Revealed were thousands of coins dated 1816 to 1820, with the 1818 and

1820 being the most numerous. Today, the Randall hoard accounts for most known Mint State examples of these particular dates.

• **Col. Cohen Hoard of 1773 Virginia Halfpennies (1870s):** Sometime in the 1870s or earlier, Col. Mendes I. Cohen, a Baltimore numismatist, obtained a cache of at least 2,200 Uncirculated specimens of the 1773 Virginia halfpenny. These passed through several hands, and many pieces were dispersed along the way. As a result, today these are the only pre-colonial (pre-1776) American coins that can be easily obtained in Mint State.

• **Exeter Hoard of Massachusetts Silver (1876).** During the excavation of a seller near the railroad station in Exeter, New Hampshire, a group of 30 to 40 Massachusetts silver shillings was found in the sand, amid the remains of what seemed to be a wooden box. All bore the date 1652 and were of the Pine Tree and Oak Tree types, plus, possibly, a rare Willow Tree shilling.

• **Economite Treasure (1878):** In 1878 a remarkable hoard of silver coins was found in a subterranean at Economy, Pennsylvania, in a building erected years earlier by the Harmony Society, a utopian work-share community. The March 1881 issue of *The Coin Collector's Journal* gave this inventory: Quarter dollars: 1818 to 1828: 400 pieces. Half dollars: 1794: 150, 1795: 650, 1796: 2, 1797: 1, 1801: 300, 1802: 200, 1803: 300, 1805 over '04: 25, 1805: 600, 1806: 1,500, 1807: 2,000, 1815: 100, Common half dollars 1808-1836: 111,356 pieces. Silver dollars: 1794: 1, 1795: 800, 1796: 125, 1797: 80, 1798 Small Eagle reverse: 30, 1798 Large Eagle reverse: 560, 1799 5 stars facing: 12, 1799: 1,250, 1800: 250, 1801, '02, and '03: 600. Foreign silver (French, Spanish, and Spanish-American), total face value: $12,600. Total face value of the hoard: $75,000.00. Other information indicates that most of the coins had been taken from circulation and showed different degrees of wear.

• **Hoard of Miser Aaron White (before 1888)** • Aaron White, a Connecticut attorney, distrusted paper money and even went so far as to issue his own token inscribed, "NEVER KEEP A PAPER DOLLAR IN YOUR POCKET TILL TOMORROW." He had a passion for saving coins and accumulated over 100,000 pieces. After his death the coins were removed to a warehouse. Later the were placed in the hands of dealer Édouard Frossard, who sold most of them privately and others by auction on July 20, 1888, billed as "18,000 American and foreign copper coins and tokens selected from the Aaron White hoard." An overall estimate of the White hoard, as it existed before it was given to Frossard, was made by Benjamin P. Wright, and included these: "250 colonial and state copper coins, 60,000 copper large cents [which were mainly "rusted" and spotted; 5,000 of the nicest ones were picked out and sold for 2¢ each], 60,000 copper-nickel Flying Eagle and Indian cents [apparently most dated 1862 and 1863], 5,000 bronze two-cent pieces, 200 half dollars, 100 silver dollars, 350 gold dollars, and 20,000 to 30,000 foreign copper coins.

• **The Collins Find of 1828 Half Cents (1894):** Circa 1894 Benjamin H. Collins, a Washington, D.C., numismatist, acquired a bag of half cents dated 1828, of the 13-stars variety. It is believed that about 1,000 coins wee involved, all bright Uncirculated. By the early 1950s all but a few hundred had been distributed in the marketplace, and by now it is likely that all have individual owners.

• **Chapman Hoard of 1806 Half Cents (1906):** About 1906 Philadelphia dealer Henry Chapman acquired a hoard of 1806 half cents. Although no figure was given out at the time, it is estimated that a couple hundred or so coins were involved. Most or all had much original mint red color, with toning to brown, with light striking at the upper part of the wreath.

• **Baltimore Find (1934):** One of the most storied hoards in American numismatics is the Baltimore Find, a cache of at least 3,558 gold coins, all dated before 1857. On August 31, 1934, two young boys were playing in the cellar of a rented house at 132 South Eden Street, Baltimore, and found these coins hidden in a wall. Later, more were found in the same location. On May 2, 1935, many of the coins were sold at auction, by which time others had been sold privately, some unofficially. This hoard included many choice and gem coins dated in the 1850s.

• **New Orleans Bank Find (1982):** A few minutes past noon, October 29, 1982, a bulldozer unearthed a cache of long-hidden silver coins, believed to have been stored in three wooden boxes in the early 1840s. The pieces, mostly Spanish-American issues, but hundreds of United States coins, including 1840-O and 1841-O Liberty Seated quarters were minted in quantity. A scramble in the dirt and mud ensued, and men in business suits, ladies in dresses, and others scrambled to find treasure. The latest dated coin found was from 1842. This must have been a secret reserve of some long-forgotten merchant or bank.

• **Wells-Fargo Hoard of 1908 $20 (1990s):** In the 1990s dealer Ron Gillio purchased a hoard of 19,900 examples of the 1908 No Motto double eagle. For a time these were stored in a Wells Fargo Bank branch, giving the name to the cache. All were Mint State, and many were choice and gem quality. Offered in the market, these were dispersed over a period of several years.

• **Gold coins from abroad (turn of the 21st century):** In the late 1990s and in the first years of the twenty-first century some exciting finds of Mint State double eagles were located in foreign banks. Involved were high-grade examples of some Carson City issues in the Liberty Head series and hundreds of scarce mintmark varieties of double eagles after 1923. As is often the case when hoards are found, pieces were filtered into the market without any publicity or an accounting of specific varieties found.

SUNKEN TREASURE

Throughout American history tens of thousands of ships have lost at sea and on inland waters. Only a handful of these vessels were reported as having had significant quantities of coins aboard.

In the late 20th and early 21st centuries, numismatist were front row center as coins from several sidewheel steamers lost in the 1850s and 1860s yielded rare coins. Sketches of four of these ships are given here. Two of these, the *S.S. Yankee Blade* and the *S.S. Central America,* carried coins from the California Gold Rush.

The other two treasure ships, the *S.S. Brother Jonathan* and the *S.S. Republic,* lost off the coast of California and the coast of Georgia, respectively; each had double eagles and other coins on board.

S.S. YANKEE BLADE, Lost on October 1, 1854

The *S.S. Yankee Blade,* launched in 1853, and was in the service of the Independent Steamship Co. in 1854. On October 1 she was on a run from San Francisco south to Panama, carrying about 900 passengers and crew and an unknown amount of gold, but including about $152,000 in coins consigned by the banking house of Page, Bacon & Co. In heavy fog Captain Randall, believing he was in deep water far at sea, proceeded at full speed ahead, trying to establish a speed record—certain to be beneficial in advertising.

The captain was wrong, and the steamer was amidst the rockbound Channel Islands, off the coast of Santa Barbara, California. The ship smashed onto a rock, and was stranded at a rakish angle. In time, she sank, but not before most people escaped. In the ensuing confusion, an estimated 17 to 50 passengers lost their lives.

As to what happened to the gold coins aboard, seemingly some were recovered soon after the disaster, in circumstances shrouded in mystery. Perhaps other coins were found later, over a long period of time. In any event, in 1948 the hull was found again, and afterward various divers visited the wreck. Circa 1977 extensive recoveries were made, and an estimated 200 to 250 1854-S double eagles came on the market. All showed microscopic granularity, possibly from the action of sea-bottom sand, and all had die cracks on the reverse. Little in the way of facts has ever reached print.

——— *S.S. CENTRAL AMERICA,* Lost September 12, 1857 ———

In contrast to the preceding, in the annals of undersea treasure hunting the *S.S. Central America* has been extremely well documented. On August 20, 1857, more than 400 people, plus crew, and about $2,600,000 in gold treasure left San Francisco aboard the steamer *S.S. Sonora,* headed for Panama. The destination was reached in due course, the passengers and gold crossed 58 miles of land on the Panama Railroad, and arrived at the port city of Aspinwall on the Atlantic side.

On Thursday, September 3, *S.S. Central America* left Aspinwall. A stop was made at Havana on Monday the 7th. On the next morning the ship continued north toward New York City, its destination, where the gold coins and ingots would be received.

On Wednesday the 9th, a day out of Havana, the second officer noted in his records that a fresh breeze was kicking up swells. A tropical storm was in progress, surely to fade in a day or so. Meanwhile the large ship could handle any type of weather. However, matters went from bad to worse, and on Thursday the *S.S. Central America* was in the grip of a monster hurricane, one of the strongest on record.

On Friday the storm still raged, and the ship developed leaks in several places, flooding the lower areas. On the lower deck the rising water and the violent tossing of the vessel made it virtually impossible to continue feeding coal to the boilers. At 11 o'clock in the morning, Captain Herndon enlisted the aid of male passengers to form a bucket line to bail water, which proved to be futile. The ship became swamped and was at the mercy of the waves hitting broadside. By the next morning the decks were awash, and it was feared that the ship would be lost. The captain directed that the American flag be flown upside-down, a signal of distress.

Early in the afternoon the sail of the brig *Marine* came into sight, and soon the small ship drew near. In the following hours nearly all of the women and children were transferred to the *Marine,* and some crew members went also. A few minutes after 8:00 in the evening a huge wave hit the ship, she shuddered, timbers splintered, and with Captain Herndon standing on the paddle box, the *S.S. Central America* slipped below the waves. Although some passengers and crew were later rescued from the water, about 435 lives were lost. The hull settled at the bottom 7,200 feet below the surface.

With the Panic of 1857, the Civil War, and other matters of national importance the *S.S. Central America* was largely forgotten. Its location was not known, except that it had gone down somewhere along the planned route. In 1980 Tommy Thompson, a Columbus, Ohio scientist, directed his efforts to finding the wreck, and in 1985 a group of entrepreneurs and investors formed the Columbus-America Discovery Group. After much effort, including the guidance of scientist Bob Evans, the long-lost ship was found, and recovery of gold coins and ingots was accomplished through the aid of the *Nemo,* a remote controlled underwater device with arms that could retrieve the treasure carefully. When all was said and done, over 5,000 mint-fresh 1857-S double eagles, several hundred gold ingots, and other coins were recovered.

The California Gold Marketing Group, under the direction of Dwight Manley, began the sale of the treasure coins and ingots in 2000, and within the next few years all were sold, for an estimated $100,000,000. As part of the project, the present writer created the 1,050-page book, *A California Gold Rush History,* with extensive illustrations and information. As no larger Gold Rush era treasure was ever lost, by definition no greater treasure can ever be found, making the *S.S. Central America* find a unique event.

—— *S.S. BROTHER JONATHAN,* Lost on January 30, 1865 ——

In 1865 the sidewheel steamer *S.S. Brother Jonathan* was important in the coastwise trade from California north to Oregon and Washington. Shortly before noon on Friday, July 28, the 1,360-ton vessel headed from San Francisco to Portland, carrying 150 or more passengers, a crew of about 60, and a 500-ton cargo ranging from machinery for a woolen mill to casks of whiskey. Gold coins were aboard, of an unknown value.

Heading along the coast the ship ran into high winds and waves, and Capt. DeWolf put the vessel into the harbor at Crescent City to spend the night. In the morning the sea would be calm, it was thought. On Sunday the 30th, the ship resumed the trip, but the open sea was still rough, and the captain ordered the ship to turn around and go back to Crescent City. Unexpectedly, the ship struck a hidden rock, a pinnacle hidden just below the waves. Only a few passengers survived. In the best seafaring tradition, the captain went down with the ship.

In following years many efforts were made to find the lost ship, but without success. Finally, in the 1990s a group of investors and entrepreneurs formed Deep Sea Research, Inc., found the ship, and were able to recover over 1,000 gold coins, a find dominated by Mint State 1865-S double eagles.

———————— *S.S. REPUBLIC,* Lost October 25, 1865 ————————

In high winds off the coast of Georgia the *S.S. Republic,* on its way from New York to New Orleans, was wrecked off the coast of Georgia, carrying an estimated $400,000 in gold coins to the bottom. All but 21 passengers were rescued.

In 2003 the numismatic world was startled and delighted to learn that Odyssey Marine Exploration, Inc., had located the wreck of the long-lost ship, in about 1,700 feet of water. Strewn on the sea floor was an array of gold coins along with bottles and other artifacts. Recovery began in November.

By this time the recovery included more than 900 *silver* coins, some of which were well preserved, a highly unusual situation—as, normally, seawater is very destructive to silver. However, many of these pieces must have been protected in some way.

The gold coins comprised $10 and $20 coins, a mixture of dates from 1865 and earlier times. Included were many exceptionally well- preserved specimens from the 1860s. As the *Guide Book* goes to press, recovery is ongoing, and no inventory has been published. More excitement is in the offing!

Great Collectors and Collections of the Past
By Ron Guth and Jeff Garrett

Appleton, William Sumner

William Sumner Appleton was an active buyer in the latter half of the 19th century, purchasing J.J. Mickley's 1804 silver dollar, Mickley's entire gold coin collection, and virtually all of Lorin G. Parmelee's collection. He authored several works, including one on Washington-related coins and medals.

Bass, Harry W.

Harry W. Bass, Jr. did what most collectors can only dream of—he built a nearly complete collection of United States gold coins, with an emphasis on superb quality. A true numismatist in the classic sense, Bass collected by die variety, both major and minor. The bulk of his collection was sold over a series of four auctions from 1999 to 2000, but the core collection of gold types and $3 gold pieces (including the unique 1870-S) is now on display at the Money Museum of the American Numismatic Association in Colorado Springs, Colorado.

Boyd, Frederick C.C.

F.C.C. Boyd was active as a coin dealer and collector during the first half of the 20th century. He acquired many great rarities, including an 1894-S dime, an 1876-CC twenty-cent piece, a 1927-D double eagle, and many others; for a short time, he owned an 1804 silver dollar. His silver and gold coins were sold at action in 1946, with the silver portion billed as "The World's Greatest Collection." His U.S. colonial coins are just now coming onto the market, via the John J. Ford collection.

Brand, Virgil M.

Virgil Brand was a Chicago brewer, who used his fortune to amass one of the largest coin collections of all time. Active from 1879 until his death in 1926, Brand was not averse to buying multiple items of great rarities (he owned six of the ten 1884 trade dollars, 30 $4 Gold "Stellas," five 1792 Silver-Center cents, etc.) but only one 1804 silver dollar. At his death, his collection contained over 350,000 coins, which required several decades to disperse completely.

Browning, Jeff

Jeff Browning was the name behind the Dallas Bank Collection of gold coins, sold at auction in 2001. Collecting during the 1960s and 1970s, Browning acquired a complete set of Liberty Head double eagles, a complete set of $4 Stellas, and a 1907 Ultra High Relief double eagle.

Carter, Amon, Sr. and Jr.

Amon Carter, Sr. was a Texas oilman and co-founder of American Airlines. In the 1930s, he was introduced to coins by B. Max Mehl and went on a two-decade buying binge that netted him fabulous rarities such as an 1804 silver dollar, an 1884 trade dollar, an 1885 trade dollar, an 1822 half eagle, and many other rarities. Upon his death, Carter's collection passed to his son, who developed his own reputation as a top-ranked collector of United States currency.

Dunham, William F.

William Dunham was a Chicago druggist who was an active collector in the first half of the 20th century. His collection included one of the finest known 1802 half dimes, an 1804 silver dollar, and an 1822 half eagle. Following Dunham's death, the Texas coin dealer, B. Max Mehl, purchased the collection intact. Mehl's 1941 Mail Bid Sale of the Dunham collection, offered in a lavish catalogue, was a deception as many of the best coins had already been sold privately!

Eckfeldt, Adam

A Mint employee for many years, Adam Eckfeldt was instrumental in building the Mint Cabinet that is now part of the National Numismatic Collection at the Smithsonian Institution. Beginning with the Mint's inception in 1792, Eckfeldt set aside coins each year with an eye to someday establishing a conservatory of coins. His dream was realized in 1838, when Mint Director Robert Maskell Patterson established a national collection at the Philadelphia Mint. Thanks to Adam Eckfeldt's foresight, collectors of today can enjoy many rarities that might otherwise have been lost forever.

Eliasberg, Louis E., Sr.

Louis Eliasberg is famous in numismatic circles for having assembled the only complete collection of federally-issued United States coins. In 1942, Eliasberg purchased John Clapp's comprehensive collection intact, reducing his want list to a mere handful of coins. In 1950, Eliasberg achieved his goal of completion with the purchase of the unique 1873-CC No Arrows dime. His gold coins were sold at auction in 1982 and the balance of the collection was sold at auction in 1996 and 1997. The combined sales reached a total of $44 million.

Ellsworth, Colonel James W.

James Ellsworth's collection, built during the late 1800s through 1923, included many important rarities, such as a 1787 Brasher doubloon and two (!) 1804 silver dollars. Unlike most collectors, Ellsworth sold his collection during his lifetime, sharing many of the most significant coins with another famous collector, John Work Garrett.

King Farouk of Egypt

Farouk was a flamboyant king who used the Egyptian treasury to build a fabulous collection of U.S. and world coins. Farouk was deposed in 1952 and the sale of his collection in 1954 was one of the great numismatic events of history. The 1933 double eagle he once held reappeared in 2002, selling for a record price of $7.59 million!

Garrett, John Work

In 1919, John Work Garrett acquired a collection built by his father and brother that was already one of the most celebrated in America. While not as complete as Louis Eliasberg's U.S. coin collection, Garrett's included U.S. colonial and pre-federal issues, plus rarities from around the world. The sale of his U.S. coins (from 1979-1981) realized over $25 million, setting a modern record for a single coin collection. In adjusted dollars, it would still be the most valuable collection today.

Green, Colonel Edward Howland Robinson

Col. E.H.R. Green was a prolific collector thanks to the fortune left him by his mother, Hetty Green (the "Witch of Wall Street"). He once owned all five of the 1913 Liberty Head nickels, an 1804 silver dollar, several 1838-O half dollars, and over 200 1796 Draped Bust quarter dollars. In 1939, his coin collection was appraised at over $1.2 million, a staggering figure at the time.

Lilly, Josiah K.

Josiah K. Lilly amassed a huge collection of U.S. and world gold coins during the 1950s and 1960s. After his death, the Smithsonian Institution accepted the donation of the collection in exchange for a $5 million estate tax credit (worth roughly $50 million today). The U.S. section was virtually complete and included such rarities as the 1787 Brasher half doubloon, an 1822 half eagle, and a 1907 Ultra-High Relief $20 gold piece. His collection, which has been exhibited in a special room in the National Museum of American History since the early 1970s, may be taken down in August 2004.

Mickley, Joseph J.
Joseph Mickley was one of the pioneer collectors of American coins, beginning a quest for a cent of his birth year (1799) in the early 1800s. Legend had Mickley visiting the U.S. Mint in 1827 to purchase four of the rare quarter dollars of that date; however, that legend has been debunked in recent years. Mickley is best known for the restrikes that he made of certain U.S. coins (1811 half cent, 1804 large cent, and 1823 large cent) using dies that the Mint had sold years earlier as scrap metal. Most of Mickley's dies were bought back by the U.S. government when they appeared in an auction of Mickley's estate in 1878.

Mitchelson, John C.
In December 1911, Joseph Mitchelson donated his collection of over 10,000 U.S. and world coins to the Connecticut State Library in Hartford, Connecticut, where the bulk of the collection remains to this day. Provisions were made for the addition of new U.S. coins as they were minted in subsequent years. Highlights of the collection include a 1907 Ultra High Relief double eagle, a 1737 Higley copper, and many other fabulous rarities, few of which have been seen by the general public. In 1995, selected duplicates from the Mitchelson collection were sold at auction, including a 1927-D double eagle.

Newcomer, Waldo
Waldo Newcomer began collecting in the 1890s and quickly built one of the largest and most complete collections of American colonial and federal coins. His collection of U.S. gold coins was said to be complete except for one half eagle and one double eagle. Newcomer also owned examples of great rarities such as two 1787 Brasher doubloons, an 1802 half dime, an 1838-O half dollar, an 1853 half dollar (without rays and arrowheads), and an 1804 silver dollar. Newcomer's coins were sold at auction over nearly a decade from 1932 to 1941.

Norweb, Mrs. R. Henry
Over the course of many decades in the late 1800 and throughout the 20th century, the Norweb family built an extensive collection of rare colonials and superb quality U.S. coins. Mrs. Norweb acquired the love of numismatics at her father's feet and continued adding coins after his death. Highlights of the collection included a 1787 Brasher doubloon, a 1792 Pattern quarter dollar, a 1913 nickel, an 1815 half eagle, and the finest known 1861 Paquet Reverse double eagle. The Norweb collection realized $20 million at auction in 1987 and 1988, despite the previous gifting-away of the Brasher doubloon and the 1913 nickel!

Parmelee, Lorin G.
Lorin Parmelee, a Boston bean baker, started collecting coins in the 1850s, when U.S. colonial copper coins and large cents still circulated at face value. As his taste and fortunes advanced, he began purchasing coins at auction, then began buying entire collections, taking what he wanted, and selling off the duplicates. The remainders, from the Charles Bushnell collection (purchased by Parmelee in 1880) alone, represented one of the finest coin auctions of the 19th century. In its time, Parmelee's collection was generally perceived to be the finest and most complete collection of coins ever assembled. Included were great rarities such as the 1796 and 1797 half dollars, and 1804 silver dollar, and a set of 1783 Nova Constellatio pattern coins in silver.

Pittman, John Jay
Unlike most of the collectors in this section, John Jay Pittman had limited resources with which to buy rare coins. However, through shrewd purchases, Pittman amassed a collection that realized more than $30 million when it was sold between 1997 and 1998. Some of his best purchases were made at the 1954 sale of King Farouk's coin collection.

Reed, Byron
Byron Reed was a real estate tycoon from Omaha, Nebraska, who built a fine collection of American coins, books, and autographs. Reed worked on his collection from the 1880s until his death in 1891. Reed bequeathed his coins and library to the city of Omaha, along with a plot of land for a building that would eventually house both collections. In 1996, selections from his coin collection were sold at auction to raise money for the city. However, the majority of Reed's collection, including his 1804 silver dollar and rare U.S. patterns, remains largely intact, with many of the coins now on display at the Western Heritage Museum in Omaha.

Sheldon, Dr. William H.
Dr. Sheldon collected large cents by die variety and, in 1949 he wrote *Early American Cents* (renamed *Penny Whimsy* in 1958), the standard reference book on the 1793-1814 cent varieties. He was accused (posthumously, and some say unfairly) of switching coins at the American Numismatic Society, but his scholarship remains undisputed. The 70-point grading system used by numismatist today was developed by Sheldon.

Snowden, James Ross
James Snowden served as Director of the Mint from 1853 to 1861, and was a serious numismatist, as well. He built the cabinet of Washington coins, tokens, and medals that went on display at the Philadelphia Mint in 1860. Snowden acquired many of the items in the display by trading restrikes of rare United States coins.

Stickney, Matthew Adams
Matthew Stickney was a contemporary of Joseph J. Mickley and, thus, among the first truly serious collectors of American coins. Stickney acquired many of his best coins directly from the Mint: some through trades and some through an annual purchase of Proof coins beginning in 1845. Other rarities came from his special relationship with a New York bullion firm, which sent him gold rarities for their intrinsic metal value. Around 1843, Stickney traded a gold 1785 Immune Columbia colonial coin for one of the Mint's 1804 silver dollars! Other highlights from his collection include the unique 1776 New Hampshire cent and a 1776 Massachusetts "Janus Head" copper.

Trompeter, Ed
Ed Trompeter built a collection of Proof U.S. gold coins, complete for the period from 1860-1915, plus extra rarities such as an 1855 Proof gold dollar, a complete set of $4 gold "Stellas," a Quintuple "Stella," a 1907 Ultra High Relief double eagle, and more. Trompeter's Proof gold dollars through three dollar gold pieces were sold at auction in 1992; his Proof half eagles through double eagles were sold privately for over $15 million in 1998. The Trompeter pedigree is one of the most desirable of modern times.

Wilkison, John
John Wilkison built the finest collection of U.S. gold pattern coins ever assembled outside the Mint. His collection included unique rarities such as the 1907 Indian Head double eagle and the complete set of gold 1872 "Amazonian" patterns ($1 through $20). The collection formed the basis for David Aker's 1975 book *United States Gold Patterns*, a modern numismatist's "wish book."

Woodin, William H.
William Woodin once owned the unique 1870-S $3. In 1909, he acquired the two known gold 1877 $50 "half unions," prompting an outrage that the government had allowed them to be released. Shortly thereafter, Wooding traded them for a "trunkful" of patterns that served as the basis for the first book on U.S. Pattern coins. The half unions are now in the Smithsonian Institution and Woodin's patterns represent the majority of the pieces that appear on the market today.

GLOSSARY

Over the years coin collectors have developed a special jargon to describe their coins. The following list includes terms that are used frequently by coin collectors or that have a special meaning other than their ordinary dictionary definitions. You will find them useful when you want to discuss or describe your coins.

Alloy — A combination of two or more metals.

Altered Date — A false date on a coin; a date altered to make a coin appear to be one of a rarer or more valuable issue.

Bag Mark — A surface mark, usually a small nick, acquired by a coin through contact with others in a mint bag.

Billon — Base silver, usually a low-grade mixture of silver and copper.

Blank — The formed piece of metal on which a coin design will be stamped.

Bronze — An allow of copper, zinc, and tin.

Bullion — Uncoined gold or silver in the form of bars, ingots, or plate.

Business Strike — An Uncirculated coin intended for eventual use in commerce as opposed to a Proof coin.

Cast Coins — Coins that are made by pouring molten metal into a mold instead of in the usual manner of striking with dies.

Cent — One one-hundredth of the standard monetary unit. Also called Centabo in Mexico and some Central and South American countries.

Certified Coin — A coin that has been graded, authenticated, and encapsulated in plastic by an independent grading service.

Cherrypicker — A collector who finds scarce and unusual coins by carefully searching through old accumulations or dealer's stocks.

Clad Coinage — Issues of the United States dimes, quarters, halves, and dollars made since 1965. Each coin has a center core and a layer of copper–nickel or silver on both sides.

Collar — The outer ring, or die chamber that holds a blank in place in the coinage press while the coin is impressed with the obverse and reverse dies.

Contact marks — Minor abrasions on an uncirculated coin, made by contact with other coins in a bag or roll.

Countermark — A stamp or mark impressed on a coin to verify its use by another government or to indicate revaluation.

Crack-out — A coin that has been removed from an encapsulated grading service holder.

Crown — A dollar-size silver coin; specifically one from Great Britain.

Designer — The artist who creates a coin's design. An engraver is the person who cuts a design into a coinage die.

Die — A piece of metal engraved with a design and used for stamping coins.

Die Crack — A fine, raised line on a coin caused by a broken die.

Die Defect — An imperfection on a coin caused by a damaged die.

Die Variety — Any minor alteration in the basic design of a coin.

Dipped, Dipping — Refers to chemical cleaning of a coin with diluted acid.

Double Eagle — The United States $20.00 gold coin.

Double Die — A die that that been given two misaligned impressions from a hub; also, a coin made from such a die.

Doubloon — Popular name for a Spanish gold coin originally valued at $16.00.

Eagle — A United States $10.00 gold coin; also refers to U.S. silver, gold, and platinum bullion pieces made from 1986 to the present.

Edge — Periphery of a coin containing a series of reeds, lettering, or other decoration.

Electrotype — A reproduction of a coin or medal made by the electrodeposition process. Electrotypes are frequently used in museum displays.

Electrum — A naturally occurring mixture of gold and silver. Some of the world's first coins were made of this alloy.

Encapsulated Coins — Coins that have been authenticated, graded, and sealed in plastic by a professional service.

Engraver — The person who cuts the design into a coinage die.

Error — A mismade coin not intended for circulation.

Exergue — That portion of a coin beneath the main design and separated by a line.

Field — The background portion of a coin's surface not used for a design or inscription.

Filler — A coin in worn condition but rare enough to be included in a collection.

Fineness — The purity of gold, silver, or any other precious metal, expressed in terms of one thousand parts. A coin of 90 percent pure silver is expressed as .900 fine.

Flan — A blank piece of metal in the size and shape of a coin; also called a planchet.

Gem — A coin of exceptionally high quality.

Half Eagle — The United States $5.00 gold coin.

Hub — A positive-image punch to impress the coin's design into a die for coinage.

Incuse — The design of a coin which has been impressed below the coin's surface. A design raised above the coin's surface is in relief.

Inscription — The legend or lettering on a coin.

Intrinsic Value — Bullion/melt value of the actual precious metal in a numismatic item.

Investment Grade — Generally a coin in grade MS-65 or better.

Junk Silver — Common-date silver coins taken from circulation; worth only bullion value.

Key Coin — The scarcest or most valuable coin in a series.

Laureate — Head crowned with a laurel wreath.

Legal Tender — Money that is officially issued and recognized for redemption by an authorized agency or government.

Legend — The principal inscription on a coin.

Lettered Edge — The narrow edge of a coin bearing an inscription, found on some foreign and most older United States coins.

Luster — Shiny "frost" on the surface of an Uncirculated or Mint State coin.

Milled Edge — The raised rim around the outer surface of a coin, not to be confused with the reeded or serrated narrow edge of a coin.

Mint Error — Any mismade or defective coin produced by a mint.

Mint Luster — Shiny "frost" on the surface of an Uncirculated or Mint State coin.

Mint Mark — A small letter, indicating which mint struck the coin.

Mint Set — A set of Uncirculated coins packaged and sold by the Mint. Each set contains one each of the coins made for circulation at each of the mints.

Motto — An inspirational word or phrased used on a coin.

Mule — A coin struck from two dies not originally intended to be used together.

Obverse — The front or face side of a coin.

Overdate — Date made by superimposing one or more numbers on a previously dated die.

Over Graded — A coin in poorer condition than stated.

Overstrike—Impression made with new dies on a previously struck coin.

Patina — The green or brown surface film found on ancient copper and bronze coins caused by oxidation over a long period or time.

Pattern — Experimental or trial coin, generally of a new design, denomination, or metal.

Pedigree — The record of previous owners of a rare coin.

Planchet — The blank piece of metal on which a coin design is stamped.

Proofs — Coins struck for collectors by the Mint using specially polished dies and planchets.

Proof Set — A packaged set of each of the Proof coins made during that year and sold by the Mint to collectors.

Quarter Eagle — The United States $2.50 gold coin.

Raw — A coin that has not been encapsulated in plastic by any grading service.

Reeded Edge — The edge of a coin with grooved lines that run vertically around its perimeter as seen on modern United States silver and clad coins.

Relief — Any part of a coin's design that is raised above the coin's field is said to be in relief. The opposite of relief is incuse, meaning sunk into the field.

Restrike — A coin struck from genuine dies at a later date than the original issue.

Reverse — The back side of a coin.

Rim — The raised portion of a coin that protects the design from wear.

Round — A round one-ounce silver medal or bullion piece.

Series — A set of one coin of each year issued from each mint of a specific design and denomination. For example, Lincoln cents from 1909 to 1959.

Slab — A hard plastic case containing a coin that has been graded and encapsulated by a professional service.

Spot Price — The daily quoted market value of precious metals in bullion form.

Token — A privately issued piece that has an exchange value for goods or services, but is not an official government coin.

Trade Dollar — Silver dollar issued especially for trade with a foreign country. In the United States, trade dollars were first issued in 1873 to stimulate trade with the Orient. Many other countries have also issued trade dollars.

Truncation — The sharply cut-off bottom edge of a bust or portrait.

Type — A coin's basic distinguishing design.

Type Set — One of each coin of a particular design, series, or period.

Uncirculated — A coin that has never been used or worn in any way and has retained its original new surface and luster; also called Mint State.

Unique — An item of which only one specimen is known to exist.

Variety — A coin's design that sets it apart from the normal issue of that type.

Wheaties — Lincoln cents with the wheat reverse issued from 1909 to 1958.

Year Set — A set of coins for any given year consisting of one of each denomination from each year.

TOP 250 COIN PRICES REALIZED
(from auctions since 1994)

RANK	DEN	DATE/VAR	GRADE	PRICE	DATE	FIRM
1	G$20	1933	GEM BU	$7,590,020	Jul-02	Sothebys/Stack's
2	S$1	1804 Original	PCGS PR68	$4,140,000	Aug-99	Bowers & Merena
3	10C	1873-CC Arrows	NGC MS65	$2,300,000	Jan-04	Goldberg
4	5C	1913 Liberty	NGC PR66	$1,840,000	Mar-01	Superior
5	S$1	1804 Original	PCGS PR64	$1,840,000	Oct-00	Stack's
6	S$1	1804 Original	PR63	$1,815,000	Apr-97	Bowers & Merena
7	5C	1913 Nickel	GEM PR66	$1,485,000	May-96	Bowers & Merena
8	G$20	1907 EX-HR Lt Edg PR	PCGS PR67	$1,210,000	May-99	Goldberg
9	G$20	1907 EX-HR Lt Edg PR	PCGS PR68	$1,150,000	Feb-03	Goldberg
10	S$1	1870-S	BU PL	$1,092,500	May-03	Stack's
11	50C	1797 O-101a	NGC MS66	$966,000	Mar-04	ANR
12	T$1	1885 Trade	NGC PR61	$920,000	May-03	Stack's
13	S$1	1804 Restrike PR	PCGS PR58	$874,000	Nov-01	Bowers & Merena
14	G$20	1907 EX-HR Lt Edg PR	PR	$825,000	Dec-96	Sotheby's
15	G$20	1907 EX-HR Lt Edg PR	PR	$690,000	Oct-01	Sotheby's/Stack's
16	G$10	1839 Type of 38 PR	NGC PR67	$690,000	Sep-99	Goldberg
17	G$20	1907 EX-HR Lt Edg PR	PCGS PR67	$660,000	Jan-97	Bowers & Merena
18	50C	1861 Original	VF (35)	$632,500	Oct-03	Stack's
19	10C	1873-CC No Arrows	PCGS MS64	$632,500	Apr-99	Heritage
20	G$2.5	1796 No Stars	BU	$605,000	Nov-05	S/R/A
21	G$20	1927-D	PCGS MS65	$577,500	May-98	Akers
22	G$10	1838 PR	PR	$550,000	May-98	Akers
23	S$1	1889-CC	PCGS MS68	$529,000	Jan-01	Bowers & Merena
24	G$20	1927-D	GEM BU	$522,500	Mar-91	Stack's
25	T$1	1884 Trade	PCGS PR67	$510,600	Oct-00	Goldberg
26	G$10	1795 13 Leaves B-1-A T-1	PCGS MS65	$506,000	Jul-03	Bowers & Merena
27	G$5	1833 Large Date PR	GEM PR	$467,500	Oct-97	Akers
28	50C	1796 16 Stars	BU	$460,000	May-99	Stack's
29	G$4	1880 Coil Hair PR	PCGS PR66	$440,000	Aug-91	Superior
30	$20	Humbert 1852/1	NGC PR64	$434,500	Oct-90	Superior
31	10C	1894-S	GEM PR	$431,250	Oct-00	Stack's
32	$1	1776 Continental Cur. Silver.N-3-D H-3-B	EF (45)	$425,500	Oct-03	Stack's
33	P1C	J-1 1792 Silver Center Cent	BU	$414,000	Jan-02	Stack's
34	S$1	1893-S	SUPERB GEM BU	$414,000	Nov-01	Stack's
35	G$20	1927-D	MS	$402,500	Oct-01	Sotheby's/Stack's
36	$20	J-452 Transitional 1865 Gold	PCGS PR64	$400,000	Aug-90	A/S/R/S
37	G$10	1857 PR	NGC PR66	$396,000	May-99	Goldberg
38	50C	1792 Getz Silver	GEM Brilliant UNC	$391,000	May-04	Stack's
39	G$20	1927-D	NGC MS66	$390,500	Jun-95	Heritage
40	G$4	1880 Coil Hair PR	NGC PR61	$379,500	Mar-04	Bowers & Merena
41	G$5	1909-O	GEM UNC	$374,000	May-98	Akers
42	G$5	1829 Small Size	MS	$374,000	Oct-96	Spink America
43	$20	Humbert 1852/1	PCGS PR65	$374,000	May-92	Superior
44	G$20	1870-CC	PCGS AU53	$368,000	Jan-04	Heritage
45	G$4	1880 Coil Hair PR	NGC PR65	$368,000	Oct-00	Stack's
46	$5	J.H. Bowie K-1, Owens	PCGS AU58	$353,000	Jan-01	Stack's
47	$50	Wass Mol 1855 K-9	GEM BU	$345,000	Oct-03	Stack's
48	P$10	J-1579 1878 Gold	GEM PR	$345,000	Oct-03	Stack's
49	S$1	1795 Off-Center Bust B-14 BB-51	NGC MS67	$345,000	Jul-02	Bowers & Merena
50	G$4	1879 Coil Hair PR	PR	$345,000	Oct-01	Sotheby's/Stack's
51	G$20	1861 Paquet	MS	$345,000	Oct-01	Sotheby's/Stack's
52	NJersy	1786 Date Below M.7-E	CH AU (55)	$322,000	Oct-03	Stack's
53	G$4	1880 Flow Hair PR	PCGS PR65	$310,500	Mar-04	Bowers & Merena
54	G$20	1856-O	NGC MS63	$310,500	Jan-02	Heritage
55	G$4	1879 Coil Hair PR	NGC PR66	$310,500	Oct-00	Stack's
56	G$5	1835 PR	GEM PR	$308,000	Oct-97	Akers
57	G$4	1880 Coil Hair PR	PR	$308,000	Oct-95	Stack's
58	G$20	1869 PR	NGC PR65	$308,000	May-90	Superior
59	$50	Kellogg 1855 K-4	GEM PR	$304,750	Oct-03	Stack's
60	H10C	1792	PCGS MS64 PQ	$299,000	Jan-04	Goldberg
61	P$5	J-1575 1878 Gold	GEM PR	$299,000	Oct-03	Stack's
62	G$2.5	1796 No Stars	BU	$299,000	May-99	Stack's
63	G$5	1832 12 Stars	MS	$297,000	Oct-96	Spink America
64	G$4	1879 Flow Hair PR	PCGS PR67	$293,250	Jul-03	ANR

RANK	DEN	DATE/VAR	GRADE	PRICE	DATE	FIRM
65	G$2.5	1798 Close Date	PCGS MS65	$291,500	Aug-91	Superior
66	50C	1794	PCGS MS63	$288,500	Jan-99	Bowers & Merena
67	$1	1776 Cont. Cur. Sil. N-1-C H-1-A.3	F/VG (or better)	$287,500	Oct-03	Stack's
68	50C	1796 16 Stars O-102	NGC MS64	$276,000	Mar-04	ANR
69	P$10	J-1373 1874 Gold	GEM PR	$276,000	Oct-03	Stack's
70	G$10	1798/7 7X6 Stars B-2-A T-10	PCGS MS62	$276,000	Jul-03	Bowers & Merena
71	G$5	1798 Sm Eagle	PCGS EF40	$275,000	May-99	Goldberg
72	G$2.5	1866 PR	PCGS PR66	$275,000	Jul-96	RARCOA/Akers
73	G$2.5	1798 Close Date	PCGS MS65	$268,500	Jun-00	Sotheby's
74	Denarium	(ca. 1659) Maryland Copper, Pl. ed.	AU	$218,500	May-04	Stack's
75	G$4	1880 Coil Hair PR	PR	$264,500	Mar-99	Stack's
76	S$1	1795 3 Leaves B-5 BB-27	NGC MS65	$264,500	Mar-04	ANR
77	S$1	1884 Trade	PCGS PR65	$264,500	Oct-00	Superior
78	G$5	1798 Sm Eagle	PCGS EF40	$264,500	Jun-00	Goldberg
79	G$5	1835 PR	PR	$264,000	May-98	Akers
80	G$10	1933	Very CH UNC	$264,000	May-98	Akers
81	G$4	1880 Coil Hair PR	PR	$264,000	Feb-92	Superior
82	G$5	1894-S	NGC MS69	$264,000	Aug-90	Akers
83	T$1	1884 Trade	NGC PR63	$258,750	May-03	Stack's
84	Copper	ND Confed, Wash/Shield M.4-C	AU (53)	$253,000	Oct-03	Stack's
85	G$4	1880 Coil Hair PR	NGC PR64	$253,000	Jan-00	Bowers & Merena
86	G$10	1839/8 Type of 1838	MS65	$253,000	Feb-98	Superior
87	G$20	1908 Motto Roman Finish PR	PR	$253,000	Dec-97	Sotheby's
88	50C	1792 Getz Silver	Choice AU	$241,500	May-04	Stack's
89	1C	1793Wreath Vine and Bars S-9	NGC MS66BN	$241,500	Mar-04	ANR
90	G$10	1920-S	PCGS MS66	$241,500	Jan-04	Stack's
91	G$2.5	1837 PR B-6145	PCGS PR66DC	$241,500	Jul-03	ANR
92	G$5	1795 Large Eagle B-5W B-6422	PCGS MS64	$241,500	Jan-03	Bowers & Merena
93	G$4	1880 Flow Hair PR	PR	$241,500	Oct-01	Sotheby's/Stack's
94	G$5	1829 Large Size	PCGS MS65	$241,500	Oct-99	Bowers & Merena
95	S$1	1794	AU58	$241,500	May-99	Bowers & Merena
96	G$5	1825/4	NGC AU50	$241,500	Feb-99	Superior
97	G$2.5	1796 Stars	AU	$231,000	Oct-96	Spink America
98	G$4	1879 Coil Hair PR	PCGS PR65	$231,000	Jul-97	Bowers & Merena
99	G$4	1880 Flow Hair PR	NGC PR65	$231,000	Nov-90	Bowers & Merena
100	G$5	1795 Sm Eagle	NGC MS65	$230,000	Mar-00	Superior
101	G$4	1879 Coil Hair PR	PR	$222,000	Oct-95	Stack's
102	3 Pence	1737 Higley Copper	EF	$218,500	May-04	Stack's
103	Copper	1786 Non Vi Virtute Vice Small Head	Choice AU	$218,500	May-04	Stack's
104	1C	1793Chain AMERI. S-1	NGC MS62BN	$218,500	Mar-04	ANR
105	G$10	1798/7 7X6 Stars B-2-A T-10	PCGS MS62	$218,500	Jan-04	Heritage
106	S$1	1871-CC	V CH BU PL	$218,500	May-03	Stack's
107	E$20	J-1643 1879 Gold	PR62/63	$214,500	May-96	Bowers & Merena
108	Sm1C	1943-D Copper w/cert #50035362	PCGS MS64BN	$212,750	Feb-03	Goldberg
109	G$5	1795 Sm Eagle	PCGS MS65	$212,750	Mar-01	Goldberg
110	P$2 1/2	J-1566 1878 Gold	PCGS PR65	$210,000	Aug-90	A/S/R/S
111	P$10	J-1581 1878 Gold	PCGS PR64	$210,000	Aug-90	A/S/R/S
112	G$20	1925-S	GEM UNC	$209,000	May-98	Akers
113	25C	1873-CC No Arrows	PCGS MS64	$209,000	Feb-98	Superior
114	G$5	1866 Motto PR	PR	$209,000	Oct-96	Spink America
115	G$5	1829 Large Size	PCGS MS64	$209,000	Jan-96	Superior
116	G$2.5	1836 PR B-6143	NGC PR66CAM	$207,000	Oct-03	Stack's
117	Shilng	1652 Willow Tree N.2-A, Cr 2-A	EF	$207,000	Jan-02	Stack's
118	S$1	1794	NGC MS61	$207,000	Nov-01	Bowers & Merena
119	G$10	1933	PCGS MS65	$207,000	Jun-00	Heritage
120	G$5	1795 Sm Eagle	NGC MS65	$207,000	Sep-99	Goldberg
121	G$20	1921 Special Striking	PR (Spec. Striking)	$203,500	Jun-00	Sotheby's
122	G$20	1862 PR	GEM PR	$203,500	May-98	Akers
123	G$20	1856-O	PCGS MS63	$203,500	Jan-95	Superior
124	G$4	1879 Flow Hair PR	PR66	$201,250	Sep-03	Goldberg
125	PS$1	J-88 Restrike 1838 Silver	NGC PR64	$201,250	May-03	Stack's
126	G$5	1836 PR	GEM PR	$198,000	Oct-97	Akers
127	G$4	1879 Coil Hair PR	PR	$198,000	Feb-92	Superior
128	$10	Miners Bnk K-1	CH BU (MS64)	$195,500	Oct-03	Stack's

RANK	DEN	DATE/VAR	GRADE	PRICE	DATE	FIRM
129	PS$1	J-61 Restrike 1836 Silver	PCGS PR63	$195,500	May-03	Stack's
130	P$10	J-1774A P-1996 1907 Gold PE B-7095	NGC PR62	$195,500	Jan-03	Heritage
131	50C	1794 O-101a	CH BU	$195,500	Oct-02	Stack's
132	G$20	1854-O	NGC AU58	$189,750	Jan-04	Heritage
133	S$1	1893-S	NGC MS65	$189,750	May-03	Stack's
134	P$5	J-1570 P-1764 1878 Gold	PCGS PR65	$189,750	Aug-02	Superior
135	S$1	1895-O	PCGS MS65DMPL	$189,750	May-01	Heritage
136	G$10	1798/7 7X6 Stars	PCGS MS61	$189,750	Feb-99	Superior
137	$50	RE Humbert RE 1852 887	NGC MS64	$189,500	Jan-99	Bowers & Merena
138	G$10	1933	PCGS MS64	$187,000	Jan-96	Superior
139	G$20	1875 PR	NGC PR64	$187,000	Aug-90	Akers
140	G$20	1924-S	GEM UNC	$187,000	May-98	Akers
141	G$10	1907 Rolled Edge	NGC MS67	$184,000	Jan-04	Stack's
142	PS$1	J-108 Restrike 1839 Silver	PCGS PR64	$184,000	Jan-04	ANR
143	$1	1776 EG FECIT, Pewter N-3-D H-3-B	Sup.GEM BU MS66	$184,000	Oct-03	Stack's
144	G$10	1797 Sm Eagle B-1-A B-6833 T-7	NGC MS61	$184,000	Jul-03	Heritage
145	PS$1	J-65 Restrike 1836 Silver	NGC PR64	$184,000	May-03	Stack's
146	50C	1838-O	PRBM	$184,000	Oct-02	Stack's
147	G$5	1828/7	NGC MS64	$184,000	Feb-99	Superior
148	50C	1817/4	PCGS AU50	$184,000	Feb-99	Superior
149	G$20	1927-S	NGC MS67	$181,500	Jun-95	Heritage
150	G$5	1909-O	NGC MS65	$178,500	Nov-98	Bowers & Merena
151	G$2.5	1854-S	PCGS AU50	$178,250	Jan-04	Superior
152	G$10	1798/7 7X6 Stars B-2A B-6837	PCGS MS61	$178,250	Jan-03	Bowers & Merena
153	S$1	1797 10X6 Stars	NGC MS65	$178,250	Nov-01	Bowers & Merena
154	G$2.5	1841 PR	PCGS PR64	$178,250	May-00	Bowers & Merena
155	G$2.5	1796 No Stars	NGC MS63	$178,250	Mar-00	Superior
156	G$5	1864-S	PCGS MS65	$178,250	Oct-99	Bowers & Merena
157	G$10	1795 9 Leaves	PCGS MS61	$178,500	Mar-98	Heritage
158	G$2.5	1834 Classic PR	PR	$176,000	May-98	Akers
159	G$2.5	1835 PR	PR	$176,000	May-98	Akers
160	G$10	1848 PR	PR	$176,000	May-98	Akers
161	G$10	1907 Wire Edge	GEM UNC	$176,000	May-98	Akers
162	25C	1852	GEM PR	$176,000	May-98	David Akers
163	G$1	1854 Type 2 PR	PCGS PR65	$176,000	Oct-97	Akers
164	G$3	1875 PR	NGC PR64	$174,900	Aug-90	Akers
165	Shilng	1783 Chalmers Rings	Choice VF	$172,500	May-04	Stack's
166	G$10	1933	PCGS MS64	$172,500	Jan-04	Stack's
167	G$20	1883 PR	PCGS PR65DC	$172,500	Jan-04	Heritage
168	Sm1C	1856 Fly. Eagle S-3 w/Eagle Eye P.S.	PCGS MS66	$172,500	Jan-04	Heritage
169	G$20	1870-CC	NGC AU50	$172,500	Sep-03	Heritage
170	Shilng	N England N.II-A, Cr ill	EF	$172,500	Jan-02	Stack's
171	Shilng	1652 Willow Tree N.3-D, Cr 3-D	EF	$172,500	Jan-02	Stack's
172	1C	1793 Wreath Vine and Bars	PCGS MS69BN	$172,500	Mar-01	Superior
173	$50	Wass Mol 1855	BU	$170,500	Dec-96	Sotheby's
174	G$20	1861	GEM BU	$170,500	Aug-90	RARCOA
175	S$1	1893-O	PCGS MS66PL	$166,750	Jan-04	Heritage
176	G$4	1880 Flow Hair PR	PCGS PR66CA	$166,750	Apr-02	Heritage
177	1C	1793 Chain AMERI. S-1 B-1	AU50	$166,750	Jan-02	Stack's
178	G$20	1891 PR	PCGS PR67	$166,750	Oct-99	Bowers & Merena
179	DT50C	J-1960 P-2031 1915 Pan-Pac Gold	NGC PR64	$165,000	Nov-03	Heritage
180	G$5	1815	NGC MS62	$165,000	May-99	Goldberg
181	G$20	1926-D	GEM UNC	$165,000	May-98	Akers
182	G$20	1854-O	PCGS AU50	$161,000	Jan-04	Heritage
183	G$2.5	1848 CAL.	NGC MS67	$161,000	Jan-04	Heritage
184	G$10	1795 9 Leaves B-4-C T-3	PCGS MS60	$161,000	Jan-04	Heritage
185	50C	1853-O No Arrows	VF	$161,000	Oct-02	Stack's
186	50C	1870-CC	CH BU	$161,000	Oct-02	Stack's
187	50C	1878-S	GEM BU PL	$161,000	Oct-02	Stack's
188	S$1	1893-S	PCGS MS64	$161,000	Feb-02	Goldberg
189	Shilng	N England N.II-A, Cr ill	EF	$161,000	Jan-02	Stack's
190	S$1	1795 Silver Plug B-7	CH AU	$161,000	Jan-02	Stack's
191	G$20	1854-O	AU	$161,000	Oct-01	Sotheby's/Stack's

RANK	DEN	DATE/VAR	GRADE	PRICE	DATE	FIRM
192	20C	1876-CC	NGC MS66	$161,000	Mar-01	Superior
193	G$2.5	1837 PR	PCGS PR65	$161,000	May-00	Bowers & Merena
194	S$1	1851 Restrike (over a New Orleans dol)	ANACS PR62	$161,000	Feb-00	Goldberg
195	G$10	1803 Sm St Rev	PCGS MS65	$161,000	Sep-99	Goldberg
196	10C	1796	BU	$161,000	May-99	Stack's
197	G$4	1879 Coil Hair PR	NGC PR63	$161,000	Sep-98	Heritage
198	G$5	1828/7	NGC MS63	$159,500	May-99	Goldberg
199	G$2.5	1848 CAL.	PCGS MS66	$156,500	Aug-98	Bowers & Merena
200	G$5	1832 12 Stars	NGC EF45	$159,500	May-98	Akers
201	$50	RE Humbert RE 1852 887	BU	$159,500	Dec-96	Sotheby's
202	G$5	1828/7	MS	$159,500	Oct-96	Spink America
203	G$10	1899 PR	PCGS PR67	$159,500	Jan-90	Superior
204	G$5	1913-S	PCGS MS66	$156,500	Jan-99	Bowers & Merena
205	$10	Baldwin 1850 K-3	PCGS MS64	$155,250	Nov-02	Bowers & Merena
206	5C	1918/7-D	NGC MS65	$155,250	Apr-02	Heritage
207	G$10	1848-O	GEM BU	$154,000	Oct-94	Stack's
208	P$10	J-1373 1874 Gold	PCGS PR64	$154,000	Jul-93	Superior
209	50C	1792 Getz Copper w/circles & Squares	Choice EF	$149,500	May-04	Stack's
210	G$20	1884 PR	NGC PR66CAM	$149,500	Jan-04	Heritage
211	PS$1	J-63 Restrike 1836 Silver	PCGS PR63	$149,500	May-03	Stack's
212	G$20	1870-CC	PCGS EF40	$149,500	Jul-02	Bowers & Merena
213	S$1	1896-O	PCGS MS65	$149,500	Apr-02	Heritage
214	G$10	1933	MS	$149,500	Oct-01	Sotheby's/Stack's
215	$10	Baldwin 'Horseman' 1850	PCGS MS64	$149,500	May-00	Bowers & Merena
216	25C	1918/7-S	PCGS MS64FH	$149,500	Jan-00	Heritage
217	G$2.5	1804 13 Star Rev	PCGS AU55	$149,500	Aug-99	Bowers & Merena
218	G$1	1855 PR	GEM PR	$148,500	Feb-92	Superior
219	G$2.5	1831	PCGS MS66	$148,500	Aug-90	Akers
220	G$20	1860 PR	PCGS PR64	$148,500	May-90	Superior
221	G$5	1872-C W-1A	PCGS EF45	$146,100	Jan-04	Heritage
222	$10	Wass Mol Large Head	PCGS AU58	$145,220	Jun-98	Kingswood
223	$10	Ormsby	PCGS AU50	$145,000	May-99	Goldberg
224	G$20	1856-O	NGC AU50	$143,750	Jan-04	Heritage
225	G$10	1913-S	NGC MS67	$143,750	Jan-04	Stack's
226	25C	1852	NGC PR65	$143,750	Jan-04	Superior
227	G$20	1872 PR	PCGS PR66	$143,750	Jun-02	Stack's
228	G$4	1880 Flow Hair PR	NGC PR65	$143,750	Oct-00	Stack's
229	G$10	1839 Type of 1840	BU	$143,000	May-98	Akers
230	25C	1850	GEM PR	$143,000	May-98	David Akers
231	50C	1850	CH PR	$143,000	May-98	David Akers
232	G$10	1920-S	NGC MS65	$143,000	Jul-96	RARCOA/Akers
233	G$20	1907 EX-HR Lt Edg PR	Impaired PR	$143,000	Dec-92	Sotheby's
234	G$4	1879 Flow Hair PR	NGC PR66	$143,000	Oct-90	Superior
235	G$10	1875 PR	NGC PR64	$143,000	Aug-90	Akers
236	G$2.5	1796 No Stars	PCGS AU58	$141,100	Aug-98	Heritage
237	50C		PCGS MS65	$140,875	Jan-04	Superior
238	S$1	1795 Center Bust	PCGS MS65	$140,875	Nov-01	Bowers & Merena
239	Sm1C	1943-S Copper	PCGS AU58	$138,000	Mar-04	ANR
240	G$2.5	1796 No Stars	NGC MS62	$138,000	Jan-04	Heritage
241	S$1	1895-O	NGC MS65DMPL	$138,000	Jan-04	Heritage
242	T$1	1884 Trade	NGC PR63	$138,000	Jan-03	Bowers & Merena
243	G$5	1876-CC	PCGS MS65	$138,000	Jul-02	Bowers & Merena
244	Sm1C	1864 L on Ribbon Die Pair 3	PCGS PR64RD	$138,000	Jun-02	Heritage
245	T$1	1884 Trade	PCGS PR63	$138,000	Apr-02	Heritage
246	Shilng	1652 Willow Tree N.1A, Cr 1-A	EF	$138,000	Jan-02	Stack's
247	G$20	1907 HR-Flat Edge PR	NGC PR68	$138,000	Dec-00	Stack's
248	G$5	1795 Sm Eagle	PCGS MS63	$138,000	Oct-99	Bowers & Merena
249	G$10	1795 13 Leaves	PCGS MS64	$138,000	Aug-99	Bowers & Merena
250	50C	1796 15 Stars	BU	$138,000	May-99	Stack's

[384]